"Amazingly easy to use. Very portable, very complete."

—*Booklist*

♦

"Complete, concise, and filled with useful information."

—*New York Daily News*

♦

"Hotel information is close to encyclopedic."

—*Des Moines Sunday Register*

♦

"The only mainstream guide to list specific prices. The Walter Cronkite of guidebooks—with all that implies."

—*Travel & Leisure*

Virginia

by Bill Goodwin

Macmillan • USA

ABOUT THE AUTHOR

Born and raised in North Carolina, **Bill Goodwin** has lived in northern Virginia since 1979. He was an award-winning newspaper reporter before becoming a legal counsel and speech writer for two U.S. Senators, Sam Nunn of Georgia and the late Sam J. Ervin, Jr., of North Carolina. Now a full-time travel writer, Goodwin is the author of *Frommer's South Pacific,* co-author of *Frommer's Florida,* and editor of *Frommer's USA.* He also served as editor for the first edition of *Frommer's America on Wheels Mid-Atlantic.*

MACMILLAN TRAVEL

A Simon & Schuster Macmillan Company
1633 Broadway
New York, NY 10019

Find us online at **www.frommers.com**.

ISBN 0-02-862018-6
ISSN 1058-4943

Editor: Leslie Shen
Production Editor: Lori Cates
Design by Michele Laseau
Digital Cartography by Ortelius Design

SPECIAL SALES

Bulk purchases (10+ copies) of Frommer's and selected Macmillan travel guides are available to corporations, organizations, mail-order catalogs, institutions, and charities at special discounts, and can be customized to suit individual needs. For more information write to Special Sales, Macmillan General Reference, 1633 Broadway, New York, NY 10019.

Manufactured in the United States of America

Contents

List of Maps

AN INVITATION TO THE READER

In researching this book, we discovered many wonderful places—hotels, restaurants, shops, and more. We're sure you'll find others. Please tell us about them, so we can share the information with your fellow travelers in upcoming editions. If you were disappointed with a recommendation, we'd love to know that, too. Please write to:

Frommer's Virginia, 4th edition
Macmillan Travel
1633 Broadway
New York, NY 10019

AN ADDITIONAL NOTE

Please be advised that travel information is subject to change at any time—and this is especially true of prices. We therefore suggest that you write or call ahead for confirmation when making your travel plans. The authors, editors, and publisher cannot be held responsible for the experiences of readers while traveling. Your safety is important to us, however, so we encourage you to stay alert and be aware of your surroundings. Keep a close eye on cameras, purses, and wallets, all favorite targets of thieves and pickpockets.

WHAT THE SYMBOLS MEAN

✪ Frommer's Favorites

Our favorite places and experiences—outstanding for quality, value, or both.

The following abbreviations are used for credit cards:

AE	American Express	EURO	Eurocard
CB	Carte Blanche	JCB	Japan Credit Bank
DC	Diners Club	MC	MasterCard
DISC	Discover	V	Visa

FIND FROMMER'S ONLINE

Arthur Frommer's Outspoken Encyclopedia of Travel (**www.frommers.com**) offers more than 6,000 pages of up-to-the-minute travel information—including the latest bargains and candid, personal articles updated daily by Arthur Frommer himself. No other Web site offers such comprehensive and timely coverage of the world of travel.

The Best of Virginia

America's first permanent English-speaking colonists had a rough start at Jamestown in 1607, but within a few years the beautiful and bountiful land they called Virginia had greatly rewarded them for their courageous efforts. They first set foot on a sandy Atlantic Ocean beach at Cape Charles, at the mouth of one of the world's great estuaries, the Chesapeake Bay. Beyond them lay a varied, rich, and highly scenic land. They settled beside one of the great tidal rivers whose tributaries led their descendants through the rolling hills of the Piedmont, over the Blue Ridge Mountains, and into the great valleys beyond.

Almost 400 years later, the history-loving Commonwealth of Virginia rewards today's traveler with glimpses back to the colonial era, to the stirrings of revolution and the great victory that sealed independence for the United States, and to the bloody battles that nearly tore the young nation apart during the Civil War. The state literally abounds with historic homes and plantations, buildings that rang with revolutionary oratory, museums that recall the nation's storied past, and small towns that seem little changed since the earliest days of colonial times.

Fortunately, preservation hasn't been limited to historical landmarks. Conservation efforts have kept a great deal of Virginia's wilderness looking much as it did in 1607, making the state a virtual paradise for lovers of the great outdoors. Whether you like to hike, bike, bird watch, fish, canoe, or boat—or just lie on a sandy beach—Virginia has a place to indulge your passion.

This chapter gives you descriptions of some of the best experiences Virginia has to offer. Bear in mind that it's just an overview, and you'll surely come up with your own "bests" as you travel through the state. Be sure to see the destination chapters later in this book for full details on the places mentioned below.

1 The Best of Colonial Virginia

- **Old Town Alexandria:** Although Alexandria is today very much part of metropolitan Washington, D.C., the historic district known as "Old Town" evokes the time when the nation's early leaders strolled its streets and partook of grog at Gadsby's Tavern. See chapter 5.
- **Mount Vernon:** When he wasn't off surveying, fighting in the French and Indian Wars, leading the American Revolution, or

serving as our first president, George Washington made his home at a northern Virginia plantation 8 miles south of Alexandria. Restored as it was in Washington's day, Mount Vernon is America's second most visited historic home. See chapter 5.

- **Fredericksburg & the Northern Neck:** Not only did the Fredericksburg area play a role in the birth of a nation, it was also the birthplace of George Washington, the father of that new nation. Also born here was James Monroe, who as president kept European powers out of the Americas by promulgating the Monroe Doctrine. A generation later, the great Confederate leader Robert E. Lee was born here. Fredericksburg still retains much of the charm it possessed in those early days, and the birthplaces of Washington and Lee stand not far from town on the Northern Neck. See chapter 6.

- **Charlottesville:** Although Washington was the father of the United States, Thomas Jefferson was its intellectual genius. This scholar, lawyer, writer, and architect built two monuments to himself—his lovely hilltop home, Monticello, and the University of Virginia. Both still evoke memories of this great thinker and patriot. See chapter 7.

- **Richmond:** Although Richmond is best known as the capital of the Confederacy, it played a major role in events leading up to the American Revolution. It was in Richmond's St. John's Church that Patrick Henry shouted "Give me liberty, or give me death," thus inciting Virginia to join the rebellion. See chapter 10.

- **Williamsburg, Jamestown & Yorktown:** Known as the Historic Triangle, these three towns are the finest examples of colonial America to be found anywhere. Thanks to an infusion of cash from the Rockefeller family, Colonial Williamsburg has been restored and rebuilt exactly as it appeared when it was the capital of Virginia from 1699 to 1780. The site of the original Jamestown settlement is now a national historical park, as is Yorktown, where George Washington bottled up Lord Cornwallis and won the American Revolution. See chapter 11.

- **James River Plantations:** America's first great wealth was created by colonists who fanned out from Jamestown and hacked huge tobacco plantations out of Virginia's virgin forests. Today, you can visit some of the great manses they built along the James River between Williamsburg and Richmond. Descendants of the colonial planters still occupy some of these mansions. See chapter 11.

2 The Best of Civil War Virginia

Some historians think the Civil War actually began in 1859 with John Brown's aborted anti-slavery raid on Harpers Ferry, then in Virginia. When the real fighting broke out in 1861 and the Confederacy moved its capital to Richmond, the state became the prime target of the Union armies. Consequently, Virginia saw more battles than any other state, as Robert E. Lee's Army of Northern Virginia turned back one assault after another aimed at Richmond. Today's peaceful visitor can visit the sites of many key battles, all of them national historical parks.

- **Harpers Ferry:** Now just over the West Virginia line, Harpers Ferry National Historical Park is dedicated to John Brown's raid. The forces that captured and hung him were led by Robert E. Lee, then a Union officer. The old stone town has been preserved, and the historical park has lovely hiking trails overlooking the gorge where the Potomac and Shenandoah rivers join and cut their way through the Blue Ridge. See chapter 5.

- **Manassas:** The first battle of the war occurred along Bull Run near Manassas in northern Virginia, and it was a shock to the Union when the rebels engineered a

Virginia

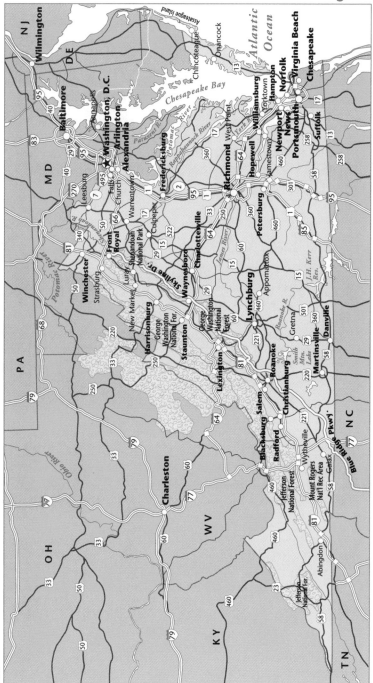

surprising victory over a disorganized Union force. They won again here at the Second Battle of Manassas. See chapter 5.

- **Fredericksburg:** No other town in Virginia has as many significant battlefields as does Fredericksburg. Lee used the Rappahannock River as a natural line of defense, and he fought several major battles against Union armies trying to cross it near Fredericksburg and advance on Richmond. Today, you can visit the battlefields in town and at Chancellorsville and the Wilderness all in an afternoon. See chapter 6.

- **Appomattox Court House:** After the fall of Petersburg in April 1865, Lee fled for little more than a week until realizing that continuation of the war was fruitless. On April 9, he met Grant at Wilbur McLean's farmhouse and surrendered his sword. America's bloodiest conflict was over. The farmhouse is preserved as part of Appomattox Court House National Historical Park. See chapter 7.

- **New Market:** While Lee was fending off the Union near Fredericksburg, the war was ebbing and flowing up and down the Shenandoah Valley, the Confederacy's breadbasket. The town of Winchester actually changed hands 72 times. Perhaps the war's most poignant battlefield is at New Market, where the corps of cadets from Virginia Military Institute marched up from Lexington and helped stop a larger Union force. Ten of the teenagers were killed, and 47 were wounded. See chapter 8.

- **Richmond:** The capital of the Confederacy, Richmond is loaded with reminders of the great conflict, including the Museum of the Confederacy and its adjacent White House of the Confederacy, home of President Jefferson Davis. The city's Monument Avenue is lined with statues of the rebel leaders. Now suburbs, the city's eastern outskirts are ringed with battle sites, part of the Richmond National Battlefield Park. See chapter 10.

- **Petersburg:** After nearly 4 years of frustration in trying to capture Richmond, Union Gen. Ulysses S. Grant finally bypassed the southern capital in 1864 and headed for the important railroad junction of Petersburg, the lifeline of the Confederate capital. Even there he was forced into a siege situation, but finally, in April of 1865, Grant broke through and forced Lee into retreat westward. See chapter 10.

3 The Best of the Great Outdoors

Virginia has hundreds of thousands of acres preserved in national and state parks, national forests, and national recreation areas. Especially in the mountains, you can find more than 1,000 miles of trails for hiking, biking, and horseback riding. The Chesapeake Bay offers fabulous boating and fishing, and the Atlantic beaches are among the best on the East Coast.

- **The W&OD Trail:** Even in Virginia's metropolitan areas, it's possible to get away from it all. One fine example is the Washington & Old Dominion (W&OD) Trail, which begins in Arlington and runs 45 miles across northern Virginia to Purcellville at the edge of the Blue Ridge Mountains. A rails-to-trails park, it follows an old railroad bed through the Washington, D.C., suburbs into the gorgeous Hunt Country. See chapter 5.

- **Shenandoah National Park:** Nearly 2 million visitors a year venture into the Shenandoah National Park, which straddles the crest of the Blue Ridge Mountains from Front Royal to Rockfish Gap between Charlottesville and Waynesboro. Many visitors merely ride along the 105-mile Skyline Drive, one of America's most scenic routes. Others come to walk more than 500 miles of hiking trails, including 101 miles of Virginia's 450-mile share of the Maine-to-Georgia Appalachian Trail. Many trails start at the Skyline Drive and drop down into hollows and canyons, some of them with waterfalls. Even on the Skyline Drive, you are likely to encounter deer, and you might even see bear, bobcat, and wild turkey. See chapter 8.

- **Running the Rivers (Front Royal, Luray, Lexington, Richmond):** The South Fork of the Shenandoah River twists and turns its way between the valley towns of Front Royal and Luray, making it a perfect place for river rafting, canoeing, and kayaking—or just floating along in an inner tube. Likewise, the James River can be swift and turbulent as it crosses the Shenandoah Valley, cuts through the Blue Ridge Mountains, and courses its way across the Piedmont to Hampton Roads. Depending on the amount of rain, you can even raft down the James through metropolitan Richmond. See chapters 8 and 10.

- **Mount Rogers National Recreation Area:** While you won't be alone in Shenandoah National Park, you could have a hiking, mountain-biking, horseback-riding, or cross-country skiing trail all to yourself in Mount Rogers National Recreation Area. This wild wonderland in the Southwest Highlands occupies some 117,000 forested acres, including its namesake, Virginia's highest peak. Two of Virginia's finest rails-to-trails hiking, biking, and riding paths serve as bookends to the 60-mile-long recreation area: the New River Trail near Wytheville, and the Virginia Creeper Trail, from Abingdon to White Top Mountain. See chapter 9.

- **Back Bay National Wildlife Refuge/False Cape State Park:** You can't sunbathe or swim on the beach of Back Bay National Wildlife Refuge, a mere 15 miles south of the heavily developed resort area of Virginia Beach, but you can hike through the dunes or take a canoe into the marshes, an Atlantic Flyway landing zone for migrating birds. You can sunbathe and swim at the adjoining False Cape State Park, but it's so out-of-the-way that you'll have to bring your own drinking water. See chapter 12.

- **Assateague Island:** Of all the natural areas in Virginia, none surpasses Assateague Island, which keeps the Atlantic Ocean from the back bays of Chincoteague. Here you will find the famous wild ponies grazing in Chincoteague National Wildlife Refuge, and relatively tame humans strolling some 37 miles of pristine beach. Assateague Island is also one of the nation's prime places to watch birds, for it, too, is situated directly on the Atlantic Flyway. See chapter 12.

4 The Best Scenic Drives

The best way—some of us think the *only* way—to see Virginia is by car, and with very good reason: the Old Dominion has some of America's most scenic drives.

- **George Washington Memorial Parkway:** Stay away from this route during rush hour, when it becomes a major commuter artery into and out of Washington, D.C. But any other time, the "G.W. Parkway" is a great scenic drive along the Potomac River from I-495 at the Maryland line all the way to Mount Vernon. The river views of Washington's monuments are unparalleled. See chapter 5.

- **Skyline Drive:** Few roads anywhere can top the Skyline Drive, which twists and turns 105 miles along the Blue Ridge crest in Shenandoah National Park. The views down over the rolling Piedmont to the east and the Shenandoah Valley to the west are nothing short of spectacular, especially during spring, when the wildflowers are in bloom, and in fall, when the leaves change color from green to brilliant hues of rust, orange, and yellow. See chapter 8.

- **Interstate 81 and U.S. 11:** Few interstate highways are as beautiful as I-81, which runs the entire length of Virginia from the Shenandoah Valley all the way through the Southwest Highlands to Tennessee. Alongside, the old Valley Pike (now U.S. 11) is a scenic excursion back to the 1950s, complete with old-fashioned gas stations, clapboard houses, and small-town restaurants. See chapters 8 and 9.
- **Lexington to Hot Springs:** While I-81 runs down the floor of Virginia's great valleys, other roads offer a very different scenic treat by cutting across the mountains. One of these is Va. 39, which runs from Lexington to Hot Springs via the Goshen Pass, a picturesque gorge cut by the Maury River. You can make a loop by continuing north from Hot Springs via U.S. 220 to the beautiful village of Monterey in "Virginia's Switzerland." From Monterey, you can cross the mountains via U.S. 250 to Staunton and I-81. See chapter 8.
- **Blue Ridge Parkway:** Actually a continuation of the Skyline Drive, this road continues along the Blue Ridge crest all the way south to the Great Smoky Mountains National Park in North Carolina. Of the 218 miles in Virginia, the most scenic are north of Roanoke. Here you'll find it difficult to keep your eyes on the road, as the parkway often runs right along the ridgeline, with views down both sides of the mountain at once. See chapter 9.
- **Colonial Parkway:** It's not very long, but the Colonial Parkway between Jamestown, Williamsburg, and Yorktown has its scenic merits, especially the views of the James River near Jamestown and of the York River near Yorktown. The parkway goes through a tunnel under the heart of Colonial Williamsburg. See chapter 11.
- **Chesapeake Bay Bridge-Tunnel:** One of the man-made wonders of the world, the Chesapeake Bay Bridge–Tunnel runs for 17 miles over—and under—the mouth of the Chesapeake Bay between Norfolk and the Eastern Shore. You can barely see dry land when you're out in the middle. See chapter 12.

5 The Best Small Towns

Another good reason to see Virginia by car is its many lovely small towns, the best of them capturing and keeping alive the state's storied history. This is especially true in the Shenandoah Valley, where first the Valley Pike, then U.S. 11, and now I-81 string together Winchester, Strasburg, Staunton, and Lexington, all possessed of 18th- and 19th-century brick and stone buildings.

- **Waterford Village:** Founded by Quakers in the late 1700s, the little hamlet of Waterford went into a time capsule in 1870 when the railroad bypassed it in favor of nearby Leesburg. Today it looks very much like it did then, its houses carefully preserved by private owners. See chapter 5.
- **Middleburg:** The self-proclaimed unofficial capital of Virginia's horse-loving Hunt Country, Middleburg takes up barely 6 blocks along U.S. 50, making it small enough to be digested in an afternoon. Some of the world's wealthiest individuals keep their horses near Middleburg, and the town has a host of upscale shops in buildings dating back to the 1700s. See chapter 5.
- **Monterey:** Over Shenandoah and Bull Pasture Mountains from Staunton, the little village of Monterey appears more like New England than Virginia, with its white churches and clapboard homes nestled in a picturesque valley. Thousands of visitors make the trek over the mountains during the annual Highland Maple Festival in March. See chapter 8.
- **Lexington:** Not only one of Virginia's but also one of America's best small towns, Lexington has a lively college atmosphere in addition to a host of historical sights.

It's home to Virginia Military Institute (VMI), where Gen. Thomas J. "Stonewall" Jackson taught; its student body went off to the Civil War at New Market. After the war, Robert E. Lee came here as president of Washington College, now known as Washington and Lee University. VMI was also the alma mater of Gen. George C. Marshall, winner of the Nobel Peace Prize for the post–World War II Marshall Plan to rebuild Europe. Jackson, Lee, and Marshall are buried here, and the town has three fine museums dedicated to these great leaders. On top of all that, Lexington's downtown looks so much like it did when Jackson and Lee were here that only dirt had to be added to Main Street's pavement to film the movie *Sommersby*. See chapter 8.

- **Abingdon:** Daniel Boone opened Virginia's Southwest Highlands to settlement in the 1770s, and it wasn't long before a thriving town grew up at Abingdon. Homes and buildings dating back to 1779 still line shady Main Street, making Abingdon a wonderful place for a stroll. The town's beauty has attracted a community of artists, craftspeople, and actors. The latter perform at the famous Barter Theatre, where you can still barter for a ticket. See chapter 9.
- **Onancock:** Relatively isolated on the Eastern Shore, little Onancock was incorporated in 1690 and was for more than 2 centuries an important Chesapeake Bay shipping port. The great ferries don't run anymore between Norfolk and Baltimore, and U.S. 13 passes a mile east of town, leaving Onancock as a lovely reminder of the old days of planters and merchants. See chapter 12.

6 The Best Beaches

If you want to find a great beach in Virginia, just head east. The Atlantic Ocean surf beats all along the state's shoreline, from North Carolina to Maryland. Fortunately for conservationists, however, not all of this coastline is easily accessible to travelers.

- **Virginia Beach:** Okay, it's developed, but this resort still has a seemingly unending fine-sand beach with excellent surf. The resort itself is one of Virginia's best family destinations, with much more to do than sun and swim. See chapter 12.
- **Back Bay National Wildlife Refuge/False Cape State Park:** Also among the best of the great outdoors, these two preserves are just 15 miles south of—but a developed world removed from—Virginia Beach. You can't swim or sunbathe at the refuge's deserted beach, but you can hike or bike south to False Cape State Park. Carry your own drinking water—it's that isolated and undeveloped. See chapter 12.
- **Assateague Island:** This 37-mile-long barrier island is completely within the Assateague Island National Seashore, which has prevented all development along this stretch of golden sand. The National Park Service has been kind enough to build bathhouses and rest rooms on one end of the beach; otherwise, it belongs to the seagulls and to hardy souls who don't mind a hike. The Virginia end of the island is also home to Chincoteague National Wildlife Refuge, where the famous Chincoteague wild horses roam. See chapter 12.
- **Parramore and Cedar Islands:** Parramore is partially owned and preserved by the Nature Conservancy. Although Cedar has cottages on it, there is no way to reach either island and their long, straight beaches except by boat. Those you can rent in Wachapreague. See chapter 12.

7 The Best Family Vacations

A vast majority of Virginia's visitors arrive by car, and most of them are families. Accordingly, the state's major attractions and resorts are well equipped to entertain and care for children. It's a great place for kids to learn about American history, while still enjoying a good time at the beach or at one of the state's three major amusement parks.

- **Northern Virginia:** A good place for a history lesson is in northern Virginia, especially at Mount Vernon, Old Town Alexandria, and Arlington National Cemetery. Of course, Arlington is just across the Potomac River from Washington, D.C., where the kids can roam the National Air and Space Museum and other key attractions. See chapter 5.
- **Shenandoah National Park:** Two lodges in the most popular part of Shenandoah National Park make this scenic wonderland a great place for family vacations. The kids can participate in ranger programs, hike to waterfalls, or go for a pony ride in the mountain forests. See chapter 8.
- **Richmond:** The state capital has several attractions of interest to children, including the hands-on Science Museum of Virginia. The big draws, however, are the wild rides and movie and TV characters at the huge Paramount's Kings Dominion amusement park north of the city. See chapter 10.
- **Colonial Williamsburg:** The historic area of Colonial Williamsburg is the best place of all for children to get a quick lesson in American history. On the streets, they might run into Thomas Jefferson (actually, an actor) and have a conversation about the Declaration of Independence, or perhaps practice marching and drilling with the 18th-century militia. As soon as they get bored, head for Busch Gardens Williamsburg or Water Country USA, two nearby theme parks. See chapter 11.
- **Virginia Beach:** First there's the beach, all 4 miles or so, with lifeguards during summer—but that's not all Virginia Beach has to offer. Rainy days can be spent at the local Virginia Marine Science Museum—the state's most popular museum. Norfolk's NAUTICUS, Hampton's Virginia Air and Space Center, and Colonial Williamsburg are all just short drives away. See chapter 12.
- **Chincoteague:** The little fishing village was the setting for Marguerite Henry's classic children's book *Misty of Chincoteague,* and there are plenty of wild horses (called "ponies" here) in Chincoteague National Wildlife Refuge on Assateague Island, which also has a lifeguarded beach for swimming during the summer. The best time to see the horses is during the annual pony swim the last week in July. See chapter 12.

8 The Most Unusual Travel Experiences

A museum devoted to hounds, a stalactite organ, an 18th-century version of today's Jacuzzi, a stuffed horse, and a cruise to Elizabethan times all make for unusual travel in Virginia.

- **Tally Ho! (Leesburg):** The Hunt Country gets its name from the hounds, horses, and very wealthy people who hunt foxes for sport here. You can learn all about the history of this aristocratic pastime at Leesburg's Morven Park, home to the Museum of Hounds and Hunting. See chapter 5.
- **Chimes Down Under (Luray):** There are several caverns under the Shenandoah Valley, but one of the most fascinating is at Luray. Through subterranean rooms more than 140 feet high comes beautiful organ music—but not from a man-made instrument. Well, almost not man-made. Thanks to modern technology, hammers striking million-year-old stalactites make this wonderful music. See chapter 8.
- **Ancient Hot Tubs (Warm Springs):** Eighteenth-century travelers couldn't climb into the hotel Jacuzzi after a rough day on the road—unless, that is, they pulled

into Warm Springs. Since 1761, travelers have slipped their weary bodies into these natural rock pools whose circulating waters range from 94°F to 104°F. You can, too. See chapter 8.

- **Mounting Little Sorrel (Lexington):** After he died of wounds accidentally inflicted by his own men at the Battle of Chancellorsville, Gen. Stonewall Jackson was brought home and buried in Lexington, where he had taught at Virginia Military Institute before the conflagration. One of the key exhibits at VMI's museum is the bullet-pierced raincoat Jackson was wearing that disastrous night. And thanks to taxidermy, there stands the hide of his war horse, Little Sorrel. Nearby, Robert E. Lee's horse Traveller is buried just outside Lee Chapel, his master's resting place. See chapter 8.

- **Hoi Toide Tonoit (Tangier Island):** Out in the Chesapeake Bay sits remote Tangier Island, whose residents have been so isolated over the centuries that they still speak with the Elizabethan brogue of their forebears. Out here, "high tide tonight" is pronounced *hoi toide tonoit*—as in "hoity-toity"—and narrow 17th-century lanes accommodate no modern automobiles. Cruises leave from Onancock on the Eastern Shore and from Reedville on the Northern Neck. See chapters 6 and 12.

9 The Best Country Inns

With all of its old homes and gorgeous countryside, it's no wonder that Virginia is a hotbed of country inns and bed-and-breakfasts. Some have been in business since colonial times, and a few are among the best America has to offer. Our picks barely touch the surface.

- **Tides Inn (Irvington):** Down by the Chesapeake Bay in Virginia's Tidewater, the Tides Inn is a sprawling resort complex beside a broad creek near the eastern end of the Northern Neck. The Stephens family has maintained a tradition of gracious service here since 1946. Guests can go boating on the Chesapeake Bay or play golf on a creekside course. See chapter 6.

- **Clifton, The Country Inn (Charlottesville):** You'll think you have arrived at "Tara" in *Gone With the Wind* when you first glimpse the tall white columns fronting this stately manse, built in 1790 by Thomas Mann Randolph, who married Thomas Jefferson's daughter Martha. Clifton today adds all the modern comforts, an energetic young staff, and chef Craig Hartman's gourmet cuisine to its Jefferson-era charms. See chapter 7.

- **Keswick Hall (Charlottesville):** Just a few miles from Clifton, this Italianate villa outside Charlottesville features all the trappings of an English baronial estate, plus a golf course redesigned by Arnold Palmer. The entire establishment is graced with owner Sir Bernard Ashley's antiques and wallpaper, upholstery, and curtains designed by his late wife, Laura Ashley. See chapter 7.

- **Wayside Inn (Middletown):** Located in the tiny Shenandoah Valley village of Middletown, the Wayside Inn has been serving travelers since stagecoaches started prowling the Valley Pike (now U.S. 11) in 1797. Restored by an antique collector in the 1960s, today's rooms are decorated with an assortment of 18th- and 19th-century pieces. The Wayside Theatre is virtually next door, lending entertainment to a stop here. Just down the pike is another antique-laden historic relic, the Hotel Strasburg. See chapter 8.

- **L'Auberge Provençal (White Post):** Master chef Alain Borel and his wife, Celeste, have created the look, feel, and cuisine of southern France in this 1750s farmhouse located a few miles southeast of Winchester. Alain grows many of his own ingredients, and others he buys fresh from local farmers. See chapter 8.

- **Inn at Little Washington (Washington):** For the best, you need look no further than the tiny Blue Ridge foothill village of Washington, which everyone in Virginia calls "Little Washington." The rooms here were designed by an English decorator, but it's the romantic restaurant that draws the most raves, as co-owner and chef Patrick O'Connell relies on regional products to produce wonderful French cuisine. See chapter 8.
- **Fort Lewis Lodge (Millboro):** One of Virginia's most unusual country inns, the Fort Lewis Lodge occupies an old mill and a rebuilt barn on a farm beside the Cowpasture River, just over the mountain from Warm Springs. A spiral staircase winds its way to three rooms inside the old silo beside the barn, and there are two log cabins with their own fireplaces. It's a great place to show urban kids a bit of farm life in beautiful surroundings. See chapter 8.
- **Camberly's Martha Washington Inn (Abingdon):** Gracing Abingdon's historic district, the center portion of this Greek Revival inn was built as a private home in 1832. You can sit in white-wicker rocking chairs on the front porch and watch the traffic on Main Street—or imagine Daniel Boone's dogs being attacked by wolves nearby. See chapter 9.

10 The Best Luxury Accommodations

With deep enough pockets, you can enjoy some of the Mid-Atlantic's best luxury accommodations in Virginia. Here are some of the finest the Old Dominion has to offer.

- **Ritz-Carlton Pentagon City (Arlington):** Although this Ritz-Carlton was built in 1990 as part of a modern shopping mall, massive china cabinets, graceful wing chairs, plush sofas, Oriental rugs, crystal sconces, and a $2.5-million collection of 18th- and 19th-century paintings and antiques make it seem from another era. So does the superb service. See chapter 5.
- **The Homestead (Hot Springs):** Outstanding service, fine cuisine, and a myriad of recreational activities denote this grand old establishment, in business since Thomas Jefferson's day. In fact, Jefferson was the first of seven presidents to stay here. The Homestead offers accommodations ranging from standard rooms to plush suites. PGA pro Lanny Wadkins presides over its golf course, one of Virginia's finest. See chapter 8.
- **Hotel Roanoke & Conference Center (Roanoke):** The grand, Tudor-style Hotel Roanoke stood in a wheat field when the Norfolk & Western Railroad built it in 1882 as the centerpiece of its new town called Roanoke. It was closed in 1989, but a $42-million renovation has completely restored its grand public areas to their original appearance and rebuilt all its rooms to modern standards. See chapter 9.
- **Jefferson Hotel (Richmond):** A stunning beaux arts landmark with Renaissance-style balconies and an Italian clock tower, the Jefferson was opened in 1895 by a wealthy Richmonder who wanted his city to have one of America's finest hotels. A complete 1980s restoration renewed its original splendor. See chapter 10.
- **Williamsburg Inn:** Another establishment with not one but three fine golf courses, the Williamsburg Inn was built as part of the Colonial Williamsburg restoration, but looks like it might have been here in 1750. If staying in the main inn with its superb service and cuisine won't do, you can opt for one of several restored colonial houses and taverns that have been converted into accommodations. See chapter 11.
- **Cavalier Hotel (Virginia Beach):** We were children when Vice President Richard Nixon brought his family to the Cavalier Hotel for a beach vacation in the

1950s. Situated on a hill overlooking the Atlantic, the Cavalier has been a grand beach resort since 1927, and its older section still looks like it did back then—or when the Nixons visited 30 years later. Today there's a new wing beside the beach, but stay in the old section for charm. See chapter 12.

11 The Best Moderately Priced Accommodations

Virginia has far too many fine, affordably priced lodgings to mention them all here. The following are some we like best.

- **Kenmore Inn (Fredericksburg):** George Washington's brother-in-law, Fielding Lewis, once owned the property where this 1700s mansion sits, right in Fredericksburg's Old Town historic district. A sweeping staircase leads to guest rooms furnished with four-poster beds and a mix of antiques. Four rooms have working fireplaces. See chapter 6.
- **Belle Grae Inn (Staunton):** Owner Michael Organ gave up teaching at Mary Baldwin College in the 1980s to convert an 1873 hilltop Victorian house into an inn. Today his establishment includes houses ringing an entire city block, all of them beautifully restored and furnished with period pieces. The cuisine here is the best in town. See chapter 8.
- **Linden Row Inn (Richmond):** One of the best-run hotels we've ever experienced, the Linden Row Inn consists of seven mid-19th-century row houses, all of them restored and furnished with late Empire and early Victorian pieces, beautiful wallpapers, damask draperies, flower-patterned carpets, and marble-top dressers. And it's convenient to downtown Richmond's historic sights. See chapter 10.
- **The Breakers Resort Inn (Virginia Beach):** Among the many cookie-cutter, high-rise buildings lining Virginia Beach's oceanfront, the Breakers stands out as a family-operated hotel that's friendly to families. Efficiencies here have fully equipped, money-saving kitchens. See chapter 12.
- **Hart's Harbor House (Wachapreague):** Unlike many small-town bed-and-breakfasts run by expatriates from big cities, hosts Tom and Pat Hart of Hart's Harbor House are born-and-bred Wachapreaguers. Accordingly, their knowledge of the Eastern Shore is unsurpassed, and they are experts at arranging boat trips out to Parramore and Cedar Islands along the Atlantic. Accommodations are in two Victorian houses they have restored (one's called Burton House Bed-and-Breakfast), both with charming screened porches. See chapter 12.

12 The Best Inexpensive Accommodations

Virginia has a large number of clean, comfortable motels of the Econo Lodge, Super 8, and Motel 6 variety. But for something a little more unique, check out the following inexpensive choices.

- **Americana Hotel (Arlington):** When our parents brought us to Washington, D.C., in 1955, we stayed at an old-fashioned motel, one of many that lined U.S. 1 in Arlington. The Americana was built a few years after that, but it still stands among the high-rise buildings of what's now known as Crystal City. It's run by the same family, and it's as clean and comfortable as ever. See chapter 5.
- **Laurel Brigade Inn (Leesburg):** You need to reserve at least a month in advance for a room at the Laurel Brigade Inn, a Hunt Country charmer going back to 1766 when an "ordinary" (tavern) stood here. Some of the rooms have fireplaces, just like in the old days. See chapter 5.

- **Fredericksburg Colonial Inn (Fredericksburg):** Don't be surprised to see Blues and Grays toting Civil War rifles in the lobby of the Fredericksburg Colonial Inn, so popular is this establishment with reenactment buffs. An avid collector, the owner has laden the rooms with antiques. See chapter 6.
- **Roseloe Motel (Hot Springs):** You don't have to pay a fortune to stay at the Homestead—just drive 3 miles north to the Roseloe, a clean family operation across U.S. 220 from the lovely sounds of the Garth Newel Chamber Music Center. The hot pools at Warm Springs are a short drive away, and you can pay a lot less than the cost of a room to use the Homestead's superb recreational facilities. See chapter 8.
- **Alpine Motel (Abingdon):** Another holdover from the early 1960s, the immaculate, family-run Alpine Motel has extraordinarily large rooms—common in those days when cost-per-square-foot wasn't as high as today. Most of the rooms have mountain views. See chapter 9.

13 The Best Culinary Experiences

Author William Styron, a native of southeastern Virginia, once said that the French consider strong, salt-cured Virginia hams to be America's only gourmet contribution to the world's cuisine. That may be the opinion in Paris, but Virginians are also crazy about rockfish and crabs from the Chesapeake Bay and shad and trout from their rivers. Their farms produce a plethora of vegetables during the summer, and their orchards are famous for autumn apples. And let's not forget the peanut, one of Virginia's major crops.

You can dine on all types of cuisine in Virginia, but the highlights here are produced from recipes handed down since colonial times, dishes such as peanut soup and Sally Lunn bread. Here are some of the best places to sample Virginia's unique and very historic cuisine.

- **Gadsby's Tavern (Alexandria):** George Washington said good-bye to his troops from the door of Gadsby's Tavern in Alexandria's Old Town historic district. This old rooming house and the tavern next door look much as they did then, and a wait staff in colonial garb still serve chicken roasted on an open fire, buttermilk pie, and other dishes from that period. See chapter 5.
- **The Green Tree (Leesburg):** Most of the dishes at the Green Tree are from faithfully reproduced 18th-century recipes garnered from the Library of Congress. A smoked-sausage pie, a green-herb soup, and an oyster-flavored cabbage pie are featured offerings. See chapter 5.
- **Inn at Little Washington (Washington):** Chef Patrick O'Connell constantly changes his basically French menu to take advantage of trout, Chesapeake Bay seafood, Virginia hams, and other local delicacies at the romantic dining room of the Inn at Little Washington. The service here is extraordinarily attentive and unobtrusive. See chapter 8.
- **Mrs. Rowe's Family Restaurant and Bakery (Staunton):** Every town has its favorite "local" restaurant, where you can clog your arteries with plain old Southern favorites like pan-fried chicken, sausage gravy over biscuits, and fresh vegetables seasoned with smoked pork and cooked to smithereens. In business since 1947, Mrs. Rowe's somehow manages to cook the golden oldies without all the lard you'll ingest elsewhere. See chapter 8.
- **The Roanoker Restaurant (Roanoke):** Another favorite "local" restaurant, the Roanoaker regularly changes its menu to take advantage of the freshest vegetables

available, but every day it serves the best biscuits in Virginia, hot from the oven. See chapter 9.

- **The Log House 1776 Restaurant (Wytheville):** The name is appropriate at this particular restaurant, part of which is contained in a log house built in 1776. Here you can order Thomas Jefferson's favorite, chicken marengo, or a very sweet Confederate beef-and-apple stew like the one Robert E. Lee fed his troops. See chapter 9.

- **The Frog and the Redneck (Richmond):** The "Frog" stands for the French style of cooking learned and practiced by noted chef Jimmy Sneed. The "Redneck" refers to the local ingredients he uses in his gourmet interpretations of traditional French dishes. You'll get Virginia ham and cantaloupe here, not Bayonne and melon. See chapter 10.

- **King's Barbeque (Petersburg):** Like all Southerners, Virginians love their smoked pork barbecue, and it doesn't get any better than at the two branches of King's Barbeque. Pork, beef, ribs, and chicken roast constantly over an open pit right in the dining rooms, and the sauce is served on the side, not soaking the succulent meat and overpowering its smoked flavor. See chapter 10.

- **Trellis Café, Restaurant & Grill (Williamsburg):** Chef Marcel Desaulniers has been nationally recognized for his outstanding regional cuisine, all of which emphasizes fresh local produce. Desaulniers has written three cookbooks, including *Death by Chocolate.* They don't raise cocoa in Virginia, but you can definitely die by it here. See chapter 11.

- **Old Chickahominy House (Williamsburg):** Named for a nearby river, this reconstructed, antique-filled 18th-century house is one of the best places to sample traditional Virginia fare, such as Brunswick stew and Virginia ham on hot biscuits. See chapter 11.

2 Getting to Know Virginia

No state in the nation can equal the Commonwealth of Virginia in its role as the cradle of the American republic. America originated at Jamestown and grew along the banks of the Rappahannock, the Potomac, and the James rivers. Spurred on by Virginia leaders like Patrick Henry, whose ringing denunciation of the Stamp Act inspired all 13 colonies, the desire for independence grew strong. This was the first colony to have a Bill of Rights, and Virginia aristocrat Thomas Jefferson gave voice to this revolutionary philosophy in the ringing phrases of the Declaration of Independence. The mantle of responsibility for leading the new nation in its struggle for freedom and its first years as a republic fell on the most famous of all Virginians, George Washington.

When the Civil War broke out, Virginia turned its back on the Union it had played such an important role in creating. Richmond served as capital of the Confederacy, Virginia's own Robert E. Lee commanded the Rebel army, and some 60% of the war was fought on Virginia soil.

With monuments, sites, and battlefields marking more than three centuries of American history, Virginia today is a pioneer in the field of historic preservation. There's more here than just history, though: the commonwealth's natural beauty will lure you back again and again. From the pristine beaches of the Eastern Shore to the forests and highlands of western Virginia, visitors will find boundless opportunities for hiking, freshwater and ocean fishing, swimming, boating, sailing, and skiing. Overlooking the Shenandoah Valley and southwestern highlands, two of Virginia's many fabulously scenic routes—the Skyline Drive and Blue Ridge Parkway—carry motorists along the very spine of the Blue Ridge Mountains.

To this appealing mix of living history and outdoor fun, add a vibrant cultural scene that includes the nation's oldest repertory theater company, major art and science museums, a growing wine industry, and a culinary spectrum that ranges from Virginia ham to Chincoteague oysters. And that's not even mentioning the theme parks, the steeplechase race meets in Hunt Country, and the opportunities to sample farm life or take the waters at the Homestead, the nation's oldest spa hotel.

1 The Regions in Brief

Virginia has three distinct geographic regions. Along the eastern coast, the **Tidewater** (or coastal plain) is dominated by four rivers—the Potomac, Rappahannock, York, and James—that empty into the Chesapeake, one of the world's largest estuaries. These rivers divide the Tidewater into three peninsulas, or *necks* in local parlance. To the south, the Chesapeake meets the Atlantic Ocean at the large natural harbor of Hampton Roads.

The rolling hills of the **Piedmont** run through central Virginia, from Richmond, Charlottesville, and Lynchburg to the Hunt Country and suburban sprawl of northern Virginia. This farm country gently rises to meet the foothills of the **Blue Ridge Mountains.** Between the Blue Ridge and the Allegheny Mountains to the west, a series of gorgeous valleys—including the fabled Shenandoah—extends the length of the state, from the Potomac in the north to the Southwest Highlands near the borders of Tennessee and Kentucky.

NORTHERN VIRGINIA   The fastest growing, most densely populated, and wealthiest part of the state, northern Virginia today is much more than a suburban bedroom for government workers in Washington, D.C.; areas such as Tysons Corner have become unincorporated cities in their own right, with employment in high-tech service industries outstripping that of the federal government. Long known for its famous cemetery just across the Potomac from the nation's capital, Arlington today is a melting pot of immigrants from around the world—with a marvelous mix of ethnic cuisines to show for it. Centered on its historic Old Town, Alexandria offers fascinating daytime walks as well as lively nighttime entertainment and good restaurants. Beyond are the beautiful Potomac plantations, including George Washington's Mount Vernon. In Virginia's Hunt Country, sightseers can enjoy Virginia's traditional historic inns and fine restaurants. Farther south is Manassas, site of the first major battle of the Civil War.

FREDERICKSBURG & THE NORTHERN NECK   The quaint cobblestone streets and historic houses of Fredericksburg recall America's first heroes—George Washington, James Monroe, John Paul Jones—as does the quiet Northern Neck farmland, where the birthplaces of Washington and Robert E. Lee stand. Military buffs love to explore Fredericksburg's Civil War battlefields.

CENTRAL VIRGINIA   These rolling Piedmont hills are "Mr. Jefferson's country." Charlottesville boasts his magnificent estate, Monticello, as well as the University of Virginia, which he designed. From Lynchburg, you can visit Popular Forest, his beloved retreat, as well as Patrick Henry's final home at Red Hill and Appomattox Court House, where the Civil War ended when Robert E. Lee surrendered to Ulysses S. Grant.

THE SHENANDOAH VALLEY   Some of Virginia's most striking scenery is along the Skyline Drive, which follows the crest of the Blue Ridge Mountains through Shenandoah National Park, where visitors will find a host of hiking paths, including part of the famed Appalachian Trail. Down below, towns like Winchester, Staunton, and Lexington evoke the Civil War, which ebbed and flowed over the rolling countryside of the Shenandoah Valley, the South's breadbasket. Nearby are the famous mineral waters of Warm Springs and Hot Springs.

THE SOUTHWEST HIGHLANDS   The vibrant city of Roanoke is the gateway to the highlands of Virginia's southwestern extremity, a land of untouched forests, waterfalls, and quiet streams. Here sits the state's highest point, Mount Rogers, surrounded by a national recreation area teeming with trails for hiking, mountain biking, and horseback riding. Down in the Great Valley of Virginia, the historic town of Abingdon features the famous Barter Theatre, begun during the Great Depression when its company traded tickets for hams.

RICHMOND   The state capital has few rivals among U.S. cities for its wealth of historic associations, among them St. John's Church, where Patrick Henry made his famous "Give me liberty, or give me death" speech. Fine arts and science museums, cafes, lively concerts, and theater add to Richmond's cosmopolitan ambience. Military buffs can tour the Richmond and Petersburg battlefield sites, and children can get their kicks at nearby Paramount's Kings Dominion amusement park.

WILLIAMSBURG, YORKTOWN, & JAMESTOWN   Coastal Virginia's "Historic Triangle" is one of the country's most visited areas, and with good reason. Colonial Williamsburg's 173 acres re-create Virginia's colonial capital. Yorktown commemorates the last, victorious battle of the American Revolution in 1781, and Jamestown is where America's first permanent English settlers arrived in 1607. Adding to its allure are two theme parks and world-class discount shopping.

HAMPTON ROADS & THE EASTERN SHORE   The port area of Hampton Roads includes cosmopolitan Norfolk, shipbuilding Newport News, historic Hampton, and Virginia Beach with its 20 miles of white-sand beach, boardwalk, and nearby historic homes. The 17-mile–long Chesapeake Bay Bridge-Tunnel links Norfolk to the Eastern Shore, an unspoiled sanctuary noted for the charming village of Chincoteague and nearby Assateague Island, whose wildlife refuge and national seashore have protected the famous wild ponies and prevented any development on almost 40 miles of pristine beach.

2 Virginia Today

The memory of the state's past still exerts its influence, as it surely must in all towns where descendants of America's first patriots still live and where the homes, monuments, and battlefields that shaped the country's history compose their daily landscape. But Virginians look ahead, past their historical treasures, to an exciting future, as their cities undergo dramatic downtown renewals and scenic mountains and beach resorts become vacation meccas for visitors to the Old Dominion.

TOBACCO & OTHER INDUSTRIES   Although colonist John Rolfe is best remembered today for marrying Pocahontas, the tobacco industry he helped found is still important to Virginia's economy, despite its recent troubles. Besides tobacco, other local farm income is based on the apple orchards of the Shenandoah Valley; livestock, dairy farming, and poultry raising in the Piedmont; and the state's famous Smithfield hams and peanuts from the Tidewater country. Industry continues to grow as well, notably in the manufacturing of clothes, chemicals, furniture, and transportation equipment.

Impressions

To be a Virginian, either by birth, marriage, adoption, or even on one's mother's side, is an introduction to any state in the union, a passport to any foreign country, and a benediction from the almighty God.

—Anonymous

❓ Did You Know?

- The only brothers to sign the Declaration of Independence were Richard Henry Lee and Francis Lightfoot Lee.
- Virginia Beach's innovative recycling program created "Mount Trashmore," a mountain of trash that's now a children's playground.
- Robert E. Lee's faithful horse, Traveller, is buried just outside the general's crypt on the campus of Washington and Lee University in Lexington.
- More Americans lost their lives in the Civil War than in World Wars I and II combined.
- Over 60% of the Civil War was fought in Virginia.
- Stonewall Jackson acquired his nickname in the first Battle of Manassas, when General Lee, marveling at his persistence in standing his ground, exclaimed, "There stands Jackson, like a stone wall!"
- Playwright George Bernard Shaw, when paid a ham by the Barter Theatre, returned it for spinach because he was a vegetarian.
- There are more miles of trout streams than roads in Virginia.
- Elected in 1912, Woodrow Wilson was the first southern-born president since the Civil War.
- The world's largest office building, the Pentagon, contains more than 6.5 million square feet of space and almost 18 miles of corridors.
- Virginia's motto, *Sic Semper Tyrannus,* translated from the Latin means "Thus Always to Tyrants."
- Virginia is known as the "Mother of Presidents" because eight U.S. presidents were born here: George Washington, Thomas Jefferson, James Madison, James Monroe, both William Henry and Benjamin Harrison, John Tyler, and Woodrow Wilson.
- The Norfolk Naval Base is the world's largest naval facility.

MODERN POLITICS   Prominent in Virginia Tidewater plantation society since the 1600s, the Byrd family dominated the state's politics from World War I until the 1980s. Under their conservative control, the "Mother of Presidents" virtually withdrew from national leadership. The state government vigorously fought federally mandated public school integration in the 1950s, with one county actually closing its schoolhouse doors rather than admitting African Americans to previously all-white institutions. Although racial relations have improved, many white Richmonders were incensed in 1995 when the city council's African-American majority voted to place a statue of tennis star and Richmond native Arthur Ashe among those of Confederate heroes lining Monument Avenue.

Today, Virginia's politics are about evenly split between Democrats and Republicans, with the statehouse regularly changing hands. Democrat L. Douglas Wilder became the nation's first elected African-American governor in 1989. Republican George Allen—son of the famous professional football coach—took the mansion back in 1993, but Virginia voters also handed Democrat Charles Robb—son-in-law of President Lyndon B. Johnson—a senatorial victory over controversial Iran-Contra figure Oliver North.

3 A Look at the Past

Dateline

- **1607** First permanent English settlement in New World established at Jamestown.
- **1612** John Rolfe begins cultivation of tobacco for export.
- **1619** House of Burgesses—first representative legislative body in New World—meets in Jamestown. First Africans arrive at Jamestown as indentured servants.
- **1624** Virginia becomes a royal colony.
- **1652** Burgesses affirm that only they have right to elect officers of Virginia colony.
- **1682** Tobacco riots protest falling crop prices.
- **1699** Virginia's government moves to Williamsburg.
- **1754** French and Indian War begins as George Washington leads Virginia troops against French in Ohio Valley.
- **1755** Washington takes command of Virginia army on frontier.
- **1765** Patrick Henry protests Stamp Act, saying, "If this be treason, make the most of it."
- **1774** First Virginia Convention meets and sends delegates to Continental Congress.
- **1775** Patrick Henry incites rebellion with his "Liberty or Death" oration at Virginia Convention in Richmond. Washington chosen leader of army by Continental Congress.
- **1776** Patrick Henry elected first governor of self-declared free state of Virginia. Thomas Jefferson's wording for Declaration of Independence adopted by Congress.
- **1779** State capital moved to Richmond.
- **1781** Cornwallis surrenders at Yorktown.

continues

Virginia's history began on April 26, 1607, when 104 English men and boys arrived at Cape Henry on the Virginia coast aboard the *Susan Constant,* the *Godspeed,* and the *Discovery.* The expedition—an attempt to compete with profitable Spanish encroachments in the New World—was sponsored by the Virginia Company of London and supported by King James I.

A MODEST BEGINNING   The travelers were lured by promises of wealth. Upon arrival, they were heartened to find, if not streets paved with gold, at least an abundance of fish and game. Their optimism was short-lived, however, for they were attacked by American Indians on the very day of their arrival. Fleeing Cape Henry, they settled on Jamestown Island, which offered greater protection from the Spanish and the Indians. Unfortunately, most were gentlemen, unaccustomed to work of any kind and with little inclination or aptitude for it. As one on-the-scene chronicler described it, "a world of miseries ensewed." An unfamiliar climate, contaminated water, famine, disease, and Indian attacks claimed their victims, and by autumn only 50 remained alive.

The Native Americans were ambivalent about the new arrivals. When Capt. John Smith tried to barter for corn and grain, they took him prisoner and carried him to Chief Powhatan. According to legend, they would have killed him, but Powhatan's teenage daughter, the beautiful princess Pocahontas, interceded and saved his life. However, Smith was not much of a diplomat in dealing with natives; he helped sow seeds of dissension that would result in centuries of hostility between the tribes and the European settlers.

In 1613, John Rolfe (who later married Pocahontas) took a new aromatic tobacco from the New World to England. The settlers had discovered not the glittery gold they expected, but the "golden weed" that would be the foundation of Virginia's fortunes.

The year 1619 was marked by several important happenings: The Virginia Company sent a shipload of 90 women to suitors who had paid their transportation costs, 22 burgesses were elected to set up the first legislative body in the New World, and 20 Africans arrived in a Dutch ship to work as indentured servants, a precursor of slavery.

In 1699, the capital of the colony was moved from Jamestown, which had suffered a disastrous fire, to the planned town of Williamsburg, and it was from

Williamsburg that colonial patriots launched some of the first strong protests against Parliament.

COLONIAL LIFE By the mid-18th century, the growth of vast tobacco plantations along Tidewater Virginia's rivers brought with it a concurrent increase in the importation of slaves from Africa as the base for the "plantation economy."

The French and Indian War in the 1750s proved to be a training ground for America's Revolutionary forces. When the French built outposts in territory claimed by Virginia, the Colonial Governor sent George Washington to protect Virginia's claims. In the field, Washington acquitted himself with honor, and after General Braddock's defeat, he was appointed commander-in-chief of Virginia's army on the frontier.

UNREST GROWS Expenses from the war and economic hardships led the British to increase taxes in the colonies, and protests in Virginia and Massachusetts escalated. The 1765 Stamp Act met with general resistance. Patrick Henry inspired the Virginia House of Burgesses to pass the Virginia Resolves, setting forth colonial rights according to constitutional principles. The young orator exclaimed, "If this be treason, make the most of it." The Stamp Act was repealed in 1766, but the Townshend Revenue Acts of 1767, which included the hated tax on tea, exacerbated tensions.

Ties among the colonies were strengthened when Virginia's burgesses, led by Richard Henry Lee, created a standing committee to communicate their problems in dealing with England to similar committees in the other colonies. When the Boston Post Bill closed that harbor in punishment for the Boston Tea Party, the Virginia General Assembly moved swiftly. Although Governor Dunmore had dissolved the legislature, it met at Raleigh Tavern and recommended that a general congress be held annually. Virginia sent seven representatives to the First Continental Congress in 1774, among them Lee, Patrick Henry, and George Washington.

The following year, Patrick Henry made a fiery plea for arming Virginia's militia. He concluded his argument with these now-familiar words: "Is life so dear, or peace so sweet, as to be purchased at the price of chains and slavery? Forbid it, Almighty God! I know not what course others may take; but as for me, give me liberty, or give me death!"

Later in 1775, upon hearing news of the battles of Lexington and Concord, the Second Continental Congress in Philadelphia voted to make the conflict

- **1787** Washington elected president of Constitutional Convention.
- **1788** Virginia ratifies Constitution.
- **1789** Washington inaugurated as first president. Virginia cedes area to U.S. for seat of government.
- **1801** Thomas Jefferson inaugurated president.
- **1803** Jefferson sends James Monroe to France for purchase of Louisiana Territory.
- **1809** James Madison inaugurated president.
- **1814** President and Dolley Madison flee to Virginia as British enter Washington.
- **1831** Nat Turner's slave rebellion.
- **1832** House of Delegates bill to abolish slavery in Virginia loses by seven votes.
- **1859** John Brown hanged after failed raid on Harpers Ferry Arsenal.
- **1861** Richmond chosen as Confederate capital. First battle of Manassas.
- **1862** First ironclad ships, *Monitor* and *Merrimac,* battle in Hampton Roads harbor. Confederate victories at Second Manassas and Fredericksburg.
- **1863** Stonewall Jackson fatally wounded at Chancellorsville.
- **1864** Confederacy wins Battle of the Wilderness at Spotsylvania Court House near Fredericksburg. Grant's siege of Petersburg begins.
- **1865** Richmond evacuated. Lee surrenders at Appomattox.
- **1867** Virginia put under military rule of Reconstruction Act. Confederate president Jefferson Davis imprisoned for treason in Fort Monroe.
- **1870** Virginia readmitted to Union.

continues

- **1900** Legislature passes "Jim Crow" segregation laws.
- **1902** Poll tax in new state constitution effectively keeps African Americans from voting.
- **1913** Woodrow Wilson inaugurated president.
- **1917** Wilson leads America into war against Germany. Growth of Hampton Roads naval and military installations.
- **1954** Supreme Court school integration ruling leads to school closings to avoid compliance with law.
- **1989** L. Douglas Wilder, nation's first African-American governor, takes office in Richmond.
- **1994** Senator Charles Robb defeats challenge from controversial Republican Oliver North.

near Boston a colony-wide confrontation and chose Washington as commander of the Continental Army. War had begun.

BIRTH OF THE NATION   On June 12, 1776, the Virginia Convention, meeting in Williamsburg, adopted George Mason's Virginia Declaration of Rights and instructed Virginia's delegates to the Continental Congress to propose independence for the colonies. Mason's revolutionary document stated that "all power is vested in, and consequently derived from, the people," and that "all men are created free and independent, and have certain inherent rights . . . : among which are the enjoyment of life and liberty, with the means of acquiring and possessing property." He also firmly upheld the right of trial by jury, freedom of the press, and the right of all people to freedom of religion. When the Congress meeting in Philadelphia adopted Thomas Jefferson's Declaration of Independence (based on Mason's declaration) on July 4, 1776, the United States of America was born.

The Revolution was a bloody 7-year conflict marked by many staggering defeats for the patriots. Historians believe it was only the superb leadership and determination of Gen. George Washington that inspired the Continental Army (a ragtag group of farmers, laborers, backwoodsmen, and merchants) to continue so long in the face of overwhelming odds.

VICTORY AT YORKTOWN   Although many Virginians were in Washington's army, it was not until the war's final years that the state became a major battleground. The turning point came in March 1781, when British General Lord Cornwallis established a base at the York River.

Two weeks after Cornwallis settled into Yorktown for the winter, General Washington received word from a French admiral, the Comte de Grasse, that he was taking his squadron to the Chesapeake Bay and that his men and ships were at Washington's disposal through October 15. After conferring with the Comte de Rochambeau, commander of the French troops in America, Washington decided to march 450 miles to Virginia with the object of defeating Cornwallis.

Meanwhile, on September 5, 1781, a fleet of 19 British ships under Adm. Thomas Graves appeared at the entrance to Chesapeake Bay with the aim of reinforcing Cornwallis's Yorktown entrenchment. They were met by 24 French ships under de Grasse. Though the battle ended in a stalemate, Graves was forced to return to New York to repair his ships. The French remained to block further British reinforcements or the possibility of their escape by water, while the French and American armies under Washington neared Yorktown to block aid or escape by land.

The siege began on September 28 when 17,000 men under Washington occupied a line encircling the town. The allied army, spread out in camps extending 6 miles, dug siege lines and bombarded the redcoats with heavy cannonfire. British defeat was inevitable. On October 17, a cease-fire was called, and a British officer was led to American lines, where he requested an armistice. Although the war was not officially over until the Treaty of Paris was signed 2 years later, Cornwallis's defeat effectively marked the colonists' victory.

FRAMING THE CONSTITUTION   The new nation's governmental powers were weak, resting on the inadequate provisions of the Articles of Confederation. To remedy the situation, a Constitutional Convention met in Philadelphia, and Washington was elected president of the Convention. He and fellow Virginian James Madison fought to have the new Constitution include a Bill of Rights and gradual abolition of the slave trade. Although both measures were defeated, the two Virginians voted to adopt the Constitution, feeling that its faults could be amended later.

In 1788, Virginia became the 10th state to ratify the Constitution, and by 1791 the first 10 amendments—the Bill of Rights—had been added. Madison was author of the first 9 amendments, and Richard Henry Lee, the 10th.

THE COUNTRY'S EARLY VIRGINIAN PRESIDENTS   Washington was elected president under the new Constitution and took office on April 30, 1789.

As third president of the United States, Jefferson nearly doubled the size of the country by purchasing the Louisiana Territory from Napoleon.

James Madison took office as president in 1809. Unable to maintain Jefferson's peacekeeping efforts in the face of continued provocations by England, Madison was swayed by the popular demand for armed response, and in 1812 Congress declared war. Although some coastal plantations were attacked by British warships, the only suffering Virginia witnessed was the burning of nearby Washington, D.C.

James Monroe followed, having already served Virginia and the nation in many capacities. During his two terms as president, the nation pushed westward, and he faced the first struggle over the slavery question (which resulted in the Missouri Compromise), established the Monroe Doctrine, and settled the nation's boundary with Canada.

THE CIVIL WAR   It was not long before the United States became a nation divided. The issues were states' rights, slavery, and the conflicting goals of an industrial North and an agricultural South. In 1859, John Brown and his small band of followers raided the arsenal at Harpers Ferry (now West Virginia) to procure arms for a slave revolt he hoped to instigate. Brown was captured and hanged. In the North, his execution rallied support for the abolitionist cause; in the South, people shuddered at the threat of a slave revolt.

The election of 1860 was crucial. The Republicans nominated Abraham Lincoln, whom the South vowed it would not accept, but the Democrats split and Lincoln was elected. Seven states seceded—Texas, Louisiana, South Carolina, Alabama, Georgia, Florida, and Mississippi. At his inauguration, Lincoln declared, "In your hands, my dissatisfied fellow countrymen, and not in mine, is the momentous issue of civil war. You can have no oath registered in heaven to destroy the government, while I have the solemn one to preserve, protect, and defend it."

On April 12, 1861, guns sounded at Fort Sumter in Charleston harbor. Secession had become war.

FIRST MANASSAS   In May 1861, the Confederate capital was transferred to Richmond, only 100 miles from Washington. Virginia was doomed to become the first major battleground of the Civil War. The first of six heavy offensives by the North against Richmond was decisively repulsed on July 21, 1861, at the battle of First Manassas (Bull Run). Union Gen. Irvin McDowell's 35,000 ill-trained federal volunteers marched southward to the cry "Onward to Richmond," and the following Union attacks were successful. Later, however, a stonewall-like stand by the Virginia Brigade of Gen. Thomas J. Jackson swept McDowell's forces back to Washington. In addition to the victory, the South had found a new hero—"Stonewall" Jackson. Total casualties in this first major engagement of the war: 4,828 men! It was apparent that this would be a long and bitter conflict.

THE PENINSULAR CAMPAIGN   The second major offensive against Richmond, the Peninsular Campaign, devised by Union Gen. George B. McClellan, was the setting for the most famous naval engagement in the western hemisphere. On March 9, 1862, two ironclad vessels, the U.S.S. *Monitor* and the C.S.S. *Virginia* (formerly the *Merrimac*), pounded each other with cannons. Although the battle was a draw, the advent of ironclad warships heralded a new era in naval history.

Two months later, Yorktown was reduced to rubble and the Union army advanced up the peninsula. The Confederates retreated until they were only 9 miles from Richmond. At that point they fought, and the Confederate leader, General Johnson, was badly wounded. Robert E. Lee was appointed head of the army of Virginia. Personally opposed to secession, Lee had sadly resigned his commission in the U.S. Army when Virginia joined the Confederacy, saying, "My heart is broken, but I cannot raise my sword against Virginia." In a series of victories beginning on June 26, 1862, Lee finally defeated the Union armies. Richmond had again been saved.

SECOND MANASSAS, FREDERICKSBURG & CHANCELLORSVILLE
The third Union drive against Richmond was repulsed at Manassas, where Gen. Robert E. Lee secured his place in history by soundly defeating 70,000 Union troops under Gen. John Pope with a Confederate army of 55,000 men in 3 days. On December 13, 1862, Gen. Ambrose Burnside, newly chosen head of the Army of the Potomac, crossed the Rappahannock and struck Fredericksburg while Lee's army was scattered in northern Virginia. The federal advance was so slow that by the time the Union armies moved, Lee's forces were firmly entrenched in the hills south of the city. Burnside was unsuccessful, and the fourth Union drive against Richmond was turned back.

Gen. Joseph Hooker took command of the Union army early in 1863, and, once again, federal forces attempted to take Richmond. Fighting raged for 4 days. The Union army retreated, and the fifth drive on Richmond failed. But Lee's victory was costly. In addition to heavy casualties, Stonewall Jackson was wounded by his own troops and died of complications resulting from the amputation of his arm. Without Jackson, Lee began his second invasion of the North, which would end in the small Pennsylvania town of Gettysburg.

A WAR OF ATTRITION   In March 1864, Grant was put in command of all federal armies. His plan for victory called for "a war of attrition"—total unrelenting warfare that would put constant pressure on all points of the Confederacy. The first great confrontation between Lee and Grant, the Battle of the Wilderness, resulted in a Confederate victory, but the South's casualties were high—11,400. The Richmond campaign was the heaviest fighting of the Civil War. Three times Grant tried and failed to interpose his forces between Lee and Richmond. More than 80,000 men were killed and wounded.

LAYING SIEGE TO PETERSBURG   Still determined, Grant secretly moved his army across the James River toward Petersburg, an important rail junction south of Richmond. Improvised Southern forces managed to hold the city until Lee arrived. Grant then resorted to ever-tightening siege operations. Blocked in his trenches, Lee could not leave Grant's front. To do so would be to abandon Petersburg and Richmond. Subjected to hunger and exposure, the Confederate will to resist began to wane, and periodic skirmishes further weakened Confederate morale.

Lee, hoping to divert Grant's attention, dispatched a small army under Jubal Early to the menaced Shenandoah Valley. Grant instructed Union Gen. Philip Sheridan: "The Shenandoah is to be so devastated that crows flying across it for the balance of the season will have to bring their own provender." The second valley campaign resulted in the destruction of Early's army and the Shenandoah Valley.

LAST DAYS OF WAR   Back in Petersburg, Grant's attrition strategy was succeeding. For the Army of Northern Virginia, the 10-month siege of that city meant physical hardship, disease, filth, dwindling morale, and tedious waiting for the inevitable onslaught. It came on April 1, 1865, when federal forces smashed through weakened Confederate lines at Five Forks; Petersburg fell, and Richmond was occupied by federal forces. Lee's last hope was to rendezvous with Joe Johnson's army, which was retreating through North Carolina before Sherman's advance. On April 8, however, the vanguard of Grant's army succeeded in reaching Appomattox Court House ahead of Lee, thus blocking the Confederates' last escape route.

On April 9, 1865, the Civil War ended in Virginia at Appomattox, in Wilbur McLean's farmhouse. Grant, so uncompromising in war, proved compassionate in peace. All Confederate soldiers were permitted to return home on parole, cavalrymen could keep their horses, and officers could retain their sidearms. Rations were provided at once for the destitute Southerners. Accepting these generous terms, Lee surrendered his 28,000 soldiers, the ragged remnants of the once-mighty Army of Northern Virginia. Lee's farewell was moving in its simplicity: "I earnestly pray that a merciful God will extend to you his blessing and protection. With an unceasing admiration of your constancy and devotion to your country, and a grateful remembrance of your kind and generous consideration for myself, I bid you all an affectionate farewell."

RECOVERY & RENEWAL   To a state devastated by a conflict that pitted brother against brother, recovery was slow. Besides the physical and psychological damages of the conflict, the Reconstruction era brought Virginia under federal military control until 1870.

By the turn of the century, however, Virginia's economic growth was characterized by new railroad lines connecting remote country areas in the west with urban centers. Factories were bringing more people to the cities, and the economy, once based entirely on agriculture, now had a growing industrial base. The great ports enjoyed growing importance as steamship traffic carried an increasing volume of commercial freight. During this period, the scholar, author, and educator Booker T. Washington, who had been born in slavery, studied at Virginia's Hampton Institute and achieved fame as an advisor to presidents.

Virginia-born Woodrow Wilson was serving as governor of New Jersey at the time he was elected president in 1912. Although noted for his peace-loving ideals, Wilson saw the entry of the United States into World War I in 1917. War brought prosperity to Virginia with new factories and munitions plants and the expansion of military-training camps throughout the state.

World War II brought a population explosion, with men and women of the armed forces flocking to northern Virginia suburbs near Washington, D.C., and the port area of Hampton Roads. Many of these people stayed after the war, and by 1955 the majority of Virginians were urban dwellers. Today, the state's population is about 6.5 million.

4 Recommended Books, Films, Videos & Recordings

BOOKS
BIOGRAPHIES & AUTOBIOGRAPHIES

Brodie, Fawn M., *Thomas Jefferson: An Intimate Portrait,* (Norton, 1974).
Freeman, Douglas Southall, *George Washington,* (7 vols., 1948–57; abridged 1-vol. edition, Macmillan, 1985).

Freeman, Douglas Southall, *Lee,* (4 vols., 1935; abridged 1-vol. edition, Macmillan, 1985).

Malone, Dumas, *Jefferson and His Times,* (6 vols.; Little, Brown, 1948–81).

Van Woodward, C., ed, *Mary Chestnut's Civil War,* (Yale University Press, 1982). Pulitzer Prize–winning autobiography.

Washington, Booker T., *Up from Slavery,* (1903; reprinted by Doubleday, 1963).

NOVELS

Adams, Richard, *Traveller* (Dell, 1989). About General Lee's horse.

Bontemps, Arna, *Black Thunder* (1936; reprinted by Beacon, 1968). Based on Gabriel Prosser's slave uprising in Richmond in 1800.

Cather, Willa, *Sapphira and the Slave Girl* (1940; reprinted by Vintage, 1975).

Crane, Stephen, *Red Badge of Courage* (1895; Bantam, 1981).

Glasgow, Ellen, *The Voice of the People* (1900; Irvington, 1972).

Styron, William, *The Confessions of Nat Turner* (1967; Bantam, 1981).

HISTORY

Dabney, Virginius, *Virginia, The New Dominion* (University Press of Virginia, 1971).

Foote, Shelby, *The Civil War* (3 vols., 1963–74; Vintage, 3 vols., 1986).

Ward, Geoffrey C., with Ric Burns and Ken Burns, *The Civil War* (Knopf, 1990).

Wheeler, Richard, *Witness to Appomattox* (HarperCollins, 1991).

GENERAL

Dillard, Annie, *Pilgrim at Tinker Creek* (Harper & Row, 1974).

Hume, Ivor Noel, *Martin's Hundred* (Knopf, 1982).

Jefferson, Thomas, *Notes on the State of Virginia* (1787; reprinted by Norton, 1982).

Loth, Calder, *The Virginia Landmarks Register* (3rd ed.; University Press of Virginia, 1986).

Peters, Margaret T., comp, *A Guidebook to Virginia's Historical Markers* (University Press of Virginia, 1985).

FILM & VIDEO

Brother Rat (1938), with Jane Wyman and Ronald Reagan, depicting cadet life at the Virginia Military Institute.

The Civil War (1990), with Colleen Dewhurst, Morgan Freeman, Jason Robards, and Sam Waterston; PBS series directed by Ken Burns.

Dirty Dancing (1987), with Jennifer Grey and Patrick Swayze; filmed at Mountain Lake Resort.

Silence of the Lambs (1990), with Jodie Foster and Anthony Hopkins; filmed at Quantico, Va.

Sommersby (1993), with Jodie Foster and Richard Gere; filmed in Lexington, Warm Springs, and Bath County.

Trail of the Lonesome Pine (1936), with Fred MacMurray, Henry Fonda, and Sylvia Sidney; based on John Fox's romantic tale set in an Appalachian mining village.

RECORDINGS

The Civil War: Its Music and Its Sounds, Philip's Mercury (1991).

Original Sound-track Recordings: The Civil War, Elektra Nonesuch (1991).

Planning a Trip to Virginia

This chapter is devoted to the where, when, and how of your trip to Virginia. Whether you plan to stay a day, a week, 2 weeks, or longer, there are many choices you'll need to make *before* leaving home. All this, and more, can be found in the sections that follow.

1 Visitor Information

The **Virginia Tourism Corporation,** 901 E. Byrd St. (P.O. Box 798), Richmond, VA 23219 (☎ **800/VISIT-VA** or 804/786-2051; fax 804/786-1919; www.virginia.org; e-mail: vainfo@vedp.state. va.us), is the best source for information about the entire state. It publishes or distributes a host of information, including a statewide travel planner; official state highway maps showing all roads or just the scenic routes; an up-to-date calendar of events; lists of all hotels and motels and those that accept pets; a list of country inns and bed-and-breakfasts; an outdoor guide to the state; a golf directory; a state park directory; a list of Virginia wineries and wine festivals; and a guide for travelers with disabilities.

The corporation also operates information offices in **Washington, D.C.,** at 1629 K St. NW (☎ 202/659-5523); in the **United Kingdom** at Department WS, 1st Floor, 182/184 Addington Road, Selsdon, Surrey CR2 8LB (☎ 0181-651-4743; fax 0181-651-5702); in **Germany** at Fremdenverkehrsamt Virginia, Department 102, Steinweg 3, D-60313 Frankfurt (☎ 069-291923; fax 069-291904); and in **Japan** at Grand Spot No. 203, 22-17 Sakuragaokacho, Shibuya-ku, Tokyo 150 (☎ 03/3462-4493; fax 03/3462-4494).

If you're driving into Virginia, you can stop at roadside **Welcome Centers** in Bracey, on I-85 near the North Carolina border; Bristol, on I-81 near the Tennessee border; Clear Brook, on I-81 near the West Virginia border; Covington, on I-64 near the West Virginia border; New Church, on U.S. 13 at the Maryland border; Fredericksburg, on I-95 southbound; Lambsburg, on I-77; Manassas, on I-66; Rocky Gap, on I-77; and Skippers, on I-95.

2 When to Go

Virginia is a gorgeous place in October, when the Indian summer weather is at its finest and the turning leaves blaze orange, red, and yellow across the state. Throngs of visitors mob the mountains to see the autumn foliage during this "leaf season." (You can find out the approximate dates for peak color by calling ☎ **800/434-5323** for the Shenandoah Valley, ☎ **540/999-3500** for Shenandoah National Park and the Skyline Drive, and ☎ **704/298-0398** for Virginia's portion of the Blue Ridge Parkway.)

Otherwise, Virginia is busiest during summer, when the historic sites, theme parks, and beaches draw millions of visitors from around the world—and hotel rates are at their highest. The least crowded—and least expensive—time to visit is in spring. Fortunately, that's when the dogwoods, azaleas, and wildflowers are in a riot of bloom from one end of Virginia to the other.

THE CLIMATE

Virginia enjoys four distinct seasons, with some variations in temperature from the warmer, more humid coastal areas to the cooler climate in the mountains. Wintertime snows are usually confined to northern Virginia and the mountains. In summer, extremely hot and humid spells can last several weeks, but are normally short-lived. Spring and autumn are long seasons, and in terms of natural beauty and heavenly climate, they're optimum times to visit. Annual rainfall averages 46 inches; annual snowfall, 18 inches.

Virginia's Average Temperatures

	Jan	Feb	Mar	Apr	May	June	July	Aug	Sept	Oct	Nov	Dec
High (°F)	44	46	56	68	75	84	90	88	81	69	57	47
Low (°F)	26	27	38	45	54	62	66	65	59	48	39	28

VIRGINIA CALENDAR OF EVENTS

January

- **Historic Birthday Parties,** Lexington. The historic town throws a birthday bash for its Civil War heroes, Robert E. Lee and Stonewall Jackson. Call ☎ **540/643-3777.** Mid-January.
- **Wildlife Arts Festival,** Newport News. Artists display and sell stained glass, carvings, oils, watercolors, and photography, all with a wildlife theme. Call ☎ **757/595-1900.** Mid-January.
- **Lee Birthday Celebrations,** Alexandria. Period music, plus house tours at Lee-Fendall House and Lee's boyhood home. Call ☎ **703/548-1789.** Fourth Sunday in January. Also, open house at Stratford Hall on the Northern Neck, Lee's birthplace. January 19.

February

- **Antiques Forum,** Williamsburg. Lectures and workshops on 18th-century life. Call ☎ **800/603-0948.** First week in February.
- **Maymont Flower and Garden Show,** Richmond. A breath of spring, with landscape exhibits, vendors, and speakers. Call ☎ **804/358-7166.** Early February.
- ✪ **George Washington Birthday Events,** Alexandria. Black-tie or colonial-costume Saturday evening dinner, followed by birth-night ball at Gadsby's Tavern, where George and Martha Washington attended balls in 1798 and 1799. On Sunday, Revolutionary War encampment at Fort Ward, featuring a skirmish between British and colonial uniformed troops. Parade on Monday. Call ☎ **703/838-5005** for information and tickets. Presidents' Day weekend.
- **George Washington's Birthday Party,** Fredericksburg. Reduced rates at attractions. Call ☎ **540/373-1569.** Monday of Washington's Birthday weekend.

March

- **James Madison's Birthday,** Montpelier. Ceremony at cemetery and reception at house. Call ☎ **540/672-2728.** March 16.
- **Patrick Henry Speech Reenactment,** St. John's Church, Richmond. "Give me liberty or give me death," he said here. Call ☎ **804/648-5015.** Closest Sunday to March 23.
- ✪ **Highland Maple Festival,** Monterey. See maple syrup produced, pour it over pancakes, and visit one of the state's largest crafts shows. Call ☎ **540/468-2550** for information. Second and third weekends in March.

April

- **Thomas Jefferson's Birthday Commemoration,** Monticello, Charlottesville. Wreath-laying ceremony at gravesite, fife-and-drum corps, and a speaker. Call ☎ **804/984-9822.** April 13.
- ✪ **International Azalea Festival,** Norfolk. The brilliant beauty of azaleas in bloom is the backdrop for ceremonies in the Norfolk Botanical Garden saluting NATO countries, including the crowning of a queen who reigns at a parade and other festivities. Also features a military display that includes an air show, visiting of ships, and aircraft ground exhibits. Call ☎ **757/622-2312.** Second to third week in April.
- **Virginia Horse Festival,** Virginia Horse Center, Lexington. All breeds are showcased with demonstrations, events, seminars, sales, and equine art and merchandise. Call ☎ **540/463-2194.** Third weekend in April.
- ✪ **Historic Garden Week in Virginia,** statewide. The event of the year—a celebration with tours of the grounds and gardens of some 200 Virginia landmarks, including plantations and other sites open only during this week. For information contact the **Garden Club of Virginia,** 12 E. Franklin St., Richmond, VA 23219 (☎ **804/644-7776** or 804/643-7141; www.vagardenweek.org). Last full week in April.

May

- ✪ **Shenandoah Apple Blossom Festival,** Winchester. Acres of orchards in blossom throughout the valley, plus 5 days of music, band competitions, parades, coronation of the queen, footraces, arts and crafts sale, midway amusements, and a carnival, with a celebrity grand marshal. Contact **Festival,** 5 N. Cameron St., Winchester, VA 22601 (☎ **703/662-3863**). Usually first weekend in May.
- **Virginia Gold Cup Race Meet,** Great Meadow Course, The Plains. Everyone dresses to the nines for the state's premier steeplechase event. Call ☎ **540/347-2612.** First Saturday in May.
- **Seafood Festival,** Tom's Cove, Chincoteague. All you can eat—a seafood lover's dream come true. Must get tickets in advance from **Eastern Shore Chamber of Commerce,** P.O. Drawer R, Melfa, VA 23410 (☎ **804/787-2460**). First weekend in May.
- **George Mason Day,** Gunston Hall, Lorton. All-day celebration with music and costumed role-players portraying Mason's daily life and concern for the Bill of Rights. Call ☎ **703/550-9220.** May 5.
- **Jamestown Landing Day,** Jamestown. Militia presentations and sailing demonstrations celebrate the first settlers. Call ☎ **757/253-4838.** Early May.
- **New Market Battlefield Historical Park,** New Market. Reenactment of battle. Call ☎ **540/740-3101.** Second Sunday in May.
- **New Market Day,** Virginia Military Institute Campus, Lexington. Annual roll call for cadets who died in the battle. Call ☎ **540/464-7207.** May 15.
- **Oatlands Sheepdog Trials,** Leesburg. Dogs compete in sheepherding contests. Crafts, food, and house and garden tours. Call ☎ **703/777-3174.** Late May.

○ **Virginia Hunt Country Stable Tour,** Loudon County. A unique opportunity to view prestigious Leesburg, Middleburg, and Upperville horse farms and private estates. Ticket information at **Trinity Church,** Upperville (near Middleburg) (☎ **703/592-3711**). Late May.

• **Shenandoah Valley Music Festival,** Orkney Springs. Classical to country-and-western fill the mountain air. Call **Orkney Springs Hotel** at ☎ **800/459-3396.** Starts Memorial Day weekend, then weekends through August.

June

• **Vintage Virginia Wine Festival,** Great Meadows Steeplechase Course, The Plains. Taste the premium vintages from 35 wineries at this Hunt Country festival. Arts and crafts displays, food, and jazz, reggae, and pop music. Call ☎ **800/277-CORK** for information about this and many other wine festivals statewide. First weekend in June.

• **Harborfest,** Norfolk. Tall ships, sailboat races, air shows, military demonstrations, and fireworks. Call ☎ **757/627-5329.** First full weekend in June.

• **Boardwalk Art Show,** Virginia Beach. Works in all mediums, between 14th Street and 28th Street along the boardwalk. Call ☎ **757/425-0000.** Mid-June.

○ **James River Bateaux Festival,** Lynchburg. Old-fashioned "bateaux" boats race to Richmond. Music at the riverfront, footraces, games, and historic crafts exhibits and demonstrations. The 8-day festival moves along the James, stopping each night at a historic town along the 200-year-old river route. Call ☎ **804/845-2604.** Second to third week in June.

○ **Ash Lawn-Highland Summer Festival,** Charlottesville. James Monroe's home is the setting for opera, musicals, concerts, and a traditional bonfire finale. Tickets from the box office or in town (☎ **804/293-9539**). End of June to August.

• **Hampton Jazz Festival,** Hampton. Big names perform at Hampton Coliseum. Call ☎ **757/838-4203.** Late June.

July

• **Independence Day Celebrations,** statewide. Every town parties and shoots fireworks in honor of the nation's birthday. Contact local tourist information offices. July 4.

• **Happy Birthday USA,** Staunton. Free concert hosted by the Statler Brothers in Gypsy Hill Park. Call ☎ **540/885-7927.** July 4.

• **Stratford Hall Open House.** Honoring Richard Henry Lee and Francis Lightfoot Lee, the only two brothers to sign the Declaration of Independence. Call ☎ **804/493-8038.** July 4.

○ **Pony Swim and Auction,** Chincoteague. Famous wild horses swim the Assateague Channel, and are later herded to carnival grounds and auctioned off. Return swim to Assateague on Friday. Call ☎ **757/336-6161.** Festival is last 2 weeks in July; swim on last Wednesday in July.

○ **Virginia Highlands Festival,** Abingdon. Appalachian Mountain culture showcase for musicians, artists, artisans, and writers. Area's largest crafts show has antique market and hot-air balloons. Call ☎ **540/623-5266.** Last 2 weekends in July.

August

• **Old Time Fiddlers' Convention,** Galax. Dating to 1935, one of the largest and oldest such conventions in the world. It also coincides with the Fiddlefest street festival. Call ☎ **703/236-8681** for information. Early August.

• **Hot Air Balloon Festival and Flying Circus Airshows,** Bealeton. One of the largest regional conventions of hot-air balloons, plus biplanes barnstorm and offer

---

Virginia's Vinos

When Thomas Jefferson returned home to Charlottesville in 1789 after 5 years in Paris as minister to France, he brought with him a keen appreciation for fine wine. Although Virginians had grown grapes since the early 1600s, there just wasn't enough good wine made here to satisfy Mr. Jefferson's tastes.

Too bad he can't come back to life today, for Jefferson would find his beloved commonwealth dotted with 140 vineyards, with about 10 more springing up every year. Some 50 of them are successful commercial operations, and their vintages are getting better all the time.

You'll find Virginia wines served in many of the state's restaurants, or you can visit the wineries during your tour of the state (look for wine-logo road signs). You can also taste them at wine festivals held in various locations in Virginia almost every weekend, especially in October, the state's official Wine Month.

The Virginia Division of Wine Marketing, P.O. Box 1163, Richmond, VA 23218 (☎ **800/828-4637**), publishes an annual directory of wineries and wine festivals. It's also available from the Virginia Tourism Corporation (see "Visitor Information," above).

---

open-air cockpit rides. Call ☎ **540/439-8661.** Balloon Festival is mid-month; flying circus, weekends May to October.

September

- **American Music Festival,** Virginia Beach. Top entertainers perform on the sand. Tickets are first come, first served. Call ☎ **800/VA-BEACH.** Labor Day weekend.

- **Miller Genuine Draft/Autolite Platinum 200 Auto Race,** Richmond. Two-day stock-car event at the International Raceway. Call ☎ **804/345-7223.** Early September.

- **Budweiser River Ribfest,** Town Point Park, Norfolk. One of the largest free festivals in the east features national, regional, and local artists. Call ☎ **757/441-2345.** Weekend after Labor Day.

- **Southwest Blue Ridge Highlands Storytelling Festival,** Historic Crab Orchard Museum and Pioneer Park, Tazewell. You will hear it all here, or learn to spin your own yarn in workshops. Also, find music for tired ears. Call ☎ **540/988-6755.** Early September.

- **Apple Harvest Arts & Crafts Festival,** Winchester. Bookend to Winchester's apple festival; the fruits are made into butter, pies, and cobblers, but arts and crafts take the spotlight. Square dancing, mountain music, and food, too. Call ☎ **540/662-3996.** Third weekend in September.

- **Northern Neck Seafood Extravaganza,** Ingleside Winery, Oak Grove. Oysters, crabs, shrimp, and clams, all washed down with fine vintages. Call ☎ **804/333-4083.** Third Saturday in September.

- **State Fair of Virginia,** Richmond. Rides, entertainment, agricultural exhibits, pioneer farmstead, and flower shows. At Strawberry Hill Fairgrounds. Call ☎ **804/228-3283.** Ten days in late September.

October

- **Chincoteague Oyster Festival,** Chincoteague. A feast of oysters—but for advance ticket holders only. Call ☎ **804/336-6161.** Early October.

- **Michelob Championship at Kingsmill,** Williamsburg. PGA golfers compete in Virginia's top pro golf tournament. Call ☎ **757/253-3985.** Early October.
- ✪ **Waterford Homes Tour and Crafts Exhibit,** Waterford Village. The tiny Quaker town grows to some 40,000 on this one weekend. Call ☎ **540/882-3085** for tickets. First weekend in October.
- **Yorktown Day.** British surrender in 1781 celebrated with a parade, historic house tours, colonial music and dress, and military drills. Call ☎ **757/253-4838.** October 19.
- **International Gold Cup,** Great Meadows Course, The Plains. Fall colors provide a backdrop to one of the most prestigious steeplechase races. Call ☎ **540/ 253-5001.** Third Saturday in October.
- **Marine Corps Marathon,** Arlington. More than 18,000 men and women run a 26.2-mile course from Arlington through Washington, D.C., and back. The U.S. Marine Corps' "People's Marathon" is open to all (there's even a wheelchair division). Call ☎ **800/786-8762** or 703/784-2225. Third or fourth Sunday in October.

November

- **The First Thanksgiving,** Charles City. Reenactment at Berkeley Plantation. Call ☎ **804/829-6018.** Early November.
- ✪ **Assateague Island Waterfowl Week,** Chincoteague. The only time of the year when visitors can drive to the northern end of Chincoteague National Wildlife Refuge on Assateague Island. Guided walks for pedestrians. Call ☎ **757/ 336-6122.** Thanksgiving weekend.

December

- **Mount Vernon by Candlelight,** Mount Vernon. See Washington's mansion as he would have, by the light of candles. Tickets required. Call ☎ **703/780-2000.** First week in December.
- **Grand Illumination,** Williamsburg. Gala opening of holiday season with fife-and-drum corps, illumination of buildings, caroling, dancing, and fireworks. Call ☎ **800/246-2099.** First Saturday in December.
- **Christmas Candlelight Tour,** Fredericksburg. Call ☎ **540/371-4504.** First weekend in December.
- **Christmas Open House at Point of Honor,** Lynchburg. Call ☎ **804/847-1459.** First Saturday in December.
- **Monticello Candlelight Tour,** Charlottesville. Call ☎ **804/984-9822.** Early December.
- **Historic Michie Tavern Feast and Open House,** Charlottesville. The old tavern puts on two Christmastime feasts. Reservations required. Call ☎ **804/ 977-1234.** Second weekend in December.
- **Jamestown Christmas,** Jamestown. Call ☎ **757/253-4838.** Second to fourth week in December.

3 The Active Vacation Planner

Although Virginia is best known for its multitude of historic sites, it's also home to a host of outdoor activities. You'll find them described in the chapters that follow, but here's a brief overview of the best places to move your muscles, with tips on how to get more detailed information.

The Virginia Tourism Corporation publishes an annual *Virginia Outdoors* magazine that gives a comprehensive rundown of the activities available, a calendar of outdoor events, and a list of the many outfitters and tour companies operating in the state (see "Visitor Information," above).

BICYCLING & MOUNTAIN BIKING   Bicycling is popular throughout Virginia, and with very good reason. Most of the state's scenic highways are open to bicycles: the 105-mile Skyline Drive above the Shenandoah Valley, the 218-mile Blue Ridge Parkway in the Southwest Highlands, and the 22-mile Colonial Parkway between Jamestown and Yorktown, to name the most popular. A bike path follows the scenic George Washington Memorial Parkway for 17 miles along the Potomac River from Arlington to Mount Vernon, the first president's home. Also in northern Virginia, the Washington & Old Dominion Trail begins in Arlington and ends 45 miles away at Purcellville in the rolling hills of the Hunt Country. Two other rails-to-trails parks follow old railroad beds in the Southwest Highlands: the 55-mile New River Trail near Wytheville, and the 34-mile Virginia Creeper Trail in the Mount Rogers National Recreation Area. They go through some of the state's finest mountain scenery. Even in busy Hampton Roads, bikers can ride on their own path along the Virginia Beach boardwalk, then through the natural beauty of First Landing/ Seashore State Park and Back Bay National Wildlife Refuge (and even into the heart of the Great Dismal Swamp). Every road on the flat Eastern Shore is bicycling heaven, especially at Chincoteague and Assateague Island.

Statewide, Virginia is crossed by sections of three major bicycling routes: 150 miles of the Maine-to-Virginia route from Arlington to Richmond (Interstate Bike Route 1); 500 miles of the TransAmerican Bicycle Trail from the Kentucky line to Yorktown (Route 76); and 130 miles of the Virginia-to-Florida route from Richmond to the North Carolina line at Suffolk (Route 17). For strip maps of these routes, contact **Adventure Cycling Association,** P.O. Box 8308, Missoula, MT 59807 (☎ **406/721-1776**).

Mountain bikers can find plenty of trails, especially in Mount Rogers National Recreation Area and in the George Washington and Jefferson National Forests, which occupy large parts of the Shenandoah Valley and the Southwest Highlands. For details about the latter, contact the **George Washington and Jefferson National Forests,** 210 Franklin Rd. SW, Roanoke, VA 24004 (☎ **540/265-6054**). *Mountain Bike Virginia,* by Scott Adams (Beachway Press, 1995), is a very handy atlas to Virginia's best trails, with excellent maps.

For statewide information, contact the **Virginia Department of Transportation's Bicycle Coordinator,** 1401 E. Broad St., Richmond, VA 23219 (☎ **804/ 786-2964**).

BIRD WATCHING   The big bird-watching draws in Virginia are the water-fowl nesting in the flatlands and marshes of the Eastern Shore, all of them on the Atlantic Flyway. Chincoteague National Wildlife Refuge on Assateague Island, the Eastern Shore National Wildlife Refuge (just north of the Chesapeake Bay Bridge-Tunnel), and Back Bay National Wildlife Refuge below Virginia Beach all offer first-rate bird-watching opportunities.

BOATING, CANOEING, KAYAKING & RAFTING   The Chesapeake Bay and its many tributaries, including the Potomac, Rappahannock, York, and James rivers, are perfect for boating. In fact, you can come away from eastern Virginia with the impression that every other home has a boat and trailer sitting in the yard. Marinas also abound in the region, especially on the Northern Neck and in Hampton Roads. Over on the Eastern Shore, you can rent boats to explore the back bays of Chincoteague and Wachapreague. A detailed map showing public access to the Chesapeake and its tributaries is available from the **Virginia Department of**

Conservation and Recreation, 203 Governor St., Suite 302, Richmond, VA 23219 (☎ 804/786-1712).

Canoeing and kayaking enthusiasts can indulge their zeal on the quiet backwaters of the Eastern Shore or on the swiftly running Shenandoah, James, and Maury rivers. The Southern Fork of the Shenandoah River near Front Royal is the state's most popular venue, with the James and Maury rivers near Lexington a close second. During periods of heavy rain—usually spring and late fall—these rivers also have white-water rafting. In fact, the James River makes Richmond the only city in the country with white-water rafting right in town. When the water is low and the weather hot during summer, multitudes cool off by floating down the Shenandoah and other rivers in inner tubes.

FISHING The same waters that are so great for boating also have just about every species of fresh- and saltwater fish imaginable. The best rivers for fishing include the South Fork of the Shenandoah for smallmouth bass and redbreast sunfish; the James for smallmouth bass and catfish; the New for walleye, yellow perch, musky, and smallmouth bass; the Rappahannock for smallmouth bass and catfish; and the Chickahominy for largemouth bass, chain pickerel, bluegill, white perch, and channel catfish. Many of these same species are found in reservoirs such as Lake Anna between Richmond and Fredericksburg; Gaston and Buggs Island lakes on the North Carolina line; Lake Moomaw west of Staunton and Lexington; and Claytor Lake, off I-81 near Pulaski in the Southwest Highlands. The mountains have 2,800 miles of trout streams, many of them stocked annually. From Virginia Beach, Chincoteague, and Wachapreague, you can go on charter and party boats in search of bluefish, flounder, cobia, gray and spotted trout, sharks, and other saltwater fish.

The **Virginia Department of Game and Inland Fisheries,** 4010 W. Broad St., Richmond, VA 23230 (☎ 804/367-1000), publishes an annual freshwater-fishing guide and a regulations pamphlet detailing licensing requirements and regulations. Available at most sporting-goods stores, marinas, and bait shops, licenses are required except on the first Saturday and Sunday in June, which are free fishing days throughout Virginia. The most comprehensive book on the subject is *Virginia Fishing Guide* by Bob Gooch (University Press of Virginia, 1988, 1993).

GOLF You can play golf almost anytime and anywhere in Virginia, given the state's mild climate and more than 130 courses. Williamsburg has some of the best, including the Golden Horseshoe, Green, and Gold courses at the Williamsburg Inn, and the links at Kingsmill Resort, home of the annual PGA Michelob Classic in October. The Homestead's beautiful course in Hot Springs has the nation's oldest first tee, in continuous use since 1890. Wintergreen Resort near Charlottesville also has one of the nation's best courses.

The Virginia Tourism Corporation publishes an annual golf guide listing all the state's courses (see "Visitor Information," above). Another good source is *Virginia Fairways Annual Golf Guide,* published by Richmond Newspapers, Inc., 333 E. Grace St., Richmond, VA 23219 (☎ 804/755-8079; fax 804/775-8019). It costs $4.95.

HIKING & BACKPACKING The same trails that make Virginia so popular with bicyclists (see "Bicycling & Mountain Biking," above) also make it a hiker's heaven. Some 450 miles of the Appalachian Trail snake through Virginia, nearly climbing Mount Rogers and paralleling the Blue Ridge Parkway and the Skyline Drive in many places. The best backcountry trails are in Shenandoah National Park and Mount Rogers National Recreation Area, with less-traveled trails in the George Washington and Jefferson national forests. The state also has several rails-to-trails paths along old railroad beds, the best of which are the Washington & Old Dominion Trail in northern Virginia, and the Virginia Creeper Trail and the New River Trail, both in the Southwest Highlands.

For information and maps of the Appalachian Trail, contact the **Appalachian Trail Conference,** P.O. Box 807, Harpers Ferry, WV 25425-0807 (☎ **304/ 535-6331**). Three good books give trail-by-trail descriptions. *The Trails of Virginia: Hiking the Old Dominion,* by Allen de Hart (University of North Carolina Press, 1995), is the most comprehensive guide to Virginia's trails. *The Hiker's Guide to Virginia,* by Randy Johnson (Falcon Press, 1992), is a slimmer, easier-to-carry volume, as is *Hiking Virginia's National Forests,* by Karin Wuertz-Schaeffer (Globe Pequot Press, 1994), which covers trails in the George Washington and Jefferson National Forests in the Shenandoah Valley and Southwest Highlands.

HORSEBACK RIDING & RACING   Equestrians will find hundreds of miles of public horse trails in Virginia, the majority of them in the Hunt Country of northern Virginia and in the Southwest Highlands. The granddaddy of them all, Virginia Highlands Horse Trail, runs the length of Mount Rogers National Recreation Area, which has campgrounds especially for horse owners. Horses are also permitted on the Virginia Creeper Trail and the New River Trail. You can rent horses at the Mount Rogers National Recreation Area and along the New River Trail. Shenandoah National Park has guided trail rides. For a list of public horse trails and stables statewide, write the **Virginia Horse Council,** P.O. Box 72, Riner, VA 24149.

The Hunt Country and the Piedmont have 25 steeplechase races from spring to fall. The biggest are the Virginia Gold Cup in May and International Gold Cup in October, both at The Plains, in the Hunt Country (see "Virginia Calendar of Events," above). For an annual schedule, write the **Virginia Steeplechase Association,** P.O. Box 1158, Middleburg, VA 22117.

Colonial Downs, in New Kent County between Richmond and Williamsburg (see chapter 10), is the state's only thoroughbred track, with pari-mutuel betting and simulcast racing.

HOT-AIR BALLOONING   The rolling hills of the Hunt Country and central Virginia are beautiful—especially during leaf season in October—when seen from a basket suspended under a hot-air balloon. Among several operators, **United Balloon Ventures** in Bealeton (☎ 540/439-8621) operates weekends from May to October. **Balloons Unlimited** (☎ 540/554-2002) and **Rise and Shine Ballooning** (☎ 540/ 729-0055) both fly over the Hunt Country. You can also go up for a quiet ride from Charlottesville's **Boar's Head Inn** (☎ 800/476-1988 or 804/296-2181). Call the companies well in advance, since reservations are essential and schedules depend on weather conditions.

HUNTING   Believe it or not, Virginia's turkey and white-tail deer populations are now larger than when Capt. John Smith hunted them to feed the Jamestown settlers. The state also has squirrel, grouse, bear, bobcat, fox, rabbit, pheasant, and quail, and the marshes of Chincoteague and the Eastern Shore are world famous for their geese, duck, and brant (a type of wild goose). In other words, you can hunt for something almost anywhere outside Virginia's metropolitan areas. Special seasons allow hunting with muzzleloaders and bows and arrows. Licenses are required. Contact the **Virginia Department of Game and Inland Fisheries,** 4010 W. Broad St., Richmond, VA 23230 (☎ 804/367-1000), for details.

SKIING   You may glide over more man-made snow than the real thing, but Virginia has four downhill ski areas. Two are resorts mentioned in this book: The Homestead in Hot Springs (☎ **800/838-1766;** see chapter 8) and Wintergreen near Charlottesville (☎ **800/325-2200;** see chapter 7). Two others are condominium developments with golf courses and tennis courts as well as ski slopes: Massanutten, P.O. Box 1227, Harrisonburg, VA 22801 (☎ **540/289-9441**); and Bryce Resort, P.O. Box 3, Bayse, VA 22810 (☎ **540/856-2121**).

WATER SPORTS   To indulge your passion for surfing, jet skiing, wave running, sailing, or scuba diving, head for Virginia Beach, which has it all in abundance. Jet skis also rip up the waters of Chincoteague's back bays.

PACKAGE TOURS   Among the adventure tour companies offering outdoor tours to the state are the following:

All Adventure Travel, 5589 Arapahoe, Suite 208, Boulder, CO 80303 (☎ **800/ 537-4025**), has cycling and hiking tours to the Hunt Country, Shenandoah Valley, and the Piedmont of central Virginia.

Atlantic Canoe & Kayak Company, P.O. Box 405, Oakton, VA 22124 (☎ **800/ 297-0066** or 703/838-9072), has kayaking packages to the Northern Neck and Assateague Island on the Eastern Shore.

Backroads, 1516 5th St., Suite L101, Berkeley, CA 94710-1740 (☎ **800/ 462-2848**), has 5-day cycling and country-inn tours of the Shenandoah Valley.

Classic Adventures, P.O. Box 153, Hamlin, NY 14464-0153 (☎ **800/777-8090** or 716/964-488), has 5-night bike tours from Fredericksburg to the Hunt Country.

Highland Adventures, P.O. Box 151, Monterey, VA 24465 (☎ **540/468-2722**), has caving, rock-climbing, and mountain-bike trips to "Virginia's Switzerland" west of Staunton near the West Virginia border.

Hiking Holidays, P.O. Box 750, Bristol, VT 05443 (☎ **802/453-4816**), and **New England Hiking Holidays,** P.O. Box 164B, North Conway, NH 03860 (☎ **800/869-0949**), both have hiking trips to the Shenandoah National Park and the Blue Ridge Mountains.

Vermont Bicycle Touring, P.O. Box 711, Bristol, VT 05445 (☎ **800/ 245-3868**), has bike trips in the Shenandoah Valley, the Hunt Country, and Williamsburg area.

4 Health, Insurance & Safety

HEALTH

Malaria may have been a curse of the colonists who settled Virginia, but today the state poses no unusual health threats. Although they don't carry malaria, mosquitoes are still rampant in the Tidewater during summer, especially in the marshes of Chincoteague and the Eastern Shore, so take plenty of insect repellent if you're going there. Hospitals and emergency-care facilities are widespread in the state, so unless you're in the backcountry mountains, help will be close at hand.

INSURANCE

Many travelers buy insurance policies providing health and accident, trip-cancellation and -interruption, and lost-luggage protection. The coverage you need will depend on the extent of protection in your existing policies. Some credit-card companies also insure their customers against travel accidents if the tickets were purchased with their cards. Read your policies and credit-card agreements over carefully before buying additional insurance.

Many health insurance companies and health maintenance organizations provide coverage for illness or accidents for their patients while away (don't forget to bring your identification card), but you may have to pay the local provider upfront and file for a reimbursement when you get home. You will need adequate receipts, so collect them at the time of treatment.

Trip-cancellation insurance covers your loss if you have made nonrefundable deposits, bought airline tickets that have no or partial refunds, or paid for a charter flight, but can't travel for some good reason. Trip-interruption insurance, on the other hand, offers refunds in case an airline or tour operator goes bankrupt or out of business.

Lost-luggage insurance covers your loss over and above the limited amounts for which the airlines are responsible, and some policies provide instant payment so that you can replace your missing items on the spot.

Your travel agent should know of a company that offers traveler's insurance. Here are some American companies:

Travel Assistance International (TAI), ☎ 800/821-2828 or 202/347-2025. The American agent for Europ Assistance Worldwide Services, Inc.

Travel Guard International, ☎ 800/782-5151 or 715/345-0505.

Access America, ☎ 800/284-8300 or 804/285-3300.

Health Care Abroad (Wallach & Co., Inc.), ☎ 800/237-6615 or 703/687-3166.

Divers Alert Network (DAN), ☎ 800/446-2671 or 919/684-2948.

SAFETY

Most areas of Virginia are relatively free of street crime, but this is not the case in some areas of Richmond, Norfolk, Roanoke, and other large cities. Ask your hotel staff or the local visitor information office whether neighborhoods you intend to visit are safe. Avoid deserted streets and alleys, and always be especially alert at night. Arlington and Alexandria have low crime rates compared to Washington, D.C., across the Potomac River, but they aren't entirely free of it, either. Anywhere you go, it's your responsibility to be on the alert and to safeguard your valuables. Never leave anything of value visible in your parked car; it's an invitation to theft anywhere.

When heading into the great outdoors, keep in mind that injuries often occur when people fail to follow instructions. Believe the experts who tell you to stay on the established ski trails. Hike only in designated areas, follow the marine charts if piloting your own boat, carry rain gear, and wear a life jacket when rafting. Mountain weather can be fickle at any time of the year. And watch out for summer thunderstorms that can leave you drenched and send bolts of lightning your way.

For more information, see "Fast Facts: For the Foreign Traveler" in chapter 4.

5 Tips for Special Travelers

FOR TRAVELERS WITH DISABILITIES

The *Virginia Travel Guide for the Disabled,* a 300-page guide for persons with disabilities, is well worth the $5 cost. Its listings supply information on accessible hotels, restaurants, shops, and attractions. For a copy, contact the Virginia Tourism Corporation (see "Visitor Information," above). The corporation's TTD number for the hearing impaired is **☎ 804/371-0327.**

Other resources include **Mobility International USA (☎ 503/343-1284)**, which offers its members travel-accessibility information and has many interesting travel programs for the disabled; the **Travel Information Service (☎ 215/456-9600)**; and the **Society for the Advancement of Travel for the Handicapped (☎ 212/447-7284)**. In addition, **Twin Peaks Press,** P.O. Box 129, Vancouver, WA 98666 (**☎ 360/694-2462**), specializes in travel-related books for people with disabilities.

Companies offering tours for those with physical or mental disabilities include **Accessible Journeys (☎ 800/TINGLES** or 610/521-0339), **Flying Wheels Travel**

(☎ 800/535-6790 or 507/451-5005), **The Guided Tour, Inc.** (☎ 215/782-1370), and **Wilderness Inquiry** (☎ 800/728-0719 or 612/379-3858).

In addition, both **Amtrak** (☎ 800/USA-RAIL) and **Greyhound** (☎ 800/752-4841) offer special fares and services for the disabled. Call at least a week in advance of your trip for details.

The **National Park Service** issues "Golden Access Passports" that admit a disabled person and companion into a national park, forest, or wildlife refuge for free. Buy them at park entrances.

FOR SENIORS

Many Virginia hotels, motels, and attractions offer discounts to senior citizens. Always ask about senior discounts when making air or hotel reservations.

Choice Hotels, which includes Clarion, Comfort Inn, Econo Lodge, Friendship Inn, Rodeway Inn, Sleep Inn, and Quality Inn, gives a 30% discount to anyone 50 or over who books a room in advance through its toll-free reservations phone numbers (see appendix for numbers). Rooms are limited, and the discount doesn't apply if you reserve directly with the hotels.

The **American Association of Retired Persons (AARP),** 601 E St. NW, Washington, D.C. 20049 (☎ 800/424-3410 or 202/434-2277), offers its members discounts on hotels, car rentals, air travel, and tours. The AARP Travel Service sponsors group worldwide tours and cruises; members must be 50 years or older.

Other helpful organizations include the nonprofit **National Council of Senior Citizens,** 1331 F St. NW, Washington, D.C. 20004 (☎ 202/347-8800), part of whose magazine is devoted to travel tips. **Mature Outlook,** 6001 N. Clark St., Chicago, IL 60660 (☎ 800/336-6330), offers discounts at select hotels, restaurants, and car-rental firms. **Golden Companions,** P.O. Box 5249, Reno, NV 89513 (☎ 702/324-2227), helps travelers ages 45 and over find compatible companions through a personal voicebox mail service. Contact them for more information. **Elderhostel,** 75 Federal St., Boston, MA 02110-1941 (☎ 617/426-7788), sponsors vacations on college campuses. Participants must be 55 or older; however, if two people go as a couple, only one has to be of the required age.

Companies specializing in travel for seniors include **Grand Circle Travel,** 347 Congress St., Suite 3A, Boston, MA 02210 (☎ 800/221-2610 or 617/350-7500); and **SAGA International Holidays,** 222 Berkeley St., Boston, MA 02115 (☎ 800/343-0273).

The National Park Service issues a **"Golden Age Passport"** to any citizen or person who lives in the United States and is 62 or older, providing free admittance to all national parks. Get this lifetime admission permit for $10 at any Park Service property; proof of age is necessary.

FOR FAMILIES

Virginia has a host of activities ideal for families with children, from learning American history at Williamsburg to riding the exciting rides at Paramount's Kings Dominion. We won't begin to tell you how to raise your children, but you might give them a stake in your trip by letting them help plan it. And since much of your travel in Virginia is likely to be by car, think about carrying a few simple games to relieve potential boredom. Many Virginia hotels offer baby-sitting services, and most resorts have children's programs.

Below are some of the highlights of the state that are particularly good for children.

HISTORIC ATTRACTIONS   Virginia will bring history to life for your kids (and you, too) with myriad associations involving America's first heroes—Washington,

Jefferson, Madison, Monroe, and Patrick Henry among them. Be sure to take them to the first English settlement at **Jamestown;** to the picturesque village of **Colonial Williamsburg** and its craft demonstrations, militia reviews, and tours designed especially for kids; and to **Yorktown,** where they can climb over the ramparts where Washington defeated Cornwallis. Other possibilities are the presidential homes of **Mount Vernon, Monticello,** and **Ash Lawn-Highland** (Monroe's home). **Civil War battlefield** tours portray crucial events with fascinating exhibits, scenic walks and drives, and multimedia programs.

THEME PARKS　Theme parks offer thrills and chills, not to mention food, fun, and entertainment, at **Paramount's Kings Dominion, Busch Gardens Williamsburg,** and **Water Country USA.**

MUSEUMS　In Arlington, kids and adults alike will get a kick out of seeing themselves on TV at the **Newseum,** a state-of-the-art museum that shows the history of journalism and how it works. Roanoke's museums, especially the **Museum of Transportation,** with its railroad cars, and **Science Museum,** featuring all sorts of interactive exhibits, rate high with kids. Richmond's **Children's Museum** and the **Science Museum of Virginia** will keep children enthralled with participatory activities and "touch me" exhibits.

Another family favorite is Virginia Beach's **Marine Science Museum,** where computers, exhibits, and the museum's own waterside setting explore the marine environment. Nearby in Norfolk, the new **NAUTICUS** has interactive and "virtual adventures" featuring make-believe U.S. Navy ships. Across the harbor in Hampton, they can see real spaceships at the **Virginia Air and Space Center.**

It's not a museum, but after reading the story of the pony in *Misty of Chincoteague,* kids will adore a chance to see the action themselves at the **wild ponies' swim across Assateague Channel.** The wildlife refuge there also offers hikes, nature programs, and a sandy beach.

THEATER　Theater for young people is sponsored by **TheatreVirginia** (☎ 804/367-0831) in the Virginia Museum of Fine Arts, Richmond. Outdoor theater is appealing to kids of all ages—in Lexington, the **Theater at Lime Kiln** (☎ 540/463-3074) has folk music and other concerts, as well as musicals that kids will enjoy.

6　Getting There & Getting Around

BY PLANE

Most international visitors will arrive at **Washington Dulles International Airport** (☎ 703/661-2700), in northern Virginia about 25 miles west of Washington, D.C. Dulles is also a major regional hub for domestic flights.

Also in northern Virginia, **Ronald Reagan Washington National Airport** (☎ 703/685-8000), located on the Potomac River midway between Arlington and Alexandria, is the region's busiest airport, but because of space and noise limitations, it takes no international flights and only domestic flights originating no more than 1,250 miles away.

Other major Virginia gateways are **Richmond International Airport** (☎ 804/226-3000), **Norfolk International Airport** (☎ 804/857-3351), **Newport News/Williamsburg Airport** (☎ 804/877-0221), **Charlottesville/Albemarle Airport** (☎ 804/973-8341), and **Roanoke Regional Airport** (☎ 703/362-1999).

You can get around the state by air, but depending on the airline, you might have to change planes along the way. For example, US Airways offers the most flights around the state, but you may have to fly through its headquarters at Ronald Reagan

Washington National Airport to get, say, from Charlottesville to Norfolk. Check with the airlines or your travel agent for the most efficient and cost-effective routing.

THE AIRLINES Most domestic carriers serve Washington Dulles or Ronald Reagan Washington National, with many going to both. **US Airways** (☎ 800/428-4322) has more flights—especially using jet aircraft—to Virginia airports than any other airline. Other major carriers serving the state's airports are **American** (☎ 800/433-7300), **Continental** (☎ 800/525-0280), **Delta** (☎ 800/221-1212), **Northwest** (☎ 800/225-2525), **TWA** (☎ 800/221-2000), and **United** (☎ 800/241-6522). **AirTran** (☎ 800/AIR-TRAN), the cut-rate successor to ValuJet, flies to both Washington airports and to Norfolk and Newport News. Other discount airlines serving the Washington airports are **Midway** (☎ 800/44-MIDWAY), **Vanguard** (☎ 800/826-4827), and **Western Pacific** (☎ 800/930-3030).

Among the **international airlines** serving Washington Dulles Airport are **Aeroflot** (☎ 888/340-6400, or 202/429-4922 in Washington, D.C.), **Air Canada** (☎ 800/776-3000), **Air France** (☎ 800/237-2747), **All Nippon Airways** (☎ 800/235-9262), **British Airways** (☎ 800/247-9297), **Icelandair** (☎ 800/223-5500), **Japan Airlines** (☎ 800/525-3663), **KLM Royal Dutch Airlines** (☎ 800/374-7747), **Korean Airlines** (☎ 800/438-5000), **Lufthansa** (☎ 800/645-3880), and **Virgin Atlantic** (☎ 800/862-8621).

For more information, see "Getting to the United States" in chapter 4.

MONEY-SAVING TIPS Always shop among the airlines, and don't forget the cut-rate carriers such as AirTran, Midway, Vanguard, and Western Pacific. Ask for the lowest fare and if it's cheaper to book in advance, fly in midweek, or stay over a Saturday night. Don't stop at the 7-day advance purchase; ask how much the 14- and 30-day plans cost. Decide when you want to go before you call, since many of the best deals are nonrefundable. Also check travel sections of your local newspaper for special promotional fares or packages. Your travel agent can find out all available options.

Travel agents offer hundreds of **package tour** options, especially to Washington, D.C., and to Williamsburg. Quite often, a package tour will result in savings not just on airfares, but on hotels and other activities as well. You pay one price for a package that varies from one tour operator to the next. Airfare, transfers, and accommodations are always covered, and sometimes meals and specific activities are thrown in. The specifics vary a great deal, so consult your travel agent to find out the best deals at the time you want to travel.

BY TRAIN & BUS

Amtrak trains are better for getting to and from Virginia than for getting around. Its Metroliner and other northeast corridor trains connect New York to Union Station in Washington, D.C., where riders can board the Metrorail subway to Arlington and Alexandria. All Amtrak trains between New York and Florida stop at Washington, D.C., and Richmond; some also stop at Alexandria, Quantico, and Fredericksburg. Another train follows this route from New York to Richmond, then heads east to Newport News via Williamsburg. From Newport News, Amtrak's Thruway bus service connects to Norfolk and Virginia Beach. Some east- and westbound trains to and from Washington stop at Charlottesville, Staunton, and Clifton Forge. From Clifton Forge, a Thruway bus connects to Roanoke.

Call Amtrak (☎ **800/USA-RAIL**) for schedules and fares.

Generally, you'll find **Greyhound/Trailways** bus service available to and from— as well as between—all Virginia cities and most towns (☎ **800/231-2222**).

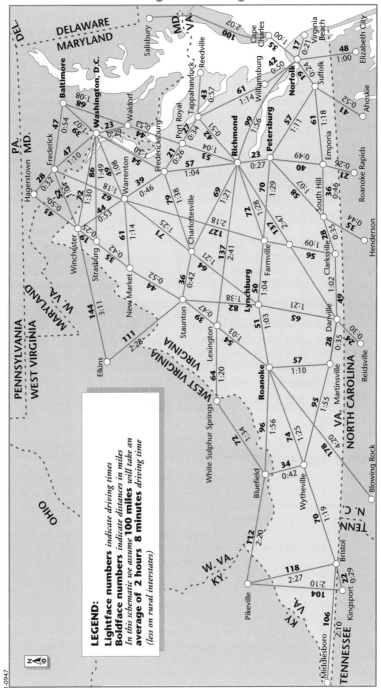

LEGEND:
Lightface numbers indicate driving times
Boldface numbers indicate distances in miles
In this schematic we assume **100 miles** *will take an*
average of **2 hours 8 minutes** *driving time*
(less on rural interstates)

1-0947

BY CAR

If at all possible, see Virginia by car. You'll have optimum flexibility to visit the rural beauties of the state, including the plantations and Civil War battlefields. And, of course, two of the state's most scenic attractions, the Skyline Drive and Blue Ridge Parkway, are motoring destinations.

Visitors arriving in Virginia by car from the northeast do so via **I-95,** which runs north-south across the state (note that I-95 will be undergoing several major construction projects until the year 2000, especially at the Capital Beltway [I-495] junction in northern Virginia, between Richmond and Petersburg, and south of Petersburg near the North Carolina line). From western Maryland and eastern Tennessee, the major highway is **I-81,** which runs north-south the entire length of the state through the Shenandoah Valley and Southwest Highlands. Major western entrance points are from West Virginia via **I-77** and **I-64.** The latter runs east-west across the state between Covington and Norfolk. In northern Virginia, **I-66** traverses the state east-west between Arlington and I-81 at Strasburg.

The state maintains a **highway helpline** (☎ **800/367-ROAD**) for road emergencies. The Virginia Tourism Corporation distributes a detailed **state road map** as well as one that highlights the scenic drives (see "Visitor Information," above).

Most **car-rental companies** operate in Virginia's major metropolitan areas and at all but the smallest of airports. See the appendix for their toll-free phone numbers.

7 Tips on Accommodations

Virginia has a vast array of accommodations, from rock-bottom roadside motels to some of the nation's finest resorts. Whether you spend a pittance or a bundle depends on your budget and your tastes. In the words of that well-worn phrase, you can enjoy "champagne tastes on a beer budget"—if you plan carefully and possess a little knowledge of how the hotel industry works.

The Virginia Tourism Corporation (see "Visitor Information," above) publishes a directory of all the state's accommodations. If you plan to take your pet along, ask the corporation for a list of hotels and motels that accept animals.

MONEY-SAVING TIPS

The rates quoted in this book are "rack," or published, rates—that is, the highest regular rates charged by a hotel or motel. Not long ago the rack rate was what you paid, unless you were part of a tour group or had purchased a vacation package. Today, most hotels give discounts to corporate travelers, government employees, senior citizens, automobile club members, active duty military personnel, and others. Most hotels usually don't advertise these discounted rates or even volunteer them at the front desk, but you can take advantage of them by asking politely if there's a special rate that might apply to you.

One company that does advertise a major discount is Choice Hotels, which gives a 30% discount to anyone over 50 at its chains (see "For Seniors" under "Tips for Special Travelers," above).

Computerized reservations systems have also permitted many larger properties to adjust their rates on an almost daily basis, depending on how much business they anticipate having. Even if they don't officially reduce their rates, they may drop them rather than have beds go empty. Don't hesitate to ask if a less expensive rate is available on the days you plan to be there.

Most rack rates include commissions of 20% or more for travel agents, which many hotels will knock off if you make your own reservations and bargain a little.

Downtown hotels catering to business travelers during the week usually offer big discounts on Friday, Saturday, and Sunday nights. If you're staying in a city over a weekend, always ask about a weekend rate or package deal. Weekend rates don't apply in the resort areas such as Virginia Beach, nor in college towns like Charlottesville, but you should ask there about weekday or week-long vacation packages.

Parking fees can run up the cost at downtown hotels, especially for long-term stays, and many hotels jack up the price of long-distance phone calls made from your room. Accordingly, always inquire about the costs of parking, and use a pay phone if the hotel tacks a hefty surcharge on calls.

BED & BREAKFASTS

Bed-and-breakfast inns can offer added value when you consider that room rates include breakfast and often afternoon tea, as well. Virginia has several first-rate country inns and scores of bed-and-breakfasts, far too many to mention them all in this book. For further information, contact the **Bed & Breakfast Association of Virginia,** P.O. Box 791, Orange, VA 22960 (www.symweb.com/bbav; e-mail: bbav@symweb.com), the state's largest group of B&B properties. It inspects and approves all the establishments it promotes. In addition, most local visitor centers will send you a list of bed-and-breakfasts in their area.

The Virginia Division of Tourism operates a **reservation service** for many country inns and bed-and-breakfast accommodations (☎ **800/934-9184**).

FAST FACTS: Virginia

American Express   Call customer service (☎ **800/528-4800**) to report lost or stolen traveler's checks or for locations of representatives in Virginia. The main Virginia office is in Richmond at 1412A Starling Dr. (☎ **804/740-2030**).

Car Rentals   See "Getting There & Getting Around" earlier in this chapter.

Climate   See "When to Go" earlier in this chapter.

Embassies and Consulates   See chapter 4, "For Foreign Visitors."

Emergencies   Call ☎ **911** (no charge) for police, fire, and ambulance.

Information   See "Visitor Information" earlier in this chapter.

Liquor Laws   In Virginia, many grocery and convenience stores sell beer and wine, but only state-licensed Alcoholic Beverage Control (ABC) stores are permitted to sell bottles of hard liquor. Any licensed establishment (restaurant or bar) can sell drinks by the glass. The legal drinking age is 21, and a photo identification may be requested if you appear to be underage.

Newspapers/Magazines   Each major city in Virginia has its own daily newspaper, and the *Washington Post* is available at newsstands and coin boxes as far south as Richmond and as far west as Lexington.

Pets   Many hotels and motels accept small, well-behaved pets. However, a small fee is often charged to allow them into guest rooms. Many places, in particular bed-and-breakfast inns, do not allow pets at all. The Virginia Tourism Corporation publishes a list of the state's hotels and motels that accept pets (see "Visitor Information," earlier in this chapter). Two good resources for pet owners are *Frommer's On the Road Again with Man's Best Friend: Mid-Atlantic States* and *Frommer's America on Wheels: Mid-Atlantic* (both by Macmillan Travel), which will steer you toward dog-friendly accommodations. Pets are usually restricted in national parks, so check with each park's ranger station before setting out.

Police   To reach the police, dial ☎ **911** from any phone (no charge).

Taxes   The Virginia state sales tax is 4.5% for most purchases, and a few local jurisdictions add another 0.5% to bring the total sales tax to 5%. Hotel taxes vary from town to town; in most communities it's 5%, which makes the total tax on your hotel bill 9.5% or 10%. Some local jurisdictions also add a restaurant tax, bringing the total tax on meal and drink bills to anywhere from 8% to 10%.

Time Zone   Virginia is on eastern standard time (EST), the same as New York and other East Coast cities. When it's noon in Virginia, it's 11am in Chicago, 10am in Detroit, 9am in Los Angeles, 8am in Anchorage, and 7am in Honolulu.

Weather   In northern Virginia, call ☎ **703/936-1212;** in Richmond, call ☎ **804/ 268-1212;** in Roanoke, call ☎ **540/982-2303.** Elsewhere, check the front pages of the telephone directory for the local number.

For Foreign Visitors   4

Although the United States may seem like familiar territory to foreign visitors au courant with U.S. fads and fashions, you might still encounter many uniquely American situations. In this chapter, we will point out some of the unexpected differences from what you are used to at home and explain some of the more confusing aspects of daily life in the United States.

1 Preparing for Your Trip

ENTRY REQUIREMENTS

DOCUMENT REGULATIONS   Immigration laws have been a hot political issue in the United States recently, so it's wise to check at any U.S. embassy or consulate for current information and requirements. You can also plug into the U.S. State Department's Internet site at **www.state.gov**.

Canadians may enter the U.S. without passports or visas; you need only proof of residence. The U.S. State Department has a **Visa Waiver Program** allowing citizens of certain countries to enter the United States without a visa for stays of up to 90 days. At press time, these countries included Andorra, Australia, Austria, Belgium, Brunei, Denmark, Finland, France, Germany, Iceland, Ireland, Italy, Japan, Liechtenstein, Luxembourg, Monaco, the Netherlands, New Zealand, Norway, San Marino, Spain, Sweden, Switzerland, and the United Kingdom. Citizens from these visa-exempt countries need only a valid passport and a round-trip air or cruise ticket in their possession upon arrival. Once here, they may then visit Mexico, Canada, Bermuda, and/or the Caribbean islands and return to the United States without needing another visa. Further information is available from any U.S. embassy or consulate.

Citizens of other countries must have (1) a valid **passport** with an expiration date at least 6 months later than the scheduled end of their visit to the United States; and (2) a **tourist visa** that's available from any U.S. embassy or consulate.

To get a visa, you must submit a completed application form (either in person or by mail) with a 1½-inch-square photo and must demonstrate binding ties to a residence abroad. Usually you can obtain a visa at once or within 24 hours, but it may take longer during the summer rush from June to August. If you cannot go in person, contact the nearest U.S. embassy or consulate for directions on applying by mail. Your travel agent or airline office may also be able to supply visa applications and instructions. The U.S. embassy or consulate that processes your application will determine whether you will be issued a multiple- or single-entry visa and any restrictions on the length of your stay.

MEDICAL REQUIREMENTS   No inoculations are needed to enter the United States, unless you are coming from or have stopped over in areas known to be suffering from epidemics, particularly cholera or yellow fever. If you have a condition requiring treatment with medications containing narcotics or drugs requiring a syringe, carry a valid signed prescription from your physician to allay any suspicion that you are smuggling drugs.

CUSTOMS REQUIREMENTS   Every adult visitor may bring free of duty 1 liter of wine or spirits; 200 cigarettes or 100 cigars (but no cigars from Cuba) or 3 pounds of smoking tobacco; and $100 worth of gifts. These exemptions are offered to travelers who spend at least 72 hours in the United States and who have not claimed them within the preceding 6 months. It is altogether forbidden to bring into the country foodstuffs (particularly cheese, fruit, cooked meats, and canned goods) and plants (vegetables, seeds, tropical plants, and so on). Foreign tourists may bring in or take out up to $10,000 in U.S. or foreign currency with no formalities; larger sums must be declared to Customs on entering or leaving.

INSURANCE

Unlike most other countries, the United States does not have a national health-care system, and the cost of medical care is extremely high. Accordingly, we strongly advise every traveler to secure health coverage before setting out.

You may want to take out a comprehensive travel policy that covers (for a relatively low premium) sickness or injury costs (medical, surgical, and hospital); loss or theft of your baggage; and costs of accident, repatriation, or death. Such packages (for example, Europ Assistance Worldwide Services in Europe) are sold by automobile clubs at attractive rates, as well as by insurance companies and travel agencies. The United States agent for Europ Assistance is **Travel Assistance International,** 1133 15th St. NW, Suite 400, Washington, D.C. 20005 (☎ **800/821-2828** or 202/331-1690).

MONEY

CURRENCY   The U.S. monetary system has a decimal base: 1 American **dollar** ($1) = 100 **cents** (100¢).

Dollar notes ("bills") are all the same size and are green on one side, gray on the other. They come in $1 (a "buck"), $5, $10, $20, $50, and $100 denominations. The six denominations of coins—with their American nicknames—are 1¢ ("penny"), 5¢ ("nickel"), 10¢ ("dime"), 25¢ ("quarter"), 50¢ ("half-dollar"), and the rare $1 piece.

CURRENCY EXCHANGE   Foreign-exchange bureaus, so common in Europe, are rare even at airports in the United States and are nonexistent outside major cities. Try to avoid having to change foreign currency or traveler's checks denominated in other than U.S. dollars at small-town banks or even at branches in big cities. In fact, you should change your home currency into U.S. dollars before leaving home.

TRAVELER'S CHECKS   Traveler's checks in U.S. dollars are easily changed in banks and are also accepted at most hotels, motels, stores, and restaurants. Sometimes a passport or other photo identification is necessary.

CREDIT CARDS   The method of payment most widely used in the United States is credit and charge cards: Visa (BarclayCard in Britain, Chargex in Canada),

MasterCard (EuroCard in Europe, Access in Britain, Diamond in Japan), American Express, Diners Club, and Carte Blanche. You must have a credit or charge card to rent a car. It can also be used as proof of identity or as a "cash card," allowing you to draw money from banks that accept it. Automatic teller machines (ATMs) are widespread throughout the United States.

SAFETY

GENERAL   While tourist areas are generally safe, crime is on the increase everywhere, and U.S. urban areas tend to be less safe than those in Europe or Japan. Virginia is generally a safe state, especially in rural areas, but you should be careful in the downtown areas of the larger cities, particularly at night.

As a general rule, you should always stay alert, particularly in large U.S. cities. It's wise to ask the city's or area's tourist office which neighborhoods are safe, if you're in doubt. Avoid deserted areas, especially at night. Don't go into any city park at night unless there's an occasion that attracts crowds. Generally speaking, you can feel safe in areas where there are many people and many open establishments.

Avoid carrying valuables with you on the street, and don't display expensive cameras or electronic equipment. Hold on to your pocketbook, and place your billfold in an inside pocket. In restaurants, theaters, and other public places, keep your possessions in sight.

Remember also that hotels are open to the public, and in a large hotel, security may not be able to screen everyone entering. Always lock your room door; don't assume that once inside your hotel, you are automatically safe and need no longer be aware of your surroundings.

For more information, see "Health, Insurance & Safety" in chapter 3.

DRIVING   Safety while driving is particularly important. Question your rental agency about personal safety or ask for a brochure on traveler safety tips when you pick up your car. Ask the agency for written directions or a map with the route clearly marked showing how to get to your destination. And, if at all possible, arrive and depart during daylight hours.

Recently, more and more crime has involved cars and drivers. If you drive off a highway into a doubtful neighborhood, leave the area as quickly as possible. If you have an accident, even on the highway, stay in your car with the doors locked until you assess the situation or until the police arrive. If you are bumped from behind on the street or are involved in a minor accident with no injuries and the situation appears to be suspicious, motion to the other driver to follow you. *Never* get out of your car in such situations. You can also keep a sign in your car: PLEASE FOLLOW THIS VEHICLE TO REPORT THE ACCIDENT. Show the sign to the other driver and go directly to the nearest police precinct, well-lighted service station, or all-night store.

If you see someone on the road who indicates a need for help, do not stop. Take note of the location, drive on to a well-lighted area, and telephone the police by dialing ☎ **911.**

Park in well-lighted, well-traveled areas if possible. Always keep your car doors locked, whether the car is attended or unattended. Look around you before you get out of your car, and never leave any packages or valuables in sight. If someone attempts to rob you or steal your car, do not try to resist the thief or carjacker; report the incident to the police department immediately.

Also, make sure you have enough gasoline (petrol) in your tank to reach your intended destination so that you're not forced to look for a service station in an unfamiliar and possibly unsafe neighborhood—especially at night.

2 Getting to the United States

Travelers from overseas can take advantage of the **APEX (advance-purchase excursion) fares** offered by all the major U.S. and European carriers. If you're coming from the United Kingdom or Europe, **Virgin Atlantic Airways** (☎ 800/662-8621 in the U.S. or 01/293-74-77-47 in the U.K.) has cut-rate fares on its flights from London and Manchester to Washington Dulles International Airport, in northern Virginia.

Some large American airlines (for example, TWA, American Airlines, Northwest, United, and Delta) offer special discount tickets under the name **Visit USA** to travelers on their transatlantic or transpacific flights, allowing travel between any U.S. destinations at minimum rates. Tickets must be purchased before you leave your foreign point of departure. This system is the best, easiest, and fastest way to see the United States at low cost. You should get information well in advance from your travel agent or the office of the airline concerned, since the conditions attached to these discount tickets can be changed without advance notice.

The visitor arriving by air, no matter what the port of entry, should cultivate patience and resignation before setting foot on U.S. soil. Getting through immigration control can take as long as 2 hours, especially on summer weekends. Make very generous allowance for delay in planning connections between international and domestic flights—an average of 2 to 3 hours at least.

In contrast, travelers arriving by car or by rail from Canada will find border-crossing formalities streamlined to the vanishing point. Air travelers from Canada, Bermuda, and some places in the Caribbean can sometimes go through Customs and Immigration at the point of departure, which is much quicker.

For more information about travel to and within Virginia, see "Getting There & Getting Around" in chapter 3.

FAST FACTS: For the Foreign Traveler

Automobile Organizations   Auto clubs will supply maps, suggested routes, guidebooks, accident and bail-bond insurance, and emergency road service. The **American Automobile Association (AAA)** is the major club in the United States, with almost 1,000 offices nationwide. Members of some foreign auto clubs have reciprocal arrangements with the AAA and enjoy its services at no charge (ask your home club if it has an agreement with AAA). You may be able to join AAA even if you're not a member of a reciprocal club. Check the phone book for local offices. The AAA's nationwide emergency road service number is ☎ 800/AAA-HELP.

Business Hours   Public and private **offices** are usually open Monday through Friday from 9am to 5pm. **Banking** hours vary by establishment in Virginia; most are open Monday through Thursday from 9am to 2pm, with extended hours on Friday. A few banks are open Saturday morning until noon. Most **post offices** are open Monday through Friday from 8:30am to 5pm, Saturday from 8:30am to 12:30pm. **Store** hours are usually Monday through Friday from 10am to 6pm; some shopping centers operate 7 days a week, usually Monday through Saturday from 10am to 9pm, Sunday from noon to 6pm. **Museum** hours vary widely, with many closed Monday.

Currency Exchange   See "Money" under "Preparing for Your Trip," above.

Customs   See "Entry Requirements" under "Preparing for Your Trip," above.

Drinking Laws   Every state has its own laws governing the sale of liquor. The only federal regulation restricts the consumption of liquor in public places to people ages 21 or over. For laws specific to Virginia, see "Liquor Laws" under "Fast Facts: Virginia" in chapter 3.

Electric Current   The United States uses 110 to 120 volts, 60 cycles, compared to the 220 to 240 volts, 50 cycles, used in most of Europe. In addition to a 100-volt converter, small appliances of non-American manufacture, such as hair dryers and shavers, will require a plug adapter with two flat, parallel pins.

Embassies/Consulates   All embassies are located in the national capital, Washington, D.C. Some consulates are located in major U.S. cities, and most nations have a mission to the United Nations in New York City. Foreign visitors can find telephone numbers for their embassies and consulates by calling directory assistance in Washington, D.C. (☎ **202/555-1212**).

Emergencies   Call ☎ **911** for **fire, police,** and **ambulance.** If you encounter such traveler's problems as sickness, accident, or lost or stolen baggage, call **Traveler's Aid,** an organization that specializes in helping all distressed travelers, whether American or foreign. Check the local telephone directory for the nearest office.

Holidays   Banks, government offices, schools, many stores, and some museums and restaurants are closed for the following national holidays: January 1 (New Year's Day), third Monday in January (Martin Luther King, Jr. Day), third Monday in February (Presidents' Day), last Monday in May (Memorial Day), July 4 (Independence Day), first Monday in September (Labor Day), second Monday in October (Columbus Day), November 11 (Veterans Day/Armistice Day), last Thursday in November (Thanksgiving), and December 25 (Christmas).

Mail   You can receive mail at the main post office of the city or region where you expect to be. It should be addressed "c/o General Delivery" and must be picked up in person with proof of identity (passport or driver's license). U.S. mailboxes are found at intersections; they're blue with a red-and-white stripe and carry the inscription U.S. MAIL. First-class domestic mail **stamps** cost 32¢ at press time but were expected to rise to 33¢. Air-mail postcards and letters (up to half an ounce) cost 46¢ to send to Canada and Mexico, 60¢ to all other countries, but these prices may increase slightly, too.

Newspapers/Magazines   The *New York Times, USA Today,* and *Washington Post* newspapers and *Newsweek* and *Time* magazines cover world news and are widely available throughout Virginia. A few European magazines and newspapers are available in large cities.

Post   See "Mail," above.

Radio/Television   There are many local radio stations throughout Virginia, each broadcasting particular types of talk shows and/or music—classical, country, pop, jazz, and gospel—punctuated at least hourly by news, traffic, and weather updates. Television, dominated by four coast-to-coast networks (ABC, CBS, NBC, and Fox), plays an important role in American life. In recent years, the Public Broadcasting System (PBS) and a growing number of cable channels, notably CNN, have widened program choices.

Safety   See "Safety" under "Preparing for Your Trip," above.

Taxes   There is no VAT (value-added tax) or other indirect tax at a national level in the United States. Every state, and each city in it, has the right to levy its own local tax on all purchases, including hotel and restaurant checks and airline tickets. These taxes are added to your bill, so be prepared for the shock of having to pay an additional 4.5% or 5% sales tax on most purchases. Hotel taxes vary from town to town; most will add a total tax of 9.5% or 10% to your hotel bill. Some local jurisdictions also add a restaurant tax, bringing the total tax on meal and drink bills to 8% to 10%.

Telephone/Fax/Telegraph   The telephone system in the United States is run by private corporations, so rates, especially for long-distance service, operator-assisted calls, and even public pay phones, can vary widely. Generally, hotel surcharges on long-distance and local calls are astronomical, so you're usually better off using a **public pay telephone,** which you'll find clearly marked in most public buildings and private establishments as well as on the street. Convenience grocery stores and gas stations usually have them. Many convenience groceries and packaging services sell prepaid calling cards in denominations up to $50; they are often the least expensive way to call home. Many public phones at airports now accept American Express, MasterCard, and Visa. Local calls made from public pay phones usually cost 25¢.

Most **long-distance and international calls** can be dialed directly from any phone. For calls within the United States and to Canada, dial 1, followed by the area code and the 7-digit number. For other international calls, dial 011, followed by the country code, city code, and the telephone number of the person you are calling.

Calls to area codes 800 and 888 are **toll free.** However, calls to numbers in area codes 700 and 900 (chat lines, bulletin boards, "dating" services, and so forth) can be very expensive—usually a charge of 95¢ to $3 or more per minute, and they sometimes have minimum charges that can run as high as $15 or more.

For **reversed-charge or collect calls,** and for **person-to-person calls,** dial 0 (zero, *not* the letter *O*), followed by the area code and number you want. An operator will then come on the line, and you should specify that you are calling collect, or person-to-person, or both. If your operator-assisted call is international, ask for the overseas operator.

For local **directory assistance** ("information"), dial 411; for **long-distance information,** dial 1, then the appropriate area code and 555-1212.

Telegraph and **telex** services are provided primarily by Western Union, which has hundreds of offices across the country (☎ **800/325-6000** for the nearest location). You can also telegraph money, or have it telegraphed to you, very quickly over the Western Union system, but this service can cost as much as 15% to 25% of the amount sent.

Most hotels have **fax** machines available for guest use (be sure to ask about the charge to use it), and many hotel rooms are even wired for guests' fax machines. A less expensive way to send and receive faxes may be at stores such as **Mail Boxes Etc.,** a national chain of packing service shops (look in the Yellow Pages directory under "Packing Services").

There are two kinds of telephone directories in the United States. The **White Pages** lists private and business subscribers in alphabetical order. The inside front cover lists emergency numbers for police, fire, ambulance, the Coast Guard, poison-control center, crime-victims hotline, and so on. The first few pages will tell you how to make long-distance and international calls, complete with country codes and area codes. Government numbers usually are on pages printed on blue paper. The **Yellow Pages,** printed on yellow paper, lists all local services, businesses, and industries by type, with an index at the front or back. The Yellow Pages also includes city plans or detailed area maps, often showing postal ZIP codes and public transportation routes.

Time   The United States is divided into six time zones. From east to west, they are eastern standard time (EST, 5 hours behind Greenwich mean time), central standard time (CST), mountain standard time (MST), pacific standard time (PST), Alaska standard time (AST), and Hawaii standard time (HST). All of Virginia is on eastern standard time. Always keep in mind the changing time zones if you are traveling (or even telephoning) long distances in the United States. For example, noon in New York City (EST) is 11am in Chicago (CST), 10am in Detroit (MST), 9am in Los Angeles (PST), 8am in Anchorage (AST), and 7am in Honolulu (HST).

Daylight Savings Time is in effect in Virginia from 1am on the first Sunday in April until 2am on the last Sunday in October. Daylight savings time moves the clock 1 hour ahead of standard time.

Tipping   Wait staff and taxi drivers are tipped between 15% and 20% (in Virginia, doubling the sales taxes added to restaurant bills will equal the approximate tip). Bellhops should be tipped $1 per bag they carry to your room; airport porters should get at least 50¢ for a small bag, $1 for a larger one.

Toilets   You won't find public toilets (euphemistically referred to as "rest rooms") on the streets in most U.S. cities, but you can find them in hotel lobbies, bars, restaurants, museums, department stores, railway and bus stations, and service stations. Note, however, that restaurants and bars in resort or heavily visited areas may display a notice that TOILETS ARE FOR THE USE OF PATRONS ONLY. You can ignore this sign or, better yet, avoid arguments by paying for a cup of coffee or soft drink, which will qualify you as a patron. Some public places are equipped with pay toilets that require you to insert one or two dimes (10¢) or a quarter (25¢) into a slot on the door before it will open. In rest rooms with attendants, a tip of at least 25¢ is customary.

THE AMERICAN SYSTEM OF MEASUREMENTS

Length

1 inch (in.)			=	2.54cm			
1 foot (ft.)	=	12 in.	=	30.48cm	=	.305m	
1 yard (yd.)	=	3 ft.			=	.915m	
1 mile	=	5,280 ft.					=	1.609km

To convert miles to kilometers, multiply the number of miles by 1.61 (for example, 50 mi. × 1.61 = 80.5km). Note that this conversion can be used to convert speeds from miles per hour (m.p.h.) to kilometers per hour (kmph).

To convert kilometers to miles, multiply the number of kilometers by .62 (for example, 25 km × .62 = 15.5 mi.). Note that this same conversion can be used to convert speeds from kilometers per hour to miles per hour.

Capacity

1 fluid ounce (fl. oz.)			=	.03 liter		
1 pint (pt.)	=	16 fl. oz.	=	.47 liter		
1 quart (qt.)	=	2 pints	=	.94 liter		
1 gallon (gal.)	=	4 quarts	=	3.79 liters	=	.83 Imperial gal.

To convert U.S. gallons to liters, multiply the number of gallons by 3.79 (for example, 12 gal. × 3.79 = 45.48 liters).

To convert liters to U.S. gallons, multiply the number of liters by .26 (for example, 50 liters × .26 = 13 U.S. gal.).

To convert U.S. gallons to Imperial gallons, multiply the number of U.S. gallons by .83 (for example, 12 U.S. gal. × .83 = 9.96 Imperial gal.).

To convert Imperial gallons to U.S. gallons, multiply the number of Imperial gallons by 1.2 (for example, 8 Imperial gal. × 1.2 = 9.6 U.S. gal.).

Weight

1 ounce (oz.)		=	28.35g				
1 pound (lb.)	= 16 oz.	=	453.6g	=	.45 kg		
1 ton	= 2,000 lb.	=			907kg	=	.91 metric ton

To convert pounds to kilograms, multiply the number of pounds by .45 (for example, 90 lb. × .45 = 40.5kg).
To convert kilograms to pounds, multiply the number of kilograms by 2.2 (for example, 75kg × 2.2 = 165 lb.).

Area

1 acre		=	.41 ha				
1 square mile	=	640 acres	=	2.59 ha	=	2.6km^2	

To convert acres to hectares, multiply the number of acres by .41 (for example, 40 acres × .41 = 16.4ha).
To convert hectares to acres, multiply the number of hectares by 2.47 (for example, 20ha × 2.47 = 49.4 acres).
To convert square miles to square kilometers, multiply the number of square miles by 2.6 (for example, 80 sq. mi × 2.6 = 208km^2).
To convert square kilometers to square miles, multiply the number of square kilometers by .39 (for example, 150km^2 × .39 = 58.5 sq. mi.).

Temperature

°C	−18°	−10		0		10		20		30		40
°F	0°	10	20	32	40	50	60	70	80	90	100	

To convert degrees Fahrenheit to degrees Celsius, subtract 32 from °F, multiply by 5, then divide by 9 (for example, 85°F − 32 × $^5/_9$ = 29.4°C).
To convert degrees Celsius to degrees Fahrenheit, multiply °C by 9, divide by 5, and add 32 (for example, 20°C × $^9/_5$ + 32 = 68°F).

Northern Virginia 5

America's past and present meet in northern Virginia. Linked by bridges and three subway lines to the nation's capital, Arlington is very much in Washington's international, cosmopolitan orbit. Yet in nearby Alexandria, the cobblestone streets of the 18th-century Old Town historic district still ring with the footsteps of George Washington, James Monroe, and Robert E. Lee. South of Old Town on the Potomac, more visitors go through the doors of George Washington's beloved Mount Vernon than of any American home except the White House.

Northern Virginia is a vast suburban area stretching west and south from the nation's capital. Not long ago, Arlington, Alexandria, and the region's other municipalities were primarily bedroom communities for workers who headed across the river each morning. However, a boom of high-tech service industries and the arrival of major corporate headquarters have given this region its own thriving economy. Now its residents are just as likely to work in fast-growing Fairfax County, which wraps around Arlington and Alexandria and has one million residents, making it the most populous single jurisdiction in Virginia—almost twice the size of the District of Columbia. If it were incorporated, the Fairfax area known as Tysons Corner would be Virginia's wealthiest city, and the strip running west through Reston and Herndon to Washington Dulles International Airport is one of the nation's leading high-tech corridors.

Of course, the downside to this rapid growth is some of the nation's most horrendous traffic, as you will quickly discover if you drive northern Virginia's overburdened roads during rush hour. But if you continue west past Dulles, the crowded highways quickly give way to the winding country roads, beautiful rolling hills, picturesque horse farms, charming country inns, and quaint villages of Loudon and Fauquier counties, heart of Virginia's renowned Hunt Country.

1 Arlington

Across the Potomac River from Washington, D.C.; 100 miles N of Richmond

Easy access to Washington, D.C., and its tourist attractions is Arlington's main draw for visitors, who can stay in less expensive digs here and still be only minutes away from the capital via Metrorail, the region's clean and efficient subway system. Even visitors who stay across the Potomac River in D.C. eventually find their way here, too,

Arlington

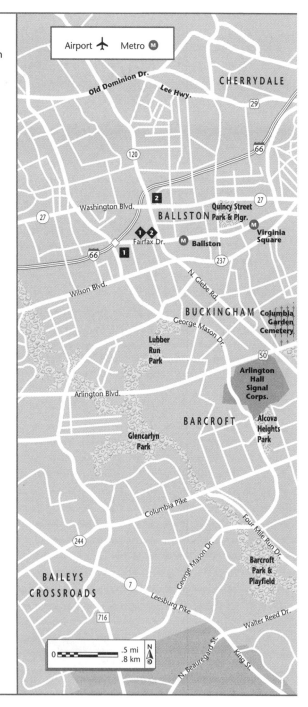

1-0948

52

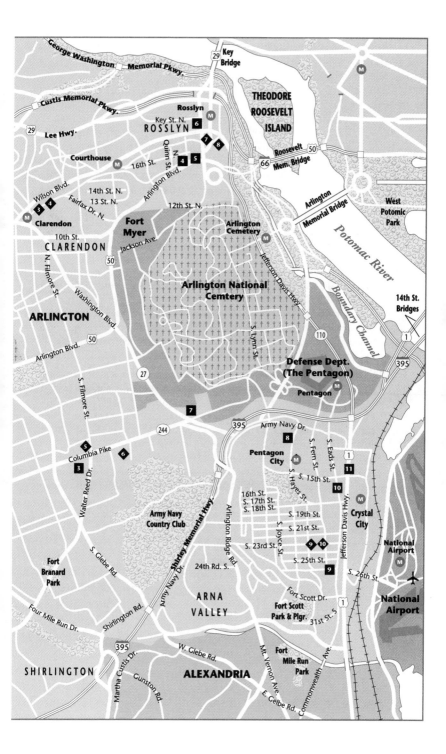

for Arlington is home to the Pentagon, our national military headquarters; the Newseum, an interactive museum dedicated to journalism; and Arlington National Cemetery, our most hallowed national shrine.

As its straight land borders will attest, Arlington was once part of the District of Columbia, originally a square flanking the Potomac. Unneeded in the final planning, Arlington was returned to the state of Virginia in 1847.

Although it has always provided housing for federal government civilian workers and military personnel, Arlington in recent years has developed a lively life of its own. Its subway stations, safe neighborhoods, and more affordable housing have attracted the type of young folk who used to live in the now-troubled capital city. Some of the friendly pubs that have sprung up to offer libation and entertainment to these young residents have even put the county on the music map.

Nor do Arlingtonians have to cross the river for good food these days, for immigrants from overseas have not only given it Virginia's most diverse population, but have also opened many ethnic restaurants serving cuisines from around the world.

ESSENTIALS

VISITOR INFORMATION   Contact the **Arlington Visitor Center,** 735 S. 18th St., Arlington, VA 22202 (☎ **800/677-6267** or 703/358-5720 for information, or 888/743-8292 for hotel reservations; fax 703/892-9469), for maps and information about events, accommodations, and restaurants, as well as answers to any questions about the area. The center is 2 blocks south of Pentagon City Metro station (go south on South Hayes Street, which becomes South 18th Street).

GETTING THERE   By Plane   Recently renovated and expanded to the tune of $1 billion, **Ronald Reagan Washington National Airport** (☎ **703/685-8000**) is located on the Potomac River in Arlington. **SuperShuttle** (☎ **800/BLUE-VAN**) operates frequent van service daily from 6am to 11pm to locations in D.C. and northern Virginia. Shuttle fares start at $6 one-way. Metrorail's Yellow and Blue lines stop at the airport's new main terminal (see "Getting Around," below).

International and long-distance domestic flights arrive at **Washington Dulles International Airport** (☎ **703/661-2700**), about 25 miles west of Arlington via I-66 and the Dulles Access Road. **Washington Flyer** (☎ **703/685-1400**) operates buses between Dulles and National airports, and also shuttles between Dulles and the West Falls Church Metro stop, from which you can access all Metrorail route locations ($8 one-way, $14 round-trip).

All of the major car-rental companies are represented at both airports.

By Car   I-95 and **I-395** are the major highways to Arlington from the north and south. From the north, follow I-95 south to Exit 19, for U.S. 50 west and Washington, D.C. Follow U.S. 50 west (John Hanson Highway), which will turn into New York Avenue. Follow signs for I-395 south toward Richmond and cross the 14th Street Bridge, leaving Washington, D.C. From the northwest, take I-270 to I-495 south to the **George Washington Memorial Parkway,** which runs through Arlington to Alexandria along the south bank of the Potomac River. In addition, **I-66, U.S. 50** (Arlington Boulevard), and **U.S. 29/211** (Lee Highway) run east-west through Arlington. **U.S. 1** (Jefferson Davis Highway) passes north-south through the county.

By Train   Visitors arriving on Amtrak at Washington's **Union Station,** 50 Massachusetts Ave. NE (☎ **800/USA-RAIL**), can easily switch to the Metro stop there for a quick ride to Arlington. Alexandria also has an Amtrak station with adjacent Metrorail stop (see "Getting There" in section 2, below).

By Bus   The **Greyhound/Trailways** bus station is at 3860 S. Four Mile Run Dr., near South Walter Reed Drive (☎ **800/321-2222**).

COUNTY LAYOUT   The main thoroughfares radiate from the Potomac River bridges. I-395 runs southwest through the county from the 14th Street Bridge to Alexandria, where it connects with I-95. I-66 begins at the Theodore Roosevelt Bridge and runs from Rosslyn due west. Paralleling I-66, Wilson Boulevard begins at the Key Bridge in Rosslyn and runs due west. Jefferson Davis Highway (U.S. 1) extends due south from the 14th Street Bridge (I-395) to Alexandria. Columbia Pike starts at the Pentagon and heads southwest into Fairfax County.

THE NEIGHBORHOODS IN BRIEF   Arlington is a county, not a city, and has no single downtown area. Instead, it's a place of neighborhoods. **Crystal City** and **Pentagon City** straddle Jefferson Davis Highway (U.S. 1) between National Airport and the Pentagon on the county's eastern side. Both are home to office buildings, apartments, and hotels that have sprung up like glass-and-steel forests over and around the Metro stations. Roughly cutting the county in half, **Columbia Pike** is lined with older apartment buildings and small shops. Although it doesn't have its own Metro subway line, Columbia Pike is one of the most populous—and least expensive—areas of the county. To the west, just across the Key Bridge from Georgetown in D.C., **Rosslyn** is another center of office and condominium towers. From there, the Metro's Orange line runs under Wilson Boulevard to Clarendon and Ballston. Often called "Little Saigon" because of its many Vietnamese restaurants, **Clarendon** now offers a wide variety of cuisines and lively neighborhood bars, most of them housed in older storefronts. Easy to find if you're arriving via I-66, **Ballston** was once a weekend getaway for Washingtonians, but its older buildings are quickly giving way to new office towers and condos centered on its Metro station and modern shopping mall.

GETTING AROUND   Washington's **Metrorail** subway system offers efficient transport within Arlington and to Washington, D.C. The Orange line runs under Wilson Boulevard from Rosslyn west through Clarendon and Ballston. The Blue line runs southeast from Rosslyn to Arlington National Cemetery, the Pentagon, Pentagon City, Crystal City, and Ronald Reagan Washington National Airport to Alexandria. Sharing tracks with the Blue line in Arlington, the Yellow line also connects the Pentagon, Pentagon City, Crystal City, and National Airport to Alexandria. Metrorail operates Monday to Friday from 5:30am to midnight, Saturday from 8am to midnight, and Sunday from 10am to midnight. For information, call ☎ **202/ 637-7000.** You can also call that number for **Metrobus,** which has extensive (and complicated) 24-hour service throughout Arlington.

The best taxi company here is **Red Top Cab** (☎ **703/522-3333**).

WHAT TO SEE & DO

If you're in Arlington, you probably want to take the Metro over to D.C. and see some of the many attractions in the nation's capital. For complete descriptions, see either *Frommer's Washington, D.C.,* or *Frommer's Washington, D.C., from $50 a Day,* available at your local bookstore.

ATTRACTIONS

✪ **Arlington National Cemetery.** Va. 110 at Memorial Circle. ☎ **703/607-8052.** Free admission. Tourmobile $4 adults, $2 children 3–11. Apr–Sept daily 8am–7pm; Oct–Mar daily 8am–5pm. Parking $1 per hour first 3 hours, $2 per hour thereafter. Metro: Blue line to Arlington Cemetery. From I-395 or I-66 take Va. 110 to entrance signs.

Arlington National Cemetery

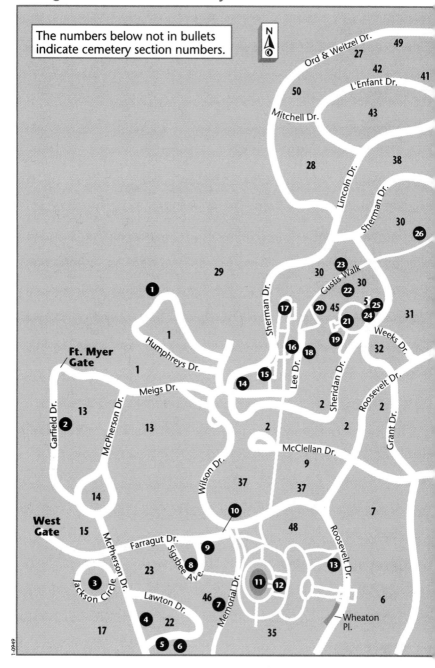

The numbers below not in bullets indicate cemetery section numbers.

N

Ord & Weitzel Dr.
49
27
42
41
L'Enfant Dr.
50
43
Mitchell Dr.
28
38
Lincoln Dr.
Sherman Dr.
30
26
29
23 Custis Walk
30
30
1 22
Sherman Dr.
17 20 45 5 25
Humphreys Dr.
21 24
Ft. Myer Gate
1
16 19 31
18
Weeks Dr.
1
Meigs Dr.
14 15
32
Garfield Dr.
13
2
McPherson Dr.
13
Lee Dr.
Sheridan Dr.
2
Roosevelt Dr.
2
Grant Dr.
2
13
2
2
14
McClellan Dr.
Wilson Dr.
37
9
37
7
West Gate
15
10
48
Roosevelt Dr.
Farragut Dr.
9
McPherson Dr.
Sigsbee Ave.
8
13
23
Jackson Circle
3
Lawton Dr.
46
7
6
4
22
Memorial Dr.
Wheaton Pl.
17
5 6
35

1-0949

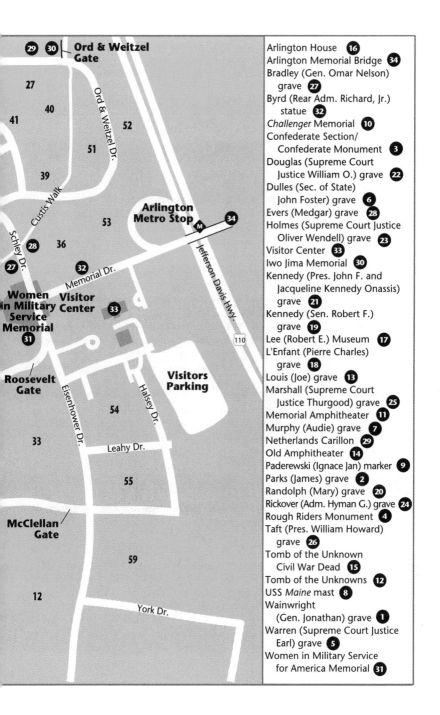

Arlington House **16**
Arlington Memorial Bridge **34**
Bradley (Gen. Omar Nelson) grave **27**
Byrd (Rear Adm. Richard, Jr.) statue **32**
Challenger Memorial **10**
Confederate Section/ Confederate Monument **3**
Douglas (Supreme Court Justice William O.) grave **22**
Dulles (Sec. of State) John Foster) grave **6**
Evers (Medgar) grave **28**
Holmes (Supreme Court Justice Oliver Wendell) grave **23**
Visitor Center **33**
Iwo Jima Memorial **30**
Kennedy (Pres. John F. and Jacqueline Kennedy Onassis) grave **21**
Kennedy (Sen. Robert F.) grave **19**
Lee (Robert E.) Museum **17**
L'Enfant (Pierre Charles) grave **18**
Louis (Joe) grave **13**
Marshall (Supreme Court Justice Thurgood) grave **25**
Memorial Amphitheater **11**
Murphy (Audie) grave **7**
Netherlands Carillon **29**
Old Amphitheater **14**
Paderewski (Ignace Jan) marker **9**
Parks (James) grave **2**
Randolph (Mary) grave **20**
Rickover (Adm. Hyman G.) grave **24**
Rough Riders Monument **4**
Taft (Pres. William Howard) grave **26**
Tomb of the Unknown Civil War Dead **15**
Tomb of the Unknowns **12**
USS *Maine* mast **8**
Wainwright (Gen. Jonathan) grave **1**
Warren (Supreme Court Justice Earl) grave **5**
Women in Military Service for America Memorial **31**

For more than a century, this famous cemetery on a ridge overlooking the Potomac River and Washington, D.C., has been a cherished shrine commemorating the lives given by members of the U.S. armed forces. Its seemingly endless graves mark the mortal remains of the honored dead, both the known and the unknown, who served in conflicts from the Revolutionary War through the Persian Gulf War.

This quiet expanse of green is a walker's paradise. Head first for the **Arlington Cemetery Visitor Center,** where you can get a free map—and if you have family buried here, find out where. If you're not hoofing it, you can purchase a **Tourmobile** ticket for a cemetery tour. Service is continuous, and the narrated commentary interesting. At the visitor center you can also purchase Tourmobile combination tickets ($12 for adults, $6 for children) that include Arlington and major Washington, D.C., sights, allowing you to stop and reboard when you're ready.

At the cemetery's ceremonial entrance, you'll come to a fountain emptying into a reflecting pool backed by an imposing granite wall. This is the **Women in Military Service for America Memorial,** dedicated in 1997 to honor all women who have served in the military, from the Revolution to the present. The memorial's Hall of Honor has a block of Colorado marble virtually identical to that of the Tomb of the Unknowns (see below). On the terrace roof, 11 glass panels are etched with quotations about women who have served, and inside, there's a computerized registry of more than 250,000 women veterans.

Follow the paved pathways to the **John F. Kennedy and Robert F. Kennedy gravesites,** which are marked by an eternal flame. Jacqueline Kennedy Onassis is buried next to her first husband. Nearby stands a simple white cross at the grave of Robert F. Kennedy. Looking north, you'll have a spectacular view of the capital city across the river (during his presidency Kennedy once remarked of this spot, "I could stay here forever"). A few steps below the gravesite is a wall inscribed with JFK quotations, including the one he's most remembered for: "And so my fellow Americans, ask not what your country can do for you—ask what you can do for your country. My fellow citizens of the world, ask not what America will do for you, but what together we can do for the freedom of man."

Sitting atop the ridge above the Kennedy graves, the Greek Revival **Arlington House** (☎ 703/557-0613) was built by George Washington Parke Custis, grandson of Martha Washington by her first marriage, after his daughter married a dashing young Virginian named Robert E. Lee. The Lees were residing in the mansion in April 1861, when General Lee received word of the dissolution of the Union and Virginia's secession (see the "Born of Vengeance" box, below). After it was acquired by the U.S. government in 1883, Arlington House was used for several decades as office space and living quarters for cemetery staff. In 1925, Congress empowered the Secretary of War to restore the house to its pre–Civil War appearance and furnish it with original pieces (as much as possible) and replicas. Since 1955, it has served as a permanent memorial to Robert E. Lee. There's a self-guided tour, with volunteers in period dress on hand to give an introductory talk, hand out brochures, and answer questions. Servants' quarters and a small museum adjoin. Admission is free. Hours are October to March, daily from 9:30am to 4:30pm; until 6pm April to September (closed Christmas and New Year's Day).

Beyond the mansion, America's most distinguished honor guard slowly marches before the **Tomb of the Unknowns,** a tribute to all members of the armed forces who have given their lives for their country in war. The 50-ton white-marble tomb rests above the remains of unidentified combatants slain during World War I. Unknowns from World War II, the Korean War, and Vietnam are in the crypts on the plaza in front of it. Plan your visit to coincide with the changing of the guard

Born of Vengeance

On April 20, 1861, Robert E. Lee crossed the Potomac River to a meeting at Blair House, opposite the White House in Washington, D.C. There he was offered command of all Union forces that would fight the Civil War. A distinguished career soldier and patriot, Lee nevertheless turned down President Abraham Lincoln and went home to his Custis-Lee mansion across the Potomac River in Arlington. Two days later he left for Richmond, where he took command of his native Virginia's rebel army.

The Union soon turned the Custis-Lee estate into a bivouac area for troops headed to war. Outraged at Lee's inflicting an unexpected defeat on them at the first Battle of Manassas, Quartermaster General Montgomery Meigs ordered that Union dead be buried in the front yard of Lee's mansion. Thus was America's most hallowed national cemetery born of an act of vengeance.

Robert E. Lee never returned to Arlington. After many years and lengthy litigation, the U.S. Supreme Court finally returned ownership to his son. In 1883, George Washington Custis Lee sold the estate to the U.S. government for $150,000. Today you can visit Lee's old home, which has been restored and furnished to reflect its appearance during the Lee family's time of residence.

ceremony—an impressive ritual of rifle maneuvers, heel clicking, and military salutes. It takes place daily every hour on the hour October through March, every half hour the rest of the year.

Adjoining the tomb is the Greek Revival outdoor **Memorial Amphitheater,** used for special holiday services, particularly on Memorial Day when the sitting president or vice president attends. Free Tourmobile transportation from the visitor center parking lot is provided on these occasions.

On the northern periphery of Arlington National Cemetery, just off Va. 110 about 1¹/₂ miles north of the Kennedy graves, stands the **U.S. Marine Corps War Memorial,** better known as the Iwo Jima Memorial. The famous statue of Marines raising the American flag over Iwo Jima in February 1945 symbolizes the nation's esteem for the honored dead of the U.S. Marine Corps. News photographer Joe Rosenthal won a Pulitzer Prize for his photo of the flag-raising on Mount Suribachi, and sculptor Felix W. de Weldon, then on duty, was moved to create a sculpture based on the scene Rosenthal had captured.

The Memorial grounds are used for military parades on Tuesday from 7 to 8:30pm in summer, and at all times many visitors picnic on the grass. There is a free shuttle from the visitor center starting at 6pm.

Near the Iwo Jima statue is the **Netherlands Carillon,** a gift from the people of Holland, with 50 bells, each carrying an emblem signifying a segment of Dutch society; for instance, the smallest bells represent Dutch youth. Verses cast on each bell were composed by poet Ben van Eysselsteijn. The carillon was officially dedicated on May 5, 1960, the 15th anniversary of the liberation of the Netherlands from the Nazis. The 127-foot-high open steel tower housing it stands on a plaza with steps guarded by two bronze lions. Thousands of tulip bulbs are planted on the surrounding grounds, creating a colorful display in spring. Carillon concerts are presented on Easter Sunday and every Saturday thereafter in April, May, and September, from 2 to 4pm. Concerts are held from 6 to 8pm June through August. Visitors are permitted into the tower after the carillonneur performs, to enjoy spectacular views of Washington.

⊙ **Newseum.** 1101 Wilson Blvd. (at N. Kent St.), Rosslyn. ☎ **888/NEWSEUM** or 703/284-3544. www.newseum.org. Free admission. Audio guides $4. Wed–Sun 10am–5pm. Metro: Rosslyn.

If you've ever envisioned being Dan Rather or Barbara Walters on television, you *can* be at this state-of-the-art museum dedicated to journalism and journalists. Its interactive newsrooms let you be a momentary anchorperson, reporter, editor, interviewer, or sportscaster. The control room staff will even make a tape of your "on the air" performance and sell it to you for $10 at the gift shop. You'll also learn how journalists facing deadlines decide what's news and what isn't, and how they get it to you. You can explore a host of exhibits ranging from a 660 B.C. statue of Thoth, the ancient Egyptian god of scribes, to a huge "Video News Wall" with live TV news feeds coming in from around the world. It's best to rent a headset and audio guide at the front desk and make a tour of the three-story, 72,000-square-foot premises first, with public radio's Susan Stamberg and Bob Edwards speeding you along. Then you can watch a 10-minute video about the news, shown on a 20-by-40-foot high-definition screen in the dome-topped main theater, and return to the areas that interest you most. There are also constantly changing exhibits and appearances by well-known journalists (call ahead for the schedule).

The interactive newsrooms are on the second story; the exhibits, on the third. Outside, Freedom Park has a memorial to all journalists who have died in the line of duty, plus a piece of the Berlin Wall, the door from Martin Luther King, Jr.'s, jail cell in Birmingham, Ala., and other mementos of famous news stories.

The Pentagon. I-395 at Boundary Channel Dr. ☎ **703/695-1776.** Free admission. Open for tours only, June 1–Labor Day every half hour Mon–Fri 9:30am–3:30pm; Labor Day–May 31 on the hour Mon–Fri 9am–3pm. Closed federal holidays. Metro: Blue or Yellow line to Pentagon. Visitor parking south of I-395 on Army Navy Dr. at South Hayes St., opposite Macy's.

Hawk or dove, you'll find it interesting to tour the immense five-sided headquarters of the American military establishment. Built during the early years of World War II, it's the world's largest office building, housing approximately 24,000 employees—as well as, for their convenience, a post office, an Amtrak ticket office, a beauty salon, a dry cleaner, two banks, clothing boutiques, a jeweler, a florist, and more. Many mind-boggling statistics underscore the vastness of the Pentagon—for example, the building contains enough phone cable to gird the globe three times!

The only way to see the Pentagon is on a 1$^1/_2$-hour tour of certain corridors. No reservation is necessary for groups of fewer than nine people, but you must get a ticket at the tour window in the Concourse area near the Metro station. In tourist season, avoid a long wait in line by arriving by 9am. You must bring a photo ID (a driver's license or passport) to be admitted. You'll have to go through a metal detector and have your bags searched before the tour, so leave at your hotel any articles that would arouse protective suspicion. Also be aware that there are no food facilities or public rest rooms at the Pentagon.

A SCENIC DRIVE ALONG THE POTOMAC RIVER

Skirting the south bank of the Potomac River from Mount Vernon to the Capital Beltway (I-495), the **George Washington Memorial Parkway** is one of Virginia's most scenic drives. It's best driven from south to north, since you can pull off at designated areas (perhaps for a picnic) beside or overlooking the river. Thrill-seekers congregate at **Gravelly Point,** just north of Ronald Reagan Washington National Airport, where jet planes roar overhead just a few feet off the ground. Another good spot is north of Key Bridge at **Potomac Overlook Regional Park,** where you'll have a view down over Washington, D.C. As noted in "Outdoor Activities," below, you can also hike, run, or bike along part of the parkway.

OUTDOOR ACTIVITIES

Two first-rate hiking, biking, and running trails begin in Arlington. A 17-mile paved trail starts at Memorial Bridge and borders the **George Washington Memorial Parkway** 17 miles south to Mount Vernon, passing through Old Town Alexandria on the way (see "A Scenic Drive Along the Potomac River," above). Beginning in the Shirlington area, on I-395, the **Washington & Old Dominion (W&OD) Trail** follows Four Mile Run Drive and Glencarlyn Park northwest to an old railroad bed, which then proceeds 45 miles to Purcellville in the Hunt Country. There are access points with parking at Walter Reed Drive and at Columbia Pike. Horses can be ridden on 30$^1/_2$ miles of the W&OD, from Vienna to Purcellville.

You'll have to drive about 15 miles northwest of Arlington to **Great Falls Park,** on Old Dominion Drive in Great Falls, Va. (☎ **703/285-2966**), but you'll be rewarded with easy hiking trails along the rim of the dramatic Mather Gorge, cut by the Potomac River as it roars its way through the foothills before emerging as the broad tidal river separating Arlington from D.C. Some trails are open to mountain bikes, the cliffs are one of northern Virginia's best rock-climbing venues, and kayakers love these rushing waters (bring your own bike, ropes, or kayak). The park is open from 8am to dusk. Admission is $4 per car, good for 3 days. To reach the park, go west on I-66, north on I-495, west on Georgetown Pike (Va. 193), and north on Old Dominion Drive (Va. 738).

SHOPPING

Arlington's prime shopping area sits almost directly over the Pentagon Center Metro station, at South Hayes Street and Army Navy Drive, between I-395 and U.S. 1. Anchored by Macy's and Nordstrom, the plush four-level **Fashion Centre at Pentagon City** (☎ **703/415-2400**) has more than 150 shops, including branches of Ann Taylor, Crate & Barrel, Banana Republic, Brentano's, Scribner's, the Disney Store, Record World, Crabtree & Evelyn, Godiva Chocolates, Hoffritz, Laura Ashley, Victoria's Secret, Lane Bryant, the Limited, the Body Shop, and the Gap. It's built around a soaring atrium that covers a food court and entry to a six-screen movie theater, and it adjoins the Ritz-Carlton Pentagon City (see "Where to Stay," below). Pay parking is available in a six-level garage, but you can park free for 2 hours on weekdays and all day weekends across South Hayes Street at **Pentagon Centre** (☎ **703/415-7612**), which houses Borders Books & Records, a Best Buy discount electronics and appliance store, a Marshall's discount clothing store, Linens 'N' Things, a huge Costco Wholesale, and three very good chain restaurants (California Pizza Kitchen, Chevy's Mexican Restaurant, and Sgt. Pepper's Market). Both complexes are open Monday to Saturday from 10am to 9:30pm and Sunday from 11am to 6pm (Costco's hours vary).

The county's other mall, the much smaller **Ballston Common,** Wilson Boulevard at North Glebe Road (☎ **703/243-8088**), is anchored by J.C. Penney and Hecht's. There's a food court, two restaurants, and a multilevel pay parking garage. Mall shops are open Monday to Saturday from 10am to 9:30pm, Sunday from noon to 5pm.

Potomac Mills, about 20 miles south of Arlington in Dale City, Va. (☎ **800/VA-MILLS** or 703/643-1770), is not only one of the nation's largest outlet malls, but also one of Virginia's most visited tourist attractions. This huge complex of 250 factory and discount shops includes the Swedish retailer Ikea and a large branch of Waccamaw Pottery. Virtually every factory outlet store is represented here, as well as clearance outlets for the likes of Nordstrom, J.C. Penney, Saks Fifth Avenue, and Levi's. The mall is open Monday to Saturday from 10am to 9:30pm, Sunday from 11am to 6pm. It's 30 minutes south of Arlington at Exit 143 off I-95. A shuttle bus runs between the mall and the Rosslyn and Pentagon City Metro stations in Arlington, Wednesday to Sunday. Round-trip fare is $12. Call ☎ **703/551-1050** for schedule and reservations.

Closer are **Tysons Corner Center** (☎ **703/893-9400**) and **Tysons Galleria** (☎ **800/950-7467** or 703/827-7730), two upscale malls across the road from each other at Tysons Corner, at Leesburg Pike (Va. 7) and Chain Bridge Road (Va. 123), just west of I-495. The tenth-largest mall in the country, Tysons Corner Center has more than 230 specialty shops anchored by Bloomingdale's, Nordstrom, Lord & Taylor, Hecht's, and J.C. Penney. Hours are Monday to Saturday from 10am to 9:30pm, Sunday from noon to 5pm. The even more upmarket Tysons Galleria sports a Nordstrom and Macy's among its 120 stores. Hours are Monday to Saturday from 10am to 9pm, Sunday from noon to 6pm. Both malls offer food courts and free parking, and Tysons Corner Center has an eight-screen movie theater. A shuttle bus connects Tysons Corner to the West Falls Church Metrorail station every 30 minutes during business hours.

WHERE TO STAY

Generally a room is easy to come by here, even at the last minute, except perhaps during the height of the spring season, during an occasional large convention, or on Marine Corps Marathon weekend in mid- to late October. The Arlington Visitors Center's **reservations service** will help you find a place to stay (☎ **888/743-8292**).

CRYSTAL CITY & PENTAGON CITY

Adjacent to National Airport, the Crystal City and Pentagon City neighborhoods have the vast majority of Arlington's 9,000-plus hotel rooms. In addition to those listed below, you can choose among the **Courtyard by Marriott Crystal City,** 2899 Jefferson Davis Hwy. (☎ 800/847-4775 or 703/549-0320), which actually lacks a courtyard but does offer a clublike elegance; the **Days Inn Crystal City,** 2000 Jefferson Davis Hwy. (☎ 800/DAYS-INN or 703/920-8600), a mid-rise building actually on South Eads Street at South 20th Street; the **Doubletree Hotel National Airport,** 300 Army Navy Dr. (☎ 800/222-TREE or 703/416-4126), with more than 600 rooms and suites in twin towers; the **Holiday Inn National Airport,** 1489 Jefferson Davis Hwy. (☎ 800/HOLIDAY or 703/416-1600), with 308 rooms right over the Crystal City Metro stop; or the **Hyatt Regency Crystal City,** 2799 Jefferson Davis Hwy. (☎ 800/233-1234 or 703/418-1289), a 685-room highrise that caters to groups. All units at the **Residence Inn by Marriott,** 550 Army Navy Dr. (☎ 800/331-3131 or 703/413-6630), have kitchens.

✪ **Americana Hotel.** 1400 Jefferson Davis Hwy., Arlington, VA 22202. ☎ **800/548-6261** or 703/979-3772. Fax 703/979-0547. 102 rms. A/C TV TEL. $70–$75 double. Seasonal rates available. AE, DC, DISC, MC, V. Free parking. Entry is on S. Eads St. at S. 15th St. Metro: Crystal City.

A holdover from the days when Crystal City had only roadside motels instead of the high-rises that now make a canyon of Jefferson Davis Highway, this modest hotel is a block from the Metro and Crystal Underground's numerous restaurants and shops. Although the Americana has been around since the 1960s, you'll find it clean, extraordinarily well maintained, and equipped with all standard hotel features. Complimentary coffee, orange juice, and pastries are served in the lobby each morning. Free shuttle service to National Airport is available.

✪ **Crystal Gateway Marriott.** 1700 Jefferson Davis Hwy. (U.S. 1), Arlington, VA 22202. ☎ **703/920-3230.** Fax 703/979-6332. 700 rms, including 46 suites. A/C TV TEL. $229–$249 double. Children under 18 stay free in parents' room. Weekend and other packages available.

AE, DC, DISC, MC, V. Parking $10 per night. Entry is on S. Eads St. at S. 18th St. Metro: Crystal City.

Just 5 minutes from National Airport, this first-rate Marriott is connected by a short passageway under U.S. 1 to a subterranean mall with a Metro stop and some 75 shops, restaurants, and facilities such as a bank and hair salon. A six-story atrium skylight lobby is adorned with Oriental art objects. Almost up to Ritz-Carlton quality (see below), rooms here have elegant dark wood furniture, including armoires housing satellite-fed TVs. The 15th and 16th floors are the concierge level, where a private lounge (closed some weekends) serves a complimentary breakfast and evening cocktails with hors d'oeuvres. A concierge is on duty, and additional in-room amenities include nightly turndown, bathroom scales, electric shoe polishers, and magazines.

Dining: Plushest of the hotel's three restaurants is the romantic Tuscany's, serving Northern Italian cuisine under the stars (through the skylight). Not quite as posh is the Terrace, with cushioned wicker furnishings amid lush greenery overlooking the pool. Off the Atrium Lounge, light fare (lunch and dinner) is featured at Teams Sports Bar, equipped with billiard tables and numerous TVs.

Services: Concierge, room service (from 7am to midnight), free newspaper delivery, nightly turndown on request, complimentary airport shuttle.

Facilities: Indoor/outdoor pool, health spa, Jacuzzi, saunas, business center, lobby gift shop plus underground concourse shops.

Howard Johnson Plaza National Airport. 2650 Jefferson Davis Hwy., Arlington, VA 22202. ☎ **800/654-2000** or 703/684-7200. Fax 703/684-3217. 279 rms. A/C TV TEL. $90–$159 double. Weekend rates available. AE, DC, DISC, MC, V. Parking $9 per night. Metro: Crystal City.

Attractively decorated rooms and a good location convenient to the Metro and National Airport make this HoJo a good choice. Its first four floors are used for parking, so the rooms are at least six stories up, and many offer views of D.C. or the Potomac. A Bob's Big Boy family restaurant is open daily from 6am to 11pm, and a McDonald's stands next door. An outdoor pool is on site, and there's free airport shuttle service.

✪ Ritz-Carlton Pentagon City. 1250 S. Hayes St. (at S. 12th St.), Arlington, VA 22202. ☎ **800/241-3333** or 703/415-5000. Fax 703/415-5061. 345 rms, including 41 suites. A/C TV TEL. $249–$279 double; $299–$500 suite. Weekend and other packages available. AE, DC, DISC, MC, V. Parking $22 per night. Metro: Pentagon City.

Across from the Pentagon, the Ritz-Carlton is located in the upscale Fashion Centre retail-office complex. It's hard to believe that this traditional-looking hostelry—decorated with massive polished china cabinets, graceful wing chairs, plush sofas, Oriental rugs, crystal sconces, and a $2.5-million collection of 18th- and 19th-century paintings and antiques—was built as late as 1990. The impeccable service also hearkens back to another era. Rooms are spacious and airy, with beautiful mahogany pieces (some have four-poster beds) and every amenity imaginable: TVs concealed in armoires, plush terry bathrobes, marble bathrooms (complete with phone), and in-room safes.

Guests on Club floors have a private lounge where complimentary breakfast, light lunch, afternoon tea, and hors d'oeuvres and cocktails are served. Club guests also have a private concierge staff.

Dining: The hotel's highly acclaimed Sunday brunch is served in the Grill, which feels like an English club with its green-marble mantel, equestrian-themed oil paintings and bronzes, and shaded table lamps and wall sconces. A popular luncheon buffet and afternoon tea are served daily in the Lobby Lounge.

Services: Multilingual concierge staff, 24-hour room service, nightly turndown, baby-sitting, complimentary shoeshine, and airport shuttle.

Facilities: Indoor pool, fitness and exercise center, Jacuzzi, steam room, sauna, business center, gift shop.

COLUMBIA PIKE

✪ Arlington/Cherry Blossom Travelodge. 3030 Columbia Pike (between Walter Reed Dr. and S. Glebe Rd.), Arlington, VA 22204. ☎ **800/578-7878** or 703/521-5570. Fax 703/271-0081. 76 rms. A/C TV TEL. $62–$76 double. Additional person $7 extra; children under 18 stay free in parents' room. AE, DC, DISC, MC, V. Free parking. Metro: Pentagon, then any no. 16 bus. From I-395, go north on Glebe Rd., turn right on Columbia Pike to motel on right.

Set back from the street so there's little traffic noise, this clean, well-run property is built of glass, steel, and brick. Flowerpots hang on exterior walkways, leading to clean, fairly spacious guest rooms for the money. Rincome, a Thai restaurant open from 11am to 11pm, adjoins the motel. Nearby on Columbia Pike are several fast-food and ethnic restaurants, including the excellent Matuba Japanese restaurant and the very popular Bob & Edith's Diner (see "Where to Dine," below).

Sheraton National Hotel. 900 S. Orme St. (at junction of Columbia Pike & Arlington Blvd.), Arlington, VA 22204. ☎ **800/325-3535** or 703/521-1900. Fax 703/521-2122. 417 rms, including 17 suites. A/C TV TEL. $179–$209 double. Weekend packages available. AE, DC, DISC, MC, V. Parking $5 per night.

Situated in a small residential neighborhood near the huge Navy Annex office building, this 16-story Sheraton manages to avoid the sterile personality projected by so many large hotels. The two-story lobby is an airy contemporary concourse with lots of plants, cheerful by day with the bright light of skylight windows and lit at night by a rectangular fixture that looks like a modernist light sculpture. Guest rooms are spacious, and many have fabulous views of the Potomac and Washington, D.C. Concierge-level suites on the 14th floor each come with luxuries such as a separate living room, a wet bar, a refrigerator, two TVs, and a second bathroom, plus a private lounge offering complimentary continental breakfast, afternoon snacks, and an honor bar. All accommodations are handsomely appointed and of exceptional value.

Dining/Entertainment: Stars, an intimate 16th-floor dining room, offers spectacular nighttime views of the river and Washington. A pianist performs nightly in the adjacent Stars Lounge. Off the lobby, the gardenlike Café Brasserie serves a breakfast buffet, lunch, and dinner. Adjoining the cafe, the Quarterdeck Lounge invites relaxation with drinks, light fare, and sports TVs.

Services: Room service (from 7am to 11pm); same-day laundry/valet; complimentary shuttle to airport, Pentagon, and Pentagon City Mall.

Facilities: Rooftop indoor pool and outdoor sundeck with panoramic views, exercise room with sauna, newsstand.

ROSSLYN

Right across Key Bridge from Georgetown in D.C., Rosslyn has several chain hotels in addition to the properties mentioned below. About half the 584 rooms at the **Marriott Key Bridge,** 1401 Lee Hwy. (☎ **800/331-3131** or 703/524-6400), overlook the river and Washington, as do its rooftop restaurant and lounge. Also here are the **Best Western Key Bridge,** 1850 N. Fort Myer Dr. (☎ **800/528-1234** or 703/522-0400), and the **Hyatt Arlington,** 1325 Wilson Blvd. (☎ **800/233-1234** or 703/525-1234). Both are high-rise properties that cater primarily to groups and business travelers.

Holiday Inn Rosslyn Westpark. 1900 N. Fort Myer Dr. (at I-66), Arlington, VA 22209. ☎ **800/368-3408** or 703/807-2000. Fax 703/522-8864. 276 rms, 24 suites. A/C TV TEL. $109–$119 double; $135 suite. Children 18 and under stay free. Weekend packages available. AE, DC, DISC, MC, V. Free parking. Metro: Rosslyn.

Here's a property that offers good value and great convenience. This Holiday Inn is just a block from the Rosslyn Metro station and a 10-minute walk across the Key Bridge to Georgetown restaurants and nightlife. Many rooms in the 17-story property have balconies overlooking the Potomac and/or the Washington Monument. Amenities include in-room safes and irons and ironing boards; local calls are free. In addition, king rooms offer stocked minibars, coffeemakers, and hair dryers.

The hotel's glass-enclosed rooftop restaurant, Vantage Point, features American fare, including moderately priced all-you-can-eat buffet lunches. Additional facilities include a coffee shop, swimming pool with sundeck, whirlpool, sauna, exercise room, coin-operated laundry, and gift shop. Room service is available during restaurant hours.

Motel 50 Rosslyn. 1601 Arlington Blvd. (U.S. 50), Arlington, VA 22209. ☎ **800/504-4888** or 703/524-3400. Fax 703/524-0220. 38 rms. A/C TV TEL. $45–$75 double, for up to 4 people. Rates include continental breakfast. AE, MC, V. Free parking. Metro: Rosslyn.

Owned and operated by the same family as the Americana Hotel (see above), Motel 50 is located right on U.S. 50, so you're going to hear traffic from most of the rooms. But otherwise, it's a clean, well-run, and friendly property. An extensive continental breakfast is served in the lobby each morning, and free transport is provided to and from National Airport on request. Many popular restaurants are nearby.

Quality Inn Iwo Jima. 1501 Arlington Blvd. (U.S. 50), Arlington, VA 22209. ☎ **800/228-5151** or 703/524-5000. Fax 703/522-5484. 141 rms. A/C TV TEL. $79–$110 double. Children under 18 stay free. Weekend packages available. AE, DC, DISC, MC, V. Free parking. Metro: Rosslyn.

This pleasant Quality Inn, with a brick and white stucco facade, offers attractive and exceptionally comfortable rooms. Though this property is also situated on U.S. 50, it's set back a bit, which makes a big difference in terms of traffic noise. In-room amenities include hair dryers and coffeemakers; some rooms also offer irons and ironing boards. Facilities include an indoor/outdoor swimming pool, coin-operated laundry, and a small fitness room. MacArthur's Café, a moderately priced restaurant serving American and Italian fare, is decorated with World War II memorabilia. *USA Today* is available free in the lobby, and room service is offered during restaurant hours. The Metro is about 3 blocks from the hotel.

BALLSTON

Comfort Inn Ballston. 1211 N. Glebe Rd. (at Washington Blvd.), Arlington, VA 22201. ☎ **800/221-2222** or 703/247-3399. Fax 703/524-8739. 126 rms. A/C TV TEL. $100–$120 double. Children under 18 stay free in parents' room. Weekend and other packages available. AE, DC, DISC, MC, V. Free parking. From I-66, take Glebe Rd. exit and turn left. Metro: Ballston.

Housed in a three-story red-brick building, this Comfort Inn offers a convenient location off I-66, just 10 minutes from National Airport and a 5-block walk to the Metro and Ballston Common Mall. Rooms are exceptionally bright and spacious, with dark polished-wood furnishings and all the standard motel amenities. There's a gift shop in the lobby and an adjoining Italian restaurant.

Holiday Inn Arlington at Ballston. 4610 N. Fairfax Dr. (at N. Wakefield St.), Arlington, VA 22203. ☎ **800/HOLIDAY** or 703/243-9800. Fax 703/527-2677. 221 rms. A/C TV TEL. $139 double. Weekend packages available. AE, DC, DISC, MC, V. Free parking. From I-66 eastbound, take Exit 71 to hotel on right. From I-66 westbound, take Exit 71, turn left on Glebe Rd., right on Fairfax Dr. to hotel on left. Metro: Ballston.

Although it lacks charm, this nine-story, utilitarian hotel is just 2 blocks from the Ballston Metro station and the many restaurants surrounding it (the hotel provides a free shuttle to the station). Entered from interior corridors, the long rooms come equipped with two double beds or one king-size bed, plus either a sofa or a table and chairs. The Lacey Station Dining Car Restaurant at the lobby level serves three meals daily and provides room service during restaurant hours, while the Side Track Lounge features a cozy, U-shaped bar. Facilities include an outdoor pool, fitness center with sauna, jogging trail, and gift shop.

WHERE TO DINE
CRYSTAL CITY

A row of old storefronts in the 500 block of South 23rd Street, between Jefferson Davis Highway (U.S. 1) and South Fern Street, now houses a good selection of Chinese, Italian, Mexican, Thai, and Vietnamese restaurants, most with sidewalk seating in fine weather. In addition to those listed below, the moderately priced **Cafe Italia,** 519 S. 23rd St. (☎ 703/521-2565), is notable for its traditional pastas and other dishes from the old country. You can get inexpensive chow while watching the action at two sports bars, **Crystal City Sports Pub** (☎ 703/521-8215) and **The Fox Hole** (☎ 703/685-0555).

Chez Froggy. 509 S. 23rd St. (at S. Eads St.). ☎ **703/979-7676.** Reservations recommended. Main courses $12.50–$21. DC, DISC, MC, V. Mon–Fri 11am–2pm and 5:30–10pm; Sat 5:30–10pm. Metro: Crystal City. FRENCH.

The food at this cozy bistro is maintained with consistency by chef Jean-Claude Lelan. In good weather, there's outdoor dining at the sidewalk. Indoors, the decor is pleasant but unpretentious, with ceramic and glass frogs, large and small, scattered about to add a note of whimsy. At dinner, appetizers of homemade pâté or half a dozen snails in garlic butter deserve consideration, as does the salad of fresh spinach and chèvre with almonds. You can always get fresh frog's legs sautéed in butter and garlic. Daily specials include fresh items such as soft-shell crabs with either garlic or almonds. From the regular menu comes veal scallopine in creamy mushroom-and-Calvados sauce, steamed salmon with fresh basil beurre blanc, and roast rack of lamb with garlic and thyme. Potatoes, assorted vegetables, French bread, and sweet butter accompany all entrees. Dessert offerings include *la coupe Froggy* (vanilla ice cream, fresh strawberries, whipped cream, and Curaçao). The lower-priced lunch menu offers salads and omelets as well.

Ristorante Portofino. 526 S. 23rd St. (at S. Eads St.). ☎ **703/979-8200.** Reservations recommended. Main courses $14–$19. AE, DC, MC, V. Mon–Fri 11am–2pm; daily 5–10pm. Metro: Crystal City. ITALIAN.

A pretty downstairs garden room is just one of the dining spaces in this bustling Italian restaurant, a family-owned institution since 1970. The entrance is at the rear of the converted three-story residence, and you'll know when you hear the taped arias of such famous tenors as Enrico Caruso and Luciano Pavarotti that you're in for a home-style Italian meal. Dinner begins with some tasty specialties, including fried calamari, ricotta-filled baked eggplant with creamy tomato sauce, and prosciutto with fresh mozzarella. Any of the pastas on the menu can be ordered as a half portion for an appetizer—linguine with green pesto sauce, fettuccine Alfredo, and spaghetti carbonara are a few of the possibilities. Entrees include veal in all expected guises (parmigiana, piccata, marsala), plus a good variety of chicken and fish dishes. The house special dessert is a wonderful rum cake with whipped cream.

COLUMBIA PIKE

Bob & Edith's Diner. 2310 Columbia Pike (at S. Wayne St.). ☎ **703/920-6130.** Reservations not accepted. Breakfasts $3–$8.50; sandwiches and burgers $2–$5; meals $5–$8. No credit cards. Daily 24 hours. DINER.

This family-operated institution was here long before the explosion of new, polished-chrome diners popped up all over the nation, and it's still *the* place for local residents to have breakfast any time of day—or a late-night snack when every other restaurant has closed. It's extremely popular for breakfast on weekends, when a horde of young customers cranks up rock music on the high-decibel jukebox; during the week, however, you'll find everyone from business executives to plumbers sitting at the counter or in the booths. Breakfast ranges from steak and eggs to thick, light waffles and pancakes, or you can choose from 28 sandwiches and burgers, all cooked to order on the grills behind the counter. Entrees are plain and simple American, such as steaks, meat loaf, roast beef, and liver and onions.

If the wait's too long here, you can mosey up the street to **America's Best Diner,** 2820 Columbia Pike, at Walter Reed Drive (☎ **703/521-1566**), a modern restaurant built to look like a 1950s-style diner.

✪ **Matuba Japanese Restaurant.** 2915 Columbia Pike (at Walter Reed Dr.). ☎ **703/521-2811.** Reservations not accepted. Sushi $2–$4.50 per 2 items; main courses $7–$12. AE, MC, V. Mon–Thurs 11:30am–2pm and 5:30–10pm; Fri 11:30am–2pm and 5:30–10:30pm; Sat 5:30–10:30pm; Sun 5:30–10pm. JAPANESE.

In a row of shops adjacent to the Arlington Cinema & Drafthouse, this narrow storefront is usually packed with Arlingtonians dining at natural wood tables and chairs or at the bar in the rear, where young Japanese chefs turn tuna, shrimp, salmon, eel, and other fresh ingredients into fine sushi. The cooked items are equally good, particularly the chicken teriyaki prepared over a charcoal grill and the tempura shrimp and vegetables wrapped in a light, delicate batter. Prices here are a bargain, especially the $4.95 daily lunch special, which includes miso soup, green salad, cooked meat or seafood, steamed rice, six pieces of sushi, and a cube of bean curd topped by a slightly sweet sauce.

ROSSLYN

✪ **Red Hot & Blue.** 1600 Wilson Blvd. (at N. Pierce St.). ☎ **703/276-7427.** Reservations not accepted. Sandwiches $5–$6; main courses $7–$17.50. AE, MC, V. Sun–Thurs 11am–10pm; Fri–Sat 11am–midnight. Metro: Rosslyn. AMERICAN.

Condé Nast Traveler magazine picked Red Hot & Blue as one of the best barbecue joints in the country, so join the line of hungry diners waiting for tables at this casual, fun-filled, high-energy eatery. Some of the crowd gravitates to the bar for frosted steins of beer under the jolly eye of a blue-neon pig strumming a red guitar. The late Lee Atwater, chairman of the Republican National Committee, along with a group of Tennessee politicians and a TV reporter, opened the restaurant and named it for a Memphis radio show. The decor is a jumpy black, white, and red, and seating is in banquettes and at small tables jammed rather close together. But the food is just fine—ribs wet (with sauce) or dry (secret spices), barbecued beef brisket, smoked chicken and ham, fried catfish, and homemade trimmings like beans, coleslaw, potato salad, and fries. For dessert, try the Southern-style banana pudding or an Oreo cookie sundae. Naturally, the speakers play the blues, and occasionally nationally known blues artists perform here.

Red Hot & Blue has a **carryout branch** at 3014 Wilson Blvd. in Clarendon (see below). The menu and prices are the same at both branches.

Tom Sarris' Orleans House. 1213 Wilson Blvd. (at N. Lynn St.). ☎ **703/524-2929.** Reservations not accepted. Main courses $8–$15. AE, DC, DISC, MC, V. Mon–Fri 11am–11pm; Sat 4–11pm; Sun 4–10pm. Metro: Rosslyn. PRIME RIB/STEAKS.

Almost hidden by the surrounding high-rises, this white pseudo-antebellum building, trimmed in wrought iron, has been the home of the area's best beef bargain for more than 3 decades. The interior resembles a New Orleans garden, with iron chairs and railings, leaded-glass fixtures, and ceiling fans. The menu offers steaks, baked chicken, and seafood, but locals and visitors alike flock here for the prime rib, especially the regular cut: It's ample for most appetites and costs just $7.95—a great value anywhere and an absolute steal here. Heartier appetites can opt for the larger Louis XIV cut ($10.95) or the mammoth portion ($13.95). The meat is tender and well seasoned, served in its own juices. With it, you get an oven-roasted potato and offerings from an exceptional salad bar that's decorated like a riverboat. Wine and other drinks are available.

CLARENDON

Centered on North Highland Street and Wilson, Clarendon, and Washington boulevards, this area is now one of the prime places to dine in the Washington area, so diverse and so good are its multitude of inexpensive ethnic restaurants. You'll emerge from the Clarendon Metro station in the median strip dividing Wilson and Clarendon boulevards; the restaurants are on either side of the station, or within a block's walk.

In addition to those mentioned below, you can eat Greek food alfresco under a grapevine at **Aegean Taverna,** 2950 Clarendon Blvd., at North Garfield Street (☎ 703/841-9494), which also has Greek music on weekend evenings. **Atami,** 3155 Wilson Blvd. (☎ 703/522-4787), sets an appropriately Japanese scene for fine sushi. **Cafe New Delhi,** 1041 N. Highland St., at North 11th Street (☎ 703/528-2511), dispenses high-quality North Indian–style chicken and lamb from a tandoori oven, while the small and simple **Madhu Ban,** 3217 N. Washington Blvd. (☎ 703/528-7184), is cheap and strictly vegetarian (its crispy, crepe-like masala dosas are among the best in town). **A Taste of Casablanca,** 3211 Washington Blvd. (☎ 703/527-7468), will take you to Morocco, while **La Cantinita's Havana Cafe,** 3100 Clarendon Blvd. (☎ 703/524-3611), will transport you to Miami's South Beach and its Cuban fare. If the wait at Queen Bee (see listing below) is too long, you can get almost-as-good Vietnamese cuisine at several other restaurants, including **Cafe Dalat,** 3143 Wilson Blvd. (☎ 703/276-0935); **Cafe Saigon,** 1135 N. Highland St. (☎ 703/243-6522); and **Little Viet Garden,** 3012 Wilson Blvd. (☎ 703/522-9686), which has adorned part of a parking lot with potted trees and shrubs for outdoor dining.

For some ethnic cuisine hailing from closer to home, a carryout branch (with tables and counter seating, but no table service) of **Red Hot & Blue** (see above) serves its Memphis-style barbecue at 3014 Wilson Blvd. (☎ 703/243-1510). You can get all the old American favorites at the **Silver Diner,** 3200 Wilson Blvd., at Washington Boulevard (☎ 703/812-8600).

The two most popular neighborhood pubs are **Witlow's on Wilson,** 2854 Wilson Blvd., at North Fillmore Street (☎ 703/276-9693), and the more yuppiefied **Clarendon Grill,** 1101 N. Highland St., between Clarendon Boulevard and North 11th Street (☎ 703/524-7455). Both have bands playing on weekend evenings.

Note: At night, Hard Times Cafe, Queen Bee, and many other Clarendon restaurants have free **validated parking** in the lot on North Highland Street in the block north of Wilson Boulevard.

Hard Times Cafe. 3028 Wilson Blvd. (at N. Highland St.). ☎ **703/528-2233.** Reservations not accepted. Main courses $5–$6.50. AE, MC, V. Mon–Thurs 11:30am–10pm; Fri–Sat 11:30am–11pm; Sun noon–10pm. Metro: Clarendon. CHILI.

A casual, laid-back hangout, the Hard Times Cafe is the kind of chili parlor you'd find in Texas. The bar is always crowded, the jukebox plays country music, and the "bowls of red" are first-rate. The Lone Star State decor features Texas flags, plus a longhorn steer hide and historic photos of the Old West on the walls. Seating is in roomy oak booths as well as at tables. The restaurant cooks up three styles of chili: Texas (ground chuck simmered with secret spices and *no* tomatoes), Cincinnati (with hot and sweet spices, including cinnamon), and spicy vegetarian with peanuts. You can request your chili with beans or spaghetti. Homemade cornbread is included in the price; cheese and onions cost slightly more. Sandwiches, burgers, salads, and sides of onion rings and steak fries round out the offerings. Pecan pie is the logical dessert.

✪ **Queen Bee.** 3181 Wilson Blvd. (near Washington Blvd.). ☎ **703/527-3444.** Reservations not accepted. Main courses $6–$9. MC, V. Daily 11am–10pm. Metro: Clarendon. VIETNAMESE.

Locals flock to this friendly and unpretentious eatery directly across the street from the Clarendon Metro station. Etched-glass sconces provide soft lighting, and mirrors line one of the walls, adding an illusion of depth to the room. At lunch or dinner, start with the Queen Bee platter, a sampler of appetizers including a spring roll, shrimp tempura, charcoal-grilled pork, and house salad. Among the entrees, specials include steamed rice-flour meat rolls and shrimp cakes. Chicken is prepared in several delicious ways—curried, in ginger sauce, or with lemongrass. Roast duck and quail are also stellar entrees. Vegetarians can choose from a mélange of vegetables sautéed in oyster sauce or fresh tofu sautéed with tomato and scallions. Meal-size Vietnamese-style *pho* (noodle soups) are a house specialty.

BALLSTON

Food Factory. 4221 N. Fairfax Dr. (entry at rear, off N. Stuart St.). ☎ **703/527-2279.** Reservations not accepted. Main courses $4–$7. MC, V. Mon–Fri 11am–10pm; Sat–Sun noon–10pm. Metro: Ballston. SOUTH ASIAN.

Plain and simple, with cafe chairs set at family-style tables, the Food Factory is famous hereabouts for its fine kabobs cooked in a tandoori oven. You can opt for Afghani-style sticks of beef, chicken, lamb, or spicy *chapli* (ground beef), or pick one of the Northern Indian–style samosas or meat and vegetable curries displayed at a cafeteria table.

✪ **Rio Grande Cafe.** 4301 N. Fairfax Dr. (at N. Taylor St.). ☎ **703/528-3131.** Reservations not accepted. Main courses $7–$17. AE, DC, DISC, MC, V. Mon–Thurs 11am–10:30pm; Fri–Sat 11:30am–11:30pm. Metro: Ballston. MEXICAN.

Part of an excellent small chain (George Bush was a regular at the Bethesda, Maryland, branch when he lived in the White House), this casual, north-of-the-border roadhouse consistently serves some of the best Tex-Mex fare in northern Virginia. The dining room sets an appropriate scene with crumbling adobe walls bearing old advertising signs and photos from southwest Texas—although in warm weather you might want to wait for an umbrella table out on the sidewalk. You can start with old standbys such as nachos, quesadillas, or *ceviche* (South American–style marinated raw fish), then go on to tacos, enchiladas, burritos, or fajitas. Or you can choose from chicken, frog's legs, or quail grilled over mesquite, or perhaps a nightly special, such as rainbow trout sautéed with cilantro, white wine, and lemon butter.

NEARBY DINING

Evans Farm Inn and the Sitting Duck Pub. 1696 Chain Bridge Rd. (at Dolly Madison Blvd. [Va. 123]), McLean. ☎ **703/356-8000.** Reservations recommended. Main courses $15–$25; lunch buffet $12 ($8 for children under 6). AE, DC, DISC, MC, V. Mon–Sat noon–2:30pm and 5–11pm; Sun noon–9pm (Sunday brunch 11am–2pm in the pub). Free parking. Easiest entrance to find is on Dolly Madison Blvd. (Va. 123) about half a mile east of I-495. AMERICAN.

A 40-acre working farm, complete with horses, goats, pigs, a donkey, and all sorts of fowl, is the setting for Ralph and Maria Evans' charming 18th-century–style building erected in the 1950s with timbers, old bricks, and early glass salvaged from nearby colonial sites. Their award-winning restaurant has large dining rooms decorated with old farm implements, carousel horses, and spinning wheels. Downstairs, the Sitting Duck Pub evokes an old Tudor inn with a dartboard, Hogarth drawings, copper pitchers, and, in winter, a roaring fire. Also on the property are a cookhouse that displays colonial cooking items, a mill and mill pond, a country store and doll shop, and a large duck pond. There's a whole afternoon's entertainment here.

The lunch buffet includes a trip to the bounteous salad bar, an entree, vegetables, and home-baked bread. Dinner entrees, such as roast prime rib, half a chicken, sirloin steak, or barbecued baby-back ribs, come with vegetables, spoon bread, and salad bar. The Evans Farm garden provides all the floral decorations and much of the produce used at the inn. On Friday and Saturday nights, there's piano playing and singing in the pub, which also serves Sunday brunch.

ARLINGTON AFTER DARK

The best source of up-to-the-minute nighttime entertainment information is the daily "Style" and the Friday "Weekend" sections of the *Washington Post,* available at newsstands all over northern Virginia.

THE PERFORMING ARTS   All of northern Virginia is very much in the orbit of the John F. Kennedy Center for the Performing Arts, the National Theater, and other such first-rate venues across the Potomac in Washington, D.C. See *Frommer's Washington, D.C.,* or *Frommer's Washington, D.C., from $50 a Day* for details.

On this side of the Potomac, ✪ **Wolf Trap Farm Park,** 1624 Trap Rd., Vienna, Va. (☎ **703/255-1868**), is the nation's only national park dedicated to the performing arts, with a star-studded summer season. Performances are held in the open-air, 6,900-seat Filene Center II, but many patrons choose to picnic and watch the show from under the stars out on the sloping lawn (the sound system is great, but bring binoculars, and arrive early for a prime spot). A smaller venue, the **Barns of Wolf Trap,** offers performances indoors during the spring and fall. Tickets range from $12 to $20 on the lawn and up to $40 or more inside, depending on who's playing. The lawn opens 90 minutes before the performance. Take I-66 west and follow the signs for I-495 north to the Dulles Toll Road; stay on local exits (you'll see a sign) until you come to Wolf Trap. Toll is 50¢. Metro: West Falls Church, then take the Wolf Trap Express Shuttle ($3.50), which runs every 30 minutes beginning 2 hours before showtime.

THE BAR & MUSIC SCENE   Lively pubs along Wilson Boulevard have made Arlington a center of music for the entire national capital area. "Arlington's Wilson Boulevard used to be way out there, but now it's definitely in," the *Washington Post* said recently in describing this hip scene. Indeed, a number of bands have formed here, including the nationally known hard-core punk group Fugazi; the county even has its own record label, Dischord.

You can catch the tunes every weekend night along Wilson Boulevard between Rosslyn and Clarendon. Working west, alternative and pop prevail at the sprawling **Bardo Rodeo,** in a former automobile dealership at 2100 Wilson Blvd., near the Courthouse Metro station (☎ **703/527-9399**). In Clarendon, the pierced set takes in alternative and indie rockers at **Galaxie Hut,** a tiny hole-in-the-wall at 2711 Wilson Blvd. (☎ **703/525-9399**). **IOTA,** a block west at 2832 Wilson Blvd. (☎ **703/522-8340**), showcases roots rock, a blend of country, folk, and rock. Across the street, **Witlow's on Wilson,** 2854 Wilson Blvd., at North Filmore Street (☎ **703/**

276-9693), specializes in frat rock and blues. More upscale is **Clarendon Grill,** a block south of the boulevard at 1101 N. Highland St. (☎ **703/524-7455**), which offers a mix of music.

Also on the strip, **Ireland's Four Courts,** 2051 Wilson Blvd., near the Courthouse Metro stop (☎ **703/525-3600**), features Gaelic musicians Tuesday through Saturday.

Elsewhere, **Cowboy Cafe South,** in the Adams Square shopping center at 2421 Colombia Pike (☎ **703/486-3467**), features country and western groups Saturday and some other evenings, as does **Whitey's,** 2761 N. Washington Blvd., at Pershing Drive (☎ **703/525-9825**).

2 Alexandria

5 miles S of Washington, D.C.; 95 miles N of Richmond

Founded by a group of Scottish tobacco merchants, the seaport town of Alexandria came into being on a sunny day in July 1749, when a 60-acre tract of land was auctioned off in half-acre lots. Although Alexandria addresses today include a large chunk of nondescript suburbia, George Washington and Robert E. Lee would still recognize the streets of their hometown, now known as **Old Town.** As you stroll the brick sidewalks and cobblestone streets of this highly gentrified historic district, you'll see more than 2,000 18th- and 19th-century buildings. You can visit Gadsby's Tavern, where 2 centuries ago the men who created this nation discussed politics, freedom, and revolution over tankards of ale. You can stand in the doorway of the tavern where Washington reviewed his troops for the last time, visit Lee's boyhood home, and sit in the pews of Christ Church where both men worshipped.

In this "mother lode of Americana," the past is being ever-increasingly restored in an ongoing archaeological and historical research program. Although the present is manifested by an abundance of quaint shops, boutiques, art galleries, and restaurants capitalizing on the volume of tourism (not to mention hordes of young people just hanging out on Friday and Saturday nights), it's still easy to imagine yourself in Colonial times and picture the bustling waterfront where fishermen brought in the daily catch and foreign vessels unloaded exotic cargo.

ESSENTIALS

VISITOR INFORMATION   The **Alexandria Convention & Visitors Association** at Ramsay House, 221 King St., at Fairfax Street (☎ **703/838-4200;** 703/838-5005 for 24-hour Alexandria events recording; fax 703/838-4683), is open daily from 9am to 5pm (closed New Year's Day, Thanksgiving, and Christmas). Here you can pick up maps and brochures, find out about special events taking place during your visit, and get information about accommodations, restaurants, sights, shopping, and whatever else. If you come by car, get a free **1-day parking permit** here for gratis parking at any 2-hour meter for up to 24 hours (the permits don't apply to 2-hour zones without meters).

GETTING THERE   By Plane   Ronald Reagan Washington National Airport (☎ **703/685-8000**) is just 2 miles north of Alexandria via the George Washington Memorial Parkway. Washington's Metrorail (see below) provides easy transport to Alexandria via its Blue and Yellow lines. SuperShuttle (☎ **800/BLUE-VAN**) operates frequent van service daily from 6am to 10pm.

By Car   Going south from Washington, cross the 14th Street Bridge (I-395) and go south on the scenic George Washington Memorial Parkway, which becomes Washington Street, Alexandria's main thoroughfare. A left turn on King Street will take you into the heart of Old Town. I-95 crosses the Potomac River at Alexandria; take Exit 1 (U.S. 1) and go north into Old Town.

By Train   The Amtrak passenger **rail station** (☎ **703/836-4339**) is at 110 Callahan Dr., near King Street.

By Washington Metrorail   From Arlington or Washington, take the Blue or Yellow lines to the King Street station (it's across the tracks from Amtrak's Alexandria station). From the Metro station, board DASH buses numbered AT-2 or AT-5 (85¢) to King and Fairfax—right to the door of the visitor center. Take a transfer, and you can board any DASH bus for 4 hours. It's a short ride from the station; in fact, you could walk it, but better to save your feet for sightseeing.

CITY LAYOUT   Old Town Alexandria is laid out in a simple grid system. Going west from the Potomac River, Union to Lee Street is the 100 block, Lee to Fairfax the 200 block, and so on. Numbers on the cross streets (more or less going north and south) are divided north and south by King Street. King to Cameron is the 100 block north, Cameron to Queen the 200 block north, and so on. King to Prince is the 100 block south, and so on.

As a glance at the walking-tour map later in this chapter will indicate, Old Town is contained within several blocks. Park your car for the day, don comfortable shoes, and start walking—it's the easiest way.

GETTING AROUND   Old Town is compact, so you can easily see its historic sights on foot. Alexandria's bus system, known as **DASH,** provides service from 5am to 11pm daily except New Year's Day, Thanksgiving, and Christmas. Buses numbered AT-2 and AT-5 run between the King Street Metro station and the Ramsay House visitor center (which gives away route maps and sells DASH tokens). Base fare is 85¢, with exact fare or tokens required. Call ☎ **703/370-3274** for schedules.

All the major **car-rental firms** are based at Ronald Reagan Washington National Airport. For a taxi, call **Alexandria Yellow Cab Company** (☎ **703/549-2500**) or **Alexandria White Top Cab Company** (☎ **703/683-4004**).

WHAT TO SEE & DO
ATTRACTIONS

Whenever you come, you're sure to run into some activity or other—a jazz festival, a tea garden or tavern gambol, a quilt exhibit, a wine tasting, or an organ recital. It's all part of Alexandria's *cead mile failte* (100,000 welcomes) to visitors.

The visitor center at Ramsay House (see above) sells a money-saving **block ticket** for discounted admission to five historic Alexandria sites: Gadsby's Tavern, Lee's Boyhood Home, the Carlyle House, Stabler-Leadbeater Apothecary Shop, and the Lee-Fendall House. The ticket, which can also be purchased at any of the five buildings, costs $12 for adults, $5 for students 11 to 17, and is free for children under 11.

Note: Many Alexandria attractions are closed on Monday. The Potomac plantations (described later in this chapter) are just 14 miles south of Alexandria and are most logically visited on day trips from Old Town.

Alexandria Black History Resource Center. 638 N. Alfred St. ☎ **703/838-4356.** Free admission. Tues–Sat 10am–4pm.

Located in a 1940s building that originally housed the black community's first public library, the Black History Resource Center exhibits historical objects, photographs, documents, and memorabilia relating to African Americans in Alexandria from the 18th century on. In addition to the permanent collection, the museum presents rotating exhibits.

The Athenaeum. 201 Prince St. (at Lee St.). ☎ **703/548-0035.** Free admission (donations appreciated). Wed–Fri 11am–3pm; Sun 1–4pm. Call for Sat hours. Gallery shows Sept–June.

A handsome Greek Revival building with a classic portico and unfluted Doric columns, the Athenaeum is home to the Northern Virginia Fine Arts Association. Art exhibits here run the gamut from Matisse lithographs to shows of East Coast artists. The building, which dates from 1851, originally contained the Bank of the Old Dominion. The bank's operations were interrupted by the Civil War, when Yankee troops turned the building into a commissary.

Boyhood Home of Robert E. Lee. 607 Oronoco St. ☎ **703/548-8454.** Admission $4 adults, $2 children 11–17, free for children under 11. Tours Mon–Sat 10am–3:30pm; Sun 1–3:30pm.

Revolutionary cavalry hero Gen. Henry "Light-Horse Harry" Lee brought his wife, Ann Hill Carter, and five children to this early Federal-style mansion in 1812 when the future commander of the Confederate army was just 5 years old. A tour of the house, built in 1795, gives you a glimpse into the gracious lifestyle of Alexandria's gentry. George Washington was an occasional guest of earlier occupants, Col. and Mrs. William Fitzhugh. In 1804, the Fitzhughs' daughter, Mary Lee, married Martha Washington's grandson, George Washington Parke Custis, in the drawing room, and the Custises' daughter married Robert E. Lee. General Lafayette, a comrade-in-arms of Light-Horse Harry Lee during the American Revolution, honored Ann Hill Carter Lee with a visit to the house in October 1824. The drawing room is now called the "Lafayette Room" to commemorate that visit. The current furnishings are of the Lee period but did not belong to the family.

Carlyle House. 121 N. Fairfax St. ☎ **703/549-2997.** Admission $4 adults, $2 children 11–17, free for children under 11. Tues–Sat 10am–4:30pm; Sun noon–4:30pm.

Not only is Carlyle House regarded as one of Virginia's most architecturally impressive 18th-century homes, but it also figured prominently in American history. Patterned after Scottish-English manor houses, it was completed in 1753 by Scottish merchant John Carlyle for his bride, Sara Fairfax of Belvoir, who hailed from one of Virginia's most prominent families. A waterfront property with its own wharf, it became a social and political center visited by many great men of the time—George Washington among them. But its most important moment in history occurred in April 1755, when Maj. Gen. Edward Braddock, commander-in-chief of His Majesty's forces in North America, met here with five colonial governors and asked them to tax colonists to finance a campaign against the French and Indians. Colonial legislatures refused to comply, one of the first instances of serious friction between America and Britain. Nevertheless, Braddock made Carlyle House his headquarters during the campaign.

The house is furnished with period pieces, and the original large parlor and adjacent study have survived intact. An upstairs room houses an exhibit called "A Workman's View," which explains 18th-century construction methods with hand-hewn beams and hand-wrought nails. **Tours,** lasting about 40 minutes, leave every half hour between 10am and 4:30pm.

✪ **Christ Church.** 118 N. Washington St. (at Cameron St.). ☎ **703/549-1450.** Free admission. Mon–Sat 9am–4pm; Sun 2–4:30pm. Closed all federal holidays.

This sturdy red-brick Georgian-style church, in continuous use since 1773, would be an important national landmark even if its two most distinguished members were not Washington and Lee. There have, of course, been many changes since Washington's day. The bell tower, church bell, galleries, and organ were added by the early 1800s; the "wineglass" pulpit, during an 1891 restoration. But much of what was changed later has since been unchanged. The pristine white interior with wood moldings and gold trim is colonially correct, though modern heating has obviated the need for charcoal braziers and hot bricks. For the most part, the original structure remains, including the handblown glass in the windows. The town has grown up around the building that was first called the "Church in the Woods" because of its rural setting.

Christ Church has had its share of historic moments. Washington and other early members fomented revolution in the churchyard, and Robert E. Lee met here with Richmond representatives, who offered him command of Virginia's army at the beginning of the Civil War. You can sit in either the Lee family pew or the pew where George and Martha sat with her two Custis grandchildren. In 1991, the **Old Parish Hall** was completely restored to its original appearance; it now houses a gift shop and an exhibit on the history of the church. Do walk in the weathered graveyard, Alexandria's first and only burial ground until 1805. The remains of 34 Confederate soldiers are also interred here.

Fort Ward Museum and Historic Site. 4301 W. Braddock Rd. ☎ **703/838-4848.** Free admission. Fort, daily 9am–sunset; museum, Tues–Sat 9am–5pm, Sun noon–5pm. From Old Town, follow King St. west, go right on Kenwood St., then left on W. Braddock Rd. Continue for ³/₄ mile to the entrance on the right.

A short drive from Old Town, this 45-acre museum, park, and historic site take you a leap forward in Alexandria history to the Civil War. The action here centers, as it did in the early 1860s, on an actual Union fort that Lincoln ordered erected as part of a system called the "Defenses of Washington." About 90% of the earthwork walls are preserved, and the Northwest Bastion has been restored, with six mounted guns (there were originally 36) facing south waiting for the Confederates who never came. Visitors can explore the fort as well as replicas of the Ceremonial Entrance Gate and an officer's hut. A museum on the premises houses Civil War memorabilia. Tours of the fort are given by guides in Union soldier costumes on selected Sundays.

Picnic areas with barbecue grills are located in the park surrounding the fort, and evening concerts are presented from June to mid-September in the outdoor amphitheater.

Friendship Firehouse. 107 S. Alfred St. ☎ **703/838-3891** or 703/838-4994. Free admission. Fri–Sat 10am–4pm; Sun 1–4pm.

Alexandria's first fire-fighting organization, the Friendship Fire Company, was established in 1774. As the city grew, the company attracted increasing recognition, not only for its firefighting efforts but also for its ceremonial and social presence at parades and other public occasions. In 1855, Friendship's building at 107 S. Alfred St. was destroyed by fire, and a new brick building (today the restored museum) in the fashionable Italianate style was erected on the same spot. A strong local tradition centers on George Washington's involvement with the firehouse as a founding member, active firefighter, and purchaser of its first fire engine, although extensive research does not bear out these stories. This interesting museum not only exhibits firefighting paraphernalia dating back to the 18th century, but also documents the Friendship Company's efforts to claim Washington as one of their own.

Gadsby's Tavern Museum. 134 N. Royal St. ☎ **703/838-4242.** Admission $4 adults, $2 children 11–17, free for children under 11. Apr–Sept, Tues–Sat 10am–5pm, Sun 1–5pm; Oct–Mar, Tues–Sat 11am–4pm, Sun 1–4pm. Last tour begins 45 min. before closing.

Alexandria was at the crossroads of colonial America, and the center of life in Alexandria was Gadsby's Tavern. Consisting of two buildings—a tavern dating to about

1770 and the City Tavern and Hotel (ca. 1792)—it's named today for a memorable owner, Englishman John Gadsby, whose establishment was a "gentleman's tavern" renowned for elegance and comfort. The rooms have been restored to their 18th-century appearance. The second-floor ballroom with its musicians' gallery was the scene of Alexandria's most lavish parties, and since 1797 George Washington's birthday ball and banquet have been an annual tradition here.

Thirty-minute **tours** depart 15 minutes before and after the hour. A special tour called Gadsby's Time Travels is offered periodically. To cap off the experience, you can dine at Gadsby's colonial-style restaurant (see "Where to Dine," below).

George Washington Masonic National Memorial. 101 Callahan Dr. (at King St.). ☎ **703/683-2007.** Free admission. Daily 9am–5pm. Guided tours available about every 45 min. between 9:15am and 3:45pm.

Visible for miles around, this imposing neoclassical shrine is modeled on the design of the lighthouse at Alexandria, Egypt, and dedicated to the most illustrious member and first Worshipful Master of Alexandria Lodge No. 22. It sits atop Shooter's Hill, overlooking the city. Emphasizing the panoramic view is an overlook with a wide-angle photograph pinpointing Civil War battle sites in Alexandria, taken by Matthew Brady during the Civil War. President Coolidge and former president Taft spoke at the cornerstone-laying in 1923. The pink-granite memorial was dedicated in 1932, with President Hoover assisting in the rites.

Visitors enter the ornate Memorial Hall, dominated by a colossal 17-foot-high bronze of Washington sculpted by Bryant Baker. On either side are 46-foot-long murals by Allyn Cox: One depicts Washington laying the Capitol cornerstone, and the other shows him and his officers in Christ Church, Philadelphia. A stained-glass window in the hall honors 16 patriots associated with Washington. A fourth-floor museum displays many valuable items, including the Washington family Bible, the bedchamber clock stopped by Washington's physician at 10:20pm (the time of his death), and a key to the Paris Bastille presented to the lodge by the Marquis de Lafayette. On the ninth floor, an observatory parapet offers a 360-degree view that takes in the Potomac, Mount Vernon, the Capitol, and the Maryland shore.

Lee-Fendall House. 614 Oronoco St. (at Washington St.). ☎ **703/548-1789.** Admission $4 adults, $2 children 11–17, free for children under 11. Tues–Sat 10am–3:45pm; Sun 1–3:45pm.

This handsome Greek Revival–style house is a veritable Lee family museum of furniture, heirlooms, and documents. Light-Horse Harry Lee never actually lived here, although he was a frequent visitor, as was his good friend George Washington. He did own the original lot, but sold it to Philip Richard Fendall (himself a Lee on his mother's side), who built the house in 1785. From 1785 to 1903, the house was home to 37 Lees of Virginia. John L. Lewis, the American labor leader, was its last private owner.

Thirty-minute guided **tours** interpret the 1850s era of the home and offer insight into Victorian family life. You'll also see the colonial garden with its magnolia and chestnut trees, roses, and boxwood-lined paths.

The Lyceum. 201 S. Washington St. ☎ **703/838-4994.** Free admission. Mon–Sat 10am–5pm; Sun 1–5pm.

Another distinguished Greek Revival building, the Lyceum is a museum focusing on Alexandria's history from colonial times through the 20th century. It features changing exhibits and an ongoing series of lectures, concerts, and educational programs. An adjoining nonprofit shop carries 18th-century reproductions and crafts.

Even without its manifold offerings, however, the brick-and-stucco Lyceum itself merits a visit. Built in 1839, it was designed in the Doric temple style (with imposing white columns) to serve as a lecture, meeting, and concert hall. The first floor originally contained the Alexandria Library and natural-science and historical exhibits. It was an important center of Alexandria's cultural life until the Civil War, when Union forces took it over for use as a hospital.

Old Presbyterian Meeting House. 321 S. Fairfax St. (at Duke St.). ☎ **703/549-6670.** Free admission. Mon–Fri 9am–4:30pm; services Sun at 8:30 and 11am.

Presbyterian congregations have worshipped in Virginia since Jamestown days, when the Rev. Alexander Whittaker converted Pocahontas. This brick church was established by Scottish pioneers in 1774. Though it wasn't George Washington's church, the Old Meeting House bell tolled continuously for 4 days after his death in December 1799, and memorial services were preached from the pulpit here by Presbyterian, Episcopal, and Methodist ministers.

Many famous Alexandrians are buried in the church graveyard—John and Sara Carlyle, Dr. James Craik (the surgeon who treated Washington, dressed Lafayette's wounds at Brandywine, and ministered to the dying Braddock at Monongahela), and William Hunter, Jr., founder of the St. Andrew's Society of Scottish descendants (bagpipers pay homage to him the first Saturday of each December). It's also the site of the Tomb of an Unknown Revolutionary Soldier. The original parsonage, or *manse,* is still intact. There's no guided tour, but there are recorded narratives in the church and graveyard.

Stabler-Leadbeater Apothecary. 105–107 S. Fairfax St. ☎ **703/836-3713.** Admission $2.50 adults, $2 students 11–17, free for children under 11. Mon–Sat 10am–4pm; Sun 1–5pm. Closed New Year's Day, Thanksgiving, and Christmas.

When it went out of business in 1933, this landmark drugstore was the second-oldest in continuous operation in America. Beginning in 1792, it was run for five generations by the same family, and its early patrons included George Washington and Robert E. Lee, who purchased the paint for Arlington House here. Gothic Revival decorative elements and Victorian-style doors were added in the 1860s.

Today the apothecary shelves are lined with about 900 of the original handblown gold-leaf–labeled bottles (the most valuable collection of antique medicinal bottles in the United States), old scales stamped with the royal crown, patent medicines, and equipment for bloodletting. Among the shop's documentary records is an 1802 epistle from Mount Vernon: "Mrs. Washington desires Mr. Stabler to send by the bearer a quart bottle of his best Castor Oil and the bill for it."

Docent **tours** are offered Sundays from 1 to 5pm; other times, a 10-minute recording guides you around the displays.

The Torpedo Factory. 105 N. Union St. (between King and Cameron sts., on the Potomac River). ☎ **703/838-4565.** Free admission. Shops and galleries daily 10am–5pm; archaeology exhibits Tues–Fri 10am–3pm, Sat 10am–5pm, Sun 1–5pm.

Built by the U.S. Navy in 1918 and operated as a torpedo shell-case factory until the early 1950s, then used as storage for dinosaur bones and various artifacts of the Smithsonian Institution, this block-long, three-story waterfront building now houses six galleries and 85 studios for artists and craftspeople, who create and sell their own works on the premises. Here you can see artists at work—potters, painters, printmakers, photographers, sculptors, and jewelers, among others.

Exhibitions in the art galleries change monthly. On permanent display are exhibits on Alexandria history provided by Alexandria Archaeology (☎ **703/838-4399**), headquartered here and engaged in extensive city research.

GUIDED TOURS

Though it's easy to see Alexandria on your own, you may find your experience enhanced by a comprehensive walking tour. **Doorways to Old Virginia** (☎ 703/548-0100) and **Old Town Experience** (☎ 703/836-0694) offer tours daily during the summer months, less often during the off-season ($4 per person). Check with them or the visitor center for schedules and tickets. Doorways to Old Virginia charges $4 per person; Old Town Experience, $5 per person. Doorways to Old Virginia also offers ghost tours on weekend evenings from May through October.

POTOMAC RIVER CRUISES

Sightseeing cruises of both the Alexandria and Washington, D.C., waterfronts and down the river to Mount Vernon aboard the **_Admiral Tilp_** and the **_Matthew Hayes_** depart from the city pier behind the Torpedo Factory, 105 N. Union St. (☎ 703/548-9000). Tour guides provide an entertaining commentary on the cities' history, legends, and sights. There are snack stands on the passenger boats, or you can bring your own lunch. The schedules change from year to year and season to season, so check at the boats' wharfside booth or call for information and reservations. Prices range from $7 to $22 for adults, $6 to $20 for seniors, and $4 to $10 for children 2 to 12.

The **_Dandy,_** a 100-ton restaurant cruise ship berthed at the foot of Prince Street (☎ 703/683-6090), sails up the Potomac to Washington, D.C., affording passengers super views of the city and its monuments, on 2¹/₂-hour luncheon and 3-hour dinner cruises. Reservations are imperative, since you'll choose your entree when you call. Lunches have three courses; dinner is a multi-course affair. Lunch cruises range from $28 to $32 per person, and dinner trips from $50 to $58 per person, depending on the day of the week. Prices include the meal but not bar drinks, coffee, or gratuities. Music and a small dance floor round out the dinner cruise. The _Dandy_ also offers midnight cruises.

WALKING TOUR
Old Town Alexandria

Start: Ramsay House visitor center, King Street and Fairfax Street.
Finish: Torpedo Factory, Waterfront at Cameron Street.
Time: Allow approximately 2¹/₂ hours, not including museum and shopping stops.
Best Times: Anytime.
Worst Times: Monday, when many historic sites are closed.

You'll feel as though you've stepped back into the 18th century as you stroll Alexandria's brick-paved sidewalks, lined with colonial residences, historic houses and churches, museums, shops, and restaurants. This walk ends at the waterfront, no longer a center of commercial shipping but now home to a vibrant arts center along the Potomac riverfront park.

Begin your walk at the:

1. **Ramsay House visitor center,** 221 King St., at Fairfax Street, in the heart of the Historic District. It's a historic structure itself, with a Dutch barn roof and an English garden. After perusing the wealth of information offered here about Alexandria, go north on Fairfax to:

2. **Carlyle House,** an elegant 1753 manor house set off from the street by a low wall. Continue north on Fairfax to the corner. Turn left on Cameron, past the back of the old city hall, to the red-brick buildings across Royal Street, known as:

3. Gadsby's Tavern. The original 18th-century tavern now houses a museum of 18th-century antiques, while the hotel portion is an Early American–style restaurant.

☕ **TAKE A BREAK**   If you're ready for lunch, the 18th-century atmosphere at Gadsby's Tavern is the perfect place for a sandwich or salad.

From Gadsby's, continue west on Cameron Street and turn right on St. Asaph Street. At Queen Street, you can see:

4. No. 523, the smallest house in Alexandria. Continuing north on St. Asaph, you'll come to:

5. Princess Street. The cobblestones that pave the street are original; heavy traffic is banned here. One block farther north on St. Asaph, turn left at Oronoco Street. On your right is:

6. Robert E. Lee's Boyhood Home, where he lived before he went to West Point in 1825. Across Oronoco Street, at the corner of Washington, is the:

7. Lee-Fendall House, a gracious white clapboard residence that was home to several generations of Lees. Enter through the pretty colonial garden. Head south (left) on Washington, a busy commercial thoroughfare, to Queen Street and cross over to:

8. Lloyd House, a beautiful late-Georgian residence (1797) that is now part of the Alexandria Library and houses a fascinating collection of old documents, books, and records on the city and state. From here, proceed south on Washington Street to the quiet graveyard entrance behind:

9. Christ Church, where the Washingtons and Lees worshipped. Leave by the front entrance, on Columbus Street, and turn left to King Street.

☕ **TAKE A BREAK**   A cappuccino-and-pastry break at **Bread & Chocolate,** 611 King St., is guaranteed to revive flagging spirits. Sandwiches and salads are also available at this casual spot.

From King Street, turn left on Alfred Street, to the:

10. Friendship Firehouse, on South Alfred Street. This historic firehouse has an extensive collection of antique fire-fighting equipment. Turn left at the corner of Prince Street and proceed to Washington. At the corner is the Greek Revival:

11. Lyceum, built in 1839 as the city's first cultural center. Today it's a city historical museum. The museum shop has a lovely selection of crafts, silver, and other gift items. At the intersection of Washington and Prince stands:

12. *The Confederate Soldier,* a sadly dejected bronze figure modeled after a figure in the painting *Appomattox* by John A. Elder. From here, continue walking east on Prince to Pitt Street, then turn left to King. Turn right and you'll see the fountain in the large open area called:

13. Market Square, along King Street from Royal to Fairfax in front of the Williamsburg-style Town Hall, which has been used as a town market since 1749. Today the market is held once a week, on Saturday mornings. From here, turn right on Fairfax to the quaint:

14. Stabler-Leadbeater Apothecary Shop, housing a remarkable collection of early medical ware and handblown glass containers. Proceed south on Fairfax to Duke Street, to the:

15. Old Presbyterian Meeting House, the 18th-century church where George Washington's funeral sermons were preached in 1799. The graveyard has a marker

Walking Tour—Old Town Alexandria

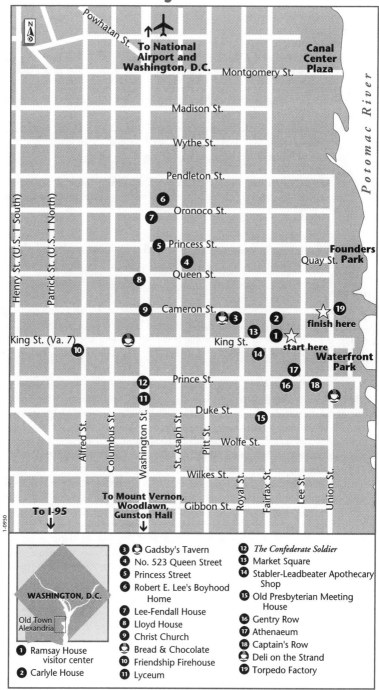

1 Ramsay House visitor center
2 Carlyle House
3 🌀 Gadsby's Tavern
4 No. 523 Queen Street
5 Princess Street
6 Robert E. Lee's Boyhood Home
7 Lee-Fendall House
8 Lloyd House
9 Christ Church
🌀 Bread & Chocolate
10 Friendship Firehouse
11 Lyceum
12 *The Confederate Soldier*
13 Market Square
14 Stabler-Leadbeater Apothecary Shop
15 Old Presbyterian Meeting House
16 Gentry Row
17 Athenaeum
18 Captain's Row
🌀 Deli on the Strand
19 Torpedo Factory

commemorating the Unknown Soldier of the Revolutionary War. Retrace your steps back to Prince Street and turn right. Between Fairfax Street and Lee Street you'll see:

16. Gentry Row, named for the local leaders who made their homes in these three-story town houses in the 18th and 19th centuries. At the corner of Prince and Lee is the:

17. Athenaeum, a handsome Greek Revival structure that now houses contemporary art shows. Cross Lee Street to:

18. Captain's Row, a pretty cobblestone section of Prince Street. You're now in sight of the Potomac riverfront and may want to stroll down to the little waterfront park at the foot of Prince Street for a panoramic view of the river.

☕ **TAKE A BREAK**   The **Deli on the Strand,** on Union Street between Prince and Duke, has delicious salads and sandwiches you can eat at picnic tables on their porch or carry out to the park.

Continue north on Union Street to the:

19. Torpedo Factory, an arts-and-crafts center with studios and galleries open to the public.

SHOPPING

Old Town has hundreds of charming boutiques, antiques stores, art galleries, and gift shops selling everything from souvenir T-shirts to 18th-century reproductions. Plan to spend a fair amount of time browsing between visits to historic sites. A guide to antiques stores is available at the visitor center. Here are some suggestions to get you started.

KING STREET   Take your time as you stroll along King Street between the river and Washington Street. Beginning with the art galleries and studios in the Torpedo Factory at the water's edge (see "Attractions," above), this main drag has many fascinating shops interspersed among its restaurants and offices.

One highlight here is the **Winterthur Museum Store,** 207 King St., between Lee and Fairfax streets (☎ 703/684-6092), an off-site venture of the renowned museum of decorative arts on the magnificent country estate of horticulturist Henry Francis du Pont, in Delaware's Brandywine Valley. It's a delightful browse, including the back garden, which features all sorts of garden plants and ornaments. You'll come across fine reproductions from the Winterthur collections, including lamps, prints, ceramics, brassware, jewelry, garden furniture, and statuary. At the corner of King and Lee streets, **The Pineapple, Inc.** (☎ 703/836-3639), has two floors of gorgeous things for the home, including exquisite door handles and knobs, handmade antique quilts, period reproduction furnishings, candlesticks, hurricane lamps, picnic baskets, and the like.

UNION STREET NEAR THE RIVER   Near the river on South Union Street between Duke and Prince streets, you'll come to the **Christmas Attic** (☎ 703/548-2829), where it's always the holiday season, complete with toy train sets choo-chooing along a track overhead and 20 or more decorated trees. Christmas decorations, gifts, toys, and ornaments are sold year-round, with festive items for other holidays available in their appropriate months. The **Carriage House,** 215 S. Union St., houses two interesting shops: **Rocky Road to Kansas** (☎ 703/683-0116) has on display more than 200 vintage and 20th-century patchwork quilts, antiques, gift items, and collectibles; and **Old Town Coffee, Tea & Spice** (☎ 703/683-0856) carries about 50 kinds of coffee and 175 varieties of tea, plus gourmet imports like

German cornichons, Dundee preserves from Scotland, and imported cheeses and pâtés. Accessories such as teapots and cosies and coffeepots are sold here, too.

Around the corner on Prince Street, between South Union and Strand streets, you'll find **Olde Towne Gemstones** (☎ **703/836-1377**), where rock and fossil enthusiasts Pat, Mike, and Marvin Young actually make jewelry from petrified dinosaur bones that come from their collection of fossils, some up to 500 million years old. There's also a wide-ranging collection of minerals, gemstones, petrified wood, and objets d'art. Banded-agate clocks are a popular item.

ANTIQUING NORTH OF KING STREET There's good antiques shopping north of King Street on North Lee Street, between Cameron and Queen streets. The building known as **Old Town Market and Antique Mall,** 210 N. Lee St., houses **Teacher's Pet/Trojan Antiques** (☎ **703/549-9766**), two adjoining shops offering a highly browsable mix of collectible dolls and stuffed animals, hand-painted birdhouses, antique and reproduction furnishings, antique silver, old books and postcards, and much more. While you're here, peek into two other antiques/collectibles shops: **Time Juggler** (☎ **703/836-3594**) and **Old Town Antiques** (☎ **703/519-0009**).

Also in this block, **Crilley Warehouse Mall,** 218 N. Lee St. (☎ **703/548-3330**), is a mini-mall housing several shops on two levels in a turn-of-the-century bakery. **Hunt's III** (☎ **703/548-1111**) has three showrooms filled with antiques and collectibles—furniture, Herend hand-painted porcelain china and figurines, silver, jewelry boxes, crystal, and more. Also noteworthy is **Monday's Child** (☎ **703/548-3505**), featuring lovely imported and domestic clothing for children.

Now walk west on Cameron to the corner of North Royal Street, where **La Cuisine** (☎ **703/836-4435**) offers a seemingly endless supply of copperware, cookbooks, terrines, cooking implements, and hard-to-find ingredients, and **Gossypia** (☎ **703/836-6969**) carries Mexican and Latin American fold art—masks, textiles, Nativity scenes, and jewelry. Some clothing is sold here as well.

WHERE TO STAY

The properties listed below are located in the historic district. In addition, the **Holiday Inn Hotel & Suites,** 625 1st St. (☎ **800/HOLIDAY** or 703/548-6300), is on the north end of Old Town, next to the Best Western Old Colony (see below). The nearby **Executive Club Suites,** 610 Bashford Lane (☎ **800/535-CLUB** or 703/739-2582), is a converted apartment building, so all units have kitchens. Another good bet if you want a kitchen is **Embassy Suites,** 1900 Diagonal Rd. (☎ **800/EMBASSY** or 703/684-5900), across the street from the King Street Metro station on the western edge of Old Town. The high-rise **Ramada Plaza Hotel Old Town,** 901 N. Fairfax St., at Madison Street (☎ **800/2-RAMADA** or 703/683-6000), stands near the river, giving some of its 258 rooms water views.

The Alexandria Hotel Association provides a **reservation service** (☎ **800/296-1000**) to help you find a room at these and other properties, including several chain motels near I-95 and I-395.

Best Western Old Colony. 615 1st St. (at Washington St.), Alexandria, VA 22314. ☎ **800/528-1234** or 703/739-2222. Fax 703/549-2568. 151 rms. A/C TV TEL. $89 double. Rates include continental breakfast. AE, DC, DISC, MC, V. Free parking.

Encompassing some 7 acres, this Best Western is on the northern edge of Old Town, a 15-minute walk from the prime attractions. It's a rambling two-story red-brick motel built in 1958 but greatly improved over the years. Although the grounds are predominately parking lots, the covered walkways, English ivy, and large shade trees break up the black-top and lend a colonial ambience. The rooms are spacious, although the baths are dated and small. Limited facilities include an outdoor pool.

Econo Lodge Old Town. 700 N. Washington St. (between Madison and Wythe sts.), Alexandria, VA 22314. ☎ **800/237-2243** or 703/836-5100. Fax 703/597-7015. 39 rms. A/C TV TEL. $50–$65 double. Additional person $5 extra. AE, DISC, MC, V. Free parking.

This very plain but clean Econo Lodge is just a few blocks from the center of Old Town activity. The rooms are on the old side by today's standards but nevertheless good-sized, and some come equipped with refrigerators. All units in this two-story brick building face a small parking lot. The motel offers free shuttle service to National Airport.

✪ **Holiday Inn Select Old Town.** 480 King St. (between Pitt and Royal sts.), Alexandria, VA 22314. ☎ **800/368-5047** or 703/549-6080. Fax 703/684-6508. 227 rms. A/C TV TEL. $169–$179 double. Weekend and other packages available. AE, DC, DISC, MC, V. Parking $6 per night.

Right in the heart of Old Town (just a block from the visitor center), this six-story red-brick building is one of the finest of all Holiday Inns; in fact, it even feels more like an inn than a hotel. Entered via a quiet brick courtyard and Williamsburg-look lobby, the hotel occupies an entire block. Complimentary morning coffee and Danish and afternoon English tea are served in the lamp-lit lobby. Guest rooms are colonial in feel, and come with safes and hair dryers. Rooms with king-size beds have small seating areas with couches and coffee tables.

Dining: 101 Royal Restaurant features seafood and steaks. Annabelle's, an intimate lounge off the courtyard, is open for afternoon and evening drinks and light snacks.

Services: Concierge, room service (from 6:30am to midnight), same-day laundry, nightly turndown, complimentary baby-sitting and airport and Metro shuttles.

Facilities: Heated indoor pool, exercise room, sauna, beauty salon, gift shop.

✪ **Morrison House.** 116 S. Alfred St. (between King and Prince sts.), Alexandria, VA 22314. ☎ **800/367-0800** or 703/838-8000. Fax 703/684-6283. 42 rms, 3 suites. A/C TV TEL. $150–$240 double; $295 suite. Weekend and holiday packages available. AE, DC, MC, V. Parking $10 per night.

Designed after the grand manor houses of the Federal period, Morrison House, in the heart of Old Town, is enchanting from the moment you ascend the curving staircase to its white-columned portico, where a butler greets you at the door of the marble foyer. The residential-style lobby divides into a series of beautifully appointed, cozy rooms: a mahogany-paneled library, a formal parlor, and two intimate restaurants. Afternoon tea is served daily from the sideboard in the library. Guest rooms are charmingly furnished with fine Federal-period reproductions, including mahogany four-poster beds, brass chandeliers, and decorative fireplaces. In-room amenities include two phones, TV and VCR, fresh flowers, and imported terry robes. The plush Italian marble baths are equipped with hair dryers.

Dining/Entertainment: The Dining Room, with antique prints on the walls and fresh bouquets at every table, serves all three meals. The Elysium, with the look of an English club, is the inn's showpiece, offering fine Mediterranean-influenced cuisine. Serving both restaurants, the Grill bar offers more than 20 different wines and champagnes by the glass. A resident pianist performs on the baby grand in the lounge on Thursday, Friday, and Saturday.

Services: 24-hour butler, concierge, and room service; indoor valet parking; free newspaper delivery; nightly turndown; complimentary shoeshine.

Facilities: Privileges at nearby health club.

Sheraton Suites. 801 N. St. Asaph St. (between Madison and Montgomery sts.), Alexandria, VA 22314. ☎ **800/325-3535** or 703/836-4700. Fax 703/548-4514. 247 suites. A/C TV TEL. $125–$159 double. Weekend and holiday packages available. AE, DC, DISC, MC, V. Parking $7 per night.

Old Town Alexandria Accommodations & Dining

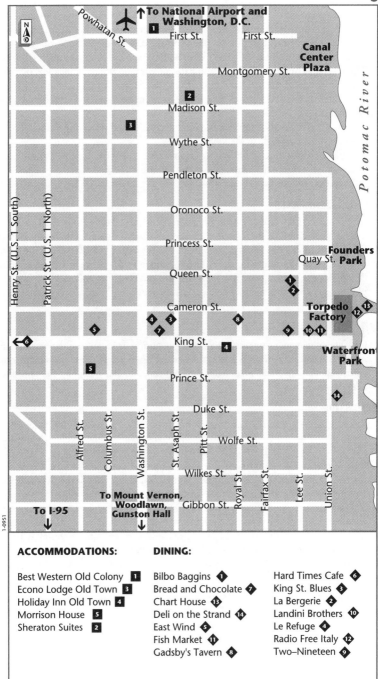

ACCOMMODATIONS:

Best Western Old Colony **1**
Econo Lodge Old Town **3**
Holiday Inn Old Town **4**
Morrison House **5**
Sheraton Suites **2**

DINING:

Bilbo Baggins ◆**1**
Bread and Chocolate ◆**7**
Chart House ◆**13**
Deli on the Strand ◆**14**
East Wind ◆**5**
Fish Market ◆**11**
Gadsby's Tavern ◆**8**

Hard Times Cafe ◆**6**
King St. Blues ◆**3**
La Bergerie ◆**2**
Landini Brothers ◆**10**
Le Refuge ◆**4**
Radio Free Italy ◆**12**
Two–Nineteen ◆**9**

Recently renovated to the tune of $2.5 million, this very hospitable all-suite hotel provides a luxurious residential atmosphere. Each spacious suite has a full living room with a wet bar and fridge, an extra phone on the desk (equipped with call waiting), a comfortable convertible sofa, big TVs in both rooms, and irons and ironing boards. Those on the corporate club level also have fax-copy-printer machines and two-line portable phones. Bedrooms are set off from the living rooms by curtained French doors, and most have king-size beds. Other in-room amenities include coffeemakers and hair dryers.

Dining: The Fin and Hoof Bar & Grill offers steaks and seafood specialties. Breakfast is served buffet-style in the lobby.

Services: Concierge, room service (from 6:30am to 11pm), same-day laundry/valet, complimentary newspaper and airport shuttle.

Facilities: Indoor pool, health club, Jacuzzi, gift shop.

BED & BREAKFASTS

Thirty private Old Town homes, all historic properties dating from 1790 to 1895, offer B&B accommodations under the aegis of Evelyn Boxley of **Princely Bed & Breakfast Ltd.,** 2822 Avenham Ave., Roanoke, VA 24014 (☎ **800/470-5588**). The best time to call for reservations is Monday through Friday between 10am and 6pm. Rooms are nicely furnished, most with antiques and fireplaces, and cost $85 to $100, plus tax, per room per night. There's a $20 surcharge on those rates if you stay only 1 night.

WHERE TO DINE

Old Town has more fine restaurants, serving cuisines from around the world, than it does historic attractions. A few of the best are listed below. You'll pass many others as you walk up King Street from the Potomac, and along Union Street south of King Street.

EXPENSIVE

Chart House. 1 Cameron St. (on the Potomac River). ☎ **703/684-5080.** Reservations advised. Main courses $18–$29; Sun brunch $13–$22. AE, DC, DISC, MC, V. Mon–Thurs 5–10:15pm; Fri–Sat 5–11pm; Sun 11am–2:30pm and 5–10pm. AMERICAN.

One of the few Washington-area restaurants actually on the Potomac River, this member of the national Chart House chain gives diners a view of the river, with alfresco patio dining in good weather. Under a soaring cathedral ceiling, the interior is decidedly tropical, featuring rattan furniture, potted palms, and a copper-covered salad bar. The straightforward American fare includes steaks, prime rib, and seafood, supplemented by daily specials and the salad bar. All entrees come with freshly baked squaw and sourdough breads and unlimited salad-bar selections. For dessert, try the house specialty of mud pie—Kona coffee ice cream in an Oreo cookie crust, topped with fudge, whipped cream, and diced almonds.

✪ **Gadsby's Tavern.** 138 N. Royal St. (at Cameron St.). ☎ **703/548-1288.** Reservations advised. Main courses $17–$21. DC, DISC, MC, V. Mon–Sat 11:30am–3pm and 5:30–10pm; Sun 11am–3pm and 5:30–10pm. AMERICAN.

In the spirit of history, pass through the portals where Washington reviewed his troops for the last time and dine at the famous Gadsby's Tavern, where the period furnishings, wood-plank floors, fireplace, and gaslight-style lamps re-create an authentic colonial atmosphere. You'll dine off the same kind of pewter and china our ancestors used and be served by appropriately costumed wait staff. The coachyard serves as an outdoor dining area. All the fare is homemade, including the Sally Lunn bread baked daily. Lunch might consist of an appetizer of shrimp and clams in puff pastry, chicken roasted on an open fire and served with fried potatoes, and a dessert of buttermilk pie. In winter, warm yourself with drinks like hot buttered rum and Martha's Remedy—coffee, cocoa, and brandy. Dinner entrees usually include roast turkey, crabcakes, stuffed flounder, and colonial game pie. Entertainers perform 18th-century style during dinner and at Sunday brunch.

La Bergerie. 218 N. Lee St. (in Crilley Shops, between Cameron and Queen sts.). ☎ **703/683-1007.** Reservations required. Main courses $15–$24. AE, DC, DISC, MC, V. Mon–Sat 11:30am–2:30pm and 5:30–11pm. FRENCH/SPANISH.

Alexandria's fanciest restaurant features Basque specialties in a fittingly provincial setting, with crystal chandeliers and oil paintings of the Pyrenees countryside on exposed-brick walls. White-linened tables, each adorned with a pink rose in a silver vase, add an elegant note. Exquisite desserts and a large floral arrangement grace an antique dresser up front, and there are many hanging and potted plants. Owner-chef Jean Champagne-Ibarcq's lunch fare includes hors d'oeuvres of pâté, escargots, and avocado stuffed with crabmeat, plus main courses of chicken in white wine and filet of fresh sole sautéed with apples. His dinner entrees include wine-braised salmon, swordfish with tomato and basil over pasta, or roast duck. A fresh plum tart with homemade plum ice cream is a delicious finish.

☺ Landini Brothers. 115 King St. (between Lee and Union sts.). ☎ **703/836-8404.** Reservations recommended. Main courses $13.50–$24. AE, DC, DISC, MC, V. Mon–Sat 11:30am–11pm; Sun 4–10pm. NORTHERN ITALIAN.

The classic, delicate cuisine of Tuscany is featured at this rustic, almost grotto-like restaurant with stone walls, a flagstone floor, and rough-hewn beams overhead. It's especially charming at night by candlelight. There's additional seating in a lovely upstairs dining room. Everything is homemade—the pasta, the desserts, and the crusty Italian bread. Things might get underway with prosciutto and melon or Top Neck clams on the half shell, followed by prime aged beef tenderloin medallions sautéed with garlic, mushrooms, and rosemary in a Barolo wine sauce. Dessert choices include tiramisu and custard-filled fruit tarts.

Two-Nineteen. 219 King St. (between Fairfax and Lee sts.). ☎ **703/549-1141.** Reservations suggested, especially for dinner in the formal dining rooms. Main courses $15–$24. AE, DC, DISC, MC, V. Mon–Thurs 11am–10:30pm; Fri–Sat 11am–11pm; Sun 5–10:30pm. AMERICAN/CREOLE.

Two-Nineteen comprises three formal Victorian-style dining rooms, a covered sidewalk patio, and the Bayou Room, a Rathskeller-like basement. Crystal chandeliers, rose-velvet upholstery, and a floral-patterned carpet highlight these elegant dining rooms in which New Orleans cuisine is featured. Begin with oysters Bienville (baked in cream sauce with shrimp and crab) or crabmeat royale (with artichoke bottoms and hollandaise sauce). Seafood entrees include blackened gulf fish with blue crab claws, *poisson en papillote* (fish baked in parchment paper), and seafood-stuffed rainbow trout. The covered patio, reminiscent of a New Orleans courtyard, is a delightful alternative in warm weather.

In the Bayou Room, you'll find many of the same items featured upstairs, plus sandwiches and salads. The setting is highly atmospheric, with stone and brick walls, oak beams, a bar of leaded glass and oak, and a ceiling plastered with a collection of business cards from all over the country.

MODERATE

☺ Bilbo Baggins. 208 Queen St. (between Fairfax and Lee sts.). ☎ **703/683-0300.** Reservations suggested, especially for dinner on weekends. Main courses $12–$16. AE, DC, DISC, MC, V. Mon–Sat 11:30am–2:30pm and 5:30–10:30pm; Sun 4:30–9:30pm. AMERICAN.

Named for a character in Tolkien's *The Hobbit,* this charming two-story restaurant offers fresh homemade fare. The downstairs area has rustic wide-plank floors, wood-paneled walls, oak tables, and a brick oven centerpiece. Upstairs is another dining room with stained-glass windows and seating on old church pews. It adjoins a skylit wine bar with windows overlooking Queen Street treetops. Candlelit at night, it becomes an even cozier setting. The eclectic menu changes daily to reflect seasonal specialties, but lunch entrees usually include quiche Lorraine, gnocchi pesto, and spinach/bacon/mushroom salad. At dinner, we've enjoyed entrees such as salmon topped with crabmeat and red and black caviar, and lamb chops brushed with Dijon mustard and sautéed in bread crumbs. An extensive wine list is available (more than 30 boutique wines are offered by the glass and another 150 by the bottle), as are all bar drinks and excellent homemade desserts like steamed dark-chocolate bread pudding topped with sliced bananas.

East Wind. 809 King St. ☎ **703/836-1515.** Reservations suggested. Main courses $8–$15. AE, DC, DISC, MC, V. Mon–Thurs 11:30am–2:30pm and 6–10pm; Fri 11:30am–2:30pm and 5:30–10:30pm; Sat 5:30–10:30pm; Sun 5:30–9:30pm. VIETNAMESE.

The decor of this Vietnamese restaurant is very appealing: Sienna stucco and knotty-pine–paneled walls are adorned with works by talented Vietnamese artist Minh Nguyen. There are planters of greenery, a lovely floral arrangement on each table, and a large floral display up front. An East Wind lunch might begin with an appetizer of *cha gio* (delicate Vietnamese egg rolls). One of our favorite entrees is *bo dun*—beef tenderloin strips marinated in wine, honey, and spices, then rolled in fresh onions and broiled on bamboo skewers. Also excellent is grilled lemon chicken, or try the charcoal-broiled shrimp and scallops served on rice vermicelli. Vegetarians will find many selections here.

✪ **Fish Market.** 105 King St. (at Union St.). ☎ **703/836-5676.** Reservations not accepted. Main courses $10–$16. AE, DC, MC, V. Sun–Thurs 11:15am–1am; Fri–Sat 11:15am–2am (kitchen closes at midnight). SEAFOOD.

So popular is the Fish Market that its original seven dining rooms were expanded to include the building next door. The original corner location is a warehouse that's over 200 years old, with heavy beams, terra-cotta tile floors, exposed-brick and stucco walls adorned with nautical antiques, copper pots suspended over a fireplace, copper-topped bars, and saloon doors. The newer Sunquest Room is bright, with light streaming in through floor-to-ceiling windows; its white walls are graced with musical instruments. At lunch or dinner you might have a crabcake sandwich, rich seafood stew, or a platter of fried oysters. On weekends, there's live entertainment in the upstairs Main Dining Room and the Sunquest Room.

✪ **Le Refuge.** 127 N. Washington St. (at Cameron St.). ☎ **703/548-4661.** Reservations recommended, especially at dinner. Main courses $15–$25; special 3-course dinner $17. AE, DC, MC, V. Mon–Sat 11:30am–2:30pm and 5:30–10pm (early-bird dinner, Mon all evening, Tues–Thurs 5:30–7pm and 9–10pm). FRENCH.

A wicker model of the Eiffel Tower sits in the bowfronted window of this charming little restaurant. The intimate setting is typically French—stucco walls adorned with wine labels and provincial ceramics, bentwood chairs, black-leather banquettes, and tables covered with beige-and-brown napery. The special three-course dinner is a great buy: It includes soup or salad; fresh catch of the day, leg of lamb, or calf's liver; and crème brûlée or peach Melba for dessert. There's a lunch version for $11. Regular house specialties include bouillabaisse, classic rack of lamb, rainbow trout amandine, and chicken Dijonnaise, and nightly specials feature produce fresh from the market.

INEXPENSIVE

It's a bit of a hoof from the Old Town historic attractions, but there's a **Hard Times Cafe** chili parlor at 1404 King St., near West Street (☎ 703/683-5340). It has the same menu, hours, and low prices as the Arlington branch (see "Where to Dine" under "Arlington," above).

Bread & Chocolate. 611 King St. (between Washington and St. Asaph sts.). ☎ **703/ 548-0992.** Breakfast $2.50–$6; sandwiches and salads $2–$6; main courses $5–$7. AE, DC, DISC, MC, V. Mon–Sat 7am–7pm; Sun 8am–6pm. CONTINENTAL.

Modeled after a Swiss *Konditorei,* this cheerful place has a counter up front displaying an array of fresh-baked breads, croissants, napoleons, chocolate truffle cakes, Grand Marnier cakes, Bavarian fruit tarts, and other goodies. The interior features a changing art show on white walls lit by gallery lights. At breakfast, you can get a café mocha and an almond croissant or opt for a 3-minute egg with a selection of cheeses and a basket of bread. The rest of the day, entrees—like a salad of grilled portobello mushrooms with baby greens in blue cheese dressing, or a fresh fruit plate with raspberry-yogurt sauce—are served with fresh breads.

✪ **King Street Blues.** 112 N. St. Asaph St. (between King and Cameron sts.). ☎ **703/ 836-8800.** Reservations not accepted. Sandwiches $6.50–$8; main courses $7.50–$12. AE, DC, DISC, MC, V. Mon–Thurs 11:30am–10:30pm, Fri–Sat 11:30am–11:30pm, Sun 10:30am–10pm; bar stays open later. AMERICAN/SOUTHERN.

This re-creation of a Virginia roadhouse is one of Alexandria's most charming eateries. It's easy to find, for it occupies all three floors of a small brick building with windows painted on its exterior brick wall, and has a blue entrance canopy adorned with a pig trumpeting the words "Good Food." Blue neon outlines the real window panes. Brian McCall, a local artist whose studio (called "The Barking Dog") is in the Torpedo Factory, has covered almost every inch of the interior walls with papier-mâché figures and murals. His colorful work is reminiscent of Red Grooms's constructions, created with a sly tongue-in-cheek good humor. A young crowd usually packs the place for the house beef stew (with a memorable accompaniment of garlic mashed potatoes), barbecued pork and chicken in a sweet yet spicy sauce, southern-fried catfish filet, baked meat loaf, and house-smoked baby-back ribs. For something unusual, order the "American nachos"—they come with cheese, scallions, and either chicken or pork barbecue over potato chips instead of tortilla chips. The daily blue-plate special, served Monday through Thursday at both lunch and dinner, is an excellent value at $4.95.

Radio Free Italy. 5 Cameron St. (behind the Torpedo Factory). ☎ **703/683-0361.** Reservations not accepted. Main courses $5–$10. AE, DC, DISC, MC, V. Daily 11:30am–midnight. CONTEMPORARY.

Anchor of the Torpedo Factory's pleasant but limited Food Pavilion, Radio Free Italy has a downstairs carryout counter and a fancier dining area on the mezzanine, which offers views of the boat-filled marina (in fact, this is a poor person's version of the very expensive Chart House, which blocks part of the view). Both levels offer outdoor waterfront seating in good weather. A salad of chilled seafood marinated in lemon and olive oil leads the appetizers, while oak-fired pizzas feature California-style toppings, such as grilled chicken, goat cheese, spinach, and marinara. There's a full bar, with Italian wines available by the glass.

PICNIC FARE

Buy the fixings for a picnic at the **Deli on the Strand,** a pleasant establishment on Union Street between Prince and Duke streets, a block south of King Street (☎ 703/

548-7222). They bake bread on the premises, so the aroma is divine, and you can get reasonably priced cold-cut sandwiches as well as croissants, muffins, and, on weekends, bagels. Also available are luscious homemade salads, cheeses, beer, and wine. There are a few picnic tables outside. Hours are daily from 8am to 6pm, until 7pm in summer.

ALEXANDRIA AFTER DARK

Like Arlington, Alexandria falls under the aegis of Washington, D.C., when it comes to the performing arts (see "Arlington After Dark" under "Arlington," above).

King Street restaurants are the center of Alexandria's ongoing club and bar scene. Especially noteworthy are **Two-Nineteen,** 219 King St. (☎ **703/549-1141**), which features live jazz every night in the Basin Street Lounge; **Murphy's,** 713 King St. (☎ **703/548-1717**), where live bands lead Irish and Welsh sing-alongs on weekends; and the **Fish Market,** 105 King St. (☎ **703/836-5676**), with either a pianist or a guitarist from Thursday to Saturday nights.

For bluegrass, country, and folk, head out to the **Birchmere,** 3901 Mount Vernon Ave., just south of Glebe Road (☎ **703/549-5919**), a showcase for nationally known stars.

The **Laughing Lizard Lounge Comedy Club,** 1322 King St. (☎ **703/ 548-CLUB**), features improv comedy, with open-mike nights and scheduled performers in the nightclub; there's music in the bar and out on the patio.

3 Mount Vernon & the Potomac Plantations

Mount Vernon: 8 miles S of Alexandria

It's easy to picture Scarlett O'Hara saying "fiddle-dee-dee" to Rhett Butler on the spacious lawns of the Potomac River plantations at Mount Vernon, Woodlawn, and Gunston Hall. Dating from colonial times, these are the homes of the people who shaped our government and its institutions. To visit them is an education in early American thought, politics, sociology, art, architecture, fashion, and the decorative arts.

ESSENTIALS

GETTING THERE   You will need a car to get to Woodlawn and the other attractions south of Mount Vernon, but you can get to the first president's home by public transportation.

By Car   It's a pleasant drive 8 miles south of Alexandria via the George Washington Parkway/Mount Vernon Memorial Highway. The same highway connects to U.S. 1 and the nearby attractions.

By Tourmobile & Bus   From Arlington National Cemetery or the Washington Monument in Washington, D.C., you can take the Tourmobile (☎ **202/554-5100**) to Mount Vernon from April to October daily at 10am and noon. The fare is $20 for adults; $10 for children 3 to 11; and free for children under 3. The trip takes about 4 hours; reservations are required in person at least 30 minutes before departure. Call for off-season departure times.

Grey Line tour buses depart from the Lyceum, 201 S. Washington St. in Old Town Alexandria, at 9:45am daily, with return at 12:15pm. The fare is $18 for adults, $9 for children, including Mount Vernon admission. Call Mount Vernon (☎ **703/289-1995**) for reservations, which are required.

By Boat   From April to October, the **Potomac Riverboat Company,** at Union and Cameron streets behind the Torpedo Factory (☎ **703/548-9000**), offers cruises down the river to Mount Vernon, departing Tuesday to Sunday at 11:30am and 2pm. Fares are $22 for adults, $20 for seniors, and $10 for children, including admission to Mount Vernon.

WHAT TO SEE & DO

✪ **Mount Vernon.** End of George Washington Parkway, 8 miles S of Old Town Alexandria and I-95. ☎ **703/780-2000.** Admission $8 adults, $7.50 seniors, $4 children 6–11. Mar–Aug daily 8am–5pm; Sept–Oct daily 9am–4pm; Nov–Feb daily 9am–4pm.

In 1784, George Washington wrote the Marquis de Lafayette, "I am become a private citizen on the banks of the Potomac, and under the shadow of my own Vine and my own Fig-tree, free from the bustle of a camp and the busy scenes of public life . . . I am not only retired from all public employments, but I am retiring within myself; and shall be able to view the solitary walk, and tread the paths of private life with heartfelt satisfaction."

Alas, Washington's announcement of retirement to his beloved ancestral plantation home was premature. In 1787, he once again heeded the call to duty, presiding over the Constitutional Convention in Philadelphia. In 1789, he became the first president of the United States and managed to visit Mount Vernon only once or twice a year during his 8-year term. It wasn't until 1797, 2 years before his death, that Washington was finally able to devote himself fully to the "tranquil enjoyments" of Mount Vernon.

The home and final resting place of George and Martha Washington has been one of America's most-visited shrines since 1858, when a group of women, led by Ann Pamela Cunningham, banded together to raise money to rescue the sadly deteriorated mansion. The organization they formed, the Mount Vernon Ladies Association of the Union, purchased the estate from Washington's great-grandnephew, John Augustine Washington, Jr., and continues to own and maintain the mansion and its beautifully kept grounds. For more than 100 years, there's been an ongoing effort to locate and return the estate's scattered contents and memorabilia, thus enhancing its authentic appearance (ca. 1799).

There's no formal tour of Mount Vernon, but attendants stationed throughout the house and grounds offer explanatory commentary that provides a unique glimpse into 18th-century plantation life.

The house itself—an outstanding example of Georgian architecture—is constructed of beveled pine painted to look like stone. You'll enter by way of the "large dining room," which contains many of the original chairs, Hepplewhite mahogany sideboards, and paintings. Step outside and enjoy the view that prompted Washington to declare, "No estate in United America is more pleasantly situated than this."

A key to the Paris Bastille, which Lafayette presented to Washington in 1790 via messenger Thomas Paine, hangs in the central hall, the social center of the house in Washington's day. The "little parlor" contains the English harpsichord of Martha Washington's granddaughter, Nelly Custis. Martha's china tea service is laid out on the table in the "west parlor." In the "small dining room," the sweetmeat course set up on the original mahogany dining table is based on a description of an actual Mount Vernon dinner in 1799. The "downstairs bedroom" was used to accommodate the many overnight guests Washington mentions in his diary. Washington's study contains its original globe, desk, and dressing table.

Upstairs are five bedchambers, including the "Lafayette Room," named for its most distinguished occupant, and George and Martha's bedroom, in which Washington died.

After leaving the house, you can tour the outbuildings, including the kitchen, smokehouse, overseer's and slave quarters, and the Washingtons' graves. A museum on the property has many interesting exhibits and memorabilia, and a 4-acre exhibition area focuses on Washington's accomplishments off the battlefield and outside the government.

Allow at least 2 hours to tour the entire house and grounds. A detailed map is supplied at the entrance. The best time to visit is off-season, when the crowds are sparser. If you must visit in spring or summer, come early on weekends and holidays or you may encounter long lines. On Washington's Birthday, by the way (the federal holiday, not the actual date), admission is free and a wreath-laying ceremony is held at his tomb.

Note: There's an ongoing schedule of special activities at Mount Vernon, especially in summer. They run the gamut from special garden and history tours to colonial crafts demonstrations and treasure hunts for children. Call to find out what's going on during your visit.

WHERE TO DINE AT MOUNT VERNON   A **snack bar** at the entrance serves light fare daily. There are picnic tables outside. If you pack your own picnic, consider driving about a mile north on the George Washington Memorial Parkway to **Riverside Park,** where picnic tables overlook the Potomac.

The **Mount Vernon Inn** (☎ 703/780-0011), to the right of the gift shop at the entrance to the plantation, is a quaintly charming colonial-style restaurant complete with wait staff in 18th-century costumes, period furnishings, working fireplaces, and a menu that includes Virginia peanut-and-chestnut soup and colonial *pye* (a crock of meat or fowl and garden vegetables with a puff-pastry top). There's a full bar, and premium Virginia wines are offered by the glass. A fixed-price dinner costs $14, including soup or salad, entree, homemade breads, and dessert. Reservations are suggested at dinner. Main courses cost $5.50 to $8.50 at lunch, $12 to $24 at dinner. American Express, Discover, MasterCard, and Visa are accepted. Open daily from 11am to 3:30pm, and for dinner Monday to Saturday from 5 to 9pm.

Gunston Hall. 10709 Gunston Rd. (Va. 242). ☎ **703/550-9220.** Admission $5 adults, $4 seniors, $1.50 students through 12th grade, free for children under 6. Daily 9:30am–5pm. Closed New Year's Day, Thanksgiving, and Christmas. From Woodlawn, drive 6 miles south on U.S. 1, turn left on Gunston Rd. (Va. 242).

Yet another meticulously restored 18th-century plantation awaits exploration if you continue south on U.S. 1 to Va. 242. Some 550 acres remain of the original 5,000 acres belonging to George Mason (1725–92), a statesman and political thinker who, while shunning public office, played an important behind-the-scenes role in founding our nation. Mason drafted the Virginia Declaration of Rights, model for the Bill of Rights. Thomas Jefferson based the famous sentence of the Declaration of Independence on Mason's statement that "all men are by nature equally free and independent and have certain inherent rights . . . namely, the enjoyment of life and liberty, with the means of acquiring and possessing property, and pursuing and obtaining happiness and safety." A staunch believer in human rights, Mason refused to sign the Constitution (which he helped write) because it didn't abolish slavery or, initially, contain a Bill of Rights.

At the reception center, an 11-minute film introduces visitors to Mason and his estate. En route to the house, you'll pass a small museum of Mason family memorabilia. Inside the house, a guide is on hand to answer questions.

A highlight is the Palladian Room, the chef d'oeuvre of Gunston Hall's brilliant young creator, an indentured English craftsman in his early 20s named William Buckland, who worked here from 1755 to 1759. The room's intricately carved woodwork was inspired by the 16th-century Italian architect Andrea Palladio. Another room features a chinoiserie interior, the latest London rage in the mid-18th century.

In Mason's library and study is the writing table on which he penned the Virginia Declaration of Rights.

Containing only plants found in colonial days, the formal gardens focus on the 12-foot-high English boxwood allée planted by Mason. A nature trail leads down the Potomac past the deer park and woodland area. Also on the premises is the family graveyard where George and Ann Mason are buried.

Gunston Hall borders Pohick Bay Regional Park (see below).

Pohick Bay Regional Park. 6501 Pohick Bay Dr. (off Gunston Rd. [Va. 242]). ☎ **703/339-6104.** Admission $4 per car; use of pool $4 adults, $3.50 seniors and children 2–11, free for children under 2. Park daily 8am–dark; pool Memorial Day–Labor Day daily 10am–8pm.

Close to Gunston Hall, this 1,000-acre park focusing on water-oriented recreation occupies a spectacular bayside setting on the historic 100,000-acre Mason Neck peninsula. It offers one of the largest swimming pools on the East Coast; boat access to the Potomac (sailboat and paddleboat rentals are available); 200 campsites available on a first-come, first-served basis; a 4-mile bridle path; scenic nature trails; an 18-hole golf course and pro shop; miniature golf; and sheltered picnic areas with grills. It's the perfect place to refresh yourself after a morning spent traipsing around old plantations.

Pohick Church. 9301 Richmond Hwy. (U.S. 1). ☎ **703/339-6572.** Free admission. Daily 9am–4pm; services Sun 8, 9:15, and 11:15am. From Woodlawn, drive 5 miles south on U.S. 1.

Located about 4^1/$_2$ miles south of the grist mill, Pohick Church was built in the 1770s from plans drawn up by George Washington. The interior was designed by George Mason, owner of Gunston Hall (see above), with box pews like those prevalent in England at the time. During the Civil War, Union troops stabled their horses in the church and stripped the interior. The east wall was used for target practice. Today the church is restored to its original appearance and houses an active Episcopal congregation.

Woodlawn Plantation. 9000 Richmond Hwy. (U.S. 1) (at Mount Vernon Memorial Pkwy. [Va. 235]). ☎ **703/780-4000.** Admission $6 adults, $4 students and seniors, free for children under 5. Admission may be higher during special events. Mon–Sat 10am–4pm; Sun noon–4pm. Tours on the half hour. Closed New Year's Day, Thanksgiving, and Christmas. From Mount Vernon, drive 2 miles west on Mount Vernon Memorial Parkway (Va. 235) to U.S. 1.

Originally a 2,000-acre section of the Mount Vernon estate (today some 130 acres remain), Woodlawn was a wedding gift from George Washington to his adopted daughter (and Martha's actual granddaughter), the beautiful Eleanor "Nelly" Parke Custis, and his nephew, Maj. Lawrence Lewis, who married in 1799. Three years later, they moved into the house designed by William Thornton, first architect of the Capitol, and furnished it primarily with pieces from Mount Vernon.

Under the auspices of the National Trust for Historic Preservation, the restored mansion and its elegant formal gardens reflect many periods of history. Post-Lewis occupants included antislavery Quaker and Baptist settlers from the North (1846–89); New York City playwright Paul Kester (1901–05); and Elizabeth Sharpe of Pennsylvania (1905–25), who commissioned noted architect Waddy Wood to restore the house to a semblance of its original appearance. Finally, Sen. Oscar Underwood of Alabama and his wife, Bertha, retired here in 1924. The Underwood family occupied the house through 1948, retaining Waddy Wood to continue its restoration. With nature trails designed by the National Audubon Society, the grounds are representative of many periods in the estate's history and include the largest East Coast collection of 19th-century species of roses.

Allow at least an hour to see the house and grounds, including a 30-minute guided tour.

Also on the premises are two other houses: **Grand View,** built about 100 yards from the mansion in 1858, and Frank Lloyd Wright's **Pope-Leighey House,** designed in 1940 for the Loren Pope family of Falls Church. The Pope-Leighey House was rescued from highway construction and moved to the Woodlawn grounds in 1964. Built of cypress, brick, and glass, the house was created as a prototype of well-designed architectural space for middle-income people. "The house of moderate cost," said Wright in 1938, "is not only America's major architectural problem but the problem most difficult for her major architects." In 1946, the house was purchased by the Robert A. Leigheys—hence the double name. After living in the house for 17 years, the Leigheys donated to the National Trust both the house and the money to dismantle and move it.

Woodlawn and the Pope-Leighey House have the same opening hours and can been seen via a combination ticket. Grand View is not open to the public.

4 The Hunt Country

Leesburg: 35 miles NW of Washington, D.C.; 115 miles NW of Richmond
Middleburg: 45 miles W of Washington, D.C.; 95 miles NW of Richmond

The colonial tradition of fox hunting continues today in Virginia's Hunt Country, the rolling hills between the Washington, D.C., metropolitan area and the Blue Ridge Mountains. The Hunt Country is studded with expansive horse farms bordered by stone fences, plantations with elegant manses, picturesque villages, historic country inns, and fine restaurants. You can see the rich and famous strolling the streets or having a bite of lunch in picturesque Leesburg and Middleburg, for some of the world's wealthiest people keep their thoroughbreds here.

In addition to attracting horse lovers, the area's picturesque back roads and the 45-mile Washington & Old Dominion Railroad (W&OD) Trail bring bicyclists from all over the mid-Atlantic states. Horses, too, can be ridden on the W&OD Trail, which follows an old railroad bed through the Horse Country, crossing South King Street in downtown Leesburg.

ESSENTIALS

VISITOR INFORMATION   For information about **Leesburg** and **Loudon County,** contact the Loudon Tourism Council, 108-D South St. SE, Leesburg, VA 22075 (☎ **800/752-6118;** www.state.va.us/loudon). The Leesburg **tourist office** is on Loudon Street in Market Station, a renovated complex of shops and restaurants. It's open daily from 9am to 5pm, to 6pm during summer.

Middleburg has an information center in the Pink Box, 12 Madison St., Middleburg, VA 22117 (☎ **540/687-8888**). It's open Monday to Friday from 11am to 3pm, Saturday and Sunday from 11am to 4pm. (Note the public pavilion next door: It's dedicated to the late Jacqueline Kennedy Onassis in honor of the contributions she made to the town while residing here.)

GETTING THERE   By Plane   Washington Dulles Airport is on the eastern edge of the Hunt Country, 14 miles east of Leesburg and 21 miles east of Middleburg.

By Car   Leesburg: There are two routes from the Capital Beltway (I-495) to Leesburg. The free but slow route is Va. 7 to Leesburg. The fast way is via the Dulles Toll Road (Va. 267), between both I-495 and I-66 and Washington Dulles Airport; it feeds into the Dulles Greenway, a privately financed toll expressway connecting Dulles to Leesburg. The total toll from the I-495 to Leesburg is $1.50. **Middleburg:**

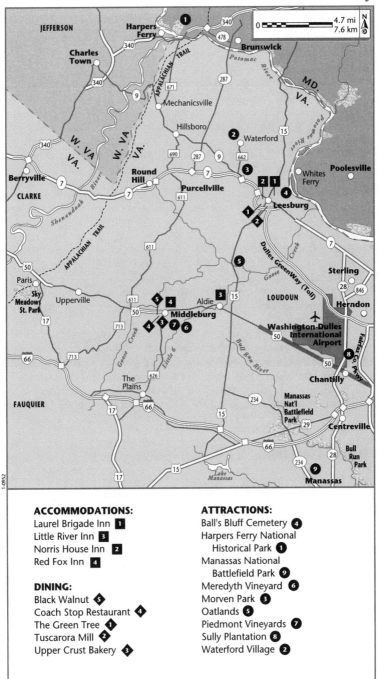

ACCOMMODATIONS:
Laurel Brigade Inn **1**
Little River Inn **3**
Norris House Inn **2**
Red Fox Inn **4**

DINING:
Black Walnut **5**
Coach Stop Restaurant **4**
The Green Tree **1**
Tuscarora Mill **2**
Upper Crust Bakery **3**

ATTRACTIONS:
Ball's Bluff Cemetery **4**
Harpers Ferry National
   Historical Park **1**
Manassas National
   Battlefield Park **9**
Meredyth Vineyard **6**
Morven Park **3**
Oatlands **5**
Piedmont Vineyards **7**
Sully Plantation **8**
Waterford Village **2**

From Arlington or I-495, follow I-66 west to Va. 28 north to U.S. 50 west into town. U.S. 15 south from Leesburg intersects with U.S. 50 westbound 10 miles east of Middleburg.

LEESBURG

The largest town in the Hunt Country, Leesburg is a good base for exploring the region. It has considerable charm, with architecture ranging from pre-Revolutionary to late 19th century. The center of Leesburg and its historic district is at the intersection of Market Street (Va. 7 Business) and King Street (U.S. 15 Business). Everything you will want to see is within 2 blocks of this key crossroads, including one of the largest collections of **antiques dealers** in Virginia. The visitor center (see above) has lists of the shops, both in town and throughout the Hunt Country.

EXPLORING LEESBURG

At the Market Street–King Street intersection stands the brick **Loudon County Court House,** built in 1894 and a mix of Roman Revival and classical elements. The **Loudon Museum,** 16 W. Loudon St., at Wirt Street (☎ **703/777-7427**), is a small regional museum housing memorabilia about the county from American Indian days to the present. It's open Monday through Saturday from 10am to 5pm and Sunday from 1 to 5pm.

The little circle of stone markers in **Ball's Bluff Cemetery** and the adjacent **Civil War battlefield** are located at the edge of the Potomac River in northeast Leesburg, off U.S. 15 Bypass.

On the northwest edge of town, the 1,200-acre estate of ✪ **Morven Park** (☎ **703/777-2414**) is home to the Museum of Hounds and Hunting, the Winmill Carriage Collection, and a Greek Revival mansion. To reach Morven Park, take Va. 7 Business west 1 mile from the center of town, then turn right onto Morven Park Road, left onto Old Waterford Road. The estate is open April 1 to October 31, Tuesday to Friday from noon to 5pm; April 1 through November, Saturday and Sunday from 10am to 5pm. Call for special December hours. Admission is $6 for adults, $5 for seniors, and $3 for children.

NEARBY ATTRACTIONS

✪ **Harpers Ferry National Historical Park.** Harpers Ferry, WV. ☎ **304/535-6298.** Admission $5 per car; $3 per pedestrian, bicyclist, bus passenger, and people ages 17–61. Daily 8am–5pm. Closed Christmas. From Leesburg, it's about 12 miles to Harpers Ferry. Take Va. 7 west, turn right at Va. 9. Take another right at C.R. 671. Turn left at the intersection of U.S. 340 and go west to Harpers Ferry.

Thomas Jefferson wrote of Harpers Ferry in 1783, "the view is worth a voyage across the Atlantic." The National Historical Park that now preserves much of that breathtaking view at the confluence of the Potomac and Shenandoah rivers is worth a visit from anyone interested in discovering a wealth of American history—and not just John Brown's famous raid against slavery in 1859, for Harpers Ferry also saw the arrival of the first successful American railroad, the first application of interchangeable parts, the largest surrender of Union troops during the Civil War, and the education of former slaves in one of the earliest integrated schools in the United States.

Nevertheless, Harpers Ferry is best remembered for John Brown's raid, which presaged the Civil War. After his friend, abolitionist editor Elijah Lovejoy, was murdered by a mob in 1837, Brown dedicated his life to the destruction of slavery. When the Supreme Court decreed in its infamous Dred Scott decision that Congress could not deprive slave owners of their human property, Brown led a raid into Missouri and freed 11 slaves. Seeking weapons, he captured the federal arsenal at Harpers Ferry on

October 16, 1859. The next day, 90 U.S. Marines under the command of Col. Robert E. Lee surrounded the arsenal, and Col. J. E. B. Stuart twice delivered surrender demands to Brown. When he refused, a party of 12 Marines smashed the door and captured Brown and the surviving raiders. Brown was tried for treason and hanged in Charles Town on December 2.

You can hop a free shuttle bus from the **visitor center** and parking lot to the Historic Area, a half mile away, where the **John Brown Museum** vividly recounts the story with photographs, documents, and a slide show. Many original stone buildings are open, including a restored dry-goods store, a blacksmith shop, and an armorer's house. In addition, the area is a terrific place for **hiking,** since several scenic walking tracks lead to less congested areas of the park. The most popular crosses the Potomac River and scales the mountain to the top of a cliff, where you'll see the view so loved by Jefferson.

While here, enjoy a country-style lunch or dinner at the **Hilltop House Hotel,** on Ridge Street (☎ **800/338-8319** or 304/535-2132). Overlooking the Potomac, this historic hostelry dates from 1888 and has hosted Mark Twain, Alexander Graham Bell, Pearl S. Buck, Woodrow Wilson, and other luminaries.

Oatlands. U.S. 15, 6 miles south of Leesburg. ☎ **703/777-3174.** House and garden tours, $6 adults, $5 seniors and children 6–18, free for children under 12. Garden tours only, $3 per person. Apr–Dec, Mon–Sat 10am to 4:30pm; Sun 1–4:30pm.

An 1803 Greek Revival mansion with a Corinthian portico and beautiful gardens, Oatlands hosts numerous events, such as the Hunt Country Antiques Show in January, annual sheepdog trials in May, a Celtic festival in June, and a Civil War weekend in August. Oatlands is open to the public from early April to late December, when it's all decked out in Victorian-era Christmas decorations, and tours are given by candlelight.

Sully Plantation. Va. 28, Chantilly. ☎ **703/437-1794.** Admission $4 adults, $3 students, $2 seniors and children under 16. Mar–Dec, Wed–Mon 11am–4pm; Jan–Feb, Sat–Sun 11am–3:30pm. Closed New Year's Day, Thanksgiving, and Christmas. Sully is on Va. 28, $^3/_4$ mile north of U.S. 50, 9 miles south of Va. 7 in Leesburg.

Sully Plantation, a $2^1/_2$-story farmhouse, was built in 1794 by Richard Bland Lee (brother of "Light-Horse Harry" Lee and northern Virginia's first congressman) for his wife, Elizabeth Collins Lee. The original plantation had more than 3,000 acres. Washington Dulles International Airport now occupies most of the land, leaving a small plot for the main house, dairy, smokehouse, kitchen building, and slave quarters. Today the house is furnished with antiques of the Federal period and looks much as it would have during the 1795–1842 era. Mahogany furniture, Wilton carpets, and imported silver approximate the style in which the Lees lived. Living-history programs further re-create the era.

✪ Waterford Village. On C.R. 662. ☎ **540/882-3018.** Free admission. Daily 24 hours. From Leesburg, take Va. 7 west, turn right onto Va. 9, then turn right on C.R. 662 into Waterford.

Reached by one of this area's most scenic drives, the enchanting hamlet of Waterford, with numerous 18th- and 19th-century buildings, is a National Historic Landmark. Surrounded by a lush landscape of 1,420 acres, it offers vistas of farmland and pasture that unfold behind barns and churches. You'll feel as though you've entered an English country scene painted by Constable. A Quaker from Pennsylvania, Amos Janney, built a mill here in the 1740s. Other Quakers followed, and by 1840, most of the buildings now on Main Street and Second Street were in place. In 1870, the railroad bypassed Waterford, and because the pace of change slowed, much of the town was preserved. The population swells to some 40,000 on the first weekend in October, however, when local residents stage the annual **Waterford Arts and Crafts Fair,** one of the best in the region.

HORSEBACK RIDING

Although there are horse farms throughout these hills, few of them rent mounts. One that does is **Greenway Stables,** P.O. Box 211, Leesburg, VA 22075 (☎ **703/ 327-6117**), which offers unguided trail rides over its property on Racefield Road, off U.S. 50 between I-66 and C.R. 629. Reservations are required; let them know your level of experience and whether you prefer English or Western.

WHERE TO STAY

A mansion built atop a knoll in 1773 is the centerpiece of the unique **Ramada Inn at Carradoc Hall,** on Va. 7 about 2 miles east of downtown (☎ **800/522-6702** or 703/771-9200). Also on Va. 7 but only half a mile east of downtown are the **Best Western Leesburg-Dulles** (☎ **800/528-1234** or 703/777-9400) and the **Leesburg Days Inn** (☎ **800/DAYS-INN** or 703/777-6622).

✪ **Laurel Brigade Inn.** 20 W. Market St., Leesburg, VA 22075. ☎ **703/777-1010.** 8 rms. A/C. $60–$90 double. AE, DISC, MC, V.

The history of this popular, two-story Federal-period charmer goes back to 1766, when town records show that a tavern operator named John Miller became the owner of an "ordinary" (the colonial equivalent of a British pub) on this lot. In 1817, it was purchased by Eleanor and Henry Peers and became the Peers Hotel. The hotel's kitchen was so highly regarded it was chosen to prepare the food for the collation on the courthouse green when Lafayette visited Leesburg in 1825. In 1949, the building became Laurel Brigade Inn, named for the Civil War brigade led by local Col. Elijah V. White. Rooms today are pleasantly furnished with wing chairs, chenille spreads, and hooked rugs, and some have fireplaces. Although there are no phones in the rooms, a pay phone is available in the lobby. Rooms facing the back overlook a lovely garden stretching back to a gazebo that's been the setting for weddings.

The **Laurel Brigade Restaurant** is open for lunch and dinner. The price of a three-course lunch ($10.75 to $14.50) brings you a full meal: appetizer, entree (perhaps chicken potpie, crabcakes, or grilled pork chop with spiced apple), vegetable and hot rolls, dessert (such as apple dumpling with hard sauce), and coffee or tea. At dinner, the three-course meals ($12.50 to $25) feature entrees like crab imperial, baked scallops, and strip steak. You can also order à la carte at either meal.

To secure a room at this very popular inn, reserve at least 4 to 6 weeks in advance for weekends, 7 to 10 days otherwise.

Norris House Inn. 108 Loudon St. SW, Leesburg, VA 20175. ☎ **800/644-1806** or 703/ 777-1806. Fax 703/771-8051. www.norrishouse.com. E-mail: inn@norrishouse.com. 6 rms (none with bath). $75–$145 double. Rates include breakfast. AE, DC, DISC, MC, V.

A charming 2¹⁄₂-story red-brick 1806 home, Norris House was renovated in the Eastlake style in the Victorian era. Its facade is bedecked with green shutters and a white-columned entrance porch, the whole capped by three pedimented dormer windows. The common rooms include a parlor and library, the former with an oak fireplace. A full breakfast, served in the formal dining room, might feature fresh fruit or juice, quiche, home-baked muffins, and coffee or tea. Guest-room furnishings are a charming mix of antiques. All share three baths and have fireplaces, stenciled fireplace surrounds, four-poster beds (some with lace canopies), rockers, and framed botanical prints on the walls.

WHERE TO DINE

✪ **The Green Tree.** 15 S. King St., Leesburg. ☎ **703/777-7246.** Reservations recommended, especially for dinner on weekends. Main courses $14–$23. AE, DC, DISC, MC, V. Summer daily 11:30am–10pm. Off-season Mon–Thurs 11:30am–9:30pm; Fri–Sat 11:30am–10pm; Sun 11:30am–10pm. COLONIAL AMERICAN.

Not only is the decor colonial at this downtown restaurant: most of the dishes are made from faithfully reproduced 18th-century recipes gathered from the Library of Congress and the National Archives. Recipes for green-herb soup, Sally Lunn bread, roast prime rib with Yorkshire pudding, and rum-and-black-walnut pie are among the stellar results of this research. Both dining rooms have wide-plank floors, harvest dining tables, ladderback chairs, brass chandeliers, working fireplaces, and walls hung with hunting prints; servers are in period dress. A full dinner might start with cabbage pie or a sampling platter of smoked-sausage pie, seafood, mushroom canapés, pâté with rusks (a crusty colonial bread), and English beer cheese. Among the entrees are rabbit fricassee, crab, roast chicken, and broiled brook trout.

Tuscarora Mill. 203 Harrison St. (in Market Station), Leesburg. ☎ **703/771-9300.** Reservations recommended, especially at dinner. Main courses $12–$22. AE, MC, V. Daily 11:30am–2:30pm and 5:30–9:30pm; cafe serves light fare until 11pm Sun–Thurs, until midnight Fri–Sat. AMERICAN.

Housed in a renovated turn-of-the-century mill, one of the six historic buildings that make up the Market Station shopping and dining complex, this simpatico restaurant has a casual ambience—a combination of light jazz music, flourishing plants suspended from wood-beamed high ceilings, skylights, fresh bouquets, and black wrought-iron street lamps. Red-metal exterior siding, grain bins, old belts and pulleys, and a grain scale evoke the mill's past. Delicious luncheon fare includes sandwiches, omelets, and hot entrees like sautéed shrimp over angel-hair pasta. At dinner, standouts include the house-smoked chicken with mushrooms, brandy, and cream over fettuccine, or the basmati-crusted yellowfin tuna with salsa of red curry and pineapple. À la carte vegetables such as braised endive and garlic mashed potatoes are tempting extras. For dessert, warm strawberry napoleon with zabaglione is a seasonal favorite; chocoholics may opt for the double-chocolate torte with raspberry sauce.

MIDDLEBURG

One of Virginia's most beautiful small towns, Middleburg likes to call itself the unofficial capital of the Hunt Country. Indeed, jodhpurs and riding boots are *de rigeur* in this town that is home to those interested in horses, horse breeding, steeplechase racing, and fox hunting.

EXPLORING THE TOWN

Middleburg is included on the National Register of Historic Villages, and it's about the same size today as when it was settled in 1731. You can't get lost here, for the entire town occupies just 6 blocks along Washington Street (U.S. 50). Park anywhere on Washington Street and buy a copy of a walking tour brochure for $1 from the **Pink Box Visitor Information Center,** 12 N. Madison St. (☎ **540/687-8888**). Then stroll along Middleburg's brick sidewalks, poke your head into upscale shops with names like the Finicky Filly that sell "home embellishments," have lunch at one of several fine restaurants, or stop for a cone at Scruffy's Ice Cream Parlor. Note the small Gothic Revival **Emmanuel Episcopal Church** (1842) at Liberty Street; it was the first example of mid-19th-century architecture in the village.

NEARBY ATTRACTIONS

Adding to the area's interest are a number of wineries. Just 5 minutes south of Middleburg on Logan's Mill Road (C.R. 628), **Meredyth Vineyard** (☎ 540/687-6277) enjoys a beautiful setting in the Bull Run Mountains. Tours are given daily from 11am to 4pm. The 58-acre farm winery also has a picnic area and gift shop. **Piedmont Vineyards,** on Halfway Road (C.R. 626) about 3 miles south of town (☎ 540/687-5528), was formerly a dairy farm. Its barn now houses a winery, tasting room, and gift shop. Tours are given daily from 10am to 4pm. Both wineries are closed New Year's Day, Thanksgiving, and Christmas.

✪ **Manassas National Battlefield Park.** 6511 Sudley Rd. (Va. 234), Manassas. ☎ **703/361-1339.** Admission $2 adults, free for children under 17. Battlefield, daily dawn to dusk. Visitor center, summer daily 8:30am–6pm; winter daily 8:30am–5pm. From Middleburg (about 11 miles), take U.S. 50 east, turn right onto U.S. 15 south, turn left at Va. 234, and continue southeast to Manassas. From I-66, take Exit 47B and go half a mile north on Va. 234.

The first massive clash of the Civil War took place here on July 21, 1861. A well-equipped but poorly trained Union army of 35,000 under Gen. Irvin McDowell had marched from Washington, where cheering crowds expected them to return victorious within several days. Most of the men were 90-day volunteers who had little knowledge of what war would mean. Their goal was Richmond, but to meet the on-coming army, Gen. P. G. T. Beauregard deployed his Confederate troops along a stream known as Bull Run to the north and west of the important railroad junction of Manassas. The 10 hours of heavy fighting on the first day stunned soldiers on both sides as well as onlookers who had ridden out from Washington to watch the fray. A surprise Confederate victory shattered any hopes that the war would end quickly. Historians later conjectured that had the Confederates not been too disorganized to follow the fleeing Union troops, an even more decisive victory perhaps could have ended the war, with the South victorious.

Union and Confederate armies met here again on August 28–30, 1862. The Second Battle of Manassas secured Gen. Robert E. Lee's place in history as his 55,000 men soundly defeated the Union army under Gen. John Pope.

The two battles are commemorated at the 5,000-acre battlefield park. Start your tour here at the visitor center, where a museum, a 13-minute slide show, and a battle map program tell the story. There are a number of self-guided walking tours that highlight Henry Hill, Stone Bridge, and the other critical areas of the two battles. A 12-mile driving tour covers the sites of Second Manassas, which raged over a much larger area.

WHERE TO STAY

Red Fox Inn. 2 E. Washington St. (P.O. Box 385), Middleburg, VA 22117. ☎ **800/223-1728** or 540/687-6301. Fax 540/687-6053. 25 rms and suites. A/C TV TEL. $135–$245 single or double. Rates include continental breakfast. AE, DC, DISC, MC, V.

The historic Red Fox Inn in the center of Middleburg maintains the romantic charm of early Virginia in its original 1728 stone structure. Later additions include the Stray Fox Inn building, so called because a misfired cannonball struck its foundation in the Civil War, and the McConnell House Inn building. The Red Fox has three rooms and three suites, all with wide-plank floors and 18th-century furnishings; several have working fireplaces. Rooms in the Stray Fox and McConnell also preserve a traditional character with hand-stenciled floors and walls, canopy beds, hooked rugs, and original fireplace mantels. Continental breakfast is served in the rooms, and extra amenities include terry bathrobes, bedside sweets, fresh flowers, and a morning Washington newspaper.

The dark, cozy **Red Fox Inn Restaurant** occupies the first floor of the inn. It features a Hunt Country ambience—low beamed ceilings, pewter dishes, and equestrian prints lining the walls. The seasonal menu runs the gamut from pastas (such as angel-hair with smoked salmon, smoked scallops, green onion, dill, and shiitake mushrooms) to dinner entrees ($16.50 to $19.50) like chicken breast stuffed with Boursin cheese. Across the back street, you'll find **Mosby's Tavern,** an English-style drinking establishment with a mixed menu for lunch and dinner, which you can enjoy at one of the wooden booths or, in good weather, on the small outdoor patio.

A Nearby Country Inn

✪ **Little River Inn.** U.S. 50 (P.O. Box 116), Aldie, VA 22001. ☎ **703/327-6742.** 5 rms (2 with bath), 3 cottages (with bath). A/C TV. $80–$210 double. Rates include full breakfast. AE, MC, V. Aldie is 5 miles east of Middleburg on U.S. 50.

The peaceful setting of this country inn is so appealing, it's almost worth coming to Aldie just to stay here. Farm animals, a small garden, and a patio are behind the main building, an early-19th-century farmhouse. The living room has polished wide-plank floors; in front of the fireplace are two antique wing chairs and a sofa, all upholstered in colonial-print fabrics. Fresh flowers, a basket of magazines, and a few decorative pieces of china add warmth to the setting. Accommodations range from one room to a cottage of your own. The main house has five bedrooms, all charmingly furnished with antique pieces and pretty quilts; one has a working fireplace. Three small houses are also on the property—both the log cabin and the Patent House, a small late-1700s domicile, have working fireplaces. Hill House (ca. 1870) sits on 2 acres of landscaped gardens and can be rented in its entirety, or its two bedrooms may be rented separately. The full breakfast includes home-baked goodies like poppy-seed muffins and giant popovers filled with cooked apples, raisins, and cinnamon sauce.

WHERE TO DINE

You may want to buy the fixings for a gourmet picnic before you set out on a day's excursion in Hunt Country. Try **Black Walnut,** 20 E. Washington St. (☎ **540/ 687-6833**), or the **Upper Crust Bakery,** 2 N. Pendleton St. (☎ **540/687-5666**).

Coach Stop Restaurant. 9 E. Washington St., Middleburg. ☎ **540/687-5515.** Reservations not necessary. Main courses $12–$17. AE, DC, MC, V. Mon–Sat 7am–9pm; Sun 8am–9pm. AMERICAN.

Locals flock here for good old-fashioned American fare—everything from a delicious breakfast of Virginia country ham and eggs or creamed chipped beef to a dinner of honey-dipped fried chicken. Seating is at the counter or at tables and booths set with hunting-themed place mats. Ceiling fans keep the breezes moving as you tuck into a hearty meal. Lunchtime sandwiches, including turkey, bacon, avocado, or a grilled Reuben, are served with french fries or pasta salad. Dinner entrees—comfort foods like pork chops or roast turkey with stuffing and gravy—are served with two vegetables.

6 Fredericksburg & the Northern Neck

Like other early Virginia towns, Fredericksburg is steeped in American history, with a heritage spanning 3 centuries of colonial, Revolutionary, and Civil War events. It came into being in 1728 as a 500-acre frontier settlement on the banks of the Rappahannock River. George Washington, James Monroe, Thomas Jefferson, and George Mason are among the great names who walked Fredericksburg's cobblestoned streets. During the Civil War, military heroes such as Stonewall Jackson fought one major battle in the town and three others nearby. Remarkably, Fredericksburg survived, though the scars of war are still visible; a 40-block area of the town has been designated a National Register Historic District. Each year hundreds of thousands of visitors come to the battlefields, now part of a national military park.

Both George Washington and Robert E. Lee were born east of Fredericksburg on the bucolic Northern Neck, a peninsula set apart by the broad Potomac on one side and the winding Rappahannock River on the other. At the end of the peninsula sits the Tides Inn, one of Virginia's finest resorts, and the tiny fishing village of Reedville, built in the Victorian era and still making its living from the Chesapeake Bay. Large and small creeks crisscross the neck, and bald eagles, blue heron, flocks of waterfowl, and an occasional wild turkey inhabit the unspoiled marshland.

1 Fredericksburg

50 miles S of Washington, D.C.; 45 miles S of Alexandria; 50 miles N of Richmond

Though George Washington always called Alexandria his hometown, he spent his formative years in the Fredericksburg area at Ferry Farm (where he supposedly never told a lie about chopping down the cherry tree). His mother later lived in a house he purchased for her on Charles Street, and she is buried on the former Kenmore estate, home of his sister, Betty Washington Lewis.

The town was a hotbed of revolutionary zeal in the 1770s. Troops drilled on the courthouse green on Princess Anne Street, and it was in Fredericksburg that Thomas Jefferson, George Mason, and other founding fathers met in 1777 to draft what later became the Virginia Statute of Religious Freedoms, the basis for the First Amendment guaranteeing separation of church and state. James Monroe began his law career in Fredericksburg in 1786.

Old Town Fredericksburg

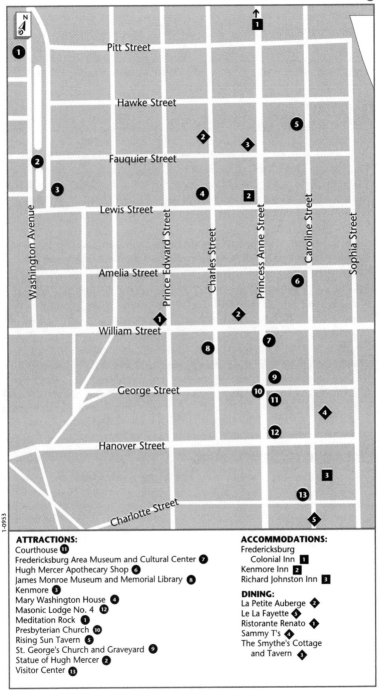

ATTRACTIONS:
Courthouse ⑪
Fredericksburg Area Museum and Cultural Center ⑦
Hugh Mercer Apothecary Shop ⑥
James Monroe Museum and Memorial Library ⑧
Kenmore ❸
Mary Washington House ❹
Masonic Lodge No. 4 ⑫
Meditation Rock ❶
Presbyterian Church ⑩
Rising Sun Tavern ❺
St. George's Church and Graveyard ❾
Statue of Hugh Mercer ❷
Visitor Center ⑬

ACCOMMODATIONS:
Fredericksburg
    Colonial Inn ▪1
Kenmore Inn ▪2
Richard Johnston Inn ▪3

DINING:
La Petite Auberge ◆2
Le La Fayette ◆5
Ristorante Renato ◆1
Sammy T's ◆4
The Smythe's Cottage
    and Tavern ◆3

During the Civil War, its strategic location—equidistant from two rival capitals, Richmond and Washington—made Fredericksburg a fierce battlefield, scene of one of the war's bloodiest conflicts. Clara Barton nursed wounded Federal soldiers in the still-extant Presbyterian church. Cannonballs embedded in the walls of some prominent buildings, as well as the graves of 17,000 Civil War soldiers in the town's cemeteries, are grim reminders of that tragic era.

ESSENTIALS

VISITOR INFORMATION   The **Fredericksburg Visitor Center,** at 706 Caroline St. (at Charlotte Street), Fredericksburg, VA 22401 (☎ **800/678-4748** or 540/373-1776), offers free maps, menus of many restaurants, and a walking tour brochure following the 1862 Battle of Fredericksburg. It also sells a block ticket to the major sites (see "Exploring Fredericksburg," below). The center is open Memorial Day to Labor Day, daily from 9am to 7pm; the rest of the year, 9am to 5pm. Closed New Year's Day and Christmas.

GETTING THERE   By Car   Fredericksburg is about an hour's drive from Richmond or Arlington, a little less from Alexandria. From I-95, take Exit 130A and follow Va. 3 east. Bear left on William Street (Va. 3 Business), which takes you to the heart of town.

By Plane   The nearest airports are Ronald Reagan Washington National and Washington Dulles International (see "Getting There" in the Arlington section of chapter 5) and Richmond International (see "Orientation & Getting Around" in chapter 10).

By Train   Fredericksburg's **Amtrak** station (☎ **800/872-7245**) is at Lafayette Boulevard and Princess Anne Street, 3 blocks south of the visitor center. Several Amtrak trains arrive daily from Washington, D.C., and New York City to the north, Richmond and Newport News to the south. **Virginia Railway Express** (☎ **800/743-3843** or 703/497-7777) operates a commuter rail link between Fredericksburg and Union Station in Washington, D.C., with stops at Arlington (Crystal City), Alexandria, Lorton, Woodbridge, Quantico, and Stafford.

EXPLORING FREDERICKSBURG

Make your first stop in town the **Fredericksburg Visitor Center** (see "Essentials," above), which is housed in a historic 1824 house on Caroline Street at Charlotte Street. Here you can see a 12-minute slide presentation on Fredericksburg's colonial history and get a pass for free parking anywhere in the city (including lots beside the center and across the street).

The center also sells a **Hospitality Pass** ticket for seven main attractions. It costs $19.50 for adults, $7 for students 6 to 18. For adults, that's a savings of 30% over individual admissions. The pass includes the Hugh Mercer Apothecary, the Rising Sun Tavern, the James Monroe Museum, the Mary Washington House, Belmont, the Fredericksburg Area Museum, and Kenmore. **Pick Four,** another discount ticket, allows adults to choose any four of the seven main attractions for $13.75, students 6 to 18 for $5.50. Children under 6 are admitted free to all attractions. (Tickets can also be purchased at any of these attractions.)

Note: The seven block-ticket attractions listed below are closed New Year's Day, Thanksgiving, and December 24, 25, and 31. All except Belmont are within walking distance of the visitor center.

The visitor center also sells tickets for **Trolley Tours of Fredericksburg** (☎ **540/898-0737**), an easy way to see 35 historic sights. The 1¼-hour tours leave the visitor center at 10am, noon, 1:30pm, and 3:30pm from June through September. During April, May, and October, they depart at 10:30am and 1:30pm. Fares are $10 for adults, $5 for children 6 to 12, and free for kids under 6.

THE BLOCK-TICKET ATTRACTIONS

Belmont. Washington St. (Va. 1001), Falmouth. ☎ **540/654-1015.** Admission (without block ticket) $4 adults, $1.50 children 6–18, free for children under 6. Mar–Nov, Mon–Sat 10am–5pm, Sun 1–5pm; Dec–Feb, Mon–Sat 10am–4pm, Sun 1–4pm. From the visitor center, take U.S. 1 north across the Falmouth Bridge, turn left at the traffic light in Falmouth, and go a quarter of a mile up the hill; turn left on Washington St. (Va. 1001) to Belmont.

Situated on 27 hillside acres overlooking the falls of the Rappahannock River, Belmont began as an 18th-century farmhouse (the central six rooms of the house date to the 1790s) and was enlarged to a 22-room estate by a later owner. The house is furnished with the art treasures, family heirlooms, and European antiques of famed American artist Gari Melchers, who lived here from 1916 until his death in 1932. His wife, Corinne, gave Belmont to the Commonwealth of Virginia in 1955. In addition to Melchers's own works, there are many wonderful paintings in the house—a watercolor sketch by Jan Brueghel, 19th-century paintings by Morisot, and works by Rodin. **Tours** (about an hour long) are given on the hour and half hour. They begin in the Stroh Visitor Center (Melchers's former carriage house), where you can also view an orientation video.

Fredericksburg Area Museum and Cultural Center. 907 Princess Anne St. (at William St.). ☎ **540/371-5668.** Admission (without block ticket) $4 adults, $1.50 children 6–18, free for children under 6. Mar–Nov, Mon–Sat 10am–5pm, Sun 1–5pm; Dec–Feb, Mon–Sat 10am–4pm, Sun 1–4pm.

This municipal museum and cultural center occupies the 1816 Town Hall located in Market Square. In existence since 1733, Market Square was the center of trade and commerce in Fredericksburg for over a century, while Town Hall served as the city's social and legal center. Lafayette was entertained at Town Hall in 1824 with lavish parties and balls, and the building continued to serve its original function until 1982.

The first level is a changing exhibit area for displays relating to regional and cultural history. The second floor houses permanent exhibits on Native American settlements and pre-English explorers (the earliest years); natural history; colonial settlement; the Revolution and Federal Fredericksburg, including architectural and decorative aspects of the period; the antebellum period (1825–61), focusing on the development of canals, early industry, railroads, and the cholera epidemic of 1833; the Civil War and its aftermath, graphically depicting the reality of the war as experienced by the local citizenry; Fredericksburg's evolution from town to city (1890–1920); and, finally, 20th-century Fredericksburg. Exhibits are enhanced by audiovisual presentations, crafts demonstrations, and symposiums. The hall's 19th-century Council Chamber on the third floor is also used for changing exhibits.

Hugh Mercer Apothecary Shop. 1020 Caroline St. (at Amelia St.). ☎ **540/373-3362.** Admission (without block ticket) $4 adults, $1.50 children 6–18, free for children under 6. Mar–Nov, daily 9am–5pm; Dec–Feb, daily 10am–4pm.

Dr. Hugh Mercer practiced medicine and operated this shop from 1761 to 1776. A much-admired patriot and scholar, he followed his close friend George Washington into the Revolution as a brigadier-general. His soldiering career was short-lived, for he met a violent death at the Battle of Princeton in 1776. The warrior tradition continued in his family, however—Gen. George S. Patton was his great-great-great-grandson. A fascinating **tour** is given by a hostess in colonial dress, who explains how the doctor treated patients in those days.

Little Shop of Horrors

You've only to visit Dr. Hugh Mercer's Apothecary Shop to realize the ghastliness of getting sick in the 18th century.

Patients didn't read magazines while waiting to see this doctor, for Mercer's waiting room doubled as his operating room. Since opium, the only known anesthesia, was too expensive and too difficult to obtain, those waiting for treatment were often put to work holding down the screaming wretch under the knife.

Even minor treatment seems ghoulish by today's standards, as displays in Mercer's shop attest. Leeches and other devices were used to bleed patients (George Washington may well have bled to death while undergoing treatment in his final days). A heated cup removed boils and carbuncles, a knife cut out cataracts, and an ominous-looking key extracted teeth (Dr. Mercer did it all).

You can also see Mercer's saw, used to amputate limbs. Such instrument gave rise to the early slang term for doctors: *sawbones*.

James Monroe Museum and Memorial Library. 908 Charles St. (between William and George sts.). ☎ **540/654-1043.** Admission (without block ticket) $4 adults, $1.50 children 6–18, free for children under 6. Mar–Nov, daily 9am–5pm; Dec–Feb, daily 10am–4pm.

James Monroe came to Fredericksburg in 1786 to practice law and went on to become a senator; minister to France, England, and Spain; governor of Virginia; Secretary of State; Secretary of War; and fifth president of the United States. His shingle hangs outside, while within, all the furnishings are originals from either the Monroes' White House years or their retirement home.

In a cozy office much like one Monroe might have used, you can peruse correspondence from Thomas Jefferson (a letter partially in code), James Madison, and Benjamin Franklin. Here, too, are the gun and canteen Monroe used in the American Revolution. Other than Washington, he was the only president to actually fight in the War of Independence and to experience the grim winter at Valley Forge as well.

Also on display are two Rembrandt Peale portraits of Monroe, the outfits the Monroes wore at the court of Napoleon, silhouettes of the Monroes by Charles Willson Peale, his wife's teensy wedding slippers, his dueling pistols, and other memorabilia. The library of some 10,000 books is a reconstruction of Monroe's own personal collection. Thirty-minute **tours** are given throughout the day.

✪ **Kenmore.** 1201 Washington Ave. (between Lewis and Fauquier sts.). ☎ **540/373-3381.** Admission (without block ticket) $6 adults, $3 children, free for children under 6. Mar–Dec, Mon–Sat 10am–5pm, Sun noon–5pm; Jan–Feb, Mon–Fri by reservation only, Sat and Presidents' Day 10am–4pm, Sun noon–4pm.

This stately Georgian mansion was built in the 1770s for Betty Washington (George's sister) and her husband, Fielding Lewis, one of the wealthiest planters in Fredericksburg. According to legend, George involved himself considerably in the building, decoration, and furnishings of the estate. During the Revolution, Lewis financed a gun factory and built vessels for the Virginia navy. As a result of his large expenditures in the cause of patriotism, he eventually had to sell Kenmore to liquidate his debts. He died soon after the victory at Yorktown.

Today the house is meticulously restored to its colonial appearance. The original exquisitely molded plaster ceilings and cornices are its most outstanding features. Most of the floors and all the woodwork and paneling are also original, and the authentic 18th-century English and American furnishings include several Lewis family pieces.

After touring the house, take a walk through the famous boxwood gardens, the Wilderness Walk, and the cutting garden, all restored and maintained according to the original plans by the Garden Club of Virginia. A museum shop is also on the premises.

Mary Washington House. 1200 Charles St. (at Lewis St.). ☎ **540/373-1569.** Admission (without block ticket) $4 adults, $1.50 children 6–18, free for children under 6. Mar–Nov, daily 9am–5pm; Dec–Feb, daily 10am–4pm. Closed New Year's Day, Thanksgiving, and Dec 24–25.

George Washington purchased this house for his mother, Mary Ball Washington, in 1772, and added a two-story extension. She was then 64 years old and had been living at nearby Ferry Farm since 1739. Lafayette visited during the Revolution to pay respects to the mother of the greatest living American, and Washington came in 1789 to receive her blessing before going to New York for his inauguration as president. He never saw her again, for she died later that year. Thirty-minute **tours** are given by hostesses in colonial garb throughout the day.

The Rising Sun Tavern. 1306 Caroline St. (at Fauquier St.). ☎ **540/371-1494.** Admission (without the block ticket) $4 adults, $1.50 children 6–18, free for children under 6. Mar–Nov, daily 9am–5pm; Dec–Feb, daily 10am–4pm.

The Rising Sun was originally a residence, built in 1760 by Charles Washington, George's youngest brother, but it served as a tavern for some 30 years, beginning in the early 1790s. The building is preserved, not reconstructed, though the 17th- and 18th-century furnishings are not all originals. Thirty-minute tours are led by a tavern wench—an indentured servant sentenced to 7 years for stealing a loaf of bread in England. The Rising Sun Tavern was a proper high-class tavern, she explains, not for riffraff. The gentlemen congregated over Madeira and cards in the Great Room or had a rollicking good time in the Taproom over multicourse meals and many tankards of ale (the tavernkeeper's son will serve you wassail—a delicious spiced drink—during the tour). Meanwhile, ladies were consigned to the Retiring Room, where they would spend the entire day gossiping, doing needlework, and reading the Bible (novels were verboten).

OTHER TOP ATTRACTIONS

Chatham. 120 Chatham Lane. ☎ **540/371-0802.** Free admission. Daily 9am–5pm. Closed New Year's Day and Christmas. Take William St. (Va. 3) east across the river and follow the signs.

This pre-Revolutionary mansion built between 1768 and 1771 by wealthy planter William Fitzhugh has figured prominently in American history. Fitzhugh was a fourth-generation American who supported the Revolution both politically and financially. In the 18th century, Chatham was a center of Southern hospitality, often visited by George Washington. During the Civil War, the house, then belonging to J. Horace Lacy, served as headquarters for Federal commanders and as a Union field hospital. Lincoln visited the house twice, and Clara Barton and Walt Whitman nursed the wounded here. Exhibits on the premises tell about the families who have owned Chatham and detail the role the estate played during the war. Plaques on the grounds identify battle landmarks. Five rooms and the grounds can be viewed on a self-guided tour, with National Park Service employees on hand to answer questions. A picnic area is on the premises.

The Courthouse. Princess Anne and George sts. ☎ **540/372-1066.** Free admission. Mon–Fri 9am–4pm.

If you're interested in architecture, be sure to see this Gothic Revival courthouse, built in 1853. Its architect, James Renwick, also designed St. Patrick's Cathedral in New York and the original Smithsonian "Castle" and Renwick Gallery in Washington,

D.C. Exhibits in the lobby include copies of Mary Ball Washington's will and George Washington's address to the city council in 1784.

Masonic Lodge No. 4. 803 Princess Anne St. (at Hanover St.). ☎ **540/373-5885.** Admission $2 adults, $1 students, 50¢ children under 13. Mon–Sat 9am–4pm; Sun 1–4pm.

Not only is this the mother lodge of the father of our country, it's also one of the oldest Masonic lodges in America, established, it is believed, around 1735. Although the original building was down the street, Masons have been meeting at this address since 1812. On display are all kinds of Masonic paraphernalia and memorabilia, among them the Masonic punchbowl used to serve Lafayette, a Gilbert Stuart portrait of Washington in its original gilt Federalist frame, and the 1668 Bible on which Washington took his Masonic obligation (oath). **Tours** are given throughout the day.

Presbyterian Church. George and Princess Anne sts. ☎ **540/373-7057.** Free admission. Services Labor Day–June, Sun 8:30 and 11am; July–August, Sun 8:30 and 10am (go to church office at other times).

This Presbyterian church dates to the early 1800s, although the present Greek Revival building was completed in 1855—just in time to be shelled during the Civil War, and, like St. George's (see below), to serve as a hospital where Clara Barton nursed Union wounded. Cannonballs in the front left pillar and scars on the walls of the loft and belfry remain to this day. The present church bell replaced one that was given to the Confederacy to be melted down for making cannons.

St. George's Episcopal Church. Princess Anne St. (between George and William sts.). ☎ **540/373-4133.** Free admission. Mon–Sat 9am–5pm (unless a wedding is taking place Sat); Sun services Labor Day–May at 8 and 10:30am, June–Labor Day at 8 and 10am.

Martha Washington's father and John Paul Jones's brother are buried in the graveyard of this church, and members of the first parish congregation included Mary Washington and Revolutionary War generals Hugh Mercer and George Weedon. The original church on this site was built in 1732; the current Romanesque structure, in 1849. During the Battle of Fredericksburg, the church was hit at least 25 times, and in 1863 it was used by General Lee's troops for religious revival meetings. In 1864, when wounded Union soldiers filled every available building in town, it served as a hospital. Note the three signed Tiffany windows.

WASHINGTON AVENUE

Washington Avenue, just above Kenmore, is the site of several notable monuments. A brochure detailing its historic buildings is available at the visitor center. Mary Washington is buried at **Meditation Rock,** a spot where she often came to pray and meditate; there's a monument there in her honor. Just across the way is the **Thomas Jefferson Religious Freedom Monument,** commemorating Jefferson's Fredericksburg meeting with George Mason, Edmond Pendleton, George Wythe, and Thomas Ludwell Lee in 1777 to draft the Virginia Statute of Religious Freedom. The **Hugh Mercer Monument,** off Fauquier Street, honors the doctor and Revolutionary War general.

WHERE TO STAY

Every major chain has motels just off I-95. The strip along Va. 3 at Exit 130 is Fredericksburg's major shopping area, with the Spotsylvania Mall, several strip centers, and an inexpensive Morrison's Cafeteria among a host of chain family restaurants. Here you'll find the **Best Western Fredericksburg** (☎ 800/528-1234 or 540/371-5050), the **Best Western Thunderbird** (☎ 800/528-1234 or 540/373-0000), the **Econo Lodge Central** (☎ 800/55-ECONO or 540/786-8374), a **Hampton Inn**

(☎ 800/HAMPTON or 540/371-0330), a **Ramada Inn** (☎ 800/2RAMADA or 540/786-8361), the **Sheraton Fredericksburg Inn & Conference Center** (☎ 800/682-1049 or 540/786-8321), and a **Super 8** (☎ 800/800-8000 or 540/786-8881).

Another concentration of motels, restaurants, and shops is at Exit 126 (U.S. 1) south of town, where you'll find the Massaponax Factory Outlet Center (including Bass Shoes, Bugle Boy, Corning Revere, Dress Barn, and Oneida). Sitting among the factory shops, the new **Comfort Inn Southpointe** (☎ 800/228-5151 or 540/898-5550) and **WyteStone Suites Hotel** (☎ 800/794-5005 or 540/891-1112) both sport indoor pools. On U.S. 1 just north of I-95 are **Days Inn Fredericksburg South** (☎ 800/DAYS-INN or 540/373-5340), **Econo Lodge South** (☎ 800/55-ECONO or 540/898-5440), a new **Fairfield Inn by Marriott** (☎ 800/348-6000 or 540/891-9100), the independent and inexpensive **Heritage Inn** (☎ 800/787-7440 or 540/898-1000), and **Holiday Inn Fredericksburg South** (☎ 800/HOLIDAY or 540/898-1102).

The following inns are located in Old Town.

✪ Fredericksburg Colonial Inn. 1707 Princess Anne St., Fredericksburg, VA 22401. ☎ **540/371-5666.** 30 rms, 10 suites. A/C TV TEL. $60 double; $80 2-room family unit for 4. Rates include light continental breakfast. AE, MC, V. Free parking.

Victorian furnishings from the Civil War era make this attractive spot a natural hub for Civil War buffs, and people participating in local Civil War reenactments often drop by; don't be surprised to see musket-toting Blues and Grays in the lobby. In the Conference Room, you'll find a display of Civil War weaponry and Confederate dollars. The rooms are furnished with antiques (owner Alton Echols, Jr., is an avid collector), such as a marble-top walnut dresser, rag rugs, a canopied bed, a Victorian sofa, and a bed that belonged to George Mason's son. The spacious lobby is furnished with comfortable wicker rocking chairs and a player piano.

✪ Kenmore Inn. 1200 Princess Anne St., Fredericksburg, VA 22401. ☎ **800/437-7622** or 540/371-7622. Fax 540/371-5480. 14 rms, including 1 suite. A/C TEL. $95–$125 double; $150 suite. Additional person $10 extra. Rates include continental breakfast. Packages available. AE, DC, MC, V. Street parking with free card from visitor center.

An elegant white pediment supported by fluted columns and a front porch with wicker chairs welcome you to this late 1700s mansion in Old Town on property originally owned by George Washington's brother-in-law, Fielding Lewis. Crystal chandeliers, Oriental rugs, polished Georgian side tables, and an enormous gold-framed mirror enhance the foyer. A sweeping staircase leads to the guest rooms—a handsome assortment of both cozy and spacious accommodations furnished with a mix of antiques, many in Regency style. Expect to find four-poster beds with pretty coverlets and lacy canopies, draperies framing louver-shuttered windows, antique chests, and walls hung with botanical prints and engravings. The house has eight working fireplaces, four in the bedrooms.

The inn serves lunch Tuesday through Saturday and dinner Monday through Saturday. On Sunday, brunch is served from 11:30am to 2:30pm. The Pub, a convivial spot, offers live music Friday and Saturday nights.

Richard Johnston Inn. 711 Caroline St., Fredericksburg, VA 22401. ☎ **540/899-7606.** 6 rms, 2 suites. A/C. $90–$130 double. Additional person $10 extra. Rates include continental breakfast. AE, MC, V. Free parking.

Two 18th-century brick row houses have been joined to form this elegantly restored inn directly across the street from the visitor center. The downstairs sitting rooms and dining room, where continental breakfast is served, are invitingly furnished. The Oriental rugs and mahogany furniture in the second-floor rooms in one house create a more formal atmosphere, while in the other house, braided rugs, rockers, oak dressers, and four-poster beds lend a country charm. Third-floor dormer rooms are cozy, with low ceilings. The inn's original summer kitchen exudes rural charm, with brick floors, two antique beds, and a private entrance off the courtyard. The spacious and comfortable suites each offer a private courtyard entrance as well as a separate living room with TV, wet bar, and refrigerator. The owners have dogs in the house, but your pets aren't allowed.

WHERE TO DINE
EXPENSIVE

Le La Fayette. 623 Caroline St. (at Charlotte St.). ☎ **540/373-6895.** Reservations recommended. Main courses $9–$24; special prix-fixe dinner $14; Sunday brunch $17.50. AE, DC, DISC, MC, V. Tues–Sat 11:30am–2:30pm and 6–9pm; Sun 11:30am–2:30pm and 5:30–9pm. FRENCH.

Owners Pierre and Edith Muyard have restored a Georgian-style private home, once called the Chimneys, to create an elegant restaurant named for the famed French marquis. The interior retains much of its period character, with original wide-plank flooring, paneling, and dining-room fireplaces. Tables are set with white cloths, gleaming china, and silver. During the day, sunlight pours in through the many-paned windows; at night, lamps on each table glow in crystal holders. Traditional French cuisine dominates the menu, but you'll also note many nouvelle innovations. Dinner might start with hearty onion soup gratinée. Specialties among the entrees are poached salmon filet with sea scallops in lobster bouillon; fresh trout sautéed with shrimp, tomatoes, and toasted almonds; and sautéed veal scallopine with morel and dry-sherry cream sauce. Duck l'orange or catfish thermidor are the main-course choices for a special three-course dinner served Tuesday to Friday evenings. An extensive wine list includes both French and domestic selections. The homemade desserts vary, but usually include a delectable chocolate mousse cake. Sunday brunch offers a bountiful buffet.

MODERATE

La Petite Auberge. 311 William St. (between Princess Anne and Charles sts.). ☎ **540/371-2727.** Reservations recommended, especially at dinner. Main courses $10–$19; early-bird dinner $14. AE, CB, DC, MC, V. Mon–Fri 11:30am–2:30pm and 5:30–10pm; Sat 5:30–10pm; early-bird dinner Mon–Thurs 5:30–7pm. FRENCH.

The delightful La Petite Auberge was designed to look like a garden, an effect enhanced by white latticework and garden furnishings. Unpainted brick walls are hung with copper pots and cheerful oil paintings, and candlelit tables are adorned with fresh flowers. A cozy lounge adjoins.

The menu changes daily. A recent visit included a salade Niçoise, tortellini in cream sauce, *poulet aux champignons*, and avocado stuffed with curried chicken salad. The early-bird dinner here is an attractive offering—soup, salad, a choice of seven entrees from the regular dinner menu, and homemade ice cream.

Ristorante Renato. 422 William St. (at Prince Edward St.). ☎ **540/317-8228.** Reservations recommended, especially on weekends. Main courses $10–$22 (most under $16); lunch special $6; early-bird dinner $22 for 2 people. AE, MC, V. Mon–Fri 11:30am–2pm and 4:30–10pm; Sat–Sun 4:30–10pm; early-bird dinner Mon–Fri 4:30–7pm. ITALIAN.

This very good, reasonably priced Italian eatery offers homey decor—candlelit (at night) white-linened tables adorned with fresh flowers, ceramic candelabra chandeliers, oil paintings of Italy lining the walls, and a working fireplace. The booths in a small room to one side are especially cozy. In addition to its regular menu, Renato offers a complete luncheon featuring salad, home-baked bread, and a choice of such entrees as eggplant parmigiana, fettuccine Alfredo, or steamed mussels in white sauce. A similar early-bird dinner adds dessert and a demicarafe of wine; a three-course meal with a bottle of wine is also available anytime Monday through Thursday evenings, at a cost of $50 for two persons.

The Smythe's Cottage and Tavern. 303 Fauquier St. (at Princess Anne St.). ☎ **540/ 373-1645.** Reservations suggested on weekends. Main courses $11–$18. MC, V. Mon and Wed–Thurs 11am–9pm; Fri–Sat 11am–10pm; Sun noon–9pm. TRADITIONAL SOUTHERN.

At quaintly charming Smythe's Cottage, you can dine on the site of a blacksmith's stable once operated by George Washington's brother. The current building dates back to 1840. The original owner hailed from an old Virginia family, hence the photograph of General Grant upside down next to a photo of her great-great-grandfather, who was hanged by the Union army in the Civil War. The low-ceilinged interior is extremely cozy, decorated with colonial-style furnishings, old oil portraits, and family memorabilia. In summer, there's alfresco dining in a flower-bordered garden.

The menu offers traditional Virginia fare like peanut soup, Brunswick stew, and delicious chicken potpie. The entrees are served with a basket of oven-fresh bread, soup or salad, and vegetable. The homemade desserts include hot cherry or apple turnovers. Lunch here is very reasonably priced.

INEXPENSIVE

Sammy T's. 801 Caroline St. (at Hanover St.). ☎ **540/371-2008.** Reservations not accepted. Sandwiches $2.50–$5.50; main courses $4.50–$8. DISC, MC, V. Mon–Sat 8am–10pm; Sun 8am–9pm. AMERICAN/NATURAL FOOD.

Located right in the middle of the historic business district, this simpatico eatery is one of the most popular pubs in town, offering a relaxed, tasteful setting and a creative health-food orientation. It has a rustic feel, with large overhead fans, a pressed-tin ceiling, roomy knotty-pine booths, a long oak bar, and painted wood walls adorned with framed art posters. Everything on the menu is made from scratch, with an emphasis on natural ingredients. Breakfast, served until 11am, features Belgian waffles and buckwheat pancakes with a choice of toppings, ham or sausage biscuits, and a fresh fruit bowl with yogurt and granola. The lunch and dinner menu offers many vegetarian items, such as a baked potato stuffed with mushrooms, tomatoes, walnuts, sunflower seeds, three cheeses, and sprouts, all topped with sour cream and served with soup. Entrees like broiled salmon steak, vegetarian lasagna, and chicken Parmesan over fettuccine are other enticing possibilities.

2 The Civil War Battlefields

Fredericksburg has never forgotten its Civil War victories and defeats. In **Fredericksburg and Spotsylvania National Military Park,** you can take all or part of a 75-mile-long self-guided auto tour of 16 important sites relating to four major battles.

The starting point is the **Fredericksburg Battlefield Visitor Center,** 1013 Lafayette Blvd. (U.S. 1 Business), at Sunken Road (☎ **540/373-6122**), where you can get detailed tour brochures and rent 3-hour-long auto-tour tapes ($2.75 per battlefield for cassette player and tape, $4.25 to buy each tape). We strongly recommend the tapes, since they definitely enhance the experience, and renting a player along with them will allow you to get out of your car and still hear the informative commentary. The center offers a 12-minute slide-show orientation and related exhibits; it's open daily from 9am to 5pm, with extended hours in summer determined annually. There were no entrance fees when we recently visited the battlefields, but this could change.

For advance **information,** write to the Superintendent, Fredericksburg and Spotsylvania National Military Park, 120 Chatham Lane, Fredericksburg, VA 22405.

BATTLE OF FREDERICKSBURG

Lee used the Rappahannock River as a natural line of defense for much of the war, while the Union army's goal was to cross it and head for Richmond. The Battle of Fredericksburg took place from December 11 to 15, 1862, when the Union army under Gen. Ambrose E. Burnside crossed the river into Fredericksburg via pontoon bridges. Burnside made a major mistake when he sent the main body of his 100,000 men uphill against Lee's 75,000 troops, most of them dug in behind a stone wall along Sunken Road at the base of Marye's Heights. Then open space, the ground below the heights became a bloody killing field as Lee's cannon, firing from the hill, mowed down the Yankees like shooting ducks in a barrel. The stone wall—some parts original, some reconstructed—stands beside the visitor center at the base of Marye's Heights. The driving tour begins here at the visitor center, but before you go, examine the wall and climb up the heights for a fine view over the town.

BATTLE OF CHANCELLORSVILLE

President Lincoln fired Burnside after the Marye's Heights massacre. Under his replacement, Gen. Joseph Hooker, the Union forces crossed the river above Fredericksburg in late April 1863, and advanced to Chancellorsville, a crossroads 10 miles west of Fredericksburg on the Orange Turnpike (now Va. 3). When Lee rushed westward to meet him, Hooker dug in. In a surprise attack, Stonewall Jackson flanked Hooker's line on May 2 and won a spectacular victory. Unfortunately, Jackson was inadvertently shot by his own men that same night. Field surgeons amputated his left arm and moved him to Guinea Station, 27 miles away, where he could be evacuated by train. Pneumonia set in, however, and Jackson died there on May 10. By then, Lee had driven the Union army back across the Rappahannock.

The **Chancellorsville Visitor Center** (☎ **540/786-2880**) is on Va. 3. Stop there to see another 12-minute audiovisual orientation and related exhibits. Once again, an auto-tour tape is available. The center is open daily from 9am to 5pm.

Now part of the park, the **Jackson Shrine,** where the general died, is at the junction of C.R. 606 and C.R. 607, about 27 miles southeast of Chancellorsville. From I-95, take Exit 118 at Thornburg and follow the signs east on C.R. 606.

BATTLE OF THE WILDERNESS

A year later, now under the direction of the aggressive Ulysses S. Grant, Union forces once again crossed the Rappahannock and advanced south to Wilderness Tavern, 5 miles west of Chancellorsville near what is now the junction of Va. 3 and Va. 20. Lee advanced to meet him, thus setting up the first battle between these two great generals. For the 2 days of May 5 and 6, 1864, the armies fought in the tangled thickets of the Wilderness. The battle was a stalemate, but instead of retreating as his predecessors had, Grant backed off and then went around Lee toward his ultimate target, Richmond.

BATTLE OF SPOTSYLVANIA COURT HOUSE

Lee next tried to stop Grant on May 12 at Spotsylvania Court House, on the shortest road south (now Va. 208). Taking advantage of thick fog and wet Confederate gunpowder, Union troops breached the Southerners' line. When Lee's reinforcements arrived, the two sides spent 20 hours in the war's most intense hand-to-hand combat at a site known as Bloody Angle. During the fighting, Lee built new fortifications to the rear, which he successfully defended. Instead of pushing the fight to the finish, however, Grant again backed off and moved his entire army around Lee's toward Richmond. It was the end of major fighting in the Fredericksburg area, as the war moved progressively south to its ultimate conclusion 11 months later at Appomattox.

3 The Northern Neck

A long, narrow strip of land stretching east from Fredericksburg, the Northern Neck is bounded by the Potomac and Rappahannock rivers and Chesapeake Bay. This picturesque country is a blend of venerable colonial history and saltwater vitality. The Pope's Creek Plantation, site of George Washington's birthplace, and Stratford Hall, the magnificent ancestral home of the Lee family, are both located on the Potomac riverfront. Nearby, the Ingleside Plantation Vineyards offer tours and tastings.

In the riverfront town of Irvington sits the Tides Inn, one of the premier resorts in the country. Nearby stands Christ Church, which has been described as the most perfect example of colonial church architecture in the United States. From Victorian Reedville, you can fish or depart on cruises to remote Tangier Island out in the Chesapeake.

ESSENTIALS

VISITOR INFORMATION   For information, contact the **Northern Neck Tourism Council,** P.O. Box 326, Wicomico Church, VA 22579 (☎ **800/453-6167** or 804/580-9058; fax 804/453-3915).

GETTING THERE   By Car   You'll need a car to get here. From Fredericksburg, take Va. 3 East, which traverses the length of the peninsula. From Fredericksburg, Washington's Birthplace is 40 miles; Irvington, 95 miles. You can make a scenic loop tour of the peninsula by taking Va. 3 to Irvington, Va. 200 to Reedville, then U.S. 360, Va. 202, and Va. 3 back to Fredericksburg. Alternatively, you can drive directly west to Richmond via U.S. 360.

WHAT TO SEE & DO
ATTRACTIONS
✪ George Washington Birthplace National Monument. Va. 204, off Va. 3, Washington's Birthplace, VA. ☎ **804/224-1732.** Admission to farm $2 adults, free for children under 17. Free admission to beach, picnic area, nature trail, and cemetery. National Park Service passports accepted. Daily 9am–5pm. Closed New Year's Day and Christmas.

Encompassing some 500 acres along a tributary of the Potomac, Pope's Creek Plantation is a living-history display, complete with a charming re-creation of George Washington's first home, costumed guides, and crafts demonstrations. The first child of Augustine and Mary Ball Washington, the first president was born on February 22, 1732, and lived here until he was $3^1/_2$, when the family moved to the Mount Vernon estate. The land was first settled by Washington's great-grandfather, John, in the mid-17th century. The farmhouse burned down in 1779 and was never rebuilt. The re-created building we see today is called Memorial House. There are no historic records detailing what the house looked like, so this memorial, operated by the National Park Service, is a representation of a typical farmhouse of Washington's childhood, with antique furnishings appropriate to the period.

At the visitor center, a 14-minute film called *A Childhood Place* evokes life at the plantation. There is an uphill walk of some 300 yards to the historic area; transportation is provided for those unable to walk that distance. In the historic area are the birthplace site, an herb garden, a separate building housing the plantation's kitchen (cooking demonstrations are often in progress here), and a weaving room. Graves of some Washington family members, including George's father, are in a small burial ground on the property.

Tours are offered throughout the day. Children will particularly enjoy the colonial farm, with its horses, chickens, and cows. A picnic area is available, but no refreshments, except for soda and vending-machine snacks, are sold at the park.

✪ **Historic Christ Church.** C.R. 646, off Va. 200, 1 mile north of Irvington. ☎ **804/ 438-6855.** Free admission. Church, daily 9am–5pm. Carter Reception Center, Apr–Thanksgiving, Mon–Fri 10am–4pm; Sat 10am–4pm; Sun 2–5pm. Closed Christmas.

Elegant in its simplicity and virtually unchanged since it was completed in 1735, Christ Church, listed on the National Register of Historic Places, was the gift of Robert "King" Carter. Carter offered to finance the building of the church if his parents' graves remained in the chancel. Today, the bodies of John Carter, four of his five wives, and two infant children are interred in the chancel. Robert Carter's tomb is on the church grounds. Among the descendants of the Carters are eight governors of Virginia; two presidents of the United States (the two Harrisons); Gen. Robert E. Lee; and Edward D. White, a chief justice of the U.S. Supreme Court.

The building is cruciform in shape, its brick facade laid in a pleasing Flemish bond pattern, with a three-color design that saves the expanse of brick from monotony. Inside, the three-decker pulpit is in excellent condition, and all 26 original pews remain. The building has no artificial heat or light and is now used for services only during the summer.

Ingleside Plantation Winery. Oak Grove. ☎ **804/224-8687.** Free admission. Mon–Sat 10am–5pm; Sun noon–5pm. Closed major holidays. Traveling east from Fredericksburg on Va. 3, turn right in Oak Grove on Va. 638 and continue about 2¹/₂ miles south.

The rich soil and mild climate of the Northern Neck provide ideal grape-growing conditions for this 2,500-acre plantation winery. In addition to winery tours, tastings, and a gift shop selling wine-related items, Ingleside has a small exhibit area displaying colonial wine bottles, Chesapeake waterfowl carvings, and Native American artifacts.

Reedville Fishermen's Museum. Main St., Reedville. ☎ **540/453-6529.** Admission $2 adults, free for children under 12. May–Oct, Wed–Mon 10:30am–4:30pm; Nov–late Dec and mid-Feb to Apr, Fri–Mon 10:30am–4:30pm; late Dec to mid-Feb, by appointment only. From Va. 3 east, take U.S. 360 east to Reedville.

The small village of Reedville on Cockrell's Creek, an inlet of Chesapeake Bay, provides a living image of the past with its Victorian mansions and seafaring atmosphere. The Fishermen's Museum consists of the 1875 William Walker House, restored to appear as it did in 1900, and the Covington Building, which houses a permanent collection and special exhibits. It commemorates the watermen who participated in the town's leading industry, based on a small, toothless fish, the menhaden, which is of little use for human consumption but extremely valuable for its byproducts: meal, oil, and protein supplements used in animal feeds. Capt. Elijah Reed, who came to this area from Maine in 1874, built a menhaden factory, a steamboat wharf, and a home.

✪ **Stratford Hall Plantation.** Va. 214, 2 miles north of Va. 3, Stratford. ☎ **804/493-8038.** Admission $7 adults, $6 seniors, $3 children 6–18, free for children under 6. Daily 9am–4:30pm. Closed New Year's Day, Thanksgiving, and Christmas.

This is one of the great houses of the South, magnificently set on 1,600 acres above the Potomac, renowned not only for its distinctive architectural style but also for the illustrious family who lived here. Thomas Lee (1690–1750), a planter who later served as governor of the Virginia colony, built Stratford in the late 1730s. Five of his sons played major roles in the forming of the new nation, most notably Richard Henry Lee, who made the motion for independence in the Continental Congress in 1776. He and Francis Lightfoot Lee were the only brothers to sign the Declaration of Independence. Gen. Henry "Light-Horse Harry" Lee, a cousin and hero of the Revolution, married into this family. He was a friend of George Washington and father of the most famous Lee child born at Stratford—Robert E. Lee.

The H-shaped manor house, its four dependencies, coach house, and stables have been brilliantly restored. On approaching the imposing two-story-high stone entrance staircase, you'll meet a costumed guide who will point out one of the mansion's most striking features—the brick chimney groupings that flank the roofline.

The paneled Great Hall, one of the finest rooms to have survived from colonial times, runs the depth of the house and has an inverted tray ceiling. On the same floor are bedrooms and a nursery, where you can see Robert E. Lee's crib. The fireplace in the nursery is trimmed with sculpted angels' heads.

Tours conclude in the kitchen and estate offices. You can then stroll the meadows and gardens of this 1,600-acre estate, still operated as a working farm.

Also on the estate is a rustic log cabin–style public dining room with a screened-in terrace; it offers breakfasts; light snacks; a plantation lunch with fried chicken, crabcakes, or ham ($8 adults, $4 children); and its own vintage chardonnay and cabernet sauvignon wines.

A CRUISE TO TANGIER ISLAND

Out in the Chesapeake Bay lies quaint and still relatively remote ✪ **Tangier Island,** whose inhabitants own no cars and still speak in the Elizabethan brogue of their colonial ancestors (see "Onancock" under "Chincoteague & the Eastern Shore" in chapter 12 for more information). **Tangier Island Cruises** (☎ **800/598-2628** or 804/453-2628) leave from Buzzards Point Marina, off U.S. 360 near Reedville, at 10am daily from May to October 15. The narrated voyage takes 90 minutes each way. Fares are $18.50 for adults, $9.25 for children 4 to 13, and free for kids 3 and under. Reservations are required.

WHERE TO STAY

Cedar Grove Bed & Breakfast Inn. 2743 Fleeton Rd., Reedville, VA 22539. ☎ **800/497-8215** or 804/453-3915. Fax 804/453-2650. www.virginia.org/cedargrove. E-mail: tiptons@crosslink.net. 2 suites. A/C. $100–$125 double. Rates include full breakfast. No credit cards. Free parking. From Reedville, follow Fleeton Rd. (C.R. 657) approximately 3 miles to Cedar Grove.

Surrounded by farm fields, Cedar Grove is a stately 1913 Colonial Revival house built by a sea captain for his daughter. It looks out over Chesapeake Bay and the lighthouse at the mouth of the Great Wicomico River. Arctic swans spend the winter here in the coves and marshes of the bay, and ospreys nest on nearby Big Fleet's Pond. In this tranquil setting, hosts Susan and Bob Tipton run an appealing B&B, with two spacious guest suites with private decks and Victorian furniture. Downstairs, relax in the formal parlor or in the sunroom, a pleasant spot to read or watch TV. Outdoors is a croquet court, and bicycles are available for touring the area. Less active types can kick back in a hammock or the rocking chairs on the porch or sun themselves on the Tiptons' private sandy beach.

✪ **The Tides Inn.** King Carter Dr. (P.O. Box 480), Irvington, VA 22480. ☎ **800/TIDES INN** or 804/438-5000. Fax 804/438-5552. 110 rms. A/C TV TEL. $125–$200 per person double. Family rate for 2 rooms $310 per couple plus $43 for each child 4–15, $53 for each child 16 and over (no charge for children under 4). Rates include breakfast and dinner. Golf packages available. Pets $10 per animal (in some rooms). AE, DC, DISC, MC, V. Closed early Jan to mid-Mar. Free parking. From Va. 3, take Va. 200 south 2 miles to Irvington, turn right at the sign to end of King Carter Dr.

Recently rated one of America's top 20 resorts by *Condé Nast Traveler* magazine, the Tides Inn has maintained a tradition of gracious service under the auspices of the Stephens family since 1947. The sprawling resort complex consists of several low-rise buildings encircling a nicely landscaped entrance. Guests can choose accommodations in the Main Building, where the dining room and gift shop are located, or in the Windsor or Lancaster Houses, where the rooms are more spacious and feature dressing rooms, living areas, and, in some cases, balconies overlooking Carter's Creek. All rooms contain coffeemakers.

Dining/Entertainment: For the duration of their stay, guests are assigned to a table in the lovely main dining room, which overlooks the creek. Food is also available at Cap'n B's, at the Golden Eagle golf course, and at Commodore's, an airy glass-enclosed room adjacent to the pool that serves informal buffet luncheons. Menus feature seafood items like soft-shell crabs and fried-oyster sandwiches, along with prime rib and pork tenderloin. The Chesapeake Club lounge, next to the dining room, has exquisite wood paneling, panoramic views, music, and dancing.

Services: Morning newspaper, nightly turndown, no surcharge for local or long-distance phone calls.

Facilities: Heated saltwater pool; complimentary nearby health club with aerobics classes, weights, sauna, and racquetball; unlimited tennis, sailing, paddleboating, canoeing, bicycling, croquet; two 18-hole golf courses, one 9-hole par-three course plus driving range and putting green; game room with Ping Pong, billiards, electronic games, and shuffleboard; gift and resort-wear shops; yacht cruises.

The Tides Lodge Resort & Country Club. P.O. Box 309, Irvington, VA 22480. ☎ **800/ 248-4337** or 804/438-6000. Fax 804/438-5950. 60 rms, 1 cottage. A/C TV TEL. $100–$130 double (room only); $99–$151 per person double occupancy (including breakfast and dinner); $200–$250 cottage. $7–$14 per person daily service charge in lieu of tipping. Golf and other packages available. MC, V. Free parking. From Va. 3, take Va. 200 south 2 miles to Irvington, follow signs.

Another branch of the Stephens family operates this less expensive version of the Tides Inn across Carter's Creek. A Scottish motif prevails here, in both the public areas and the comfortable, motel-style rooms, whose walls are adorned with hunting and fishing scenes. Jackets are suggested for men dining in the Royal Stewart Dining Room, but they can get away with shirts with collars in the casual Binnacle Restaurant, which overlooks the creek. There's also a sandwich bar and cafe beside the saltwater swimming pool. The Royal Stewart has dancing 3 nights a week, and McD's Pub offers weekend entertainment. Guests here can share the Tides Inn's Golden Eagle golf course and cruises, but have their own Tartan Course and pools, tennis courts, and exercise room.

Charlottesville & Lynchburg: Central Virginia

With the serene Blue Ridge Mountains on the horizon to the west, the rolling hills of central Virginia reveal a scenic pastoral landscape. No wonder Peter Jefferson, coming here to survey the land, decided to settle and amassed hundreds of acres. His son Thomas Jefferson, America's third president, inherited not only his father's property but also an abiding attachment to the land where he, too, spent much of his life, and where he associated with two other future presidents, James Madison and James Monroe.

Today Charlottesville is a lively town, filled with visitors drawn by the monuments to Thomas Jefferson's genius and the University of Virginia he founded. The historic tobacco town of Lynchburg, on the James River, has interesting sights of its own, including Jefferson's beloved country retreat and the tiny village of Appomattox Court House, where Robert E. Lee surrendered to Ulysses S. Grant.

1 Charlottesville

72 miles W of Richmond; 120 miles SW of Washington, D.C.

It was in Charlottesville that Thomas Jefferson, one of America's most passionate believers in freedom and human rights, built his famous mountaintop home, Monticello; selected the site for and helped plan James Monroe's Ash Lawn-Highland house; designed his "academical village," the University of Virginia; and died at home. "All my wishes end where I hope my days will end," he wrote, "at Monticello."

Established in 1762 as the county seat for Albemarle, the town had its Court Square complete with courthouse, jail, whipping post, pillory, and stocks to keep fractious citizens in line. The courthouse doubled as marketplace in those early days and served as a church as well, with rotating services for different denominations (Jefferson called it the "Common Temple"). Elections were held in Court Square followed by raucous political celebrations. Needless to say, the taverns across the street were well patronized.

Along with neighbor James Madison, Jefferson and Monroe were instrumental in developing the emerging nation. In addition to writing the Declaration of Independence, Jefferson advocated freedom of religion, public education, and the abolition of slavery. Madison was instrumental in developing the Constitution and its Bill of Rights. One of the two American presidents who actually fought in the Revolution, Monroe nearly doubled the new nation's size by negotiating the Louisiana Purchase, and he kept colonial powers out of the Americas by declaring the Monroe Doctrine.

Although Charlottesville today is a growing cosmopolitan center, attracting an increasing number of rich and famous folks like author John Grisham, its historic and pastoral atmosphere still enables visitors to imagine themselves back in colonial times, when Jefferson would ride 2 miles on horseback to visit his friend Monroe.

ESSENTIALS

VISITOR INFORMATION   For information, contact the **Monticello Visitor Center,** P.O. Box 178, Charlottesville, VA 22902 (☎ **804/977-1783;** fax 804/ 295-2176; monticello.avenue.gen.va.us/Tourism/CRTC; e-mail: caccbb@comnet. net). The center is on Va. 20 at Exit 121 off I-64. It's open daily from 9am to 5:30pm, to 5pm from December to March. The center sells tickets to Monticello and other key attractions (see "Seeing Charlottesville," below). It also provides maps and literature about local and state attractions, and can make same-day, walk-in hotel/ motel reservations for you.

GETTING THERE   By Car   Charlottesville is immediately accessible by I-64 from east or west and by U.S. 29 from north or south. I-64 connects with I-81 at Staunton and with I-95 at Richmond.

By Plane   US Airways, Delta, and United fly to **Charlottesville-Albemarle Airport,** 201 Bowen Loop (☎ **804/973-8341**).

By Train   The **Amtrak** station is at 810 W. Main St. (☎ **800/872-7245**).

CITY LAYOUT   Charlottesville has not one but two commercial centers, both on Main Street (U.S. 250 Business). On West Main Street, opposite the University of Virginia between 13th Street and Elliewood Avenue, the **Corner** neighborhood is a typical campus enclave, with student-dominated restaurants, bookstores and clothing stores, and a dearth of parking spaces. A mile to the east, **Historic Downtown Charlottesville** is centered on the Downtown Mall, an 8-block, pedestrian-only strip of Main Street between 2nd Street West and 8th Street East. The major suburban growth is along U.S. 29 north, which is lined with shopping centers, chain motels, and fast-food and family restaurants.

GETTING AROUND   Charlottesville Transit Service (☎ **804/296-RIDE**) provides bus service Monday through Saturday from 6:30am to 6:30pm throughout the city (but not to Monticello). Routes 2, 3, and 7 run along West Main Street between downtown and the university. Base fare is 75¢, with exact change required.

PARKING   On-street parking is extremely limited here. In the historic downtown area, you can park free for 2 hours with merchant validation in the garage on Market Street between 1st and 2nd streets, or in any of the lots and two garages along Water Street. The university's visitor parking garage is on the western side of the campus, on Emmet Street (U.S. 29 Business) a block south of University Avenue (which is the continuation of West Main Street). On the eastern side of campus, two public garages are located opposite the University Hospital on Lee Street, off Jefferson Park Avenue. The Corner has public parking on Elliewood Avenue, Wertland Street at 14th Street, and down the alleys behind the businesses fronting West Main Street. Most garages and lots cost $1 per hour.

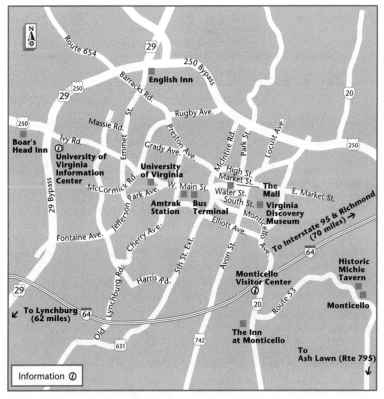

Information ⓘ

SEEING CHARLOTTESVILLE

Make your first stop in town the **Monticello Visitor Center** (see "Essentials," above). In addition to welcoming visitors, the center houses a marvelous permanent exhibit called "Thomas Jefferson at Monticello."

The center sells a **Presidents' Pass,** a discount block ticket combining admission to Monticello, Michie Tavern, and Ash Lawn-Highland. The cost is $22 for ages 12 to 59 and $20 for those over 59. Don't buy it for children under 12—they pay less at each attraction. The center is open March through October, daily from 9am to 5:30pm; the rest of the year, daily until 5pm.

THE BLOCK-TICKET ATTRACTIONS

✪ **Ash Lawn-Highland.** C.R. 795. ☎ **804/293-9539.** Admission $7 adults, $6.50 seniors, $4 children 6–11, free for children under 6. Mar–Oct, daily 9am–6pm; Nov–Feb, daily 10am–5pm. Follow the directions to Monticello. Ash Lawn is 2¹/₂ miles past Monticello on James Monroe Parkway (C.R. 795).

Fifth president James Monroe fought in the Revolution, was wounded in Trenton, and went on to hold more public offices than any other president. Monroe's close friendship with Thomas Jefferson brought him to the Blue Ridge Mountains of Charlottesville, where Jefferson wished to create "a society to our taste." In 1793, Monroe purchased 1,000 acres adjacent to Monticello and built an estate he called "Highland" (the name *Ash Lawn* dates to 1838). Before he could settle in, however,

Washington named him minister to France and sent him to Paris for 3 years. During his absence, Jefferson sent gardeners over to start orchards, and the Madisons made agricultural contributions as well. Nevertheless, by the time Monroe returned, he was suffering financial difficulties, and his "cabin castle" developed along more modest lines than originally intended. When he retired from office in 1825, his debts totaled $75,000, and he was forced to sell the beloved farm where he had hoped to spend his last days. A later owner, John Massey, built a two-story addition to the main house in 1884.

Today Monroe's 535-acre estate is owned and maintained as a working farm by his alma mater, the College of William and Mary. Livestock, vegetable and herb gardens, and colonial crafts demonstrations recall the elements of daily life on the Monroes' plantation. Horses, sheep, and cattle graze in the fields, while peacocks roam the boxwood gardens. Five of the original rooms remain, along with the basement kitchen, the overseer's cottage, restored slave quarters, and the old smokehouse. On a 40-minute **house tour,** you'll see some of the family's original furnishings and artifacts and learn a great deal about the fifth president. On the grounds are a gift shop and picnic tables.

Many special events take place at Ash Lawn-Highland: The outdoor **Summer Festival** features opera and contemporary music performances; a major colonial arts festival, **Plantation Days,** which takes place in July, showcases dozens of 18th-century crafts, historic reenactments, period music performances, and dressage.

Historic Michie Tavern. 683 Thomas Jefferson Pkwy. (Va. 683). ☎ **804/977-1234.** Admission $6 adults, $5.50 seniors, $2 children 6–11, free for children under 6. Daily 9am–5pm (last tour 4:20pm). Guided tours, Apr–Oct. Self-guided tours with recorded narratives, Nov–Mar. Closed New Year's Day and Christmas. From the visitor center, go south on Va. 20, turn left at Thomas Jefferson Pkwy. (Va. 683); Michie Tavern is about 1 mile farther.

In 1746, Scotsman "Scotch John" Michie (pronounced "Mickey") purchased 1,152 acres of land from Patrick Henry's father, and in 1784, Michie's son, William, built this historic tavern on a well-traveled stagecoach route at Earlysville, 17 miles northwest of Charlottesville. A wealthy businesswoman, Josephine Henderson, saw its value as a historic structure and in 1927 had it moved to its present location and painstakingly reconstructed. Michie Tavern stands today as a tribute to early preservationists.

Behind the tavern are reproductions of the "dependencies"—log kitchen, dairy, smokehouse, ice house, root cellar, and "necessary" (note the not-so-soft corncobs). The general store has been re-created, along with an excellent crafts shop, and the **Virginia Wine Museum** is on the premises. Behind the store is a grist mill that has operated continuously since 1797.

Unless you're picnicking at Monticello, plan your visit to Michie Tavern to coincide with lunchtime, for hot meals are still served to weary travelers for reasonable pence in the "Ordinary," a converted log cabin with original hand-hewn walls and beamed ceilings. An all-you-can-eat buffet of Southern fare costs about $10.50 for adults and $6 for children 6 to 11 (free for children under 6). You'll dine off pewter plates at rustic oak tavern tables, and in winter there's a blazing fire. The meal is served daily from 11:30am to 3pm.

✪ Monticello. Off Va. 53. ☎ **804/984-9822** or 804/984-9800. Admission $9 adults, $8 seniors, $5 children 6–11, free for children under 6. 25-minute guided tours offered Mar–Oct, daily 8am–5pm; Nov–Feb, daily 9am–4:30pm. From the visitor center on Va. 20, go south to Va. 53 and turn left, then 2 miles to Monticello's entrance.

Pronounced "Mon-ti-*chel*-lo," the home Thomas Jefferson built over 40 years from 1769 to 1809 is one of the highlights of any visit to Virginia. Considered an architectural masterpiece, it was the first Virginia plantation manse to sit atop a

Jefferson Survives

The phrase "Renaissance man" might have been coined to describe Thomas Jefferson. Perhaps our most important founding father, he was a lawyer, an architect, a scientist, a musician, a writer, an educator, and a horticulturist.

After writing the Declaration of Independence, Jefferson served as governor of Virginia, ambassador to France, secretary of state, and president for two terms, during which he nearly doubled the size of the United States by engineering the Louisiana Purchase from France. He also helped found of one of America's first political parties.

Yet despite all his national and international achievements, Jefferson ordered that his gravestone be inscribed: "Here Was Buried Thomas Jefferson/Author Of The Declaration Of American Independence/Of The Statute Of Virginia For Religious Freedom/And Father Of The University Of Virginia."

Jefferson was 83 when he died at Monticello on July 4, 1826, exactly 50 years to the day after his Declaration of Independence was signed at Philadelphia.

Ironically, his fellow revolutionary—but later heated political enemy—John Adams lay on his own deathbed in Massachusetts. Unaware that Jefferson had died a short time earlier, Adams's last words were: "Jefferson survives."

---

mountain rather than beside a river. Rejecting the Georgian architecture that characterized his time, Jefferson opted instead for the 16th-century Italian style of Andrea Palladio. Later, during his 5-year term as minister to France, he was influenced by the homes of nobles at the court of Louis XVI, and after returning home in 1789, he enlarged Monticello, incorporating features of the Parisian buildings he so admired.

Today the house has been restored as closely as possible to its appearance during Jefferson's retirement years. Nearly all its furniture and other household objects were owned by Jefferson or his family. The garden has been extended to its original 1,000-foot length, and Mulberry Row—where slaves and free artisans lived and labored in light industrial shops such as a joinery, smokehouse-dairy, blacksmith shop-nailery, and carpenter's shop—has been excavated. Guided tours of the gardens and Mulberry Row are available from April through October.

Jefferson's grave is in the family burial ground, which is still in use. After visiting the graveyard, you can take a shuttle bus back to the visitor parking lot or walk through the woods via a delightful path. There is a lovely wooded picnic area with tables and grills on the premises, and, in summer, lunch fare can be purchased.

It's best to avoid weekends, when the tourist traffic is heaviest; the 8am tour is recommended during summer.

MORE ATTRACTIONS IN TOWN

Albemarle County Court House. 501 E. Jefferson St. (at 5th St. E.). ☎ **804/296-5822.** Free admission. Mon–Fri 9am–5pm.

The center of village activity in colonial days, the Court House in the historic downtown area features a facade and portico dating from the Civil War. There's no tour offered, but you can take a glance at Jefferson's will in the County Office Building. It's easy to imagine Jefferson, Madison, and Monroe talking politics under the lawn's huge shade trees.

The Downtown Mall. Main St. between 2nd St. W. and 6th St. E. ☎ **804/296-8548** for mall events.

Impressions

Both the natural beauty of the surrounding countryside and the man-made beauty of Charlottesville combine to weave a tapestry of American history which few other towns or cities can boast.

—John F. Kennedy, 1962

Stroll into the 20th century along a charming pedestrian brick mall extending for about 8 blocks on downtown Main Street. Plan to spend an afternoon browsing and eating here, for the mall is home to a host of boutiques and restaurants. On the west end, you'll find a six-screen movie theater and the Charlottesville Ice Park, which offers ice-skating and pick-up hockey games. It's all enhanced by fountains, park benches under shade trees, outdoor cafes, and buskers making music both day and night.

McGuffey Art Center. 201 2nd St. NW (at 2nd St. W.). ☎ **804/295-7973.** Free admission. Tues–Sat 10am–5pm; Sun 1–5pm.

At the center, in an early-20th-century school building a block north of the Mall, local artists and craftspeople hold studio exhibits and sell their creations. The **Second Street Gallery,** showing contemporary art from all over the United States, is also located here.

✪ **University Of Virginia.** University Ave. ☎ **804/924-0311** for general information, 804/924-7231 for parking information. 45-minute tours given daily at 10 and 11am and 2, 3, and 4pm. Self-guided walking tour brochures available. Closed 3 weeks around Christmas.

Jefferson's University of Virginia is graced with spacious lawns, serpentine-walled gardens, colonnaded pavilions, and a classical rotunda inspired by the Pantheon in Rome. Jefferson regarded its creation as one of his three greatest achievements—all the more remarkable since it was begun in his 73rd year. He was in every sense the university's father, since he conceived it, wrote its charter, raised money for its construction, drew the plans, selected the site, laid the cornerstone in 1817, supervised construction, served as the first rector, selected the faculty, and created the curriculum. His good friends Monroe and Madison sat with him on the first board, and Madison succeeded him as rector, serving for 8 years.

The focal point of the university and starting point for **tours** is the Rotunda (at Rugby Road), today restored as Jefferson designed it. Some 600 feet of tree-dotted lawn extends from the south portico of the Rotunda to what is now Cabell Hall, designed at the turn of the 20th century by Stanford White. On either side of the lawn are pavilions still used for faculty housing, each of a different architectural style "to serve as specimens for the Architectural lecturer." Behind are large gardens (originally used by faculty members to grow vegetables and keep livestock) and the original student dormitories, used—and greatly coveted—by students today; though centrally heated, they still contain working fireplaces. The room Edgar Allan Poe occupied when he was a student here is furnished as it would have been in 1826 and is open to visitors.

Paralleling the lawn are more rows of student rooms called the Ranges. Equally spaced within each of the Ranges are "hotels," originally used to accommodate student dining. Each hotel represented a different country, and students would have to both eat the food and speak the language of that country. Although a wonderful idea on Jefferson's part, it lasted only a short while since everyone wanted to eat French but not German.

The university's **visitor information center** is located not on campus but in the University Police Headquarters, on Ivy Road (U.S. 250 Business) just east of the U.S. 29/U.S. 250 bypass. It's open 24 hours a day. See "Essentials," above, for parking information.

Virginia Discovery Museum. East end of Downtown Mall. ☎ **804/977-1025.** Admission $4 adults, $3 seniors and children 1–13. Tues–Sat 10am–5pm; Sun 1–5pm.

The Virginia Discovery Museum is a place of enchantment, offering numerous hands-on exhibits and programs for young people. Here kids can dress up as firefighters, soldiers, police, and other grownups. The Colonial Log House, an authentic structure that once stood on a site in New Bedford, Virginia, is outfitted with the simple furnishings appropriate to an early-19th-century lifestyle. A series of fascinating exhibits deals with the senses, and the Fun and Games exhibit offers a wonderful array of games, including bowling and giant checkers. An arts and crafts studio, an active beehive, and a changing series of traveling and made-on-site exhibits round out the fun.

MONTPELIER & OTHER NEARBY ATTRACTIONS

✪ **Montpelier.** 11407 Constitution Hwy. (Va. 20), Montpelier Station. ☎ **540/672-2728.** Admission $7.50 adults, $6.50 seniors, $2.50 children 6–11, free for children under 6. Apr–Oct, daily 10am–4pm; Jan–Mar and Nov–Dec, daily 10am–3:30pm. Closed New Year's Day, Race Day in early Nov, Thanksgiving, and Christmas. Montpelier is 25 miles northeast of Charlottesville. Take U.S. 29 north to U.S. 33 east at Ruckersville. At Barboursville, turn left onto Va. 20 north.

This 2,700-acre estate facing the Blue Ridge Mountains was home to President James Madison and his wife, Dolley. Madison was just 26 when he ensured that the 1776 Constitutional Convention in Williamsburg would include religious freedom in the Virginia Declaration of Rights, and his efforts at the federal Constitutional Convention in 1787 earned him the title "Father of the Constitution." Madison became secretary of state under his good friend Thomas Jefferson in 1801, and succeeded Jefferson as president in 1809. He and Dolley fled the White House in the face of advancing British troops during the War of 1812. Madison inherited what was then a modest two-story red-brick Georgian residence from his father, who built it around 1760, and with architectural advice from Jefferson, expanded its proportions.

James and Dolley are buried here in the Madison family cemetery. Two structures remain from their time: the main house and the "Ice House Temple" (built over a well and used to store ice). William du Pont, Sr., bought the estate in 1900. He enlarged the mansion and added barns, staff houses, a sawmill, a blacksmith shop, a train station, a dairy, and greenhouses, and his wife created a 2¹/₂-acre formal garden. Daughter Marion du Pont Scott later built a steeplechase course and initiated the **Montpelier Hunt Races,** which are still held here every November. The National Trust acquired the property following her death in 1984 and opened it to the public in 1987.

Check in at the visitor center, which has an exhibit about Madison's life and times and shows a short film about him and the estate. From there, guided tours will take you through the mansion, where there's another exhibit about our fourth president and his role in framing the Constitution. You can use an audio tour to cover the grounds, including the formal gardens, the family cemetery, and ongoing archaeological excavations. Call ahead for a schedule of special events, such as the races in early November, birthday celebrations for James (March 16) and Dolley (May 20), and the Montpelier Wine Festival in May.

Oakencroft Vineyard. Barracks Rd. ☎ **804/296-4188.** Admission $1 per person. Apr–Dec, daily 11am–5pm; Jan–Mar, Sat–Sun 11am–5pm. Drive 3^1/$_2$ miles west of U.S. 29 on Barracks Rd.

There have been vineyards in the Piedmont since the 18th century, and Jefferson hoped to someday produce quality wines in Virginia. Today his dream is a reality, and many area wineries offer tours and tastings. A case in point is Oakencroft Vineyard, set on 17 acres of rolling farmland with a lake and views of the Blue Ridge Mountains. Hand-hewn beams adorn the tasting room, where visitors can sample 10 different varieties for free, and trestle tables are available for alfresco lunching (bring your own picnic). A tour takes about 20 minutes.

For a list of other Charlottesville-area wineries, pick up a brochure at the visitor center.

Walton's Mountain Museum. Schuyler. ☎ **804/831-2000.** Admission $5 adults, $4 seniors, free for children under 13. Mar–Nov, daily 10am–4pm. Closed Easter Sunday, second Sat in Oct, and Thanksgiving. From I-64 take U.S. 29 south 18 miles. Turn left on Va. 6, go east 6 miles to C.R. 800, turn right on C.R. 800, and go south 2 miles to Schuyler and follow signs.

There is no real "Walton's Mountain," but Hollywood screenwriter Earl Hamner, Jr., based characters of the popular TV series *The Waltons* on real folks he knew growing up during the Depression in the picturesque hamlet of Schuyler (pronounced *Sky-*lar). Hamner worked closely with hometown residents to create this charming museum in the old elementary school across the street from his boyhood home. Photos of the real characters are displayed beside those of the actors who played them on television, and fans of the warm-hearted series will get a kick out of seeing the set of John-Boy's bedroom. All profits are given back to the community, funding such things as a computer learning center in the old school.

While here, you can get a meal or refreshment at **Schuyler Family Restaurant,** in what used to be a Victorian hotel next door to the museum (☎ **804/831-3333**).

WHERE TO STAY

Wherever you choose to stay, make your reservations as far in advance as possible; during University of Virginia events such as graduation, football games, and parents' weekends, every property here will be full.

The commercial strip along U.S. 29 north of the U.S. 250 bypass has an abundance of chain motels, including a comfortable **Courtyard by Marriott** (☎ 800/321-2211 or 804/973-7100), which abuts the Fashion Square Mall. Others along U.S. 29 north include **Best Western Mount Vernon** (☎ 800/528-1234 or 804/296-5501), **Comfort Inn** (☎ 800/228-5150 or 804/293-6188), **Econo Lodge North** (☎ 800/55-ECONO or 804/295-3185), **Hampton Inn** (☎ 800/HAMPTON or 804/978-7888), **Holiday Inn North** (☎ 800/HOLIDAY or 804/293-9111), **Knights Inn** (☎ 800/843-5644 or 804/973-8133), **Sheraton Inn Charlottesville** (☎ 800/325-3535 or 804/973-2121), and **Super 8** (☎ 800/800-8000 or 804/973-0888).

EXPENSIVE

Boar's Head Inn at the University of Virginia. 200 Ednam Dr. (P.O. Box 5307), Charlottesville, VA 22905. ☎ **800/476-1988** or 804/296-2181. Fax 804/971-5733. 175 rms and suites. A/C TV TEL. $125–$185 double. Additional person $10 extra. Weekend and golf packages available. AE, DC, DISC, MC, V. Free parking. Resort is on U.S. 250 1 mile west of U.S. 29/250 bypass.

Named for the traditional symbol of hospitality in Shakespeare's England, this university-operated resort is a combination of rural charm and sophisticated facilities. The focal point is a reconstructed historic gristmill that was dismantled and brought here in the early 1960s. It houses the Tavern, the Garden Room, the Old Mill dining room, and some guest rooms. Adjoining low-rise wings are more modern, though furnishings throughout are colonial reproductions. Some rooms offer lake views; some have working fireplaces. Each suite has one bedroom and one sitting room, with either a kitchenette or a wet bar.

The Boar's Head is one of the best places in the region to take off on a hot-air balloon ride.

Dining/Entertainment: Open for all three meals, the Old Mill Room offers candlelit dining in a historic setting with beamed ceilings, multi-paned windows, and plank floors. Among its offerings are Virginia-accented dishes such as hunter's chili with beef and venison. The adjacent Terrace Lounge offers indoor and outdoor seating, an appetizer menu, and piano music from Wednesday to Saturday. Racquets Restaurant and Lounge offers healthy salads, sandwiches, and daily specials.

Services: Concierge, room service, complimentary morning newspaper, nightly turndown, free airport shuttle, in-room coffee/tea service. Concierge section has bathrobe, hair dryer, and computer hookup.

Facilities: Four pools (including an Olympic-size model), health club, indoor and outdoor tennis, squash, platform tennis, fishing, jogging trail, bicycles, adjacent 18-hole golf course, massages, facials, gift shop.

The Omni Charlottesville Hotel. 235 W. Main St. (at McIntire St.), Charlottesville, VA 22901. ☎ **800/THE-OMNI** or 804/971-5500. Fax 804/979-4456. 204 rms. A/C TV TEL. $124–$154 double. AE, DC, DISC, MC, V. Free parking. From I-64, take Exit 120 and follow Fifth Ridge St. (C.R. 631) north to McIntire St. and hotel on the right.

You can't miss this seven-story, brick-and-glass structure—the sharp edge of its triangular shape towers above the western end of the Downtown Mall. Rooms are medium-size; those on the upper floors have views over the city.

At the street level, a fountain bubbles amid a tropical forest in the atrium lobby. With a garden-like setting and a view of the mall, 235, a Virginia wine country restaurant, specializes in regional cuisine and local wines. You can get your exercise in the health club, which has both indoor and outdoor pools. The Omni has extensive meeting space and draws more conventions and groups than most hotels here.

MODERATE

✪ **Hampton Inn & Suites.** 900 W. Main St. (P.O. Box 0) (at 10th St.), Charlottesville, VA 22903. ☎ **800/HAMPTON** or 804/923-8600. Fax 804/923-8601. 75 rms, 25 suites. A/C TV TEL. $82–$92 double; $125–$135 suite. Rates include continental breakfast. AE, DC, DISC, MC, V.

Charlottesville's newest hotel, this five-story brick structure stands just east of the campus near the university's medical center. Murals of Monticello, the Rotunda, and other local scenes overlook a gas fireplace that stands in the center of an elegant, two-story lobby. Eight of the suites here also contain gas fireplaces, and all of them have separate bedrooms, VCRs, and kitchens complete with microwave ovens and dishwashers. The medium-size rooms also come well-equipped, with two data-port phones, desks, irons and ironing boards, and hair dryers. Guests are treated to an extensive continental breakfast in a room off the lobby. Other facilities include an exercise room and free guest laundry.

INEXPENSIVE

Best Western Cavalier. 105 Emmet St. (P.O. Box 5647) (at W. Main St.), Charlottesville, VA 22905. ☎ **800/528-1234** or 804/296-8111. Fax 804/296-3523. 118 rms. A/C TV TEL. $75 double. Rates include continental breakfast. AE, DC, DISC, MC, V. Free parking. From U.S. 29 bypass, go east on Ivy Rd. (U.S. 250 Business) 1 mile to hotel on the left.

Exactly half a mile west of the Rotunda, this five-story, glass-and-steel motel is popular with visiting athletic teams, since it's also close to Scott Stadium and University Hall, the two major sports venues here. Enter the spacious rooms through external walkways bordered by wrought-iron railings. Guests are served a basic continental breakfast in the small lobby with colonial decor, and there's a restaurant on the premises. The hotel provides complimentary shuttle service to and from the airport and the Amtrak and bus stations.

Econo Lodge University. 400 Emmet St. (U.S. 29 Business), Charlottesville, VA 22903. ☎ **800/55-ECONO** or 804/296-2104. Fax 804/296-2104. 60 rms. A/C TV TEL. $45–$55 double. AE, DC, DISC, MC, V.

This Econo Lodge sits 2 blocks north of West Main Street and across Emmet Street from University Hall, the indoor sports arena. Recently renovated, the rooms are small but comfortable, and 15 of them are especially equipped for seniors (with special phones with oversized buttons, grab-bars in the bathtubs, and so forth). The best rooms, in the rear of the L-shaped building, face a hillside and get less street noise than those in the front. There's a small outdoor swimming pool here, and reasonably good Italian and Chinese restaurants are next door.

English Inn of Charlottesville. 2000 Morton Dr., Charlottesville, VA 22901. ☎ **800/786-5400** or 804/971-9900. Fax 804/977-8008. 88 rms. A/C TV TEL. $60–$89 double. Additional person $7 extra; children under 12 stay free in parents' room. Rates include continental breakfast. AE, CB, DC, MC, V. Free parking. Follow U.S. 29 north to just south of the U.S. 250 bypass.

A traditional English Tudor–style building houses this hospitable inn. You'll feel as though you're in an English club when you enter the comfortable wood-paneled lobby, its floors strewn with Oriental rugs. Step down into the Conservatory, where cozy seating areas and an oversize fireplace make a perfect setting for the continental breakfast served daily. Rooms are variously decorated, many with Queen Anne–style reproduction pieces; others have more of a contemporary look. The hotel offers no food service other than breakfast. Facilities include a pool, exercise room, and sauna.

Holiday Inn Monticello. 1200 5th St., Charlottesville, VA 22902. ☎ **800/HOLIDAY** or 804/977-5100. Fax 804/293-5228. 131 rms. A/C TV TEL. $75–$90 double. Additional person $8 extra; children under 18 stay free in parents' room. Rates include continental breakfast. AE, CB, DC, DISC, MC, V. Free parking. Take Exit 120 from I-64 and drive north (you'll be on 5th St.) over the highway; the hotel is on the right.

The most convenient accommodation to Monticello, Ash Lawn-Highland, and Historic Michie Tavern, this pleasant high-rise offers an easygoing atmosphere, a hospitable staff, and spacious accommodations. The more expensive executive-level rooms also have hair dryers, data-port phones, and access to a business center and lounge serving complimentary continental breakfast and evening hors d'oeuvres. A large outdoor pool is open seasonally. The on-premises restaurant serves a complimentary continental breakfast and has full-service dining nightly.

Red Roof Inn. 1309 W. Main St. (at 13th St.), Charlottesville, VA 22903. ☎ **800/THE-ROOF** or 804/295-4333. Fax 804/295-2021. 135 rms. A/C TV TEL. $52–$100 double. AE, DC, DISC, MC, V. Free parking. From U.S. 29 bypass, go east on Ivy Rd. (U.S. 250 Business) 1 1/2 miles to hotel on the left.

At the eastern edge of the Corner and right across West Main Street from the university, this former Howard Johnson's underwent such massive renovations recently that it feels brand-new—all new carpets, furniture, and bathroom fixtures were installed throughout the seven-story building. Interior hallways lead to medium-size guest rooms, which contain cherry-wood furniture. Despite being a bit small, the bathrooms have surprisingly ample vanity space. There are two restaurants in the building, and the Corner's multitude of food outlets are mere steps away.

BED & BREAKFAST ACCOMMODATIONS

Bed-and-breakfast accommodations in elegant homes and private estate cottages are handled by **Guesthouses Reservation Service, Inc.,** P.O. Box 5737, Charlottesville, VA 22905 (☎ **804/979-7264;** fax 804/293-7791; www.va-guesthouses.com; e-mail: guesthouses_bub_reservations@compuserv.com). You can write, fax, or e-mail for a brochure, but reservations must be made by phone. Rates range from $68 for double rooms to $200 for cottages. Credit cards can be used for deposits. The office is open Monday through Friday from noon to 5pm.

NEARBY COUNTRY INNS

✪ **Clifton, The Country Inn.** 1296 Clifton Inn Dr., Charlottesville, VA 22911. ☎ **888/ 971-1800** or 804/971-1800. Fax 804/971-7098. 7 rms, 7 suites. A/C TEL. $125–$195 double; $165–$315 suite. Rates include full breakfast and afternoon tea. MC, V. From Charlottesville take U.S. 250 east 5 miles, turn right on C.R. 789 to Clifton Inn Dr. on the left.

You'll think you've arrived at "Tara" in *Gone With the Wind* when you first glimpse the tall white columns fronting this stately manse, a combination of Federal and Colonial Revival styles. It was built in 1790 by Thomas Mann Randolph, who married Thomas Jefferson's daughter Martha and served as both congressman and governor of Virginia. Clifton today combines Jefferson-era charms with all the modern comforts. You can relax in the main house's formal parlor, browse through hundreds of titles shelved in its cozy library, or partake of homemade cookies and pastries in its tea room. Although Clifton is not as grand physically as Keswick Hall (see below), you'll be attended by a young staff whose energy and informality make a stay here seem more casual.

Guest rooms and suites upstairs in the main house all have working fireplaces, with wood stacked and ready to burn; most have clawfoot tubs with separate showers as well. Also located on this 48-acre estate are the whitewashed stables, which now house three other units, and the old carriage house and another outbuilding, which have been converted into romantic outposts. The split-level carriage house sports a grand piano, while the even more remote honeymoon cottage has a glass-walled bathroom. Feather pillows, down comforters, plush robes, and other such amenities are *de rigeur* in all rooms and suites.

Dining: Both the mansion's dining room and its slate-floor sunroom across the back showcase chef Craig Hartman's gourmet cuisine. Dinner guests arrive at 6:30pm for a cocktail reception, during which Craig and his assistants explain the preparation of the meal they will serve during one seating at 7:30pm. They present five courses Sunday through Thursday ($48 per person) and six courses on Friday and Saturday ($58 per person). Reservations are required. Wine comes from one of Virginia's finest collections, kept in a 5,000-bottle cellar beneath the house.

Services: Nightly turndown with Perrier and roses; early morning coffee and tea delivered to rooms daily, plus newspapers on weekends; complimentary cookies and soft drinks available at all hours.

Facilities: Swimming pool (romantically lit at night); tennis and croquet; 20-acre lake stocked for fishing; hiking trails.

✪ **The Inn at Monticello.** 1188 Scottsville Rd. (Va. 20), Charlottesville, VA 22902. ☎ **804/ 979-3593.** Fax 804/296-1344. 6 rms, including 2 suites (all with bath). A/C. $110–$140 double. Rates include full breakfast. MC, V. Free parking. From I-64, take Va. 20 south and continue past the visitor center for about a third of a mile. The inn is on your right.

This beautiful two-story white-clapboard country house sits well back from the road on a manicured lawn ornamented in spring with blooming dogwood trees and azaleas. Boxwoods, tall shade and evergreen trees, shrubs, and a bubbling brook provide an exceptionally lovely setting. Guests enter via the front porch into a double sitting room, dramatically furnished with crimson walls, two fireplaces, and a handsome collection of antiques. Guest rooms are individually decorated and have such special features as a working fireplace, private porch, or four-poster canopy bed. Guests can relax outdoors on the hammock or on the front verandah lined with wicker rockers. There's a croquet course on the sweeping lawn.

✪ **Keswick Hall.** 701 Country Club Dr. (P.O. Box 68), Keswick, VA 22947. ☎ **800/274-5391** or 804/979-3440. Fax 804/979-3457. www.keswick.com. 48 rms and suites. $195–$595. Rates include full breakfast. AE, CB, DC, MC, V. Free parking. From Charlottesville take U.S. 250 or I-64 east to Shadwell (Exit 124), then Va. 22 east and follow signs to Keswick.

Thomas Jefferson might explode with anger were he to see the grand lounge of this super-luxury estate, for hanging there is an original oil painting of Augusta, Princess of Wales—mother of the mad King George III against whom Jefferson and his pals rebelled in 1776. It's all part of Sir Bernard Ashley's highly successful effort to create an authentic English-style country inn smack in the middle of "Mr. Jefferson's Country." Sir Bernard restored and expanded this 1912 vintage Italianate Crawford Villa to house 48 rooms and suites, all furnished with his own extensive collection of antiques and his late wife Laura Ashley's prints on wallpaper, upholstery, and curtains. Many of the units have fireplaces, clawfoot tubs, and views over a golf course redesigned by Arnold Palmer, but don't expect to find these in the 14 least expensive "house rooms." All guests can roam around the vast public rooms on the main level, including a main lounge with fireplace and terrace with golf course view.

Dining: Dining here is gourmet, with such offerings as a saddle and leg of local rabbit with morel flan, potato fondant, and a white bean–tomato ragout (you get the picture). Dinners are fixed price at $58, while lunches are à la carte. English afternoon tea is free to guests, who can dine at the adjoining Keswick Club's bistro.

Services: Concierge, masseur, twice-daily maid service, social director, baby-sitting.

Facilities: Guests have complimentary use of the private Keswick Club's indoor/outdoor heated pool, Olympic-size outdoor pool, fitness center, tennis courts, and golf course.

✪ **Silver Thatch Inn.** 3001 Hollymead Dr., Charlottesville, VA 22911. ☎ **804/978-4686.** Fax 804/973-6156. 7 rms. A/C. $115–$150 double. Additional person $25 extra. Rates include continental breakfast. AE, CB, DC, MC, V. Free parking. Hollymead Dr. is just off U.S. 29 (right turn), about 8 miles north of town.

Occupying a rambling white-clapboard house, a section of which dates back to Revolutionary days, this charming hostelry is located on a quiet road and set on nicely landscaped grounds. Attractively decorated with authentic 18th-century pieces, the original part of the building now serves as a cozy common room, where guests are invited for afternoon refreshments. The 1812 center part of the house is now one of the dining rooms. Guest rooms are lovely, with down comforters on four-poster canopied beds, antique pine dressers, carved walnut-and-mahogany armoires, and exquisite quilts. Several rooms have working fireplaces. Hosts Vince and Rita Scoffone are on hand to help make arrangements for nearby activities—trail rides, jogging, tennis, swimming, golf, fishing, and biking. Telephones and TVs are available in the common areas.

Gourmet dinners are served in candlelit rooms open to the public (inn guests should reserve a table in advance, since this is one of the area's most popular dining venues). Nightly specials might include grilled breast of duck basted with a beer barbecue sauce or sautéed Texas antelope. The list of Virginia and California wines has been cited for its excellence.

A MOUNTAIN GETAWAY

Wintergreen Resort. Wintergreen, VA 22958. ☎ **800/325-2200** or 804/325-2200. Fax 804/325-8004. 300 units. A/C TV TEL. $115–$155 double. Weekly rates and packages available. AE, MC, V. Take I-64 west to Exit 107 and follow U.S. 250 west; turn left onto C.R. 151 south, then right on C.R. 644 for 4^1/$_2$ miles to resort. It's about 43 miles from Charlottesville.

With 6,700 of its 11,000 acres dedicated to the remaining undisturbed forestland, Wintergreen offers year-round vacation activities in a magnificent Blue Ridge Mountain setting. While the big draws here include skiing, golf, horseback riding, mountain biking, swimming in the lake, and canoeing, Wintergreen also has a Nature Foundation that offers guided hikes, seminars, and camps for children.

The resort's focal point is the tastefully lodge-like Inn, which has a huge gristmill wheel occupying the two-story registration area. Most accommodations are in small enclaves scattered throughout the property, but there are also two- to seven-bedroom homes, one- to four-bedroom condos, and studios and lodge rooms. Since the homes and condos are privately owned, furnishings are highly individual, ranging from country quaint to sleek and sophisticated. Each condo is appointed with a modern kitchen, living area, bathroom for each bedroom, and balcony or patio (the mountain views are superb); most have working fireplaces.

Dining/Entertainment: Wintergreen has several full-service restaurants. The Copper Mine Restaurant and Lounge, at the Inn, offers noteworthy American cuisine in a relaxed casual setting. The Garden Terrace Restaurant in the sports center offers healthy cuisine in a smoke-free environment. Cooper's Vantage is a casual spot for family dining and features live entertainment. The Rodes Farm Inn serves family-style country meals. The Verandah specializes in Virginia regional items, and the Trillium House offers fine dining in a charming country inn.

Services: Baby-sitting.

Facilities: Skiing (17 slopes and trails), indoor and outdoor pools, health club, spa, massage, tennis, mountain biking, 36 holes of championship golf, hiking, nature programs, horseback riding, lake swimming and canoeing, fishing, children's center, hair salon, shops, grocery store.

WHERE TO DINE

This area's most exceptional dining is at its country inns, especially the Old Mill Room in the Boar's Head Inn; Clifton, The Country Inn; the main dining room at Keswick Hall; and the Silver Thatch Inn (see "Nearby Country Inns," above).

In addition to some of those listed below, the Downtown Mall has several restaurants proffering a variety of cuisines, from expensive classical French served on china to cheap Indian curries ladled onto plastic plates. During the warm months, some of them offer outdoor seating under the Mall's shade trees. Likewise, the Corner opposite the university has several restaurants catering to the college crowd. Just stroll along the main drags of these neighborhoods and pick your place. You can tell by the crowds which are "in" and which aren't.

✪ **C&O Restaurant.** 515 E. Water St. (at 5th St. E.). ☎ **804/971-7044.** Reservations accepted for nonsmoking tables. Main courses $14.50–$19. MC, V. Mon–Thurs 11:30am–3pm and 5:30–10pm; Fri 11:30am–3pm and 5:30–11pm; Sat 5:30–11pm; Sun 5:30–10pm. INTERNATIONAL.

The unprepossessing brick front, complete with a faded Pepsi sign, might make you think twice, but don't be deterred. Located a block south of the Mall's eastern end, this establishment has received kudos from major critics. Raved a *Food & Wine* reviewer: "I can assure you that not since Jefferson was serving imported vegetables and the first ice cream at Monticello has there been more innovative cooking in these parts." Changing daily, the menu ranges across the globe—from France to Thailand, from New Mexico to Louisiana. Many patrons stop downstairs, a rustic setting of exposed brick and rough-hewn barnwood, while others proceed upstairs to a more formal venue. Both dining areas have candlelight, white-clothed tables adorned with attractive flower arrangements, the same excellent menu choices, and premium wines by the glass.

Eastern Standard Restaurant and ESCAFE. 102 Old Preston Ave. (west end of the Downtown Mall). ☎ **804/295-8668.** Reservations accepted in restaurant. Main courses $15–$22 in restaurant, $7–$13 in cafe. AE, DC, DISC, MC, V. Restaurant, Thurs–Sat 5:30–10pm; cafe, Sun, Tues, Wed 5:30–10pm, Thurs–Sat 5pm–2am. AMERICAN/MEDITERRANEAN/ASIAN.

Ironically, the Eastern Standard is the last building on the western end of the Downtown Mall. The downstairs cafe has black-leather booths, a cream-colored pressed-tin ceiling, and cartoon murals of partying customers. The upstairs restaurant sports oak floors with antique carpets, potted birds of paradise, gold walls, and big arched windows overlooking the Mall. Warm-weather seating is available on the Mall or out back.

Menus change seasonally, but appetizers might include pesto–sun-dried tomato polenta wrapped with roasted eggplant, or perhaps Jeanne Moreau's spicy sesame noodles. There are usually 10 or so entree choices, such as New York strip au poivre or a stuffed chicken breast with raspberry Dijon sauce. Desserts, made on the premises, include such delectables as Belgian chocolate truffles. The downstairs cafe features salads, sandwiches, and blue-plate specials like roasted eggplant rollatini and spicy Thai seafood.

The Hardware Store. 316 E. Main St. (Downtown Mall). ☎ **804/977-1518.** Sandwiches and salads $3.50–$9; main courses $9–$12.50. AE, DC, MC, V. Mon 11am–5pm; Tues–Thurs 11am–9pm; Fri–Sat 11am–10pm. AMERICAN.

Old rolling ladders; stacks of oak drawers that once held screws, nuts and bolts; and vintage advertising signs—all display the old-time origins of this high-energy spot popular with the college crowd. A long, narrow space with an upstairs gallery, it provides comfortable seating in spacious leather-upholstered booths. Specialties include quiches and crêpes, crabcakes, salads, an enormous variety of hamburgers, sandwiches, baked potatoes with great toppings, platters of fried fish, and barbecued ribs. There are soda-fountain treats, and pastries and cakes run the gamut from dense double-chocolate truffle cake to Southern pecan pie. The Hardware Store has a fully stocked bar.

Miller's. 109 W. Main St. ☎ **804/971-8511.** Main courses $5.50–$9.50; sandwiches $3.50–$4.95. AE, MC, V. Mon–Fri 11:30am–2am; Fri–Sat 5pm–2am. AMERICAN.

Miller's is a converted old-time pharmacy with the original white-tile floor, pressed-tin ceiling, mahogany soda fountain serving as a back bar, and cherry woodwork and shelving. Walls display historic photos of old Charlottesville drugstores. Out front on the Mall, tree-shaded tables are enclosed by planters with flowers. Roast beef and turkey, roasted and carved on the premises and served on home-baked French bread, are available at lunch and dinner. Dinner entrees might include fresh seafood, chicken, vegetable stir-fry, and fettuccine marinara. Desserts are homemade. Wine, beer, and mixed drinks are served until 2am. There's nighttime entertainment—jazz or blues—with a nominal cover charge after 9:30pm.

✪ **Northern Exposure.** 1202 W. Main St. (at 12th St.). ☎ **804/977-6002.** Reservations not accepted. Lunch $4.50–$10; main courses $9–$17. AE, DC, DISC, MC, V. Sun 10am–10pm; Mon–Thurs 11am–10pm; Fri–Sat 11am–11pm. ITALIAN/NEW AMERICAN.

You may have to wait for a table at this sophisticated bistro a block east of the Corner district, for it's Charlottesville's most popular dining spot. Patrons sit in one of four areas: a dining room decorated with old photos of New York City and a huge map of Gotham's subway system (guess where the owners are from); an enclosed patio; an open-air but heated patio; and a rooftop deck. Both lunch and dinner feature individual-size pizzas, either "red" with tomato sauce or "white" with olive oil, garlic, and cheese, with a choice of toppings both traditional and inventive. Likewise, you can order pasta with standard sauces like Alfredo or marinara, but the emphasis here is on creative concoctions like ginger sesame shrimp over linguini or Maine lobster ravioli with a cream sauce. The dinner menu offers main courses such as Cajun-style marinated steak with a pepper and Cognac cream sauce, Greek-style chicken, or a house special filet of salmon with sea salt, lemon juice, soy, and Dijon mustard. Big salads and burgers are available at all hours.

The Virginian. 1521 W. Main St. ☎ **804/984-4667.** Reservations not accepted. Sandwiches and burgers $5–$7; main courses $7–$13. AE, MC, V. Mon–Fri 9am–2am; Sat–Sun 10am–2am. AMERICAN.

Dating from 1921, Charlottesville's oldest restaurant is the best of the student hangouts lining West Main Street in the Corner neighborhood opposite the university. This simpatico spot has roomy oak booths and an always well-populated bar. Good jazz or rock is played at a low-decibel level, and shaded wall sconces supply subdued lighting. All the fare is homemade, including yummy fresh-baked breads. At lunch or dinner, you can't go wrong with a heaping bowl of pasta, whose proportions will stuff a voracious student, or perhaps a slab of home-style meat loaf. A children's menu is available.

2 Lynchburg

66 miles S of Charlottesville; 112 miles W of Richmond; 52 miles E of Roanoke

A large white-granite rock on the riverbank at 9th Street in Lynchburg marks where John Lynch, Quaker son of an Irish immigrant, began operating a ferry across the river in 1757. The town that grew up near the spot became a rich and important shipping point in the late 18th and 19th centuries, as nearby farmers brought their tons of tobacco here to be hauled downstream by shallow-draft "bateaux" to Richmond's cigarette factories and deepwater port.

Today the Lynchburg area offers visitors a look at Poplar Forest, Jefferson's country home, and Red Hill, the plantation where Patrick Henry spent his last years. For Civil War buffs, the principal attraction is nearby Appomattox Court House, where Lee surrendered to Grant, thus ending the nation's bloodiest conflict.

ESSENTIALS

VISITOR INFORMATION The **Lynchburg Visitors Information Center,** 216 12th St., at Church Street (P.O. Box 2027), Lynchburg, VA 24505 (☎ **800/ 732-5821** or 804/847-1811; fax 804/522-9592; www.speidellgroup.com/lynchburg or www.inmind.com/lynchburg; e-mail: realva@aol.com), is open daily from 9am to 5pm and provides maps, brochures, and self-guided walking tours of historic districts. From the U.S. 29 Expressway, take Exit 1A, follow Main Street west to 12th Street, and turn left.

GETTING THERE   By Car   From Charlottesville and I-64, the shortest route is U.S. 29 south. From Richmond, follow U.S. 360 west to U.S. 460, which goes directly to Lynchburg. From Roanoke, take U.S. 460 east. U.S. 29 and U.S. 501 together form the Lynchburg Expressway, a freeway that crosses the James River and nearly forms a beltway around the eastern and southern sides of the city.

By Plane   The **Lynchburg Regional Airport,** U.S. 29, 8 miles south of downtown (☎ 804/847-1632), is served by US Airways, Delta, and United.

By Train   The daily "Crescent" between New York City and New Orleans stops at the **Amtrak** station, Kemper Street and Park Avenue (☎ 800/872-7245).

ATTRACTIONS IN TOWN

Start your sojourn in Lynchburg at the visitor center (see "Essentials," above), where you can get free walking-tour guides to the Court House Hill historic district downtown and to other distinctive Federal- and Victorian-period residential neighbors.

Downtown, begin at **Monument Terrace,** on Court Street between 9th and 10th streets. This imposing 139-step staircase was built as a memorial to soldiers of all of America's wars. At the base of the staircase on Church Street stands a statue of a World War I doughboy. At the top of the steps, on Court Street between 8th and 10th streets, you'll see the imposing Greek Revival facade of the **Old Court House,** built in 1855 and an outstanding example of civic architecture. Inside, the **Lynchburg Museum** (☎ 804/847-1459) houses artifacts and displays tracing the city's history. It's open daily from 10am to 4pm; admission is $1 for adults, free for children ages 12 and under when accompanied by an adult. An alternative to climbing the steps is riding up on the **Lynchburg Public Elevator,** on Church Street between 9th and 10th streets; it runs Monday to Friday from 7am to 7pm.

West of downtown, **Point of Honor,** 112 Cabell St. (☎ 804/847-1459), was built around 1815 for Dr. George Cabell, Sr., whose most famous patient was Patrick Henry but who made most of his fortune shipping tobacco. Aside from its architectural interest (the house has an unusual octagonal bay facade, one of only a pair remaining in the United States), Point of Honor is a showcase for decorative arts of the period, and tours of the premises are packed with fascinating information about how the rich lived during the Federal period. The gardens, grounds, and auxiliary buildings have also been restored. It's open daily from 1 to 4pm; admission is $3 for adults and $1 for students (children 12 and under are free when accompanied by an adult).

A designated historic landmark, the home and garden cottage of Harlem Renaissance poet **Anne Spencer,** 1313 Pierce St. (☎ 804/845-1313), is open by appointment with a $2 suggested donation. The red-shingled house, built by Edward Spencer for his family in 1903, was her home until her death in 1975.

The **Pest House Medical Museum** is a tiny 1840s doctor's office; it was moved to the site where Lynchburg residents suffering from contagious diseases like smallpox and measles were quarantined in the early 1800s. It's not open, but you can look through the windows and see the tools of medical science as they existed between 1860 and 1900. The Pest House is in the Confederate soldiers' section of the **Old City Cemetery,** 4th Street and Taylor Street (☎ 804/847-1811). The visitor center has a free guide to the cemetery, which is open daily from 8am to 6pm.

NEARBY ATTRACTIONS

✪ **Appomattox Court House National Historical Park.** Appomattox Court House. ☎ 804/352-8987. Admission Memorial Day–Labor Day, $4 adults, free for children under 17; rest of year, $2 adults, free for children under 17. Daily 9am–5pm. The park is on Va. 24, about 3 miles north of U.S. 460 and about 22 miles east of Lynchburg.

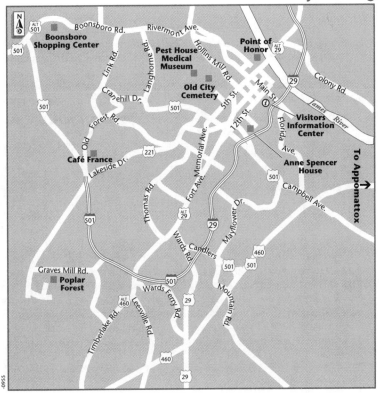

Here, in the parlor of Wilmer McLean's home, Robert E. Lee surrendered the Army of Northern Virginia to Ulysses S. Grant on April 9, 1865, thus ending the bitter Civil War. Today the 20 or so houses, stores, courthouse, and tavern that made up the little village called Appomattox Court House have been restored, and visitors can walk the country lanes in the rural stillness where these events took place. At the visitor center, pick up a map of the park. Upstairs, slide presentations and museum exhibits include fascinating excerpts from the diaries and letters of Civil War soldiers.

Buildings open to the public include McLean's house, Clover Hill Tavern, Meeks' Store, the Woodson Law Office, the courthouse (totally reconstructed), jail, and Kelly House. Surrender Triangle, where the Confederates laid down their arms and rolled up their battle flags, is outside Kelly House.

There are picnic tables at the Appomattox Wayside. No cars are allowed in the village.

Booker T. Washington National Monument. Hardy. ☎ **540/721-2094.** Free admission. Daily 9am–5pm. From Lynchburg, take U.S. 460 west to Va. 122 south.

At this memorial to one of America's great African-American leaders, visitors can conjure up the setting of Booker T. Washington's childhood in reconstructed farm buildings and demonstrations of farm life and slavery in Civil War–era Virginia. Although Washington called his boyhood home a plantation, the Burroughs farm was small, with just 207 acres and never more than 11 slaves. His mother was the cook, and the cabin where he was born was also the kitchen. His family left the farm in 1865, when he was 9. He determinedly sought an education and actually walked most of the 500 miles from his new home in West Virginia to Hampton Institute. He worked his way through school and achieved national prominence as an educator, founder of Tuskegee Institute in Alabama, author, and advisor to presidents. In 1956, a century after he was born, this national monument was established to honor his life and work.

Begin at the visitor center, which offers a slide show and a map with a self-guided plantation tour and nature walks that wind through the original Burroughs property.

Red Hill, Patrick Henry National Memorial. Brookneal. ☎ **804/376-2044.** Admission $3 adults, $2 seniors over 65, $1 students. Apr–Oct, daily 9am–5pm; Nov–Mar, daily 9am–4pm. Closed New Year's Day, Thanksgiving, and Christmas. Red Hill is 35 miles from Lynchburg. Take U.S. 501 south to Brookneal, then Va. 40 east and follow the brown signs.

The fiery orator's last home and burial place, Red Hill is a modest frame farmhouse with several dependencies, including the overseer's cottage that Patrick Henry used as a law office. Henry retired to Red Hill in 1794 after serving five terms as governor of Virginia. Failing health forced him to refuse numerous posts, including chief justice of the United States, secretary of state, and minister to Spain and France. He died here on June 6, 1799, and is buried in the family graveyard.

Begin your tour at the visitor center, where you can see an enlightening 15-minute video about Henry's years here and visit the museum with the world's largest assemblage of Henry memorabilia. The centerpiece is Peter Rothermel's famous painting *Patrick Henry before the Virginia House of Burgesses,* depicting his "If this be treason, make the most of it" speech against the Stamp Act in 1765. The site contains a reconstruction of his 18th-century plantation, which consists of his actual law office, the main house reconstructed on the original foundation, the carriage house, and other small buildings. You can't miss the most striking feature of the landscape: Standing 64 feet high and spanning 96 feet, the Osage Orange Tree is listed in the American Forestry Hall of Fame.

Thomas Jefferson's Poplar Forest. Va. 661, Forest. ☎ **804/525-1806.** Admission $6 adults, $1 children 6–16, free for children under 6. Apr–Nov, Wed–Sun 10am–4pm (last tour begins at 4pm). Closed Dec–Mar. The main entrance is on Va. 661, 1 mile from U.S. 221 via Va. 811 and about 6 miles southwest of Forest.

At Thomas Jefferson's retreat home, you can see the restoration of a National Historic Landmark in progress. Opened to the public in 1985, octagonal Poplar Forest is now undergoing archaeological research and architectural restoration, and visitors can see relics from the buildings and grounds as they are brought to light and exhibited. At one time the seat of a 4,819-acre plantation and the source of much of Jefferson's income, Poplar Forest was designed to utilize light and air flow to the maximum in as economical a space as possible. In 1806, while he was president, Jefferson himself assisted the masons in laying the foundation for the dwelling. It was his final private architectural masterpiece.

WHERE TO STAY

Several national chain motels sit near the U.S. 29 expressway. At Odd Fellows Road (Exit 7), the sprawling **Ramada Inn & Conference Center** (☎ 800/2-RAMADA or 804/847-4424) was built in the late 1950s as a Holiday Inn but recently changed ownership and names after being renovated and upgraded; it surrounds a large courtyard with outdoor pool. There's also a modern **Comfort Inn** on Odd Fellows Road (☎ 800/228-5150 or 804/847-9041). At Chandler's Mountain Road (Exit 8), an area of shopping malls and chain restaurants, you'll find the **Best Western Lynchburg** (☎ 800/528-1234 or 804/237-2986), **Days Inn** (☎ 800/325-2525 or

804/847-8655), **Hampton Inn** (☎ 800/HAMPTON or 804/237-2704), an inexpensive **Innkeeper** (☎ 804/237-7771), and the **Lynchburg Hilton** (☎ 800/HILTONS or 804/237-6333).

Holiday Inn Select. 601 Main St., Lynchburg, VA 24504. ☎ **800/465-4329** or 804/528-2500. Fax 804/528-0062. 238 rms. A/C TV TEL. $79–$85 double. AE, CB, DC, DISC, MC, V. Free parking. From U.S. 29, take Main St. (Exit 1-A) west.

Although primarily a business hotel, this eight-story brick building is just 5 blocks from Court House Square and the downtown sights. An impressive, colonial-style lobby with fountain leads to Jefferson's Restaurant, which offers all three meals at reasonable prices. The medium-size rooms have wing chairs, dark wood desks and armoires, and baths equipped with hair dryers and coffeemakers. Upper-level rooms have great views over the town. On the second floor, a weight room opens to an outdoor pool.

Lynchburg Mansion Inn Bed & Breakfast. 405 Madison St., Lynchburg, VA 24504. ☎ **800/352-1199** or 804/528-5400. 5 rms. A/C TV TEL. $109–$177 double. Rates include full breakfast. AE, DC, MC, V. Free parking. From U.S. 29 take Main St. (Exit 1-A) west. Turn left on 5th St. and right on Madison St.

This two-story Spanish Georgian mansion, set behind a cast-iron fence in downtown Lynchburg between 4th and 5th streets, fits right in with the other Victorian mansions on Quality Row in the Garland Hill Historic District. A massive two-story, six-columned portico heralds the entrance, and guests drive up past the carriage house to the porte-cochère side entrance. The front door opens to a 50-foot great hall, with soaring ceilings and polished cherry-wood columns and wainscoting. The extremely spacious guest rooms have private baths and are beautifully furnished in a variety of stunning styles—Victorian, French country, and nautical. You'll find a morning newspaper at your door, and a fresh-brewed pot of coffee and pitcher of juice set out to tide over early risers until the full, silver-service breakfast. There's a hot tub on the back porch.

WHERE TO DINE

✪ **Café France.** 3225 Old Forest Rd. (in Forest Plaza West Shopping Center). ☎ **804/385-8989.** Reservations suggested. Main courses $10–$20. AE, MC, V. Tues–Sat 11:30am–3pm and 5:30–10pm. From downtown, take the Lynchburg Expressway (U.S. 29/U.S. 501) to Old Forest Rd. The shopping center is half a mile north on the right. INTERNATIONAL.

Entry to this casual, very popular storefront eatery is through a deli with an immense selection of imported wines and beers, all available for table service. The very modern dining room, with unusual V-shaped mirrors along one wall, has table, booth, and even some counter seating. Despite the name, locals flock here for an interesting variety of well-prepared cuisines, from Caribbean chicken in a mango salsa sauce to Chesapeake crabcakes sautéed in wine and butter. The changing menu is bound to offer something to pique your palate.

The Farm Basket. 2008 Langhorne Rd. ☎ **804/528-1107.** Box lunch $6.50; sandwiches $3.50–$8. MC, V. Lunch counter, Mon–Sat 10am–3pm; shops, Mon–Sat 10am–5pm. AMERICAN.

A charming little complex of shops backing onto a creek, the Farm Basket specializes in freshly made box lunches you can carry out or eat in the shop or on the back deck overlooking the stream. The menu changes daily, but the box lunch always includes a choice of sandwich, salad, dessert, and drink—for example, sandwich choices of chicken-salad roll, ham hoecake, and beef biscuit; salads like tomato aspic or three bean; and, for dessert, lemon bread with cream cheese or apple-dapple cake. Fresh fruit and yogurt, barbecue sandwiches with coleslaw, smoked turkey croissant, crabcakes with roasted tomato chutney, shrimp salad with homemade tomato aspic, and country pâté are à la carte options.

☺ Meriwether's Market Restaurant. 4925 Boonsboro Rd. (U.S. 501 Business) (in Boonsboro Shopping Center). ☎ **804/384-3311.** Reservations recommended. Lunch $6–$7.50; main courses $9–$22. AE, MC, V. Mon–Thurs 11am–2:30pm and 5:30–10pm; Fri–Sat 11am–2:30pm and 5:30–11pm. From downtown, go 3 miles west on Main St., which becomes first Rivermont Ave. and then Boonsboro Rd. Shopping center is on the left. NEW AMERICAN.

Housed in Lynchburg's most upscale shopping center, this chic establishment is usually populated by professionals unwinding at the bar or enjoying some of the town's finest cuisine. Two of the terra-cotta–colored walls here are festooned with large cartoon murals, one featuring overfed patrons partying, the other depicting the owners and their staff. Elsewhere you'll see floral watercolors by artists Annie Massie and Taylor Harbison.

Changing seasonally, the menu features gourmet twists on Southern fare, such as an appetizer of sweet corn pancakes and smoked salmon with baby greens, and a medium-size course of grilled barbecued shrimp with grits, corn cake, and fried green tomatoes. Bottles from the award-winning wine list are also available from a small market at the front of the restaurant. Children get their own menu, as well as crayons to use on the butcher paper covering the table linen. Adults will enjoy the live jazz music here on Wednesday evenings.

Percival's Isle Coffee & Tea, Ltd. 1208 Main St. (at 12th St.). ☎ **804/847-3059.** Reservations not accepted. Breakfast $3–$5; salads and sandwiches $4–$6; pizza $7–$9. MC, V. Mon–Thurs 7am–11pm; Fri–Sat 7am–1am; Sun 9am–10pm. AMERICAN.

In the middle of a row of old storefronts a block north of the visitor center, this lively coffeehouse/tavern draws working folks for breakfast and lunch, then a pack of twenty-somethings when the nightly live music cranks up at 8pm. You can take in this lively scene from the big oak bar or at tables (some of them chest-high, a few others in alcoves formed by the storefront windows). Breakfasts run the gamut from bacon-and-eggs to lox-and-bagels, but the freshly brewed coffee also goes well with Belgian waffles and the pastries baked on the premises. Later in the day, the menu switches to sandwiches, burgers, small pizzas, and a special chicken salad seasoned differently each day.

Silver Pig Barbecue. 4835 S. Amherst Hwy. (U.S. 29) (at Seminole Dr.), Madison Heights. ☎ **804/846-5676.** Reservations not accepted. Sandwiches $2; main courses $4–$5. No credit cards. Mon–Sat 10:30am–8:30pm. From downtown, go north on U.S. 29. Restaurant is next to Shell station on the right, 1 1/2 miles north of the James River. NORTH CAROLINA BARBECUE.

This is the best place in Virginia to try that unique delicacy known as North Carolina barbecue. If you've never experienced it, it may seem a bit strange on first sight and taste. It's made by cooking pork shoulders over hickory coals for several hours, then chopping the gray meat and dousing it with a sharp, spicy sauce of vinegar and red pepper. Owner Jim Moore learned how to cook the Carolina version down in Greensboro, and that's all he serves here, either topped with vinegary coleslaw in sandwiches, or on platters trimmed with slaw, French fries, and absolutely wonderful hushpuppies (locals buy these long, thin cornbread morsels by the bagful).

The Shenandoah Valley   8

Native Americans called the 200-mile-long valley in northwestern Virginia "Shenandoah," meaning "Daughter of the Stars." Today the Shenandoah National Park offers spectacular landscapes and a plethora of hiking and riding trails, and protects the beauty and peace of the Blue Ridge Mountains along the eastern boundary of the valley. Along the Blue Ridge crest, the 105-mile-long Skyline Drive—one of America's great scenic drives—runs the full length of the park and connects directly with the Blue Ridge Parkway, which continues south into North Carolina.

Down on the rolling valley floor lay picturesque small towns steeped in American history dating to the early 1700s, when pioneers moved west from the Tidewater. Scottish-Irish and German emigrants from Pennsylvania later settled this rich farming country and built their farmhouses of stone. Lord Fairfax sent George Washington west to survey the valley, and reminders of his visit are visible at Natural Bridge, where he carved his initials, and in Winchester, which has preserved the office he occupied during the French and Indian Wars.

The Shenandoah Valley played a major role in the Civil War. Stonewall Jackson left his home and work at Lexington's Virginia Military Institute to become one of the leading figures of the Confederacy. Major valley engagements included the legendary battle at New Market, when the entire VMI Corps of Cadets fought heroically. After the war, Robert E. Lee settled in Lexington as president of what is now Washington and Lee University, and both he and Jackson are buried there.

Woodrow Wilson was born in Staunton in 1856, and a museum adjoining his restored birthplace pays tribute to this president's peace-loving ideals.

Visit the Shenandoah Valley to discover its picturesque and historic towns; to hike the Appalachian Trail and other tracks that crisscross the mountains; to enjoy the sights, colors, and aromas of the changing seasons; to marvel at the subterranean landscapes of stalagmites and stalactites in one of its many caverns; to rough it at a mountain camp or enjoy the luxury of a great resort; to raft, canoe, kayak, or just lazily float down the river in an inner tube; or to shop for antiques at some of Virginia's largest and best shops.

EXPLORING THE VALLEY

VISITOR INFORMATION   For information about attractions, accommodations, restaurants, and services in the entire region, contact the **Shenandoah Valley Travel Association (SVTA),** P.O. Box 1040, New Market, VA 22844 (☎ **540/740-3132;** fax 540/740-3100). The SVTA operates a visitor center in New Market, just off I-81 at U.S. 211 (Exit 264). The center, open daily from 9am to 5pm, has a free phone line for hotel reservations.

GETTING THERE & GETTING AROUND   The gorgeous scenery of the Shenandoah is best seen by car, since public transportation in the valley is almost nonexistent. At least part of your trip should include the spectacular Skyline Drive. The fast way to and through the region is via ✪ **I-81,** which runs the entire length of the valley floor and has been designated one of America's 10 most scenic interstates. Running alongside I-81, the legendary ✪ **Valley Pike (U.S. 11)** is like a trip back in time at least 50 years, with its old-fashioned gas pumps, small motels, shops, and restaurants. Likewise, the old U.S. 340 follows the scenic western foothills of the Blue Ridge.

I-66 enters the valley from Washington, D.C., before ending at Strasburg. I-64 comes into the valley from both east and west, running contiguous with I-81 between Staunton and Lexington. Other major east-west highways crossing the valley are U.S. 50, 211, 33, 250, and 60.

Valley roads are open year-round, but snow and ice can close the Skyline Drive in midwinter.

Amtrak offers direct service to Staunton. While there are regional airports in Charlottesville (see chapter 7) and Roanoke (see chapter 9), the nearest major airport is Washington Dulles, 50 miles east of Front Royal.

1 Shenandoah National Park & the Skyline Drive

Running for 105 miles down the spine of the Blue Ridge Mountains, Shenandoah National Park is a haven for plants and wildlife. Although long and skinny, the park encompasses some 300 square miles of mountains, forests, waterfalls, and rock formations. It has more than 60 mountain peaks higher than 2,000 feet, with Hawksbill and Stony Man exceeding 4,000 feet. From overlooks along the Skyline Drive, you can see many of the park's wonders and enjoy panoramic views over the Piedmont to the east and the Shenandoah Valley to the west. The drive gives you access to the park's visitor facilities and to more than 500 miles of glorious hiking and horse trails, including the Maine-to-Georgia Appalachian Trail.

Europeans began settling these slopes and hollows in the early 18th century. Plans for establishment of a national park got under way 200 years later, and it was President Franklin D. Roosevelt's Depression-era Civilian Conservation Corps that built the recreational facilities, guard walls, cabins, and many hiking trails. The corps completed the Skyline Drive in 1939, thus opening this marvelously beautiful area to casual visitors.

Today, over two-fifths of the park is considered wilderness. Animals like deer, bear, bobcat, and turkey have returned, and sightings of deer and smaller animals are frequent; the park also boasts more than 100 species of trees.

JUST THE FACTS

ACCESS POINTS & ORIENTATION   The park and its Skyline Drive have four entrances. Most frequently used is the northernmost **Front Royal** entry on U.S. 340 near the junction of I-81 and I-66, about 1 mile south of Front Royal and

Shenandoah Valley

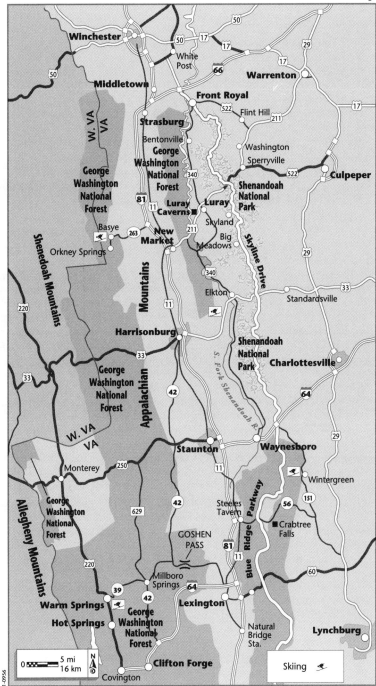

Winchester
White Post
50
17
17
17
29
50
50
66
Warrenton
Middletown
Strasburg
Front Royal
522
Flint Hill
211
17
Bentonville
Washington
Sperryville
522
Culpeper
W. VA
VA
George
Washington
National
Forest
George
Washington
National
Forest
340
81
11
Luray
Caverns
Luray
Shenandoah
National
Park
Skyland
Basye
263
Skyline Drive
New
Market
Big
Meadows
Orkney Springs
Shenedoah Mountains
211
340
29
Elkton
Standardsville
33
Mountains
11
Harrisonburg
33
George
Washington
National
Forest
Appalachian
42
Shenandoah
National
Park
Charlottesville
S. Fork Shenandoah R.
33
64
W. VA
VA
29
Monterey
250
Staunton
11
Waynesboro
George
Washington
National
Forest
629
42
Wintergreen
Blue Ridge Parkway
Steeles
Tavern
56
151
Allegheny Mountains
220
Crabtree
Falls
GOSHEN
PASS
81
11
Millboro
Springs
64
60
39
42
Warm Springs
George
Washington
National
Forest
Lexington
Natural
Bridge
Sta.
Lynchburg
Hot Springs
0   5 mi
     16 km
N
Clifton Forge
Covington
Skiing

137

1-0956

90 miles west of Washington, D.C. The two middle entrances are at **Thornton Gap,** 33 miles south of Front Royal on U.S. 211 between Sperryville and Luray, and at **Swift Run Gap,** 68 miles south of Front Royal on U.S. 33 between Standardsville and Elkton. The southern gate is at **Rockfish Gap,** 105 miles south of Front Royal at I-64 and U.S. 250, some 21 miles west of Charlottesville and 18 miles east of Staunton.

The Skyline Drive is marked with **Mile Posts,** starting at zero at the Front Royal entrance and increasing as you go south, with Rockfish Gap on the southern end at Mile 105.

DISTRICTS   The access roads divide the park into three areas: Northern District, between Front Royal and U.S. 211 at Thornton Gap (Mile 0 to Mile 31.5); Central District, between Thornton Gap and U.S. 33 at Swift Run Gap (Mile 31.5 to Mile 65.7); and Southern District, between Swift Run Gap and I-64 at Rockfish Gap (Mile 65.7 to Mile 105).

INFORMATION   For free information, call or write Superintendent, Shenandoah National Park, 3655 U.S. Hwy. 211 East, Luray, VA 22835 (☎ **540/999-3500;** www.nps.gov/shen). The headquarters is 4 miles west of Thornton Gap and 5 miles east of Luray on U.S. 211.

The best source from which to purchase information is the **Shenandoah Natural History Association,** at the same address and phone number as the park headquarters. The association has a bookstore at the park headquarters, where it sells maps, guidebooks, and other publications about the park's cultural and natural history (they are also available at the park's visitor centers, see below). The association regularly updates the enormously informative *Guide to Shenandoah National Park and Skyline Drive* by the late Henry Heatwole. The book sells for $7.50 and is an indispensable aid for anyone who wants to thoroughly explore Shenandoah, as it gives a mile-by-mile description of the park, including most hiking trails.

For guide books and detailed topographic maps of the park's three districts, write or call the **Potomac Appalachian Trail Club (PATC),** 118 Park St., Vienna, VA 22180 (☎ **703/242-0315,** or 703/242-0965 for a recording of the club's activities). The PATC helps build and maintain the park's portion of the Appalachian Trail, including trail cabins (see "Hiking & Other Sports," below). The PATC is part of the **Appalachian Trail Conference,** P.O. Box 807, Harpers Ferry, WV 25425-0807 (☎ **304/535-6331**), which covers the entire trail from Maine to Georgia.

FEES, REGULATIONS & BACKCOUNTRY PERMITS   Entrance permits good for 7 consecutive days are $10 per car, $5 for each pedestrian or bicyclist. A Shenandoah Passport ($25) is good for 1 year, as is the National Park Service's Golden Eagle Passport ($50). Park entrance is free to holders of Golden Access (for disabled U.S. citizens) and Golden Age (U.S. citizens 62 or older) passports. The former is free; the latter is available at the entrance gates for $10.

Speed limit on the Skyline Drive is a strictly enforced 35 m.p.h. Plants and animals are protected, so all hunting is prohibited. Pets must be kept on a leash at all times and are not allowed on some trails. Wood fires are permitted only in fireplaces in developed areas. The Skyline Drive is a great bike route, but neither bicycles nor motor vehicles of any sort are allowed on the trails.

Most of the park is open to backcountry camping. Permits, which are free, are required; get them at the entrance gates, visitor centers, or by mail from park headquarters (see "Information," above). Campers are required to leave no trace of their presence. No permits are necessary for backcountry hiking, but the same "no-trace" rule applies.

VISITOR CENTERS   There are two park visitor centers. The **Dickey Ridge Visitor Center,** at Mile 4.6, is usually open daily from April through November and on an intermittent schedule in December. **Byrd Visitor Center,** at Mile 51 in Big Meadows, is open daily from early April through October and on an intermittent schedule through December. Both provide information, maps of nearby hiking trails, interpretive exhibits, films, slide shows, and nature walks. There is a small information center at **Loft Mountain** (Mile Post 79.5). In addition, the privately run **Rockfish Gap Information Center,** on U.S. 211 outside the park's southern gate, has information about the park and the surrounding area.

SEASONS   The park is most popular from mid- to late October, when the gorgeous fall foliage peaks and weekend traffic on the Skyline Drive reaches bumper-to-bumper proportions. Days also tend to be clearer in fall than in summer, when lingering haze can obscure the views. In spring, the green of leafing trees moves up the ridge at the rate of about 100 feet a day. Wildflowers begin to bloom in April, and by late May the azaleas are brilliant and the dogwood is putting on a show. Nesting birds abound, and the normally modest waterfalls are at their highest during spring, when warm rains melt the highland snows. You'll find the clearest views across the distant mountains during winter, but many facilities are closed then, and snow and ice can shut down the Skyline Drive.

AVOIDING THE CROWDS   With its proximity to the sprawling Washington, D.C., metropolitan area, the park is at its busiest on summer and fall weekends and holidays. The fall foliage season in October is the busiest time, however, and reservations for October accommodations in or near the park should be made as much as a year in advance. The best time to visit, therefore, is during the spring and on weekdays from June through October. When the Central District around Big Meadows and Skyland is packed, there may be more space available in the Northern and Southern Districts.

RANGER PROGRAMS   The park offers a wide variety of ranger-led activities— nature walks, interpretive programs, cultural and history lectures, campfire talks. Most are held at or near Dickey Ridge Visitor Center in the north; Byrd Visitor Center and the Big Meadows and Skyland lodges and campground in the center; and Loft Mountain campground in the south. Schedules are published seasonally in the *Shenandoah Overlook,* available at the entrance gates, visitor centers, and from park headquarters.

SEEING THE HIGHLIGHTS

Unless you're caught in heavy traffic on fall foliage weekends, you can drive the entire length of the **Skyline Drive** in about 3 hours without stopping. But why rush? Give yourself at least a day for this drive, so lovely are the views from its 75 designated scenic overlooks. Stop for lunch at a wayside snack bar, lodge, or one of seven official picnic grounds (for that matter, any of the overlooks will do for an impromptu picnic). Better yet, get out of your car and take at least a short hike down one of the hollows to a waterfall.

If you have only a day, head directly to the **Central District** between Thornton Gap and Swift Run Gap, the most developed but also most interesting part of the park. It has the highest mountains, best views, nearly half of the park's 500 miles of hiking trails, and the park's only stables and overnight accommodations. Most visitors make Big Meadows or Skyland their base of operations for stays of more than a day, but if you plan to do this, place your lodge reservations early (see "Accommodations," below).

SCENIC OVERLOOKS   Among the more interesting of the 75 designated over-looks along the drive are the **Shenandoah Valley Overlook** (Mile 2.8), with views west to the Signal Knob of Massanutten Mountain across the south fork of the river; **Range View Overlook** (Mile 17.1; elevation 2,800 feet), providing fine views of the central section of the park, looking south; **Stony Man Overlook** (Mile 38.6), offering panoramas of Stony Man Cliffs, the valley, and the Alleghenies; **Thoroughfare Mountain Overlook** (Mile 40.5; elevation 3,595 feet), one of the highest overlooks, with views from Hogback Mountain south to cone-shaped Robertson Mountain and the rocky face of Old Rag Mountain; **Old Rag View Overlook** (Mile 46.5), dominated by Old Rag, sitting all by itself in an eastern extremity of the park; **Franklin Cliffs Overlook** (Mile 49), offering a view of the cliffs and the Shenandoah Valley and Massanutten Mountain beyond; and **Big Run Overlook** (Mile 81.2), which looks down on rocky peaks and the largest watershed in the park.

WATERFALLS   Only one waterfall is visible from the Skyline Drive, at Mile 1.4, and it's dry part of the year. On the other hand, 15 other falls are accessible via hiking trails (see "Hiking," below).

HIKING & OTHER SPORTS

HIKING   The number-one outdoor activity here is hiking. The park's 112 hiking trails total more than 500 miles, varying in length from short walks to a 101-mile segment of the Appalachian Trail running the entire length of the park. Access to the trails is marked along the Skyline Drive. There are parking lots at the major trailheads, but they fill quickly on weekends.

We strongly recommend that you get maps and trail descriptions before setting out—even before leaving home, if possible. Free maps of many trails are available at the visitor centers, which also sell the topographic maps, published by the Potomac Appalachian Trail Conference, as well as a one-sheet map of all the park's walks published by *Trails Illustrated* ($8). Also, the Shenandoah Natural History Association's *Guide to Shenandoah National Park and Skyline Drive* provides detailed descriptions of all the major hikes. (See "Information," above, for addresses and phone numbers.)

At the minimum, take one of the short hikes on nature trails at Dickey Ridge Visitor Center, Byrd Visitor Center/Big Meadows, and Loft Mountain. There's also an excellent 1.6-mile nature hike at Stony Man (Mile 41.7).

Here are a few of the more popular trails:

Limberlost Accessible Trail: Opened in 1997 at Mile 43 south of Skyland, Limberlost is the park's first trail accessible to visitors in wheelchairs. The 1.3-mile loop runs through an old-growth forest of ancient hemlocks. The trail has a 5-foot-wide, hard-packed surface; crosses a 65-foot bridge; and includes a 150-foot boardwalk.

White Oak Canyon: Beginning at Mile 42.6 just south of Skyland, this steep gorge has been described as the park's "scenic gem." The 7.3-mile trail goes through an area of wild beauty, passing no less than six waterfalls and cascades. The upper reaches to the first falls are relatively easy, but further down the track can be rough and rocky. Total climb is about 2,160 feet, so allow 6 hours.

Cedar Run Falls: Several trails begin at Hawksbill Gap (Mile 45.6). A short but steep trail leads 1.7 miles round-trip to the summit of Hawksbill Mountain, the park's highest at 4,050 feet. Another is a moderately difficult 3¹/₂-mile round-trip hike down to Cedar Falls and back. You can also connect from Cedar Run to White Oak Canyon, a 7.3-mile loop that will take all day.

Dark Hollow Falls: One of the park's most popular hikes is the 1.4-mile walk to Dark Hollow Falls, the closest cascade to the Skyline Drive. The trail begins at Mile 50.7 near the Byrd Visitor Center. Allow 1¹/₄ hours for the round-trip.

Camp Hoover/Mill Prong: Starting at the Milam Gap parking area (Mile 52.8), this 4-mile round-trip hike drops down the Mill Prong to the Rapidan River, where President Herbert Hoover, an avid fisherman, had a camp during his administration (sort of the Camp David of his day). The total climb is 850 feet; allow 4 hours.

South River Falls: Third-highest in the park, South River Falls drops a total of 83 feet in two stages. From the parking lot at South River Overlook (Mile 62.7), the trail is a moderately easy 2.6 miles round-trip, with a total climb of about 850 feet. Allow 2¹/₂ hours.

Doyles River Falls: Starting at a large parking lot at Mile 81.1, a trail drops to a small waterfall in a natural amphitheater surrounded by large trees. Continue another quarter of a mile to see an even taller falls (63 feet). This hike is 2.7 miles round-trip, with a few steep sections in its 850-foot climb; allow 3 hours.

Appalachian Trail: Access points to the Appalachian Trail are well marked at overlooks along the Skyline Drive. Along the trail, five backcountry shelters for day use each offer only a table, fireplace, pit toilet, and water. The **Potomac Appalachian Trail Club,** 118 Park St. SE, Vienna, VA 22180 (☎ **703/242-0693**), maintains seven huts and six fully enclosed cabins that can accommodate up to 12 people. Use of the huts is free, but they are intended for long-distance hikers only. Cabins cost $12 on weekdays, $20 on weekends, and must be reserved in advance through the park or by calling PATC Monday through Friday between 7 and 9pm Eastern time.

FISHING   The park's streams are short, with limited fishing. Only native brook trout may be taken, and some streams are "catch-and-release," meaning you must release your catch back into the water. Only artificial lures are allowed, and you must get a Virginia fishing license (5-day licenses are available at the entry gates, visitor centers, wayside facilities, and camp stores inside the park, or at sporting-goods stores outside). The park publishes a free recreational fishing brochure and an annual list of streams open for fishing; both are available at the Big Meadows and Loft Mountain waysides or at sporting-goods stores outside the park.

HORSEBACK RIDING   Horses are allowed only on trails marked with yellow, and even then only via guided expeditions with **Skyland Stables** (☎ **540/999-2210**), on the Skyland Lodge grounds (Mile 41.8). Rides cost $20 per hour. Pony rides for children are $3 for 15 minutes. Children must be 4 feet, 10 inches tall to ride the horses. The stables operate from April to November, depending on the spring and fall weather.

CAMPING

The park has four campgrounds with tent and trailer sites: **Mathews Arm** (Mile 22.2), **Big Meadows** (Mile 51.2), **Lewis Mountain** (Mile 57.5), and **Loft Mountain** (Mile 79.5). The Lewis Mountain and Loft Mountain campgrounds offer overnight sites on a first-come, first-served basis at $14 per site per night. They are open from mid-May to late October. Big Meadows costs $6 per night and is open from early April to the end of October.

The **Shenandoah Valley Travel Association,** P.O. Box 1040, New Market, VA 22844 (☎ **540/740-3132**), publishes a list of private campgrounds outside the park.

ACCOMMODATIONS

The park concessionaire is **Aramark Virginia Sky-Line Co.,** P.O. Box 727, Luray, VA 22835 (☎ **800/999-4714** or 540/743-5108), which operates food, lodging, and other services for park visitors. Reservations should be made well in advance—up to a year ahead for the peak fall season.

In addition to the two lodges mentioned below, housekeeping cottages are available at Lewis Mountain. Contact Aramark Virginia Sky-Line Co. for information.

See the sections that follow for accommodations in nearby towns.

Big Meadows Lodge. Mile 51.2. ☎ **800/999-4714** or 540/999-2221. 92 rms. $79–$93 main lodge; $60–$93 motel; $120–$130 suite; $68–$79 cabin rm. Additional person $5 extra. Highest rates charged in Oct. Weekday packages available. MC, V. Free parking. Closed Nov to early May.

Accommodations at Big Meadows consist of rooms in the main lodge and in rustic cabins, and multi-unit lodges with modern suites. Big Meadows is a major recreational center; many hiking trails start here, and it's also the site of the Byrd Visitor Center. The resort is built near a large grassy meadow where families of deer often come to graze at dawn and dusk. A grocery store is nearby.

The dining room features traditional regional dishes like fried chicken, mountain trout, and country ham. Blackberry–ice cream pie with blackberry syrup is a dessert specialty. Wine, beer, and cocktails are available. During the season, live entertainment keeps the Taproom busy.

Skyland Lodge. Mile 41.8. ☎ **800/999-4714** or 540/999-2211. 177 rms, including 20 cabins and 6 suites. $79–$102 lodge; $46–$84 cabin; $112–$160 suite. Highest rates charged in Oct. Weekday packages available. AE, DC, DISC, MC, V. Free parking.

Skyland was built by naturalist George Freeman Pollock in 1894 as a summer retreat atop the highest point on the drive. Encompassing 52 acres, the resort offers rustic wood-paneled cabins as well as modern motel-type accommodations with wonderful views. Some of the buildings are dark-brown clapboard, others fieldstone, and all nestle among the trees. The central building has a lobby with a huge stone fireplace, TV (also in some, but not all, rooms), and comfortable seating areas.

Complete breakfast, lunch, and dinner menus are offered at reasonable prices. Dinner entrees include vegetarian lasagna, steak, roast turkey, and pan-fried rainbow trout. There's a fully stocked taproom.

DINING

In addition to Big Meadows and Skyland lodges, there are daytime restaurants and snack bars at Elkwallow Wayside (Mile 24.1), Panorama-Thornton Gap (Mile 31.5), and Loft Mountain (Mile 79.5).

Picnic areas with tables, fireplaces, water fountains, and rest rooms are at Dickey Ridge (Mile 4.6), Elkwallow (Mile 24.1), Pinnacles (Mile 36.7), Big Meadows (Mile 51), Lewis Mountain (Mile 57.5), South River (Mile 62.8), and Loft Mountain (Mile 79.5).

2 Winchester: Apple Capital

76 miles W of Washington, D.C.; 189 miles NW of Richmond

Virginia's present-day "Apple Capital," Winchester was the site of a Shawnee Indian campground before it was settled by Pennsylvania Quakers in 1732. Thanks to its strategic location at the northern end of the Shenandoah Valley, it changed hands no fewer than 72 times during the Civil War. In more recent years, Winchester was

I Fall to Pieces

Early life wasn't easy for a Winchester native named Virginia Hensley. Her family was poor, and she had to quit high school and take a job in a drugstore to make ends meet. But she had a great voice—a voice that would someday propel her into the Country Music Hall of Fame.

Only die-hard country music fans know her by her real name, of course, for at age 21 she married a man named Gerald Cline. It was under the name Patsy Cline that Virginia Hensley sang "Walkin' After Midnight" on the nationally televised "Arthur Godfrey's Talent Scouts." The record of that song sold a million copies.

Difficult times set in again, however, and Patsy Cline disappeared from the charts. Her marriage to Gerald Cline failed, she remarried, and she took 2 years off to have a baby. But then, in 1960, she won a spot on the Grand Ole Opry and recorded one of country music's all-time hits, "I Fall to Pieces."

Her career took off, and songs like "Crazy," "Leavin' on Your Mind," and "Imagine That" will forever be linked to Patsy Cline.

It all came to an abrupt end in March 1963, when she, Hawkshaw Hawkins, and the Cowboy Copas were killed in a plane crash on their way back to Nashville. Winchester's own Patsy Cline was brought home and buried in Shenandoah Memorial Park, 3 miles south of town on U.S. 511.

The Winchester/Frederick County Visitors Center (see "Essentials," below) has a Patsy Cline Corner that includes her very own jukebox. Pick up a brochure that points the way to important sites in her life, including her home, Gaunt's Drug Store (where she worked), the high school she attended, GNM Music (where she cut her first record), the house where she married second husband Charlie Dick, and her grave.

the birthplace of novelist Willa Cather and the hometown of country music great Patsy Cline. It's also famous for the Shenandoah Apple Blossom Festival in May, one of the region's most popular events.

ESSENTIALS

VISITOR INFORMATION   The **Winchester/Frederick County Visitors Center,** 1360 S. Pleasant Valley Rd., Winchester, VA 22601 (☎ **800/662-1360** or 540/662-4135; fax 540/722-6365; www.winch.va.com), is open daily from 9am to 5pm; closed major holidays. Take Exit 313 off I-81, go west on U.S. 50, and follow the signs. Another source of information is the **Kurtz Cultural Center** (☎ **540/ 722-6367**), at Cameron and Boscawen streets in the heart of Winchester's historic district. It's open Monday through Saturday from 10am to 5pm, Sunday from noon to 5pm. Both centers distribute free maps and walking-tour brochures of the Old Town historic district. The Kurtz Cultural Center also has small museum sections devoted to the valley's role in the Civil War and to Patsy Cline, Winchester's contribution to country music (see "I Fall to Pieces," above). Both centers sell books about the Civil War.

GETTING THERE   Winchester is on I-81, U.S. 11, U.S. 522, U.S. 50, and Va. 7.

EXPLORING THE TOWN

Begin your tour at the Winchester/Frederick County Visitors Center (see "Essentials," above), where you can pick up a detailed map and see an 18-minute film about Winchester and Frederick County.

After you've been through Abram's Delight next to the visitor center (see "The Block-Ticket Museums," below), drive into Winchester's historic district. Start your tour at the visitor information desk in the **Kurtz Cultural Center,** at the corner of Cameron and Boscawen streets (see "Essentials," above).

The heart of the historic area is the **Old Town Mall,** a 4-block-long pedestrian mall along Loudon Street between Piccadilly and Cork streets. Here you can explore a number of boutiques and enjoy refreshment at a bookstore-cum-coffeehouse, a Swiss pastry shop, or several restaurants, some of which offer outdoor seating under the mall's shade trees in warm weather (see "Where to Dine," below). Facing the mall, the imposing **Frederick County Court House** was built in 1840.

While walking between the George Washington and Stonewall Jackson museums (see below), you can't miss the elaborate, Beaux Arts–style **Handley Library,** at the corner of Braddock and Piccadilly streets (☎ 540/662-9041). Built between 1907 and 1912, it's adorned with a full panoply of Classic Revival statues. A copper-covered dome covers the rotunda, which symbolizes the spine of a book, with the two flanking wings representing its open pages.

Across the street from the library is the white-columned **Elks Building,** head-quarters of Union Gen. Philip Sheridan from 1864 to 1865.

If you don't believe this northern end of the valley was fought over during the Civil War, visit **Mt. Hebron Cemetery,** on Woodstock Lane east of downtown. Some 8,000 men killed in the battles are buried here—the Rebels in Stonewall Confederate Cemetery on the south side of the street, the Yankees in the National Cemetery on the north side.

On the west side of town, **Glen Burnie Manor House and Gardens,** 801 Amherst St. (U.S. 50) (☎ **540/662-1473**), is a lovingly restored, red-brick Georgian plantation home with sections dating to 1755. It's appointed with a remarkable collection of 18th-century furniture and art—including paintings by Rembrandt Peale and Gilbert Stuart—amassed by the late Julian Wood Glass, Jr., whose family owns Glen Burnie. You shouldn't miss a stroll though the magnificent formal gardens. The house and gardens are open from April through October, Tuesday to Saturday from 10am to 4pm, Sunday from noon to 4pm. Admission is $8 for adults and students, $6 for seniors, and free for children 6 and under.

If you're in Winchester on a Saturday from mid-May to mid-October, you can take one of the weekly **walking tours** of Old Town, which depart from the Kurtz Cultural Center. A Civil War tour departs at 10:15am, while a general historical walk leaves at 10:45am; both cost $8 per person. Call ☎ **540/722-6367** for information and reservations.

THE BLOCK-TICKET MUSEUMS

Both the visitor center and the Kurtz Cultural Center sell **block tickets** to the town's three major museums for $7.50 for adults, $6.50 for seniors, and $4 for children 6 to 12 (free for children under 6).

Abram's Delight. 1340 S. Pleasant Valley Rd. ☎ **540/662-6519.** Admission (without the block ticket) $3.50 adults, $3 seniors, $1.75 children. Apr–Oct, Mon–Sat 10am–4pm; Sun noon–4pm. Closed Nov–Mar.

Adjoining the visitor center is this native-limestone residence built in 1754 by Quaker Isaac Hollingsworth on a pretty site beside a lake. The house is fully restored and furnished with simple 18th- and 19th-century pieces.

Stonewall Jackson's Headquarters. 415 N. Braddock St. (between Peyton St. and North Ave.). ☎ **540/667-3242.** Admission (without block ticket) $3.50 adults, $1.75 children, $8.75 family. Apr–Oct, Mon–Sat 10am–4pm; Sun noon–4pm. Closed Nov–Mar.

Stonewall Jackson used this Victorian home as his headquarters in the winter of 1861–62. It's filled with maps, photos, and memorabilia, making it a must for Civil War buffs. Plan on taking a guided tour, as you aren't allowed to just walk through.

Washington's Office Museum. 32 W. Cork St. (at Braddock St.). ☎ **540/662-4412.** Admission (without block ticket) $2 adults, $1 children. Apr–Oct, Mon–Sat 10am–4pm; Sun noon–4pm. Closed Nov–Mar.

George Washington used this small log cabin (since covered with clapboard) as his office in 1755 and 1756 when he was a colonel in the Virginia militia, charged with building Fort Loudon to protect the colony's frontier from the French and Native Americans. The building itself is the highlight of this charming little museum, which contains some relics from the French and Indian War period and a good many more from the Civil War a century later.

WHERE TO STAY

On the southeast side of town, the area along Millwood Avenue (U.S. 50) at I-81 (Exit 313) has Winchester's major shopping mall and several national restaurants and chain motels. About half the rooms at the **Holiday Inn** (☎ **800/HOLIDAY** or 540/667-3300) face a pleasant courtyard with outdoor pool; the hotel is also home to Jimmy's Restaurant, one of the town's most popular lunch spots. Another winner here is the inexpensive **Budgetel Inn** (☎ **800/4-BUDGET** or 540/678-0800), a member of the fine little chain that provides extra-long beds and phone cords, free local calls, a desk, a coffeemaker, and juice and a Danish hung on your doorknob before dawn.

Also nearby are the **Best Western Lee-Jackson Motor Inn** (☎ 800/528-1234 or 540/662-4154); **Comfort Inn** (☎ 800/228-5150 or 540/667-5000); **Hampton Inn** (☎ 800/HAMPTON or 540/667-8011); **Quality Inn East** (☎ 800/221-2222 or 540/667-2250); **Shoney's Inn** (☎ 800/222-2222 or 540/665-1700), which has an indoor pool; the inexpensive **Super 8** (☎ 800/800-8000 or 540/665-4450); and **Travelodge of Winchester** (☎ 800/255-3050 or 540/665-0685).

A NEARBY COUNTRY INN WITH A FRENCH FLAVOR

✪ **L'Auberge Provençale.** U.S. 340 (P.O. Box 119), White Post, VA 22663. ☎ **800/638-1702** or 540/837-1375. Fax 703/837-2004. 11 rms, including 2 suites. A/C. $150–$275 double. Rates include full breakfast. AE, DC, MC, V. From I-81, take U.S. 50 east 7 miles, turn right on U.S. 340. The inn is 1 mile on the right.

Master chef Alain Borel and his vivacious wife, Celeste, have managed to re-create the look, feel, and cuisine of Provence in a 1750s fieldstone farmhouse romantically set in the eastern foothills of the Blue Ridge. In the original main house are three intimate dining rooms and a comfortable parlor to which guests are invited for pre-dinner drinks in front of the fireplace. Three of the 10 guest rooms are in this building; antiques and beautiful fabrics complement the colonial farmhouse's fine features. The remaining cozy accommodations, in an adjoining gray-clapboard addition, are individually decorated with Victorian and European pieces and lovely French provincial–print fabrics. A hospitable plate of inn-baked buttery cookies and fresh fruit is set out in each room. Exceptional works of fine art—including prints by renowned artists and a unique selection of carved wooden animals and small handcrafted bird sculptures—adorn the guest rooms.

Dining: Chef Borel uses the finest-quality ingredients, many from his own garden or local farmers, to create his superb Provençal cuisine. The five-course prix-fixe dinner ($58 per person) might begin with foie gras with orange tomato melange, followed by a seared lamb salad with grilled peppers, tomatoes, and eggplant with a creamy mint vinaigrette dressing. After a refreshing sorbet, diners are offered such main courses as roast guinea fowl stuffed with wild game sausages, or perhaps smoked salmon with a compote of tomatoes, shallots, garlic, and broccoli with pesto toast. Even breakfast is a splendid repast at L'Auberge Provençale, and Alain will provide a gourmet picnic lunch on request.

WHERE TO DINE

The Old Town Mall along Loudon Street in the heart of downtown has a number of coffeehouses, bakeries, and restaurants. Best of the lot are **Violino Ristorante Italiano** (☎ 540/667-8006) and the pub-like **T. Jefrey's** (☎ 540/667-0429), both on the north end of the mall at Piccadilly Street. They offer outdoor seating in good weather. For inexpensive down-home fare, check out **Vivian's Country Cooking**, on the mall at 103 N. Loudon St. (☎ 540/667-7612).

Cork Street Tavern. 8 W. Cork St. (at S. Loudon St.). ☎ **540/667-3777.** Reservations not accepted. Main courses $7.50–$14. AE, DC, DISC, MC, V. Mon–Sat 11am–midnight; Sun noon–10pm. AMERICAN.

Just around the corner from South Loudon Street—the pedestrian mall at the heart of Winchester—this ancient pub with small, dark rooms, fireplace, trophies, and photos of modern movie stars makes a fine place for lunch or a snack while touring the downtown sites. The house specialty is barbecued ribs, but the menu offers a wide range of other main courses, sandwiches, burgers, and salads. A newer wing offers outdoor patio seating in warm weather.

3 Middletown & Strasburg: Antiques Galore

Middletown: 13 miles S of Winchester; 174 miles NW of Richmond; 76 miles W of Washington, D.C.
Strasburg: 6 miles S of Middletown

Middletown's historic sites will interest both history and architecture buffs, while its Wayside Theatre will entertain theater enthusiasts. An extraordinary collection of shops makes Strasburg seem like heaven to antiques shoppers. Both hamlets have exceptional country inns offering antique-filled accommodations and fine dining.

It was to Strasburg that Gen. Stonewall Jackson brought the railroad locomotives he stole from the Union during his daring Great Train Raid on Martinsburg, West Virginia. He rolled the iron beasts down the Valley Pike to the existing station at Strasburg, which is now a local museum.

ESSENTIALS

VISITOR INFORMATION The **Winchester/Frederick County Visitors Center** (see "Essentials" under "Winchester: Apple Capital," above) has in-depth information about Middletown. For Strasburg, contact the **Chamber of Commerce,** P.O. Box 42, Strasburg, VA 22657 (☎ 540/465-9197). The chamber has an information booth in the Strasburg Emporium (see "Antiquing," below).

GETTING THERE From I-81, take Exit 302 west to U.S. 11 into Middletown. Take Exits 298 or 300 into Strasburg.

A PLANTATION MANSE & MUSEUM OF PRESIDENTS

✪ **Belle Grove Plantation.** U.S. 11 South, Middletown. ☎ **540/869-2028.** Admission $5 adults, $4.50 seniors, $2.50 students 13–17, free for children under 13. Mon–Sat 10:15am–3:15pm; Sun 1:15–4:15pm. Closed mid-Nov to mid-Mar except candlelight tours at Christmas. From Winchester, take I-81 south to Exit 302 at Middletown, then U.S. 11 south 1 mile.

One of the finest homes in the Shenandoah Valley, this beautiful stone mansion was built in 1794 by Maj. Isaac Hite, whose grandfather, Joist Hite, first settled here in

1732. At the request of James Madison, brother-in-law of Isaac Hite, Thomas Jefferson was actively involved in Belle Grove's design. The columns and Palladian-style front windows are just two examples of Jefferson's influence.

Now owned by the National Trust, Belle Grove is at once a working farm, a restored 18th-century plantation house, and a center for the study and sale of traditional rural crafts. The interior is furnished with period antiques. Below the front portico is the entrance to the crafts center and gift shop, featuring an outstanding selection of locally made quilts, pillows, small rugs, and other handworked items. You must see the house via guided tour, so allow 1 hour.

Belle Grove suffered considerable damage in 1864 during the Battle of Cedar Creek, which was fought on 4,000 acres surrounding the manor house. Across U.S. 11, the **Cedar Creek Battlefield Visitors Center** (☎ 540/869-2064) honors the fight with Civil War weapons, a diorama depicting the Napoleonic tactics used, and changing exhibits such as reproductions of the works of James Taylor, an artist who followed the Union troops. The battle is re-enacted each year on the weekend closest to October 19.

The Museum of American Presidents. 130 N. Massanutten St. (U.S. 11), Strasburg. ☎ **540/465-5999.** Admission $3 adults, seniors, and children 6–16, free for children under 6. Mon–Sat 10am–5pm; Sun noon–5pm.

Leo M. Bernstein, a former Washington, D.C., lawyer and banker who restored the Wayside Inn (see "Where to Stay & Dine," below), displays his monumental collection of presidential memorabilia at this well-designed small museum in the heart of Strasburg. Among the highlights are a lock of George Washington's hair, James Madison's writing desk from his bedroom at Montpelier, and doors removed from the White House when it was restored during the Truman administration. Kids can don costumes and play educational games in a room set up like a colonial-era schoolhouse, complete with a potbelly stove.

ANTIQUING

After perusing the shops along U.S. 11 at Middletown, antiques lovers will want to continue their hunt in nearby Strasburg, which has a bevy of fine outlets at the intersection of U.S. 11 and Va. 55. The ✪ **Great Strasburg Antiques Emporium,** 110 N. Massanutten St. (☎ **540/465-3711**), is one of the state's largest shops, an enormous warehouse open daily from 10am to 5pm, to 7pm Friday and Saturday from May to October; closed New Year's Day, Easter, Thanksgiving, and Christmas.

You can't buy them, but there are plenty of antiques to inspect across Va. 55 at the **Strasburg Museum** (☎ **540/465-3175**), in the old train station where Stonewall Jackson brought his stolen locomotives. Admission is $2 for adults, $1 for teenagers, 50¢ for children under 12. The museum is open May through October, daily from 10am to 4pm.

WHERE TO STAY & DINE

Hotel Strasburg. 213 Holliday St., Strasburg, VA 22657. ☎ **800/348-8327** or 540/465-9191. Fax 540/465-4788. 19 rms, 9 suites. A/C TV TEL. $75–$87 single or double; $99–$199 Jacuzzi suite. Weekend and other packages available. AE, DC, MC, V. Parking on street. From I-81, take Exit 298 and go south on U.S. 11 1¹/₂ miles to the first traffic light; turn right 1 block, left at the light (Holliday St.).

Strasburg likes to call itself the Antiques Capital of Virginia, and this restored Victorian hotel, built as a hospital in 1895, is furnished with an impressive collection of period pieces. Most are supplied by the Strasburg Emporium (see "Antiquing," above), and are for sale. Hence, the decor changes constantly. Some rooms have Jacuzzis.

Known for its Russian sauerkraut soup, the dining room is open for all three meals. Dinner entrees might include shrimp-and-scallop cassoulet, chicken breast with walnuts and bacon in cream sauce, or Bavarian pork chops with onions, apples, and sauerkraut. A first-floor pub offers friendly conversation and libation.

✪ **Wayside Inn.** 7783 Main St., Middletown, VA 22645. ☎ **540/869-1797.** Fax 540/869-6038. 24 rms and suites. A/C TV TEL. $95–$145 single or double. Weekend and other packages available. AE, DC, MC, V. Free parking. From I-81, take Exit 302 to U.S. 11 (Main St.).

This rambling roadside inn first offered bed and board to Shenandoah Valley travelers in 1797. It became a stagecoach stop some 20 years later when the Valley Pike was hacked out of the wilderness, and has continued to function as an inn ever since. In the 1960s, a Washington financier and antiques collector restored it, and today rooms are beautifully decorated with an assortment of 18th- and 19th-century pieces. Each room's decor reflects a period style, from colonial to elaborate Victorian Renaissance Revival. Expect to find canopied beds, armoires, highboys, writing desks, antique clocks, and stenciled or papered walls adorned with fine prints and oil paintings.

Regional American cuisine is served in seven antiques-filled dining rooms. Dinner entrees include whole stuffed valley trout and smothered chicken in white wine. Breakfast and lunch are also available. Cocktails are served in the Coachyard Lounge.

MIDDLETOWN AFTER DARK

Since 1961, the **Wayside Theatre,** on U.S. 11 in Middletown (☎ **540/869-1776**), has staged fine productions by contemporary dramatists, including Peter Shaffer, Neil Simon, Wendy Wasserstein, Garson Kanin, and Alan Ayckbourn. Peter Boyle, Susan Sarandon, Jill Eikenberry, and Donna McKechnie began their careers here. The Curtain Call Café offers light post-theater fare and a chance for audience members to mingle with the performers. Admission is $16 to the Wednesday and Saturday matinees; $18 to Wednesday, Thursday, and Sunday evening performances; and $22 on Friday and Saturday nights. Senior and student discounts are available. The box office is open Monday and Tuesday from noon to 4pm, Wednesday through Saturday from 11am to 9pm, and Sunday from 3 to 8pm.

4 Front Royal: A Spy's Home

20 miles SE of Strasburg; 174 miles NW of Richmond; 70 miles W of Washington, D.C.

At the northern end of the Skyline Drive, the Front Royal area offers easy access to the Shenandoah National Park and its many outdoor activities. During the summer months, it's also a hotbed for canoeing, rafting, kayaking, and inner-tubing on the sometimes lazy, sometimes rapid South Fork of the Shenandoah River (see "River Rafting & Canoeing" box, below). Front Royal was named for a royal oak that stood in the town square during the Revolutionary War. In those days, it was a wild and woolly frontier waystation at the junction of the two trails that later became U.S. 340 and Va. 55. During the Civil War, it was home to the infamous Confederate spy Belle Boyd, whose close contact—to say the least—with Union officers led to a surprise Southern victory at the Battle of Front Royal in 1862.

Across the mountains to the east are two fine inns and dining choices, including a nationally famous, five-star inn and restaurant in "Little" Washington.

ESSENTIALS

VISITOR INFORMATION Contact the **Front Royal/Warren County Chamber of Commerce Visitors Center,** 414 E. Main St., Front Royal, VA 22630

(☎ **800/338-2576** or 540/635-3185; fax 540/635-9758; www.frontroyalchamber. com; e-mail: coc@frontroyal.com). The chamber's visitor center is located in the old yellow train station and is open daily from 9am to 5pm. From I-66, follow U.S. 340 into town and turn left on Main Street at the Warren County Courthouse.

GETTING THERE   From I-66, take Exit 6, U.S. 340/U.S. 522 south; it's 5 minutes to town. Front Royal is also easily reached from I-81 by taking I-66 east to Exit 6.

EXPLORING THE TOWN & THE CAVERNS

Begin your tour at the Front Royal/Warren County Chamber of Commerce Visitors Center (see "Essentials," above), which supplies free walking-tour brochures.

Highlights in historic downtown are both on Chester Street, a block north of the visitor center. The **Warren Rifles Confederate Museum** (☎ **540/636-6982**) has a collection of Civil War firearms, battle flags, uniforms, letters, diaries, and other personal effects; it's open mid-April through October, Monday to Saturday from 9am to 4pm, Sunday from noon to 4pm. Next door is the restored **Belle Boyd Cottage** (☎ **540/636-1446**), where the infamous Confederate spy pillow-talked with her unsuspecting Union lovers. It's open April through October, Monday to Friday from 11am to 4pm, weekends by appointment. Admission to either the museum or the cottage is $2 per person, free for children under 12 accompanied by an adult.

There are many caverns beneath the Blue Ridge Mountains, but the first one you'll encounter coming from the north is **Skyline Caverns,** on U.S. 340 a mile south of the Shenandoah National Park's northern entrance (☎ **800/296-4545** or 540/ 635-4545). The highlights here are unique rock formations called *anthodites*— delicate white spikes that spread in all directions from their positions on the cave ceiling. Their growth rate is only about 1 inch every 7,000 years. A sophisticated lighting system dramatically enhances formations like the Capitol Dome, Rainbow Trail, and Painted Desert. A miniature train covering about half a mile is a popular attraction for kids. The temperature in the caverns is a cool 54°F year-round, so take a sweater even in summer. Admission is $10 for adults, $9 for seniors, $5 for children 7 to 13, and free for children under 13. The caverns are open June 15 to Labor Day, daily from 9am to 6:30pm; March 15 to June 14 and Labor Day to November 14, Monday through Friday from 9am to 5pm, weekends from 9am to 6pm; November 15 to March 14, daily from 9am to 4pm.

SPORTS & OUTDOOR ACTIVITIES

HORSEBACK RIDING   The 4,500-acre **Marriott Ranch,** 5305 Marriott Lane, Hume, VA 22639 (☎ **540/364-2627**), offers 1¹/₂-hour guided trail rides, buggy rides, summer sunset rides, full-moon rides, and Saturday-night "Steak Bakes." Serious equestrians can stay over in the ranch's 10 rooms (7 with bath), with breakfast included. You can also rent horses and take lessons at **Massanutten Trail Rides, Inc.,** on C.R. 619 south of Front Royal (☎ **540/636-6061**).

GOLF   Duffers are welcome at **Shenandoah Valley Golf Club** (☎ **540/635-3588**) and **Bowling Green Country Club** (☎ **540/635-2095**). Call for directions, starting times, and greens fees.

WHERE TO STAY

On U.S. 522 east of U.S. 340, the **Quality Inn Skyline Drive** (☎ **800/228-5151** or 540/635-3161) is the largest and best-equipped motel here. The inexpensive **Scottish Inn** (☎ **800/251-1962** or 540/636-6168) and **Super 8** (☎ **800/800-8000** or 540/636-4888) are both at the junction of U.S. 340 and Va. 55. In addition, the

---

River Rafting & Canoeing

The streams flowing west down from Shenandoah National Park end up in the South Fork of the Shenandoah River, which winds its way through a narrow valley between the Blue Ridge and Massanutten Mountains.

The switchbacks of the South Fork are the region's main center for river rafting, canoeing, and kayaking from mid-March to mid-November. The amount of recent rain will determine whether you go white-water rafting, canoeing, kayaking, or just lazily floating downstream in an inner tube.

Several outfitters are based along U.S. 340, which parallels the river between Front Royal and Luray. **Front Royal Canoe Company** (☎ **540/635-5440**) provides equipment and guides from its location south of Front Royal. In Bentonville, a small village about 8 miles south of Front Royal, you'll find **Downriver Canoe Company** (☎ **800/338-1963** or 540/635-5526) and **River Rental Outfitters** (☎ **800/RAPIDS-1** or 540/635-5050). Near Luray, you can go with **Shenandoah River Outfitters** (☎ **800/6CANOE2** or 540/743-4159). All require advance reservations.

---

modest **Twin Rivers Motel,** on U.S. 340 south of I-66 (☎ **540/635-4101**), is well-maintained and mindful of families.

Chester House Inn. 43 Chester St., Front Royal, VA 22630. ☎ **800/621-0441** or 540/635-3937. Fax 540/636-8695. www.chesterhouse.com. E-mail: chesthse@rma.edu. 6 rms and suites (5 with bath), 1 carriage house. A/C. $65–$110 double room or suite; $180 carriage house. Rates include continental breakfast. AE, MC, V. Free parking in on-site lot.

A stately 1905 Georgian Revival mansion set on two pretty acres of gardens, Bill and Ann Wilson's B&B is a friendly place, attractively furnished with a mix of antiques and reproductions. The premier accommodation is the Royal Oak Suite, a spacious high-ceilinged unit with a fireplace, separate sitting room, and private bath; it overlooks formal boxwood gardens. Another charmer is the Blue Ridge Room, which has a wrought-iron king bed and an old coal stove. Or you can opt for the restored Carriage House, which has its own kitchen. The inn has a dining room, game room, and TV parlor, as well as terraced gardens adorned with a fountain, statuary, and brick walls.

TWO FINE NEARBY COUNTRY INNS

The two establishments below are located in the eastern foothills of the Blue Ridge Mountains, but within an easy (and very picturesque) drive from Front Royal via U.S. 522.

Caledonia Farm-1812. 47 Dearing Rd., Flint Hill, VA 22627. ☎ **800/262-1812** or 540/675-3693. Manual-start fax on both numbers. 2 rms, 2 suites. A/C. $80 single or double with shared bath; $140 suite. Rates include full breakfast. DISC, MC, V. From Front Royal, take U.S. 522 south 12 miles to Flint Hill and turn right onto C.R. 641, to C.R. 606 to C.R. 628; look for a sign indicating a right turn to the farm about 1 mile past the last intersection.

This 1812 Federal-style stone farmhouse is a delightful B&B set on a 52-acre working cattle farm. Scenic old barns, livestock and domestic animals, and open pastureland make for a bucolic setting. The common rooms are furnished with country charm. In the spacious Captain John's Room, a double bed is beautifully made up with floral sheets and a quilt, while blue-velvet wing chairs and Oriental rugs add to the cozy decor. A breezeway connects the main house with the romantically private 2¹/₂-room guesthouse. All accommodations offer working fireplaces and lovely views of the Blue Ridge. TVs and VCRs are available on request.

✪ **Inn at Little Washington.** Middle and Main sts. (P.O. Box 300), Washington, VA 22747. ☎ **540/675-3800.** Fax 540/675-3100. 9 rms, 5 suites. A/C TEL. $260 double; $420–$545 suite. Rates include continental breakfast. MC, V. Free parking. From Front Royal, take U.S. 522 south 16 miles, then west on U.S. 211 to Washington.

As glowing notices in the *New York Times, Washington Post,* and *San Francisco Chronicle* attest, the Inn at Little Washington is simply one of America's finest country inns. Located in the sleepy village of Washington, Virginia (population about 160), it was opened as a restaurant in 1978 by owners Patrick O'Connell, who is the chef, and Reinhardt Lynch, who serves as maître d'hôtel.

Rooms are magnificently furnished according to the design of an English decorator; her original sketches are framed and hanging in the inn's upstairs hallways. The two bi-level suites have loft bedrooms, balconies overlooking the courtyard garden, and bathrooms with Jacuzzi tubs. Sumptuous amenities include terry robes, thick towels, hair dryers, and elegant toiletries. Antiques and Oriental rugs add warmth to the rooms, distinguished by extravagantly canopied beds and hand-painted ceiling borders.

Dining: The 65-seat restaurant pays homage to French cuisine but relies on regional products—trout, Chesapeake Bay seafood, wild ducks, cheese from nearby dairies—for culinary inspiration. Patrick O'Connell constantly changes the menu for his fabulous fixed-price dinners ($88 per person Sunday through Thursday, $98 Friday, $118 Saturday). They might begin with a timbale of Virginia lump crabmeat and spinach mousse, continuing with an entree such as veal Shenandoah with local cider, apples, and apple brandy; barbecued grilled boneless rack of lamb in pecan crust with shoestring sweet potatoes; or Canadian salmon baked in strudel leaves with mushroom duxelles. Desserts might include warm custard bread pudding with Jack Daniels sauce and swans of white-chocolate mousse in passion-fruit purée. Make your reservations for Saturday and Sunday evenings at least 3 weeks in advance; for Friday evenings, at least 2 weeks in advance. Other evenings, reservations are suggested.

WHERE TO DINE

Main Street Mill Restaurant & Pub. 500 E. Main St. (next to visitor center). ☎ **540/636-3123.** Reservations not necessary. Sandwiches $4–$6; main courses $7–$18. AE, MC, V. Mon–Thurs 10:30am–9pm; Fri 10:30am–10pm; Sat 7am–10pm; Sun 7am–9pm. AMERICAN.

Occupying a picturesque 1922 mill building, this establishment has massive supporting columns and ceiling beams of chestnut. The distinctive trompe l'oeil murals representing Front Royal's pioneer and 19th-century eras were executed by local artist Patricia Windrow. Lunch fare includes soups, spicy chili, salads, and overstuffed deli sandwiches. Main courses, served with salad, vegetables, potato, and homemade breads, range from pastas to bacon-wrapped filet mignon to a Virginia ham dinner. Hearty breakfasts are served on weekend mornings.

5 Luray: An Underground Organ

6 miles W of Shenandoah National Park; 91 miles SW of Washington, D.C.; 135 miles NW of Richmond

Established in 1812 and named for Luray Caverns, the most visited caves in the East, this small town is surrounded by the lush, rolling farmlands of a picturesque valley between the Blue Ridge and Massanutten Mountains, and serves as the main gateway to the Shenandoah National Park's popular Central District. The park headquarters and the Thornton Gap entry are up U.S. 211 just a few miles east of town.

ESSENTIALS

VISITOR INFORMATION The **Page County Chamber of Commerce,** 46 E. Main St., Luray, VA 22835 (☎ **540/743-3915;** fax 540/743-3944; e-mail: pagecofc@shentel.net), will supply information in advance and make same-day hotel reservations at its visitor center, which is open daily 9am to 7pm from Memorial Day through October, daily 9am to 5pm the rest of the year.

GETTING THERE From Shenandoah National Park, take U.S. 211 west. From I-81, follow U.S. 211 east. From Front Royal, take U.S. 340 south (one of the valley's more scenic drives).

EXPLORING THE CAVERNS

In addition to monumental columns in rooms more than 140 feet high, ✪ **Luray Caverns,** on U.S. 211 east of town, is noted for the beautiful cascades of natural colors found on its interior walls. A U.S. Registered Natural Landmark, it also combines the works of man and nature into an unusual organ with a sound system directly connected to stalactites. Music is produced when the stalactites are electronically tapped by rubber-tipped plungers controlled by an organist or an automated system.

Admission is $13 for adults, $11 for seniors, $6 for children 7 to 13, and free for children under 7. From June 15 to Labor Day, hours are daily from 9am to 7pm; from March 15 to June 14 and from the day after Labor Day to November 14, daily from 9am to 6pm; from November 15 to March 14, Monday through Friday from 9am to 4pm, weekends from 9am to 5pm. Guided tours follow a system of brick and concrete walkways and take about an hour. For more information, call ☎ **540/743-6551** or check out the Web site at **www.luraycaverns.com**.

Admission to the caverns includes the **Historic Car and Carriage Caravan,** a collection of antique carriages, coaches, and cars—including actor Rudolph Valentino's 1925 Rolls Royce. The complex also contains a snack bar, gift shop, and fudge kitchen.

WHERE TO STAY

Just as bed-and-breakfasts proliferated during the 1980s and early 1990s, **mountain cabins** are the latest trend around Luray. Most require at least a week's rental. The visitor center (see "Essentials," above) can provide information about the area's many rental cabins and B&Bs, as well as assist in making reservations.

The **Ramada Inn,** on U.S. 211 northeast of town (☎ **800/2-RAMADA** or 540/743-4521), is surrounded by acres of farmland, giving most rooms mountain views. The **Best Western,** on West Main Street (U.S. 211 Business) in town (☎ **800/528-1234** or 540/743-6511), is an older motel that was recently refurbished. Both have outdoor swimming pools.

The Cabins at Brookside. U.S. 211 East (P.O. Box 346), Luray, VA 22835. ☎ **800/299-2655** or 540/743-5698. Fax 540/743-1326. 8 cabins. A/C. $75–$180 double. AE, DC, DISC, MC, V. From Luray, go east 4¹/₂ miles on U.S. 211. From Shenandoah National Park Headquarters, go west half a mile on U.S. 211.

Owners Bob and Cece Castle remodeled this 1940s roadside service station/motel into a collection of log-look cabins with comfortable Williamsburg-style furnishings throughout. This is the closest accommodation to the Shenandoah National Park. Although located along busy U.S. 211, the rear of the cabins open to decks or sunrooms overlooking a bubbling brook, and road noise dies down after dark. Three "honeymoon" units have Jacuzzis, four have fireplaces, and one has a kitchen (the others, refrigerators only). Morning coffee is delivered to the cabins. The rustic **Brookside Restaurant** on the premises serves inexpensive home cooking.

Luray Caverns Motel West. U.S. 211 Bypass West (P.O. Box 748), Luray, VA 22835. ☎ **540/743-4536.** Fax 540/743-6634. 19 rms, 1 apt. A/C TV TEL. $57–$74 double; $114 apt. AE, DISC, MC, V.

Operated and spotlessly maintained by Luray Caverns, this older one-story motel with a plantation facade sits just across the road from the entrance to the caverns. Although dated, the spacious rooms all have pleasant views across pastureland to the Blue Ridge Mountains.

A sister establishment, the less appealing but equally clean **Luray Caverns Motel East** (☎ **540/743-4531**), is a short distance to the east on U.S. 211 Business.

The Mimslyn Inn. 401 W. Main St. (U.S. 211 Business), Luray, VA 22835. ☎ **800/296-5105** or 540/743-5105. Fax 540/743-2632. 33 rms (all with bath), 13 suites. A/C TV TEL. $64–$84 double; $94–154 suite. AE, DISC, MC, V.

This three-story, colonial-style country inn has been well maintained but not substantially changed since it was built in 1931 on 14 acres of lawns and trees west of the business district. The brick building is fronted by a portico and porch with tall white columns and high-back rockers. New darkwood furniture and modern amenities such as TVs and phones have been added to the medium-size rooms, but they still have their original floor-to-ceiling windows and 1930s bathroom fixtures. Although wear shows here and there, the Mimsyln retains a kind of old-fashioned charm, and the rooms are clean and comfortable. A few suites have living rooms with two walls of paned windows, letting in lots of light. "Family units" have a single bath between two bedrooms. A stunning dining room with large fan-topped windows offers regional fare for breakfast, lunch, and dinner. On the third floor, you'll find a sunroom opening onto a rooftop deck. In the basement, the **Mimsyln Gallery** exhibits the works of noted artist P. Buckley Moss; it's open daily from 10am to 6pm.

A NEARBY EQUESTRIAN INN WITH FINE DINING

Jordan Hollow Farm Inn. 326 Hawksbill Park Rd., Stanley, VA 22851. ☎ **888/418-7000** or 540/778-2285. Fax 540/778-1759. www.jordanhollow.com. 20 rms (all with bath). A/C TV TEL. $110–$154 double. AE, DC, DISC, MC, V. Closed first 2 weeks in Jan. From Luray, take U.S. 340 south 6 miles, turn left on C.R. 624, left on C.R. 689, right on Hawksbill Park Rd. (C.R. 629).

Both equestrians and hikers will enjoy this working farm and inn, which has a stable of horses and ponies and 5 picturesque miles of trails in the foothills of the Blue Ridge. Two types of rooms are offered here: those in the vine-entangled Arbor View are traditional motel-style with an eclectic mix of furnishings, while the units in the log-sided Mare Meadow Lodge are more spacious and sport heavy pine furniture. Trail rides on horseback cost $20 for guests and non-guests alike, while the kids can take 15-minute pony rides for $7. Even if you don't ride, you can visit the barns and pet the horses and ponies.

✪ **The Farmhouse Restaurant,** housed in the original clapboard homestead with wraparound porches upstairs and down, offers some of this area's finest cuisine, along with the best vintages from Virginia wineries. The changing menu may include gourmet-quality tender beef Wellington, fine crab-stuffed shrimp, and mountain trout topped with almonds and a grape butter sauce. Main courses range from $13 to $22. The restaurant serves breakfast to house guests and is open to the public daily from 5:30 to 9:30pm, with a Sunday champagne brunch from 11am to 2:30pm. Reservations are recommended on Friday and Saturday.

WHERE TO DINE

Gulliver's. 55 E. Main St. ☎ **540/743-4460.** Reservations accepted only for Sat dinner. Breakfast and lunch $3.50–$5.50; dinner $6–$14. DISC, MC, V. Mon–Thurs 8am–5pm; Fri–Sat 8am–10:30pm; Sun noon–5pm (summer only). AMERICAN.

Across the street from the visitor center, this converted store dating from Victorian times still has its pressed-tin ceiling and old shelves, now holding books and knick-knacks. With the only cappuccino machine in town, it's the business district's favorite place for morning coffee and fresh-baked pastries, or for a lunch of sandwiches, salads, and admittedly "totally fattening" desserts. Fridays and Saturdays see a limited dinner menu, usually a chicken or fish plate and a light pasta, as well as live entertainment. A rather long climb leads upstairs to a gallery featuring paintings and crafts produced by regional artists and artisans.

Parkhurst Restaurant. U.S. 211, 2^1/$_2$ miles west of Luray Caverns. ☎ **540/743-6009.** Reservations recommended. Main courses $9–$21. AE, DISC, MC, V. Tues–Sat 5–10pm. INTERNATIONAL.

An inn-like ambience pervades Chef George Weddleton's cozy establishment, built in 1938 as a country motel but operated as a restaurant since 1978. A small central dining room has knotty pine paneling, but the choice tables here are in an enclosed veranda with views across the parking lot to the mountains. Plants and quiet music create a romantic atmosphere in which to enjoy a mix of cuisine ranging from Southern fried chicken to veal Oscar (with king crab). Colonial steak is a house variation on prime rib: partially roasted, then finished on the grill with seasoned butter.

A TRIP UP MASSANUTTEN MOUNTAIN

Between Luray and New Market, U.S. 211 climbs over Massunutten Mountain, which splits this part of the Shenandoah Valley in two. Most of the mountain is preserved from development by the **George Washington National Forest,** which has hiking, mountain-biking, and horseback-riding trails, plus campgrounds. You can get information at the **Massanutten Visitors Center,** atop the mountain on U.S. 211 (☎ 540/740-8310). It's open from April 15 to early November, daily from 8am to 4:30pm. For advance information, contact the forest's Lee Ranger District, 109 Molinue Rd., Edinburg, VA 22824 (☎ **540/984-4101**).

From the visitor center, a driving tour begins on C.R. 678, which runs down to Va. 55 via long, narrow Fort Valley, which splits the northern half of Massanutten Mountain into a fork-like shape. The first 7 miles are over hardpacked gravel; the rest of C.R. 678 is paved.

Down in the valley, the privately owned **Fort Valley Riding Stable,** on C.R. 678 (☎ 540/933-6633), offers horseback-riding excursions, and you can camp at the adjacent **Twin Lakes Campground** (same address and phone number).

Not so protected is the mountain's southern end, where **Massanutten Resort,** P.O. Box 1227, Harrisonburg, VA 22801 (☎ **800/207-MASS** or 540/289-9441; www.massresort.com), has installed an 18-hole golf course, numerous tennis courts and swimming pools, and luxury homes and condos, many of them for rent. Massanutten Resort is also one of four places in Virginia with downhill skiing.

6 New Market: A Civil War Battlefield & the Endless Caverns

16 miles W of Luray; 110 miles SW of Washington, D.C.

The little village of New Market holds a hallowed place in the hearts of all Civil War buffs, for it was here in 1864 that the cadets of Virginia Military Institute distinguished themselves in battle against a much larger and more experienced Union force. New Market has been a waystation on the Valley Pike (U.S. 11) since frontier times, and many buildings from that era still stand along Congress Street, the main drag. Congress Street is also a good place to browse for antiques.

ESSENTIALS

VISITOR INFORMATION   The **Shenandoah Valley Travel Association,** P.O. Box 1040, New Market, VA 22844 (☎ **540/740-3132;** fax 540/740-3100), operates a visitor center across I-81 from New Market (Exit 264). The center has a free phone line for hotel reservations, and is open daily from 9am to 5pm.

GETTING THERE   New Market is on U.S. 11 at the junction of U.S. 211 and I-81 (Exit 264).

EXPLORING THE BATTLEFIELD

Even if your knowledge of the Civil War doesn't extend much beyond distinguishing the troops in gray from the troops in blue, you'll be fascinated by the exposition of the Civil War in the Hall of Valor Museum in ✪ **New Market Battlefield Historical Park,** across I-81 from New Market (☎ **540/740-3101**). The park commemorates 257 Virginia Military Institute teenagers, whom Gen. John Breckenridge ordered to New Market in a desperate move to halt advancing Union troops. The boys marched in the rain for 4 days to reach the front line. They charged the enemy on May 15, 1864, won the day, and returned home victorious, with only 10 cadets killed and 47 wounded. Hearing of the battle, Grant exclaimed, "The South is robbing the cradle and the grave."

At the visitor center you can see two films—one about the battle, the other about Stonewall Jackson's Shenandoah campaign. The final Confederate assault on the Union line is covered in a self-guided 1-mile walking tour of the grassy field. In the center of the line of battle was the Bushong farmhouse, today a museum of 19th-century valley life.

The park is open daily from 9am to 5pm. Admission is $5 for adults, $2 for children 6 to 15, and free for children under 6, and includes the battlefield, Hall of Valor Museum, and Bushong Farm. To reach the museum from I-81, Exit 264, take U.S. 211W, then an immediate right onto C.R. 305 (George Collins Parkway); the battlefield park is 1³/₄ miles away, at the end of the road. From Luray, follow U.S. 211W, as above.

EXPLORING THE TOWN & THE CAVERNS

Begin your visit at the Shenandoah Valley Travel Association's visitor center (see "Essentials," above), where you can pick up a walking-tour brochure. Most of the historic buildings, some of them dating to before 1800, are situated along Congress Street (U.S. 11), so you can walk down one side of the street and return on the other.

Be sure to poke your head into the many relic-filled shops you'll pass, including the multi-dealer **Nickelodeon Antique Mall,** in the old firehouse (☎ **540/ 740-3424**).

On the south end of town, off Fairway Drive, the **Shenvalee** was originally part of a plantation whose name is a contraction of Shenandoah, Virginia, and Lee. During World War II, the U.S. State Department used the manor house to keep Italian detainees who had diplomatic rank. The 18-hole golf course, built in 1926, is now open to the public (☎ **540/740-8931**).

The awesome natural beauty of **Endless Caverns,** 3 miles south of town on U.S. 11 (☎ **540/740-3993**), is enhanced by the dramatic use of lighting to display spectacular rooms, each boasting a variety of stalactites, stalagmites, giant columns, and limestone pendants orchestrated into brilliant displays of nature's work. Endless Caverns maintains a year-round temperature of 56°F. **Tours** are given March 15 to June 14, daily from 9am to 5pm; June 15 to Labor Day, daily from 9am to 7pm; the day after Labor Day to November 14, daily from 9am to 5pm; and November

Gentlemen . . . I trust you will do your duty.
                    —Gen. John Breckenridge, Battle of New Market, May 15, 1864
I look back upon that orchard as the most awful spot on the battlefield.
                    —Cadet John C. Howard, Battle of New Market, May 15, 1864

15 to March 14, daily from 9am to 4pm. Admission is $10 for adults, $5 for children 3 to 12, and free for children under 3.

WHERE TO STAY & DINE

The **Quality Inn Shenandoah Valley,** at Exit 264 off I-81 (☎ **800/228-5151** or 540/740-3141), is New Market's only national chain motel. **A Touch of Country Bed & Breakfast** is in a restored old home at 9329 Congress St. (☎ **540/740-8030**).

You'll find the usual national fast-food restaurants at the I-81 interchange. You can also get your arteries hardened in a hurry at the **Southern Kitchen,** U.S. 11 about half a mile south of the interchange (☎ **540/740-3514**), which has green leatherette booths and jukeboxes installed when the place was built in the 1950s. Except for salads, there isn't a single non-fattening item on the menu, but the peanut soup, pan-fried chicken, and cream pies warrant a caloric splurge. Main courses range from $6 to $11; Discover, MasterCard, and Visa are accepted. It's open Sunday through Thursday from 7am to 9pm, Friday and Saturday from 7am to 10pm.

7 Staunton: A Presidential Birthplace

42 miles S of New Market; 142 miles SW of Washington, D.C.; 92 miles NW of Richmond

Settled well before the Revolution, Staunton (pronounced " *Stan*-ton") was a major stop for pioneers on the way west. It was Virginia's capital for 17 days during June 1781, when then-Governor Thomas Jefferson fled Richmond in the face of advancing British troops. When the Central Virginia Railroad arrived in 1854, Staunton became a booming regional center.

Today the town is noted as the birthplace of Woodrow Wilson, our 28th president. Along with Wilson's first home, many of Staunton's 19th-century downtown buildings have been restored and refurbished, including the train station and its adjacent Wharf District (now a shopping and dining complex). The town is also home to a fascinating museum that explains the origins of the unique Shenandoah Valley farming culture. And country music lovers will find another shrine here in the hometown of the Statler Brothers.

ESSENTIALS

VISITOR INFORMATION   Contact the **Staunton/Augusta County Travel Information Center,** P.O. Box 810, Staunton, VA 24404 (☎ **800/332-5219** or 540/332-3972; www.staunton.va.us). There are two visitor centers here: at the Frontier Culture Museum, on U.S. 250 west of Exit 222 of I-81; and at Exit 99 off I-64. Both are open daily from 9am to 5pm. Downtown, the **Staunton Welcome Center** is on the grounds of Woodrow Wilson Birthplace, 24 N. Coalter St. (☎ **540/332-3971**). The centers provide free walking-tour maps to Staunton's historic downtown. You can also tune your radio to AM 1620 for information.

GETTING THERE   Staunton is at the junctions of I-64 and I-81 and U.S. 11 and U.S. 250. Amtrak trains serve Staunton's station at 1 Middlebrook Ave. (☎ **800/872-7245**).

EXPLORING THE TOWN

Downtown Staunton is a treasure trove of Victorian architecture, from stately residences to the commercial buildings downtown and in the adjacent Wharf District (actually along the railroad, not a river). Pick up a walking-tour brochure from one of the visitor centers (see "Essentials," above), and set out on your own. The brochure describes five tours, but be sure to take the "Beverly" and "Wharf" tours, which cover all of historic downtown.

Art lovers, too, will enjoy downtown, which has several galleries and working studios. Be sure to go upstairs at **The Frame Gallery,** 21 N. Market St. (☎ **540/ 885-2697**), which has works by many Virginia artisans. You can see painters, potters, porcelain artists, and glass blowers working at **Avery Studio Gallery,** 115 E. Beverly St. (☎ **540/885-3415**); **Naked Creek Pottery Gallery,** 112 S. New St. (no phone); **Heyward Cutting Jr. Porcelain,** 172-A Greenville Ave. (☎ **540/ 885-4500**); and **Trout Studios Glass,** 162 Greenville Ave. (☎ **540/885-3208**).

Frontier Culture Museum. Richmond Rd. (U.S. 250), half a mile west of I-81. ☎ **540/ 332-7850.** Admission $8 adults, $7.50 seniors, $4 children 6–12, free for children under 6. Mid-Mar to Nov, daily 9am–5pm; Dec to mid-March, daily 10am–4pm.

In light of its history as a major stopping point for pioneers, Staunton is a logical location for this museum, which consists of 17th-, 18th-, and 19th-century working farmsteads representing the origins of the Shenandoah's early settlers—Northern Irish, English, and German—and explaining how aspects of each were blended into a fourth farm, the typical colonial American homestead. Staff members in period costumes plant fields, tend livestock, and do domestic chores.

Statler Brothers Complex. 501 Thornrose Ave. (near Norfolk Ave.). ☎ **540/885-7927.** Free admission. Tours Mon–Fri 2pm. Souvenir shop Mon–Fri 10:30am–3:30pm.

The singing Statler Brothers grew up in Staunton, and after they made it big in Nashville, they bought the old neighborhood elementary school and turned it into their office complex. One tour a day takes visitors through the building and lets them see the brothers' awards and a mass of memorabilia sent to them by adoring fans.

✪ **Woodrow Wilson Birthplace.** 24 N. Coalter St. ☎ **540/885-0897.** Admission $6.50 adults, $5.75 seniors, $2 children 6–12, free for children under 6. Mar–Nov, daily 9am–5pm; Dec–Feb, daily 10am–4pm.

This handsome Greek Revival building, built in 1846 by a Presbyterian congregation as a manse for their ministers, stands beside an excellent museum detailing Wilson's life. As a minister, Wilson's father had to move often, and so the family left Staunton when the future president was only 2. The house is furnished with many family items, including the crib Wilson slept in and the chair in which his mother rocked him. The galleries of the museum next door trace Wilson's Scottish-Irish roots, his academic career as a professor and president at Princeton University, and, of course, his 8 presidential years (1913–21). America's entry into World War I and Wilson's unsuccessful efforts to convince the U.S. Senate to participate in the League of Nations are also explored. Don't overlook the beautiful garden or the carriage house that shelters Wilson's presidential limousine, a shiny Pierce-Arrow.

WHERE TO STAY

On U.S. 250 at Exit 222 off I-81, you'll find the **Best Western Staunton Inn** (☎ 800/528-1234 or 540/885-1112), **Comfort Inn** (☎ 800/228-5150 or 540/ 886-5000), **Econo Lodge** (☎ 800/446-6900 or 540/885-5158), **Hampton Inn** (☎ 800/HAMPTON or 540/886-7000), **Shoney's Inn of Historic Staunton** (☎ 800/222-2222 or 540/885-9193), and **Super 8** (☎ 800/800-8000 or 540/

886-2888). Near Exit 225 (Woodrow Wilson Parkway), the **Holiday Inn Golf & Conference Center** (☎ 800/HOLIDAY or 540/248-6020) is adjacent to the Country Club of Staunton, where guests can play. There also are several bed-and-breakfasts in the area; ask the visitor center for a list.

✪ **Belle Grae Inn.** 515 W. Frederick St., Staunton, VA 24401. ☎ **888/541-5151** or 540/886-5151. Fax 540/886-6641. 18 rms, including suites and small cottage. A/C. $75–$135 double; $135–$155 suite. Packages available. Rates include full breakfast. AE, MC, V. Free parking. From I-81, take Exit 222 west and follow signs to Wilson Birthplace; once there, turn left on Frederick St. to inn.

This beautifully restored 1873 Victorian house, with white gingerbread trim and an Italianate wraparound front porch, sits well back from the street atop a sloping lawn. The property now occupies an entire city block, and most accommodations are in the adjoining 19th-century houses, all of them beautifully restored. Rooms throughout are furnished with period antiques and reproductions, Oriental rugs, wicker pieces, and canopied four-poster, sleigh, and brass beds. Some rooms have fireplaces, and most have phones and TVs. There are also TVs in the Garden Room and the main-house sitting room.

Staunton's finest cuisine is served in the Garden Room and in an adjoining dining room in the main house. "You can eat fried chicken at home," says proprietor Michael Organ. "Here you can have quail." A light-fare menu is also available.

Frederick House. 28 N. New St. (at Frederick St.), Staunton, VA 24401. ☎ **800/334-5575** or 540/885-4220. Fax 540/885-5180. www.frederickhouse.com. E-mail: ejharmon@ frederickhouse.com. 9 rms (all with bath), 8 suites. A/C TV TEL. $75–$115 double; $95–$170 suite. Rates include full breakfast. AE, DC, DISC, MC, V. From I-81, take Exit 222 west and follow the signs to Wilson Birthplace; once there, turn left on Frederick St., left on Augusta St., and left into municipal parking lot to hotel entrance.

Innkeepers Joe and Evy Harmon began converting these five historic town houses—dating from between 1810 and 1910—into a low-key, European-style hotel back in 1984. The rooms and suites are individually decorated with authentic antiques and reproductions from the Victorian era. Five units have fireplaces. Guests are treated to a full breakfast, which might include Evy's apple-raisin quiche, ham and cheese pie, or layers of sausages, cheese, and eggs. Frederick House is across the street from Mary Baldwin College and just 2 blocks from the Wilson Birthplace.

WHERE TO DINE

Staunton's finest dining is at the Belle Grae Inn (see "Where to Stay," above). At the other extreme, **Wright's Dairy Rite,** 346 Greenville Ave. (U.S. 11), a block south of Richmond Road (☎ **540/886-0435**), is a classic drive-in that has had car-hop service since it opened in 1952. Even if you dine inside this brick building, you must lift a phone to place your order with the kitchen and wait for it to be delivered to your red leatherette booth. Nothing here costs more than $5, and no credit cards are accepted. It's open Sunday through Thursday from 10am to 10pm, Friday and Saturday from 10am to 11pm.

✪ **The Beverly Restaurant.** 12 E. Beverly St. (between Augusta and New sts.). ☎ **540/886-4317.** Reservations accepted. Sandwiches $2.50–$4; main courses $3.50–$6.50. MC, V. Mon–Fri 6:30am–7pm; Sat 6:30am–4pm. AMERICAN.

Family-owned and -operated since 1961, this storefront eatery in the heart of the business district hearkens back to that nearly bygone era when even hash-house cooks made everything from scratch. You won't find prepackaged mashed potatoes among the home cooking here. Says co-owner Paul Thomas: "We've got a potato peeler back there that came over on the *Mayflower*." The fresh fare is typically small-town

Southern: rib-eye steaks, fried shrimp or fish, veal cutlets, and roast beef. The Beverly is famous hereabouts for high English tea at 3pm Wednesday and Friday.

The Depot Grille. In Staunton Station, 42 Middlebrook Ave. (at S. Augusta St.). ☎ **540/ 885-7332.** Reservations not necessary. Sandwiches and salads $5.50–$9; main courses $9–$15. AE, DC, DISC, MC, V. Sun–Thurs 11am–10:30pm; Fri–Sat 11am–11:30pm. AMERICAN.

In the Wharf District's restored train station, this popular steak-and-seafood house has a festive atmosphere, highlighted by a long Victorian bar and railroad memorabilia. Seating is in spacious wood-paneled booths or Windsor chairs at small wooden tables. A seasoned crabcake sandwich, with French fries or coleslaw, is $7; a grilled chicken-breast sandwich, $5. Black Angus sirloin for two makes a hearty dinner and comes with salad, fresh bread, potato, and vegetable. A children's menu offers a choice of four entrees, each just $2.

Also in Staunton Station, **The Pullman Restaurant,** 36 Millbrook Ave. (☎ **540/ 885-6612**), is a similar establishment. Nearby in the Wharf District, **J. Ruggles Warehouse** (☎ **540/886-4399**) is a lively restaurant-bar fronting a municipal parking lot on Johnson Street at Central Avenue. Locals describe a visit to these three institutions as pub crawling.

L'Italia Restaurant. 23 E. Beverly St. (between Augusta and New sts.). ☎ **540/885-0102.** Reservations recommended. Lunch $5.50–$9; main courses $7.50–$11. AE, DISC, MC, V. Tues–Thurs 11am–10pm; Fri–Sat 11am–11pm; Sun noon–10pm. ITALIAN.

Next to the dining room at the Belle Grae Inn (see "Where to Stay," above), locals consider the fare at L'Italia to be the best in town, and with good reason, for this pleasant establishment is run by accomplished cooks who moved here from Italy. Guests enter through a nondescript foyer in front of a small bar, but French doors lead to a sophisticated storefront dining room with modern art hung in lighted alcoves. Ceiling spots highlight the black tables and chairs set far apart for privacy. The well-prepared offerings range from Sicilian-style veal parmigiana to northern Italian veal piccata in a sauce of white wine, lemon, and capers.

✪ **Mrs. Rowe's Family Restaurant and Bakery.** Richmond Rd. (U.S. 250), just east of I-81. ☎ **540/886-1833.** Reservations not accepted. Sandwiches $5–$7; main courses $5.50– $14. DISC, MC, V. May–Oct, Mon–Sat 7am–9pm; Sun 7am–7pm. Nov–Apr, Mon–Sat 7am– 8pm; Sun 7am–7pm. Breakfast daily 7–11am year-round. AMERICAN.

Opened in 1947 by Mildred Rowe and still run by her family today, this is one of the better home-style restaurants in Virginia. Made from recipes from Mrs. Rowe's own cookbook, dishes here are very much in the Southern tradition, but tend to be lighter than the usual fare cooked elsewhere with ample portions of lard. Grilled steaks, country ham, pork chops, and fried chicken lead the regular items, but you can also choose from daily specials such as meat loaf and gravy or fried flounder filet, served with two veggies (corn pudding, spoon bread, baked tomatoes, and cucumber-and-onion salads are notable here). The freshly baked pies are so good that locals order slices along with their main courses, just to make sure they get their favorite flavors.

A Picnic Stop

A good place to stop for a picnic lunch midway between Staunton and Lexington is the picturesque **Cyrus McCormick Farm** (☎ **540/377-2255**). From I-81, Exit 205 is well marked to the village of Steele's Tavern and the McCormick Birthplace, but the scenic way to get there from Staunton is via U.S. 11 South. In a lovely rural setting, it contains a small blacksmith shop and other log cabins, where exhibits include a model of McCormick's invention, the first reaper. Hours are daily from 8am to 5pm; admission is free.

OVER THE MOUNTAINS TO MONTEREY

You can scoot along I-81 from Staunton to Lexington, but a scenic detour will take you west across the mountains into Highland County, whose rugged beauty has given it the nickname "Virginia's Switzerland." In fact, the 50-mile drive on U.S. 250 from Staunton to the little town of **Monterey** is one of the state's most scenic excursions. The road first climbs over Shenandoah Mountain (elevation 3,760 feet), at the top of which you'll find a scenic hiking trail in the Confederate breast works park. The winding, two-lane highway then scales Bull Pasture Mountain (elevation 3,240 feet) before descending into Monterey, whose white clapboard churches and Victorian homes conjure up images of New England hamlets. Sitting at more than 2,500 feet elevation, Monterey enjoys a comfortable, springlike climate during summer.

Start your visit here at the **Highland County Chamber of Commerce,** P.O. Box 223, Monterey, VA 24465 (☎ **540/468-2550;** www.cfw.com/~highcc/; e-mail: highcc@cfw.com), whose office is on Main Street next to the Highland Inn. It's open Monday through Friday from 10am to 5pm. There's also an information board in front of the Highland County Court House on Main Street.

Pick up a walking-tour brochure, and then stroll along picturesque Main Street (U.S. 250) past the likes of **H&H Cash Store,** a holdover from the days when general stores sold a little bit of everything, and **Landmark House,** built of logs around 1790. You can also poke your head into several good arts and crafts stores.

The best (and most crowded) time to be here is on the second and third full weekends in March, when Monterey hosts the **Highland Maple Festival,** one of Virginia's top annual events. A smaller version, the Hands and Harvest Festival, is held on Columbus Day weekend in October.

Outdoor enthusiasts can contact **Highland Adventures,** P.O. Box 151, Monterey, VA 24465 (☎ **540/468-2722**), a company specializing in caving, rock climbing, mountain biking, and other outdoor adventures in the Allegheny Highlands of Virginia and West Virginia (reservations are essential).

Accommodations are available in several B&Bs (the chamber has a list) and at the charming **Highland Inn,** on Main Street (☎ **888/466-4682** or 540/468-2143), a veranda-fronted resort hotel built in 1904 but significantly renovated in recent years. Rooms and suites range from $55 to $85. Dinner is served Wednesday through Saturday from 6 to 8pm, and the rustic Black Sheep Tavern has its own menu. Even less expensive is the **Montvalle Motel,** also on Main Street (☎ **540/468-2500**), a plain but comfortable 1950s facility.

From Monterey, another marvelously scenic drive on U.S. 220 takes you 30 miles south along the Jackson River to Warm Springs (see below). From there you can drive back across the mountains to Lexington via Va. 39 and the dramatic Goshen Pass.

8 Warm Springs & Hot Springs: Taking the Waters

Hot Springs: 220 miles SW of Washington, D.C.; 160 miles W of Richmond
Warm Springs: 5 miles N of Hot Springs

At temperatures ranging from 94°F to 104°F, thermal springs rise throughout the mountains and valleys of Bath County, making this highlands region a retreat since the 18th century. (The Homestead, one of the nation's premier spas at Hot Springs, has been in operation since 1766.)

ESSENTIALS

VISITOR INFORMATION   Contact the **Bath County Chamber of Commerce,** Hot Springs, VA 24445 (☎ **800/628-8092** or 540/839-5409). The visitor center is on U.S. 220 near the junction with Main Street, and is open Memorial Day to Labor Day, Monday through Friday from 9am to 5pm, to 4:30pm off-season.

GETTING THERE   U.S. 220 runs north and south through Hot Springs and Warm Springs, with easy access to I-64 at Covington, 20 miles south of Hot Springs. The scenic route is via Va. 39 from Lexington, a 42-mile drive that follows the Maury River through Goshen Pass. You can also take the scenic loop through "Virginia's Switzerland," described in the Staunton section, above.

The nearest place with regular air service is Roanoke Regional Airport; **Woodrum Livery Service** (☎ **540/345-7710**) offers connecting transportation. The nearest Amtrak station is in Clifton Forge. (☎ **800/872-7245**).

TAKING THE WATERS & ENJOYING AN ACCLAIMED SUMMER MUSIC FESTIVAL

The most famous of the thermal springs are the **Jefferson Pools,** which sit in a grove of trees at Warm Springs, at the intersection of U.S. 220 and Va. 39. Opened in 1761, they're still using the octagonal white clapboard bathhouses built in the 19th century (one for men, one for women). The crystal-clear waters of these natural rock pools circulate gently and offer a wonderfully relaxing experience. Hours are mid-April through October, daily from 10am to 6pm; closed November to mid-April. The charge is $12 per 1-hour session. Call ☎ **540/839-5346** for information.

There's music in the mountain air on summer weekends at the **Garth Newel Chamber Music Center,** P.O. Box 240, Warm Springs, VA 24484 (☎ **540/ 839-5018;** fax 540/839-3154), on U.S. 220 between the villages of Warm Springs and Hot Springs. This annual summer chamber music festival has been drawing critical acclaim since the early 1970s. Tickets cost $15. Garth Newell also sponsors a series of unique Music Holiday Weekend Retreats in spring, fall, and winter, including Christmas and New Year's. Accommodations and dining at the on-site Manor House are part of the package. Call or write for details.

WHERE TO STAY & DINE
In Hot Springs

This tiny village lives to serve the Homestead resort (see below). Main Street begins where U.S. 220 circles around the resort and runs for 2 blocks south; here you'll find a country grocery store, several upscale art and clothing dealers (some in the old train depot), an interesting crafts outlet called the Bacova Guild Showroom (☎ **540/ 839-2105**), and the Homestead-owned Sam Snead's Tavern (see below).

✪ **The Homestead.** Hot Springs, VA 24445. ☎ **800/838-1766** or 540/839-1776. Fax 540/ 839-7670. 440 rms, 81 suites. A/C MINIBAR TV TEL. $125–$186 double per person; $199–$473 suite per person. Children under 5 stay free in parents' rm, children 5–12 pay $34 per day extra, children 13–18 pay $56 extra. Higher rates charged during holidays. Weekend, golf, and other packages available. Rates include breakfast, dinner, and afternoon tea. AE, DC, DISC, MC, V. Free parking. The main entrance is off U.S. 220.

With a prodigious reputation dating back to 1766, this famous spa and golf resort has been host to Presidents Jefferson, Wilson, Hoover, F.D.R., Truman, Eisenhower, Carter, and Reagan, plus social elites like the Henry Fords, John D. Rockefeller, the Vanderbilts, and Lord and Lady Astor.

Two mountains flank the hotel's main building of red Kentucky brick with white-limestone trim. Guests enter via the magnificent Great Hall, lined with 16 Corinthian columns and a 211-foot floral carpet. Two fireplaces, wing chairs, Chippendale-reproduction tables with reading lamps, and deep sofas create a warm atmosphere.

Afternoon tea is served here daily to the classical music of the piano in the background.

Guests have a variety of accommodations in rooms and suites with a Virginia country-manor ambience and custom-designed mahogany furniture. Most units offer spectacular mountain views, and the 81 suites in the South Wing have working fireplaces, private bars, sun porches, two TVs, and two phones.

Dining/Entertainment: The Homestead's historic Dining Room is a lush palm court, in which an orchestra performs every evening during six-course dinners. The adjoining Commonwealth Room is adorned with murals of Virginia landmarks, such as Mount Vernon and Monticello. Tables throughout are elegantly appointed. Under the supervision of European-trained chefs, the cuisine features regional favorites like fresh rainbow trout, grilled lamb chops, and roast beef with Armagnac sauce. Cocktails, hors d'oeuvres, and after-dinner espresso are served in the View Lounge. Other dining options include the Homestead's signature restaurant, The Grille, and casual dining in the Casino and in Café Albert (named for the head chef, Albert Schnarwyler, who's been here since 1962). Across Main Street from the hotel, Sam Snead's Tavern is a lively pub serving traditional American fare (open Wednesday through Monday from 5 to 10pm). Evening entertainment includes live music, dancing, and free movies.

Guests may don casual resort wear during the day, including shorts of respectable length, but men must wear jackets and long pants after dark, with both jackets and ties required in the Dining Room.

Services: Concierge, room service, travel agency, children's programs.

Facilities: Three outstanding golf courses (Lanny Wadkins is the resident PGA pro), indoor and outdoor pools, spa with full health club facilities, 12 tennis courts, bowling, fishing, hiking trails, horseback and carriage rides, ice-skating on an Olympic-size rink, lawn bowling and croquet, billiards, sporting clays and skeet trap, downhill and cross-country skiing mid-December to March, warm springs pools, horseshoes, volleyball, video game room, board games, beauty salon, 21 boutique and specialty shops. *Note:* Non-guests can pay to use all of the Homestead's facilities except the indoor pool, provided they reserve a day in advance.

✪ **Roseloe Motel.** U.S. 220 N. (Route 2, Box 590), Hot Springs, VA 24445. ☎ **540/ 839-5373.** 14 rms. A/C TV TEL. $46–$53 double. AE, DC, DISC, MC, V. Free parking. From Hot Springs, go north 3 miles on U.S. 220.

At the opposite extreme from the Homestead, this brick-fronted, family-owned motel offers inexpensive, well-maintained, and clean rooms virtually across the highway from the Garth Newel Chamber Music Center. Four units have full kitchens, while two have kitchenettes. The others have refrigerators.

In Warm Springs

A charming little community with many historic homes, Warm Springs revolves around its thermal pools, described above. There's an unstaffed visitor center kiosk, on U.S. 220 just south of the Va. 39 junction, which usually has copies of a walking-tour brochure to the little village (if it doesn't, the Bath County Chamber of Commerce in Hot Springs does).

Anderson Cottage Bed & Breakfast. Old Germantown Rd. (Box 176), Warm Springs, VA 24484. ☎ **540/839-2975.** 2 rms (1 with shared bath), 2 suites, separate guest cottage. $60– $125 per night double. Rates include full breakfast. No credit cards. From Va. 39, turn left onto Old Germantown Rd. (C.R. 692), to fourth house on the left.

One of Bath County's oldest buildings, this log-and-white-clapboard cottage has been in owner Jean Randolph Bruns's family since the 1870s. The setting is an expansive lawn with a warm stream flowing through the property in the heart of the picturesque village. The house has appealing country charm, with many family heirloom pieces and photos, wide-board floors, Oriental rugs, working fireplaces, and lots of loaded bookcases. Accommodations are individually decorated and exceptionally spacious. Originally an 1820s brick kitchen, the Guest Cottage is ideal for families, with two bedrooms, two baths, a full kitchen/dining/sitting room with fireplace, and a living room.

Inn at Gristmill Square. C.R. 645 (Box 359), Warm Springs, VA 24484. ☎ **540/839-2231.** Fax 540/839-5770. E-mail: grist@va.tds.net. 16 rms, 1 suite. A/C TV TEL. $80–$100 double. Rates include continental breakfast. Modified American Plan (also including 5-course dinner and gratuities) $155–$165 double. DISC, MC, V. Free parking. From U.S. 220N, turn left onto C.R. 619 and right onto C.R. 645.

Five restored 19th-century buildings, including an old mill, make up this unique hostelry. It includes the Blacksmith Shop, which houses a country store; the Hardware Store, with seven guest units; the Steel House, with four units; and the Miller's House, with four rooms. Furnishings are charming period pieces, with comfortable upholstered chairs, brass chandeliers, quilts on four-poster beds, marble-top side tables, and working fireplaces. Breakfast is served in your room in a picnic basket. Other facilities include an outdoor pool, three tennis courts, and sauna.

The rustic Waterwheel Restaurant and Simon Kenton Pub are cozy spots in the old mill building. The restaurant features notably good American cuisine, with entrees like grilled trout, pork Calvados, and filet of salmon with béarnaise sauce. Wines are displayed among the gears of the waterwheel. The restaurant also serves Sunday brunch.

A NEARBY COUNTRY INN

✪ **Fort Lewis Lodge.** HCR 3, Box 21A, Millboro, VA 24460. ☎ **540/925-2314.** Fax 540/925-2352. 13 rms, 2 cabins. $135–$155 double. MC, V. Free parking. From Warm Springs, go 13 miles east on Va. 39, turn left on Indian Draft Rd. (C.R. 678) and drive north 10.8 miles, then turn left on Indian Rd. (C.R. 625) to entrance.

You'll discover one of Virginia's most unusual country inns at John and Caryl Cowden's farm beside the Cowpasture River, which cuts a north-south valley over the mountain from Warm Springs. Most guest quarters here are in a reconstructed barn, but an outside spiral staircase leads to three rooms inside the attached silo. One end of the rough-look barn is now a comfortable lounge with stone fireplace and large windows looking out to a Jacuzzi-equipped deck to the farmland and mountains beyond. Other guests stay in hand-hewn log cabins, each with a fireplace.

The Cowdens' summertime garden supplies flowers and vegetables for excellent meals served in the old Lewis Mill, whose upstairs has been turned into a game room. A screened porch to one side shelters Buck's Bar, which serves beer and wine. Activities include biking, hiking, and swimming and fishing for trout in the Cowpasture River. Fort Lewis Lodge is very popular with families getting away from Washington, D.C., and other nearby cities, so book early.

9 Lexington: A College Town with a Slice of American History

36 miles S of Staunton; 180 miles SW of Washington, D.C.; 138 miles W of Richmond

A lively college atmosphere prevails in Lexington, which consistently ranks as one of America's best small towns. Fine old homes line tree-shaded streets, among them the house where Stonewall Jackson lived when he taught at Virginia Military Institute.

A beautifully restored downtown looks so much like it did in the 1800s that scenes for the recent movie *Sommersby* were filmed on Main Street (Richard Gere was "hanged" behind the Jackson House while Jodie Foster looked on). After the Civil War, Robert E. Lee came to Lexington to serve as president of what was then Washington College; he and his horse Traveller are buried here. And Gen. George C. Marshall, winner of the Nobel Peace Prize for his post–World War II plan to rebuild Europe, graduated from VMI, which has built a fine museum in his memory.

Washington and Lee University has one of the oldest and most beautiful campuses in the country. Built in 1824, Washington Hall is topped by a replica of a masterpiece of American folk art, an 1840 carved-wood statue of George Washington. The massive trees dotting the campus are believed to have been planted by Lee.

Sometimes called the West Point of the South, VMI opened in 1839 on the site of a state arsenal, abutting the Washington and Lee campus (one school has brick walkways; the other, concrete). The most dramatic episode in VMI's history took place during the Civil War at the Battle of New Market on May 15, 1964, when the corps of cadets helped turn back a larger Union army (see the New Market section, above). A month later, Union Gen. David Hunter got even, bombarding Lexington and burning down VMI.

If you have time to stop in only one Shenandoah Valley town, make it lovely Lexington.

ESSENTIALS

VISITOR INFORMATION   The **Visitor Center,** 106 E. Washington St., Lexington, VA 24450 (☎ **540/463-3777;** fax 540/463-1105; e-mail: lexington@rockbridge.net), is a block east of Main Street. Begin your tour of Lexington at this excellent source of information, for it offers museum-like displays about the town's history, distributes free walking-tour brochures, and can make same-day hotel reservations. Be sure to see the engrossing slide show on Lexington's history. The center is open daily from 8:30am to 6pm June through August, from 9am to 5pm the rest of the year.

GETTING THERE   Lexington is on both I-81 and I-64, and U.S. 60 and U.S. 11 go directly into town.

EXPLORING THE TOWN

Be sure to pick up a free **walking-tour** brochure at the visitor center. It explains Lexington's many historic buildings and contains one of the best maps of downtown.

Ghost Tour of Lexington (☎ **540/348-1080**) conducts 1¼-hour nighttime walks through the streets, back alleys, and Stonewall Jackson Cemetery from late May to October. Cost is $8 for adults, $6 for children 4 to 10, and free for children under 4. Purchase tickets in advance at Shear Timing Hair Salon, 17 S. Randolph St.

Seeing the sights is easy and enjoyable via **Lexington Carriage Company** (☎ **540/463-5647**), whose horse-drawn carriages depart from the visitor center for 45-minute narrated tours daily from 9am to 5pm during the summer, from 10am to 4:30pm during April, May, September, and October. Fares are $10 for ages 14 to 64, $9 for seniors, $6 for ages 7 to 13, $3 for ages 4 to 6, and $1 for kids under 4.

You also can get around on bicycles rented from **Rockbridge Outfitters Ltd.,** 112 W. Washington St. (☎ **540/463-1947**), across the street from the W&L campus. Rates are $4 per hour with a 3-hour minimum, or $24 for a full day.

✪ **George C. Marshall Museum.** VMI Campus. ☎ **540/463-7103.** Admission $3 adults, $2 seniors, $1 children. Mar–Oct, daily 9am–5pm; Nov–Feb, daily 9am–4pm.

This impressive white building houses the archives and research library of General of the Army George C. Marshall. A 1901 graduate of VMI, Marshall had an illustrious career, including service in France in 1917, when he was aide-de-camp to General Pershing. In World War II, he was army chief of staff, then secretary of state and secretary of defense under President Truman. He is best remembered for the Marshall Plan, which fostered the economic recovery of Europe after the war. For his role in promoting peace, he became the first career soldier to be awarded the Nobel Peace Prize.

✪ Lee Chapel and Museum. Washington and Lee University. ☎ **540/463-8768.** Free admission. Mid-Oct to mid-Apr, Mon–Sat 9am–4pm. Mid-Apr to mid-Oct, Mon–Sat 9am–5pm; Sun 2–5pm. Washington and Lee University borders Washington St., Jefferson St., and Letcher Ave. The chapel is closest to Letcher Ave.

This magnificent Victorian-Gothic chapel of brick and native limestone, today used for concerts and other events, was built in 1867 at the request of General Lee. A white-marble sculpture of Lee by Edward Valentine portrays the general recumbent. Lee's remains are in a crypt below the chapel. His office was in the lower level of the building, now part of the chapel museum and preserved just as he left it on September 28, 1870. His beloved horse, Traveller, is buried in a plot outside the office.

Among the museum's most important possessions are Charles Willson Peale's portrait of George Washington wearing the uniform of a colonel in the British Army and the painting of General Lee in Confederate uniform by Theodore Pine. The two portraits hang in the chapel auditorium.

Museum of Military Memorabilia. 122$^{1}/_{2}$ S. Main St. (in the alley beside the Presbyterian Church). ☎ **540/464-3041.** Admission $4 adults and children, $3 seniors. Tours May–Oct, Wed–Sat 11am–4:15pm. Closed Nov–Apr.

This small but fascinating museum displays a collection of military uniforms and various bits of soldiers' gear, with the oldest dating from 1740 in Prussia and the newest from the 1991 Persian Gulf War. The uniforms come from several different countries and represent a number of conflicts. You'll also see insignia, flags, a few weapons, trench art from World War I, and a piece of the Berlin Wall. You must take the 45-minute guided tour in order to view the exhibits.

✪ Stonewall Jackson House. 8 E. Washington St. (between Main and Randolph sts.). ☎ **540/463-2552.** Admission $5 adults, $2.50 children 6–12, free for children under 6. Mon–Sat 9am–5pm, Sun 1–5pm; open until 6pm in summer. Guided tours begin on the hour and half hour (last tour at 4:30pm). Closed New Year's Day, Easter, Thanksgiving, and Christmas.

Maj. Thomas Jonathan Jackson came to Lexington in 1851 to take a post as teacher of natural philosophy (physics) and artillery tactics at VMI. Jackson lived here with his wife, Mary Anna Morrison, from early 1859 until he answered General Lee's summons to Richmond in 1861; it was the only house he ever owned. Photographs, text, and a slide show tell the story of the Jacksons' stay here. Appropriate period furnishings duplicate the items on the inventory of Jackson's estate made shortly after he died near Chancellorsville in 1863. His body was returned to Lexington and buried in Stonewall Jackson Memorial Cemetery on South Main Street.

Virginia Horse Center. Va. 39, west of U.S. 11 and north of I-64. ☎ **540/463-7060.** Admission varies by event; most are free. Open year-round. From downtown, take U.S. 11 north, turn left on Va. 39 a tenth of a mile north of I-64. The center is 1 mile on the left.

Sprawling across nearly 400 acres, the Virginia Horse Center offers horse shows, educational seminars, and sales of fine horses. Annual events include draft pulls, rodeos, various competitions, and competitive breed shows. In April, the center holds a Horse

Impressions

Let us cross the river and rest under the shade of the trees.
— Stonewall Jackson's last words, May 10, 1863

Festival showcasing the entire Virginia industry. For a full program of events, contact the center at P.O. Box 1051, Lexington, VA 24450.

✪ **Virginia Military Institute Museum.** Jackson Memorial Hall, VMI Campus. ☎ **540/464-7232.** Free admission. Daily 9am–5pm.

The VMI Museum displays uniforms, weapons, and memorabilia from cadets who attended the college and fought in numerous wars. Of special note: the world-famous H.M. Steward Antique Firearm Collection; the VMI *coatee* (or tunic) that belonged to Gen. George S. Patton, Jr., VMI 1907; Stonewall Jackson's uniform coat worn at VMI and the bullet-pierced raincoat he was wearing when accidentally shot by his own men at Chancellorsville; and, thanks to taxidermy, Jackson's unflappable war horse, Little Sorrel.

THE NATURAL BRIDGE

Thomas Jefferson called this hugely impressive limestone formation "the most sublime of nature's works . . . so beautiful an arch, so elevated, so light and springing, as it were, up to heaven." The bridge was part of a 157-acre estate Jefferson acquired in 1774 from George III. It was included in the survey of western Virginia carried out by George Washington, who carved his initials into the face of the stone. This geological oddity rises 215 feet above Cedar Creek; its span is 90 feet long and spreads at its widest to 150 feet. The Monocan Indian tribes worshipped it as "the bridge of God." Today it is also the bridge of man, as U.S. 11 passes over it.

The Natural Bridge is now a small tourist-industry enclave, with a cavern, department-store–size souvenir shop, restaurant, hotel, campground, wax museum, and zoo. During summer, a 45-minute sound-and-light show called *The Drama of Creation* begins at dusk beneath the bridge.

The bridge is 12 miles south of Lexington on U.S. 11 (take Exit 175 off I-81). Admission to the bridge is $8 for adults, $4 for children 6 to 15. Combination tickets including the bridge, wax museum, and caverns cost $15 for adults, $7.50 for children 6 to 15. The bridge itself is open daily from 8am to dusk. For more information, call ☎ **800/533-1410** or 540/291-2121.

SHOPPING

Lexington's charming 19th-century downtown offers many interesting shops, most of them on Main and Washington streets. **Artists in Cahoots,** in the Alexander-Witherow House, at the corner of Main and Washington (☎ **540/464-1147**), a co-operative venture run by local artists and craftspeople, features an outstanding selection of paintings, sculptures, wood and metal crafts, hand-painted silk scarves, handblown glass, Shaker-style furniture, photographs, prints, decoys, stained glass, and jewelry. **Virginia Born & Bred,** 16 W. Washington St. (☎ **540/463-1832**), has made-in-Virginia gifts.

Antiques hunters will find fascinating browsing at the **Lexington Antique & Craft Mall** (☎ **540/463-9511**), in which 250 dealers occupy 40,000 square feet of space. They offer country and formal furniture, glassware, books, quilts, folk art, and much more. The mall is located in the Kroger Shopping Center on U.S. 11, about half a mile north of downtown. It's open Monday through Thursday from 10am to 6pm,

Friday and Saturday from 10am to 8pm, Sunday from 12:30 to 5pm; winter hours vary.

OUTDOOR PURSUITS

CANOEING, KAYAKING & RAFTING   The Maury River, which runs through Lexington, provides some of Virginia's best white-water rafting and kayaking, especially through the Goshen Pass, on Va. 39 northwest of town. The visitor center has information about several put-in spots, or you can rent equipment or go on expeditions on the Maury and James rivers with **James River Basin Canoe Livery,** U.S. 60 East (Route 4, Box 125), Lexington, VA 24450 (☎ 540/261-7334; www.virtualcities.com/ons/va/r/varb501.htm; e-mail: canoeva@rockbridge.net). Call, write, or e-mail for schedules and reservations.

HIKING   Two linear parks connect to offer hikers and joggers nearly 10 miles of gorgeous trail between Lexington and Buena Vista, a railroad town 7 miles to the southeast. The major link is the **Chessie Nature Trail,** which follows an old railroad bed along the Maury River between Lexington and Buena Vista. No vehicles (including bicycles) are allowed, but you can cross-country ski the trail during winter. The Chessie trail connects with a walking path in **Woods Creek Park,** which starts at the Waddell School on Jordan Street and runs down to the banks of the Maury. Both trails are open from dawn to dusk. The visitor center has maps and brochures.

There are excellent hiking, mountain-biking, horseback-riding, and all-terrain-vehicle trails in the **George Washington National Forest,** which encompasses much of the Blue Ridge Mountains east of Lexington. Small children might not be able to make it, but the rest of the family will enjoy the 3-mile trail up to **Crabtree Falls,** a series of cascades tumbling 1,200 feet down the mountain (it's the highest waterfall in Virginia). Heartier hikers can scale on up to the Appalachian Trail at the top of the mountain. Crabtree Falls is on Va. 56 east of the Blue Ridge Parkway; from Lexington, go north on I-81 to Steeles Tavern (Exit 205), then east on Va. 56.

The National Forest Service has an **information office** at Natural Bridge (☎ 540/291-1806), which offers free maps of trails and campgrounds. It's open daily from 9:30am to 5:30pm, April to mid-November. Or you can contact the Glenwood Ranger District, George Washington and Jefferson National Forests, P.O. Box 10, Natural Bridge Station, VA 24579 (☎ **540/291-2188**).

WHERE TO STAY

Lexington has several chain motels, especially at the intersection of U.S. 11 and I-64 (Exit 55), 1 1/2 miles north of downtown. They include the **Best Western Inn at Hunt Ridge** (☎ 800/464-1501 or 540/464-1500), **Comfort Inn** (☎ 800/628-1956 or 540/463-7311), **Econo Lodge** (☎ 800/446-6900 or 540/463-7371), **Holiday Inn Express** (☎ 800/HOLIDAY or 540/463-7351), and **Super 8** (☎ 800/800-8000 or 540/463-7858).

✪**Hampton Inn Col Alto.** 401 E. Nelson St., Lexington, VA 24450. ☎ **800/HAMPTON** or 540/463-2223. Fax 540/463-9707. 86 rms. A/C TV TEL. $78–$122 double motel room; $150–$250 in manor house. Rates include continental breakfast. AE, DC, DISC, MC, V.

This is certainly no ordinary Hampton Inn—Col Alto is an 1827 manor house built on a plantation that was then on the outskirts of town. Recently remodeled, the mansion now houses 10 bedrooms comparable to those found in deluxe country inns or B&Bs. An interior designer individually decorated these luxurious quarters with made-in-Virginia linens, reproduction antiques, and bright, vivid paints, wallpapers, and fabrics. Accommodations range in size from huge, light-filled rooms on the front of the house to smaller but more private ones in the rear. One unit even has a round window of the style much favored by Thomas Jefferson. Two formal parlors on the first floor are available for mansion guests only, who can also choose to have breakfast and the morning newspaper delivered to their rooms. Guests in both the mansion and the new, L-shaped motel wing next door can enjoy continental breakfast in the original dining room. The motel rooms are somewhat larger than average and have microwave ovens, coffeemakers, robes, and irons and ironing boards; some have balconies overlooking a courtyard with outdoor swimming pool.

HISTORIC COUNTRY INNS

Make reservations for Alexander-Witherow House, McCampbell Inn, and Maple Hall through **Historic Country Inns,** 11 N. Main St., Lexington, VA 24450 (☎ **540/463-2044;** fax 540/463-2044; www.innbook.com).

Alexander-Witherow House and McCampbell Inn. 11 N. Main St. ☎ **540/463-2044.** 15 rms, 8 suites. A/C TV TEL. $60–$125 double; $145 suite. Rates include continental breakfast. DISC, MC, V. Free parking behind the McCampbell Inn.

The Alexander-Witherow House is a lovely late Georgian town house built in 1789 as a family residence over a store. The ground floor is occupied by Artists in Cahoots (see "Shopping," above). Accommodations are all homey suites with separate living rooms and small kitchens. Comfortable furnishings include wing chairs, four-poster beds, and hooked rugs on wide-board floors. The McCampbell Inn, across Main Street, houses the main office for Historic Country Inns; guests at both hostelries eat breakfast here. Begun in 1809, with later additions in 1816 and 1857, it occupies a rambling building, with rooms facing both Main Street and the quieter back courtyard. Furnishings are a pleasant mix of antiques and reproductions; all units have wet bars and refrigerators.

✪ **Maple Hall.** On U.S. 11. ☎ **540/463-6693.** 21 rms and suites. A/C TV. $100–$165 double. Rates include breakfast. MC, V. Free parking. Take U.S. 11, 7 miles north of town; house is near Exit 195 of I-81.

Set on 56 rolling acres, this handsome red-brick, white-columned 1850 plantation house offers a restful country retreat. Old boxwoods surround the inn, which consists of a main house, a restored Guest House, and a Pond House. Rooms are individually furnished, many with antiques, Oriental rugs, and massive Victorian pieces; 10 units have gas fireplaces. The Guest House has a living room, kitchen, and three bedrooms with baths. The Pond House, added in 1990, contains four suites and two mini-suites. Guests relax on the shaded patio, on porches with rocking chairs, and on back verandas overlooking the fishing pond and nearby hills. A pool, tennis court, and 3-mile hiking trail are on-site.

Elegant dining in pretty garden-like surroundings attracts a good following to the Maple Hall restaurant, open daily for dinner. Specialties might include grilled quail, chicken breast sauté Provençal, and filet mignon wrapped in bacon and served with béarnaise sauce.

BED & BREAKFASTS

In addition to those mentioned below, Lexington has several other bed-and-breakfasts; the visitor center offers a complete list.

Llewellyn Lodge. 603 S. Main St., Lexington, VA 24450. ☎ **800/882-1145** or 540/463-3235. Fax 540/464-3122. E-mail: LLL@rockbridge.net. 6 rms (all with bath). A/C TV. $65–$98 double. Rates include full breakfast. AE, DISC, MC, V. Free on-site parking.

A 55-year-old brick colonial-style house, the Llewellyn Lodge is within easy walking distance of all of Lexington's historic sites. On the first floor are a cozy sitting room with working fireplace and a TV room. Guest rooms are decorated in exceptionally pretty color schemes. All rooms have ceiling fans, and three have TVs. Co-host John Roberts has hiked just about every trail and fished every stream in the Blue Ridge Mountains; he is a font of information on outdoor activities.

Seven Hills Inn. 408 S. Main St., Lexington, VA 24450. ☎ **888/845-3801** or 540/463-4715. Fax 540/463-6526. 7 rms (6 with bath). A/C. $80–$125 double. Rates include full breakfast. MC, V. Free on-site parking.

Built in 1928 as a fraternity house, this three-story brick colonial was later a boys' home, then a girls' home, and since 1990 has been a luxury bed-and-breakfast. All rooms are spacious, with antique reproductions, four-poster beds, and large baths (one has a Jacuzzi tub). A plethora of English and Japanese antiques graces the public rooms on the first floor. The basement has a large paneled TV lounge, where smoking is permitted. A professional innkeeper provides gourmet breakfasts featuring such goodies as Virginia ham biscuits and deep-dish Swedish pancakes.

WHERE TO DINE

While you're walking around town, stop in at Lexington's famous **Sweet Things,** 106 W. Washington St., between Jefferson Street and Lee Avenue (☎ **540/463-6055**), for a cone or cup of "designer" ice cream or frozen yogurt. Television weatherman Willard Scott raves about the fresh pastries at **Country Kitchen Bakery,** 8 N. Main St., between Washington and Henry streets (☎ **540/463-5691**). It's open Tuesday through Friday from 7am to 5pm, Saturday from 7am to 2pm, and is a great place for breakfast.

Harbs'. 19 W. Washington St. (between Main and Jefferson sts.). ☎ **540/464-1900.** Sandwiches $3–$6; main courses $8–$13. MC, V. Summer Mon–Thurs 8am–3pm; Fri–Sat 8am–10pm; Sun 9am–3pm. Rest of year Mon 8am–8pm; Tues–Thurs 8am–10pm; Fri–Sat 8am–11pm; Sun 9am–3pm. AMERICAN.

A favorite among university students and townsfolk, Harbs' has a French bistro look, with black and white tile floors, small cafe tables, walls hung with work by local artists, and, in fine weather, alfresco dining on the back patio. Good mornings begin at Harbs' with oversize muffins, bagels, or Belgian waffles with a steaming cup of coffee. Lunch and dinner feature an array of sandwiches—hero-size or on wholewheat, Branola, or rye bread or a pita or kaiser roll. Pitas are stuffed with tangy hummus or tabbouleh and vegetables. A chicken taco salad is also a good lunchtime choice. The dinner menu changes often and might include blackened tuna with pink and green peppercorns. During the school year, Harbs' often features evening entertainment, such as classical or bluegrass music or a poetry reading.

✪ Willson-Walker House Restaurant. 30 N. Main St. (between Washington and Henry sts.). ☎ **540/463-3020.** Reservations requested at dinner. Lunch $5–$8; main courses $10–$19. AE, MC, V. Tues–Sat 11:30am–2:30pm and 5:30–9pm. Closed for Sat lunch Jan–Mar. AMERICAN.

Occupying the first floor of an 1820 Greek Revival home, this distinctive restaurant, furnished with period antiques, offers some of the valley's finest cuisine. In good weather, the most popular tables are on first- and second-floor verandas behind massive two-story white columns. At lunch, the $5 chef's special includes choice of soup or salad, entree, homemade muffins and rolls, and beverage. Changing weekly, the menu offers such tempting starters as crêpes filled with Scottish smoked salmon, dill cream cheese, capers, and red onions. Main courses might include lobster medallions with papaya crème Anglaise, sautéed sea scallops with pink grapefruit buerre blanc, or roast pork loin with Granny Smith apples and fresh ginger cream.

The Palms. 101 W. Nelson St. (at Jefferson St.). ☎ **540/463-7911.** Sandwiches and salads $5–$7; main courses $6.50–$15. DISC, MC, V. Mon–Tues 10am–1am; Wed–Sat 10am–2am; Sun 10am–11pm. AMERICAN.

With neon palms in its storefront window, this popular pub offers a congenial setting for hearty meals. Deli sandwiches run the gamut from roast beef to smoked turkey. Mexican specialties like tacos and burritos spice up the menu. Dinner entrees, served with soup or salad, vegetable, and bread, include choices like baby-back ribs, grilled mahimahi, and fettuccine Alfredo. At lunch or dinner, the hearty burgers will not disappoint. The Palms serves Sunday brunch and has a full bar with five sports TVs.

LEXINGTON AFTER DARK

The ruins of an old limestone kiln provide the backdrop for the open-air **Theater at Lime Kiln,** Borden Road off U.S. 60W (☎ **540/463-3074**), which presents musicals, plays, and concerts from Memorial Day to Labor Day at 8pm. Productions have ranged from a Civil War epic called *Stonewall Country,* based on Jackson's life, to Shakespeare, Appalachian folktales, and even water puppeteers from Vietnam. Tickets to plays and musicals are $7 to $15, and concerts run $6 to $20; seniors and students pay $2 less for plays. To reach the theater from downtown Lexington, take U.S. 11 south and turn right onto U.S. 60W.

Roanoke & the Southwest Highlands

You soon notice after leaving the vibrant, railroad-oriented city of Roanoke that I-81 begins to climb as it heads into Virginia's Southwest Highlands, the state's increasingly narrow "tail" hemmed in by West Virginia, Kentucky, Tennessee, and North Carolina. Down the center of the Highlands runs the rolling Great Valley of Virginia, whose floor averages 2,000 feet in altitude. Just as they delineate the Shenandoah Valley, the Blue Ridge Mountains form the eastern boundary of the Southwest Highlands, but here are dwarfed by the ridges to the west. While peaks above 4,000 feet are rare up in the Shenandoah, here they regularly exceed that altitude, with Mount Rogers reaching 5,729 feet, the highest point in Virginia.

Thousands of acres of this beautiful country are preserved in the Jefferson National Forest and in Mount Rogers National Recreation Area, which rivals the Shenandoah National Park with 300 miles of hiking and riding trails, including its own stretch of the Appalachian Trail. Two other major walks, the Virginia Creeper and New River Trails, lure hikers to follow old railroad beds along river banks.

The Highlanders are justly proud of their history, which includes Daniel Boone's blazing the Wilderness Road through these mountains, plateaus, and hollows to Cumberland Gap and on into Kentucky. Gorgeous Abingdon and other small towns still have log cabins from those frontier days.

The Highlanders have also preserved their ancient arts, crafts, and renowned mountain music. Abingdon hosts both Virginia's official state theater and its Highlands Festival, one of America's top annual arts and crafts shows. The coal-mining town of Big Stone Gap has its own drama about mountain life. The famous Carter family makes mountain music at tiny Maces Spring, and fiddlers from around the world gather every August for their old-time convention at Galax.

Whether you love history, drama, music, arts, crafts, the great outdoors, or all of the above, you will be enchanted with Virginia's beautiful Southwest Highlands.

EXPLORING THE SOUTHWEST HIGHLANDS

VISITOR INFORMATION A one-stop source for regional information is the **Highlands Gateway Visitor Center,** Drawer B-12, Max Meadows, VA 24360 (☎ **800/446-9670** or 540/637-6766). Funded by the National Forest Service, this state-of-the-art center is located in the Factory Merchants Outlet Mall, 10 miles northeast of

Wytheville at Exit 80 off the joint I-81/I-77. It offers brochures from all towns in the region, a touch-screen computer, and a small theater showing a video about the Highlands. It sells National Forest topographical maps, Appalachian Trail maps and guide books—even mountain music tapes and Smokey the Bear dolls. The center is open Monday through Saturday from 9am to 5pm (10am to 5pm in January and February), Sunday from noon to 5pm.

GETTING THERE & GETTING AROUND   Given the distances, the lack of public transportation, and the need to be able to explore the area's spectacular scenery at leisure, traveling by car is the only way to go. I-81 runs the entire length of the highlands and is its major thoroughfare. U.S. 11 follows I-81, and the Blue Ridge Parkway parallels it to the east. I-77 cuts north-south through the center of the region (the section from Wytheville north to Bluefield, W. Va., is one of America's most dramatically scenic interstates). Otherwise, byways in the region are mountain roads—narrow, winding, and sometimes steep—so give yourself ample time to reach your destination.

The area's only air gateway is Roanoke Regional Airport (see "Getting There By Plane" under " Roanoke: City Below a Star," below). The nearest Amtrak station is in Clifton Forge, 45 miles northwest of Roanoke on I-64. Amtrak has a Thruway bus connection from Clifton Forge to Roanoke. For information call ☎ **800/872-7245.**

1 The Blue Ridge Parkway

Maintained by the National Park Service, the 470-mile Blue Ridge Parkway links the Shenandoah National Park in Virginia to the Great Smoky Mountains National Park in North Carolina. It begins at the southern terminus of the Skyline Drive and winds southwest through the Blue Ridge Mountains. Magnificent vistas and the natural beauty of the forests, wildlife, and wildflowers combine with pioneer history to make this a fascinating route.

Consider driving between Lexington and Roanoke via the northern section. Beyond Roanoke, the parkway runs through lower country, with more meadows and less mountain scenery. On the other hand, the 62-mile stretch between Otter Creek south to Roanoke Mountain crosses the James River Gorge; climbs Apple Orchard Mountain, the highest parkway point in Virginia (elevation 3,950 feet); and has the most spectacular overlooks and the best selection of visitor activities. At times, the road here follows the ridgeline, rendering spectacular views down both sides of the mountains at once. It also leads to the Peaks of Otter Lodge, the only place actually on the parkway where you can spend the night (see "Accommodations," below).

There are also many **hiking trails,** including the Appalachian Trail, which follows the parkway from Mile 0 to about Mile 103. Most trails are at or near the visitor centers (see below), which distribute free trail maps.

JUST THE FACTS

ACCESS POINTS & ORIENTATION   The northern parkway entrance is near Waynesboro at the southern end of the Skyline Drive, on U.S. 250 at Exit 99 off I-64. The major access points in Virginia are U.S. 60 east of Buena Vista; U.S. 501 between Buena Vista and Lynchburg (Otter Creek and the James River Gorge); U.S. 460, Va. 24, and U.S. 220 near Roanoke; U.S. 58 at Meadows of Dan; and I-77 at Fancy Gap.

Unlike the Skyline Drive, which is surrounded by a national park, the parkway for most of its route runs through mountain meadows, private farmland, and forests (some

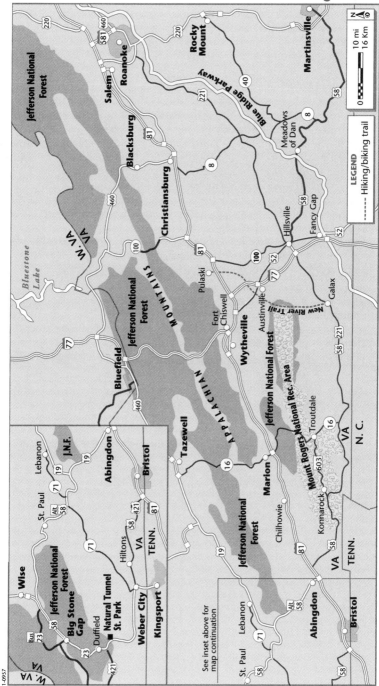

but not all of them national forests). Nature hikes, camping, and other visitor activities are largely confined to the visitor centers and to more than 200 overlooks.

Mile Posts on the west side of the parkway begin with zero at the northern Rockfish Gap entry and increase as you head south. The North Carolina border is at Mile 218.

INFORMATION   For general information, contact the **National Park Service (NPS),** 400 BB&T Building, Asheville, NC 28801 (☎ **704/298-0398**). The NPS sends out a brochure with an excellent map of the parkway, and can provide specific information about hiking trails, campgrounds, and bicycling as well. Also ask for a copy of *The Blue Ridge Parkway Directory,* published by the **Blue Ridge Parkway Association,** P.O. Box 453, Asheville, NC 28802. This booklet offers a wealth of information, including maps and descriptions of nearby attractions, shops, lodging, and restaurants. It also includes a calendar of when the wildflowers bloom.

The directory is available free at the visitor centers, which also sell the detailed *Blue Ridge Parkway: Rockfish Gap to Grandfather Mountain* by William G. Ford (Menasha Ridge Press, Birmingham, AL, $6.95), and an excellent book for hikers, *Walking the Blue Ridge: A Guide to the Trails of the Blue Ridge Parkway,* by Leonard M. Adkins (University of North Carolina Press, Chapel Hill, $12.95).

FEES, REGULATIONS & BACKCOUNTRY PERMITS   There is no fee for using the parkway. Maximum speed limit is 45 m.p.h. along the entire route. Bicycles are allowed only on paved roads and parking areas, not on any trails. Camping is permitted only in designated areas (see "Camping," below). Fires are permitted in campgrounds and picnic areas only. Hunting is prohibited. Pets must be kept on a leash. No swimming is allowed in parkway ponds and lakes.

VISITOR CENTERS   Several visitor centers are located along the parkway, including one at **Rockfish Gap** (Mile 0), which is open year-round. Others may be closed from November to March. Since the centers are the focal points of most visitor activities, here's a rundown:

Humpback Rocks Visitor Center (Mile 5.8) has picnic tables, rest rooms, and a self-guiding trail to a reconstructed mountain homestead.

James River Visitor Center (Mile 63.6) has a footbridge that crosses the river to the restored canal locks, exhibits, and a nature trail. Otter Creek wayside has a daytime restaurant and campground just up the road.

Peaks of Otter (Mile 85.9) has a 2-mile hike to the site of a historic farm, wildlife and Native American exhibits, rest rooms, and the Peaks of Otter Lodge (see "Accommodations," below), which looks across a picturesque little lake to the appropriately named Sharp Top Mountain. A trail leads to the top of this 3,875-foot peak, or you can take the campstore's **shuttle bus** to within 1,500 feet of the peak (allow 1 1/2 hours to hike to the peak and back, and wear comfortable shoes). The bus runs spring to fall, every hour daily from 10am to 5pm. Round-trip fares are $3.75 for adults, $2.25 for children under 12.

Rocky Knob (Mile 167.1) has some 15 miles of hiking trails (including the Rock Castle Gorge National Recreational Trail), a comfort station, and picnic area.

Mabry Mill (Mile 176) has a picturesque gristmill with a giant wheel spanning a little stream. Displays of pioneer life, including crafts demonstrations, are featured, and the restored mill still grinds flour. A restaurant, open May through October, adjoins it.

SEASONS   The parkway is at its best during spring, when the wildflowers bloom and young leaves are multi-hued green, and during mid-October, when changing leaves are at their blazing best (and traffic is at its heaviest).

CAMPING

Campgrounds are at **Otter Creek,** Mile 60.8; **Peaks of Otter,** Mile 86; **Roanoke Mountain,** Mile 120.4; and **Rocky Knob,** Mile 174.1. The Roanoke Mountain campground is actually on Mill Mountain, about 1 mile west of the parkway above the city of Roanoke (see "Roanoke: City Below a Star," below).

Campgrounds are open from about May 1 to early November, depending on weather conditions. Drinking water and rest rooms are available, but shower and laundry facilities are not. There are tent and trailer sites, but none have utility connections. The charge per night for each site is $9 for two adults, $2 extra for each additional adult, and free for children under 18. Golden Age and Golden Access Passport holders are entitled to a 50% discount. Daily permits are valid only at the campground where purchased.

Housekeeping cabins are available at Rocky Knob; to make reservations, write Rocky Knob Cabins, Meadows of Dan, VA 24120 (☎ **540/593-3503**).

ACCOMMODATIONS

Peaks of Otter Lodge. Milepost 86 (P.O. Box 489), Bedford, VA 24523. ☎ **800/542-5927** (in Virginia and North Carolina) or 540/586-1081. 60 rms, 3 suites. A/C. $72–$77 double; $85–$108 suite. Additional person $6.25 extra; children under 16 stay free in parents' rm. MC, V. Free parking.

At Peaks of Otter, everything is in harmony with nature, from the lakeside mountain setting to the rustic room decor of natural rough-grained wood with slate-top furnishings. Split-rail fences and small footbridges add to the picturesque beauty of this serene valley. The main lodge building has a restaurant, a crafts and gift shop, and a game and TV room with a view of the lake. Accommodations are in motel-like attached units on a grassy slope overlooking the lake. All rooms have private balconies or terraces to maximize the splendid view, but only suites have TVs and phones. Reservations are accepted beginning October 1 for the *following* year's fall foliage season. Winter and early spring are not overly crowded, but reservations should be made 4 to 6 weeks ahead for all good-weather months.

The lodge's dining room is low-key and pleasant, with a cathedral ceiling, hanging plants, and windows overlooking the lake. Reasonably priced American fare is served at all three meals; there is also a full bar. The parkway's Peaks of Otter visitor center is located here (see "Just the Facts," above).

2 Roanoke: City Below a Star

54 miles SW of Lexington; 74 miles NE of Wytheville; 193 miles SW of Richmond; 251 miles SW of Washington, D.C.

Sprawling across the floor of the Roanoke Valley, Virginia's largest metropolitan area west of Richmond likes to call itself the "Capital of the Blue Ridge." Roanoke is also known as "Star City," for the huge lighted star overlooking the city from Mill Mountain.

There was no star on the mountain when colonial explorers followed the Roanoke River gorge through the Blue Ridge Mountains in the 17th century. They established several small settlements in the Roanoke Valley, including one named Big Lick. When the Norfolk and Western Railroad arrived in the 1880s and laid out a town for future development, it decided that *Roanoke*—a Native American word for "shell money"—was a much more prosperous-sounding name for its new city than Big Lick. Although Roanoke is still a major railroad junction (as the many tracks running through downtown will attest), its economy suffered when the interstate highway system shifted most freight from boxcars to trucks in the mid-20th century. Milestones in its recovery have been the construction of the Civic Center and a convention and cultural complex, and the restoration of the now trendy Market Square area around the Historic City Market.

With its zoo and its hands-on educational museums, Roanoke has special appeal for children. Families can easily spend a full day and more exploring its sights.

ESSENTIALS

VISITOR INFORMATION   Contact the **Roanoke Convention and Visitors Bureau,** 114 Market St., Roanoke, VA 24011 (☎ **800/635-5535** or 540/342-6025; fax 540/342-7119; www.visitroanokeva.com). Just a few doors north of Market Square, the chamber's visitor center is the best place to pick up maps and brochures for walking and biking tours before starting your exploration of Roanoke. It's open daily from 9am to 5pm.

GETTING THERE   **By Car**   From I-81, take I-581 south into the heart of Roanoke. I-581 becomes U.S. 220; together, these two highways form the Roy Webber Expressway, which passes all the way through town. The Blue Ridge Parkway runs along the top of the mountains east of the city; the major Roanoke exits are at U.S. 460, Va. 24, the Mill Mountain Spur Road (at Mile 120), and U.S. 220.

By Plane   The **Roanoke Regional Airport** (☎ **540/362-1999**), 5$^{1}/_{2}$ miles northwest of downtown off Herschberger Road (Exit 3 off I-581), is served by Continental Express, Delta Connection, Northwest Airlink, and US Airways (only the latter flies jets here). The major car-rental firms have booths on-site. **Roanoke Airport Limousine Service** (☎ **800/228-1958** or 540/345-7710) runs vans to downtown and to points 100 miles away, including Lexington in the Shenandoah Valley (see chapter 8). The fare to downtown is $12 for the first passenger, $2 for each additional person.

By Train   Amtrak provides Thruway bus connections daily between Roanoke and its station in Clifton Forge, Va. (45 miles away). For information, call ☎ **800/872-7245.**

GETTING AROUND   For a taxi, call **Liberty Cab** (☎ **540/344-1776**). **Valley Metro** provides public bus service Monday through Saturday from 5:45am to 8:45pm. The downtown transfer point is Campbell Court, 17 W. Campbell Ave. Call ☎ **540/982-2222** for schedules and fares. The visitor center distributes free Ride Guide route maps.

EXPLORING DOWNTOWN

✪ **Market Square,** in the center of downtown at Market Street and Campbell Avenue, is Roanoke's answer to Georgetown in Washington, D.C., and Shockoe Slip in Richmond. As they have for more than a century, stands and shops at the **Historic City Market** display plants, flowers, fresh fruits and vegetables, dairy and eggs, and farm-cured meats. Nearby, restored Victorian-era storefronts house trendy restaurants, gift shops, art galleries, clothiers, a book-and-music emporium, an Orvis outdoor-wear outlet, plus two spiffed-up relics from the past: Agnew Seed Store, which still uses its old-fashioned oak drawers, and Wertz's Country Store, carrying a gourmet selection of local produce. The landmark **Market Building** houses a food court offering the downtown lunch crowd an international menu, from Chinese egg rolls to North Carolina–style barbecue. The market and food court are open Monday through Saturday.

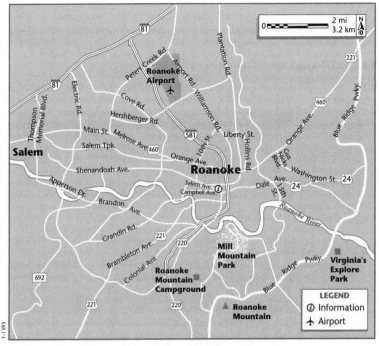

Next door on Campbell Avenue, a five-story converted warehouse known as **Center in the Square** houses the Mill Mountain Theater (see "Roanoke After Dark," below) and three museums:

- **Art Museum of Western Virginia** (☎ 540/342-5760) displays ancient and contemporary works, from tribal African to contemporary American. It's open Tuesday through Saturday from 10am to 5pm and Sunday from 1 to 5pm; admission is free.
- **Roanoke Valley History Museum** (☎ 540/342-5770) houses documents, tools, costumes, and weapons that tell the story of Roanoke from pioneer days to the present. The museum shop carries historic items, wooden and tin toys, and locally made quilts. It's open Tuesday through Friday from 10am to 4pm, Saturday from 10am to 4pm, and Sunday from 1 to 5pm; admission is $2 for adults, $1 for seniors and children 6 to 12, and free for children under 6.
- **Science Museum of Western Virginia and Hopkins Planetarium** (☎ 540/342-5710) will intrigue children with its high-tech interactive exhibits. A new weather gallery features a tornado simulator and a Weather Channel–like studio. The museum store on the ground level offers a fascinating collection of educational toys. Hours are Monday through Saturday from 10am to 5pm and Sunday from 1 to 5pm; admission is $5 for adults, $4 for seniors, $3 for children 3 to 12, and free for children under 3.

Five blocks west of Market Square in a restored freight depot, the **Virginia Museum of Transportation,** 303 Norfolk Ave., at 3rd St. (☎ 540/342-5670), gives kids a chance to climb aboard a caboose, stroll through a railway post-office car, and see the classic steam giants up close. It's open March to December, Monday through

Saturday from 10am to 5pm and Sunday from noon to 5pm; closed Mondays in January and February. Admission is $5 for adults, $4 for seniors, $3 for students 13 to 18, and free for children under 13.

ATTRACTIONS ON MILL MOUNTAIN

Situated between the city and the Blue Ridge Parkway, Mill Mountain offers panoramic views over Roanoke Valley. The two main attractions are in **Mill Mountain Park,** on the Mill Mountain Parkway Spur, a winding road that leaves the city south of downtown as Walnut Avenue and ends at Mile 120 on the parkway.

Roanoke citizens know they're home when they can see the white neon **Star on the Mountain.** Erected in 1949 as a civic pride project, it stands 88 1/2 feet tall, uses 2,000 feet of neon tubing, and is visible from most parts of the city. There's an excellent viewpoint at the base.

Nearby, kids will enjoy **Mill Mountain Zoo** (☎ 540/343-3241), a 3-acre home to 40 animal species, including monkeys, prairie dogs, hawks, red pandas, Japanese macaques, a snow leopard, and a Siberian tiger. It's open daily from 10am to 5pm (until 7pm Friday in summer). Admission is $5 for adults, $4.50 for seniors, $3 for children 3 to 11, and free for children under 2.

It's a scenic 7-mile drive from Mill Mountain to ✪ **Virginia's Explore Park** (☎ 540/427-1800), a 1,300-acre reserve in the Roanoke River gorge. The park sports a reconstructed 18th-century settlement and 8 miles of nature trails. More than 1,000 acres of its hills and wetlands have been set aside as a natural area, so humans are limited to hiking, wildlife viewing, and environmental research. The village has a blacksmith and wheelwright shop, the Brugh Tavern (appropriately pronounced "Brew"), a German-style "bank" barn, a school, a mountain church, and several houses, all of them moved to the site from elsewhere. There's also a working farm. The park is open April to October on Monday, Tuesday, Saturday, and Sunday from 9am to 5pm. Admission is $6 for adults, $4 for students, and free for children under 6. The road to the park leaves the Blue Ridge Parkway at Mile 115; follow the signs.

DIXIE CAVERNS

If you didn't go underground in the Shenandoah Valley, you can do so at **Dixie Caverns,** near Exit 132 off I-81 on U.S. 11/460 about 5 miles southwest of Salem (☎ 540/380-2085). These caves are best known for a huge dome-like structure called the Wedding Bell (yes, a few couples actually get married here each year) and an underground lake called the Magic Mirror. Guided tours take 45 minutes. Admission is $6.50 for adults, $3.50 for children 5 to 12. The caverns are open daily from 9:30am to 6pm in summer, daily from 9:30am to 5pm the rest of the year; closed Christmas Day.

You can also **camp** here, with wooded hook-up sites going for $16 for two persons, tent spaces for $5 per person.

WHERE TO STAY

Downtown Roanoke has two older chain motels that cater to groups attending functions at the adjacent Civic Center: the **Quality Inn Civic Center** (☎ 800/228-5151 or 540/342-8961) and **Days Inn** (☎ 800/325-2525 or 540/342-4551), both on Orange Avenue east of Exit 4 off I-581. If you're coming off the Blue Ridge Parkway, convenient choices include the **Holiday Inn Tanglewood** (☎ 800/HOLIDAY or 540/774-4400) and **Hampton Inn Tanglewood** (☎ 800/HAMPTON or 540/989-4000), both on Franklin Road near U.S. 220 southeast of downtown. Near the airport, Herschberger Road (Exit 3 off I-581) has the **Best Western at Valley View** (☎ 800/362-2410 or 540/362-2400), **Clarion Hotel** (☎ 800/CLARION or 540/362-4500), and **Comfort Inn Airport** (☎ 800/228-5150 or 540/563-0229). Farther out, Peters Creek Road (Exit 2 off I-581) has a **Hampton Inn** (☎ 800/HAMPTON or 540/265-2600), the **Holiday Inn Airport** (☎ 800/HOLIDAY or 540/366-8861), and an inexpensive **Super 8** (☎ 800/800-8000 or 540/563-8888).

B&B accommodation is available in town at **Walnuthill Bed & Breakfast,** 436 Walnut Ave. SE (☎ 540/427-3312; fax 540/427-0273).

✪ **Colony House Motor Lodge.** 3560 Franklin Rd. (U.S. 220 Business), Roanoke, VA 24014. ☎ **800/552-7026** or 540/345-0411. Fax 540/345-0411, ext. 459. 69 rms, 2 suites. A/C TV TEL. $58–$68 double; $85 suite. Rates include continental breakfast. AE, DC, DISC, MC, V. From I-581/U.S. 220, take Franklin Rd. (U.S. 220 Business) south to motel on left. From Blue Ridge Pkwy., take U.S. 220 Business west, exit on Franklin Rd. north to motel on right.

This clean, well-maintained motel enjoys a convenient suburban location in the Tanglewood shopping area, 2 miles south of downtown and 2 miles north of the Blue Ridge Parkway. A series of peaked roofs creates cathedral ceilings in some of the spacious rooms, all of which have unusual louvered screen doors that let in fresh air without sacrificing privacy. About half the rooms are at the rear of the property; they face a steep hillside and get less natural light but also less traffic noise. A small roadside outdoor swimming pool has a view of the K-Mart across Franklin Road. Continental breakfast is served in the lobby, and there's a 24-hour Waffle House next door.

✪ **Hotel Roanoke & Conference Center.** 110 Shenandoah Ave., Roanoke, VA 24016. ☎ **800/222-TREE** or 540/985-5900. Fax 540/853-8264. 332 rms and suites. A/C TV TEL. $79–$145 double; $159–$259 suite. Packages available. AE, DC, DISC, MC, V. Self-parking $3, valet parking $5. From I-581 south, take Exit 5, cross Wells Ave. into parking lot.

The Norfolk and Western Railroad built this grand Tudor-style hotel in a wheat field in 1882, even before it changed the name of Big Lick to Roanoke. Heated by steam from the railroad's maintenance shops and cooled by America's first hotel air-conditioning system (circulating ice water), it became a resort as well as a stopover. Some 26 passenger trains a day rolled into the station at the foot of the hill, and virtually every celebrity passing though Roanoke stayed here, among them William Jennings Bryan, Amelia Earhart, Joe DiMaggio, Jack Dempsey, Elvis Presley, and Presidents Eisenhower, Nixon, Ford, Reagan, and Bush. For the locals, it was *the* place for wedding receptions, reunions, beauty pageants, and other special events.

In 1989, the Norfolk and Western's successor corporation closed the hotel and gave it to Virginia Polytechnic Institute (VPI), the state's land-grant university at Blacksburg. With massive help from Roanokers, VPI raised and spent $42 million restoring the public areas, rebuilding the rooms and suites, and adding a 63,000-square-foot conference center and an enclosed, climate-controlled pedestrian walkway across the railroad tracks to Market Square. With much fanfare, the hotel reopened in 1995 under the management of Doubletree Hotels.

Even if you don't stay here, it's worth a walk uphill just to see the rich, black walnut–paneled lobby with its Oriental rugs and leather lounge furniture; the oval-shaped Palm Court lounge with its pineapple central fountain and four lovingly restored murals of colonial and Victorian Virginians dancing the reel, waltz, minuet, and quadrille; and the elegant Regency Room, where waiters in starched tunics deliver the hotel's signature peanut soup.

The building was gutted and rebuilt above the public areas, so all the rooms and suites are completely modern. Given the odd shape of the building, there are now 92 room configurations, many with sloping ceilings and gable windows.

Dining/Entertainment: In addition to peanut soup, the Regency Room serves venison, quail, pink speckled trout, sweet-potato chips, and other historic dishes, all at moderate prices. Pub fare is available in the knotty Pine Room, which has a large bar, sports TV, and billiard table.

Services: Concierge, room service, laundry, free newspaper, nightly turndown.

Facilities: Outdoor pool, fitness center.

The Patrick Henry Hotel. 617 S. Jefferson St. (at Bullit Ave.), Roanoke, VA 24011. ☎ **800/ 303-0988** or 540/345-8811. Fax 540/342-9908. 125 units. $99 double; $125–$185 suite. Packages available. Rates include continental breakfast. Parking $3.25 per day. AE, DC, DISC, MC, V. From I-585, take Elm St. (Exit 6) west, turn right on S. Jefferson St. to the hotel on the left.

A downtown Roanoke landmark since 1925, this mid-rise brick building is the kind of hotel where politicians once cut deals in smoke-filled rooms. The rooms and suites here are some of the largest you'll find anywhere at these prices. All rooms—not only the suites—boast kitchens and modern bathrooms, which were installed a few years ago when this was a Radisson property. A marble staircase leads into the two-story lobby, which has massive windows, polished marble floors, Oriental rugs, period furnishings, and a brilliant bas-relief frieze embellishing its ceiling.

Hunter's Grille specializes in hand-cut steaks and provides room service during lunch and dinner hours. The Patrick Henry offers free airport transportation, newspapers on weekdays, a game room, and a coin-operated laundry. Guests can use the health-club facilities at the local YMCA.

Roanoke Airport Marriott. 2801 Hershberger Rd. NW, Roanoke, VA 24017. ☎ **800/ 228-9290** or 540/563-9300. 320 rms. A/C TV TEL. $124–$134 double. Additional person $10 extra; children under 18 stay free in parents' room. Weekend rates available. AE, DC, DISC, MC, V. Free parking. From I-581 south, take Exit 3W, Hershberger Rd.; make a right U-turn at the first light; the hotel is on the service road.

This eight-story Marriott feels more Californian than Virginian. Designed like a Mediterranean villa, its spacious lobby is adorned with decorative objects from Italy, France, and Spain; brick walls, Oriental rugs, and a huge fireplace create a warm atmosphere. A concierge level offers upgraded amenities and a private lounge. Rooms are conventionally decorated with brass-trimmed traditional furnishings of dark wood.

Dining/Entertainment: Remington's, the Marriott's fine-dining spot, features beamed ceilings, stucco walls, and French provincial armchairs. Lily's, an inviting room with skylights and high ceilings, is open for all meals. There's also a lobby bar and entertainment lounge.

Services: 24-hour room service, free newspaper, courtesy airport shuttle.

Facilities: Indoor and outdoor pools, fitness center, sauna, whirlpool, two lighted tennis courts, gift shop.

WHERE TO DINE

Market Square (see "Exploring Downtown," above) is one of Virginia's most diverse dining scenes. The block of Campbell Avenue just east of Market Street offers beverages and pastries at **Mill Mountain Coffee & Tea** (☎ 540/342-9404), kebabs and curries at **Nawab Indian Cuisine** (☎ 540/345-5150), and fish and shrimp at **Awful Arthur's Seafood Company** (☎ 540/344-2997). Around the corner in the Market Building, you'll find Japanese cuisine at **Soriya Hibachi House** (☎ 540/ 345-5593). Opposite the stalls on Market Street, **Ernie's Bar & Grill** (☎ 540/ 982-1131) is a popular spot for breakfast. All are closed on Sunday evening.

✪ **Buck Mountain Grille.** 5002 Franklin Rd. (U.S. 220) (at Blue Ridge Pkwy.). ☎ **540/ 776-1830.** Reservations accepted. Main courses $8–$18. AE, DC, DISC, MC, V. Tues–Thurs

11am–3pm and 5–9pm; Fri 11am–3pm and 5–10pm; Sat 5–10pm; Sun 11am–3pm and 5–9pm. From downtown, take Franklin Rd. (U.S. 220) south 7 miles. From Blue Ridge Pkwy., exit U.S. 220 east, make a U-turn to restaurant. INTERNATIONAL.

This roadside, peaked-roof establishment is a fine place for lunch while driving the Blue Ridge Parkway or for dinner while overnighting in Roanoke. Some guests are seated at the counter or in booths, but most dine at linen-covered tables in a pleasant dining room whose white walls sport local artwork for sale. The menu offers a mix of cuisine, with innovative new American and Mediterranean dishes predominating. Nightly specials feature Roanoke's freshest seafood. Vegetarians can choose from several offerings, and a children's menu is available.

✪ Carlos Brazilian International Cuisine. 312 Market St. (in Market Square south of Campbell St.). ☎ **540/345-7661.** Reservations recommended. Lunch $6–$8; main courses $8–$18. AE, MC, V. Mon–Thurs 11am–2pm and 5–9pm; Fri–Sat 11am–2pm and 5–10pm. BRAZILIAN/SPANISH/CARIBBEAN.

Brazilian-born chef Carlos Amaral brings exceptional cuisine to downtown Roanoke's Market Square. You'll find both his bright storefront dining room and the darker spaces in the rear packed with patrons at both lunch and dinner. Small table lanterns and flower arrangements create an elegant ambience. The highlights are obviously Brazilian, and include *moquca mineira,* a blend of shrimp, clams, and fish in a slightly spicy tomato sauce and served over rice and thinly sliced onions and green peppers. Chicken sautéed with pineapple, grapes, and fried bananas is another winner. Vegetarians can pick from pastas, Brazilian black beans served with collard greens, or a meatless version of paella Valenciana (there's regular paella, too). Don't be in a hurry: Carlos prepares everything to order.

Macado's. 120 Church St. (between 1st and 2nd sts.). ☎ **540/342-7231.** Sandwiches $3.50–$5.50; main courses $5–$7. AE, MC, V. Daily 11:30am–1am. AMERICAN.

The whole family will enjoy this lively spot, part of a successful Virginia chain. The decor is eclectic—old Coke ads, beer signs, an elk head, and other odds and ends on the walls; a small airplane suspended in midair; and many hanging plants. Seating, on several levels, is divided by brass rails into intimate areas. The menu offers sandwiches, salads, soups, and hot entrees. Pita pizzas and baked potatoes topped with cheese sauces are other options. Ice-cream sodas, sundaes, apple cobbler, and pecan pie are among the desserts. There's a full bar.

✪ The Roanoker Restaurant. 2522 Colonial Ave. (south of Wonju St.). ☎ **540/344-7746.** Reservations not accepted. Main courses $7–$9. MC, V. Mon–Thurs 7am–9pm; Fri–Sat 7am–10pm; Sun and holidays 8am–9pm. From downtown, go south on Franklin Rd., turn right on Brandon Ave., left on Colonial Ave. From I-581, go south to Colonial Ave. exit, turn left at traffic light on Colonial Ave. to restaurant on left. SOUTHERN.

A very popular local restaurant since 1941, the Roanoker occupies a colonial-style building surrounded by much-needed parking lots. Several dining rooms offer booth seating arranged to provide privacy. Antique signs from Roanoke businesses adorn the walls. Every Roanoker with a car seems to have breakfast here, so fluffy are the biscuits served with spicy sausage gravy. The lunch and dinner menus change daily, depending on available produce. Fresh vegetables may include skillet-fried yellow squash, a mouth-watering Southern favorite.

ROANOKE AFTER DARK

Mill Mountain Theater, in the Center in the Square building on Campbell Avenue (☎ 800/317-6455 or 540/342-5740), offers children's productions, lunchtime readings, and year-round matinee and evening performances on two stages. Productions range from Shakespeare to minstrels. A recent season featured *Only a Kingdom; Yes,*

Virginia, There Is a Santa Claus; Inherit the Wind; Having Our Say; Fiddler on the Roof; and *Always . . . Patsy Cline.* Tickets range from $5 to $15 for the intimate Theater B, from $15 to $25 for the Main Stage. Seniors, students, and children receive discounts.

Many of the restaurants and pubs at Market Square offer live music on weekends, some during the week.

A NEARBY MOUNTAIN RESORT

Mountain Lake. Mountain Lake, VA 24136. ☎ **800/346-3334** or 540/626-7121. Fax 540/626-7172. 100 rms, including 16 cabins. TEL. Main hotel $165 double; Chestnut Lodge $195 double. Children 12 and older in parents' rm are charged $25 per day; ages 4–12, $15; ages 3 and under free. Rates include breakfast and dinner. AE, DC, DISC, MC, V. Closed Nov–Apr. From I-81, take Exit 118, U.S. 460 west; turn right onto C.R. 700 and go 7 miles to Mountain Lake.

If you saw the movie *Dirty Dancing,* you're already familiar with this rustic mountaintop resort. Surrounded by a 2,600-acre wildlife conservancy, it consists of a main building (a stately, rough-cut–stone lodge) with clusters of small white-clapboard summer cottages nearby. The lobby has thick rugs over a terra-cotta tile floor and comfortable seating in front of a massive fireplace. Complimentary tea and coffee are kept hot on the sideboard. A stone archway separates the lobby from the adjoining bar and lounge.

The popular parlor suites have Jacuzzis and fireplaces, and some rooms offer full lake views. Dark-wood Chippendale-reproduction furnishings give the decor a warm, traditional look. Cottages are more simply furnished, although guests here enjoy porches with rockers. Chestnut Lodge, a recent addition, is a three-story gray-clapboard building set on the side of a hill. Rooms here are decorated in country style, with fireplaces and private balconies.

Dining: The spacious, stone-walled dining room has large windows offering panoramic lake views—a romantic evening setting. A recent dinner here began with an appetizer of sautéed mushrooms in burgundy sauce, followed by swordfish in sour cream–dill sauce, and chocolate mousse for dessert. There's also a snack bar in the Recreation Barn.

Facilities: Health club with sauna and weight room; tennis; hiking trails; boathouse with canoes and rowboats; fishing; Recreation Barn for Ping-Pong, billiards, and evening entertainment; summer program for children; clothing, souvenir, and sporting-goods shops.

3 Wytheville: Gateway to the Highlands

74 miles SW of Roanoke; 49 miles NE of Abingdon; 306 miles SW of Washington, D.C.; 247 miles SW of Richmond

Situated on a relatively flat plateau, Wytheville's strategic position in the center of the Highlands has made it a major crossroads since trappers and hunters came into the region in the early 1700s. After a treaty with hostile Native Americans opened Kentucky for settlement in 1775, Daniel Boone built the Wilderness Road through the Highlands to Cumberland Gap. Monroe Street in downtown Wytheville was part of that route, and a few log cabins left over from those days still stand on Main Street.

The Wilderness Road is long gone, but I-81 and I-77 meet here today, giving Wytheville a motel room for every family in town, plus a host of places to dine. Since accommodations are relatively scarce elsewhere in this sparsely populated region, these facilities make Wytheville a well-equipped base from which to explore Mount Rogers National Recreation Area (see "Mount Rogers National Recreation Area," below) and other sights in the central portion of the Highlands.

ESSENTIALS

VISITOR INFORMATION   The **Wytheville/Bland Chamber of Commerce,** P.O. Box 533, Wytheville, VA 24382 (☎ **540/223-3355;** fax 540/223-3315; **www.wytheville.org**; e-mail: wacvb@naxs.com), supplies information about the town, including a walking-tour brochure to the historic district. It has a visitor information office in the Municipal Building, at Monroe Street and 1st Street. Roadside tourist information kiosks are also located at all interstate exits leading into town.

GETTING THERE   I-81 and I-77 meet on the outskirts of Wytheville. To get into town, take Exits 67, 70, or 73 off I-81. U.S. 11 (Main Street) and U.S. 21 meet in downtown.

EXPLORING THE TOWN

Stop at the chamber of commerce for a walking-tour brochure explaining the town's historic buildings (see "Essentials," above). An 1830s mayor decided Wytheville needed wide streets to keep fires from spreading, so even though the town dates back to 1757, the broad avenues deprive it of some of the quaintness and charm of other old towns like Lexington and Abingdon.

With the South's only salt mine and an important lead mine nearby (see "Outdoor Pursuits," below), Union troops attacked the crossroads village and burned many historic homes and businesses during the Civil War. One area remained untouched, however, and you will want to examine these **Old Log Houses,** on Main Street (U.S. 11) between 5th and 7th streets. Some of them now house shops and a restaurant (see "Where to Dine," below).

Another house that escaped Civil War destruction—but not bullet holes—was the **Rock House Museum,** at Monroe and Tazewell streets (☎ **540/223-3330**). A National and State Historic Landmark, this Pennsylvania-style stone structure was built in 1820. The museum has a collection of historic artifacts from the region. Admission is $2 for adults, $1 for children 6 to 12, and free for children under 6. It's open July and August, Wednesday through Saturday from 10am to 3pm; April to June and September to October, on Wednesday, Thursday, and Friday from 10am to 3pm. Just behind the house on Tazewell Street, the **Thomas J. Boyd Museum** has exhibits on Wytheville's history, including an 1850s fire truck, Civil War relics, and farm equipment. (Same phone, hours, and admission as the Rock House Museum.)

Although it's not open to the public, upstairs in the building at 145 E. Main St., in the business district, was the **Birthplace of Edith Bolling Wilson,** second wife of Staunton-born President Woodrow Wilson.

OUTDOOR PURSUITS

Wytheville is near the ✪ **New River Trail State Park,** an exceptional hiking, biking, and horse path running 57 miles between Galax and Pulaski. The trail follows an old railroad bed beside the picturesque New River, which despite its name is in geologic terms one of the oldest rivers in the United States (it predates the Appalachian Mountains).

The trail headquarters are at Foster Falls, an old mining hamlet on C.R. 608, about 20 miles northeast of Wytheville, or 2 miles north of U.S. 52 (take Exit 24 off I-77 and follow the signs). You can enter the trail here daily from 8am to 10pm. User fees are $2 for adults, $2 for children, plus a $2 per vehicle parking fee.

Other entries are at Shot Tower Historical State Park (see below); Draper, near Exit 92 off I-81; Allisonia and Hiwassee, both on C.R. 693; Barren Springs, on Va. 100; Austinville, on Va. 69; Ivanhoe, on Va. 94; Byllesby Dam, on C.R. 602; and Galax, on U.S. 58. There's also a branch trail to Fries, on Va. 94.

The trail's concessionaire, **New River Adventures, Inc.,** 1007 N. 4th St., Wytheville, VA 24382 (☎ 540/228-8311), rents bicycles, canoes, and inner tubes, and sells backpacking and fishing equipment. Bikes cost $4 per hour or $15 per day. Canoes start at $30 per day, plus $10 for a shuttle ride. Tubes go for $10 per day. Also check with **New River Bicycles** (☎ 540/980-1741), **Allisonia Trading Post** (☎ 540/980-2051), and **Cliffview Trading Post** (☎ 540/238-1530). The latter is at the Cliffview Ranger Station near Galax and also rents horses. Horse-trailer parking is permitted only at the Cliffview Ranger Station, Shot Tower State Park, and Draper.

For more information, write or call New River Trail State Park, Route 2, Box 126F, Foster Falls, VA 24360 (☎ 540/699-6778).

While in this area, you can also stop at **Shot Tower Historical State Park,** on U.S. 52 near Exit 5 off I-77, which features a stone shot tower built about 1807. Molten lead poured from the top of the tower fell 150 feet into a kettle, thus cooling and turning into round shot. The lead was mined at nearby Austinville, birthplace of Stephen Austin, the "Father of Texas." Admission to the park is free, but there's a $1 per vehicle parking fee on weekdays, $2 on weekends. The park is open April to November from 8am to dusk. Rangers conduct tours of the tower from Memorial Day to Labor Day on weekends and holidays from 10am to 6pm.

SHOPPING

Three log cabins in Old Town Square, Main Street at 7th Street, now house the **Wilderness Road Trading Post** (☎ 540/223-1198), purveyor of Appalachian crafts, pottery, toys, and a wide range of gifts.

Near Fort Chiswell, about 10 miles northeast of Wytheville on the service road between Exits 77 and 80 off I-81, you'll find **Snooper's Antique & Craft Mall** (☎ 540/637-6441) and **Old Fort Emporium Antique Mall** (☎ 540/228-GIFT). Both are cooperatives, with vendors selling a wide range of antiques, collectibles, and gifts. Both are open from Memorial Day to Labor Day, daily from 10am to 8pm, to 7pm in spring and fall, to 6pm in winter.

Across I-81 at Exit 80, **Factory Merchants of Fort Chiswell** (☎ 540/637-6214) has 35 outlet stores, including Polo Ralph Lauren, Bugle Boy, London Fog, Samsonite, Arrow, L'Eggs/Hanes/Bali, Reebok, Bass, Corning/Revere, Casual Corner, Dress Barn, and Hush Puppies. The Highlands Gateway Visitor Center is also located here (see "Exploring the Southwest Highlands" at the beginning of this chapter).

WHERE TO STAY

The Wytheville area has more than 1,200 motel rooms, most in national chain establishments along I-81 and I-77.

Exit 73 off I-81 (U.S. 11) has the largest concentration, with a **Days Inn** (☎ 800/325-2525 or 540/228-5500), **Holiday Inn** (☎ 800/HOLIDAY or 540/228-5483), **Motel 6** (☎ 800/446-8356 or 540/228-7988), and **Red Carpet Inn** (☎ 800/251-1962 or 540/228-5525). Formerly a Howard Johnson's, the **Shenandoah Inn** (☎ 800/446-4656 or 540/228-3188) sits on top of a hill above the intersection, giving many rooms fine mountain views. Rooms in the Holiday Inn were recently renovated as part of this chain's general facelift, but note that some rooms in the Motel 6 and Red Carpet Inn are virtually beside I-81 and are subject to traffic noise. You can also take Exit 73 to reach a parking lot–surrounded **Econo Lodge** (☎ 800/424-4777 or 540/228-5517), about 1 mile to the south on U.S. 11.

For less congested locations, consider Exit 70 off I-81 (N. 4th Street), which has the modern **Comfort Inn Wytheville** (☎ 800/228-5150 or 540/228-4488), and

Exit 41 off I-77 (Peppers Ferry Road), where the **Best Western Wytheville Inn** (☎ **800/528-1234** or 540/228-7300), **Hampton Inn** (☎ **800/HAMPTON** or 540/228-6990), and **Ramada Inn** (☎ **800/2-RAMADA** or 540/228-6000) are far enough away from the interstate to escape the road noise.

Boxwood Inn Bed & Breakfast. 460 E. Main St. (U.S. 11), Wytheville, VA 24382. ☎ **540/ 228-8911.** 8 rms (all with bath). A/C. $64–$74 double. Rates include full breakfast. MC, V. Take Exit 73 off I-81, go 1¹/₂ miles south on U.S. 11 to inn on the right.

This renovated Georgian colonial home is just a few doors down from the historic log cabins on East Main Street. The rooms sport Victorian antiques and reproductions, such as solid oak sleigh beds; the units on the front of the house are enormous. A full breakfast is served family-style in the sunny country kitchen.

WHERE TO DINE

✪ **The Log House 1776 Restaurant.** 520 E. Main St. (U.S. 11) (at 7th St.). ☎ **540/228- 4139.** Reservations recommended. Lunch $3–$5; main courses $9–$17. AE, DISC, MC, V. Mon– Sat 11am–3pm and 4–10pm. From I-81, take Exit 67 or 73 and follow U.S. 11 to the restaurant. AMERICAN.

Although clapboard additions to this historic building were made in 1804 and 1898, the main dining room is in a log house built in 1776. Modern gas logs now burn in the fireplaces, but antiques augment the colonial charm of the dining room. Offerings include Virginia fare such as peanut soup, Smithfield ham, Confederate beef stew (a very sweet concoction of beef, vegetables, and apples that General Lee fed his troops), and Thomas Jefferson's favorite, chicken Marengo, which he brought home from his stint as ambassador to France.

Scrooge's Restaurant. At Comfort Inn, Halston Rd. at E. 4th St. ☎ **540/228-6622.** Reservations not accepted. Main courses $9–$17. AE, DC, MC, V. Sun–Thurs 5–10pm; Fri–Sat 5– 11pm. From downtown, take 4th Ave. north across I-81, turn right on Halston Rd. From I-81, take Exit 70, follow signs to Comfort Inn. INTERNATIONAL.

Cartoons of Dickens's Ebenezer Scrooge, especially those on the sports-bar walls showing him scowling his way through such modern activities as tennis and golf, make this English-style establishment a fun place. Recommended is the "pig and pepper soup," a spicy mixture of smoked sausage, potatoes, and peppercorns that will warm the innards after a cold day on the New River Trail. Otherwise, the menu takes a stab at fine dining with the likes of charbroiled steaks, chicken, and seafood dishes like flounder Florentine and shrimp Provençal. There's a "Tiny Tim" menu for kids.

Skeeter's E.N. Umberger Store. 165 E. Main St. (between 1st and Tazewell sts.). ☎ **540/ 228-2611.** Reservations not accepted. Breakfast $1–$2.50; sandwiches and hot dogs $1.10– $2.20. No credit cards. Mon–Fri 7am–5:50pm; Sat 7am–4:50pm. AMERICAN.

Established in 1920 and housed in an ancient storefront, this simple diner is the home of "Skeeter's World Famous Hotdogs," which are grilled on rollers and served on steamed buns, Southern-style. Other offerings include breakfast items and simple sandwiches. The diner hasn't changed since the 1940s, as the old advertisements and well-worn counter will attest.

4 Mount Rogers National Recreation Area

Noted for its 300 miles of hiking, mountain-biking, cross-country skiing, and horse trails, Mount Rogers National Recreation Area includes 117,000 forested acres running some 60 miles from the New River southwest to the Tennessee line. Included is its namesake, Virginia's highest peak at 5,729 feet. Nearby White Top is the state's second-highest point at 5,520 feet. Most of the land, however, flanks Iron

Mountain, a long ridge running the area's length. Ranging the extensive upland meadows are wild ponies, introduced to keep the grasses mowed.

Not all of this remote expanse is pristine, for as part of the Jefferson National Forest, it's subject to multiple uses such as hunting and logging. Nevertheless, you'll find three preserved wilderness areas and plenty of other backcountry to explore, with mountain scenery that's among the best in Virginia. The many trails include the Virginia Creeper Trail, the Virginia Highlands Horse Trail, and a stretch of the Appalachian Trail. A spur off the Appalachian Trail leads to the summit of Mount Rogers.

JUST THE FACTS

ACCESS POINTS & ORIENTATION   Access roads from I-81 are U.S. 21 from Wytheville; Va. 16 from Marion; C.R. 600 from Chilihowie; Va. 91 from Glades Spring; and U.S. 58 from Damascus and Abingdon. C.R. 603 runs 13 miles lengthwise through beautiful highland meadows from Troutdale (on Va. 16) to Konnarock (on U.S. 58).

INFORMATION   Since the area is so vast and most facilities widespread, it's a good idea to get as much information in advance as possible. Contact the **Mount Rogers National Recreation Area,** 3714 Hwy. 16, Marion, VA 24354 (☎ **540/ 783-5196**). If you're driving from the north on I-81, stop at the **Highlands Gateway Visitor Center,** Drawer B-12, Max Meadows, VA 24360 (☎ **800/446-9670** or 540/637-6766), in the Factory Merchants Outlet Mall at Exit 80 near Fort Chiswell. Like the recreation area itself, both visitor centers are operated by the National Forest Service. They offer free brochures describing the trails, campgrounds, and wilderness areas, and they sell a one-sheet topographic map of the area. The topographic map does not show the trails, however, so if writing or calling for information, specifically request brochures on trails, campgrounds, horseback riding, and recreation areas.

FEES, REGULATIONS & BACKCOUNTRY PERMITS   There is no charge to drive through the area, but day-use fees from $1 to $3 per vehicle apply to specific recreational areas, payable on the honor system. Except for the Appalachian Trail and some others reserved for hikers, mountain bikes are permitted but must give way to horses. Bikers and horseback riders must walk across all bridges and trestles. Hikers must not spook the horses. Fishing requires a Virginia license. The "No-Trace Ethic" applies: Leave nothing behind, and take away only photographs and memories.

VISITOR CENTER   The visitor center is 6 miles south of Marion on Va. 16 (take Exit 45 off I-81 and go south). Exhibits and a 10-minute video describe the area. The center is open Memorial Day to October, Monday through Thursday from 8am to 5:30pm, weekends from 9am to 5pm. Off-season, it's open Monday through Friday from 8am to 4:30pm.

SEASONS   The area is most crowded on summer and fall weekends and holidays. Spring is punctuated by wildflowers in bloom (the calendars published by the Blue Ridge Parkway are generally applicable here), while fall foliage is at its brilliant best in mid-October. Cross-country skiers use the trails during winter. Summer thunderstorms, winter blizzards, and fog any time of the year can pose threats in the high country, so caution is advised.

SEEING THE HIGHLIGHTS

If you don't have time to camp and hike, you can still enjoy the lovely scenery from your car. From Marion on I-81, take Va. 16 south 16 miles to the country store at Troutdale. Turn right on C.R. 603 and drive 13 miles southwest to U.S. 58. Turn right there and drive 20 miles down Straight Branch—a misnomer if ever there was one—to I-81 at Abingdon.

OUTDOOR PURSUITS

HIGH-COUNTRY HIKING   Almost two-thirds of the area's 300 miles of trails are on these routes: the local stretch of the **Appalachian Trail** (64 miles), the **Virginia Highlands Horse Trail** (66 miles), and the **Iron Mountain Trail** (51 miles). Many of the other 67 trails connect to these main routes, and many can be linked into circuit hikes.

You can walk for days on the white-blaze Appalachian Trail without crossing a paved road, especially on the central stretch up and down the flanks of Mount Rogers between C.R. 603 and C.R. 600. A spur goes to the top of the mountain. The blue-blaze **Mount Rogers Trail,** a very popular alternate route, leaves C.R. 603 near Grindstone Campground; a spur from that track heads down into the pristine Lewis Fork Wilderness before rejoining the Appalachian Trail.

Running across the southern end of the area, the **Virginia Creeper Trail** offers a much easier, but no less beautiful, hike (and bike ride). This 34-mile route follows an old railroad bed from Abingdon to White Top Mountain (see "Outdoors: The Virginia Creeper Trail" under "Abingdon: A Town with Beauty & Charm," below).

HORSEBACK RIDING   Riders can use 150 miles of the area's trails, including Iron Mountain, New River, and the Virginia Highlands Horse Trail, which connects Elk Garden to Va. 94. Horse camps are at Fox Creek, on Va. 603; Hussy Mountain, near Speedwell; and Raven Cliff, about 4 miles east of Cripple Creek. They have toilets and drinking water for horses (but no water for humans).

Mount Rogers High Country Outdoor Center, on C.R. 603 near Troutdale (☎ 540/677-3900), offers day rides and overnight pack trips by horse, pack mule, or covered wagon. Reservations are required, so phone for information and current prices.

CAMPING

In addition to the horse camps mentioned above, the recreation area has several other campgrounds, all open from mid-March through December. On C.R. 603, **Grindstone** serves as a base camp for hikers heading up Mount Rogers. It has a half-mile nature trail and weekend ranger programs. **Beartree,** a popular recreation site on U.S. 58 near C.R. 603, features a sand beach on a 12-acre lake stocked with trout for fishing. Both Grindstone and Beartree have flush toilets and warm showers but no trailer hookups. Fees are $10 per site from May through September, $4 during the months of March, April, October, and November.

ACCOMMODATIONS

There are no hotels, motels, or inns within Mount Rogers National Recreation Area. The nearest motels are in Wytheville on the north end (see above); Abingdon on the south (see below); and Marion in the center, where the **Best Western Marion** (☎ 800/528-1234 or 540/783-3193) and the **Econo Lodge Marion** (☎ 800/ 55-ECONO or 540/783-6031) stand side by side on U.S. 11 north of downtown. Both were recently renovated. Opposite them on U.S. 11 is the **Virginia House Inn** (☎ 800/505-5151 or 540/783-5112), a one-story motel still operated by the same family that built it in 1952. The rooms, at $49 for a double, are small but clean and comfortable.

Fox Hill Inn. 8568 Troutdale Hwy. (Va. 16), Troutdale, VA 24378. ☎ 800/874-3313 or 540/ 677-3313. 6 rms, 1 suite (all with bath). $75 double; $130 suite. Children stay free in parents' rm. Rates include full breakfast. DISC, MC, V. From I-81, take Exit 45 at Marion, then Va. 16 south 20 miles. Inn is on the left, 2 miles south of the country store at Troutdale.

Situated on a secluded hilltop surrounded on three sides by gorgeous mountain views, this comfortable country home offers a big living room with a fireplace, a dining room and terrace with great mountain views, and a roomy country kitchen. A basement game room has Ping-Pong and board games. Very spacious guest rooms are furnished in simple country style. This is also a working farm, where cattle and sheep graze the meadows, and children can get a real feel for farm life. The hosts will arrange canoe trips on the New River, horseback riding, and mountain-biking.

5 Abingdon: A Town with Beauty & Charm

49 miles SW of Wytheville; 133 miles SW of Roanoke; 437 miles SW of Washington, D.C.; 315 miles SW of Richmond

While on his first expedition to Kentucky in 1760, Daniel Boone camped at the base of a hill near a small Halston Valley settlement known as Black's Fort. When wolves emerged from a cave and attacked his dogs, Boone named the place Wolf Hill. Boone and other pioneers opened the area for settlement, and by 1778, a thriving community named Abingdon had grown up around Black's Fort and Wolf Hill. The fort has been replaced by the Washington County Court House, but Boone's cave is still behind one of the historic homes on tree-shaded Main Street. Indeed, Abingdon today looks much as it did in those early years, making it one of Virginia's best small towns to visit.

Abingdon's beauty and historic charm have attracted more than its share of actors, artists, craftspeople, and even a few writers. Visitors drive hundreds of miles to attend shows at the Barter, Virginia's official state theater, and the town is crowded the first 2 weeks of August for the popular Virginia Highlands Festival, a display of the region's best arts and crafts.

Abingdon is also a convenient base for a scenic driving tour westward to Big Stone Gap in the Appalachian coal fields (where you'll find yet another fine theater), and for an evening drive to the little community of Maces Spring, where the famous Carter family makes mountain music every Saturday night.

ESSENTIALS

VISITOR INFORMATION   Contact the **Abingdon Convention & Visitors Bureau,** 335 Cummings St., Abingdon, VA 24210 (☎ **800/435-3440** or 540/676-2282; fax 540/676-3076; www.naxs.com/abingdon/tourism; e-mail: acvb@naxs.com). Located in a restored Victorian house, the **Abingdon Visitors Center** is on the left as you drive into town on U.S. 58; it's open daily from 9am to 5pm.

GETTING THERE & GETTING AROUND   Abingdon is at the junction of I-81 and U.S. 11, U.S. 19, and U.S. 58. From I-81, take Exit 17 and follow U.S. 58 west directly into town. U.S. 11 runs east-west along Main Street. Both the **Greyhound/Trailways** bus station (☎ **800/231-2222**) and the local **taxi depot** are at 495 W. Main St. (☎ **540/628-4409**).

WHAT TO SEE & DO

Stop at the visitor center (see "Essentials," above) and pick up a walking-tour brochure and map. With advance notice, the center can also arrange for guided tours. Horse-drawn carriage rides depart from Camberly's Martha Washington Inn (see "Where to Stay," below) on weekends during the summer, or call ☎ **540/669-6522** at other times.

Begin your sightseeing tour at the **Fields-Penn 1860 House Museum,** at the corner of Main and Cummings streets (☎ 540/676-0216), which depicts how Abingdon's elite lived in the mid-19th century. The museum is open Wednesday through Saturday from 1 to 4pm. Admission is free.

From there, stroll east along lovely Main Street, where Camberly's Martha Washington Inn, the Barter Theatre, and 30 other buildings and homes—with birthdates ranging from 1779 to 1925—wait to be observed. Lined with brick sidewalks, the historic part of Main Street runs for about three-quarters of a mile. It goes up and down two hills, so wear comfortable walking shoes.

After the second hill—where the 1869 Washington County Court House stands— you'll come to the **Cave House,** now home to a fine crafts shop (see "Shopping," below). Behind the house is the cave from whence emerged the wolves who attacked Daniel Boone's dogs. To reach it, take the alley to the left of the house to a stop sign, and turn right. You can peer through a lattice fence into the mouth of the cave, which is below a rickety old barn.

Across Main Street is **The Tavern,** considered the oldest building in Abingdon. Built around 1779 and used as a stagecoach inn and tavern, it's now home to one of the town's better restaurants (see "Where to Dine," below). You can still see the mail slot in the town's original post office, in an addition on the east side of the building.

Art lovers can head to the west side of town and the **William King Regional Arts Center,** 415 Academy Dr. (☎ 540/628-5005), where three galleries host rotating exhibits, most with a cultural heritage theme and an emphasis on visual arts produced in Southwest Virginia. There's also a very good museum shop. The center is open Tuesday, Wednesday, and Friday from 10am to 5pm, Thursday from 10am to 9pm, Saturday from 10am to 3pm, and Sunday from 1 to 5pm; it's closed Labor Day weekend. Admission is free with a suggested $3 donation. The center is housed in an old school building in an office complex (turn uphill off Main Street on Academy Street at the Chevron station and follow the signs for arts center parking).

A NEARBY GRISTMILL

A scenic 3¹/₂-mile drive leads from Abingdon through a picturesque valley to **White's Mill** (☎ 540/676-0285), built in 1790, last "restored" in 1866, now on the National Register of Historic Places, and still grinding corn into meal and grits. A sluice provides water for the 20-foot steel wheel. Admission is by donation. Open April to December, Wednesday through Saturday from 9am to dusk; January to March, weekends from 9am to 5pm. White's Mill Mercantile, an old general store across the road, now sells the meal and grits as well as locally made preserves, apple butter, black walnut syrup, rag dolls, dried flower arrangements, and other crafts. From East Valley Street in Abingdon, turn north onto White's Mill Road. It's all downhill to the mill, so you'll have an arduous bike ride coming back.

OUTDOORS: THE VIRGINIA CREEPER TRAIL

Take Pecan Street south off Main Street to the western head of the **Virginia Creeper Trail.** This 34-mile hiking, biking, and horseback-riding route follows an old railroad bed from Abingdon to White Top Station, at the North Carolina line on the southern flank of White Top Mountain, just inside Mount Rogers National Recreation Area. It starts at an elevation of 2,065 feet in Abingdon, drops to 2,000 feet at the town of Damascus (11 miles east on U.S. 58), then climbs to 3,675 feet. Now on display at the Abingdon trailhead is the old steam engine, which had such a tough time with this grade that it became facetiously known as the "Virginia Creeper."

Beginning 2 miles east of Damascus, the stretch between Green Cove Station and Iron Bridge crosses High Trestle (about 100 feet high) and has swimming holes in the adjacent stream. Green Cove is a seasonal Forest Service information post with portable toilets.

Blue Blaze Bike & Shuttle Service in Damascus (☎ **800/475-5905** or 540/ 475-5095) provides bike rentals and operates a daily shuttle along the trail during the summer months, on Saturday and Sunday during spring and fall. Fares are $12 from Abingdon to the top, $9 from Damascus. Bike rentals are $30 for a full day, $20 for a half day.

Bike rentals are also available at the Abingdon trailhead on weekends between April and October from **Highlands Bike Rentals** (☎ **540/628-9672**). During the week you can rent from **Highlands Ski Haus,** on East Main Street near I-81 (☎ **540/ 628-1329**). It's open Monday through Friday from 10am to 7pm, Saturday from 9am to 7pm. Rates at both are $25 per full day and $15 per half day.

SHOPPING

Mountain arts and crafts are for sale in the **Cave House Crafts Shop,** 279 E. Main St. (☎ **540/628-7721**), a 150-member cooperative housed in the 1858 Victorian home built in front of the famous wolf cave.

Original artworks are on display and for sale in the **Arts Depot,** located in the old freight station on Depot Square (☎ **540/628-9091**); visitors are welcome to watch artists at work in their studios Thursday, Friday, and Saturday from 11am to 3pm.

Main Street has no fewer than 10 **antiques shops,** which you will pass during your walking tour.

Dixie Pottery, 5 miles south of Abingdon on U.S. 11 (half a mile south of Exit 13 off I-81), is a huge warehouse-style store that sells decorative objects and housewares from around the world. You'll find both cheap and high-quality china, porcelain figurines, candles, dried and artificial flower arrangements, baskets, and lots of brass, copper, pewter, enamel, and cast-iron ware.

WHERE TO STAY

I-81 has three chain motels: **Comfort Inn** at Exit 14 (☎ **800/221-2222** or 540/ 676-2222), **Super 8** (☎ **800/800-8000** or 540/676-3310) at Exit 17, and **Holiday Inn Express** (☎ **800/HOLIDAY** or 540/676-2929) at Exit 19.

Abingdon has several bed-and-breakfast homes in addition to the Summerfield Inn listed below. The visitor center has a complete list. You can also stay in **Crooked Cabin,** 303 E. Main St., Abingdon, VA 24210 (☎ **540/628-9583**), a log cabin built in 1790. It has three bedrooms, a living room, and kitchen. Rates are $225 in summer, $150 off-season.

✪ **Alpine Motel.** 822 E. Main St. (P.O. Box 615), Abingdon, VA 24212. ☎ **540/628-3178.** Fax 540/628-4217. 19 rms. A/C TV TEL. $47 double. AE, DISC, MC, V.

Located just off Exit 19 of I-81 near several restaurants, this older but extraordinarily well maintained 1960s-vintage motel has mountain views from 15 of its 19 rooms. Owners Jim and Gloria Stroup keep their very spacious units spotlessly clean. Their rates are somewhat higher during the Highlands Festival.

✪ **Camberly's Martha Washington Inn.** 150 W. Main St., Abingdon, VA 24210. ☎ **800/ 533-1014** or 540/628-3161. Fax 540/628-8885. 67 rms, 10 suites. A/C TV TEL. $149–$159 double; $185–$430 suite. Children under 12 stay free in parents' rm. AE, DC, DISC, MC, V. Free parking.

In the heart of the historic district, the stately Greek Revival portico of the Martha Washington Inn creates a formal facade for this 2½-story red-brick hotel; its center portion was built as a private residence in 1832. White-wicker rocking chairs give the front porch the look of an old-time resort. The lobby and adjoining parlor are elegantly decorated, with original marble fireplaces and crystal chandeliers. Choose from regular or deluxe rooms, the latter more lavishly appointed with rich fabrics and fine antiques. Suites have museum-quality furnishings. One, decorated in red silk with gold-leaf trim, has a working fireplace. Two executive-level suites have fireplaces, Jacuzzis, and steam showers.

Dining: The dining room serves traditional Southern fare at breakfast, lunch, and dinner. The President's Club serves cocktails nightly.

Services: Concierge, room service (from 7am to 10pm), nightly turndown, shoeshine.

Summerfield Inn Bed & Breakfast. 101 W. Valley St., Abingdon, VA 24210. ☎ **540/628-5905.** www.naxs.com/abingdon/suminn. E-mail: suminn@naxs.com. 7 rms. A/C TEL. $70–$125 double. Rates include breakfast. AE, DISC, MC, V. Closed Dec–Feb. Free parking on-site.

Just 1 block from Main Street and the Barter Theatre, this gracious 1920s Colonial Revival residence is set back from the quiet street on an expansive lawn. The inviting veranda, bright with flower boxes, is lined with wicker rockers. A spacious foyer leads to a cozy library where guests can relax and watch TV. The dining room, with a handsome sideboard gleaming with a silver tea set, features a magnificent long oval table and period chairs. Adjacent is a cheerful sunroom. A portrait of hosts Don and Champe Hyatt's children graces one wall of the living room, furnished with a piano, Queen Anne–period wing chair, and plush Regency-style sofas flanking the fireplace. The guest rooms offer both the ambience of a private home and the luxurious comfort of a fine hotel; each is elegantly furnished with antique pieces and reproductions. Beside the main house, the "Cottage" houses three deluxe rooms, including a honeymoon suite with TV and Jacuzzi. Breakfast is served at guests' convenience from 7 to 9am.

WHERE TO DINE

The Abingdon General Store and Gallery. 301 E. Main St. (at Tanner St.). ☎ **540/628-8382.** Reservations not accepted. Lunches $6–$7. MC, V. Bakery and deli Mon–Sat 9:30am–5:30pm; dining room Mon–Sat 11am–3pm. DELI/SANDWICHES/SALADS.

The front part of this restored old general store houses a shop that carries gifts, crafts, and decorative pottery; for food, head to the gourmet deli and bakery at the rear. From June through September, you can eat your salad, soup, or deli sandwiches outside in the courtyard known as the Plum Alley Eatery. When the weather turns cold, sit upstairs in the Dumwaiter Restaurant, or pick up a box lunch to take with you while biking, hiking, or riding the Virginia Creeper Trail.

Biscuit Connection. 798 W. Main St. (U.S. 11). ☎ **540/676-2433.** Reservations not accepted. Breakfast, sandwiches, and burgers $1.50–$4. No credit cards. Mon–Fri 6am–2:30pm; Sat 6am–1:30pm. Closed New Year's Day, Thanksgiving, and Christmas. Located 1 mile west of historic district; look for the sign just west of the railroad overpass. AMERICAN.

This tiny (just 5 tables), down-home hole-in-the-wall specializes in big, light biscuits right out of the oven. You can order them at the counter either plain or with gravy, country ham, chicken, sausage, pork tenderloin, or bacon, egg, and cheese. This is the town's best bet for a fresh, inexpensive breakfast. Burgers and homemade sandwiches are available at lunch.

Hardware Company Restaurant. 260 W. Main St. ☎ **540/628-1111.** Reservations not accepted. Sandwiches and burgers $4–$7; main courses $12–$17. MC, V. Sun–Mon 11am–10pm; Tues–Sat 11am–midnight. AMERICAN.

The restaurant bears an appropriate name, for this building housed a hardware store from 1885 until 1983. Many of the old features remain: pressed-tin ceiling, rolling ladder, brick walls, and the old oak counter, now a long and friendly bar. The walls are hung with old-fashioned hardware-store memorabilia. Patrons sit at wooden booths upholstered in black leather or at oak tables in Windsor chairs. A balcony overlooking the main dining area and bar provides extra space. The menu offers a variety of piled-high sandwiches and assorted burgers, plus a limited list of main courses: pastas, steaks, chicken, and a moderately spicy Cajun concoction of shrimp, chicken, and crawfish. Desserts might include hot fudge cake and a candy bar–rich caramel pie.

At the rear of the building, the Main Street Yacht Club Lounge has a round fireplace, sports TVs, and food service after 4:30pm.

✪ **Starving Artist Cafe.** 134 Wall St. (Depot Square). ☎ 540/628-8445. Reservations not accepted. Main courses $12–$21. AE, MC, V. Mon 11am–2pm; Tues–Sat 11am–3pm and 5–9pm. AMERICAN.

Despite its unpretentious location at Depot Square, this charming cafe lacks nothing in the way of culinary sophistication. The food is both innovative and delicious and is prepared using only the freshest ingredients. The setting is low-key: Seating is at silver-painted ice-cream parlor chairs and tables, and walls are adorned with a changing display of local artists' work, all for sale. In summer, there's outdoor dining on the patio. The cafe doesn't lack for customers, and the small dining room is usually full; arrive off-hours or prepare for a wait—it's worth it. French onion soup and smoked salmon with Dijon-horseradish sauce and garlic bread are among the appetizer choices. The chef makes superb pan-blackened prime rib with Cajun spices (Friday and Saturday nights only), steaks, and seafood dishes such as Norwegian salmon Oscar. All entrees are served with a choice of wild rice, rosemary potatoes, twice-baked potato, or home or Cajun fries; hot bread; and a salad. Freshly baked desserts are excellent. At lunch, the menu bestows artists' names on a gallery of sandwiches: The Leonardo da Vinci, for example, features spicy Italian meatballs on a hoagie with fresh tomato-basil sauce and melted provolone.

✪ **The Tavern.** 222 E. Main St. ☎ 540/628-1118. Reservations advised for outdoor seating at dinner. Main courses $12–$21. AE, MC, V. Year-round, Mon–Sat 11am–10pm; June–Aug, Sun noon–8pm. GERMAN/AMERICAN.

The oldest building in Abingdon, the Tavern was built in 1779 as an overnight inn for stagecoach travelers. Exposed brick and stone walls, log beams, and hand-forged locks and hinges make for an appropriately rustic setting. Downstairs, you'll find an antique bar and a cozy waiting lounge with fireplace; upstairs, three dining rooms and a porch overlooking a brick terrace under huge shade trees. The menu reflects the present owners' German and American backgrounds. Lunch offers bratwurst with green peppers and onions, as well as Reubens, smoked-turkey club sandwiches, and ostrich burgers. At dinner, you can choose from Wiener schnitzel, kassler ripchen (German smoked pork loin), shrimp Provençal, veal or shrimp piccata, or Southern-fried chicken.

EVENING ENTERTAINMENT

✪ **Barter Theatre.** At the corner of W. Main and College sts. ☎ 540/628-3991. Tickets $16–$24, depending on show and time.

The official policy still permits barter for admission (with prior notice), but theatergoers now pay cash to attend the State Theater of Virginia, America's longest-running professional repertory theater. The building itself was built around 1832 as

Hams for *Hamlet*

The career of an aspiring, Virginia-born actor named Robert Porterfield came to a screeching halt during the Great Depression. Giving up on Broadway, he and 22 other unemployed actors came to Abingdon during the summer of 1933 and began putting on plays and shows.

Their first production was John Golden's *After Tomorrow,* for which they charged an admission of 40¢, or the equivalent in farm produce—thus did their little operation become known as the Barter Theatre.

Playwrights who contributed—among them Noel Coward, Thornton Wilder, Robert Sherwood, Maxwell Anderson, and George Bernard Shaw—were paid with a token Virginia ham. Shaw, a vegetarian, returned the smoked delicacy and requested spinach instead; Porterfield and his crew obliged.

The first season ended with a profit of $4.30, two barrels of jelly, and a collective weight gain of 300 pounds!

a Presbyterian church, and later served as a meeting hall for the Sons of Temperance. It functioned as the town hall and opera house when Robert Porterfield brought his unemployed actors here in 1932 (see box, above). Recent productions, now performed by an Actor's Equity company, have included *Camelot; Alice . . . through the Picture Tube; Travels With My Aunt; The Bear Facts;* and *Don't Dress for Dinner.* The theater's impressive alumni include Hume Cronyn, Patricia Neal, Fritz Weaver, Ernest Borgnine, Gregory Peck, and Ned Beatty. Across Main Street, the **Barter's First Light Theatre** specializes in the classics. The season for both stages runs from April through December.

✪ **Carter Family Fold Music Shows.** C.R. 614, Maces Spring. ☎ **540/386-9480.** Music show tickets $4 adults, $1 children 6–12, free for children under 6. From Abingdon, take I-81 south 17 miles to Bristol, U.S. 58 west 19 miles to Hiltons, C.R. 614 east 3 miles to auditorium.

Mountain-music fans consider the 78-mile round-trip from Abingdon to the Carter Family Music Center well worth it, for here they can see and hear the best regional artists every Saturday night. This is as pure as it gets—the descendants of country music legends A.P. Carter, wife Sara, and sister-in-law Maybelle won't allow electronic equipment in their unpretentious auditorium, which occupies a huge shed. Local residents are adept at traditional styles like buck dancing and clogging on a small dance floor in front of the stage. An annual festival that takes place during the first weekend in August (the same time as the Virginia Highlands Festival in Abingdon) draws many well-known singers and music groups, clog-dance performers, and local artisans who sell crafts. A family museum in A.P. Carter's country store is open on Saturday from 5 to 7pm, before the show.

AN EASY EXCURSION TO BIG STONE GAP

The mountains get steeper and the valleys narrower as you head west from Abingdon into Virginia's share of the Appalachian coal fields. Following I-81 south, U.S. 58 west, U.S. 23 north, and Alternate U.S. 58 east, you can make a scenic loop through these hollows.

From Abingdon, take I-81 south 17 miles to Bristol, then follow the winding U.S. 58 west across the mountains 40 miles to **National Tunnel State Park,** where you can take a cable-car ride down a 400-foot-deep gorge to railroad tracks emerging from the mouth of an 850-foot-long tunnel cut by an underground river. The park has nature trails, interpretive programs, a campground, a swimming pool, and a small but very good museum explaining the tunnel's geological formation. Admission to the park is free; cable-car rides cost $2 round-trip. The park is open daily from 8am to dusk; the cable car operates daily from 10am to 5pm during summer, weekends only in spring and fall. For information, contact the park at Route 3, Box 250, Duffield, VA 24244 (☎ **540/940-2674**).

From Duffield, you can make a sidetrip west 55 miles in each direction on U.S. 58 to **Cumberland Gap National Historical Park,** at the confluence of Virginia, Kentucky, and Tennessee. During the 1780s, more than 300,000 settlers followed Daniel Boone to Kentucky through the gap, at that time the only way to get wagons through the otherwise unbroken Allegheny Front. It is still a major local thoroughfare, with a four-lane highway through the gap.

After Duffield, U.S. 23 climbs north through Jefferson National Forest into the mining town of **Big Stone Gap.** Take the first U.S. 23 Business exit and follow it to the **Regional Tourist and Information Center,** where you can get a walking-tour brochure. The center is housed in Interstate Railroad Private Car Number 101, built in 1870. Visitors are welcome to poke through its staterooms and dining room. The center and car are open from Memorial Day to Labor Day, Monday through Wednesday from 9am to 5pm, Thursday through Saturday from 9am to 7pm, and Sunday from 1 to 5pm; the rest of the year, Monday through Friday from 10am to 4:30pm. For information in advance, contact the center at P.O. Box 236, Big Stone Gap, VA 24219 (☎ **540/523-2060**).

Big Stone Gap was the hometown of John Fox, Jr., author of *Trail of the Lonesome Pine.* His sentimental drama—a local lass falls for a Yankee mining engineer and becomes a worldly woman—is re-enacted every summer by **Trail of the Lonesome Pine State Outdoor Drama,** on Clinton Avenue near East 4th Street (☎ **540/ 523-1235**). Shows are at 8pm Thursday through Saturday from mid-June through August. Tickets are $10 for adults, $7 for seniors and children. The playhouse is adjacent to the **June Tolliver House & Craft Shop** (☎ **540/523-4707**), home of the heroine's real-life role model.

The **John Fox, Jr., Museum** (☎ **540/523-2747** or 540/523-1235), in his charming 1888 house on Shawnee Avenue between East 2nd and East 3rd streets, is filled with family furnishings and mementos. It's open from Memorial Day to Labor Day, Tuesday and Wednesday from 2 to 5pm and Thursday through Sunday from 2 to 6pm; admission is $3 for adults and $1 for students.

The **Southwest Virginia Museum,** West 1st Street and Wood Avenue (☎ **540/ 523-1322**), is housed in a renovated 1888 residence and displays artifacts of the history and culture of the area. The **Harry W. Meador, Jr., Coal Museum,** Shawnee Avenue at East 3rd Street (☎ **540/523-4950**), explains the industry that has been the backbone of the local economy for more than a century.

From Big Stone Gap, take U.S. 23 north, then Alternate U.S. 58 east back to Abingdon. The rest of the trip is easy, since both highways have four lanes.

AN EASY EXCURSION TO CRAB ORCHARD

About 1 hour north of Abingdon on U.S. 19/460 just west of Tazewell, the **Crab Orchard Museum and Pioneer Park of Southwestern Virginia** (☎ **540/ 988-6755**) is an exceptionally interesting museum with exhibits devoted to prehistoric times, Native Americans, the Revolutionary War, the Civil War, and the domestic life and home industries of the area. Outdoors are original farm dwellings, shops, and barns outfitted in typical pioneer fashion. Admission is $6 for adults, $5 for seniors, $3 for children 13 to 18, and free for kids under 13. The museum is open Monday through Saturday from 9am to 5pm, Sunday from 1 to 5pm.

Richmond 10

Richmond supplanted the more militarily vulnerable Williamsburg as Virginia's capital in 1780, and it has been the scene of much of the state's history ever since. It was in St. John's Church that Patrick Henry concluded his address to the second Virginia Convention with the stirring words "Give me liberty, or give me death!" The traitorous Benedict Arnold led British troops down what is now Main Street in 1781 and set fire to many buildings, including tobacco warehouses—in those days, the equivalent of banks. Cornwallis briefly occupied the town, and Lafayette came to the rescue.

It was during the Civil War, however, that Richmond made its mark on American history. Jefferson Davis presided over the Confederate Congress here, and Robert E. Lee accepted command of Virginia's armed forces. For 4 years the Union army tried to capture it. Battling troops often surrounded the city, overflowing its tobacco warehouses with prisoners of war, its hospitals with the wounded, and its cemeteries with the dead.

The city has a host of monuments, battlefields, and museums that recall its role during the Civil War, and just 30 minutes south on I-95 sits Petersburg, where the war's last great battle sealed Richmond's fate. But there are also more modern attractions to keep visitors busy, including an excellent fine arts museum, a hands-on science museum with state-of-the-art planetarium, and a lovely botanical garden.

A short drive north of the city will take you to that most modern of all attractions, Paramount's Kings Dominion theme park, while an excursion to the south leads to historic Petersburg, the vital rail junction whose loss in 1865 led to Lee's surrender a week later.

1 Orientation & Getting Around

ARRIVING

BY PLANE **Richmond International Airport,** Airport Drive off I-64, I-295, and Williamsburg Road (U.S. 60) (☎ 804/226-3052), locally known as Byrd Field, is about 15 minutes east of downtown. It's served by American, Continental, Delta, Northwest, United, and US Airways.

The major car-rental companies have desks at the airport.

Groome Transportation (☎ 800/552-7911 in Virginia, or 804/222-7222) offers 24-hour van service to downtown; the cost is

---

❓ Did You Know?

- The Houdon statue of George Washington in the Rotunda of the State Capitol is the only one ever made of the first president from life.
- Richmond is the only major metropolitan area in the country that has white-water rafting trips in the heart of the city.
- Swollen with the rainstorms of Hurricane Agnes in 1972, the James River rushed down the streets of Shockoe Bottom, causing damage in excess of $350 million. Now this area is behind a flood wall.
- The oldest lawmaking body in the western hemisphere, the General Assembly of Virginia, has convened in Richmond since 1788.

$13.50 for one person, $17.75 for two people, $21.25 for three people, and $6.50 each for four or more. Groome also runs vans to Williamsburg ($28 for one person, $18 per person for two or more going to the same place), and it sends a shuttle to Fredericksburg ($23 per person one-way) and Ronald Reagan Washington National Airport ($30 per person one-way) daily every hour on the half hour from 6:30am to 4:30pm. The return shuttle leaves Ronald Reagan Washington National Airport on the hour, so you can get from Washington, D.C., or Fredericksburg to Richmond via airport shuttle.

BY CAR   Two major interstate highways intersect in Richmond—**I-64,** traveling east-west, and **I-95,** traveling north-south. **I-295** bypasses the city on its east and north sides. **U.S. 60** (east-west) and **U.S. 1** and **U.S. 301** (north-south) are other major arteries.

BY TRAIN   Several daily **Amtrak** trains pull into the station at 7519 Staples Mill Rd., north of Exit 185 off I-64 (☎ **800/872-7245**). Bus Route 27 connects the station to downtown (see "Getting Around," below).

BY BUS   The **Greyhound/Trailways** bus terminal is at 2910 N. Boulevard (☎ **800/231-2222**), near the Metro Richmond Visitors Center (see below).

VISITOR INFORMATION

The **Metro Richmond Convention and Visitors Bureau,** 550 E. Marshall St. (Box C-250), Richmond, VA 23219 (☎ **800/365-7272** or 804/782-2777; fax 804/780-2577; www.erols.com/richmond), provides information in advance and will make hotel reservations, often at a discount (call its toll-free number).

It also operates four visitor information centers. One is in the bureau's offices on the second floor of Sixth Street Marketplace, on Marshall Street at 6th Street. The bureau is open Monday through Friday from 8:30am to 5pm.

Drivers approaching via I-95/I-64 can take Exit 78 to the **Metro Richmond Visitors Center,** 1710 Robin Hood Rd. near Boulevard (☎ **804/358-5511**), opposite the Diamond baseball park. The center occupies an old railroad station, and has a huge steam locomotive, a red caboose, and several other cars on display in a small park with picnic area. It's open September to May, daily from 9am to 5pm, and June to August, until 7pm.

A third center is in the **Bell Tower** (☎ **804/648-3146**), on the State Capitol grounds near 9th Street and Marshall Avenue. It's open April to October, Monday through Saturday from 9am to 5pm, and November to March, Monday through Friday from 9am to 4pm.

Metropolitan Richmond

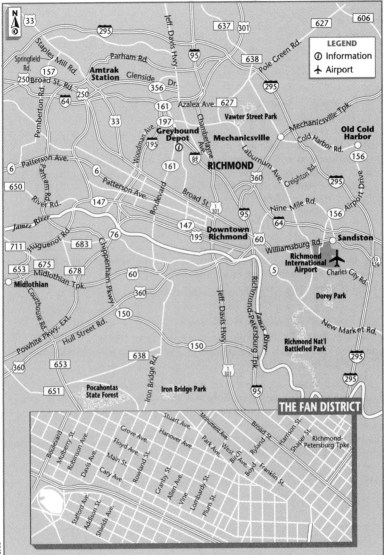

LEGEND
- ⓘ Information
- ✈ Airport

THE FAN DISTRICT

1-0958

Finally, the **Richmond International Airport Visitors Center** (☎ **804/236-3260**) is open Monday through Saturday from 9:30am to 5:30pm, Sunday from noon to 5:30pm.

CITY LAYOUT

Richmond is located at the fall line of the James River. Although the city has spread southward, all the hotels, restaurants, and historic sites of interest to visitors are north of the river. A series of bridges crosses the river, and there's also access to two islands, Brown's Island and Belle Isle. **Brown's Island** is separated from the mainland by the old **Kanawha Canal,** on which 19th-century barges carried cargo around the rapids, and is accessible by a footbridge from South 7th and Tredegar streets. It is rather flat

Impressions

Broad-streeted Richmond . . . The trees in the streets are old trees used to living with people. Family trees that remember your grandfather's name.
—Stephen Vincent Benet, *John Brown's Body*

and traversed by train tracks on its river side. **Belle Isle,** once the site of an infamous Civil War prison, is a more scenic spot. It's accessible via a footbridge under the Lee Bridge; there are signs on 3rd and 5th at Byrd Street, directing visitors to Tredegar Street and then to the bridge.

Foushee Street divides street numbers east and west, while **Main Street** divides them north and south. **Broad Street** is the major east-west thoroughfare, and it's one of the few downtown streets with two-way traffic.

NEIGHBORHOODS IN BRIEF

Metropolitan Richmond grew from east to west, along the banks of the James River. As you explore the neighborhoods described below (moving roughly from east to west), you'll get a good sense of Richmond's history.

Church Hill   This east Richmond neighborhood is largely residential, with an abundance of 19th-century Greek Revival residences. St. John's Church is the outstanding landmark of the area. Bordering Church Hill is:

Tobacco Row   Paralleling the James River for about 15 city blocks between 20th and Pear streets, this is Richmond's latest urban redevelopment area; handsome old red-brick warehouses are being converted into apartment houses here.

Shockoe Bottom   Shockoe Bottom is roughly bounded by Dock and Broad streets and 15th and 20th streets, with the heart at the 17th Street Farmer's Market between East Main and East Franklin streets. Richmond's first real business district, it once encompassed tobacco factories, produce markets (farmers still sell produce at stands on North 17th Street), slave auction houses, warehouses, and shops, and it retains much of its original character. Today, old-fashioned groceries with signs in their windows for fresh chitterlings stand alongside trendy shops and restaurants, making this Richmond's prime nightlife district. Shockoe Bottom is also home to the Edgar Allan Poe House and the old train station, whose spectacular clock tower is visible to motorists on I-95.

Shockoe Slip   This warehouse and commercial area was reduced to rubble in 1865 and rebuilt as a manufacturing center after the war. Although it has lost some of its luster to Shockoe Bottom, Shockoe Slip today is a tourist mecca, with its quaint cobblestone streets, old-fashioned street lamps, and renovated warehouses and residences housing lively restaurants, art galleries, nightspots, and fashionable shops. The Slip adjoins downtown on the east, roughly between 10th and 14th streets and Main and Canal streets.

Downtown   West and north of Shockoe Slip, downtown includes the old and new city halls, the state capitol, and other government buildings of Capitol Square; and the historic homes and museums of the Court End area, notably the Valentine Museum, Museum and White House of the Confederacy, and John Marshall House. The financial and business center of Richmond, downtown also encompasses the Coliseum, the Carpenter Center for the Performing Arts, and the Sixth Street Marketplace.

Of Swords & Tennis Racquets

Since it fell to Grant's army in 1865, Richmond has changed in many ways—especially in its demographics. Many descendants of the defeated Confederate soldiers have fled to Richmond's sprawling suburbs, while descendants of the slaves those soldiers fought so hard to keep in bondage now control the city council. Their majority set the city's remaining old-line residents on ear in 1995 by voting to place the statue of an African American among those of the Civil War heroes lining hallowed Monument Avenue.

It was a hard-fought battle, but today at the corner of Monument Avenue and Roseneath Road stands the bronze likeness of the late Arthur Ashe—Richmond's most famous modern son—holding not a sword, but a tennis racquet.

Jackson Ward   Jackson Ward, north of Broad Street, is a downtown National Historic District and home to many famous African Americans, including the first woman bank president in the United States, Maggie Walker, and legendary tap dancer Bill "Bojangles" Robinson, who donated a stoplight for the safety of children crossing the intersection of Leigh Street and Chamberlayne Avenue (where a monument to him stands today). Notable, too, is the fine ornamental ironwork gracing the facades of many Jackson Ward residences.

The Fan   Just west of downtown, the Fan is named for the shape of the streets, which "fan" out from downtown. Bordered by West Broad and Boulevard and West Main and Belvidere, it includes Virginia Commonwealth University and many turn-of-the-century town houses, now occupied by homes, apartments, restaurants, and galleries. Monument Avenue's most scenic blocks, with the famous Civil War statues down its median strip, are in the Fan.

Carytown   Just west of Boulevard, Carytown has been called Richmond's answer to Georgetown. Cafes, restaurants, boutiques, antique shops, and the restored Byrd Theater, an old movie palace, bring Saturday-afternoon crowds to stroll West Cary Street.

GETTING AROUND

BY PUBLIC TRANSPORTATION   The Greater Richmond Transit Company (☎ 804/358-GRTC) operates the **public bus** system throughout the metropolitan area and a motorized **trolley** around downtown. Pick up maps at any visitor center for the trolley, which runs Monday through Saturday, every 10 to 15 minutes between 11am and 8:30pm, every 25 minutes from 8:30 to 11pm. Trolley fare is 25¢ per ride. Base bus fare is $1.25. Service on most bus routes begins at 5am and ends at midnight. GRTC has an information booth in Sixth Street Marketplace, Marshall Street and 6th Street, where you can get trolley and bus maps.

No public bus service is available between downtown and the airport.

BY CAR   Richmond is fairly easy to navigate by car, although all but a few streets are one-way. Left turns from a one-way street onto another one-way street may be made at red lights after a full stop.

BY TAXI   Call **Yellow Cab Service Inc.** (☎ 804/222-7300) or **Veterans Cab Association** (☎ 804/329-1414). Fares are approximately $1.50 per mile.

BY BICYCLE   Bikes can be rented at **Two Wheel Travel,** 2934 W. Cary St. (☎ 804/359-2453), in Carytown 2 blocks west of Boulevard.

SAFETY

Richmond has a drug problem, so ask at the visitor centers or at your hotel desk if a neighborhood you intend to visit is safe. Avoid all deserted streets after dark. In any city, even in the most heavily visited areas, it's wise to stay alert and be aware of your surroundings, whatever the time of day.

2 Accommodations

The closest suburban chain motels to downtown are near Robin Hood Road and I-95 (Exit 78), near the Metro Richmond Visitors Center and the Diamond, home of baseball's Richmond Braves: **Days Inn North** (☎ 800/DAYSINN or 804/353-1287) and **Holiday Inn Central** (☎ 800/HOLIDAY or 804/359-9441).

The Executive Center area, on West Broad Street (U.S. 33/250) at I-64 (Exit 183), about 5 miles west of downtown, has a wide selection of much newer properties. This pleasant, campus-like area also has many chain restaurants, including an inexpensive Morrison's Cafeteria. Best of the hotels is the redwood-and-brick **Hyatt Richmond at Brookfield** (☎ 800/233-1234 or 804/285-1234). Nearby are the colonial-look **Comfort Inn Executive Center** (☎ 800/228-5150 or 804/672-1108), a comfortable **Courtyard by Marriott** (☎ 800/321-2211 or 804/282-1881), a **Days Inn** (☎ 800/DAYS-INN or 804/282-3300), a **Fairfield Inn by Marriott** (☎ 800/228-2200 or 804/755-7155), the **Hampton Inn West** (☎ 800/HAMPTON or 804/747-7777), the **Holiday Inn West** (☎ 800/HOLIDAY or 804/285-9951), a **Shoney's Inn** (☎ 800/222-2222 or 804/672-7007), and a **Super 8** (☎ 800/800-8000 or 804/672-8128).

If you arrive without a reservation, the Metro Richmond Visitors Bureau will assist you in making one, or you can call them in advance for help at ☎ **800/365-7272** (see "Visitor Information," above).

EXPENSIVE

The Berkeley Hotel. 1200 E. Cary St. (at 12th St.), Richmond, VA 23219. ☎ **804/780-1300.** Fax 804/343-1885. 55 rms. A/C TV TEL. $130–$175 double. Weekend and other packages available. AE, DC, DISC, MC, V. Complimentary valet parking.

At this elegant little Shockoe Slip hostelry, a handsome red-brick facade opens into a seemingly old-world interior. Although established in 1988, the hotel creates the illusion that it was built hundreds of years ago. Rooms are very residential in feel and luxuriously appointed with fine period-reproduction furnishings and walls hung with botanical prints; some have Jacuzzis.

Dining: Every chef in town says that the Berkeley has Richmond's finest dining. Virginia ingredients accent entrees such as venison with kale, stewed okra, and black-eyed peas, or breast of duck with creamy grits, wild mushrooms, and berries. Nightingale's Lounge adjoins.

Services: Concierge, laundry, newspaper, turndown.

Facilities: Pool and health club nearby.

✪ **Jefferson Hotel.** Franklin and Adams sts., Richmond, VA 23220. ☎ **800/484-8014** or 804/788-8000. Fax 804/225-0334. 275 rms. A/C MINIBAR TV TEL. $165–$225 double. Additional person $10 extra; children under 17 stay free in parents' rm. Weekend and other packages available. AE, DC, MC, V. Self-parking $8; valet parking $11.

A stunning Beaux Arts sightseeing attraction in its own right, the Jefferson was opened in 1895 by Maj. Lewis Ginter, who wanted his city to have one of the finest hotels in America. He hired the architectural firm of Carrère & Hastings, which had designed the monumental New York Public Library. The magnificent limestone-and-brick facade here is adorned with Renaissance-style balconies, arched porticos, and an Italian clock tower. Two-story faux-marble columns, embellished with gold leaf, encircle the Rotunda, or lower lobby. Acres of Oriental area rugs define the central seating area, furnished with elegant tufted-leather sofas amid potted palms. The marble Grand Staircase, magnificently wide and red-carpeted, leads to the Palm Court upper lobby under a stained-glass domed skylight; 9 of its 12 panes are original Tiffany glass.

Furnished with custom-made 18th-century reproduction pieces, the rooms have hosted hundreds of notables, including Charles Lindbergh, Henry Ford, Charlie Chaplin, Elvis Presley, and Presidents Harrison, McKinley, Wilson, Coolidge, and both Roosevelts. F. Scott and Zelda Fitzgerald held glamorous parties here.

Dining: Sunday brunch in the Rotunda is a bountiful all-you-can-eat feast in opulent surroundings. T.J.'s (as in Thomas Jefferson) is a restaurant, bar, and oyster bar just off the Rotunda. Off the Palm Court, there's elegant dining at Lemaire's (named for the real T.J.'s maître d'), a warren of seven handsome rooms, one with a library. Dinners here feature regional entrees such as roast pheasant stuffed with fresh oysters and Virginia ham in wine sauce.

Services: Concierge, 24-hour room service, same-day valet laundry, complimentary newspaper, nightly turndown, baby-sitting; shuttle to theaters and Shockoe Slip can be arranged.

Facilities: Access to nearby health club, business center, beauty salon, gift shop.

Omni Richmond Hotel. 100 S. 12th St. (at E. Cary St.), Richmond, VA 23219. ☎ **800/ THE-OMNI** or 804/344-7000. Fax 804/648-6704. 347 rms, 6 suites. A/C MINIBAR TV TEL. $189 double; $209–$239 suite. Additional person $15 extra; children under 12 stay free in parents' rm. Weekend and other packages available. AE, DC, DISC, MC, V. Valet parking $9.

The Omni is located in the James Center office towers, across the street from Shockoe Slip's boutiques, restaurants, and clubs. It boasts a handsome pink-marble lobby, with green-velvet–upholstered chairs and sofas around a working fireplace. Rooms are decorated in soft pastels, and some have spectacular views of the nearby James River. Club-floor rooms offer access to a private lounge, where a complimentary continental breakfast and afternoon refreshments are served on weekdays.

Dining: Caffè Gallego is a casual venue that opens to the office tower's atrium. The Market, a gourmet take-out deli, offers breakfast pastries and other bakery treats, sandwiches, and pizzas.

Services: Concierge, room service (from 7am to midnight).

Facilities: Indoor/outdoor pool with sun deck, squash and racquetball courts, and Nautilus equipment, all on the premises, are available to Omni guests for $10 per day. James Center shops adjoin the hotel lobby.

Richmond Marriott. 500 E. Broad St. (at 5th St.), Richmond, VA 23219. ☎ **800/228-9290** or 804/643-3400. Fax 804/788-1230. 401 rms, 10 suites. A/C TV TEL. $129 double; $200–$500 suite. Weekend and other packages available. AE, DC, DISC, MC, V. Self-parking $5; valet parking $7. Bus: 1, 2, or 3.

Ideally located for convention-goers at the Sixth Street Marketplace shops, the Marriott is connected via a skywalk to the Richmond Convention Center. Many of the exceptionally spacious and handsomely furnished accommodations offer panoramic city views.

Dining/Entertainment: Allie's American Grille serves breakfast, lunch, and dinner in a cheerful atmosphere. Sporting events are aired on the big TV in Triplett's, the lobby lounge and cocktail bar.

Services: Concierge, limited room service, laundry, free newspaper.

Facilities: Indoor pool, health club, game room, gift shop.

MODERATE

Crowne Plaza Hotel. 555 E. Canal St. (at 6th St.), Richmond, VA 23219. ☎ **800/HOLIDAY** or 804/788-0900. Fax 804/788-7087. 300 rms. AC TV TEL. $79–$119 double. Additional person $10 extra. AE, DC, DISC, MC, V. Self-parking $5; valet parking $8.

You won't mistake this Crowne Plaza for any other building in town—it's a starkly modern, triangular 16-story high-rise with reflecting glass windows. Formerly the Radisson Hotel Richmond, it was undergoing a $3-million renovation during a recent visit, so rates may be higher than those quoted above. Most rooms offer stunning city views. Facilities include an indoor pool, health club, sauna, Jacuzzi, and Nautilus equipment. Guests on the executive level get their own concierge and complimentary continental breakfast.

The casual Pavilion Cafe serves all three meals, while the Capital Grille offers a more formal venue for dinner.

✪ **Linden Row Inn.** 100 E. Franklin St. (at 1st St.), Richmond, VA 23219. ☎ **800/348-7424** or 804/783-7000. Fax 804/648-7504. 64 rms, 6 suites. A/C TV TEL. $99–$149 double; $149–$199 suite. Additional person $5 extra; children under 18 stay free in parents' rm. Rates include continental breakfast. AE, DC, MC, V. Valet parking $7.

This row of seven 140-year-old Greek Revival town houses and their garden dependencies (small, separate buildings) is within walking distance of Shockoe Slip, Capitol Square, and the financial center. Not only the facades have remained intact; original interior features such as fireplaces, marble mantels, and crystal chandeliers still grace the inn. In other words, the property has been renovated but not restored, so don't expect the quality—or services—you'll get at a place like the Jefferson Hotel.

Rooms in the main houses, all with windows nearly reaching the 12-foot ceilings, have a mix of late-Empire and early-Victorian pieces, with damask draperies, flower-patterned carpets, and marble-top dressers. Back rooms overlook a brick-walled garden and patio, and the garden dependencies of the original town houses have been restored and offer accommodations with private entrances, pine furniture, and handmade quilts.

The cozy dining room is not the inn's strong suit. Cheese, crackers, and drinks in the early evening and hot beverages after dinner are laid out buffet style in two parlors, handsomely furnished with leather couches and working fireplaces.

Limo service and limited room service are available, and use of the YMCA Fitness Center is free to guests.

BED & BREAKFASTS

Carefully chosen bed-and-breakfast accommodations in the downtown area are offered by **Bensonhouse of Richmond,** 2036 Monument Ave., Richmond, VA 23220 (☎ **804/353-6900;** fax 804/355-5050; www.bensonhouse.com; e-mail: be.our.guest@bensonhouse.com). Administrator Lyn Benson offers five listings, all within 5 to 15 minutes of major attractions, and all with hosts who are knowledgeable about the city. Rates range from $95 to $155 for a double; full or continental breakfast included. Ms. Benson's own B&B, **Emmanuel Hutzler House** (address above; ☎ **804/355-4885**), is an Italian Renaissance–style inn, built in the 1900s with beautiful mahogany paneling, leaded-glass windows, and a coffered-beam ceiling, all lovingly restored. Her spacious guest rooms boast handsome antique furnishings, TVs, private baths (some with Jacuzzis), and in-room telephones.

Mr. Patrick Henry's Inn. 2300–02 E. Broad St. (at 23rd St.), Richmond, VA 23223. ☎ **800/932-2654** or 804/644-1322. 4 suites. A/C TV TEL. $95–$125 double. Rates include full breakfast for two. AE, DC, DISC, MC, V.

Downtown Richmond Accommodations & Dining

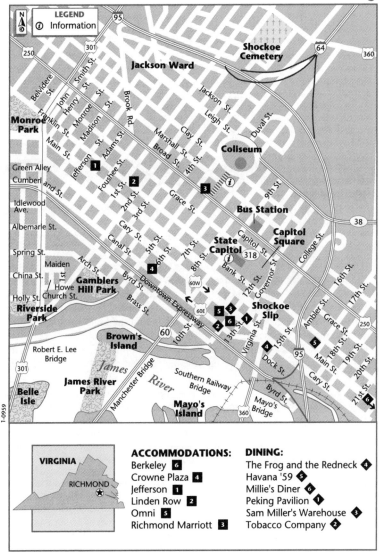

LEGEND
ⓘ Information

ACCOMMODATIONS:
Berkeley **6**
Crowne Plaza **4**
Jefferson **1**
Linden Row **2**
Omni **5**
Richmond Marriott **3**

DINING:
The Frog and the Redneck ◆4
Havana '59 ◆5
Millie's Diner ◆6
Peking Pavilion ◆1
Sam Miller's Warehouse ◆3
Tobacco Company ◆2

VIRGINIA
RICHMOND ★

One block west of historic St. John's Church, these two Greek Revival town houses are in Richmond's oldest neighborhood. Innkeepers James and Lynn News have turned their first two floors over to a tavern and colonial-style restaurant, where James's cooking has received critical acclaim. The tavern on the basement level has low-beamed ceilings and whitewashed-brick walls; it serves up light fare. The outdoor garden patio offers alfresco dining in good weather. All accommodations have working fireplaces and kitchenettes, and one has a private balcony overlooking the garden. Furnishings are a mix of antiques and reproductions, featuring four-poster beds, wing chairs, and pretty ruffled curtains. St. John's landmark church is just a block away, and the Richmond battlefield headquarters are nearby.

William Catlin House Bed & Breakfast Inn. 2304 E. Broad St. (between 23rd and 24th sts.), Richmond, VA 23223. ☎ **804/780-3746.** 5 rms (3 with bath). A/C. $95–$150 double. Rates include breakfast and taxes. DISC, MC, V. Free off-street parking.

Occupying an 1845 Greek Revival residence, this inn offers a comfortable home away from home. Sliding doors separate a plush first-floor parlor from the dining room, where breakfast is served. Guest accommodations are in the basement and on the second and third floors. They're tastefully furnished with period pieces, lace curtains, fireplaces, and charming decorative objects like spinning wheels and dried-flower arrangements. Hosts Robert and Josephine Martin provide evening snacks of sherry and mints as well as a delicious full breakfast.

3 Dining

SHOCKOE SLIP

✪ The Frog and the Redneck. 1423 E. Cary St. (between 14th and 15th sts.). ☎ **804/648-3764.** Reservations recommended. Main courses $14–$20. AE, DC, DISC, MC, V. Dining room, Mon–Fri 5:30–10pm; Sat 5–10:30pm. Cafe bar, Mon–Fri 11:30am–2pm and 5:30–10pm; Sat 5–10:30pm. FRENCH/AMERICAN.

This facetious name derives from co-owner and chef Jimmy Sneed, who grew up in the South and then worked as an under-chef at Jean-Louis Paladin's renowned French restaurant in Washington, D.C. Jimmy excellently blends the "Frog" style of cooking he learned there with local "Redneck" ingredients. For example, instead of Bayonne ham and melon, Jimmy offers Virginia ham and local cantaloupe as an appetizer. Some of the largest lumps of backfin Chesapeake crab meat we've ever seen floated in his delicious pimento-accented sweet red pepper soup. As his signature dish, Jimmy packs those giant lumps into the best sautéed crabcakes we've ever tasted. Jimmy changes his menu daily to incorporate the freshest local produce. A suggestion: Try his five-course sampler menu, a deal at $45 per person. Meanwhile, co-owner Adam Steely presides over a spacious bistro-style dining room with mirrors on the posts supporting the upper floors of a converted warehouse. As would be expected, the wine list carries a good selection of both French and Virginian vintages.

The adjoining **Frog Bar Cafe** draws a yuppie crowd for lunch (wood-fired pizzas are the specialty) and evening drinks.

Peking Pavilion. 1302 E. Cary St. (at 13th St.). ☎ **804/649-8888.** Reservations recommended. Main courses $8.75–$22.50. AE, MC, V. Sun–Thurs 11:30am–9:30pm; Fri 11:30am–10:45pm; Sat 5–10:30pm. Free parking after 5pm in Central Parking Garage, E. Cary St. at Virginia St. CHINESE.

The exquisite wood carvings and tapestries on the walls and the dragon-motif-backed chairs of this plush choice are from mainland China. Yet for all its elegance, Peking Pavilion offers surprisingly inexpensive combination lunch platters—entree with soup, spring roll, and fried rice for $5.25 to $7. House special entrees lead off with Peking duck with crispy skin and tender meat, Chinese pancakes, spring onions, and plum sauce. Or you might try Seafood Delight, a combination of shrimp, scallops, lobster, and chicken sautéed in a rich, spicy sauce.

Sam Miller's Warehouse. 1210 E. Cary St. (between 12th and 13 sts.). ☎ **804/643-1301.** Reservations suggested, especially for dinner on weekends. Sandwiches and burgers $5.50–$8; main courses $14–$25.50. AE, DC, MC, V. Daily 11:30am–4:30pm and 5–11pm; Sun brunch 10am–5pm; Fri–Sat entertainment until 2am. AMERICAN.

A popular pub since the Slip's revival in 1975, Sam Miller's seats diners in cozy booths, with small dark-green tole lamps on the tables keeping the lighting romantically low. At lunch, terrific sandwiches include beef barbecue with coleslaw, crabcakes, and a juicy 5-ounce hamburger. Chesapeake Bay seafood and prime rib are dinner-menu highlights. The seafood entrees, all served with vegetable du jour and wild rice or baked potato, include broiled or blackened fresh fish du jour; shrimp stuffed with crab imperial; and an enormous seafood platter piled high with scallops, oysters, clams, shrimp, fresh fish, and crabcakes.

The Tobacco Company. 1201 E. Cary St. (at 12th St.). ☎ **804/782-9431.** Reservations accepted. Main courses $16–$22. AE, DC, MC, V. Mon–Fri 11:30am–2:30pm and 5:30–10:30pm; Sat 11:30am–2:30pm and 5–11pm; Sun 10:30am–2:30pm and 5:30–10pm. AMERICAN.

Appropriately, this dining-entertainment complex is housed in a former tobacco warehouse that's been converted to a sunny, plant-filled three-story atrium. An exposed antique elevator carries guests from the first-floor cocktail lounge to the two dining floors above. Nostalgic touches abound—brass chandeliers, a cigar-store Indian, even an old ticket booth that now serves as the hostess desk. Tiffany-style lamps cast a glow on the seating areas, handsomely sectioned off by white porch-style banisters. Exposed-brick walls are festooned with antique collectors' items.

Contemporary American cuisine is featured. Lunch specialties could be as light as a vegetarian stir-fry or as hearty as chicken chimichangas. Also available are omelets, salads, sandwiches, and burgers. At dinner, you might begin with shrimp and Virginia ham with papaya or an innovative pairing of mushrooms and escargots, then move on to the house special: slow-roasted prime rib with seconds on the house. There's live music in the Club downstairs Tuesday through Saturday nights, with dancing Thursday through Saturday.

SHOCKOE BOTTOM

Havana '59. 16 N. 17th St. (between Main and Franklin sts.). ☎ **804/649-2822.** Reservations not accepted. Sandwiches and salads $4–$7; main courses $10–$15. AE, DC, DISC, MC, V. Sun–Thurs 5:30–11pm; Fri–Sat 5:30–11:30pm; Sat–Sun brunch 10am–3pm. CUBAN.

This lively theme restaurant presents a strange sight across the street from the covered stalls of Richmond's ancient Farmer's Market, especially during warm weather when its big, garage-style storefront windows roll up to let fresh air in—and cigar smoke out. Then you might swear you're down in Havana in 1959 when Fidel Castro marched into town. Fake palms, ceiling fans, string lights, Cuban music, and adobe walls with gaping holes (where plaster ought to be) set a festive scene. Although the quality of the Cuban cuisine doesn't live up to the overall ambience, you'll have an enjoyable time. And you'll get your fill, since both appetizers and main courses come in gargantuan-size portions. Best bets are the pizzas and pork tenderloin, both from a wood-fired oven.

CHURCH HILL

✪ **Millie's Diner.** 2603 E. Main St. (at 26th St.). ☎ **804/643-5512.** Reservations not accepted. Main courses $14.50–$22. AE, DC, DISC, MC, V. Tues–Fri 11am–2pm and 5:30–10:30pm; Sat 5:30–10:30pm; Sun 9am–3pm (brunch) and 5:30–9:30pm. ECLECTIC.

Once Millie's really was a diner, and the counter, booths, and open kitchen from those days are still here. It's not a diner anymore, however, for now a talented young chef works the gas stove, turning out a variety of tasty dishes. His spicy Thai shrimp with asparagus, red cabbage, shiitake mushrooms, cilantro, lime, peanuts, and hot chilis over fettuccine is always on the blackboard menu, which otherwise changes every 2 weeks. Sometimes he features Southern-influenced cooking, sometimes dishes from the Pacific Rim or the Caribbean. Regardless, he prepares everything from scratch—as you watch, if you grab a counter seat. Excellent fare, an entertaining wait staff, and hearty portions make this noisy eatery highly popular among Richmond's young professionals.

THE FAN

✪ **Joe's Inn.** 205 N. Shields Ave. (between Grove and Hanover sts.). ☎ **804/355-2282.** Reservations not accepted. Sandwiches $2.50–$5.50; main courses $6–$11. AE, MC, V. Mon–Thurs 9am–midnight; Fri–Sat 8am–2am; Sun 8am–midnight. ITALIAN.

This very popular neighborhood hangout has been serving terrific Greek-accented Italian fare since 1952, including veal parmigiana, fish, pizzas, and pasta. The house specialty is gargantuan portions of spaghetti. Two can easily share an order of spaghetti à la Joe, which arrives steaming hot en casserole, bubbling with a layer of baked provolone between the pasta and heaps of rich meat sauce. Soups, salads, omelets, and sandwiches are also options. Stop by for a mouth-watering stack of hotcakes or French toast at breakfast. Joe's occupies two storefronts: a dining room side and a bar side with sleek mahogany booths and ornate brass-trimmed ceiling fans.

Strawberry Street Café. 421 N. Strawberry St. (between Park and Stuart aves.). ☎ **804/353-6860.** Reservations needed only for large groups. Sandwiches and burgers $4.50–$7; main courses $6–$13; weekend brunch buffet $8. AE, MC, V. Mon–Thurs 11:30am–3pm and 5–10:30pm; Fri 11:30am–3pm and 5pm–midnight; Sat 11am–midnight; Sun 10am–10:30pm. AMERICAN.

The chic but casual Strawberry Street Café is decorated in turn-of-the-century style, with a beautiful oak bar, *Casablanca*-inspired fan chandeliers, and a plant-filled cafe-curtained window. Flower-bedecked tables (candlelit at night) add a cheerful note. At lunch or dinner, you can help yourself to unlimited offerings from a bountiful salad bar displayed in a clawfoot bathtub. At lunch, you might get a broccoli quiche or a 6-ounce burger. At dinner, the menu offers several pastas plus London broil, steaks, chicken Oscar, and homemade chicken potpie with a flaky crust. There's luscious chocolate cake for dessert. The weekend unlimited brunch bar lets you create a memorable meal from an assortment of fresh fruits, yogurt, baked ham, pastries, hot entree, salads, homemade muffins, and beverage.

Texas-Wisconsin Border Café. 1501 W. Main St. (at Plum St.). ☎ **804/355-2907.** Main courses $4.50–$8. AE, MC, V. Daily 11am–2am; brunch Sat–Sun 11am–3pm. AMERICAN.

The Texas-Wisconsin Border Café is exactly what its name evokes: a lively rustic/western/hip eatery offering cook-off–winning chili. The setting: a longhorn steer horn over the bar, fans suspended from a black pressed-tin ceiling, and pine-wainscoted cream walls hung with boar and elk heads, photos of everyone from Pancho Villa to LBJ, and works by local artists. The music is mellow rock, blues, or country. Sporting events are aired on the TV over the bar, which serves more than a dozen brands of bottled beer plus four on tap. The food is all fresh and homemade: From Texas come "widow-maker" chili and "oil field" beans, while representing Wisconsin are bratwurst stew, kielbasa, and potato pancakes. Homemade desserts like cheesecake and rich chocolate cake round things (and people) out.

CARYTOWN

✪ **Ristorante Amici.** 3343 W. Cary St. (between Freeman Rd. and S. Dooley St.). ☎ **804/353-4700.** Reservations recommended. Main courses $13–23. AE, MC, V. Mon–Thurs 11:30am–2:30pm and 5:30–10pm; Fri–Sat 11:30am–2:30pm and 5:30–11pm; Sun 5:30–10pm. NORTHERN ITALIAN.

This delightful establishment seats diners upstairs in a formal, coral-stucco room. On the street floor is a small bar and seating at several additional tables for dinner, and during good weather, patrons vie for umbrella tables on a sidewalk patio. The owners of Amici (which means "friends" in Italian) hail from Cervinia, a small resort in the Italian Alps, where they perfected their craft—and perfection in the culinary arts is certainly what they have achieved here. You might begin with grilled portobello mushroom caps with garlic, basil, and olive oil; and thin slices of veal loin with delicate tuna sauce. Among the entree highlights is a superb veal scaloppini with mushrooms and Barbera wine sauce. From the grill come fresh salmon, jumbo shrimp and scallops, chicken breast, lamb chops, steaks, and bison. Stunning desserts include a wicked tiramisu. The wine list, with many Italian vintages, is surprisingly affordable.

PICNIC FARE

In Carytown, **Coppola's Delicatessen,** 2900 W. Cary St., at South Colonial Avenue (☎ **804/359-NYNY**), evokes New York's Little Italy with an aromatic clutter of cheeses, sausages, olives, pickles, and things marinated. Behind-the-counter temptations include pasta salads, antipasti, cannoli, specialty sandwiches, and pasta dinners. Coppola's is so New York that it "imports" Thuman's low-fat, low-salt deli meats from New Jersey. Prices are low; this is a down-to-earth deli, not a pretentious gourmet emporium, though the fare is as good as any the latter might offer. There are some tables inside and a few out on the street. Hours are Monday through Wednesday from 10am to 8pm, Thursday through Saturday from 10am to 9pm.

4 Attractions

For a free overall view of the city, start at the observation deck of the **New City Hall,** 900 Broad St. at 9th Street, for a magnificent panorama of Richmond and the James River. You'll also get a fine bird's-eye view of the 1894 **Old City Hall,** diagonally across Broad Street between 9th and 10th streets, a dramatic Victorian Gothic with gray-stone walls 3 feet thick. Now a private office building, it has an interior courtyard that's a three-story marvel of painted cast iron. Visitors are welcome to enter the first floor during business hours. It's well worth the stop.

Several of Richmond's attractions are nearby, and you can buy a **Historic Downtown Richmond Ticket** to them for $15 per person, regardless of age. Among other attractions, the block ticket admits you to the Museum and White House of the Confederacy, the Valentine Museum, John Marshall House, St. John's Church, Black History Museum, Maggie L. Walker National Historic Site, Richmond National Battlefield Park, and the Edgar Allan Poe Museum. Block tickets can be purchased at any of these sights or at the Richmond visitor centers (see "Visitor Information," above). Ticket holders can also take a Sunday afternoon walking tour given April to October by **Historic Richmond Tours** (☎ **804/780-0107**).

THE TOP ATTRACTIONS

Agecroft Hall. 4305 Sulgrave Rd. ☎ **804/353-4241.** Admission $5 adults, $4.50 seniors, $3 students; half price for gardens only. Tues–Sat 10am–4pm; Sun 12:30–5pm.

In an elegant neighborhood overlooking the James River, Agecroft Hall is an authentic late-15th-century Tudor manor house built in Lancashire, England, and brought here in the 1920s. Today it serves as a museum portraying the social history and material culture of an English gentry family of the late Tudor and early Stuart eras. Typical of its period, the house has ornate plaster ceilings, massive fireplaces, rich oak paneling, leaded- and stained-glass windows, and a two-story great hall with a mullioned window 25 feet long. Furnishings authentically represent the period. Adjoining the mansion are a formal sunken garden, resembling one at the English royals' Hampton Court Palace, and a formal flower garden, an Elizabethan knot garden, and an herb garden. Visitors see a 12-minute slide show about the estate followed by a half-hour house tour. Plan time to explore the gardens as well.

Edgar Allan Poe Museum. 1914–1916 E. Main St. ☎ **804/648-5523.** Admission $6 adults, $5 seniors and students, free for children under 6. Sun–Mon noon–4pm; Tues–Sat 10am–4pm. Free parking on premises.

Enclosing an "Enchanted Garden," the Poe Museum consists of four buildings in which the poet's rather sad life and career are documented. The museum complex centers on the Old Stone House, the oldest building in Richmond, dating to about 1736. Poe didn't live in this house, but as a 15-year-old he was part of a junior honor guard that escorted Lafayette when the famous general was entertained here in 1824. Today the Old Stone House contains a shop and a video presentation that initiates guided tours of the museum. The other three buildings were added to house the growing collection of Poe artifacts and publications, now the largest in existence.

Poe was orphaned at age 2 and taken into the home of John and Frances Valentine Allan, thus his middle name. As a young man, Poe worked as an editor, a critic, and a writer for the *Southern Literary Messenger.* The desk and chair he used at the *Messenger* are among the photographs, portraits, documents, and other memorabilia on display. Most fascinating is the Raven Room displaying artist James Carling's evocative illustrations of "The Raven." Tours of the museum are given throughout the day.

Hollywood Cemetery. 412 S. Cherry (at Albemarle St.). ☎ **804/648-8501.** Free admission. Daily 8am–5pm.

Perched on the bluffs overlooking the James River not far from Maymont, Hollywood Cemetery is the serenely beautiful resting place of 18,000 Confederate soldiers, two American presidents (Monroe and Tyler), six Virginia governors, Confederate president Jefferson Davis, and Confederate Gen. J.E.B. Stuart (one of 22 Confederate generals interred here). Designed in 1847, it was conceived as a place where nature would remain undisturbed. Its winding scenic roads, flowering trees, stone-bridged creeks, and ponds are largely intact today. The section in which the Confederates are buried is marked by a 90-foot granite pyramid, a monument constructed in 1869.

John Marshall House. 818 E. Marshall St. (at 9th St.). ☎ **804/648-7998.** Admission $3, $2.50 seniors, $1.25 children 7–12, free for children under 7. Apr–Sept, Tues–Sat 10am–5pm; Oct–Dec, Tues–Sat 10am–4:30pm.

This historic property is the restored home of John Marshall, a giant in American judicial history. As its chief justice from 1801 to 1835, Marshall essentially established the power of the United States Supreme Court through his doctrine of judicial review, under which federal courts can overturn acts of Congress. Earlier, Marshall served in the Revolutionary Army, argued cases for George Washington (his close personal friend), served as ambassador to France under John Adams, and had a brief term as secretary of state. He was a political foe of his cousin, Thomas Jefferson.

Largely intact, the house Marshall built between 1788 and 1790 is remarkable for many original architectural features—exterior brick lintels, interior wide-plank pine floors, wainscoting, and paneling. Marshall's own furnishings and personal artifacts have been supplemented by period antiques and reproductions. A guided **tour** of the house takes about 20 minutes.

Lewis Ginter Botanical Garden at Bloemendaal. 1800 Lakeside Ave. ☎ **804/262-9887.** Admission $4 adults, $3 seniors, $2 children 2–12, free for children under 2. Daily 9:30am–4:30pm. Take I-95N to Exit 80 (Brook Rd.) and turn left at Hilliard Rd. to Lakeside.

In the 1880s, self-made Richmond millionaire, philanthropist, and amateur horticulturist Lewis Ginter (a founder of the American Tobacco Company) built the Lakeside Wheel Club as a summer playground for the city's elite. The resort boasted a lake, a nine-hole golf course, cycling paths, and a zoo. At Ginter's death in 1897, part of his vast fortune went to his niece, Grace Arents, who converted the property to a hospice for sick children and named it Bloemendaal for Ginter's ancestral village in the Netherlands. An ardent horticulturist, she imported rare trees and shrubs and constructed greenhouses. A white gazebo and trellised seating areas were covered in rambling roses and clematis. Large beds on the front lawn were planted with shrubs and flowers. Grace died in 1926, leaving her estate to the city of Richmond to be maintained as a botanical garden and public park. An admissions brochure suggests routes through the gardens and highlights significant aspects of the collection. There's a delightful Tea House on the premises for lunch.

Maggie L. Walker National Historic Site. 110^1/$_2$ E. Leigh St. (between 1st and 2nd sts.). ☎ **804/771-2017.** Free admission. Wed–Sun 9am–5pm. Closed New Year's Day, Thanksgiving, and Christmas.

The daughter of a former slave, Maggie L. Walker was an unusually gifted woman who achieved success in the world of finance and business and rose to become the first woman bank president in the country. Originally a teacher, Walker, after her marriage in 1886, became involved in the affairs of a black fraternal organization, the Independent Order of St. Luke, which grew under her guidance into an insurance company, and then into a full-fledged bank, the St. Luke Penny Savings Bank. The bank continues today as the Consolidated Bank and Trust, the oldest surviving African-American–operated bank in the United States. Walker also became editor of a newspaper and created and developed a department store. Her residence from 1904 until her death in 1934, this house remained in her family until 1979. It has been restored to its 1930 appearance by the National Park Service.

Maymont House and Park. Just north of the James River between Va. 161 and Meadow St. ☎ **804/358-7166.** Free admission (donations suggested). Apr–Oct, daily 10am–7pm; Nov–Mar, daily 10am–5pm. Go south 2 miles to the end of Boulevard; follow signs to the parking area. Bus: 3.

In 1886, Maj. James Henry Dooley, one of Richmond's self-made millionaires, purchased a 100-acre dairy farm and built this 33-room mansion surrounded by beautifully landscaped grounds. The house is in the Romanesque Revival style, with colonnaded sandstone facade, turrets, and towers. The architectural details of the formal rooms reflect various periods, most notably 18th-century French. The dining room has a stunning coffered oak ceiling; the library, a stenciled strapwork ceiling. A grand stairway leads to a landing from which two-story-high stained-glass windows rise. The house is elaborately furnished with pieces from many periods chosen by the Dooleys—Oriental carpets, an art nouveau swan-shaped bed, marble and bronze sculpture, porcelains, tapestries, and Tiffany vases.

The Dooleys lavished the same care on the grounds. They placed gazebos wherever the views were best, laid out Italian and Japanese gardens, and planted horticultural specimens and exotic trees culled from the world over. The hay barn today is the **Mary Parsons Nature Center.** There are outdoor animal habitats for birds, bison, beaver, deer, elk, and bear. At the **Children's Farm,** youngsters can feed chickens, piglets, goats, peacocks, cows, donkeys, and sheep. A collection of late-19th- and early-20th-century horse-drawn carriages—surreys, phaetons, hunting vehicles—is on display at the **Carriage House.** Carriage rides are a weekend afternoon option from April to mid-December.

Guided **tours** of the house are given continuously between noon and 4:30pm Tuesday through Sunday. For information on tram rides through the park, call ☎ **804/358-7167.** There's a parking lot off Spottswood Road near the Children's

Farm, and another at Hampton Street and Pennsylvania Avenue near the house and gardens.

✪ Museum of the Confederacy. 1201 E. Clay St. ☎ **804/649-1861.** Museum admission $5 adults, $4 seniors, $3 students and children 7–12, free for children under 7. Combination ticket (White House and museum) $8 adults, $7 seniors, $5 students. White House and museum, Mon–Sat 10am–5pm; Sun noon–5pm.

This fine museum houses the largest Confederate collection in the country, much of it contributed by veterans and their descendants. All the war's major events and campaigns are documented, and exhibits include period clothing and uniforms, a replica of Lee's headquarters, the role of African Americans in the Civil War, Confederate memorabilia, weapons, and art.

Next door is the **White House of the Confederacy.** When the capital of the Confederacy moved to Richmond, the city government leased this 1818 mansion as a temporary home for President Jefferson Davis. It was the center of wartime social and political activity in Richmond. In 1891, a group of civic-minded Richmond women acquired the property and began a long restoration of the White House.

Visitors begin a **tour** in the lower-level exhibit area, where there's a history of the museum. Upstairs, the entrance hall is notable for its bronzed classical Comedy and Tragedy figures holding exquisite gas lamps. Formal dinners, luncheons, and occasional cabinet meetings were held in the dining room, a Victorian chamber with ornate ceiling decoration; some of the furniture in this room is original to the Davis family. Guests were received in the center parlor, interesting now for its knickknacks produced by captured Confederate soldiers and for an 1863 portrait of Davis. Upstairs are the bedrooms and the Oval Office in which Davis conducted the business of war.

✪ Richmond National Battlefield Park. Headquarters, 3215 E. Broad St. (at 33rd St.). ☎ **804/226-1981.** Free admission. Chimborazo Visitor Center, daily 9am–5pm. Closed New Year's Day, Thanksgiving, and Christmas.

As the political, medical, and manufacturing center of the South and the primary supply depot for Lee's Army of Northern Virginia, Richmond was a prime military target throughout the Civil War. Seven major drives were launched against the city between 1861 and 1865. The bloody battlefields ring Richmond's eastern side, now mostly suburbs.

A 60-mile driving tour begins at the **Chimborazo Visitor Center** on East Broad Street at 33rd Street, at the site of one of the Confederacy's largest hospitals (about 76,000 patients were treated here). A 12-minute slide show about the Civil War is shown throughout the day, and you can rent a 3-hour auto-tape tour with cassette player that covers the Seven Days Campaign of 1862. You can also view a 25-minute film here called *Richmond Remembers;* it documents the socioeconomic impact of the Civil War on the Confederate capital. Park rangers are on hand to answer all questions.

There are smaller visitor centers at **Fort Harrison,** about 8 miles southeast, and at **Cold Harbor,** about 10 miles northeast, the former open daily during summer (check with Chimborazo for hours), the latter daily from 9am to 5pm. Cold Harbor was the scene of a particularly bloody 1864 encounter during which 7,000 of Grant's men were killed or injured in just 30 minutes. Programs with costumed Union and Confederate soldiers re-enacting life in the Civil War era take place during the summer.

It's convenient to combine a battlefield tour with visits to the James River plantations (see chapter 11), since Fort Harrison and some other sites are near Va. 5, the plantations route.

Downtown Richmond Attractions

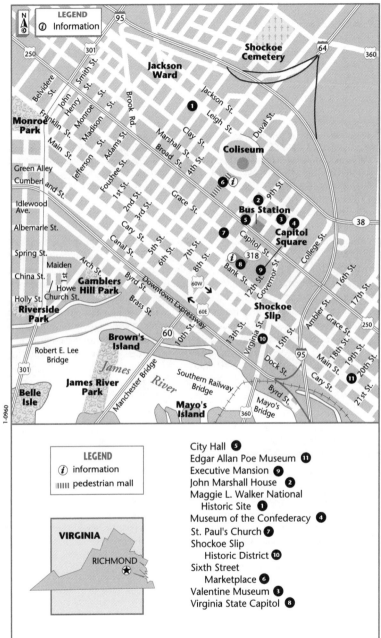

City Hall **5**
Edgar Allan Poe Museum **11**
Executive Mansion **9**
John Marshall House **2**
Maggie L. Walker National
   Historic Site **1**
Museum of the Confederacy **4**
St. Paul's Church **7**
Shockoe Slip
   Historic District **10**
Sixth Street
   Marketplace **6**
Valentine Museum **3**
Virginia State Capitol **8**

Impressions

As the sun rose on Richmond, such a spectacle was presented as can never be forgotten by those who witnessed it . . . All of the horrors of the final conflagration, when the earth shall be wrapped in flames and melt with fervent heat, were, it seemed to us, prefigured in our capital.

—An observer, April 3, 1865

Science Museum Of Virginia/Ethyl Universe Theater. 2500 W. Broad St. (3 blocks east of Boulevard). ☎ **800/659-1727** or 804/367-6552. Admission $5 adults, $4.50 seniors, $4 children 4–12. Tickets to films, $4 per person, free for children under 5. Exhibits, summer, Mon–Thurs 9:30am–5pm, Fri–Sat 9:30am–7pm, Sun 11:30am–5pm; winter, Mon–Sat 9:30am–5pm, Sun 11:30am–5pm. Theater, Mon–Thurs 11am–5pm; Fri–Sat 11am–9pm; Sun noon–5pm. Free parking.

There are few DO NOT TOUCH signs in the galleries here, for hands-on exhibits are the norm in this science museum with state-of-the-art planetarium, making it ideal for youngsters. For example, in "Computer Works," visitors create programs, discuss their problems with a computer shrink, and play "assistant" for a computer magician. One wing features exhibits on aerospace technology, energy and electricity, chemistry, and physics. Elsewhere, you'll learn about optical illusions inside a giant kaleidoscope, try to get your bearings in a full-size distorted room, and crawl into a space capsule.

Not to be missed are the shows at the 275-seat Ethyl Universe Planetarium/Space Theater, which shows spectacular Omnimax films as well as the most sophisticated special-effects multimedia planetarium shows. The building itself merits attention, too: It's the Beaux Arts former Broad Street Station, designed in 1919 by John Russell Pope (architect of the Jefferson Memorial, the National Archives, and the National Gallery of Art in Washington). With a soaring rotunda, classical columns, vaults, and arches, Pope created it to evoke a sense of wonder—very fitting for a museum of science.

St. John's Church. 2401 E. Broad St. ☎ **804/648-5015.** Admission $3 adults, $2 seniors, $1 children 7–18, free for children under 7. Tours given Mon–Sat 10am–3:30pm, Sun 1–3:30pm; services Sun at 8:30 and 11am.

Originally known simply as the "church on Richmond Hill," St. John's dates to 1741, but its congregation was established in 1611. Alexander Whitaker, the first rector, instructed Pocahontas in Christianity, baptized her, and married her to John Rolfe. The church building is best known as the 1775 meeting place of the second Virginia Convention. In attendance were Thomas Jefferson, George Wythe, George Mason, Benjamin Harrison, George Washington, Richard Henry Lee, and many other historic personages. In support of a bill to assemble and train a militia to oppose Great Britain, Patrick Henry stood up and delivered his incendiary speech: "Is life so dear, or peace so sweet, as to be purchased at the price of chains or slavery? Forbid it, Almighty God! I know not what course others may take; but as for me, give me liberty, or give me death!"

On the 20-minute guided **tour** you'll see the original 1741 entrance and pulpit, the exquisite stained-glass windows, and the pew where Patrick Henry sat during the convention. From the last Sunday in May to the first Sunday in September, there's a living-history program at 2pm re-creating the second Virginia Convention.

Valentine Museum. 1015 E. Clay St. ☎ **804/649-0711.** www.valentinemuseum.com. Admission $5 adults, $4 seniors, $3 children 7–12, free for children under 7. Mon–Sat 10am–5pm; Sun noon–5pm. Free parking on premises.

Named for Mann S. Valentine II, a 19th-century businessman and patron of the arts whose fortune was based on a patent medicine called Valentine's Meat Juice, this museum documents the history of Richmond from the 17th to the 20th centuries. It includes the elegant Federal-style Wickham House, built in 1812 by attorney John Wickham, Richmond's wealthiest citizen who had helped defend Aaron Burr in 1807. Wickham assembled the finest talents of his day to design and decorate his mansion and entertained Richmond's social elite here, along with such visiting notables as Daniel Webster, Zachary Taylor, John Calhoun, Henry Clay, and William Thackeray.

Highlights include spectacular decorative wall paintings, perhaps the rarest and most complete set in the nation; the Oval Parlor, designated as "one of the hundred most beautiful rooms in America"; and the circular Palette Staircase. Slave and servant quarters have been restored to reveal the lives of the residents who supported the Wickhams' lavish lifestyle. Guided house **tours,** included in the price of admission to the museum, are given hourly.

Valentine purchased the house in 1882, converted it into a private museum, and left it to the public when he died. Exhibits cover social and urban history, decorative and fine arts, textiles, architecture, and more. An ongoing display, "Shared Spaces, Separate Lives," uses touch-screen audiovisual elements and surround-sound special effects to explore the history of Richmond's complex race relationships. Lunch in Wickham's Garden Café is offered weekdays.

Virginia Historical Society/Center for Virginia History. 428 N. Boulevard (at Kensington Ave.). ☎ **804/358-4901.** Admission $4 adults, $3 students, $2 children. Mon–Sat 10am–5pm; Sun 1–5pm.

Housed in the neoclassical Battle Abbey, built in 1913 as a shrine to the state's Civil War dead, the South's oldest historical society (founded in 1831) has the world's largest collection of Virginia artifacts. Touring the major permanent exhibit, "The Story of Virginia, an American Experience," is like rummaging through the state's attic: You'll see gold buttons from Pocahontas's hat, Patrick Henry's eyeglasses, and much, much more. Changing exhibits cover a wide range of subjects, from Civil War armaments to a history of the Negro baseball leagues. Genealogists will find a treasure trove of family histories in the library of some 125,000 volumes and 7 million manuscripts.

✪ Virginia Museum of Fine Arts. Boulevard and Grove Ave. ☎ **804/367-0844.** Admission by suggested donation $4. Tues–Sun 11am–5pm; Thurs 11am–8pm. Free parking.

Any city would be proud of this museum, noted for the largest public Fabergé collection outside Russia—more than 300 objets d'art created at the turn of the century for Tsars Alexander III and Nicholas II. The Imperial jewel-encrusted Easter eggs evoke what art historian Parker Lesley calls the "dazzling, idolatrous realm of the last czars."

Highlights include the Goya portrait *General Nicholas Guye,* a rare life-size marble statue of Roman emperor Caligula, Monet's *Iris by the Pond,* and six magnificent Gobelin *Don Quixote* tapestries. That's not to mention the works of de Kooning, Gauguin, van Gogh, Delacroix, Matisse, Degas, Picasso, Gainsborough, and others; antiquities from China, Japan, Egypt, Greece, Byzantium, Africa, and South America; art from India, Nepal, and Tibet; and an impressive collection of contemporary American art.

The museum also contains the 500-seat **TheatreVirginia** (see "Richmond After Dark," below) and a low-priced cafeteria overlooking a waterfall cascading into a pool with a Maillol sculpture.

✪ Virginia State Capitol. 9th and Grace sts. ☎ **804/786-4344.** Free admission. Tours given Apr–Nov, daily 9am–5pm; Dec–Mar, Mon–Sat 9am–5pm, Sun 1–5pm.

Thomas Jefferson was minister to France when he was commissioned to work on a capitol building for Virginia. He closely patterned the Classical Revival building on the Maison Carrée, a Roman temple built in Nîmes during the 1st century A.D., which he greatly admired. The colonnaded wings on either side were added between 1904 and 1906. Today the building is the second-oldest working capitol in the United States, in continuous use since 1788.

The central portion is the magnificent Rotunda, its domed skylight ceiling ornamented in Renaissance style. The room's dramatic focal point is Houdon's life-size statue of George Washington, said to be a perfect likeness. "That is the man, himself," said Lafayette. "I can almost realize he is going to move." A Carrara-marble bust of Lafayette by Houdon also graces the Rotunda, as do busts of the seven other Virginia-born presidents.

Resembling an open courtyard, the old Hall of the House of Delegates, where the Virginia House of Delegates met from 1788 to 1906, is now a museum. Here, in 1807, Washington Irving took notes while John Marshall tried and acquitted Aaron Burr of treason. The room was also a meeting place of the Confederate Congress. In the former Senate chamber, now used for occasional committee meetings, Stonewall Jackson's body lay in state after his death in 1863.

Free 30-minute **tours** are given throughout the day. After the tour, explore the **Capitol grounds.** To the east is the **Executive Mansion,** official residence of governors of Virginia since 1813. Another historic building is the old **Bell Tower,** built in 1824, often the scene of lunch-hour entertainment in summer. The Bell Tower houses a visitor center, where you can get information about Richmond and other Virginia destinations.

Wilton House. S. Wilton Rd. ☎ **804/282-5936.** Admission $4 adults, $3 seniors and students, free for children under 6. Mar–Jan, Tues–Sat 10am–4:30pm, Sun 1:30–4:30pm; Feb, by appointment only. Closed national holidays. Take Va. 147 (Cary Street Rd.) west and turn south on Wilton Rd.

Originally built on the James River about 14 miles below Richmond, the stately 1753 Georgian mansion was painstakingly dismantled and reconstructed on this bluff overlooking the river in 1933. Most of the original brick, flooring, and paneling were saved. Wilton's design has been attributed to a leading Williamsburg architect, Richard Taliaferro. It was part of a 2,000-acre plantation where William Randolph III entertained many of the leading figures of the day, including George Washington, Thomas Jefferson, and Lafayette.

The house has a fine collection of period furnishings throughout. All rooms feature handsome pine paneling, some with fluted pilasters and denticulated cornices.

MORE ATTRACTIONS

The **Black History Museum & Cultural Center of Virginia,** Clay Street at Foushee Street (☎ **804/780-9093**), houses documents, limited editions, prints, art, and photos emphasizing the history of the state's African-American community. It resides in a Federal–Greek Revival–style house built in 1832 and purchased a century later by the Council of Colored Women under the leadership of Maggie L. Walker. It's open Tuesday, Thursday, Friday, and Saturday from 11am to 4pm. Admission is $2 for adults, $1 for children.

Two museums celebrate Richmond's Jewish heritage. The **Virginia Holocaust Museum,** 213 Roseneath Rd. (☎ **804/673-6341**), pays tribute to those who died in or lived through the Holocaust. Among the exhibits are a mock ghetto surrounded by barbed wire and a model of an underground hiding place. It's open by appointment only. Operated by the nation's sixth-oldest Jewish congregation, the **Congregation Beth Ahabah Museum & Archives Trust,** 1109 W. Franklin St. (☎ **804/353-2668**), houses an extensive collection of records, letters, documents, and photos relating to Jewish history. It's open Sunday through Wednesday from 10am to 3pm. Admission is free ($2 donation suggested).

Numismatists will enjoy the small but interesting **Money Museum,** in the Federal Reserve Bank lobby, 701 E. Byrd St., between 7th Street and the Manchester Bridge (☎ **804/679-8108**). Exhibits trace the history of money, from the bartering of corn to an uncut sheet of $100,000 gold certificates. Hours are Monday through Friday from 9:30am to 3:30pm; admission is free.

The lobby of the **Library of Virginia,** 800 Broad St., between 8th and 9th streets (☎ **804/692-3919**), has changing exhibits of state documents and published works, some of them more than 400 years old. "The Common Wealth," on display until September 1998, features documents from the Jamestown period, including a copy of Capt. John Smith's history of the colony published in 1624. The library is open Monday through Saturday from 9am to 5pm; admission is free.

ORGANIZED TOURS

The **Historic Richmond Foundation Tours,** 707-A E. Franklin St. (☎ **804/780-0107**), offers a variety of well-planned guided tours daily, some in comfortable, air-conditioned 24-passenger vans, others on foot. Their "Old Richmond Today," a 2¹/₂-hour tour of the historic neighborhoods plus the State Capitol, is offered daily in the morning; the cost is $16 for adults, $13 for children 6 to 12. A 1¹/₂-hour "Richmond Highlights" tour takes place Monday through Saturday afternoons. A tour of the Civil War battlefields is given from April to October on the second, third, and fourth Sundays of the month.

A RIVERBOAT CRUISE   Modern technology's answer to an 1850s riverboat, the paddle wheeler *Annabel Lee* (☎ **800/752-7093** or 804/664-5700) offers a variety of lunch, dinner, and sightseeing cruises down the James River, some as far as the famous plantations. She operates from April to mid-October. Call for all prices and departure times. Reservations are a must, especially on weekends.

NEARBY ATTRACTIONS

About 14 miles north of Richmond on I-95 is the small community of Ashland in Hanover County, which has deep historical roots. Patrick Henry once tended bar at Hanover Tavern, built in 1723, and argued cases in the Hanover County Courthouse, dating from 1735.

✪ **Scotchtown.** Rte. 2, Beaverdam. ☎ **804/227-3500.** Admission $5 adults, $4 seniors, $2 children 6–12, free for children under 6. Apr, Sat 10am–4:30pm, Sun 1:30–4:30pm; May–Oct, Tues–Sat 10am–4:30pm, Sun 1:30–4:30pm. Nov–Mar, open by appointment only. From Ashland, follow Va. 54 west, then the signs for Scotchtown at C.R. 685 north.

One of Virginia's oldest plantation houses, Scotchtown is a charming one-story white-clapboard home, located in a park-like setting of small dependencies and gardens. The house was built by Charles Chiswell of Williamsburg, probably around 1719. Patrick Henry bought the house in 1770, and from 1771 to 1778 lived here with his wife, Sarah, and their six children. Sadly, Sarah was mentally ill during much of that time and was eventually confined to a room in the basement. The manor house has been beautifully restored and furnished with 18th-century antiques, some associated with the Henry family. In the study, Henry's mahogany desk-table still bears his ink stains, and bookshelves still contain his law books. A walnut cradle used by several of his children now sits in the guest bedroom. Scotchtown also has associations with another historical figure, Dolley Madison. Her mother was a first cousin to Patrick Henry, and Dolley and her mother lived here while their family moved back to this area from North Carolina.

✪ **Paramount's Kings Dominion.** Doswell. ☎ **804/876-5000.** Admission changes from year to year, usually about $30 adults and children 7 and over; $20 children 3–6; $23 seniors 55 and over. Consecutive 2-day passes and season passes good for unlimited use at any Paramount park in the U.S. also available. Hours may vary a bit from year to year, but generally the park is open Memorial Day–Labor Day, daily 9:30am–8 or 10pm; April–May and Labor Day to early Oct, Sat–Sun 9:30am–8 or 10pm. Take Va. 30 (Exit 98) off I-95.

One of the most popular theme parks in the East, this 400-acre, family-oriented, fanciful facility offers a variety of rides and entertainment, many with themes from Paramount movies and TV shows. A ride simulator combines moving seats, a giant-screen image, digital audio technology, and other special effects with actual film footage from the movie *Days of Thunder*. A totally enclosed, multiple-inversion launch roller coaster is named "Outer Limits: Flight of Fear," after the popular TV series "Outer Limits." Another attraction, "Volcano, The Blast Coaster," uses electromagnetic energy to blast riders out of a volcano.

And that's just the beginning, for the park also has an ice-skating show featuring music from Paramount movies; a walk-of-fame salute to Paramount's movie history; several new walk-around characters, including Klingons, Vulcans, and Romulans from *Star Trek;* and an outdoor laser-and-fireworks show portraying adventure scenes from Paramount movies and TV programs such as *Mission: Impossible, Top Gun,* and *Beverly Hills Cop.* There's even an area called *Wayne's World,* featuring the aptly named "Hurler" roller coaster, and a children's fantasy area called "Hanna-Barbera Land."

White Water Canyon is a wet-and-wild ride simulating white-water rafting. Hurricane Reef offers more watery fun, with 15 water slides, a refreshing raft ride, and Splash Island, designed for younger children with a wading pool and pint-sized slides.

5　Sports & Outdoor Activities

SPECTATOR SPORTS

AUTO RACING　See NASCAR racing at **Richmond International Raceway,** located at the Virginia State Fairgrounds, between Laburnum Avenue and the Henrico Turnpike/Meadowbridge Road (☎ **804/329-6796**). The Raceway is Virginia's largest sports facility, attracting crowds of 70,000 or more.

BASEBALL　The **Richmond Braves,** the top minor-league club in the Atlanta Braves' organization, compete in the 10-team International League from April to mid-September. All home games are played at the Diamond, a 12,500-seat modern baseball stadium located at 3001 N. Boulevard (Exit 78 off I-95). Call ☎ **804/ 359-4444** for tickets or information.

COLLEGE SPORTS　The **University of Richmond's** Spiders play football and basketball in the Colonial Athletic Association (☎ **804/289-8388**). **Virginia Commonwealth University** fields a basketball team, the Rams, that plays at the Coliseum (☎ **804/282-7267**).

HORSE RACING　Virginia's first pari-mutuel racetrack, **Colonial Downs,** opened in 1997 on Va. 155, between I-64 (Exit 205) and U.S. 60 in New Kent County, 25 miles east of Richmond (☎ **804/966-7223**). Call for schedule. Admission is $5.

ICE HOCKEY　Richmond's pro hockey team, the **Renegades,** belongs to the East Coast Hockey League and plays home games October through March at the Coliseum, 601 E. Leigh St., at 7th Street (☎ **804/643-7825**).

SOCCER   The **Richmond Kickers** play professional soccer games at the University of Richmond Soccer Complex (☎ **804/282-6776**).

OUTDOOR ACTIVITIES

GOLF   Golf courses abound in the Richmond area. Among them are the **Belmont Park Recreation Center,** 1800 Hilliard Rd. (☎ **804/266-4929**), with greens fees of $11 on weekdays and $13 on weekends and holidays, when reservations are a good idea; and **Glenwood Golf Club,** Creighton Road (☎ **804/226-1793**).

WHITE-WATER RAFTING   You don't have to trek to the remote mountains to ride the rapids, for **Richmond Raft Company,** 4400 E. Main St. at Water Street (☎ **804/222-7238**), offers trips on the James through the heart of Richmond. Water levels aren't always predictable, but the James is usually high and fast enough from March to November, with spring best for fast water.

6 Shopping

Richmond's neighborhoods have a number of specialty shops, including those mentioned below. The visitor centers provide brochures that cover these and many other stores around the city and out in the suburbs.

For distinctive souvenirs, don't forget museum gift shops, especially those at the Science Museum, Art Museum, Museum and White House of the Confederacy, Valentine Museum, and Children's Museum.

✪ **CARYTOWN**   The best place in town for a shopping stroll, the 7 blocks of West Cary Street between Boulevard and Nasemond Street—known collectively as *Carytown*—are lined with a mix of small stores and interesting cafes. The old **First Baptist Church,** 3325 W. Cary St., has been transformed into an inviting retail complex, with the high-fashion Annette Dean's, Karina beauty salon, and a cafe with tables on the portico. Antiques hunting is good here, especially at **The Antiques Gallery,** 3140 W. Cary St. (☎ **840/358-0500**); **Martha's Mixture Antiques,** 3445 W. Cary St. (☎ **804/358-5827**); **Thomas-Hines Antiques,** 3027 W. Cary St. (☎ **804/355-2782**); and **Mariah Robinson Antiques,** 3455 W. Cary St. (☎ **804/355-1996**). **Ten Thousand Villages,** 2820 W. Cary St. (☎ **804/358-5170**), carries handcrafts from around the world, with lots of baskets and primitive pottery. **In the Company of Cats,** 3421 W. Cary St. (☎ **804/359-6369**), offers unusual gifts and objets d'art for feline lovers. You'll also find gourmet food shops, ethnic restaurants, secondhand clothing stores, and the landmark **Byrd Theater,** which now shows second-run films at discount prices.

MECHANICSVILLE   Four miles north of I-295 and 7 miles from downtown, this small town turned suburb is known for the Civil War battles that raged nearby. Among antiques hunters, however, Mechanicsville is famous for **Antique Village,** on U.S. 301 (☎ **804/746-8914**), where some 16 dealers purvey a treasure trove of relics.

SHOCKOE SLIP   On East Cary Street, from 12th to 14th streets, the converted warehouse district has a profusion of trendy clothing stores, restaurants, art galleries, and entertainment venues along its cobblestone streets. Among the special shops here are Toymaker of Williamsburg and Beecroft & Bull, a fine men's clothier.

WEST END   The fashionable West End neighborhood features the **Shops at Libbie and Grove,** at the intersection of the 5700 block of Grove and the 400 block of Libbie, an enclave of distinctive women's fashions and specialty shops. It's especially worth browsing here for decorative items—anything from needlepoint pillows to an abstract wall hanging. Low-scale buildings and a relaxed atmosphere give this area its casual charm.

A short drive north, **West End Antiques Mall,** 6504 Horsepen Rd. (☎ **800/ 280-1916** or 804/285-1916), has more than 85 dealers offering a wide range of antiques and collectibles. From Libbie and Grove avenues, drive north on Libbie, and turn left on Broad Street, then left on Horsepen Road. The mall is on the right.

7 Richmond After Dark

Richmond is no New York or London, so you won't be attending internationally recognized theaters and music halls here. Nevertheless, you might be able to catch visiting productions and artists at several large venues. The city also has its own ballet company and theater groups, and live music usually rocks Shockoe Bottom after dark.

Current entertainment schedules can be found in the Thursday "Weekend" section of the *Richmond Times-Dispatch,* the city's daily newspaper. The tabloid newspaper *Style Weekly* has details on theater, concerts, dance performances, and other happenings. It's free and widely available at the visitor centers and in hotel lobbies.

Tickets can be purchased through **Ticketmaster** (☎ **800/736-2000** or 804/ 262-8100).

MAJOR CONCERT HALLS & ALL-PURPOSE AUDITORIUMS

Built in 1928 as a Loew's Theater, the **Carpenter Center for the Performing Arts,** 600 E. Grace St., at Sixth Street Marketplace (☎ **804/782-3900**), was restored in 1983 to its Moorish splendor, complete with twinkling stars and clouds painted on the ceiling overhead. The center hosts national touring companies for dance, orchestra, and theater performances, including Broadway shows. The **Richmond Ballet** (see "The Performing Arts," below), the **Virginia Opera** (☎ **804/643-6004**), and the **Richmond Symphony** (☎ **804/788-1212**) perform here as well.

In the summer months, Richmond goes outdoors to **Dogwood Dell,** in Byrd Park, Boulevard and Idlewild Avenue (☎ **804/780-8683**), for free Festival of Arts music and drama performances under the stars in this tiered grassy amphitheater. Bring the family, spread a blanket, and enjoy a picnic.

Adjacent to the bustling campus of Virginia Commonwealth University, **The Mosque,** Main and Laurel streets (☎ **804/780-4213**), a 3,500-seat hall, is decorated with exotic mosaics and pointed-arch doorways. Offerings range from stage productions to nationally known musicians. The Mosque is also home to the **Richmond Forum** (☎ **804/330-3993**), which presents stimulating discussions of current topics by figures such as Gen. Norman Schwarzkopf, H. Ross Perot, and talk-show host Larry King.

The **Richmond Coliseum,** 601 E. Leigh St. (☎ **804/780-4970**), hosts everything from the Ringling Bros. and Barnum & Bailey circus to rock concerts. It's the largest indoor entertainment facility in Virginia and seats about 12,000. Major sporting events—wrestling, ice hockey, basketball—are also scheduled here.

THE PERFORMING ARTS

The state's leading professional theater is the 535-seat **TheatreVirginia,** in the Virginia Museum of Fine Arts, 2800 Grove Ave. (☎ **804/367-0831**), which offers a variety of productions such as *Gypsy, Sylvia, Arcadia, Lost in Yonkers,* and *A Closer Walk with Patsy Cline.* The season runs from October to the end of April.

You can catch family plays and musicals at **Theatre IV,** 114 W. Broad St. (☎ **804/344-8040**), which performs in the Empire Theater, at Broad and Jefferson streets.

The **Richmond Ballet** (☎ **804/359-0906**), the official State Ballet of Virginia, performs from mid-October to May. Their productions run the gamut from classical to modern, from *The Nutcracker* to commissioned world premieres. Call for schedule, prices, and locations.

THE CLUB & MUSIC SCENE

Shockoe Bottom is the city's funky nightlife district, occupying the square block beginning with the 17th Street Farmer's Market and going east along East Main and East Franklin streets to 18th Street. Its pubs go up and down in popularity, so the joints we visited recently may not be in vogue when you get there. If you can find a parking space, you can easily see for yourself what's going on by bar-hopping around Shockoe Bottom's busy block (but *do not* wander off onto deserted streets). Note that many Shockoe Bottom establishments are closed on Sunday and Monday.

The **Flood Zone,** 18th and Main streets (☎ **804/643-6006**), is Shockoe Bottom's concert hall and the state's largest nightclub, with everything from reggae to rock to country.

Up Cary Street in Shockoe Slip, **The Tobacco Company,** 1201 E. Cary St. (☎ **804/782-9555**), has acoustic jazz upstairs Tuesday through Saturday and dancing downstairs Wednesday through Saturday from 8pm to 1am.

8 An Easy Excursion to Petersburg

In the 1860s, Petersburg was a vital rail junction, which Grant recognized as the key to his quest to take Richmond. When every effort to capture the Confederate capital failed, Grant, in an inspired move, crossed the James River south of Richmond and advanced on Petersburg. Lee's forces weren't cooperative, however, and a tragic 10-month siege ensued. Finally, on April 2, Grant's all-out assault smashed through Lee's right flank, and that night Lee retreated west. A week later came the surrender at Appomattox Court House.

Today, Petersburg is a quiet southern town on the banks of the Appomattox River 23 miles south of Richmond on I-95. When you arrive, take Washington Street (Exit 52) west and follow the Petersburg Tour signs to the **visitor center,** 425 Cockade Alley (P.O. Box 2107), Petersburg, VA 23804 (☎ **800/368-3595** or 804/733-2400), where you can get a complimentary parking permit (valid for 1 day), maps, and literature. The center is open daily from 9am to 5pm.

EXPLORING THE TOWN

The visitor center is in Petersburg's historic **Old Town,** which was severely damaged by a tornado in 1993 (hence the vacant lots). There's still a flea market and restaurant in the refurbished old South Side railroad station on River Street, across from the visitor center, and the downtown attractions mentioned below have reopened. But the **Appomattox Iron Works Industrial Heritage Park,** a fine example of an Industrial Revolution factory, was still closed during a recent visit.

During the summer months, the visitor center, in the basement of the 1815 McIlwaine House, sells **block tickets** to the Siege Museum, Trapezium House, Centre Hill Mansion, Farmers Bank, and Old Blandford Church. The cost is $11 for adults, $9 for seniors and children 7 to 12. Or, choose three attractions for $7 adults, $5 seniors and children. Otherwise, admission to each is $3 adults, $2 seniors and children. Active-duty military personnel pay the seniors/children rate.

The **Siege Museum,** 15 W. Bank St. (☎ **804/733-2400**), tells the story of everyday life in Petersburg up to and during the siege in displays and an exceptionally interesting film narrated by actor Joseph Cotten, whose family lived in Petersburg during the Civil War. The museum is in the old Merchant Exchange, a magnificent Greek Revival temple-fronted building. It's open daily from 10am to 5pm.

The **Trapezium House,** at Market and High streets (☎ **804/733-2400**), is an amusing curiosity built without any right angles, supposedly because its owner was frightened by tales of ghosts who lurked in them. It's open March to October, daily from 10am to 5pm.

Centre Hill Mansion, 1 Centre Hill Circle (☎ **804/733-2400**), between Adams and Tabb streets, is a nicely restored 1823 mansion furnished with Victorian pieces. Hours are daily from 10am to 5pm.

✪ Old Blandford Church, about 2 miles south of downtown on Crater Road (U.S. 301) at Rochelle Lane (☎ **804/733-2400**), boasts one of the largest collections of Tiffany-glass windows in existence and is noted for the first observance of Memorial Day. The church was constructed in 1735 but abandoned in the early 1800s when a new Episcopalian church was built closer to the town center. During the Civil War, the building became a hospital for troops wounded in nearby battlefields, and many of them were later buried in the church graveyard. After the war, a group of Petersburg schoolgirls and their teacher came here to decorate the soldiers' graves. The ceremony inspired Mary Logan, wife of Union Gen. John A. Logan, who was head of the major organization of Union army veterans, to campaign for a national memorial day, which was first observed in 1868. The 13 Confederate states each sponsored one of the Tiffany windows as a memorial to its Confederate dead. The 14th was commissioned by the local Ladies Memorial Association. The artist himself, Louis Comfort Tiffany, gave the church the 15th window, a magnificent "Cross of Jewels" that is thrillingly illuminated at sunset. To get to the church, take Bank Street east and turn right on Crater Road (U.S. 301). It's open March to October, Monday through Saturday from 9am to 5pm, Sunday from 12:30 to 5pm; November to February, Monday through Saturday from 10am to 5pm, Sunday from 12:30 to 4pm.

Not far from the church, the **Softball Hall of Fame Museum,** 3935 S. Crater Road (U.S. 301) (☎ **804/733-1005**), celebrates the stars and history of softball throughout America. Admission is $2 for adults, $1 for seniors and students. It's open Monday through Friday from 9am to 4pm, Saturday from 10am to 4pm, Sunday from noon to 4pm.

At Fort Lee, 3 miles east of downtown on East Washington Street (Va. 36), the U.S. Army's **Quartermaster Museum** (☎ **804/734-4203**) has uniforms and equipment from all of America's wars, including a Jeep with a luxurious Mercedes car seat specially installed for Gen. George S. Patton during World War II. The Quartermaster Museum is open Tuesday through Friday from 10am to 5pm and Saturday, Sunday, and federal holidays from 11am to 5pm; admission is free. Take the first right into Fort Lee (no pass required), then the first left to the museum.

Note: The Quartermaster Museum is just half a mile east of the Petersburg National Battlefield's visitor center (see below).

THE CIVIL WAR BATTLEFIELDS

Encompassing some 2,646 acres, the **✪ Petersburg National Battlefield** preserves the key sites of the siege that lasted from mid-June 1864 to early April 1865. A multimedia presentation at the visitor center tells the story, and a 4-mile battlefield driving tour has wayside exhibits and audio stations; some stops have short walking trails. Most fascinating is the site of the Crater, literally a huge depression blown into the ground when a group of Pennsylvania volunteer infantry, including many miners, dug a passage beneath Confederate lines and exploded 4 tons of powder, creating the 170-by-60-foot crater. The carnage was sickening; thousands of men on both sides were killed or wounded during the ensuing battle. An extended 16-mile driving tour follows the entire siege line.

The park's visitor center is 2½ miles east of downtown on East Washington Street (Va. 36) (☎ **804/732-3531**). Admission is $5 per person in summer, $4 in winter. The visitor center is open daily from 9am to 5pm; battlefield, daily from 8am to dusk.

The battleground where Union troops actually broke through on April 2, 1865, to end the siege is in the privately owned **Pamplin Park Civil War Site,** on Duncan Road off U.S. 1 south (☎ **804/861-2408**). More than a mile of interpretive trails lead through some of the best-preserved Confederate earthen-work fortifications. The site also includes Tudor Hall, a plantation home built in 1812, which serves as a museum displaying Civil War relics. Plans call for a $10-million National Museum of the Civil War Soldier to be built here. Admission to the park is $3 for adults, $1.50 for children 7 to 11, free for kids under 7. Hours are daily from 9am to 5pm.

WHERE TO STAY

National chain motels near I-95 and Washington Street (Exit 52) include **Best Western** (☎ 800/528-1234 or 804/733-1776), **Howard Johnson** (☎ 800/654-2000 or 804/732-5950), **Knights Inn** (☎ 800/843-5644 or 804/732-1194), **Ramada Inn** (☎ 800/272-6232 or 804/733-0730), **Super 8** (☎ 800/800-8000 or 804/861-0793), and **Travelodge** (☎ 800/578-7878 or 804/733-0000).

Mayfield Inn. 3348 W. Washington St. (P.O. Box 2265), Petersburg, VA 23804. ☎ **800/538-2381** or 804/861-6775. Fax 804/863-1971. 2 rms, 2 suites. A/C. $69 double; $95 suite. Rates include full breakfast. AE, MC, V. From I-95 take Exit 52 and go west 3 miles on Washington St. (U.S. 1) to inn on the left.

You'll think you're in Williamsburg at this stately Georgian-style brick manse, built as a plantation home around 1750 by a member of the House of Burgesses and moved to this 4-acre plot of land in 1969. General Lee is thought to have spent the night here before going on to Appomattox. The present owners, Jamie and Dot Caudle, acquired it in 1979 and spent 5 years restoring it and furnishing it with antiques and period reproductions. Much of the interior is original, including seven working fireplaces. Rooms are spacious and luxurious; the largest has a four-poster canopied bed, dormer windows, a loveseat, and a small table with a pewter tea service cozily set in front of the fireplace. Hearty country breakfasts are served downstairs in a formal dining room. Guests can stroll in a lovely colonial herb garden or lounge at the pool or in the gazebo.

WHERE TO DINE

✪ King's Barbeque. 3221 W. Washington St. (U.S. 1 South). ☎ **804/732-5861.** Main courses $5–$9.50. AE, MC, V. Tues–Sun 7am–9pm. Follow U.S. 1 south 3 miles from downtown. AMERICAN.

Open since 1946, this Petersburg institution supplies some of the best barbecue in the entire South. The setting is a pine-paneled room with colonial-style tables and Windsor chairs. Notice the shelves over the lunch counter: They're lined with an extraordinary collection of pig dolls and figurines, including a Miss Piggy bank. Pork, beef, ribs, and chicken smoke constantly in an open pit right in the dining room. Unlike most other barbecue emporia, the pork and beef are served just as they come from the pit. Aficionados can enjoy the smoked flavor au naturel or apply vinegary sauce from squeeze bottles. The menu also offers such Southern standbys as crispy fried chicken, ham steak, and seafood items like salmon cakes and fried oysters. Side orders include barbecued beans, yam puffs, and fried potato cakes. Fluffy homemade biscuits and hot apple pie are house specialties.

If you're going to Old Blandford Church, **King's Barbeque No. 2,** 2910 S. Crater Rd. (☎ **804/732-0975**), has the same menu and is just as good.

11

Williamsburg, Jamestown & Yorktown

The narrow peninsula between the James and York rivers saw the very beginnings of colonial America and the rebellion that eventually created the United States. Visitors today can virtually relive that early history in the beautifully restored 18th-century town of Colonial Williamsburg, see the earliest permanent English settlement in North America at Jamestown, and walk the ramparts where Washington decisively defeated Cornwallis, thus turning the colonists' dream of a new nation into a reality. Along the James River, they can tour the tobacco plantations that created Virginia's first great wealth.

The area today is one of America's family vacation meccas, and not only for its historic sights. The multimillion-dollar theme park Busch Gardens Williamsburg brims with entertainment and thrilling rides, and Water Country USA offers summertime fun with watery rides and attractions. And there's also world-class shopping in the numerous factory outlet stores near Williamsburg. With so much to see and do—for all ages—you'll find this "Historic Triangle" a wonderful place to explore.

1 Williamsburg

150 miles S of Washington, D.C.; 50 miles E of Richmond

"I know of no way of judging the future," said Patrick Henry, "but by the past." That particular quotation couldn't be more apt as an introduction to Williamsburg. For one thing, Patrick Henry played a very important role here when, as a 29-year-old backcountry lawyer, he spoke out against the Stamp Act in the House of Burgesses in 1765. Many considered him an upstart and called the speech traitorous; others were inspired to revolution.

Another reason the quote is so apt: If you can judge the future by the past, you'll never have a better opportunity to do so. Williamsburg is unique even in history-revering Virginia. It has gone far beyond simply restoring and re-creating important colonial sites. Most of the year (except May 15 to July 4), a British flag flies over the Capitol. Here women wear long dresses and ruffled caps, men don powdered wigs, colonial fare is served in restaurants, blacksmiths' and harnessmakers' shops line cobblestone streets, and the local militia drills on Market Square. He may be a modern actor, but your casual conversation with "Thomas Jefferson" about the rights of man will seem almost real.

ESSENTIALS

ADVANCE INFORMATION Contact the **Williamsburg Area Convention & Visitors Bureau,** 201 Penniman Rd., Williamsburg, VA 23187 (☎ **800/368-6511** or 757/253-0192; www.visitwilliamsburg.com), for general information about both the historic attractions and the many hotels, restaurants, and activities here. The bureau sells one of the best maps of the area. It shares offices with the Williamsburg Area Chamber of Commerce.

COLONIAL WILLIAMSBURG INFORMATION About 1 million visitors come here every year, and most start at the **Colonial Williamsburg Visitor Center,** P.O. Box 1776, Williamsburg, VA 23187 (☎ **800/HISTORY** or 757/220-7645), off U.S. 60 Bypass, just east of Va. 132. You can't miss it; bright-green signs point the way from all access roads to Williamsburg.

The visitor center is operated by the Colonial Williamsburg Foundation, a non-profit, educational organization whose activities include ongoing restoration. The foundation also runs the hotels and taverns in the restored part of town, known as the Historic Area. Here you can get maps, guidebooks, and information about lodging, dining, and evening activities. Most important, the center is where you buy your **tickets** for the dozens of attractions that make up Colonial Williamsburg (see "Exploring the Historic Area," below).

The center shows a 35-minute orientation film, *Williamsburg—The Story of a Patriot,* continuously throughout the day. Be sure to pick up a copy of *Colonial Williamsburg Visitors Companion,* a tabloid newspaper telling exactly what's going on during your stay, including special evening programs.

The visitor center is open 365 days a year, from 8:30am to 7pm in summer, to 5pm the rest of the year.

The center also has two **reservations services** for Colonial Williamsburg Foundation operations: one for the foundation's **hotels** (☎ **800/HISTORY** or 757/220-7645), the other for its four colonial **taverns** (☎ **800/TAVERNS** or 757/229-2141). In summer, it's essential to make these reservations well ahead of time.

GETTING THERE **By Car** I-64 passes Williamsburg on its way between Richmond and Norfolk. For the historic area, take Exit 238 (Va. 143) off I-64 and follow the signs south to Va. 132 and Colonial Williamsburg. U.S. 60 is the old highway paralleling I-64; it's known as Richmond Road west of Williamsburg and York Street/Pocahontas Trail to the east. The scenic John Tyler Highway (Va. 5) runs between Richmond and Williamsburg, passing the James River plantations. Va. 199 forms a beltway around the southern side of the city (it will soon make a complete southern loop). Va. 199 joins I-64 at Exit 242 east of town; this is the quickest way to get to Busch Gardens Williamsburg and Water Country USA. The ✪ **Colonial Parkway,** one of Virginia's most scenic routes, connects Williamsburg to Jamestown and Yorktown (it runs through a tunnel under the Historic Area).

By Plane **Newport News/Williamsburg Airport** (☎ **757/877-0221**), 14 miles east of Williamsburg, is served by United Express, US Airways Express, and AirTran. More flights (and certainly more jets) arrive at **Richmond International Airport** (see chapter 10), about 45 miles west of town via I-64. **Norfolk International Airport** (see chapter 12) is about the same distance to the east, but traffic on I-64 can cause delays in ground transport to Williamsburg during rush hours and especially on summer weekends when heavy beach traffic funnels through the Hampton Roads Bridge-Tunnel.

CITY LAYOUT The restored **Historic Area** is at the center of Williamsburg. The 99-foot-wide **Duke of Gloucester Street** is this area's principal east-west artery, with the Capitol building at the eastern end and the Wren building of the College of William and Mary at the western end. The other two major streets are **Francis Street** and **Nicholson Street.** Merchants Square shops and services are between the Historic Area and the college, on the western end of Duke of Gloucester Street. The visitor center is north of the Historic Area.

Richmond Road (U.S. 60 West), running northwest from the Historic Area, is Williamsburg's main commercial strip, with a wide selection of motels, restaurants, and shopping centers, including the area's outlet malls. On the east side of town, **York Street/Pocahontas Trail** (U.S. 60 East) goes out to Busch Gardens Williamsburg. **By-Pass Road** joins these two highways on the north side of the Historic Area.

GETTING AROUND   Since few cars are allowed into the Historic Area between 8am and 10pm daily, you must park elsewhere. The Colonial Williamsburg Visitor Center (see "Colonial Williamsburg Information," above) has ample free parking and operates a **shuttle bus** to and from the Historic Area. The service begins at 8:50am, with frequent departures until 10pm. It's free for holders of tickets to the Historic Area attractions.

There's also a footpath from the visitor center to the Historic Area.

Since the traffic as well as the heat can be stifling here during the summer months, the easiest way to get around outside the Historic Area is via the air-conditioned **Relax & Ride Visitors Shuttle,** which runs from Memorial Day to Labor Day, daily from 9am to 9pm. These buses follow U.S. 60 from the Williamsburg Pottery Factory in the west to Busch Gardens Williamsburg in the east, with a detour to the hotels on By-Pass Road. It runs through the Historic Area on Henry and Lafayette streets. Fare is $1 per ride. Call ☎ **757/259-4111** for more information.

Bike rentals are available from Easter through October at the Williamsburg Woodlands hotel, at the Colonial Williamsburg Visitor Center (☎ **757/229-1000**). The outdoor stand is open June through August from 9am to 9pm, from 9am to 5pm in spring and fall. Rates range from $5 per hour to $18 per day.

Colonial Cab (☎ **757/220-1214**) provides taxi service, while **Colonial Rent A Car** (☎ **757/220-3399**) offers automobiles for hire at $33 to $39 per day, plus $7 insurance. Both are based at the Transportation Center, which is located at Boundary and Lafayette streets, within walking distance of the historic area.

HISTORY & BACKGROUND

In 1699, after nearly a century of famine, fevers, and battles with neighboring American Indian tribes, the beleaguered Virginia Colony abandoned the mosquito-infested swamp at Jamestown for a planned colonial city 6 miles inland. They named it Williamsburg for the reigning British monarch, William of Orange.

Royal Gov. Francis Nicholson laid out the new capital with public greens and a half acre of land for every house on the main street. People used their lots to grow vegetables and raise livestock. Most houses were whitewashed wood frame (trees being more abundant than brick), and kitchens were in separate structures to keep the houses from burning down. A "palace" for the royal governor was completed in 1720.

The town prospered and soon became the major cultural and political center of Virginia. The government met here four times a year during "Publick Times," when rich planters and politicos (one and the same in most cases) converged on Williamsburg and the population, normally about 1,800, doubled. Shops displayed their finest imported wares, and festivities included balls, horse races, fairs, and auctions.

Until the government was moved to Richmond in 1780 to be safer from British attack, Williamsburg played a major role as a seat of royal government and later as

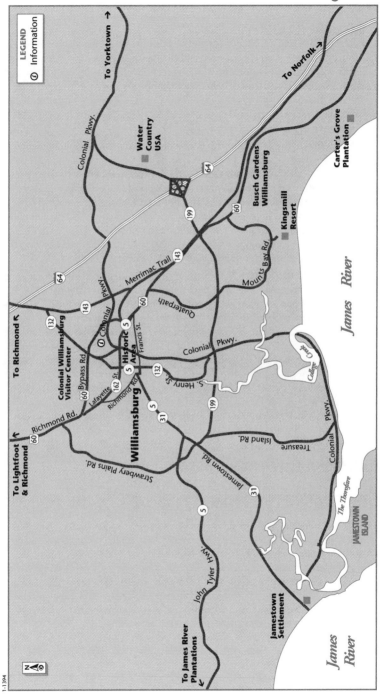

LEGEND
ⓘ Information

To Yorktown →

To Norfolk →

Colonial Pkwy.

Water Country USA

64

199

60

Busch Gardens Williamsburg

Kingsmill Resort

Carter's Grove Plantation

Merrimac Trail

143

Mounts Bay Rd.

64

Colonial Pkwy.

132

243

60

Quaterpath

Colonial Pkwy.

To Richmond ↖

ⓘ Historic 5 Area

Francis St.

College Creek

132

5

162 St.

Colonial Visitor Center

Bypass Rd.

S. Henry St.

Colonial Williamsburg Visitor Center

Lafayette

Richmond Rd.

Williamsburg

199

Richmond Rd.

5

31

Treasure Island Rd.

James River

To Lightfoot & Richmond ←

60

Strawbery Plains Rd.

Jamestown Rd.

31

Colonial Pkwy.

The Thorofare

JAMESTOWN ISLAND

5

John Tyler Hwy.

Jamestown Settlement

To James River Plantations ←

James River

N

1-1394

a hotbed of revolution. Many of the seminal events leading up to the Declaration of Independence took place here. Thomas Jefferson and James Monroe studied at the College of William and Mary. Jefferson was also the second state governor and last occupant of the Governor's Palace before the capital moved to Richmond (Patrick Henry was the first). During the Revolution, Williamsburg served as the wartime capital for 4 years and was variously the headquarters of generals Washington (he planned the siege of Yorktown in George Wythe's house), Rochambeau, and Cornwallis.

A REVEREND & A ROCKEFELLER   Williamsburg ceased to be an important political center after 1780, but it remained a quaintly charming Virginia town for another 150 years or so, unique only in that it changed so little. As late as 1926, the colonial town plan was virtually intact, including many original 18th-century buildings. Then the Rev. W.A.R. Goodwin, rector of Bruton Parish Church, envisioned restoring the entire town to its colonial appearance as a tangible symbol of our early history. He inspired John D. Rockefeller, Jr., who during his lifetime contributed some $68 million to the project and set up an endowment to help provide for permanent restoration and educational programs. Today, gifts and bequests by thousands of Americans sustain the project Goodwin and Rockefeller began.

WILLIAMSBURG REBORN   The Historic Area currently covers 173 acres of the original 220-acre town. A mile long, it encompasses 88 preserved and restored houses, shops, taverns, public buildings, and outbuildings that survived to the 20th century. More than 500 additional buildings and smaller structures have been rebuilt on their original sites after extensive archaeological, architectural, and historical research. Williamsburg set a very high standard for other Virginia restorations. Researchers investigated international archives, libraries, and museums, and sought out old wills, diaries, court records, inventories, letters, and other documents. The architects carefully studied every aspect of 18th-century buildings, from paint chemistry to brickwork; archaeologists recovered millions of artifacts while excavating 18th-century sites to reveal original foundations. The Historic Area also includes 90 acres of gardens and greens, and 3,000 surrounding acres serve as a "greenbelt" against commercial encroachment.

EXPLORING THE HISTORIC AREA

There is so much to see and do in the Historic Area that you should consider spending at least 2 days here—with evening retreats to please the kids at Busch Gardens Williamsburg or Water Country USA.

Before launching into the sights, spend some time at the Colonial Williamsburg Visitor Center (see "Essentials," above). While there, see the orientation program and the film *Williamsburg—The Story of a Patriot.*

Activities and hours change throughout the year. The best way to find out what's going on and when is the *Colonial Williamsburg Visitors Companion,* a weekly newspaper that lists the hours of operation for attractions; describes the week's special presentations, exhibits, and events; and offers a detailed map of the Historic Area. It will be invaluable in helping you make the best use of your time.

Reservations are required for the Orientation Walk (a good way to get an overview of the village) and for many tours and evening programs. Make these while you're at the visitor center.

TICKETS   It costs nothing to stroll the streets of the Historic Area, and perhaps debate revolutionary politics with the actors playing Thomas Jefferson or Patrick Henry, but you will need a ticket to enter the key buildings and all museums. Tickets are available at the Colonial Williamsburg Visitor Center and at a **ticket**

booth at the Merchants Square shops, on Henry Street at Duke of Gloucester Street.

All tickets entitle you to see the orientation film at the visitor center, use the Historic Area shuttle bus, and take a 30-minute Orientation Walk through the restored village (reservations required).

The best deal is the **Patriot's Pass,** which costs $33 for adults, $19 for children 6 to 12, and is good for 1 year of unlimited free admissions at all Colonial Williamsburg historic attractions and museums, plus a 25% discount off special programs, guided tours, exhibits, and evening programs.

If you have just a day here, the **Basic Admission Ticket** costs $25 for adults, $15 for children 6 to 12 (free for children under 6). It's good for only 1 day but provides admission to most Historic Area exhibition buildings, homes, trade sites, and shops except the Governor's Palace, plus it'll get you into the DeWitt Wallace Decorative Arts Gallery and the Abby Aldrich Rockefeller Folk Art Center. You'll have to pay extra at Carter's Grove, the Winthrop Rockefeller Archeology Museum, and Bassett Hall.

Other 1-day admission choices include a **Museums Ticket** combining the Wallace Gallery, the Folk Art Center, and Bassett Hall; it costs $10 for adults, $6.50 for children (or you can buy an annual museum pass for $17 adults, $10 kids). A **Governor's Palace Ticket** admits you to just the mansion, for $17 per person, regardless of age. The **Carter's Grove Ticket** will get you into the plantation for $15 adults, $9 children.

If you have 2 days, consider the **Colonist's Pass**—$25 for adults, $17 for children 6 to 12. It'll get you into the same sites as the Basic Admission Ticket plus the Governor's Palace on 2 consecutive days.

American Express, Diners Club, MasterCard, and Visa are accepted at all Colonial Williamsburg ticket outlets, attractions, hotels, and taverns.

HOURS   In general, attractions in the Historic Area are open from April to October daily from 9am to 5pm, to 6pm from Memorial Day to Labor Day. Some attractions are closed on specific days, and hours can vary, so check the *Colonial Williamsburg Visitors Companion* for current information.

The taverns are open during evenings, and you can stroll the streets anytime.

THE COLONIAL BUILDINGS

Brush-Everard House

One of the oldest buildings in Williamsburg, the Brush-Everard House was occupied without interruption from 1717—when Public Armorer and master gunsmith John Brush built it as a residence-cum-shop—to 1946. Charged not only with maintaining and repairing weaponry, Brush also had to take part in ceremonies requiring gun salutes, such as royal birthdays. At one of these, he wounded himself slightly and applied—without success—to the House of Burgesses for damages. Little else is known about him. He died in 1726. The most distinguished owner was Thomas Everard, clerk of York County from 1745 to 1771 and two-time mayor of Williamsburg. Though not as wealthy as Wythe and Randolph, he was in their elite circle. He enlarged the house, adding the two wings that give it a U shape. Today the home is restored and furnished to its Everard-era appearance. The smokehouse and kitchen out back are original. Special programs here focus on African-American life in the 18th century.

✪ The Capitol

Virginia legislators met in the H-shaped Capitol at the eastern end of Duke of Gloucester Street from 1704 to 1780. America's first representative assembly, it had an upper house, His Majesty's Council of State, of 12 members appointed for life by the king. The lower body, the House of Burgesses, was elected by the freeholders of each county (there were 128 burgesses by 1776). They initiated legislation, then sent it to the Council for approval or rejection. The House of Burgesses became a training ground for patriots and future governors such as George Washington, Thomas Jefferson, Richard Henry Lee, and Patrick Henry. As 1776 approached, the burgesses passed an increasing number of petitions and resolutions against acts of Parliament, particularly the Stamp Act and the levy on tea—in Henry's words, "taxation without representation," a phrase that became a motto of the Revolution.

All civil and criminal cases (the latter punishable by mutilation or death) were tried in the General Court. Since juries were sent to deliberate in a third-floor room without heat, light, or food, there were very few hung juries. Thirteen of Blackbeard's pirate crew were tried here and sentenced to hang.

The original Capitol burned down in 1747, was rebuilt in 1753, and succumbed to fire again in 1832. The reconstruction is of the 1704 building, complete with Queen Anne's coat of arms adorning the tower and the Great Union flag flying overhead. **Tours** (of about 25 minutes) are given throughout the day.

The Courthouse

An intriguing window on the criminal justice division of colonial life is offered in the courthouse, which dominates Market Square. An original building, the courthouse was the scene of widely varying proceedings, ranging from dramatic criminal trials to the prosaic issuance of licenses. Wife beating, pig stealing, and debtor and creditor disputes were among the cases tried here. Visitors can participate in the administration of colonial justice at the courthouse by sitting on a jury or acting as a defendant. In colonial times, convicted offenders were usually punished immediately after the verdict. Punishments included being publicly flogged at the whipping post (conveniently located just outside the courthouse) or being locked in the stocks or pillory, thus subjected to public ridicule. Jail sentences were very unusual—punishment was swift and drastic, and the offenders then returned to the community, often bearing lifelong evidence of their conviction.

George Wythe House

On the west side of the Palace Green is the elegant restored brick home of George Wythe (pronounced "With")—foremost classics scholar in 18th-century Virginia, noted lawyer and teacher (Thomas Jefferson, Henry Clay, and John Marshall were his students), and member of the House of Burgesses. A close friend of Royal Governors Fauquier and Botetourt, Wythe nevertheless was the first Virginia signer of the Declaration of Independence. On principle, Wythe did not sign the Constitution, however, because it did not contain a bill of rights or antislavery provisions. The house, in which he lived with his second wife, Elizabeth Taliaferro (pronounced "Tolliver"), was Washington's headquarters before the siege of Yorktown and Rochambeau's after the surrender of Cornwallis. Open-hearth cooking is demonstrated in the outbuilding.

✪ Governor's Palace

This meticulous reconstruction is of the Georgian mansion that was the residence and official headquarters of royal governors from 1714 until Lord Dunmore fled before dawn in the face of armed resistance in 1775, thus ending British rule in Virginia. As at other Williamsburg sites, where authentic period pieces were not available, reproductions have been crafted to exacting standards by artisans thoroughly schooled in 18th-century methods. The period portrayed is the final 5 years of British rule. Though the sumptuous surroundings, nobly proportioned halls and rooms, 10 acres

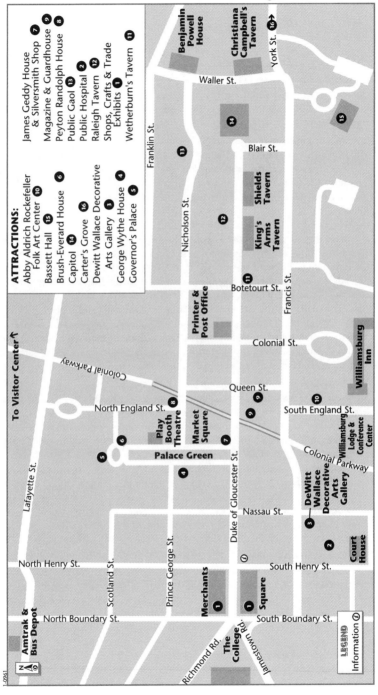

ATTRACTIONS:

Abby Aldrich Rockefeller Folk Art Center ⑩
Bassett Hall ⑮
Brush-Everard House ⑥
Capitol ⑭
Carter's Grove ⑯
Dewitt Wallace Decorative Arts Gallery ③
George Wythe House ④
Governor's Palace ⑤
James Geddy House & Silversmith Shop ⑦
Magazine & Guardhouse ⑨
Peyton Randolph House ⑧
Public Gaol ⑬
Public Hospital ②
Raleigh Tavern ⑫
Shops, Crafts & Trade Exhibits ①
Wetherburn's Tavern ⑪

LEGEND
ⓘ Information

of formal gardens and greens, and vast wine cellars all evoke splendor, the king's representative was by that time little more than a functionary of great prestige but limited power. He was more apt to behave like a diplomat in a foreign land than an autocratic colonial ruler.

Tours, given continuously throughout the day, wind up in the gardens, where you can explore at your leisure the elaborate geometric parterres, topiary work, bowling green, pleached allées, and a holly maze patterned after the one at Hampton Court. Plan at least 30 minutes to wander these stunning grounds and to visit the kitchen and stable yards.

James Geddy House & Silversmith Shop

This two-story L-shaped 1762 home (with attached shops) is an original building. Here visitors can see how a comfortably situated middle-class family lived in the 18th century. Unlike the fancier abodes you'll visit, the Geddy House has no wallpaper or oil paintings; a mirror and spinet from England, however, indicate relative affluence.

The Geddy dynasty begins with James Sr., an accomplished gunsmith and brass founder who advertised in the *Virginia Gazette* of July 8, 1737, that he had "a great Choice of Guns and Fowling Pieces, of several Sorts and Sizes, true bored, which he will warrant to be good; and will sell them as cheap as they are usually sold in England." He died in 1744, leaving his widow with eight children. His enterprising oldest sons, David and William, took over, offering their services as "Gunsmiths, Cutlers, and Founders"; on the side, they did a little blacksmithing and engraving and sold cures for "all Diseases incident to Horses." A younger son, James Jr., became the town's foremost silversmith; he imported and sold jewelry, and was a member of the city's Common Council involved in furthering the patriot cause. At a foundry on the premises, craftsmen cast silver, pewter, bronze, and brass items at a forge.

The Magazine & Guardhouse

The magazine is a sturdy octagonal brick building constructed in 1715 to house ammunition and arms for the defense of the British colony. It has survived intact to the present day. In colonial Williamsburg, every able-bodied freeman belonged to the militia from the ages of 16 to 60, and did his part in protecting hearth and home from attack by local tribes, riots, slave uprisings, and pirate raids. The high wall and guardhouse were built during the French and Indian War to protect the magazine's 60,000 pounds of gunpowder. Today, the building is stocked with 18th-century equipment—British-made flintlock muskets, cannons and cannonballs, barrels of powder, bayonets, and drums, the latter for communication purposes.

A 15-minute **horse-drawn carriage ride** around the Historic Area departs from a horse post in front of the magazine; cost is $7 per person.

Peyton Randolph House

The Randolphs were one of the most prominent—and wealthy—families in colonial Virginia. Sir John Randolph was a highly respected lawyer, Speaker of the House of Burgesses, and Virginia's representative to London, where he was the only colonial-born Virginian ever to be knighted. When he died he left his library to 16-year-old Peyton, "hoping he will betake himself to the study of law." When Peyton Randolph died in 1775, his cousin, Thomas Jefferson, purchased his books at auction; they eventually became the nucleus of the Library of Congress. Peyton Randolph did follow in his father's footsteps, studying law in London after attending the College of William and Mary. He served in the House of Burgesses from 1744 to 1775, the last 9 years as Speaker of the House. Known as the great mediator, he was unanimously elected president of 1774's First Continental Congress in Philadelphia, and though he was a believer in nonviolence who hoped the colonies could amicably settle their differences with England, he was a firm patriot as well.

The house (actually two connected homes) dates to 1715. It is today restored to reflect the period around 1770. Robertson's Windmill, in back of the house, is a post mill of a type popular in the early 18th century. The house is open to the public for self-guided tours with period-costumed interpreters in selected rooms.

The Public Gaol

They didn't coddle criminals in the 18th century, for punishments included public ridicule (stocks and pillories) as well as whipping, branding, mutilation, and hanging, the latter invoked not only for murder and treason but also for burglary, forgery, and horse stealing. Imprisonment was not the usual punishment for crime in colonial times, but persons awaiting trial (at the Capitol in Williamsburg) and runaway slaves sometimes spent months in the Public Gaol. In winter, the dreary cells were bitterly cold; in summer, they were stifling. Beds were rudimentary piles of straw; leg irons, shackles, and chains were used frequently; and the daily diet consisted of "salt beef damaged, and Indian meal." In its early days, the gaol doubled as a madhouse, and during the Revolution, redcoats, spies, traitors, and deserters swelled its population.

The gaol opened in 1704. Debtors' cells were added in 1711 (although the imprisoning of debtors was virtually eliminated after a 1772 law made creditors responsible for their upkeep), and keepers' quarters were built in 1722. The thick-walled red-brick building served as the Williamsburg city jail through 1910. The building today is restored to its 1720s appearance.

The Public Hospital

Opened in 1773, the "Public Hospital for Persons of Insane and Disordered Minds" was America's first lunatic asylum. Before its advent, the mentally ill were often thrown in jail or confined to the poorhouse. From 1773 to about 1820, "treatment" involved solitary confinement and a grisly course of action designed to "encourage" patients to "choose" rational behavior (it was assumed that patients willfully and mistakenly chose a life of insanity). So-called therapeutic techniques included the use of powerful drugs, submersion in cold water for extended periods, bleeding, blistering salves, and an array of restraining devices. On a self-guided tour you'll see a 1773 cell, with a filthy straw-filled mattress on the floor, ragged blanket, and manacles.

During what is now called the Moral Management Period (1820–65), patients were seen as having emotional disorders and were treated with kindness. The high point of the Moral Management Period was the administration of John Minson Galt II, from mid-1841 to his death in 1862. Galt created a carpentry shop, a shoemaking shop, a game room, and sewing, spinning, and weaving rooms. He conducted reading and music classes and organized evening lectures, concerts, and social gatherings. For all his good intentions, however, Galt admitted that "practice invariably falls short of theory." His rate of cure was not notable.

After Galt's death, the hospital was administered by nine different superintendents. Confidence in reform and government intervention on behalf of the unfortunate diminished in this age of Social Darwinism, when the survival of the fittest was the prevailing ethic. Although some of the improvements initiated during the Moral Management Period were extended, restraining devices once again came into vogue. This final period, when patients were essentially warehoused with little hope of cure, is known as the Custodial Care Period.

The self-guided tour sets one thinking about our often equally ineffective methods of treating the mentally ill today. The Public Hospital is open daily.

Raleigh Tavern

This most famous of Williamsburg taverns was named for Sir Walter Raleigh, who personally launched the "Lost Colony," which disappeared in North Carolina some 20 years before Jamestown was settled. After the Governor's Palace, it was the social and political hub of the town, especially during crowded Publick Times. Regular clients included George Washington and Thomas Jefferson, who met here in 1774 with Patrick Henry, Richard Henry Lee, and Francis Lightfoot Lee to discuss revolution. Patrick Henry's troops gave their commander a farewell dinner at the Raleigh in 1776.

The original tavern was destroyed by fire in 1859. The present building was reconstructed on the original site in 1932. Its facilities include two dining rooms; the famed Apollo ballroom, scene of elegant soirées; a club room that could be rented for private meetings; and a bar where ale and hot rum punch were the favored drinks. In the tavern bakery, you can buy 18th-century confections like gingerbread and Shrewsbury cake and cider to wash them down.

Wetherburn's Tavern

Though less important than the Raleigh, Wetherburn's also played an important role in colonial Williamsburg. George Washington occasionally favored the tavern with his patronage. Like the Raleigh, it was mobbed during Publick Times and frequently served as a center of sedition and a rendezvous for Revolutionary patriots. The yellow-pine floors are original, so you can actually walk in Washington's footsteps; windows, trim, and weatherboarding are a mixture of old and new; and the outbuildings, except for the dairy, are reconstructions. Twenty-five-minute **tours** are given throughout the day.

THE MUSEUMS

Abby Aldrich Rockefeller Folk Art Center

The works of folk art displayed at Bassett Hall (see below) are just a small sampling of enthusiast Abby Aldrich Rockefeller's extensive collection. This delightful museum contains more than 2,600 folk-art paintings, sculptures, and art objects. Mrs. Rockefeller was a pioneer in this branch of collecting in the 1920s and 1930s. Folk art offers aesthetic interest but also serves as visual history; since colonial times, untutored artists have creatively recorded everyday life for posterity.

The Folk Art Center collection includes household ornaments and useful wares (hand-stenciled bed covers, butter molds, pottery, utensils, painted furniture, boxes), mourning pictures (embroideries honoring departed relatives and national heroes), family and individual portraits, shop signs, carvings, whittled toys, calligraphic drawings, weavings, quilts, and paintings of scenes from daily life.

Bassett Hall

Though colonial in origin (built between 1753 and 1766 by Col. Philip Johnson), Bassett Hall was the mid-1930s residence of Mr. and Mrs. John D. Rockefeller, Jr., and it's been restored and furnished to reflect their era. The mansion's name, however, derives from the ownership of Burwell Bassett, a nephew of Martha Washington who lived here from 1800 to 1839. The Rockefellers purchased the 585-acre property in the late 1920s and moved into the restored two-story dwelling in 1936. Despite changes they made, much of the interior is original, including woodwork, paneling, mantels, and yellow-pine flooring. Much of the furniture is 18th- and 19th-century American in the Chippendale, Federal, and Empire styles. There are beautifully executed needlework rugs made by Mrs. Rockefeller herself, and six early-19th-century prayer rugs adorn the morning room. Hundreds of pieces of

---

Strange Bedfellows

Williamsburg's taverns were crowded establishments during the busy Publick Times, when they offered accommodation, food, and libation to the wealthy planters and others who thronged the town. Thomas Jefferson wrote of the Raleigh Tavern: "Last night, as merry as agreeable company and dancing with Belinda in the Apollo the Raleigh's ballroom could make me, I never could have thought the succeeding Sun would have seen me so wretched." Some things never change.

On the other hand, the degree of comfort found at Williamsburg's hostelries has changed immeasurably since Jefferson's time. In those days, the taverns' upstairs bedrooms offered nothing in the way of privacy. Often five or more grown men would share a bed, sleeping crossways in a half-sitting position. A smelly pig farmer might sleep next to a wealthy planter, thus giving rise to the expression, "Politics makes strange bedfellows."

---

ceramic and china are on display, as are collections of 18th- and 19th-century American and English glass, Canton enamelware, and folk art.

Reservations are required; make them at the Special Programs desk at the visitor center.

DeWitt Wallace Decorative Arts Gallery

The Public Hospital serves as entrance to this 62,000-square-foot museum housing some 10,000 17th- to 19th-century English and American decorative art objects. In its galleries, you'll see period furnishings, ceramics, textiles, paintings, prints, silver, pewter, clocks, scientific instruments, mechanical devices, and weapons.

In the upstairs Masterworks Gallery, you'll find a coronation portrait of George III of England and a Charles Willson Peale study of George Washington. Surrounding the atrium are some 150 objects representing the highest achievements of American and English artisans from the 1640s to 1800. At the east end of the museum, a 6,000-square-foot area with four galleries around a skylit courtyard houses changing exhibits. On the first level you'll see small displays of musical instruments, objects related to European conquest and expansion in the New World, and 18th-century dining items. A small cafe here offers light fare, beverages, and a limited luncheon menu.

The Lila Acheson Wallace Garden, on the upper level, centers on a pond with two fountains, a trellis-shaded seating area at one end, and a 6-foot gilded bronze statue of Diana by Augustus Saint-Gaudens at the other. The garden is surrounded by a 19-foot-high, plum-colored brick wall embellished (in season) with flowering vines.

Admission for Patriot's Pass holders is $5. Single admission, which includes Basic Ticket holders, costs $15.

Apart from the support of the Rockefellers, the $14 million for this project provided by *Reader's Digest* owners DeWitt and Lila Acheson Wallace represents the largest gift in the history of Colonial Williamsburg.

SHOPS, CRAFTS & TRADE EXHIBITS

Numerous 18th-century crafts demonstrations are on view throughout the Historic Area. Such goings-on were a facet of everyday life in this pre-industrial era. Several dozen crafts are practiced in cluttered shops by over 100 master craftspeople. They're an extremely skilled group, many having served up to 7-year apprenticeships both here and abroad. The program is part of Williamsburg's efforts to present an accurate picture of colonial society, portraying the average man and woman as well as more illustrious citizens. Crafts displays are open 5 to 7 days a week, with evening tours of candlelit shops available (visitors carry lanterns).

Here you can see at work a cabinetmaker, a wig maker, a silversmith, a printer and bookbinder, a maker of saddles and harnesses, a blacksmith, a shoemaker, a gunsmith, a milliner, a wheelwright, housewrights, and a candle maker, all carrying on—and explaining—their trades in 18th-century fashion.

Interesting in a morbid way is the apothecary shop, where sore feet were treated with leeches between the toes, a headache with leeches across the forehead, and a sore throat with leeches on the neck.

CARTER'S GROVE & THE ROCKEFELLER ARCHEOLOGY MUSEUM

The magnificent plantation home at ✪ **Carter's Grove** has been continuously occupied since 1755 on a site that was settled over 3½ centuries ago. Searching for traces of lost plantation outbuildings on the banks of the James, archaeologists have discovered here the "lost" 17th-century village of Wolstenholme Towne, site of a 20,000-acre tract settled in 1619 by 220 colonists who called themselves the Society of Martin's Hundred. The great Native American uprising of March 22, 1622, destroyed most of the settlement and left only about 60 living inhabitants, who fled to Jamestown.

Over a century later, Robert "King" Carter (Virginia's wealthiest planter) purchased the property for his daughter, Elizabeth. Between 1751 and 1754, Elizabeth's son, Carter Burwell, built the beautiful two-story, 200-foot-long structure that is considered "the final phase of the evolution of the Georgian mansion." The West Drawing Room—with its exquisite 1750 fireplace mantel and carved frieze panel— is often called the "Refusal Room"; legend has it that Southern belle Mary Cary refused George Washington's proposal of marriage in this room, and Rebecca Burwell said no to Thomas Jefferson here. In 1781, British cavalryman Banastre Tarleton headquartered at Carter's Grove and is said to have ascended the magnificent carved walnut stairway on his warhorse while hacking at the balustrade with his saber. Despite Tarleton's abuse, Carter's Grove remains one of the best-preserved old houses in America.

Designed by famed architect Kevin Roche, the **Winthrop Rockefeller Archeology Museum,** nestled into a hillside southeast of the mansion, identifies and interprets the Martin's Hundred clues and artifacts discovered on the site of the partially reconstructed Wolstenholme Towne. A permanent exhibit tells the story of the lost town's discovery through archaeological research. Two complete 17th-century helmets, the first intact close helmets found in North America, are displayed outside the small theater, where a film recounts the story of their recovery and preservation. The museum also displays excavation photographs, audiovisual exhibits interpreting the weapons collection, agricultural tools, ceramics, and domestic artifacts. Museum hours are the same as those of Carter's Grove plantation (see below). Admission is included in the Patriot's Pass; separate admission fee is $6.

A fascinating Carter's Grove site is the reconstruction of the slave quarters. Although the stick-and-mud chimney on one cabin and the wattled circular enclosures that housed chickens both reflect African traditions, by the 1770s (the period portrayed here) most slaves were at least second-generation Virginians. Some 24 slaves would have lived in these few pine-log cabins, sleeping on straw pallets placed on dirt floors. There are few possessions or furnishings, except in the foreman's (or senior slave's) house, wherein an actual bed, a chair and table, a mirror, and a piece of Delft china indicate favored status.

At the reception/orientation center, housed in a cedar building, visitors can view a 14-minute slide presentation on Carter's Grove and see a display of historic photographs and documents. Allow at least 3 hours to see Carter's Grove. The house is open mid-March to late November and during Christmas season, Tuesday through Sunday from 9am to 4 or 5pm; the country road, which is one-way, is open from 9am to 5pm. Admission is free for Patriot's Pass holders; Basic Ticket holders pay $15 for adults and $9 for children.

The estate is reached via U.S. 60, about 8 miles east of the Colonial Williamsburg Historic Area. Visitors may return to the Historic Area via a stunningly scenic one-way country road traversing streams, meadows, woodlands, and ravines. A re-creation of a colonial carriage pathway, the road is dotted with markers indicating old graveyards, Indian encampments, plantation sites, and other points of interest.

ESPECIALLY FOR KIDS

In addition to the excitement at Busch Gardens Williamsburg and Water Country USA (see below), families can enjoy many hands-on activities at the historic sites. At the **Powell House,** on Waller Street near Christiana Campbell's Tavern, families can participate in keeping a garden and managing a kitchen, and kids can dress up in 18th-century style. Another fun activity takes place at the **Governor's Palace,** where the dancing master gives lessons. During the summer, kids can "enlist" in the militia and practice marching and drilling at the **Magazine and Guardhouse** (I still have a snapshot of myself as a boy, holding a flintlock). Inquire at the visitor center for special themed tours in areas of your children's specific interest.

✪ **Busch Gardens Williamsburg.** 1 Busch Gardens Blvd., Williamsburg. ☎ **757/253-3350.** www.buschgardens.com. Admission and hours vary by day, season, and year, so call ahead or get brochure at visitor center. Admission about $33 adults, $26 children 3–6, including unlimited rides, shows, and attractions (free for kids under 3). Twilight discounts and 2- and 3-day Busch Gardens/Water Country USA passes available. Late Mar to mid-May, Fri 10am–6pm, Sat 10am–10pm, Sun 10am–7pm; mid-May to mid-June, Sun–Fri 10am–6pm, Sat 10am–10pm; mid-June to Aug, daily 10am–10pm; Sept–Oct, Mon and Fri 10am–6pm, Sat–Sun 10am–7pm. Also open Easter weekend and spring break. Closed Nov to late Mar. Parking $5 per car, $3 per motorcycle. From Williamsburg, take U.S. 60E for about 3 miles.

At some point you'll want to take a break from early American history, especially if you have kids in tow. That's the time to head over to Busch Gardens Williamsburg, a 360-acre family entertainment park. Here you can get a peek at European history, albeit fanciful, in authentically detailed 17th-century hamlets from England, Scotland, France, Germany, and Italy—but little mental effort is required to enjoy all the attractions you'll find here.

Each village has its own shops, crafts demonstrations, restaurants, rides, shows, and other entertainment. They are connected by trains pulled by reproductions of European steam locomotives, so you can easily skip around.

The usual starting point is the Elizabethan English hamlet of Banbury Cross, where a replica of Shakespeare's Globe Theatre presents a 3-D film trip through ancient castles. From there, you proceed to Heatherdowns, Scotland, home of the famous Anheuser-Busch Clydesdale horses and the serpentine "Loch Ness Monster," a terrifying roller coaster with two interlocking 360° loops and a 130-foot drop. Then it's back to England and Hastings, where kids can play 13th-century games and challenge King Arthur in a 3-D simulator, and the whole family can see "Rocking the Boat," a song and dance revue.

Next comes Aquitaine, France, where you and the kids can test your driving skills on the hairpin turns of Le Mans Raceway. The Royal Theatre here is the venue for the park's nighttime entertainment and special events. Then it's on to Rhinefeld,

Germany, where "Land of the Dragons" lets the kids explore a three-story tree house and ride a flume and a dragon-themed Ferris wheel. Both you and the kids can drop to your heart's content on "Alpengeist," the world's tallest and fastest inverted roller coaster (195 feet tall, 67 m.p.h.). Dancers and an oompah band entertain in Das Festhaus, a 2,000-seat festival hall.

From Germany, a 300-foot bridge crosses the "Rhine River" to San Marco, a Renaissance-style Italian village where the water ride "Escape from Pompeii" will whisk you to the smoldering ruins of the ancient Italian city destroyed by a volcano, and "Roman Rapids" will speed you to a watery splash in front of the ruins. Tamer rides pay tribute to Leonardo da Vinci's inventions.

Your one-price admission entitles you not only to unlimited rides but also to top-quality musicals, bird shows, ice-skating revues, and more. Pick up a show schedule at the entrance.

Water Country USA. Va. 199. ☎ **757/229-9300.** Admission and hours vary, so call ahead or get brochure at visitor center. Admission (including parking) about $24 adults, $17 children 3–6, free for children 2 and under. May, Sat–Sun 10am–6pm; Memorial Day to mid-June, daily 10am–6pm; mid-June to mid-Aug, daily 10am–8pm; mid-Aug to Labor Day, daily 10am–7pm; Labor Day to mid-Sept, Sat–Sun 10am–6pm. Take Va. 199 north of I-64 and follow the signs.

Virginia's largest water-oriented amusement park features exciting water slides, rides, and entertainment set to a 1950s and '60s surf theme. The largest ride—"Big Daddy Falls"—takes the entire family on a colossal river-rafting adventure. Or twist and turn on giant inner tubes through flumes, tunnels, water "explosions," and down a waterfall to "splashdown." There's much more, all of it wet and sometimes wild. It's a perfect place to chill out after a hot summer's day in the Historic Area.

SHOPPING
IN THE HISTORIC AREA

Duke of Gloucester Street is the center for 18th-century wares created by craftspeople plying the trades of our forefathers. The goods offered include hand-wrought silver jewelry from the Sign of the Golden Ball, hats from the Mary Dickenson shop, pomanders to ward off the plague from McKenzie's Apothecary, hand-woven linens from Prentis Store, leather-bound books and hand-printed newspapers from the post office, gingerbread cakes from the Raleigh Tavern Bake Shop, and everything from foodstuffs to fishhooks from Greenhow and Tarpley's, a general store.

Not to be missed is **Craft House,** also run by the Colonial Williamsburg Foundation. There are two locations, one in Merchants Square, the other near the Abby Aldrich Rockefeller Folk Art Center. Featured at Craft House are exquisite works by master craftspeople and authentic reproductions of colonial furnishings. There are also reproduction wallpapers, china, toys, games, maps, books, prints, and souvenirs aplenty.

Merchants Square "shoppes" at the west end of Duke of Gloucester Street offer a wide range of merchandise: antiques, antiquarian books and prints, 18th-century-style floral arrangements, candy, toys, handcrafted pewter and silver items, needlework supplies, country quilts, and Oriental rugs. It's not all of the "ye olde" variety, however; you'll also find a Baskin-Robbins ice-cream parlor, a drugstore that offers aspirin in lieu of leeches, a camera shop, and clothing stores. Merchants Square has free 2-hour parking for its customers.

ON RICHMOND ROAD

Shopping in the Historic Area is fun, but the biggest merchandising draws are along Richmond Road (U.S. 60) between Williamsburg and Lightfoot, an area 5 to 7 miles west of the Historic Area. If you like outlet shopping, Richmond Road will seem like paradise.

Driving west from town (or taking the Relax & Ride Visitors Shuttle during summer), you'll come first to **Patriot Plaza Premium Outlets,** between Ironbound and Airport roads (no phone), with Dansk, Fila, Leather Loft, Lenox fine china and crystal, Polo Ralph Lauren, Samsonite/American Tourister, and the Prince Michel Wine Shop, where one of Virginia's premier vintners has a tasting room and bistro. Shops here are open Monday through Saturday from 9am to 9pm, Sunday from 9am to 6pm.

Next comes **Berkeley Commons Outlet Center,** Airport and Lightfoot roads (☎ 800/866-5900 or 757/565-0702), an outdoor mall with more than 80 shops, including Anne Klein, Bass, Bose, Brooks Brothers, Capezio, Coach, Crabtree & Evelyn, Eddie Bauer, Etienne Aigner, Harvé Bernard, J. Crew, Jones New York, Jos. A. Bank, Maidenform, Mikasa, Naturalizer, Nike, Reebok/Rockport, Royal Doulton, Seiko, Van Heusen, and Waterford Wedgwood. The mall is open March to December, Monday through Saturday from 10am to 9pm; January and February, Monday through Thursday from 10am to 6pm, Friday and Saturday from 10am to 9pm, Sunday from 11am to 6pm.

Many of these same outlets are represented among the 60 stores in the area's largest enclosed mall, the **Williamsburg Outlet Mall** (☎ 888/SHOP-333 or 757/565-3378), at the intersection of U.S. 60 and Lightfoot Road (C.R. 646). It's open March to December, Monday through Saturday from 10am to 9pm, Sunday from 10am to 6pm; call for winter hours.

Just up the road is **Williamsburg Pottery Factory** (☎ 757/564-3326), a 200-acre shopping complex with over 31 tin buildings selling merchandise from all over the world. It's all bought in large volume and sold at competitive prices. Shops on the premises sell Christmas decorations, garden furnishings, lamps, art prints, dried and silk flowers, luggage, linens, baskets, hardware, glassware, cookware, candles, wine, toys, crafts, clothing, food, jewelry, plants (there's a large greenhouse and nursery)—even pottery. There's plenty of quality and plenty of kitsch. It even has its own **Pottery Factory Outlets,** with discount offerings of 20 major manufacturers under one roof. They include Black & Decker, Van Heusen, Fieldcrest-Cannon, Izod, Oneida, and Pfaltzgraff. Hours are daily from 8am to 7pm in summer, daily from 9am to 5pm the rest of the year.

Continue west 1¹/₂ miles on U.S. 60 and you'll come to the **Williamsburg Doll Factory** (☎ 757/564-9703), with limited-edition porcelain collector's dolls. You can observe the doll-making process and even buy parts to make your own. Other items sold here include stuffed animals, dollhouses and miniatures, clowns, and books on dolls. It's open daily from 9am to 5pm.

Finally we come to the **Williamsburg Soap & Candle Company** (☎ 757/564-3354). Here you can see a narrated video presentation on candle making while watching the process through viewing windows that look out on the factory. Interesting shops adjoin, and a cozy country-style restaurant is on the premises. It's open daily from 9am to 5pm, with extended hours in summer and fall.

WHERE TO STAY
COLONIAL WILLIAMSBURG FOUNDATION HOTELS

The Colonial Williamsburg Foundation operates the Williamsburg Inn, the Williamsburg Lodge, and Williamsburg Woodlands, all in the Historic Area, and the nearby Governor's Inn. For reservations at any of these, call the **visitor center reservations service** (☎ 800/HISTORY).

The room rates at the foundation's hotels can vary widely, depending on the time of year and how many guests may be booked on a given night. Try to reserve as far in advance as possible for the busy summer season. You might get a bargain during other times, especially if business is slow. And be sure to ask about a multitude of special package deals.

Governor's Inn. Va. 132 (Henry St.) (P.O. Box 1776), Williamsburg, VA 23187. ☎ **800/ HISTORY** or 757/229-1000. 200 rms. A/C TV TEL. $50–$99 double. AE, DC, DISC, MC, V. Closed Jan–Feb. Free parking.

Least expensive of the Colonial Williamsburg hotels, the Governor's Inn was recently taken over by the foundation and completely renovated and redecorated. Furnishings are clean and bright. A new wing was added as well as an outdoor swimming pool. It's near the visitor center on Va. 132, an extension of Henry Street.

✪ **Williamsburg Inn.** 136 Francis St. (P.O. Box 1776), Williamsburg, VA 23187. ☎ **800/ HISTORY** or 757/229-1000. Fax 757/220-7096. 102 rms. A/C TV TEL. $250–$375 double. AE, DC, DISC, MC, V. Free parking.

One of the nation's most distinguished hotels, this rambling white-brick Regency-style inn has played host to hundreds of VIPs, including heads of state from 17 countries and U.S. presidents Truman, Eisenhower, Nixon, Ford, and Reagan. It is considered one of the country's finest golf resorts, with three top-flight courses, including the noted Golden Horseshoe.

The lobby lounge is graced with Federal-style furnishings and two working fireplaces. Complimentary tea is served every afternoon in the East Lounge. Rooms are exquisitely furnished with Regency reproductions, and guests are pampered with French-milled soap, hair dryers, and terry-cloth robes in the bath, plus fresh flowers. A special reduced-price ticket to the Historic Area is sold at the concierge desk daily. All guests staying in official Colonial Williamsburg hotels are invited to a special 2-hour guided walking tour of the Historic Area.

In addition to accommodations in the main inn building, there are some 84 rooms close by and within the Historic Area in the perfectly charming **Colonial Houses and Taverns.** Tastefully furnished with 18th-century antiques and reproductions, they are variously equipped with canopied beds, kitchens, living rooms, fireplaces, and/or sizable gardens. The houses vary in size and can accommodate 2 to 12 comfortably. Rates range from $99 to $400.

Adjacent to the inn and golf course in a modern building called **Providence Hall,** rooms are furnished in a contemporary blend of 18th-century and Oriental style, with balconies or patios overlooking tennis courts and a beautiful wooded area. Complete services are provided by the inn. Rates, from $110 to $225, offer exceptionally good value.

Dining/Entertainment: The Regency Lounge offers cocktails, light suppers, and entertainment nightly and hosts Felicity's Tea for children each afternoon. The Regency Dining Room features classic American cuisine at its finest. After 6pm, coats and ties are required in the Regency Dining Room, jackets in the Regency Lounge. Regency Sunday brunch is served from noon to 2pm.

Services: Concierge, room service, baby-sitting.

Facilities: Two outdoor pools, Tazewell Club Fitness Center in the lodge available for inn guests, eight tennis courts, two 18-hole and one 9-hole golf course, lawn bowling, croquet, nature trail, family programs.

Williamsburg Lodge. S. England St. (P.O. Box 1776), Williamsburg, VA 23187. ☎ **800/ HISTORY** or 757/229-1000. Fax 757/220-7685. 315 rms. A/C TV TEL. $140–$235 double.

Additional person $12 extra; children under 18 stay free in parents' rm. AE, DC, DISC, MC, V. Free parking.

The Williamsburg Lodge is located near the Williamsburg Inn and offers all the sports facilities of the inn and a pleasantly rustic interior. The flagstone-floored lobby is indeed lodgelike, with cypress paneling and a large, working fireplace. A covered veranda with rocking chairs overlooks two pools and a golf course. Accommodations are contemporary but warm and homey, with polished wood floors and handcrafted furniture. American folk art—decoys, samplers, and the like—highlight the decor. West Wing rooms have windowed walls overlooking duck ponds or a wooded landscape. They're furnished in oak, cane, and bamboo, and 12 have working fireplaces. The Tazewell Wing is built around a central landscaped courtyard with informal lounge areas on all three floors. Guest rooms are attractively furnished with reproductions inspired by pieces in the Abby Aldrich Rockefeller Folk Art Center.

Dining/Entertainment: The attractive Bay Room overlooks a garden and fountain. On Friday and Saturday nights, it features a Chesapeake Bay Feast, and on Sunday an omelet brunch buffet is the draw. The Garden Lounge has drinks and musical entertainment from early afternoon.

Facilities: All inn facilities are available to lodge guests. The Tazewell Club Fitness Center is in the lodge and offers an indoor lap pool, Keiser exercise machines, and aerobics classes.

Williamsburg Woodlands. Va. 132, off U.S. 60 Bypass (P.O. Box 1776), Williamsburg, VA 23187. ☎ **800/HISTORY** or 757/229-1000. Fax 757/220-7941. 315 rms. A/C TV TEL. $70–$120 double. Additional person $8 extra; children under 18 stay free in parents' rm. AE, DC, DISC, MC, V. Free parking.

Set on 40 wooded acres with picnic tables under the pines, the Woodlands offers a lot for the money: it's conveniently located right behind the visitor center; rooms are cheerful, attractive, and equipped with all the modern amenities; and facilities include a jogging path, golf putting green, miniature golf, shuffleboard, playground, horseshoes, volleyball, badminton, and a large swimming pool complex with a toddler's pool. The Cascades restaurant serves all meals, and there's a Burger King.

OTHER ACCOMMODATIONS

The **Williamsburg Hotel/Motel Association** (☎ **800/446-9244** or 757/220-3330) will make reservations for you in any price range. The service is free, and their listings include most of the accommodations mentioned below.

Most national chains are represented here, including Best Western, Comfort Inn, Days Inn, Econo Lodge, Hampton Inn, Holiday Inn, Marriott, Quality Inn, Ramada Inn, and Travelodge. See the appendix for their toll-free numbers.

Moderate

Courtyard by Marriott. 470 McLaws Circle, Williamsburg, VA 23185. ☎ **800/321-2211** or 757/221-0700. Fax 757/221-0741. 142 rms, 9 suites. A/C TV TEL. $90–$129 double; $89–$185 suite. Children under 18 stay free in parents' rm. Weekend packages available. AE, DC, DISC, MC, V. Free parking. From Williamsburg, follow U.S. 60 east about 2 miles to Busch Corporate Center, turn right at light and bear right on McLaws Circle.

This four-story member of the fine chain designed for business travelers (and very comfortable for the rest of us) enjoys an attractively landscaped setting of trees and shrubs. A plant-filled lobby looks out to the courtyard and its good-size pool. Furnished with substantial oak pieces, the guest quarters feature large desks, separate seating areas, long phone cords, irons and ironing boards, and piping-hot faucets for instant coffee or tea. Suites have full living rooms with sofa beds and extra phones and TVs, plus wet bars with small refrigerators. The lobby restaurant offers a breakfast buffet. Facilities include an exercise room with Jacuzzi.

Fort Magruder Inn & Conference Center. U.S. 60 East (P.O. Box KE), Williamsburg, VA 23187. ☎ **800/582-1010** or 757/220-2250. Fax 757/220-9059. 287 rms, 16 suites. A/C TV TEL. $79–$139 double; $150–$250 suite. AE, DC, DISC, MC, V. From I-64, take Va. 199 west to U.S. 60 west.

Situated between the Historic Area and Busch Gardens, this modern hotel draws lots of conventions and meetings but is also a good choice for families with children who want a location convenient to both attractions. Two-story glass walls create an atrium lobby, but lots of brick and antique-look furniture remind you that this is Williamsburg and not California. Guest rooms in the curved building are spacious, with wing chairs, writing desks, and balconies looking out on gardens that surround a swimming pool and lighted tennis courts (there's also a fitness center here, and guests can play at Kingsmill Resort's excellent golf courses). Looking out on the landscaped pool area, the Veranda Room serves breakfast, lunch, and dinner, while J.B.'s Lounge provides evening cocktails and music for dancing.

Williamsburg Hospitality House. 415 Richmond Rd., Williamsburg, VA 23185. ☎ **757/ 229-4020.** 297 rms, 11 suites. A/C TV TEL. $79–$169 double; $350 one-bedrm suite; $430 two-bedrm suite. AE, DC, DISC, MC, V. Free parking.

Just 2 blocks from the Historic Area opposite William and Mary College, this four-story brick hotel is built around a central courtyard with flowering trees and plants and umbrella tables. Guest rooms and public areas are appointed with a gracious blend of 18th-century reproductions. The Colony dining room specializes in colonial cuisine. Christopher's Tavern serves lunch, dinner, and light fare. Facilities include an outdoor pool and gift shop.

Inexpensive

Budget Host Governor Spotswood Motel. 1508 Richmond Rd. (just east of Ironwood Rd.), Williamsburg, VA 23185. ☎ **800/368-1244** or 757/229-6444. Fax 757/253-2410. 78 rms, 8 cottages. A/C TV TEL. $32–$130 double. AE, DC, DISC, MC, V.

Owned and operated by the same family for two generations, this older but well-maintained motel offers rooms in one-story buildings facing a parking lot and cottages set back among magnolias, camellias, and towering pines on the property's 10 acres. The smallish but nevertheless comfortable rooms have tub-shower combination baths; some sport brass or canopy beds, and 19 of them have kitchens. Capable of accommodating up to seven people, each of the cottages has two bedrooms, a living room, a kitchen, and a bath. Kids will enjoy the outdoor pool and playground area.

If you can do without a phone in your room, the adjacent **Colonial Motel,** 1452 Richmond Rd., Williamsburg, VA 23185 (☎ **800/232-1452** or 757/ 229-3621), is another older but clean and comfortable motel still owned by the family that built it more than 3 decades ago. Rates for its 27 rooms range from $30 to $56 double. American Express, Discover, MasterCard, and Visa are accepted.

☺Heritage Inn. 1324 Richmond Rd. (at Mt. Vernon Ave.), Williamsburg, VA 23185. ☎ **800/ 782-3800** or 757/229-6220. Fax 757/228-2774. 54 rms. A/C TV TEL. $36–$82. AE, DC, DISC, MC, V.

An impressive, colonial-style brick building houses the lobby and a beautiful, light-filled dining room at this family-owned motel, convenient to the Historic Area. Although the rooms are next door in a nondescript, two-story motel block, they are both spacious and comfortable. Most contain two double beds, desks, TVs hidden in armoires, and tiled shower-tub combination bathrooms with unusual knickknack shelves built in above the vanities. Three rooms also have sitting areas. Facilities include an outdoor pool. Operated by a catering firm, the dining room offers an extensive and inexpensive breakfast buffet Tuesday through Sunday from March to December.

Motel 6. 3030 Richmond Rd., Williamsburg, VA 23185. ☎ **800/466-8356** or 757/565-3433. Fax 757/565-1013. 168 rms. A/C TV TEL. $46 single. Additional person $6 extra; children under 18 stay free in parents' rm. AE, DC, DISC, MC, V.

The only catch to snagging one of the low-priced rooms here during summer is that you usually have to reserve far in advance, even though it is one of the largest members of this budget chain. An attractive pool and sundeck are out back, and the woodsy location is a plus. There's an Outback Steakhouse in the parking lot, and the Holiday Inn next door has a coffee shop.

BED & BREAKFASTS

In addition to those mentioned below, Williamsburg has at least 16 other B&Bs. The Williamsburg Area Convention & Visitors Bureau can supply a list (see "Essentials," above).

Liberty Rose. 1022 Jamestown Rd., Williamsburg, VA 23185. ☎ **800/545-1825** or 757/253-1260. www.libertyrose.com. 4 rms (all with bath). A/C TV TEL. $135–$195 double. Rates include full breakfast. AE, MC, V. On-site parking.

Known as Williamsburg's most romantic B&B, Brad and Sara Hirz's inn has a premier location on a wooded hilltop just 1¼ miles from the Historic Area. Housed in a charming 1920s two-story white-clapboard residence with a dormered slate roof flanked by chimneys, the Liberty Rose is furnished in delightful style; you'll find Victorian, French- and English-country, and 18th-century antiques and reproductions here.

The elegant parlor has a working fireplace, comfortable chairs for relaxing, and a grand piano that guests may play. The accommodations are luxurious, each distinctively decorated. The Savannah Lace guest room has peach wallpaper, an antique carved-mahogany queen-size bed with a pink goosedown duvet, a TV, bathrobes, and a bowl of chocolates; the bathroom, tucked into the side dormer room, has a clawfoot tub (most rooms here have both a glass-enclosed shower and a clawfoot tub). A full breakfast is served on the porch or in the courtyard; a typical menu might include fresh orange juice, eggs with bacon, French toast, and coffee or tea. An overall feeling of graciousness makes the Liberty Rose a real delight, a tranquil refuge from the rigors of sightseeing.

Williamsburg Manor Bed & Breakfast. 600 Richmond Rd., Williamsburg, VA 23185. ☎ **800/422-8011** or 757/220-8011. Fax 757/220-0245. 5 rms (all with bath). A/C TV. $90 single or double. Rates include full breakfast. MC, V. On-site parking.

Right in the heart of Williamsburg, just 2 blocks from the Historic Area, this gracious 1928 Georgian Revival brick residence offers traditional comfort in nicely appointed rooms. Guests are invited to congregate in the living room, where they'll find a TV, magazines, and a great cookbook collection. In addition to the full breakfasts, host Laura Sisane offers dinners for guests, by prior reservation only. Accommodations vary in size and furnishings, but you can expect to find four-poster beds, brass lamps, Oriental rugs, and wing chairs. The breakfast table, set with fine china, might include fresh fruit, eggs in puff pastry with bacon, home-baked breads or pastries, and coffee and tea.

A NEARBY RESORT WITH CHAMPIONSHIP GOLF

Kingsmill Resort. 1010 Kingsmill Rd., Williamsburg, VA 23185. ☎ **800/832-5665** or 757/253-1703. Fax 757/253-3993. 400 units. A/C TV TEL. $115–$275 double; $155–$738 suite.

Packages available. AE, DC, DISC, MC, V. Free parking. From I-64, take Exit 242 and follow Va. 199 west past U.S. 60 to sign for Kingsmill on the James.

Nestled in a peaceful setting on beautifully landscaped grounds on the James River, the gray-clapboard Kingsmill resort complex feels very much like a country club. Its 2,900 acres of facilities include the world-famous River Course, home of the Michelob Classic; the Plantation Course, designed by Arnold Palmer; and the Bray Links Par Three (complimentary to guests). Kingsmill accommodations—guest rooms and one-, two-, and three-bedroom units—are in tastefully furnished villas overlooking the James River, golf-course fairways, or tennis courts. The decor in these individually owned and furnished condos varies from handsome colonial reproductions to sophisticated contemporary settings. Most suites have complete kitchens and living rooms with fireplaces. Daily housekeeping service, including fresh linens, is provided.

Dining: All four dining rooms feature panoramic views of the James. In the Bray dining room, breakfast, lunch buffets, and à la carte evening meals are reasonably priced. More casual dining spots are Moody's Tavern, Peyton Grille, and Kingsmill Café in the golf clubhouse.

Services: Concierge, complimentary shuttle to Colonial Williamsburg and Busch Gardens Williamsburg, children's activity programs.

Facilities: Indoor and outdoor pools, Nautilus exercise room, Jacuzzi, saunas, full-service spa, 15 tennis courts, racquetball courts, marina, pro shop, golf, billiards, children's program, gift shop.

WHERE TO DINE

Williamsburg abounds in restaurants catering to tourists. Most national fast-food and family-restaurant chains have outlets on Richmond Road (U.S. 60) on the west side of town. In addition to the restaurants located within its accommodations (see "Where to Stay," above), the Colonial Williamsburg Foundation runs four popular reconstructed colonial taverns.

COLONIAL WILLIAMSBURG FOUNDATION TAVERNS

If you're planning on dinner at one of these taverns, make your reservations first thing in the morning—if not a day or two before—by going to or calling the visitor center (☎ **800/TAVERNS** or 757/229-2141). In the spring and fall seasons, it's a good idea to reserve even before arrival (you can do so up to 60 days in advance). Business hours can vary slightly from those given below, especially in January and February when restaurants may be closed for annual upkeep.

Dine at one of the taverns for the experience, not for the finest quality cuisine. All are reconstructed 18th-century *ordinaries,* or taverns, and aim at authenticity in fare, ambience, and costuming of the staff. All offer colonial fare such as peanut soup, salad with chutney dressing, Brunswick stew, sautéed backfin crabmeat and ham topped with butter and laced with sherry, Sally Lunn bread, and deep-dish Shenandoah apple pie, and all offer alfresco dining in good weather on brick patios under grape arbors. Low-priced children's menus are available. Seasonal menus are available at the visitor center and are posted at the ticket booth on Henry Street at Duke of Gloucester Street.

Christiana Campbell's Tavern. Waller St. ☎ **757/229-2141.** Reservations essential. Main courses $19–$24. AE, DC, DISC, MC, V. Seatings Tues–Sat 5, 5:30, 7, 7:30, 9 and 9:15pm. COLONIAL.

Christiana Campbell's Tavern, near the Capitol, is "where all the best people resorted" circa 1765. George Washington was a regular (in 1772, he recorded in his diary that he dined here 10 times over a 22-month period). After the capital moved to Richmond, business declined and operations eventually ceased. In its heyday, however, the tavern was famous for seafood, and today that is once again its specialty. Campbell's is an authentic reproduction with 18th-century furnishings, blazing fireplaces, and flutists and balladeers providing musical entertainment.

Josiah Chowning's Tavern. Duke of Gloucester St. ☎ **757/229-2141.** Reservations suggested. Lunch $4–$11; main courses $5.50–$13. AE, DC, DISC, MC, V. Daily 11:30am–9pm; Gambols pub, daily 9pm–midnight. COLONIAL.

In 1766, Josiah Chowning announced the opening of a tavern "where all who please to favour me with their custom may depend upon the best of entertainment for themselves, servants, and horses, and good pasturage." It's very charming, with low-beamed ceilings, raw pine floors, and sturdy country-made furnishings. There are two working fireplaces, and at night guests dine by candlelight.

Kings Arms Tavern. Duke of Gloucester St. ☎ **757/229-2141.** Reservations required at dinner. Lunch $6–$10; main courses $20–$24. AE, DC, DISC, MC, V. Daily 11:30am–2:30pm and 5–9pm. COLONIAL.

The Kings Arms Tavern, on the site of a 1772 establishment, is actually a re-creation of the tavern and an adjoining home. Outbuildings—including stables, a barbershop, laundry, smokehouse, and kitchen—have also been reconstructed. The original proprietress, Mrs. Jane Vobe, was famous for her fine cooking, and her establishment's proximity to the Capitol made it a natural meeting place during Publick Times. Today the 11 dining rooms (8 with fireplaces) are painted and furnished following authentic early Virginia precedent. The Queen Anne and Chippendale pieces are typical appointments of this class of tavern, and the prints, maps, engravings, aquatints, and mezzotints lining the walls are genuine examples of colonial interior decoration. Balladeers wander the rooms during dinner and entertain.

Shields Tavern. Duke of Gloucester St. ☎ **757/229-2141.** Reservations essential. Breakfast $3.50–$9; lunch $6–$7; main courses $14.50–$22. AE, DC, DISC, MC, V. Daily 8:30–10am, 11:30am–3pm, and 5:15–9:30pm. Garden, daily 11:30am–dusk. COLONIAL.

With 11 dining rooms and a garden under a trumpet-vine–covered arbor that seats 200, Shields is the largest of the Historic Area's tavern/restaurants. It's named for James Shields, who, with his wife, Anne, and family, ran a much-frequented hostelry on this site in the mid-1700s. Using a room-by-room inventory of Shields's personal effects—and as a result of detailed archaeological investigation—the tavern has been furnished with items similar to those used in the mid-18th century, and many of the rooms have working fireplaces. A specially designed rotisserie unit in the kitchen allows chefs here to approximate 18th-century roasting techniques. Shields is the only tavern open for breakfast. Strolling balladeers entertain at night.

OTHER HISTORIC AREA RESTAURANTS

Berret's Restaurant & Raw Bar. 199 S. Boundary St. ☎ **757/253-1847.** Reservations recommended for dinner. Main courses $15–$19. AE, DISC, MC, V. Mar–Dec, daily 11:30am–5pm and 5:30–10pm. Jan–Feb, Tues–Sun 11:30am–5pm and 5:30–9pm. SEAFOOD.

A congenial, casual place, Berret's has a popular outdoor raw bar that seems to be busy all day long, especially on weekends, when people stop in at all hours for half a dozen oysters or clams on the half shell. The adjoining restaurant is bright and airy, with several dining rooms. Seating is at booths upholstered in a nautical-blue leather; canvas sailcloth shades and marine artifacts on the walls make an appropriate backdrop for the excellent seafood specialties. For your entree, try peanut-crusted soft-shell crabs served with peanut-bourbon butter. Lunch offerings include bouillabaisse, a vegetarian entree, and sandwiches and salads. The menu features some incredible desserts, among them chocolate-marble cheesecake with raspberry filling and whipped cream. Berret's has an interesting selection of beers and specialty wines.

A Good Place to Eat. 410 Duke of Gloucester St., Merchants Sq. ☎ **757/229-4370.** Breakfast $2.75–$4.50; lunch and dinner $2.50–$6.50. MC, V. Mid-March to Aug, daily 8am–10pm; Sept–Oct, daily 8am–8pm; Nov–Dec, daily 8am–7pm; Jan to mid-March, daily 8am–6pm. AMERICAN.

This is an especially good place for family meals. The food is high quality for a fast-food emporium—burger meat is prepared from the best cuts of chuck and round, breads and cakes are fresh-baked, even the ice cream is homemade. And the setting is rather attractive: The big indoor dining room has terra-cotta tile floors and many hanging plants. Better yet is the outdoor seating at umbrella tables on a flower-bordered brick patio. Stop by for an inexpensive breakfast of scrambled eggs and ham with homemade biscuits, or a sweet-potato muffin and coffee. At lunch or dinner you can get a ham-and-Swiss sandwich on French bread, a hamburger, or chef's salad. Leave room for a sundae with homemade ice cream and fresh whipped cream.

✪ Trellis Cafe, Restaurant & Grill. Duke of Gloucester St., Merchants Sq. ☎ **757/229-8610.** Reservations suggested at dinner. Main courses $14–$23; fixed-price dinner $22. AE, MC, V. Mon–Sat 11:30am–9:30pm; Sun 11:30am–3pm and 5–9:30pm. AMERICAN.

The *New York Times* calls the Trellis "the best restaurant in this part of Virginia." Evocative of California's delightful wine-country restaurants in both decor and cuisine, it is entered via a grapevine-covered trellis. Inside, the Garden Room is the plushest setting, with apricot velvet furnishings. The Trellis Room is country-contemporary in feel, with forest-green upholstered pine furnishings and walls minimally adorned with vineyard baskets full of dried flowers and antique French farm implements. In the Grill Room, you can watch food being prepared over an open hearth using Texas mesquite wood. Very cozy is the Vault Room, with tables under an arched ceiling of narrow heart-of-pine beams. In the Café Bar, walls are hung with antique wine-motif prints. If the weather is fine, you might dine alfresco on the planter-bordered brick terrace.

Executive chef Marcel Desaulniers has brought national recognition to the Trellis with his outstanding regional cuisine. He was the first chef from the South to be honored by the James Beard Foundation, whose awards are considered the Oscars of the culinary industry. Desaulniers was also named to *Food & Wine* magazine's honor roll of American chefs and to *Who's Who of Cooking in America*. His exciting, imaginative menu, which changes regularly to take advantage of seasonal specials, combines the best culinary aspects of different regions of the United States. Desaulniers is the author of three best-selling cookbooks: *The Trellis Cookbook, The Burger Meisters,* and *Death by Chocolate.* Needless to say, his chocolate desserts are not to be missed.

NEARBY DINING

✪ Giuseppe's Italian Cafe. 5601 Richmond Hwy. (U.S. 60) (in Ewell Station Shopping Center). ☎ **757/565-1977.** Reservations not accepted. Main courses $4.50–$17. DISC, MC, V. Mon–Thurs 11:30am–2pm and 5–9pm; Fri–Sat 11:30am–2pm and 5–9:30pm. From Historic Area, go 4 miles west on U.S. 60 to shopping center on left. ITALIAN.

This pleasant local favorite may be difficult to see from Richmond Highway (it's at the end of a strip mall with a Food Lion supermarket at its center), but it's a great place for a meal during or after a shopping expedition. Chef Dan Kennedy may have an Irish name, but he's adept at spinning out the likes of chicken Antonio in a subtly spicy pepper pesto sauce. He also offers heaping plates of spaghetti, a page full of vegetarian pastas, and individual-size pizzas with unusual toppings such as smoked oysters. All entrees come with salad or a bowl of hearty lentil-and-andouille sausage soup. There are two dining rooms here plus heated sidewalk seating.

Le Yaca. U.S. 60E (in the Village Shops at Kingsmill). ☎ **757/220-3616.** Reservations recommended. Lunch $6.50–$13.50; fixed-price dinners $21–$42. AE, DC, MC, V. Mon–Sat 11:30am–2pm and 6–9:30pm. From Historic Area, go east on U.S. 60 to Va. 199; the shops are just east of the interchange. FRENCH.

Centered on a large open hearth, on which a leg of lamb is often roasting during cold weather, Le Yaca is charmingly provincial, with glossy oak floors, rough-hewn beams overhead, and romantic soft lighting from oil candles and shaded lamps. Pale-peach walls are hung with lovely prints of Paris scenes. At lunch, a create-your-own-salad table has all you might desire: 15 scrumptious salad choices including pasta salad, cucumber in fresh cream, potato salad with lamb, carrots rapé, seafood and rice, and tomato vinaigrette; fresh-baked bread and butter is included. A fixed-price dinner might begin with mountain-style onion soup, an entree of salmon in parchment, an array of fresh vegetables, salad, and then a *marquise au chocolat*—rich chocolate truffles afloat on crème anglaise.

۞ Old Chickahominy House. 1211 Jamestown Rd. (at Va. 199). ☎ **757/229-4689.** Reservations not accepted. Breakfast $3–$7.50; lunch $3–$6.50. MC, V. Daily 8:30–10:15am and 11:45am–2:15pm. TRADITIONAL SOUTHERN.

The Old Chickahominy House is a reconstructed 18th-century residence with mantels from old Gloucester homes and wainscoting from Carter's Grove. Floors are bare oak, and walls, painted in traditional colonial colors, are hung with gilt-framed 17th- and 18th-century oil paintings. Three adjoining rooms house an antiques/gift shop. The entire effect is extremely cozy and charming, from the rocking chairs on the front porch to the blazing fireplaces within. Authentic Southern fare is featured at breakfast and lunch. The house specialty in the morning is the plantation breakfast—real Virginia ham with two eggs, biscuits, cured country bacon and sausage, grits, and coffee. At lunch, Miss Melinda's special is a cup of Brunswick stew with Virginia ham on hot biscuits, fruit salad, homemade pie, and tea or coffee. After dining, roam through the warren of antiques-filled rooms. Also check out the Shirley Pewter Shop next door.

Pierce's Pitt Bar-B-Que. Rochambeau Dr., Lightfoot (beside I-64). ☎ **757/565-2955.** Reservations not accepted. Sandwiches $2.50–$3.50; main courses $6–$13. MC, V. Sun–Thurs 7am–9pm; Fri–Sat 7am–10pm. From Historic Area, go west on Richmond Rd. (U.S. 60), right on Airport Rd. (C.R. 645) 2 miles to dead end at I-64, then left on Rochambeau Rd. 2 miles to restaurant on left. BARBECUE.

Visible from I-64, this gaudy yellow and orange barbecue joint has been dishing up pulled pork, chicken, and smoked ribs for decades, as the walls hung with old photos of the owners and their family and staff will attest. The pulled pork here comes soaked in a smoky-flavored, tomato-based sauce. All platters are accompanied by creamy coleslaw, French fries, and hushpuppies. Order at the counter and take your meal (served in plastic containers) to a table inside or outdoors under cover.

PICNIC FARE & WHERE TO EAT IT

There are benches throughout the restored area (lots of grass, too), and if you have a car you can drive to nearby scenic overlooks along Colonial Parkway (the parking areas along the James and York rivers are best, but they don't have picnic tables or other facilities).

The Cheese Shop, 424 Prince George St. in Merchants Square, between North Boundary and North Henry streets (☎ **757/220-0298**), is a good place to purchase take-out sandwiches and other fixings. It's open Monday through Saturday from

10am to 6pm, Sunday from 11am to 4pm. Out on Richmond Road, a good choice is **Padow's Hams & Deli,** in the Williamsburg Shopping Center at Monticello Avenue (☎ **757/220-4267**). It's open Monday through Friday from 10am to 8pm, Saturday from 10am to 5pm. Both delis have tables.

2 Jamestown: The First Colony

9 miles SW of Williamsburg

The story of Jamestown, the first permanent English settlement in the New World, is documented here in museum exhibits and living-history interpretations. The exploits of Capt. John Smith, leader of the colony; his legendary rescue from execution by the Native American princess Pocahontas; the arrival of the first African Americans; and a vivid picture of life in 17th-century Virginia are all part of the first chapter of American history interpreted here at the site of the first colony. Archaeologists have excavated more than 100 building frames, evidence of manufacturing ventures (pottery, wine making, brick making, and glass blowing), early wells, and old roads, as well as scores of artifacts of everyday life—tools, utensils, ceramic dishes, armor, keys, and the like.

Allow a full day for your visit and consider packing a lunch. Other than a cafe at Jamestown Settlement, there are no restaurants, so you may want to take advantage of the picnic areas at the National Park Service site.

ESSENTIALS

VISITOR INFORMATION   Two important Jamestown sites commemorate the first permanent English settlement in the New World. Jointly administered by the National Park Service and the Association for the Preservation of Virginia Antiquities, Jamestown Island is where the original colony was founded. For information about **Jamestown Island,** contact the Colonial National Historical Park, P.O. Box 210, Yorktown, VA 23690 (☎ **757/229-1733**). At the adjoining Jamestown Settlement, under the jurisdiction of the Commonwealth of Virginia, a living-history museum complex re-creates the daily life of the settlers. For **Jamestown Settlement** information, write P.O. Box 1607, Williamsburg, VA 23187 (☎ **888/593-4682** or 757/253-4838). See below for **combination ticket** information combining Settlement admission with Yorktown Victory Center admission.

GETTING THERE   From Williamsburg, follow the Jamestown Road, Va. 31S, or the Colonial Parkway.

EXPLORING THE SITES

Jamestown Island

The site of the actual colony, separated by an isthmus from the mainland, is at the western terminus of the Colonial Parkway. At the Ranger Station entrance gate, you'll pay $5 for each person over 16 years old; admission is good for 7 days. Or you can buy a Joint Jamestown-Yorktown Passport for $7 per person over 16, which will admit you for 7 days both here and at the Yorktown National Battlefield (see "Yorktown: Revolutionary Victory," below). National Park Service passports are accepted. The gate is open daily from 8:30am to 4:30pm in summer. You can stay on the grounds until dusk.

Exploration of the site of the first permanent English settlement in North America begins at the **visitor center** (☎ **757/229-1773**). Open daily from 9am to half an hour after the gate closes, it has an information desk, an exhibit area, and a theater in which a 15-minute orientation film tells the story of Jamestown from its earliest days to 1698, when the capital of Virginia moved to Williamsburg and Jamestown became a sleepy little village. Be sure to inquire at the reception desk about special programs offered on site that day; events might include a ranger-led walking tour, a costumed interpretive program, or a Young Settlers program for kids. Allow at least 2 hours for this special attraction.

From the visitor center, footpaths lead you through the actual site of **"James Cittie,"** where rubbly brick foundations of 17th-century homes, taverns, shops, and statehouses are enhanced by artists' renderings, text, and audio stations. Most complete are the remains of the tower of one of the first brick churches in Virginia (1639). Directly behind the tower is the **Memorial Church,** a 1907 re-creation built by the Colonial Dames of America on the site of the original structure, which, in 1619, housed the first legislative assembly in English-speaking North America. You can rent a recorded tour of the town site to accompany your walk.

A fascinating **5-mile loop drive** (beginning at the visitor center parking lot) winds through 1,500 wilderness acres of woodland and marsh that have been allowed to return to their natural state to approximate the landscape as 17th-century settlers found it. Illustrative markers interpret aspects of daily activities and industries of the colonists—tobacco growing, lumbering, silk and wine production, pottery making, farming, and so on.

Jamestown Settlement

This indoor/outdoor museum, operated by the Commonwealth of Virginia, is open daily except New Year's Day and Christmas. Basic hours are 9am to 5pm daily. Admission is $9.75 for adults and $4.75 for children 6 to 12 (free for children under 6).

If you're also planning to visit the Yorktown Victory Center (it doesn't have to be on the same day), buy a money-saving **combination ticket** to both museums at $13.50 for adults and $6.50 for children. A fast-food restaurant is on the premises, and parking is free.

After purchasing tickets, you can enter an orientation **theater** to watch a 20-minute film that gives you an introduction to Jamestown. Beyond the theater, three large permanent **museum** galleries feature artifacts, documents, decorative objects, dioramas, and graphics relating to the Jamestown period. The English Gallery focuses on Jamestown's beginnings in the Old World. A Powhatan Indian Gallery explores the origins and culture of the Native Americans who lived near Jamestown. The Jamestown Gallery deals with the history of the colony during its first century of existence.

Leaving the museum complex, visitors come directly into the **Powhatan Indian Village,** representing the culture and technology of a highly organized chiefdom of 32 tribes that inhabited coastal Virginia in the early 17th century. There are several mat-covered lodges, or *longhouses,* which are furnished as dwellings, as well as a garden and a ceremonial dance circle. Historical interpreters tend gardens, tan animal hides, and make bone and stone tools and pottery.

Triangular **James Fort** is a re-creation of the one constructed by the Jamestown colonists on their arrival in the spring of 1607. Inside the wooden stockade are primitive wattle-and-daub structures with thatched roofs, representing Jamestown's earliest buildings. Interpreters are engaged in activities typical of early-17th-century life, such as agriculture, animal care, carpentry, blacksmithing, and meal preparation.

A short walk from James Fort are reproductions of the three **ships,** the *Susan Constant, Godspeed,* and *Discovery,* which transported 104 colonists to Virginia in 1607. Visitors can board and explore one or more of the ships.

While here, you can take a 1¹/₂-hour narrated nature cruise on the **Jamestown Explorer,** a covered pontoon boat moored at the Jamestown Yacht Basin directly behind the settlement (☎ **757/259-0400**). The cost is $12.50 for adults, $8 for children (free for children under 4).

3 Yorktown: Revolutionary Victory

14 miles NE of Williamsburg

Yorktown was the setting for the last major battle of the American Revolution. Here, on October 19, 1781, George Washington wrote to the president of the Continental Congress, "I have the Honor to inform Congress, that a Reduction of the British Army under the Command of Lord Cornwallis, is most happily effected." Though it would be 2 years before a peace treaty was signed, and sporadic fighting would continue, the Revolution, for all intents and purposes, had been won.

Today, the decisive battlefield is a national park, and the Commonwealth of Virginia has built an interpretive museum explaining the road to revolution, the war itself, and the building of a new nation afterwards. Pre-dating the revolution, the old town of Yorktown itself is worth seeing.

ESSENTIALS

VISITOR INFORMATION   For information about the Virginia State–run **Yorktown Victory Center,** a stimulating multimedia museum with indoor and outdoor programs located on old route Va. 238, contact P.O. Box 1607, Williamsburg, VA 23187 (☎ **888/593-4682** or 757/253-4838). The National Park Service Yorktown and **Yorktown Battlefield Visitor Center** are at the terminus of the Colonial Parkway, P.O. Box 210, Yorktown, VA 23690 (☎ **757/898-3400**).

GETTING THERE   From Williamsburg, drive to the eastern end of the Colonial Parkway. From Norfolk, take I-64 west to U.S. 17 north.

HISTORY

Though tourist attention focuses to a large degree on the town's role as the final Revolutionary battlefield, Yorktown is also of interest as one of America's earliest colonial towns.

BEFORE THE REVOLUTION   Though a number of settlers lived and farmed in the area by the 1630s, Yorktown's history really dates to 1691, when the General Assembly at Jamestown (then Virginia's capital) passed the Port Act, creating a new town on the site. To encourage the development of the town, 50 acres were purchased from Benjamin Read for 10,000 pounds of "merchantable sweet-scented tobacco and cask," then broken into 85 half-acre lots and sold for 180 pounds of tobacco each. By the end of the century, Yorktown was on its way to becoming a principal mid-Atlantic port and a center of tobacco trade.

In the 18th century, Yorktown was a thriving metropolis with a population of several thousand planters, innkeepers, seamen, merchants, craftsmen, indentured servants, and slaves. After the waterfront officially became part of the town in 1738, Water Street, paralleling the river, was lined with shops, inns, and loading docks.

THE VICTORY AT YORKTOWN   The siege began on September 28, 1781, when American and French troops under Washington occupied a line encircling the town within a mile of the army led by Cornwallis. The allied army of 17,000 men, spread out in camps extending 6 miles, dug siege lines and bombarded the redcoats with cannonfire. When a French fleet sailed up from the Caribbean and defeated the

British navy off the Virginia Capes, thereby blocking any hope he had of escaping, Cornwallis's fate was sealed.

Cornwallis compounded his tactical errors by evacuating almost all his positions, except for Redoubts (forts) 9 and 10, to concentrate his troops closer to town and better defend it. Washington was thus able to move his men to within 1,000 yards of British lines. By October 9, the allies were ready to respond to British artillery—but they didn't wait to respond. The French were the first to fire. Two hours later, George Washington personally fired the first American round. By October 10, the British were nearly silenced. On October 11, the allies moved up about another 500 yards.

On October 14, the French stormed Redoubt 9 while the Continentals made short work of Redoubt 10. Both columns began their assaults at 8pm. The Americans were through by 8:10pm; the French, whose target was stronger, by 8:30pm.

On October 16, following a last-ditch and fruitless attempt to launch an attack on the allies, a desperate Cornwallis tried to escape with his troops across the York River to Gloucester Point, but a violent storm scattered his boats. On October 17 at 10am, a British drummer appeared on the rampart. He beat out a signal indicating a desire to discuss terms with the enemy. A cease-fire was called, and a British officer was led to American lines, where he requested an armistice. On October 18, commissioners met at the house of Augustine Moore (see "Exploring Yorktown," below) and worked out the terms of surrender.

At 2pm on October 19, 1781, the French and Continental armies lined Surrender Road, each stretching for over a mile on either side. The French were resplendent in immaculate white uniforms, their officers plumed and decorated; the Americans were in rags and tatters. The British army (about 5,000 British soldiers and seamen), clad in new uniforms, marched between them out of Yorktown to a band playing a tune called "The World Turned Upside Down." Gen. Charles O'Hara of the British Guards represented Cornwallis, who, pleading illness, did not surrender in person.

The battle marked the end of British rule in America and made a permanent place for Yorktown in the annals of American history.

AFTER THE REVOLUTION   Though it is doubtful that Yorktown would have recovered from the destruction and waste that accompanied the Siege of 1781, it received the coup de grace in the "Great Fire" of 1814 and declined steadily over the years, becoming a quiet rural village. In fact, like Williamsburg, it changed so little that many of the picturesque old streets, buildings, and battle sites have survived intact to this day. Today, most of Yorktown—including the surrounding battlefield areas—is part of the 9,300-acre Colonial National Historical Park.

EXPLORING YORKTOWN

✪ Yorktown Victory Center

First stop is the Yorktown Victory Center (☎ **888/593-4682** or 757/887-1776), open daily except New Year's Day and Christmas from 9am to 5pm. Set on 21 acres overlooking part of the battlefield of 1781, it offers an excellent orientation to Yorktown, including a film, a living-history program, and museum exhibits. Admission is $7.25 for adults, $3.50 for children 6 to 12 (free for children under 6); or you can buy a **combination ticket** for this and Jamestown Settlement at $13.50 for adults and $6.50 for children 6 to 12 (free for children under 6).

The Road to Yorktown, an evocative 28-minute documentary film produced by David Wolper, follows the movements of Generals Washington and Rochambeau and documents the final grueling days of the Revolution.

Visitors follow an open-air timeline walkway, **"Road to Revolution,"** which illustrates the relationship between the colonies and Britain beginning in 1750.

Aspects of the American Revolution are explored in three **gallery exhibits.** "Witnesses to Revolution" focuses on ordinary individuals who recorded their observances of the war and its impact on their lives. "At Water's Edge: The Towns of York and Gloucester" shows those towns' roles as port and urban centers in the 18th century. "Yorktown's Sunken Fleet" uses artifacts recovered from British ships sunk during the siege of Yorktown to describe shipboard life.

In the outdoor **Continental army encampment,** costumed interpreters re-create the lives of men and women who took part in the American Revolution. There are presentations on weaponry, military drills and tactics, medicine, and cookery. Nearby, an 18th-century **farmsite** demonstrates how "middling" farmers—no wealthy plantation owners here—lived and worked.

✪ Yorktown Battlefield Visitor Center

After you've seen the Yorktown Victory Center, head over to **National Park Service Visitor Center** (☎ 757/898-3400), starting point for self-guided auto tours of the battlefield and a full-service information center. Here, too, there's an orientation film. Shown on the hour and half hour, this 16-minute documentary called *Siege at Yorktown* is about the formal surrender of the British and their German mercenary allies.

Museum displays include Washington's actual military headquarters tent, a replica (which you can board and explore) of the quarterdeck of H.M.S. *Charon,* additional objects recovered from the York River in the excavations, exhibits about Cornwallis's surrender and the events leading up to it, and dioramas detailing the siege. Upstairs, an "on-the-scene" account of the Battle of Yorktown is given by a 13-year-old soldier in the Revolutionary army, his taped narrative accompanied by a sound-and-light show.

National Park Service rangers are on hand to answer questions; they also give free **tours** of the British inner defense line. The center is open daily except Christmas from 9am to 5pm, with extended hours spring through fall. Admission is $4 per person over 16, good for 7 days. Or you can buy a Joint Jamestown-Yorktown Passport for $7 per person over 16, which will admit you for 7 days here and at Jamestown Island (see "Jamestown: The First Colony," above). National Park Service passports are accepted here.

TOURING THE BATTLEFIELD

The National Park Service Visitor Center is the starting point for the 7-mile Battlefield route and the 10.2-mile Encampment route auto tours of the battlefield. You'll be given a map indicating both routes and detailing major sites. At each stop there are explanatory historical markers (sometimes taped narratives as well), but for the most interesting experience, rent a cassette player and tape at the visitor center ($2). Narrated by "British and American colonels" whose polite hostilities to each other are most amusing, the taped commentary further elucidates the battlefield sites. You won't stay in your car the whole time; it's frequently necessary to park, get out, and walk to redoubts and earthworks. A lot of the drive is very scenic, winding through woods and fields abundant with birdlife; the Encampment route is especially beautiful. If you rent the cassette, listen to the introduction in the parking lot; it will tell you when to depart. Auto-tour highlights include:

THE GRAND FRENCH BATTERY This was a large artillery area in the French section of the first siege line. Here, French soldiers manning cannons, mortars, and howitzers fired on British and German mercenary troops.

THE MOORE HOUSE   When Lord Cornwallis realized the inevitability of his defeat, he sent a message to General Washington: "Sir, I propose a cessation of hostilities for twenty-four hours, and that two officers may be appointed by each side, to meet at Mr. Moore's house, to settle terms for the surrender of the posts of York and Gloucester." General Washington granted Cornwallis just 2 hours to submit general terms. On the afternoon of October 18, 1781, two British commissioners, Col. Thomas Dundas and Maj. Alexander Ross, met in "Mr. Moore's house" with American Col. John Laurens and French representative the Vicomte de Noailles. Negotiations went on late into the evening, the British protesting terms of Article III, which required them to march out of Yorktown "with shouldered arms, colors cased that means flags furled, and drums beating a British or German march." They finally agreed to the humiliating exit, and negotiations wound up just before midnight. Washington made a few adjustments, the Articles of Capitulation were signed by Cornwallis and his senior naval officer, and the document was delivered back to Washington.

The Moore House has a long history. In the early 1700s, Lawrence Smith constructed the two-story white-frame building that would become Moore House when the property went to his daughter, Lucy, and her husband, Augustine Moore. Though surviving the battle of Yorktown unscathed, Moore House suffered considerable damage during military action in the Civil War. Shellfire destruction was aggravated by soldiers stripping away siding and other usable wood for fuel. The house was pretty much abandoned (sometimes even used as a cow barn) until John D. Rockefeller, Jr., purchased it in 1931 and the National Park Service restored it to its colonial appearance. It's now furnished with appropriate period pieces, some of which are believed to have been in the house during the surrender negotiations. It's open in summer daily from noon to 4:30pm.

SURRENDER FIELD   Here your imagination, stoked by visions from orientation films, can evoke the British march out of Yorktown. William Conrad narrates the story of the surrender scene from a pavilion overlooking the field. Cannons surrendered by the British encircle the pavilion below.

Along the Encampment route you'll come to the sites of Washington's and Rochambeau's headquarters, a French cemetery and Artillery Park, and allied encampment sites.

TOURING THE TOWN

Self-guided or ranger-led walking tours of Old Yorktown—including some places of interest not related to the famed battle—are available at the Battlefield Visitor Center. Begin your ramble close to the center at:

THE VICTORY MONUMENT   News of the allied victory at Yorktown reached Philadelphia on October 24, 1781. On October 29, Congress resolved "that the United States . . . will cause to be erected at York, in Virginia, a marble column, adorned with emblems of the alliance between the United States and his Most Christian Majesty; and inscribed with a succinct narrative of the surrender of Earl Cornwallis to his excellency General Washington, Commander in Chief of the combined forces of America and France."

All very well in theory, but due to financial difficulties, no action was taken for a century. Finally, on October 18, 1881, the cornerstone for the monument was laid by Masons as an appropriate opening to the Yorktown Centennial Celebration. The highly symbolic 98-foot marble shaft overlooking the York River was completed in 1884. The podium is adorned with 13 female figures hand in hand in a solemn dance to denote the unity of the 13 colonies; beneath their feet is the inscription ONE

COUNTRY, ONE CONSTITUTION, ONE DESTINY, a moving post–Civil War sentiment. The column itself symbolizes the greatness and prosperity of the nation, and its stars represent the "constellation" of states in the Union in 1881. Atop the shaft is the figure of Liberty.

A footpath leads from the monument into town, where you can explore:

CORNWALLIS CAVE   According to legend, Cornwallis lived here in two tiny "rooms" during the final days of the siege, when he hoped to withdraw to the river and escape overland to New York. The two rooms were carved out by various occupants of the cave—which may at one time have included the pirate Blackbeard—and Confederate soldiers later enlarged the shelter and added a roof. A taped narrative at the entrance tells the story. The cave is at the foot of Great Valley, right on the river.

THE DUDLEY DIGGES HOUSE   You can view the restored 18th-century white weatherboard house on Main Street and Smith Street only from the outside—it's a private residence, not open to the public. Its surrounding outbuildings and its dormer windows, set in the roofline, are typical of Virginia architecture in the mid-1700s. Owner Dudley Digges was a Revolutionary patriot who served with Patrick Henry, Benjamin Harrison, and Thomas Jefferson on the Committee of Correspondence. After the war, he was rector of the College of William and Mary.

THE NELSON HOUSE   Scottish merchant Thomas Nelson made three voyages between Great Britain and Virginia before deciding to settle in Yorktown in 1705. He proceeded to sire a dynasty, and by 1707 he had acquired two lots, along with a number of slaves, and built himself a house at Main and Nelson streets. Between 1711 and 1723, he obtained title to several other lots and became co-operator of a ferry, charter member of a trading company, builder of the Swan Tavern, trustee of York's port land, and a large-scale planter. By 1728, he had added 600 acres, a private warehouse and wharf, and a mill to his holdings. He died in 1745, leaving a vast estate, which his descendants—who included several prominent Revolutionary leaders, one of them a signer of the Declaration of Independence—further enlarged.

Though damaged (cannonballs remain embedded in the brickwork), the house survived the Battle of Yorktown (Cornwallis seized it for a command post during part of his occupation), and Nelson's descendants continued to occupy the house until 1907. The National Park Service acquired the house in 1968 and restored it to its original appearance.

It is open daily from 10am to 4:30pm in summer (check at the visitor center for off-season hours). Ranger-guided tours take 30 to 45 minutes.

THE SESSIONS HOUSE   Just across from the Nelson House, this is the oldest house in Yorktown, built in 1692 by Thomas Sessions. At least five U.S. presidents have visited the house, today a private residence off-limits to the public. You may, however, stare at it.

THE CUSTOMHOUSE   Dating to 1721, this sturdy brick building at the corner of Main and Read was originally the private storehouse of Richard Ambler, collector of ports. It became Gen. J. B. Magruder's headquarters during the Civil War. Today, it's maintained by the Daughters of the American Revolution as a museum.

GRACE EPISCOPAL CHURCH   Located on Church Street near the river, Grace Church dates to 1697 and has been an active house of worship ever since. Its first rector, the Rev. Anthony Panton, was dismissed for calling the secretary of the colony a "jackanapes." Gunpowder and ammunition were stored here during the siege of Yorktown. During the Civil War, the church served as a hospital. It's open to visitors daily from 9am to 5pm. The original communion silver, made in England in 1649, is still in use. Thomas Nelson II is buried in the adjacent graveyard.

THE SWAN TAVERN   For over a century, the Swan Tavern, at the corner of Main and Ballard streets (☎ **757/898-3033**), was Yorktown's leading hostelry. Originally owned by Thomas Nelson, it was in operation 20 years before Williamsburg's famous Raleigh. The Swan was demolished in 1863 by an ammunition explosion at the courthouse across the street, rebuilt, and destroyed again by fire in 1915. Today, it's reconstructed as per historical research, and the premises house a fine antiques shop. Call for hours.

WHERE TO DINE

Consider a **picnic** lunch in a large tree-shaded area at the Victory Center or at a riverside picnic area with tables and grills on Water Street at the foot of Comte de Grasse Street. There's another gorgeous area called **Ringfield,** 7 miles from Williamsburg on the Colonial Parkway.

Nick's Seafood Pavilion. Water St. ☎ **757/887-5269.** Reservations not accepted. Main courses $8–$35. AE, DC, MC, V. Daily 11am–10pm. AMERICAN/SEAFOOD.

Nick's interior is an exuberant surprise. Several spacious dining rooms are bedecked with reproductions of classic stone statuary, mosaic tiles, plants, fountains, and oil paintings. Soft-shell crabs sautéed in butter, broiled tuna or mahimahi, and broiled lobster tail are menu standbys, along with non-seafood entrees ranging from pork tenderloin Grecian-style to prime beef shish kebabs. There's baked Alaska for dessert.

4 James River Plantations

While Williamsburg was the political capital of Virginia during the 18th century, its economic livelihood depended on the great tobacco plantations like Carter's Grove. Several more of the mansions built during that period of wealthy landowners still stand today along the banks of the James River between Williamsburg and Richmond, some occupied to this day by the same families that have produced generals, governors, and two presidents. They provide an authentic feel for 18th-century plantation life.

ESSENTIALS

VISITOR INFORMATION   For information in advance, contact the individual plantations or the **Williamsburg Area Convention & Visitors Bureau,** 201 Penniman Rd., Williamsburg, VA 23187 (☎ **800/368-6511** or 757/253-0192).

GETTING THERE   The plantations are on John Tyler Highway (Va. 5) between Williamsburg and Richmond. From Williamsburg, take Jamestown Road and bear right on Va. 5. From Richmond, take Main Street east, which becomes Va. 5.

SEEING THE PLANTATIONS

The so-called Plantation Route covers a distance of 55 miles between Williamsburg and Richmond and makes an excellent scenic driving tour between the two cities. Allow a full day to visit all the plantations and to take a break for lunch. We list them here east-to-west as you come to them from Williamsburg. If you're driving from Richmond, start at Shirley and work backward.

The owners of Sherwood Forest, Evelynton, Berkeley, and Shirley offer a **block ticket** for admission to all of their homes. The cost is $28 for adults; there's no children's block ticket, as it's less expensive to simply buy individual tickets for them at each home. Block tickets can be purchased at any of the four plantations.

Sherwood Forest. Va. 5, 20 miles west of Williamsburg. ☎ 757/829-5377. Admission $8.50 adults, $8 seniors, $5.50 students, $3 grounds only. Daily 9am–5pm. Closed Thanksgiving and Christmas.

Owned by President William Henry Harrison in the 1790s, this long white-clapboard house was the home of President John Tyler after he retired from the White House in 1845. It has been continuously occupied by Tyler family members ever since. Then in his sixties, Tyler brought with him a young second wife and started a new family. The son of that marriage was in his seventies before he began a family, and his son—grandson of President Tyler—still lives upstairs. Built in 1730, the original house is now part of the Main Hall. Tyler extended the one-room-deep home to its present length of 301 feet, making it the longest wood-frame house in America. All furnishings are family heirlooms or similar period pieces. A walking tour of the grounds features many ancient trees and a number of original plantation out-buildings.

☕ **TAKE A BREAK**   You can break your driving tour of the plantations at **Indian Fields Tavern,** on Va. 5 between Sherwood Forest and Evelynton (☎ 757/829-5004). This fine restaurant, in a restored Victorian farmhouse with screened porches open in warm weather, offers tarragon chicken salad, burgers, and entrees including quiche, crabcakes, and an unusual mixed grill of local sausages and marinated duck. The signature dish at dinner is crabcakes served over Virginia ham. Reservations are required at dinner. Hours are Monday through Saturday from 11am to 3:30pm, Sunday through Thursday from 5 to 9pm, Friday and Saturday from 5 to 9:30pm. American Express, Discover, MasterCard, and Visa are accepted.

Evelynton. Va. 5, 25 miles west of Williamsburg. ☎ 800/473-5075 or 757/829-5075. Admission $7.50 adults, $6.50 seniors, $3.50 children 6–12, free for children under 6. Mar–Dec, daily 9am–5pm; Jan–Feb, Fri–Mon 9am–5pm. Closed Thanksgiving and Christmas.

Adjacent to and part of the original 1619 Westover Plantation land grant (see "Berkeley," below), this tract was named for William Byrd's daughter Evelyn (pronounced "*Eve*-lyn"). She is said to have died of a broken heart because her father refused to let her marry her chosen suitor. According to legend, her ghost still roams both houses. Since 1847, Evelynton has been home to the Ruffin family, whose patriarch, noted agriculturist Edmund Ruffin, fired the first shot of the Civil War at Fort Sumter, S.C. The original house was destroyed in 1862, when Gen. George McClellan's Union troops skirmished with Confederates led by J. E. B. Stuart and John Pelham in the fierce but short-lived Battle of Evelynton Heights. The present structure, a magnificent example of Colonial Revival style, was designed by renowned Virginia architect Duncan Lee and built in 1935.

Berkeley. Va. 5, 30 miles west of Williamsburg. ☎ 757/829-6018. Admission $8.50 adults, $4 children 6–12, free for children under 6. Daily 8am–5pm. Closed Christmas.

On December 4, 1619, 38 English settlers sent by the Berkeley Company put ashore after a 3-month voyage. They fell on their knees in a prayer of thanksgiving. If you're here on the first Sunday of November, you can participate in the annual celebration commemorating that first official Thanksgiving in the New World.

The aristocratic Harrison family bought Berkeley in 1691. Benjamin Harrison III made it a prosperous operation, and in 1726, his son, Benjamin Harrison IV, built the three-story Georgian mansion. Benjamin Harrison V was a signer of the Declaration of Independence and thrice governor of Virginia. The next generation produced William Henry Harrison, the frontier fighter whose nickname "Old

Tippecanoe" helped him get elected as our ninth president. His grandson, another Benjamin Harrison, took the presidential oath 47 years later. George Washington was a frequent guest, and every president through Buchanan enjoyed Berkeley's gracious hospitality.

Berkeley was twice occupied by invading troops. A British army under Benedict Arnold burned the family portraits, practiced target shooting on the cows, and went off with 40 slaves. Gen. George McClellan's Union army trampled the gardens and chopped up the elegant furnishings for firewood. During the Yankee occupancy, Gen. Dan Butterfield composed "Taps." After the war, the Harrisons never returned to live at Berkeley.

John Jamieson, a Scottish-born New Yorker who had served as a drummer boy in McClellan's army, purchased the disfigured manor house and 1,400 acres in 1907. His son, Malcolm, has completely restored the house and grounds to their glorious appearances of the early days of the Harrisons' tenure. Following a 10-minute slide presentation, 20-minute **tours** of the house are given throughout the day by guides in colonial dress. Allow at least another half hour to explore the magnificent grounds and gardens.

Sharing Berkeley's lane off Va. 5, **Westover** (☎ 757/829-2882) is the beautiful 1730s Georgian manor house built by Richmond's founder, William Byrd II, directly on the banks of the James. The interior is only open to the public for 5 days during Garden Week (last week in April), although visitors are invited to walk around the grounds and gardens year-round, daily from 9am to 6pm. Admission is $2.

☕ TAKE A BREAK   Berkeley is a good place to stop for lunch, for moderately priced sandwiches, soups, and salads are served in the old carriage house, now appropriately named the **Coach House Tavern** (☎ 757/829-6003). It's open Monday through Saturday from 11am to 3pm, Sunday from 11am to 4pm and 6 to 9pm. American Express, Discover, MasterCard, and Visa are accepted. There are also picnic grounds on Berkeley's premises.

Shirley. Va. 5, Charles City, 35 miles west of Williamsburg. ☎ **757/829-5121.** Admission $8.50 adults, $5.50 students 13–21, $4.50 children 6–12, free for children under 6. Mid-Feb to mid-Jan, daily 9am–5pm (last tour at 4pm); mid-Jan to mid-Feb, Sat–Sun 9am–5pm (last tour at 4pm). Closed Thanksgiving and Christmas.

Another historic James River plantation, Shirley was founded in 1613 and has been in the same family since 1660. The present mansion, built by Edward Hill III or his son-in-law, John Carter (historians are not sure), dates to 1723. Since that time, two very distinguished Virginia families—the Hills and the Carters—have occupied Shirley. Because of this continuous ownership, many original furnishings, portraits, and memorabilia remain, making this one of the most interesting plantations open to public view. The carved-walnut staircase, rising three stories with no visible means of support, is the only one of its kind in the United States. The house survived the Revolution, the Civil War, and Reconstruction, as did the dependencies—a group of superb brick outbuildings, forming a unique Queen Anne forecourt, which include a large two-story kitchen, a laundry house, and two barns. Other original structures are the stable, smokehouse, and dovecote. You can visit the house on 35-minute **tours** given throughout the day; allow at least another 30 minutes to explore the grounds and dependencies.

12

Hampton Roads & the Eastern Shore

Before they moved on to Jamestown in 1607, the 105 colonists in the *Susan Constant, Godspeed,* and *Discovery* first set foot in the New World on the sandy shores of Cape Charles. Although they didn't stay on the banks of Hampton Roads, one of the world's largest natural harbors, later generations did. Today the cities of Norfolk, Virginia Beach, Portsmouth, Chesapeake, Newport News, and Hampton—known collectively as both Hampton Roads and Tidewater—ring the harbor's southern and western shores.

Their combined population of nearly 1.5 million swells significantly during the summer months, when the sand and surf of Virginia Beach draw vacationers from around the globe. With a host of activities, a multitude of hotels, and close proximity to the other cities, "The Beach" makes a fine base of operations for a visit to this area.

The population here also goes up and down depending on deployments by the U.S. Navy, for this area has America's largest concentration of naval bases. The sailors once made Norfolk a bawdy seaport, but the city has rebuilt itself and now features an exciting "museum of the future" as well as a bustling collection of waterfront shops, restaurants, and nightclubs. A ferry crosses the Elizabeth River to the neighboring city of Portsmouth, whose architecturally rich Olde Town may remind you of Charleston and Savannah. Across the harbor, historic Hampton hosts a very modern air and space museum, and the shipbuilding city of Newport News is, fittingly, home to a terrific maritime museum.

From Virginia Beach, the 17-mile-long Chesapeake Bay Bridge-Tunnel whisks visitors north to a very different world: Virginia's rural Eastern Shore. There on the Delmarva Peninsula beckon ancient fishing villages like Chincoteague, wildlife refuges teeming with birdlife and wild horses, and the gorgeous Assateague Island National Seashore with 37 miles of pristine, totally undeveloped beach.

1 Norfolk

190 miles SE of Washington, D.C.; 93 miles E of Richmond; 17 miles W of Virginia Beach

Still a major seaport and naval base, Norfolk has replaced its notorious waterfront sailor bars and burlesque houses with high-rise offices, condominiums, marinas, museums, shops, nightspots, and a

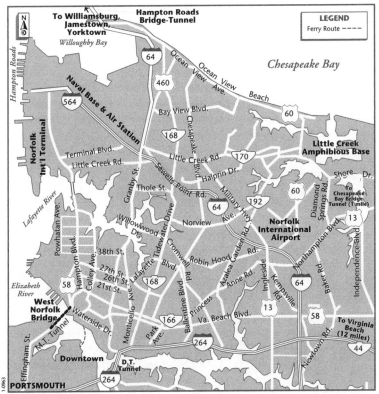

12,000-seat minor league baseball park. Interspersed in this revitalized downtown are reminders of Norfolk's past, such as historic houses and the old City Hall, now converted into a museum and memorial to World War II hero Gen. Douglas MacArthur. The city has become the region's prime dining venue as well, with hip new restaurants springing up downtown and in the restored residential neighborhoods nearby.

ESSENTIALS

VISITOR INFORMATION For advance information, contact the **Norfolk Convention & Visitors Bureau,** 252 E. Main St., Norfolk, VA 23510 (☎ **800/ 368-3097** or 757/441-1852; www.norfolk.va.us). The bureau also has a walk-in information desk at its offices, which are across Main Street from the Norfolk Marriott. If you're arriving from the west via I-64, there's an information center on Fourth View Street at Exit 273 in the Ocean View section. It's open during the summer daily from 9am to 6pm, the rest of the year daily from 9am to 5pm. Other information booths are in the Waterside and NAUTICUS (see "Attractions in Norfolk," below).

GETTING THERE By Car From the west, I-64 runs directly from Richmond to Norfolk, then swings around the eastern and southern suburbs, where it meets I-664 to form a beltway around the area. U.S. 460 also runs the length of Virginia to Norfolk, and U.S. 13 and 17 lead here from north or south. If you're coming from Virginia Beach, the Norfolk–Virginia Beach Expressway (Va. 44) becomes I-264, which goes through downtown and Portsmouth. Norfolk is linked to Portsmouth by ferry, bridge, and tunnel, and to Hampton and Newport News by the Hampton Roads Bridge-Tunnel (I-64).

By Plane   Norfolk International Airport, on Norview Avenue 1½ miles north of I-64 (☎ 757/857-3351), is served by Air South, AirTran, American, Continental, Delta, Midway, Northwest, TWA, United, and US Airways. The major car-rental firms have desks here. The **Norfolk Airport Shuttle** (☎ 800/552-7911 in Virginia, or 757/857-1231) runs vans to points between Williamsburg and Virginia Beach. One-way fares to downtown Norfolk are $13 for one passenger, $17.75 for two; to Virginia Beach or Hampton, $19 for one passenger, $25.75 for two; to Williamsburg, $28 for one passenger, $18 per passenger for two or more.

CITY LAYOUT   Norfolk occupies two peninsulas formed by the Chesapeake Bay and the Elizabeth and Lafayette rivers. **Downtown** is on the southern side of the city, on the northern bank of the Elizabeth River. Bordering downtown to the northwest, **Freemason** is Norfolk's oldest residential neighborhood, with most of its 18th- and 19th-century town houses now restored as private homes, businesses, and restaurants. You'll still find a few cobblestone streets here. Northwest of Freemason, across a semi-circular inlet known as The Hague, **Ghent** was the city's first subdivision and is now its trendiest enclave. Most houses in "old" Ghent, near The Hague and the Chrysler Museum of Art (see "Attractions in Norfolk," below), were built between 1892 and 1912. Today, it's home to everyone from well-heeled professional types to writers, aspiring artists, and college students. The heart of Ghent's business district is on **Colley Avenue** between Baldwin Avenue and 21st Street, a strip of antique shops and chic restaurants interspersed with an Irish tavern, a wine-and-cheese emporium, the NORA Cinema (first-run movies), dry cleaners, shoe-repair shops, a 7-Eleven, and a public school.

GETTING AROUND   The **Tidewater Regional Transit System (TRT)** (☎ 757/640-6300) operates public buses throughout Norfolk, Virginia Beach, Portsmouth, and Chesapeake. Bus fare is $1.50, with exact change required.

In addition, TRT operates the trolley tours of downtown Norfolk, the Norfolk Naval Base, Olde Town Portsmouth, and the Naval Air Station at Oceana; the Elizabeth River Ferry between Norfolk and Portsmouth; and the Virginia Beach trolley system—all mentioned below. Its **Discover Tidewater Passport** permits 3 days of unlimited use of the trolley tours, the ferry, and the Virginia Beach trolleys; it costs $8.50 for adults, $4.75 for seniors and children under 12. Or you can buy an **Adventure Pass,** which allows 3 days of tours and transportation and includes admission to the Chrysler Museum of Art in Norfolk, the Children's Museum of Virginia in Portsmouth, and the Virginia Science Museum in Virginia Beach. It costs $25 for adults, $20 for seniors and children under 12.

You can get schedules and buy tickets and passes at TRT's information and ticket kiosk in the Waterside (see "Attractions in Norfolk," below) and at Atlantic Avenue and 24th Street in Virginia Beach (see "Virginia Beach," below).

SEEING THE SIGHTS
ATTRACTIONS IN NORFOLK

Tidewater Regional Transit System's **Norfolk Explorers Trolley Tour** starts at the Waterside and stops at attractions downtown and in the trendy Ghent neighborhood. You can get off at any stop and reboard a later trolley. It operates from Memorial Day to Labor Day, daily at 10:30am, noon, 1:30pm, and 3pm. Departures in September are at noon, 1:30pm, and 3pm. Fare is $3.50 for adults and $1.75 for seniors and

Downtown Norfolk

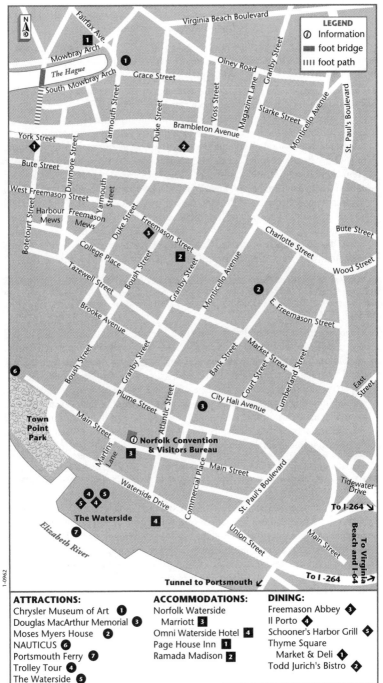

LEGEND
- ⓘ Information
- ▬ foot bridge
- ‖‖‖ foot path

Fairfax Ave.

Virginia Beach Boulevard

Mowbray Arch

The Hague

South Mowbray Arch

Grace Street

Olney Road

Granby Street

Yarmouth Street

Duke Street

Voss Street

Magazine Lane

Starke Street

Monticello Avenue

St. Paul's Boulevard

Brambleton Avenue

York Street

Bute Street

Dunmore Street

Yarmouth Street

West Freemason Street

Botetourt Street

Harbour Mews

Freemason Mews

Duke Street

Freemason Street

Charlotte Street

Bute Street

Wood Street

College Place

Boush Street

Granby Street

Monticello Avenue

Tazewell Street

Brooke Avenue

E. Freemason Street

Boush Street

Granby Street

Market Street

Bank Street

Court Street

Cumberland Street

East Street

Plume Street

Atlantic Street

City Hall Avenue

Town Point Park

Main Street

Martins Lane

ⓘ Norfolk Convention & Visitors Bureau

Commercial Place

Main Street

St. Paul's Boulevard

Tidewater Drive

Waterside Drive

To I-264

The Waterside

Elizabeth River

Union Street

Main Street

To Virginia Beach and I-64

Tunnel to Portsmouth ↙

To I-264 →

ATTRACTIONS:
- Chrysler Museum of Art ❶
- Douglas MacArthur Memorial ❸
- Moses Myers House ❷
- NAUTICUS ❻
- Portsmouth Ferry ❼
- Trolley Tour ❹
- The Waterside ❺

ACCOMMODATIONS:
- Norfolk Waterside Marriott ❸
- Omni Waterside Hotel ❹
- Page House Inn ❶
- Ramada Madison ❷

DINING:
- Freemason Abbey ❸
- Il Porto ❹
- Schooner's Harbor Grill ❺
- Thyme Square Market & Deli ❶
- Todd Jurich's Bistro ❷

259

children under 12, with free reboarding. Tickets may be purchased at the TRT kiosk at the Waterside. Call ☎ 757/640-6300 for more information.

✪ **Chrysler Museum of Art.** 425 W. Olney Rd. (at Mowbray Arch). ☎ **757/644-6200.** Admission $4 adults, $2 seniors and students, free for children under 5. Tues–Sat 10am–5pm; Sun 1–5pm. Closed New Year's Day, Independence Day, Thanksgiving, and Christmas.

Originally built in 1932 as the Norfolk Museum of Art, this imposing Italian Renaissance building on The Hague inlet was renamed in 1971 when Walter P. Chrysler, Jr., gave a large portion of his collection to the city. It spans artistic periods from ancient Egypt to the 1980s and includes one of the finest and most comprehensive glass collections in the world. Adjoining is an outstanding collection of art nouveau furniture. Other first-floor galleries exhibit ancient Indian, Islamic, Oriental, African, and pre-Columbian art. Most second-floor galleries are devoted to painting and sculpture, particularly Italian baroque and French, including works by Gauguin, Picasso, Renoir, Matisse, Braque, Bernini, and Rouault. American art holdings include 18th- and 19th-century paintings by Charles Willson Peale, Benjamin West, John Singleton Copley, and Thomas Cole, and 20th-century works by Thomas Hart Benton, Calder, Kline, Warhol, Rauschenberg, and Rosenquist. A permanent gallery is devoted solely to photography, showcasing everyone from Walker Evans to Diane Arbus.

✪ **Douglas MacArthur Memorial.** MacArthur Square (between City Hall Ave. and Plume St., at Bank St.). ☎ **757/441-2965.** Free admission. Mon–Sat 10am–5pm; Sun 11am–5pm. Closed New Year's Day, Thanksgiving, and Christmas. Validated 3-hour parking at any City of Norfolk lot.

When he arrived in Australia after suffering a crushing defeat at the hands of Japanese invaders in the Philippines, General MacArthur uttered the immortal words "I shall return." Those words, which became a rallying cry for Americans fighting in the Pacific Theater of World War II, are engraved on a bronze plaque, along with excerpts from his other speeches, at the general's final resting place in Norfolk's old city hall, an imposing domed structure with a columned front portico. Visitors can view a film that uses news footage to document the major events of MacArthur's life. Nine galleries are filled with memorabilia ranging from historic World War II surrender documents to the general's famous corncob pipe.

Moses Myers House. 331 Bank St. (at E. Freemason St.). ☎ **757/664-6283.** Admission $3 adults, $1.50 students and seniors, free for children under 5. Apr–Dec, Tues–Sat 10am–5pm, Sun noon–5pm; Jan–Mar, Tues–Sat noon–5pm.

This handsome early-Federal brick town house in Norfolk's oldest residential neighborhood was home to five generations of Myerses from 1792 to 1930. Moses Myers and his wife, Eliza, came to Norfolk in 1787. They were one of the first Jewish families to settle here, and special programs in observance of Jewish holidays are among the museum's annual events. Some 70% of the furniture and decorative arts collections displayed throughout the house is original to the first generation of the family. Two Gilbert Stuart portraits of Mr. and Mrs. Myers hang in the drawing room, which contains some distinctive Empire pieces. The fireplace surround has unusual carvings depicting a sun god—with the features of George Washington.

The **Willoughby-Baylor House,** a block away from the Moses Myers House at 601 E. Freemason St., was built in 1794 and is furnished with Georgian and Federal pieces. Admission, hours, and phone are the same for both museums.

Combination tickets for both houses and the Adam Thoroughgood House (see "Historic Attractions" in "Virginia Beach," below) cost $6 for adults, $4.50 for students and seniors, free for children 5 and under. All three houses are administered by the Chrysler Museum.

NAUTICUS, The National Maritime Center. 1 Waterside Dr. (at Boush St.). ☎ **800/ 664-1080** or 757/664-1000. Free admission to first deck and naval museum. Admission to upstairs exhibits and theaters $7.50 adults, $5 seniors and children 6–17, free for children under 6. Memorial Day–Labor Day, daily 10am–5pm; rest of year, Tues–Sat 10am–5pm, Sun noon–5pm. Closed New Year's Day, Thanksgiving, and Christmas.

It's appropriate that visitors enter this large battleship-gray building by a gangplank, since it looks like an artist's rendering of a futuristic warship. Inside, kids and adults of all ages can entertain themselves with a plethora of hands-on interactive exhibits, theaters, and a museum, all dedicated to the U.S. Navy and the sea over which it rules. Visitors can stand on the actual bridge of the U.S.S. *Preble,* or pilot a submarine in search of the Loch Ness Monster in one of the world's first virtual-reality adventures. The Aegis Theater lets you participate in running a battle aboard a destroyer, while in another area you can learn navigation by piloting a ship into San Francisco Harbor. Meanwhile, the Living Sea theater shows films about sealife in the briny depths, simulating a swim among thousands of jellyfish.

NAUTICUS also includes the **Hampton Roads Naval Museum,** operated by the U.S. Navy to tell the story of its presence in Hampton Roads. Real warships often tie up here on weekend visits, since the building sits on the old Banana Pier stretching 700 feet out into the Elizabeth River. After a day here, your school-age kids may want an appointment to Annapolis.

Moored beside the building is the **Tugboat Museum** (☎ 757/627-4884), actually the *Huntington,* a tug built in 1933 and used by the navy to dock its ships for more than 50 years. Admission is $2 for adults, $1 for children under 12. It's open Memorial Day to Labor Day, daily from 7am to 7pm; the rest of the year, Tuesday through Sunday, from 10am to 5pm.

Next to NAUTICUS in Town Point Park, you can rent **paddleboats** and pilot yourself on the river. Two-passenger models cost $5 per half hour; four-person boats rent for $7 per half hour.

✪ **Norfolk Botanical Garden.** 6700 Azalea Garden Rd. (off Norview Ave., near airport). ☎ **757/441-5385.** Admission $3.50 adults, $2.50 seniors, $1.50 children 6–18, free for children under 6. Daily 8:30am–sunset. Take I-64 to the Norview/Airport exit, pass 2 lights, and turn left onto Azalea Garden Rd. at the third light. It's about 4 miles from downtown Norfolk.

A quiet haven with more than 12 miles of floral pathways, the garden can be seen on foot, by trackless train, or by canal boat. From early April to mid-June, the grounds are brilliantly abloom with a massive display of azaleas. The Statuary Vista is a beautiful setting for Moses Ezekiel's heroic-size statues (originally intended for the Corcoran Gallery in Washington) of great painters and sculptors—Rembrandt, Rubens, Dürer, and da Vinci, among others. Notable, too, are the rose garden, with a terrace overlook; a classic Japanese hill-and-pond garden; a fragrance garden; and an Italian Renaissance garden with terraces, statuary, a fountain, and a reflecting pool. Behind the pool is the coronation court where the Azalea Queen is crowned each April. For refreshment, the Garden House Cafe is open daily from 10am to 5pm.

Norfolk Naval Base Tour. 9809 Hampton Blvd. ☎ **757/444-7955.** Admission $5 adults, $2.50 seniors and children. Tickets may be purchased at the TRT kiosk at the Waterside or at the Naval Base on Hampton Blvd. all year. Call for hours.

You can see the world's largest naval installation on this tour, enhanced by informed commentary by naval personnel. The bus goes dockside for looks at aircraft carriers, destroyers, submarines, and other naval ships. It also passes Admiral's Row, a strip of Colonial Revival houses built at the turn of the century for the Jamestown Exposition. There may be visits to selected ships on weekends from 1 to 4:30pm.

The Waterside. Waterside Dr., between the Omni Hotel and Town Point Park. ☎ **757/ 627-3300.** Free admission. Summer, Mon–Sat 10am–10pm, Sun noon–8pm; winter, Mon–Sat 10am–9pm, Sun noon–6pm.

A $23-million steel-and-glass pavilion that opened in 1983, the Waterside is the centerpiece of Norfolk's revitalized downtown waterfront. Built by the Rouse Organization—also noted for Baltimore's Inner Harbor, Boston's Faneuil Hall, and New York's South Street Seaport—the Waterside houses more than 30 international food outlets as well as several full-service restaurants and a Hooters pub. Shops offer a mix of souvenirs, jewelry, fashions, gift items, Virginia products, and crafts that make for pleasurable browsing. A short stroll along the busy waterfront and adjacent marina will bring you to the dock where cruise ships offer harbor tours (see below).

Town Point Park's amphitheater, just west of the Waterside, features a full schedule of free special events throughout the year—concerts, children's theater, magic shows, puppetry, and more. **Harbor Park,** a 12,000-seat stadium, is home to the Norfolk Tides, the New York Mets AAA International League team. For Tides information, call ☎ **757/461-5600.**

Harbor Cruises

The *Carrie B* (☎ **757/393-4735**), a reproduction of a 19th-century Mississippi riverboat, offers daytime and sunset cruises of Norfolk's harbor from the Waterside. Depending on the tour, you can see the shipyard with nuclear subs and aircraft carriers, the naval base, and the site of the Civil War battle between the *Monitor* and the *Merrimac.* It offers daily cruises from April to October. A noon sailing takes 1¹/₂ hours and costs $9.95 for adults, $4.95 for children. A 2pm tour goes out for 2¹/₂ hours and costs $11.95 for adults, $5.95 for children. From June to Labor Day, there's also a 2¹/₂-hour sunset cruise leaving at 6pm. It costs $14 for adults, $7 for children.

Also departing from the Waterside, the *Spirit of Norfolk* (☎ **757/627-7771**) is like an oceangoing cruise ship, complete with dancing, good food, and entertainment. Offerings include lunch cruises ($24 per person), sunset cocktail cruises ($15), dinner cruises ($40 weekdays, $43 weekends), and moonlight party cruises with cocktails ($20) from midnight to 2am Friday and Saturday. Call for the schedule and to make reservations.

From April to October, there are 2- and 3-hour cruises on the *American Rover* (☎ **757/627-7245**), a graceful schooner modeled after 19th-century Chesapeake Bay schooners. Prices for these sail-powered cruises along the Elizabeth River begin at $14 for adults and $7 for children. Departure point is the Waterside marina.

A FERRY RIDE TO PORTSMOUTH

When we first visited here in the early 1950s, ferries ran constantly across the Elizabeth River between Norfolk and Portsmouth. Today, the paddle-wheel **Elizabeth River Ferry** still makes that short but picturesque trip. Operated by Tidewater Regional Transit (☎ **757/640-6300**), it departs the Waterside marina every 30 minutes Monday through Thursday from 7:15am to 11:45pm, Friday from 7:15am to 11:45pm, Saturday from 10:15am to 11:45pm, and Sunday from 10:15am to 9:45pm. Fare is 75¢ for adults, 50¢ for children, and 35¢ for seniors.

When you arrive on the other side, stop first at the **Portside Visitor Center,** on Harbor Court at the ferry landing (☎ **757/393-5111**), and pick up a walking tour brochure and map. Then stroll through Portsmouth's quaint **Olde Town** section, which traces its roots back to 1752. Like those in Charleston and Savannah, the homes and buildings here present a kaleidoscope of architectural styles: Colonial,

Federal, Greek Revival, Georgian, and Victorian. Plaques mounted on imported English streetlamps point out their architectural and historical significance.

If you're not up to walking or are short on time, you can take a **Portsmouth Discovery Trolley Tour,** which departs the visitor center daily at 11am, 12:30pm, 2pm, and 3:30pm from Memorial Day to Labor Day. Fare is $3.50 for adults, $1.75 for seniors and children under 12. Check at the visitor center, or call ☎ **757/460-6300** for more information.

At the **Lightship Museum,** in Riverfront Park at the foot of London Boulevard (☎ 757/393-8741), you can tour through the *Portsmouth,* built in 1915 and anchored offshore until the 1980s to warn mariners of the dangerous shoals on the approach to Hampton Roads. Also in the park, the **Naval Shipyard Museum,** 2 High St. (☎ 757/393-8591), houses many ship models and relics of Portsmouth's military past, including a cannon mount possibly from the Confederate ironclad *Merrimac,* which fought the Union's turret-topped *Monitor* on Hampton Roads during the Civil War. Both museums are open Tuesday through Saturday from 10am to 5pm, Sunday from 1 to 5pm. Admission to either is $1 per person.

You can keep the kids busy at a number of interactive educational exhibits in **Children's Museum of Virginia,** 221 High St. (☎ 757/393-8393), but you must supervise them at all times. It's open Tuesday through Saturday from 10am to 5pm (to 7pm in summer), Sunday from 1 to 5pm. Admission is $4 per person.

Also here is the **Virginia Sports Hall of Fame,** 420 High St. (☎ 757/393-8031), whose most famous members are golfers Sam Sneed and Lanny Wadkins, tennis pro Arthur Ashe, and basketball players Ralph Sampson and Nancy Lieberman Cline. Hours are Tuesday through Saturday from 10am to 5pm, Sunday from 1 to 5pm. Admission is free.

For more information, contact the **Portsmouth Convention and Visitors Bureau,** 801 Crawford St., Portsmouth, VA 23704-3822 (☎ **800/338-8822** or 757/ 393-8481).

Attractions in Hampton

Jamestown was barely 2 years old when Capt. John Smith sent a contingent of men to build America's first fort on the Hampton River, strategically located on the western shore of Hampton Roads. Thus did Hampton become one of the nation's oldest English-speaking settlements. Blackbeard the Pirate was killed here in 1718 during a fierce battle with colonial forces (captured members of his crew were later tried and hanged at Williamsburg). Unfortunately, there are no remaining structures from those early days, for a Confederate general ordered Hampton burned to the ground rather than permit Union forces holding Fort Monroe to quarter troops and former slaves in the town. Hampton now looks purposefully to the 21st century, for it's home to a major research center of the National Aeronautics and Space Administration.

For **visitor information,** contact the Hampton Visitor Center, 710 Settlers Landing Rd., Hampton, VA 23669 (☎ **800/800-2202** or 757/727-1222). The center is on the waterfront, a block from the Virginia Air and Space Center (see below).

Casemate Museum. Fort Monroe, Hampton. ☎ **757/727-3391.** Free admission. Daily 10:30am–4:30pm. Closed New Year's Day, Thanksgiving, and Christmas. From Norfolk, take I-64 across the Hampton Roads Bridge-Tunnel to the first exit (268) and follow the Fort Monroe signs.

A must for Civil War buffs is the Casemate Museum at Fort Monroe, where Jefferson Davis was imprisoned in 1865 after the war. Located at the tip of a peninsula and surrounded by a moat, the stone fort was built between 1819 and 1834. Robert E.

Lee, a second lieutenant in the Army Corps of Engineers in 1831, was second in command of the detachment that constructed the fort. The fort was so strong that it never fell to the Confederates during the Civil War. The *casemates,* or rooms, were originally designed as storage for seacoast artillery. After 1861, they were modified to serve as living quarters for the soldiers and their families stationed at the fort. Visitors can view displays of military memorabilia and enter the sparsely furnished room where Davis was held prisoner. The accusation against Davis—that he had participated in the plot to assassinate Lincoln—was eventually found to be false, and Davis was released in 1867.

Hampton University Museum. Huntington Building, Hampton University, Hampton. ☎ **757/727-5308.** Free admission. Mon–Fri 8am–5pm; Sat–Sun noon–4pm. From Norfolk, take I-64 across the Hampton Roads Bridge-Tunnel to Exit 267, Woodland Rd.; then follow signs to the university.

Hampton University, founded in 1868 to provide an education for newly freed African Americans, boasts among its graduates Booker T. Washington, who founded Tuskegee Institute in Alabama. Four landmarks are nearby, including the imposing Memorial Chapel (1886). The museum is noted for its African collection, comprising more than 2,700 art objects and artifacts representing 887 ethnic groups and cultures. Rivaling the African collection in quality and importance, the Native American collection includes works from 93 tribes; it was established in 1878, when the federal government began sending young Native Americans from reservations in the West to be educated at Hampton. The museum also has notable holdings in works by Harlem Renaissance artists, as well as an extensive number of Oceanic and Asian objects.

✪ Virginia Air and Space Center/Hampton Roads History Center. 600 Settlers Landing Rd., Hampton. ☎ **757/727-0900.** Admission $6 adults, $4 seniors and military, $4 children 3–11, free for children under 3. Combination tickets including the IMAX film $3 more. Memorial Day–Labor Day, Mon–Wed 10am–5pm, Thurs–Sun 10am–7pm; off-season, daily 10am–5pm. From I-64, take exit 267. Follow Settlers Landing Rd. to downtown Hampton; the center will be on the left.

A stunning glass-fronted futuristic structure perched on the edge of Hampton's riverfront, this museum chronicles the history of aviation and space travel and also serves as the official visitor center for NASA's Langley Research Center. The vast interior is separated into bays that hold individual exhibits on rockets, satellites, and space exploration. The center space has about 10 air vehicles, as well as the world's largest paper airplane, suspended from its 94-foot vaulted ceiling. In the main gallery, the *Apollo 12* command module, complete with reentry burn marks, is an awe-inspiring sight. Visitors to the Space Gallery can don an astronaut's helmet and see themselves on a TV monitor. An IMAX theater shows new films about three times a year.

ATTRACTIONS IN NEWPORT NEWS

Named for Christopher Newport, skipper of the *Discovery,* which brought some of the Jamestown settlers to Virginia, Newport News dates back to the early 1600s and has a long maritime tradition. Many of America's most formidable warships have rolled down the ways of Newport News Shipbuilding & Dry Dock Company, the region's largest private employer.

For **visitor information,** contact the Newport News Tourism Development Office, 2400 Washington Ave., Newport News, VA 23607 (☎ **800/333-7787** or 757/928-6843).

Dismal Dirt & Nastiness

When the early English settlers fanned out from Jamestown, they found their way south blocked by a "vast body of dirt and nastiness." So wrote Col. William Byrd II, who in 1728 surveyed the Virginia–North Carolina border through this impenetrable region appropriately dubbed the **Great Dismal Swamp.**

George Washington came to the swamp in 1763 and organized a company to drain and log some 40,000 acres. A 5-mile ditch still bears his name, but Washington's investment went for naught. At the urging of then-governor Patrick Henry, slaves dug the 22-mile-long Dismal Swamp Canal from the Elizabeth River to North Carolina between 1793 and 1805. Still operating, it is America's oldest man-made waterway. A road constructed on the spoil is now U.S. 17 between Portsmouth and Elizabeth City, N.C.

Although much of the swamp was drained over the years, the **Great Dismal Swamp National Wildlife Refuge** still contains black bears, bobcats, white-tailed deer, otters, and a plethora of birdlife. The last of the swamp's great cypress forest stands along the haunting shores of Lake Drummond, centerpiece of the refuge.

The refuge headquarters, off Va. 32 south of Suffolk, provides a boardwalk nature walk and hiking and biking trails to Lake Drummond. For information, contact the refuge at P.O. Box 349, Suffolk, VA 23434 (☎ **757/986-3705**).

South of the North Carolina line on U.S. 17, the **Dismal Swamp Canal Welcome Center** (☎ **919/771-8333**) is open from Memorial Day through October, daily from 9am to 5pm; the rest of the year, Tuesday through Saturday from 9am to 5pm. It has a car-top boat ramp where you can launch canoes and kayaks for trips to Lake Drummond via the Federal Feeder Ditch.

In Virginia on U.S. 17, **Chesapeake Campground** (☎ **757/485-0149**) rents canoes and has camping facilities, and **Dismal Swamp Tours** (☎ **757/421-0729**) will take you into the heart of darkness by motorboat.

✪ **Mariners' Museum.** 100 Museum Dr., Newport News. ☎ **757/596-2222.** Admission $6.50 adults, $5.50 seniors, $3.25 students. Daily 10am–5pm. From I-64, take Exit 258A and follow J. Clyde Morris Blvd. south to its intersection with Warwick Blvd., go straight there on Museum Dr.

Situated in a pleasant 550-acre park setting, with a lake, picnic areas, and walking trails, the Mariners' Museum is dedicated to preserving the culture of the sea and its tributaries. Handcrafted ship models, scrimshaw, maritime paintings, decorative arts, working steam engines, and more are displayed in the spacious galleries. Particularly interesting are galleries highlighting the history and culture of the Chesapeake Bay and the Age of Exploration. An 18-minute film narrated by actor James Earl Jones discusses maritime activity the world over. From time to time, costumed historical interpreters, including an 18th-century sea captain and a model ship builder, give demonstrations.

Virginia Living Museum. 524 J. Clyde Morris Blvd., Newport News. ☎ **757/595-1900.** Museum admission $6 adults, $4 children 3–12, free for children under 3. Planetarium admission $2.50 per person. Mid-June to Labor Day, Mon–Tues and Fri–Sat 9am–6pm, Thurs 9am–9pm, Sun 10am–6pm; rest of year, Mon–Wed and Fri–Sat 9am–5pm, Thurs 9am–5pm and 7–9pm, Sun noon–6pm. Nature trail closes daily at dusk. From I-64, take Exit 258A and follow J. Clyde Morris Blvd. (U.S. 17) south.

Near the Mariners' Museum, this charming, zoo-like nature preserve and museum explains the environment of the James River area, beginning with a 60-foot cross-section simulating the river habitat from the Appalachian Mountains to the Atlantic Ocean (the latter represented by a 3,000-gallon tank of sea water filled with fish). A nearby touch-tank lets youngsters handle turtles and other small river animals. Outdoors, a boardwalk nature trail winds along the banks of a picturesque lake. Enclosures contain local wildlife such as otters, beavers, turtles, and birds (including a bald eagle grounded by a gunshot wound). A state-of-the-art planetarium presents shows explaining the southern skies.

SHOPPING FOR ANTIQUES

Norfolk is one of the best places in Virginia to search for antiques, with at least 32 shops selling a wide range of furniture, decorative arts, glassware, jewelry, and many other items, from both home and overseas. The best place to look is in Ghent, where nine shops sit along the 4 blocks of West 21st Street between Granby Street and Colonial Avenue. Granby Street has another 13 shops of its own, including the **Ghent Market & Antique Center,** which occupies an entire city block between 14th and 15th streets and Monticello Avenue (☎ **757/625-2897**). The "market" part of this huge establishment is actually a farmer's market, where you can load up on farm-fresh produce.

The visitor centers have a complete list and description of the shops, or contact **Morgan Antiques Gallery,** 242 W. 21st St., Norfolk, VA 23517 (☎ and fax **757/627-2486;** e-mail: **mhantiqu@exis.net**).

WHERE TO STAY

The hotels recommended below are within walking distance of the Waterside. A short drive east of downtown, the **Best Western Center Inn,** on Military Highway just north of I-264 (☎ **800/523-1234** or 757/461-6600), is a tasteful two-story light-gray-stucco complex set around a nicely landscaped courtyard and garden with park benches and old-fashioned street lamps. All rooms face the courtyard and Olympic-size pool. Double rooms range from $67 to $87.

In the Ocean View section, on the Chesapeake Bay near I-64 and the Hampton Roads Bridge-Tunnel, you'll find the **Days Inn Marina,** 1631 Bayville St. (☎ **800/DAYS-INN** or 757/583-4521); the **Econo Lodge Ocean View West/Naval Air Station,** 9601 Fourth View St. (☎ **800/768-5425** or 757/480-9611); and the **Quality Inn Ocean View Beach,** 1010 W. Ocean View Ave. (☎ **800/228-5151** or 757/587-8761).

✪ **Norfolk Waterside Marriott.** 235 E. Main St. (between Atlantic St. and Martins Lane), Norfolk, VA 23510. ☎ **800/228-9290** or 757/627-4200. Fax 757/628-6452. 404 rms, including 8 suites. A/C TV TEL. $134 double. Weekend packages available. AE, DC, DISC, MC, V. Self-parking $8; valet parking $10.

This luxury hotel is an elegantly appointed 24-story high-rise conveniently connected to the Waterside Festival Marketplace via a covered skywalk. Its mahogany-paneled lobby is a masterpiece of 18th-century European style, with fine paintings, a crystal chandelier, potted palm trees, comfortable seating areas with gleaming lamps, and one-of-a-kind antiques. A magnificent staircase leads to the restaurants and lounges.

Rooms are sumptuously furnished with traditional dark-wood pieces; sweeping river views are among the extras here. Guests on the concierge levels enjoy a private lounge where complimentary continental breakfast and afternoon snacks are served.

Dining/Entertainment: The second-level Dining Room is open for breakfast and dinner. Stormy's Sports Bar offers light fare and evening entertainment. The

Piano Lounge adjoining the Dining Room has a cozy fireplace and serves cocktails from 4pm.

Services: Room service, same-day laundry/valet, baby-sitting, valet parking.

Facilities: Atrium-enclosed pool, health club with Universal equipment, saunas, whirlpools and sundeck overlooking waterfront, business services, gift shop.

Omni Waterside Hotel. 777 Waterside Dr., Norfolk, VA 23510. ☎ **800/THE-OMNI** or 757/622-6664. Fax 757/625-8271. 446 rms, 20 suites. A/C TV TEL. $99–$175 double. Children under 17 stay free in parents' rm. Weekend and other packages available. AE, DC, DISC, MC, V. Self-parking $3 in adjacent Dominion Tower garage; valet parking $9.50.

Overlooking busy Norfolk Harbor, the Omni is next door to the Waterside Festival Marketplace. Its three-story atrium lobby is enhanced by stunning floral arrangements, and in the sunken Lobby Bar, 30-foot windows overlook the river. The Omni Club Level on the 10th floor offers such special amenities as complimentary continental breakfast, afternoon hors d'oeuvres, free daily newspaper, and nightly turndown with chocolates.

The Riverwalk offers American fare at all three meals, while the Lobby Bar has dancing on Friday and Saturday nights. Services include concierge, room service (from 6am to 9pm), and valet laundry. There's an outdoor pool, business center, gift and sundries shop, and a nearby health club.

✪ Page House Inn. 323 Fairfax Ave. (at Mowbray Arch), Norfolk, VA 23507. ☎ **757/625-5033.** Fax 757/623-9451. 5 rms, 2 suites. A/C TEL. $95–$100 double; $135–$150 suite. Rates include breakfast. MC, V. Free parking.

Centrally located in the historic Ghent district and across the street from the Chrysler Museum, this splendid B&B was built in 1899 by Herman L. Page, a Welsh immigrant who made good in Norfolk. It's a grand three-story brick Colonial Revival mansion with a dormered roof and double columns punctuating the expansive veranda. It stood vacant and desolate for years until New Yorkers Stephanie and Ezio DiBelardino masterfully restored its golden-oak paneling, sliding doors, and moldings on the first floor; the hand-carved fireplace in the living room; and the soaring staircase that ascends to the rooftop skylight.

Guest quarters are beautifully furnished with four-poster beds, hand-crocheted spreads, pretty wallpapers, and one-of-a-kind antiques. Five units have gas-log fireplaces. One of them also has a huge bathroom with sunken Jacuzzi and a steam shower with his-and-her heads. Stephanie serves a gourmet European-style breakfast in the large dining room, set with Lenox china. Afternoon cappuccino, served in the parlor (in front of the fireplace in winter), is another Page House ritual, giving guests a chance to meet one another and enjoy their hosts' gracious personalities.

Stephanie and Ezio also provide "boat-and-breakfast" aboard their 43-foot motor sailer *Bianca,* which can accommodate two couples who want to sail the Chesapeake. Rates are $175 for one couple, $275 for two, with a 2-night minimum stay required.

Ramada Madison Hotel. 345 Granby St. (at W. Freemason St.), Norfolk, VA 23510. ☎ **800/2-RAMADA** or 757/622-6682. Fax 757/623-5949. 124 rms. A/C TV TEL. $80–$110 double. Children 12 and under stay free in parents' rm. Weekend and other packages available. AE, DC, DISC, MC, V. Free validated city garage parking.

Built in 1906 at the corner of Granby and Freemason streets as the Southland Hotel and later known as the Madison, the Ramada was the first hostelry in Norfolk to provide indoor plumbing for its guests. Although the Marriott and Omni have eclipsed it, the lobby reflects the hotel's status as Norfolk's grande dame landmark, with polished walnut columns, wing chairs, and a medallion-printed carpet. The rooms have been renovated and decorated in colonial style with pale floral-print fabrics and mahogany furnishings. Tandom's Restaurant serves breakfast and lunch daily.

The hotel's bar opens at 5pm and serves pub fare. There is a nominal charge for use of a nearby health and racquetball club.

WHERE TO DINE
IN THE WATERSIDE

You can get an inexpensive meal at the food court in the Waterside, downtown's showpiece (see "Attractions in Norfolk," above). In addition to the two restaurants below, there's a branch of **Hooters** pub with outdoor seating in good weather (☎ 757/622-9464).

Il Porto. The Waterside. ☎ **757/627-4400.** Reservations suggested on weekends. Main courses $10–$15. AE, DC, DISC, MC, V. Daily 11am–11pm, until midnight Fri–Sun. ITALIAN.

This popular restaurant with great waterfront views has been at the Waterside since the marketplace opened, and has expanded several times since. Its candlelit interior evokes the Mediterranean with terra-cotta tile floors and stucco walls. In good weather, you can dine outdoors, overlooking the harbor. For a light lunch, try an antipasto of assorted Italian cold meats, cheeses, and marinated vegetables on salad greens. At dinner, start with mussels in white wine and parsley. Homemade pastas run the gamut from lasagna, manicotti, or linguine with clam sauce to the house special—lobster, scallops, fish, and shrimp sautéed in herb butter and tossed with broccoli and pasta. Children's plates feature spaghetti and meatballs, lasagna, or veal parmigiana.

Schooner's Harbor Grill. The Waterside. ☎ **757/627-8800.** Reservations recommended. Sandwiches and burgers $7–$8; main courses $9–$16. AE, DC, DISC, MC, V. Daily 11am–midnight. AMERICAN.

Dining at Schooner's affords a great lookout over the Waterside marina, whether you choose to sit outside on the 200-seat patio overlooking the Elizabeth River, or inside, where you can also watch the chefs prepare your meal at the gleaming brass-and-copper grill. Spacious and airy, this fun restaurant has red ceramic-tile floors, checked tablecloths, and ceiling fans with Victorian glass-shaded lamps. For lunch, you may want to indulge in spiced jumbo shrimp: A half pound is just $6. At night, the emphasis is on char-grilled burgers, steaks, fish, and a raw bar with oysters, clams, and shrimp. Barbecued ribs and chicken are also on the menu. The lively bar offers baskets of Virginia peanuts roasted in the shell.

IN FREEMASON

Freemason Abbey Restaurant & Tavern. 209 W. Freemason St. (at Boush St.). ☎ **757/622-3966.** Reservations suggested at dinner. Main courses $10–$19. AE, DISC, MC, V. Sun–Thurs 11:30am–10pm; Fri–Sat 11:30am–11:30pm. AMERICAN.

Have you ever eaten in a church? Well, you can here, in an 1873 brick-and-fieldstone building originally occupied by Norfolk's Second Presbyterian Church. The structure has been completely refurbished, exposing the massive cathedral roof trusses and adding a mezzanine that seats about 100 in a casual atmosphere. Etched-glass trim, wood-framed gothic windows, a brass chandelier, and polished wood tables and high-backed booths create a cozy tavern ambience. The specialty is lobster, and locals flock here on Wednesday nights when a 1$^1/_3$-pound lobster dinner costs only $12. A big draw for meat lovers is the Thursday-night 10-ounce prime rib dinner ($10). Try the she-crab soup for your appetizer; it's a luscious blend of crabmeat and cream with a dash of sherry. Entrees—all served with a salad, potato, oven-fresh rolls, and a steamed vegetable—include grilled salmon, New York strip steak, and seafood pasta. Finish off with Irish Cream coffee or a Freemason cappuccino, made with

Frangelico and brandy. Lighter fare for lunch or dinner includes quiches and crois-sant sandwiches.

✪ **Thyme Square Market & Deli.** 509 Botetourt St. (at York St. and Brambleton Ave.). ☎ **757/623-5082.** Reservations not accepted. Sandwiches and burgers $4.50–$6.50; main courses $8–$16. DISC, MC, V. Mon–Thurs 11am–9pm; Fri 11am–10pm. DELI/INTERNATIONAL.

Plants and wrought-iron patio chairs lend a garden ambience to this corner storefront, whose chiller cases offer a variety of gourmet deli items for stacked-high sandwiches. They go like hotcakes at lunch, but come evening, everyone's attention turns to chef Ethel Pangborn's cuisine, which ranges from her famous meat loaf to her impressive crabcakes—jumbo "hunks" of sweet backfin meat delicately seasoned with just a hint of traditional Old Bay spice. She serves them with real mashed potatoes and slices of huge, home-grown tomatoes topped with silver queen corn pared off the ear and sided by a roasted remoulade dressing.

✪ **Todd Jurich's Bistro.** 210 W. York St. (between Boush and Duke sts.). ☎ **757/622-3210.** Reservations recommended. Lunch $6–$9.50; main courses $15–$22. MC, V. Mon–Thurs 11:30am–2:30pm and 5:30–10pm; Fri 11:30am–2:30pm and 5:30–11pm; Sat 5:30–11pm. CREATIVE AMERICAN.

Actor Donald Sutherland dined regularly at this elegant, intimate bistro while film-ing a movie here recently. You'll see why when you partake of chef Todd Jurich's creative twists on Southern traditions, such as his all-lump-meat crabcakes on brioche with lemon mayonnaise—a far cry, indeed, from the fried cakes dispensed at many Chesapeake Bay seafood shacks. Todd uses only fresh produce, drawn whenever pos-sible from local farms that practice "ecologically sound agriculture." For example, the roasted chicken he serves on a seasonal risotto with crispy mustard greens was most likely allowed to range free rather than being confined to a cage. For lunch, you can choose from sandwiches such as crabcakes or Todd's own version of Smithfield barbecue.

IN GHENT

✪ **Elliot's.** 1421 Colley Ave. (between Baldwin and Shirley aves.). ☎ **757/625-0259.** Res-ervations not necessary. Main courses $6–$13.95. AE, DC, DISC, MC, V. Sun–Thurs 11am–10pm; Fri–Sat 11am–midnight. AMERICAN.

Many are the fans of Elliot's, which encompasses five former stores and a sidewalk patio in Norfolk's trendy Ghent district. An eclectic art deco decor features old photos and advertising signs on the walls, ceiling fans, hanging plants, and etched-glass par-titions. Specialties include mile-high nachos with chicken chili and delicious hot crab dip. Fresh-catch selections come broiled, blackened, or with a choice of special sauces. There are also burgers, salads, and vegetarian dishes. The children's menu is a plus for families. For dessert, you can't beat a homemade fudge brownie topped with ice cream, whipped cream, and chocolate sauce. A selection of domestic and imported beers is available—or have a bottle of house wine.

Doumar's. 19th to 20th sts. and Monticello Ave. ☎ **757/627-4163.** Sandwiches 90¢–$2.45. No credit cards. Mon–Thurs 8am–11pm; Fri–Sat 8am–12:30am. AMERICAN.

This is no modern re-creation of a 1950s drive-in with carhops, curb service, and a 1950s menu, for Doumar's has been just that since the 1930s—which makes it a hip historical attraction. The specialties here are sweet, waffle-like ice-cream cones, some of them from the original cone-making machine invented by Abe Doumar at the St. Louis Exposition in 1904. Abe's great-nephew, present owner Al Doumar, keeps his uncle's invention oiled and working. Barbecue sandwiches, burgers and hot dogs, sundaes, and milkshakes round out the menu.

Wild Monkey. 1603 Colley Ave. (between Spotswood and Brandon aves.). ☎ **757/ 627-6462.** Reservations not accepted. Lunch $5–$7.50; main courses $8–$14. AE, MC, V. Mon– Fri 11:30am–2:30pm and 5:30–10pm; Sat 5:30–10pm. AMERICAN/CAJUN.

You may have to wait on weekends to get a table at this busy storefront in the heart of the Ghent business district, so popular is Wild Monkey with Norfolk's young professional set. A huge blackboard on one side of the dining room advertises the offerings from the open kitchen in the rear, while another on the opposite side explains a limited but fine selection of California wines and displays the actual bottles. You can dine on old standbys such as "Ten Dollar" meat loaf or liver and onions, or treat your tastebuds to the spicy likes of mahimahi with a mango relish or Cajun pasta with andouille sausage. I thoroughly enjoyed a piping-hot bowl of spicy yet sweet crawfish étouffée over white and wild rice with corn-on-the-cob and slices of juicy fresh tomato on the side.

NORFOLK AFTER DARK

For a rundown on evening events, pick up a free copy of *Port Folio,* an entertainment weekly available at the visitor information offices, most hotel lobbies, and the Waterside. In addition to entertainment at hotel lounges and outdoors in Town Park on the Elizabeth River, you may be here during performances by several outstanding companies. The **Virginia Stage Company** puts on five productions annually, October through April, at the restored Wells Theatre, Monticello Avenue and Tazewell Street (☎ **757/627-1234**). The Harrison Opera House, at Virginia Beach Boulevard and Llewellyn Avenue (☎ **757/627-9545**), is home to the **Virginia Opera.**

SCOPE, Brambleton Avenue and St. Paul's Boulevard (☎ **757/441-2161**), seats 12,000 for major events—including the circus, ice shows, and concerts. Part of the SCOPE complex, **Chrysler Hall,** Charlotte Street and St. Paul's Boulevard (☎ **757/ 441-2161**), is home to the **Virginia Symphony** and the annual Pops series.

2 Virginia Beach

18 miles E of Norfolk; 110 miles E of Richmond; 207 miles S of Washington, D.C.

Given its more than 20 miles of unbroken sand and surf, it's not surprising that Virginia Beach comes alive during the summer months, when vacationers flock here. Although big hotels line the beachfront and block off ocean views from everywhere except for their own rooms, the Boardwalk boasts immaculate landscaping, wood benches, small parks, public rest rooms, and attractive white colonial-style streetlamps.

Adding to Virginia Beach's allure as a family vacation destination is the Virginia Marine Science Museum, the most popular museum in the state. History lovers will find several sites of interest, including the First Landing Cross at the spot where the Jamestown settlers first came ashore. Nature lovers can drive a few miles south to the Back Bay National Wildlife Refuge, which attracts migrating birds and protects several miles of beach and marshlands from encroaching development.

ESSENTIALS

VISITOR INFORMATION   For information on planning your trip, or assistance while you're in Virginia Beach, contact the **Visitor Information Center,** 2100 Parks Ave., Virginia Beach, VA 23451 (☎ **800/446-8038** for information or 800/ VA-BEACH for hotel reservations; www.city.virginia.beach.va.us). A large board has phones connected to the reservations desks of major hotels and resorts. Particularly helpful is a free **map** showing public rest rooms and municipal parking lots in the resort area. The center's annual "Vacation Guide" is a no-nonsense listing of every

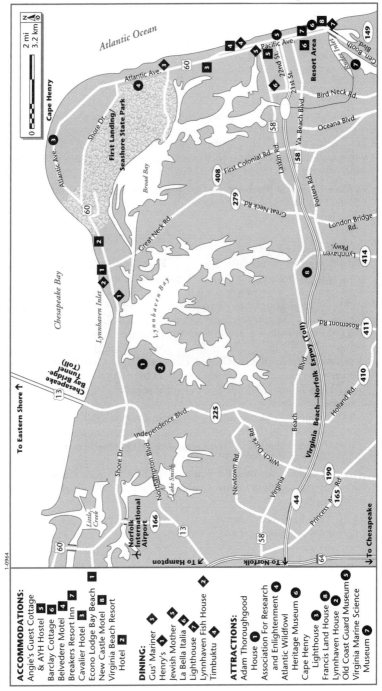

Virginia Beach

ACCOMMODATIONS:
Angie's Guest Cottage
& AYH Hostel **5**
Barclay Cottage **6**
Belvedere Motel **4**
Breakers Resort Inn **7**
Cavalier Hotel **3**
Econo Lodge Bay Beach **1**
New Castle Motel **8**
Virginia Beach Resort
Hotel **2**

DINING:
Gus' Mariner **3**
Henry's **1**
Jewish Mother **5**
La Bella Italia **6**
Lighthouse **7**
Lynnhaven Fish House **2**
Timbuktu **4**

ATTRACTIONS:
Adam Thoroughgood
House **1**
Association For Research
and Enlightenment **4**
Atlantic Wildfowl
Heritage Museum **6**
Cape Henry **9**
Lighthouse **3**
Francis Land House **8**
Lynnhaven House **2**
Old Coast Guard Museum **5**
Virginia Marine Science
Museum **7**

hotel, restaurant, and activity here. The center is at the eastern end of the Va. 44 expressway. It's open daily from 9am to 5pm, to 8pm from mid-June to Labor Day. There are **information kiosks** on Atlantic Avenue at 17th, 24th, and 30th streets. Racks at the visitor information center and elsewhere contain several slick giveaway tourist publications that are packed with information and money-saving coupons.

GETTING THERE   By Car   Follow I-64 to Va. 44 east (the "44 Expressway" in local parlance), an Interstate-grade highway that runs straight to the heart of the oceanfront resort area. Also from the west, U.S. 60 becomes the scenic Shore Drive, which dead-ends at Atlantic Avenue on the northern end of the ocean beach; a right turn takes you along this main north-south drag through the resort area. From the north or south, U.S. 13 and 17 will take you to I-64.

By Plane   Virginia Beach is served by **Norfolk International Airport,** about 30 minutes (15 miles) west of the oceanfront resort area (see "Essentials" under "Norfolk," above).

CITY LAYOUT   At the southeastern corner of the state, Virginia Beach is bordered by the Chesapeake Bay and the Atlantic Ocean. They meet at Cape Henry, home to **Cape Henry Lighthouse, Fort Story,** and **First Landing/Seashore State Park.** There's no real downtown in Virginia Beach; instead, most of the action is at the oceanfront **resort area,** where you'll find a solid line of big hotels, restaurants, beachwear and souvenir shops, video-game arcades, and the **Boardwalk,** which runs along the beach. The resort area extends from 1st Street at Rudee Inlet north to 42nd Street (the boardwalk ends at 39th Street). Behind the beachfront hotels, **Atlantic Avenue** runs north-south between Rudee Inlet and Cape Henry. It's paralleled a block inland between Rudee Inlet and 43rd Street by the wider **Pacific Avenue,** a speedier way through the resort area. At Rudee Inlet, Pacific Avenue gives way to **General Booth Boulevard,** which runs southwest past the Virginia Marine Science Museum.

A less congested area with hotels and restaurants is at **Lynnhaven Inlet,** along Shore Drive (U.S. 60) on the Chesapeake Bay 6 miles west of the oceanfront.

Some 12 miles south of the resort area, **Sandbridge** is an oceanfront enclave of cottages and a relatively undeveloped public beach. From Sandbridge south to the North Carolina line, the **Back Bay National Wildlife Refuge** and **False Cape State Park** offer undisturbed beach and marshland for hikers, bikers, bird-watchers, and sun worshippers.

GETTING AROUND   There are a few pay lots along Pacific Avenue (the visitor information center has free maps that show them), but parking spaces near the beach can be as scarce as hen's teeth between mid-June and Labor Day, especially on weekends. Your best bet then is to stay near the shore and get around on the **Beach Trolleys.**

The Atlantic Avenue Trolley runs daily from Labor Day weekend through September, every 10 to 15 minutes from noon to midnight along the entire length of Atlantic Avenue.

The North Seashore Trolley runs Monday through Friday year-round, every 30 minutes from 6:30am to 6:30pm along Pacific Avenue between 19th and 68th streets.

The Museum Express Trolley runs daily from Memorial Day to Labor Day weekends, every 15 to 30 minutes from 7:30am to 11pm, to midnight on weekends, between Atlantic Avenue at 40th Street and the Virginia Science Museum and Ocean Breeze Amusement Park on General Booth Boulevard.

Fares on any of these trolleys are 50¢ per ride for adults and children, 25¢ for seniors and disabled persons. Or you can buy a Trolley Pass, which costs $3.50 for adults and children, $1.75 for seniors and disabled persons; it's good for 3 days of unlimited rides.

In addition, the Lynnhaven Mall Trolley also runs during summer, from Atlantic Avenue at 25th Street to Lynnhaven Mall, the city's main shopping center on Lynnhaven Parkway south of Va. 44. The fare is $1.50 per person.

There's also a Naval Air Station Oceana Trolley Tour (to the home of the navy's F-14 Tomcat and F-18 Hornet fighters) from Memorial Day weekend through September. It leaves at 9:30 and 11:30am, with the latter stopping for lunch at the officers' club. Fares are $3.50 for adults and $1.75 for seniors, disabled persons, and children under 12.

The trolleys are operated by Tidewater Regional Transit (☎ 757/640-6300), which also provides public bus service in the region. TRT has a **ticket kiosk** on the oceanfront at Atlantic Avenue and 24th Street, where you can also buy its Discover Tidewater Passports and Adventure Passes (see "Getting Around" under "Norfolk," above).

OUTDOOR PURSUITS

Virginia Beach offers a wonderful variety of water sports, starting, of course, with its fine white-sand beach. But note that between Memorial Day and Labor Day, no ball playing, fishing, and other sports are allowed on the beach between 2nd Street and 42nd Street from 10am to 5pm.

Most water-sports activities are centered at Rudee Inlet, which empties into the ocean, and at Lynnhaven Inlet, where the Lynnhaven River meets the Chesapeake Bay.

BIKING, JOGGING & SKATING   You can walk, jog, or run on the Boardwalk, or bike and skate on its adjoining bike path. There are biking and hiking trails in **First Landing/Seashore State Park** and in **Back Bay National Wildlife Refuge** (see "Parks & Wildlife Refuges," below). Bikes and in-line skates are available from **Cherie's Bicycle Rentals** (☎ 757/437-8888), which has stands on the oceanfront at 8th, 22nd, 24th, and 37th streets. Cherie's also has clinics if you want to learn how to in-line skate.

FISHING   Deep-sea fishing aboard a party boat can be an exciting day's entertainment for novices and dedicated fishermen alike. Both party and private charter boats are based at the **Virginia Beach Fishing Center,** 200 Winston-Salem Ave. (☎ 757/422-5700), at the Rudee Inlet bridge. At Lynnhaven Inlet, party boats leave from the **D and M Marina,** 3311 Shore Dr. (☎ 757/481-7211).

You can also drop a line from several piers. The **Virginia Beach Fishing Pier,** between 14th and 15th streets, oceanfront (☎ 757/428-2333), open April through October, has bait for sale and rods for rent. On the Chesapeake Bay, **Lynnhaven Inlet Fishing Pier,** Starfish Road off Shore Drive (☎ 757/481-7071), open 24 hours a day in summer, rents rods and reels and sells crab cages.

GOLF   The visitor information center has a detailed list of Virginia Beach's nine public golf courses. Among them are the **Hell's Point Golf Course,** 2700 Atwoodtown Rd. (☎ 757/721-3400), designed by Rees Jones, and the **Red Wing Lake Municipal Golf Course,** 1080 Prosperity Rd. (☎ 757/437-4845).

KAYAKING   Randy Gore of **Tidewater Adventures** (☎ 757/480-1999) rents kayaks from May to September in First Landing/Seashore State Park (see "Parks &

Wildlife Refuges," below). Take the 64th Street entry off Pacific Avenue and follow the road to the beach at "The Narrows" on Broad Bay. Rentals range from $10 per hour to $80 for a full day. With at least a day's notice, Randy will also lead guided tours of Back Bay National Wildlife Refuge, into the Dismal Swamp (see the "Dismal Dirt & Nastiness" box, earlier in this chapter) or to remote villages on the upper sounds of North Carolina.

SCUBA DIVING   The Atlantic Ocean off Virginia Beach is colder and less clear than it is below Cape Hatteras, NC, but that's not to say you can't dive here. For information about dive trips, contact **Atlantic Dive Charters Ltd.,** 1324 Teresa Dr., Chesapeake, VA 23322 (☎ 757/482-9777); or **Lynnhaven Dive Center,** 1413 Great Neck Rd., Virginia Beach, VA 23454 (☎ 757/481-7949).

SWIMMING   During the summer season, lifeguards are on duty along the resort strip from 2nd to 42nd streets; they also handle raft, umbrella, and beach-chair rentals.

You can get away from the summer crowds by driving 12 miles south of Rudee Inlet to **Little Island City Park,** in the residential beach area of Sandbridge. To really escape the crowds, walk several miles to **False Cape State Park** (see "Parks & Wildlife Refuges," below).

TENNIS   The city has some 200 public tennis courts, most of which are lighted and free. If you call the city's **Parks Department** (☎ 757/437-4804), they'll be happy to steer you to the nearest one. The **Owl Creek Municipal Center,** 928 South Birdneck Rd. (☎ 757/422-4716), which has a pro shop, children's play area, 12 hard-surface and 2 tournament courts, is the major facility.

WAVE RUNNING & PARASAILING   You can rent exciting wave runners from several operators along Winston-Salem Avenue, including **Rudee Inlet Jet Ski Rentals,** which has locations at the Virginia Beach Fishing Center (☎ 757/428-4614), 31st Street at the oceanfront (☎ 757/491-1117), and 1284 Laskin Rd. (☎ 757/428-6156). At Lynnhaven Inlet, **Wave Runners Water Sports Center** (☎ 757/481-4747) rents jet skis and jet boats and also offers parasailing over the Chesapeake.

PARKS & WILDLIFE REFUGES

You don't have to go far from the busy resort area to find open spaces ideal for hiking, biking, camping, and bird watching.

FIRST LANDING/SEASHORE STATE PARK   Most convenient to the resort area, these 2,270 preserved acres run between Back Bay and the Chesapeake Bay to within 2 blocks of the ocean. Rabbits, squirrels, and raccoon are among the many species inhabiting this urban park, which boasts 28 miles of hiking trails. The main entrance is on Shore Drive (U.S. 60), where the visitor center is open daily 9am to 6pm from Memorial Day to Labor Day, daily 9am to 4pm off-season. The 64th Street entry, off Pacific Avenue, leads to a beach on Broad Bay. Admission to the park is $2 per person on weekdays, $3 on weekends; it's free at all times for hikers and bikers. The trails are open daily from 8am to sunset. Bikes are prohibited except on the paved, 6-mile Cape Henry Trail, which runs between the 64th Street entrance and the visitor center.

Twenty two-bedroom cabins can be rented for $85 a day or $520 a week during summer, or $72 a night or $371 a week off-season, with a 2-night minimum stay required. A bayside campground has 200 sites for tents and RVs (no hookups) for $20 a night in summer, $14 off-season. For reservations or more information, contact the park at 2500 Shore Dr., Virginia Beach, VA 23451 (☎ 757/481-2131).

BACK BAY & FALSE CAPE   Especially inviting for bird-watchers is ✪ **Back Bay National Wildlife Refuge,** in the southeastern corner of Virginia near the North Carolina line. Its 7,732 acres of beaches, dunes, marshes, and backwaters are on the main Atlantic Flyway for migratory birds. No swimming or sunbathing is allowed on the pristine beach here, but you can collect shells, surf-cast for fish, and bird-watch. There are also nature trails and a canoe launching spot with marked trails through the marshes. Daily admission is $4 per vehicle, $2 per pedestrian or biker. The visitor contact station (☎ 757/721-2412) is open Monday through Friday from 8am to 4pm, weekends from 9am to 4pm. It offers nature programs by reservation only. From Rudee Inlet, go south on General Booth Boulevard and follow the signs 12 miles to Sandbridge and the refuge. For more information, contact the Refuge Manager, 4005 Sandpiper Rd., Virginia Beach, VA 23456 (☎ 757/721-2412).

Swimming and sunbathing are permitted on the beach in ✪ **False Cape State Park,** 4 miles south of the Back Bay visitor contact station via hiking and biking trail. Here you'll find an interpretive trail as well as more than 3 miles of hiking trails. Primitive camping is by permit only, which you can get by calling ☎ **800/ 933-PARK.** There are no other visitor facilities here, however, so bring your own drinking water. The park is open daily from sunrise to sunset.

You can't park in the national wildlife refuge lot while visiting False Cape, so leave your vehicle at Little Island City Park in Sandbridge. From there, you can either hike or bike the 6 miles to False Cape, or take an electric tram that runs from May through October, departing daily at 9am and returning at 12:45pm (giving you 2 hours at False Cape). The tram is operated by volunteers, so call ☎ **800/933-PARK** to make sure it's running. Fares are $6 for adults, $5 for seniors and children 6 to 17, and free for kids under 6 accompanied by adults.

Sandbridge Outfitters, on the beach road north of the wildlife refuge (☎ 757/ 721-6461), offers rental equipment and nature tours of the area. You can rent bicycles and sea kayaks from **Ocean Rentals,** on Sandbridge Road 2 miles inland from the beach (☎ 757/721-6210).

AMUSEMENT PARKS

The ocean resort area between 15th and 30th streets offers the usual collection of video-game establishments and a haunted house, and at Rudee Inlet there's **Skycoaster,** where you can fly bungee-jumping style from a contraption that looks like the Gateway Arch in St. Louis, Mo.

The major amusement park here, however, is **Ocean Breeze,** 849 General Booth Blvd., south of Rudee Inlet (☎ 800/678-WILD or 757/442-0718). Next door to the Virginia Science Museum (see below), this establishment actually includes four amusements: Motor World go-kart track, Shipwreck miniature golf course with waterfalls and a sunken ship, Strike Zone baseball batting cage, and the Wild Water Rapids wave pool. There's also a bungee-jumping tower on the premises. Admission to Wild Water Rapids ranges from $8.25 to $16.50 for adults, $8.25 to $11.50 for children, depending on the day and time. Tickets to everything else are extra. Wild Water Rapids is open from Memorial Day to Labor Day, Monday through Thursday from 10am to 8pm, Friday through Sunday from 10am to 10pm.

HISTORIC ATTRACTIONS

CAPE HENRY & THE FIRST LANDING SITE   Now part of the U.S. Army's Fort Story, at the north end of Atlantic Avenue, the Jamestown colonists' **First Landing Site** is marked by a cross and plaque where they "set up a Crosse at Chesupioc Bay and named that place Cape Henry" for Henry, Prince of Wales. Also at this site are a monumental relief map showing the French and British naval engagement off Cape Henry during the Revolutionary War and a statue of the French commander. Now known as the **Battle of the Capes,** this decisive battle effectively trapped Cornwallis at Yorktown and helped end British dominion in America. When Cornwallis surrendered, George Washington expressed his gratitude to the French Admiral de Grasse: "I wish it was in my power to express to Congress how much I feel myself indebted to the Count de Grasse and his fleet."

Near the plaque commemorating the battle, visitors can enter the **Old Cape Henry Lighthouse,** the first lighthouse built by authorization of Congress, in 1791. It illuminated the entrance to Chesapeake Bay until 1881. There is no charge for visitors to enter the grounds of Fort Story. The lighthouse (☎ **757/422-9421**) is open mid-March to October 31, daily from 10am to 5pm; admission is $2 for adults, $1 for students and seniors.

MUSEUMS IN THE RESORT AREA   In the heart of the oceanfront resort area, the **Old Coast Guard Station Museum and Gift Shop,** 24th Street and Atlantic Avenue (☎ **757/422-1587**), is housed in the small white-clapboard building constructed in 1903 as a life-saving station. The museum exhibits recall rescue missions and shipwrecks along the coast. Hours are Monday through Saturday from 10am to 5pm, Sunday from noon to 5pm. Admission is $2.50 for adults, $2 for seniors, and $1 for children. An excellent gift shop carries clocks, drawings, books, and other things nautical.

The **Atlantic Wildfowl Heritage Museum,** 12th Street and Atlantic Avenue (☎ **757/437-8432**), occupies a lovely white-brick-and-clapboard beach cottage built in 1895 by Virginia Beach's first mayor. The cottage alone is worth a stop as you stroll the Boardwalk. The small but excellent museum displays a collection of intricately carved decoys, some of them a century old, plus paintings of ducks, geese, and other wildfowl. It's operated by the Back Bay Wildfowl Guild, which applies the donations and profits from the gift shop (which carries excellent decoys) to its conservation efforts. Admission is free but donations are encouraged. It's open Monday through Saturday from 10am to 5pm, Sunday from noon to 5pm (closed Mondays from November to May).

HISTORIC HOMES   One of the oldest homes in Virginia, the beautiful ✪ **Adam Thoroughgood House,** 1636 Parish Rd. (☎ **757/460-0007**), near the intersection of Pleasure House Road and Northampton Boulevard (U.S. 13), was constructed around 1680 by one of Adam Thoroughgood's grandsons (architectural historians believe its namesake never occupied the house). This picturesque medieval English–style cottage sits on 4¹/₂ acres of lawn and garden overlooking the Lynnhaven River. The interior has exposed wood beams and whitewashed walls, and although the furnishings did not belong to the Thoroughgoods, they are original to the period and reflect the family's English ancestry. Tours take about 1 hour. The house is open April to December, Tuesday through Saturday from 10am to 5pm and Sunday from 1 to 5pm; January to March, Tuesday through Saturday from noon to 5pm. Admission is free on Wednesdays; other days, $3 for adults and $1.50 for seniors and students, free for children under 5. The house is included in block tickets for the Moses Myers House and Willoughby-Baylor House in Norfolk, all administered by the Chrysler Museum (see "Attractions in Norfolk," above).

Costumed docents interpret colonial lifestyles at the **Lynnhaven House,** 4405 Wishart Rd., off Independence Boulevard (☎ **757/460-1688**). It's open June to September, Tuesday through Sunday from noon to 4pm; May and October, weekends from noon to 4pm. Admission is $3 for adults, $1 for students 6 to 18, and free for children under 6. From the beach, take Va. 44 west, then north on Independence Boulevard (Va. 225) and right on Wishart Road.

The **Francis Land House,** 3131 Virginia Beach Blvd., just west of Kings Grant Road (☎ 757/431-4000), was built as a plantation manor in the mid-18th century but now sits beside one of the area's busiest highways. It's open year-round, Tuesday through Saturday from 9am to 5pm and Sunday from noon to 5pm, with the last tour at 4:30pm. Admission is $3 for adults, $2.50 for seniors, $1.50 for students over 13, $1 for children 6 to 12, and free for children under 6.

MORE ATTRACTIONS

Association for Research and Enlightenment (A.R.E.). 67th St. and Atlantic Ave. ☎ 757/428-3588. Free admission. Mon–Sat 9am–8pm; Sun 11am–8pm.

The international headquarters carrying on the work of the late psychic Edgar Cayce offers a host of free activities daily. You can see a movie that discusses Cayce's psychic talent, which first manifested itself when, as a young man, he found he could enter into an altered state of consciousness and answer questions on any topic. His answers, or "discourses," now called "readings," number some 14,305 and have stood the test of extensive research. Guided tours begin daily at 2pm and are followed at 3pm by a 30-minute movie about Cayce's life and a lecture on such topics as health, dreams, prophecies, meditation, and reincarnation. The A.R.E. Bookstore on the first floor has an excellent selection of books and videos about holistic health, parapsychology, life after death, dreams, and even cooking. The Meditation Room on the third floor offers a spectacular view of the ocean and is painted with special colors chosen because Cayce readings suggest they can help attain higher consciousness. Outside the center is the Meditation Garden.

✪ **Virginia Marine Science Museum.** 717 General Booth Blvd. (southwest of Rudee Inlet). ☎ 757/425-FISH. Admission $7.95 adults, $6.95 seniors, $5.95 children 4–11, free for children under 4. IMAX tickets $6.95 adults, $5.95 children 4–11, free for children under 4. Daily 9am–5pm (with extended summer hours). Closed Thanksgiving and Christmas. Take Museum Express Trolley in summer, or from the resort area, go south on Pacific Ave., which becomes General Booth Blvd. across Rudee Inlet; the museum is about 1 mile south of the inlet bridge.

This entertaining and educational facility, the state's largest aquarium, focuses on Virginia's marine environment. It's fittingly located on 45 acres beside Owls Creek salt marsh, a wildlife habitat in its own right. The museum has an observation tower and a nature trail that make the marsh, its waterfowl, and other animals part of the experience. Visitors can see and touch live sea animals, plus try hands-on interactive exhibits such as oyster harvesting and weather forecasting. The tanks hold sharks, harbor seals, river otters, and other animals and sealife. Sponsored by the Christian Broadcasting Network (cable's Family Channel), a towering IMAX theater shows nature films every hour. There's also a cafe and excellent gift shop.

The museum offers offshore **dolphin-watching** cruises (daily June to October), **whale-watching** cruises (Mondays in January and February), and **ocean-collection trips** (Wednesdays from June to August). They usually cost $12 for adults, $10 for children under 12. The cruises leave from Rudee Inlet, and reservations are required (☎ 757/437-BOAT).

WHERE TO STAY

The hotels and B&Bs listed below are just the tip of the iceberg in Virginia Beach, which has more than 11,000 hotel rooms. Even with that many places to stay, you should reserve as far in advance as possible for the busy summer season, from mid-June to Labor Day weekend. Room rates rise steeply then, so both summer and off-season rates are listed below.

The visitor information center maintains a **reservations service** (☎ 800/ VA-BEACH) that will help you find accommodations in any price range. The center's annual "Vacation Guide" lists all the local hotels and their current rates. It also distributes an annual accommodations directory published by the **Virginia Beach Hotel/Motel Association,** 968 S. Oriole Dr., Virginia Beach, VA 23451.

All but a few of the major chains are represented here (see the appendix for their toll-free phone numbers). For example, there are three high-rise Holiday Inns on the oceanfront, including the **Holiday Inn Sunspree Resort on the Ocean,** Atlantic Avenue at 39th Street (☎ **800/HOLIDAY** or 757/428-1711), which is away from the maddening crowds at the north end of the boardwalk. Nearby is the **Sheraton Oceanfront Hotel,** at 36th Street (☎ **800/325-3535** or 757/425-9000), which offers Jacuzzis in some rooms. Even more removed from the busy resort scene is the **Ramada Plaza Resort,** sitting by itself beside the beach at Atlantic Avenue and 57th Street (☎ **800/365-3032** or 757/428-7025).

You can save a few bucks by staying a block off the beach. One example here is the **Comfort Inn Virginia Beach,** on Pacific Avenue at 28th Street (☎ **800/ 441-0684** or 757/428-2203), a modern, well-managed hotel with indoor and outdoor pools and an exercise room. Rates for a double room range from $90 to $140 in summer, $34 to $90 off-season.

HOTELS AT THE OCEAN

The Belvedere Motel. Oceanfront at 36th St. (P.O. Box 451), Virginia Beach, VA 23458. ☎ **800/425-0612** or 757/425-0612. Fax 757/425-1397. 50 rms. A/C TV TEL. Summer $83– $102 double; off-season $48–78 double. AE, MC, V. Closed mid-Oct to Mar.

One of the least expensive and cleanest of the smaller, family-operated oceanfront hotels, this five-story building justifiably attracts lots of repeat guests, so book early. The motel-style rooms have screen doors that swing open to balconies facing the ocean. The combo tub-shower bathrooms are small, but compensate with separate sinks and vanities. A few rooms have king-size beds (most have two doubles). The 10 units on the ends of the building are somewhat larger and have cooking facilities. Other facilities include a small swimming pool, sundeck, and the Belvedere Coffee Shop (see "Where to Dine," below); guests also get free use of bicycles.

✪ **The Breakers Resort Inn.** Oceanfront at 16th St., Virginia Beach, VA 23451. ☎ **800/ 237-7532** or 757/428-1821. Fax 757/422-9602. 57 rms and efficiencies. A/C TV TEL. Summer $120–$170 double; winter $50–$110 double. Weekend and other packages available. AE, MC, V. Free parking.

One of the more reasonably priced oceanfront hostelries, the Breakers is another small family-operated hotel. A white box-like nine-story building, its rooms are comfortably furnished with contemporary pieces. All have oceanfront balconies and refrigerators; some rooms with king-size beds contain Jacuzzis. Efficiency apartments have a bedroom with two double beds, a living room with a Murphy bed, and a sitting area. Kitchens are fully equipped. Additional amenities include an outdoor heated pool, coffee shop for poolside dining, and free bicycles.

✪ **Cavalier Hotel.** Oceanfront at 42nd St., Virginia Beach, VA 23451. ☎ **800/446-8199** or 757/425-8555. Fax 757/428-7957. 400 rms, 25 suites. A/C TV TEL. Summer $90–$185 double; winter $55–$95 double. Additional person $20 extra; children under 18 stay free in parents' room. Weekend and other packages available. AE, DC, DISC, MC, V. Self-parking free; valet parking $5–$12.

This venerable resort consists of two hotels—the original Cavalier on the hill, built in 1927, and the Cavalier on the ocean, which opened in 1973. Both were refurbished recently, but the original property still has all the gracious features you'd expect in a fine old resort, including an enclosed veranda with white-wicker furnishings, potted plants, and great ocean views; it evokes images of the days when F. Scott and Zelda Fitzgerald danced here and lunches were black-tie. The lobby is gracious, complete with colonial-style furnishings and crystal chandeliers. Some of the guest rooms feature European-style baths with black and white tile, pedestal sinks, whirlpools, lighted makeup mirrors, bidets, and hair dryers. Furnishings in these individually decorated rooms include Williamsburg-quality Chippendale reproductions, colonial-print fabrics, gilt-framed artwork, and museum-quality decorative objects. The heated indoor Olympic-size pool is magnificently tiled and illuminated by a grand skylight.

The newer building has nicely decorated contemporary-style rooms, all with oceanfront balconies.

Dining: The elegant Orion rooftop restaurant in the oceanfront hotel is open for cocktails and dinner; the dining room on the lobby floor serves all three meals. The dining room in the hotel on the hill is open seasonally.

Services: Concierge, room service, baby-sitting, valet parking, shuttle service between hotels.

Facilities: Three pools (indoor, outdoor, and kiddie), 20-station aerobic fitness course, health club, four tennis courts, bike rentals, putting green, croquet, volleyball, shuffleboard, basketball, two playgrounds, children's activities program in season, gift shop.

New Castle Motel. Oceanfront at 12th St., Virginia Beach, VA 23451. ☎ **800/346-3176** or 757/428-3981. Fax 757/491-4394. 81 rms. A/C TV TEL. Summer $125–$250; off-season $50–$250. AE, DC, DISC, MC, V.

Situated beside the Atlantic Wildfowl Heritage Museum (see "Historic Attractions," above), the 10-story, family-operated New Castle offers the most unusual mix of rooms on the beach, ranging from standard motel units to romantic deluxe models with canopy beds, gas fireplaces, his-and-her shower heads, and wooden Venetian blinds to keep passersby from watching you frolic in big Jacuzzi tubs. All units have balconies, refrigerators, microwave ovens, and spa tubs. There's an indoor pool, fitness center, free bicycles for guests' use (in summer), and a coin-operated laundry. The Cabana Cafe to one side offers reasonably priced meals under a big, beachside awning.

BED & BREAKFASTS AT THE OCEAN

Angie's Guest Cottage & AYH Hostel. 302 24th St. (between Atlantic and Pacific aves.), Virginia Beach, VA 23451. ☎ **757/428-4600.** 6 rms (1 with bath), 36 dorm beds. A/C. $54–$78 double room; $9–$12.50 dorm bed. Rates for rooms include continental breakfast. No credit cards. Closed mid-Oct to mid-Mar.

You'll find a delightful mix of American and international young folks staying at innkeeper Barbara Yates's quaint white-clapboard cottage, built a block from the beach in 1918 as family housing for the nearby life-saving station, now the Old Coast Guard Station Museum and Gift Shop (see "Historic Attractions," above). An addicted traveler (at least during the winter months, when she closes the place up), Barbara keeps her small guest rooms spotlessly clean and freshly painted. Rooms are air-conditioned but lack other modern amenities (however, she does have a portable black-and-white TV for anyone suffering from tube withdrawal). At the rear of the cottage, one of Virginia's few official AYH hostels offers three dorm rooms—men's, women's, and co-ed. They aren't air-conditioned, but lots of fans kick up a breeze. Outside, there's a covered country kitchen for guests to use, plus a sundeck and table tennis under a sprawling shade tree. Barbara rents linens to her dorm guests. Non-AYH members can stay in the dorms if space is available.

Barclay Cottage. 400 16th St. (at Arctic Ave.), Virginia Beach, VA 23451. ☎ **757/422-1956.** 5 rms (3 with bath). A/C. $65–$90 double. Rates include full breakfast. AE, MC, V. Closed Nov–Mar.

Innkeepers Peter and Claire Cantanese have turned this two-story, white-clapboard Victorian with wraparound verandas into a comfortable and charming bed-and-breakfast. Peter and Claire may hail from New Jersey, but their house is *very* coastal Southern, with rocking chairs on the porches and green shutters trimming tall windows hung with lace curtains. The guest rooms are adorned with Victorian pieces, and you'll find members of Peter's antique trunk collection placed throughout the premises. Guests gather in the lounge promptly at 9am for a full breakfast served family style. Peter and Claire have a pet dog, but don't bring yours. The beach is a 2-block walk away.

HOTELS AT LYNNHAVEN INLET

Econo Lodge Bay Beach. 2968 Shore Dr. (U.S. 60), Virginia Beach, VA 23451. ☎ **800/553-2666** or 757/481-0666. Fax 757/481-4756. 41 rms. A/C TV TEL. Summer $55–$109; off-season $35–$55 single or double. Additional person $5 extra. AE, DC, DISC, MC, V. Free parking.

This is an attractive Econo Lodge, with gray-clapboard siding and blue doors. Located about 2 miles east of the Chesapeake Bay Bridge-Tunnel, just east of Lynnhaven Inlet, it's a short walk from the Chesapeake Bay beach, or you can take a dip in the motel's heated outdoor pool. Standard motel accommodations all have microwaves and refrigerators. VCRs and tapes are available for rental. Complimentary coffee and doughnuts are served in the reception area every morning. Book well in advance for the special $55 rate during summer.

Virginia Beach Resort Hotel. 2800 Shore Dr. (U.S. 60), Virginia Beach, VA 23451. ☎ **800/468-2722,** 800/422-4747 in Virginia, or 757/481-9000. Fax 757/496-7429. 295 suites. A/C TV TEL. Summer $169–$334 double; winter $104–$289 double. Additional person $10 extra. Weekly and other packages available. AE, DC, MC, V. Free parking.

Situated $3^{1}/_{2}$ miles east of the Chesapeake Bay Bridge-Tunnel on 4 acres of beachfront property, this self-contained luxury resort is about 3 miles from the oceanfront resort area. All suites have balconies with bay views, as well as separate sleeping and living areas, furnished with sophisticated, contemporary wood pieces in pleasing pastel hues. Kitchen areas are equipped with a refrigerator and microwave. Utensils are available for a $5 charge, or you may bring your own.

　　Dining: The Tradewinds Restaurant beside the pool offers wonderful water views and good American fare; the Café by the Bay is for more casual dining.

　　Services: Room service (from 6:10am to 11pm), nightly turndown on request.

　　Facilities: Beach, indoor/outdoor pools, health club, sauna, jet-ski rental, volleyball, children's activities, business center, meeting facilities, coin-op laundry, beauty salon, gift shop.

WHERE TO DINE

Just as Virginia Beach has thousands of hotel rooms, so it also has hundreds of restaurants, especially establishments serving up bountiful harvests of seafood. We've picked a few of the best to get you started.

　　For breakfast by the sea, head for the **Belvedere Coffee Shop,** an old-fashioned diner at the Belvedere Motel, Oceanfront at 36th Street (☎ **757/425-1397**). It's small, noisy, and busy, with cooks scurrying around the stove behind the counter, but big windows look right out on the boardwalk, beach, and surf. You'll have local company for eggs, omelets, pancakes, made-to-order sandwiches, salads, and a few inexpensive hot meals such as crabcakes. Prices range from $3 to $7, but don't plan to pay by credit card. It's open daily in summer from 7am to 3pm; off-season, daily from 7:30am to 2:30pm.

If you have kids in tow, another good breakfast bet is **Pocahontas Pancake & Waffle Shop,** Atlantic Avenue at 35th Street (☎ 757/428-6352), which has plenty of reminders of the American Indian princess, including a teepee in one corner of the dining room. The menu offers a wide range of inexpensive pancakes and waffles. Hours are daily from 7am to 1pm.

AT THE OCEAN

✪ **Gus' Mariner Restaurant.** Atlantic Ave. at 57th St. (in Ramada Plaza Resort). ☎ **757/ 425-5699.** Reservations recommended. Main courses $12–$30, early-bird specials $10. AE, DC, DISC, MC, V. Summer, daily 7am–10pm; off-season, daily 7am–9pm. Early-bird specials daily 3–6pm. SEAFOOD.

One of the few hotel restaurants popular with local residents, Gus's award-winning establishment sits right beside the beach, with gorgeous sea views from its windowed walls. The crisp table linen, padded chairs, and candlelight add a touch of elegance. Seafood reigns, with old standbys like crabcakes and crab Norfolk augmented by seafood linguine and other pasta dishes. The daily catch is offered with a variety of sauces, from spicy Cajun to cucumber-dill. Early-bird specials include choices of seafood or meat entrees.

The Jewish Mother. 3108 Pacific Ave. (north of Laskin Rd.). ☎ **757/422-5430.** Reservations not accepted. Sandwiches $4–$6; other items $3–$14. AE, DISC, MC, V. Daily 8:30am–3am. DELI/AMERICAN.

A fixture on the Virginia Beach dining and nightlife scene since 1975, the Jewish Mother is well loved locally for its outstanding deli sandwiches, oversize egg and omelet platters, and fresh salads. The decor isn't fancy; in fact, it's charmingly dilapidated. The entrance looks more like a neighborhood grocery store, with take-out food items and a bakery case displaying an eclectic variety of desserts, ranging from Key lime pie to baklava to Black Forest cake. The food is top drawer, and after about 9:30pm there's solid entertainment. Live music performances run the gamut from country, bluegrass, and blues to zydeco, rock, and acoustic. Depending on the performers, there may be a cover, especially on weekends. A huge bar offers a wide selection of microbrews on tap, and arguably the largest array of bottled waters in town.

✪ **La Bella Italia.** 1065 Laskin Rd. (1 block east of Birdneck Rd.). ☎ **757/422-8536.** Reservations highly recommended for dinner. Sandwiches $4.50–$8.50; main courses $9–$17. AE, MC, V. Mon–Thurs 9am–10pm; Fri–Sat 9am–11pm. ITALIAN.

Although it's about a mile from the ocean, the deli here is an excellent place to pick up sandwiches or Italian breads, pastries, and cookies for a day at the beach. After dark, you had best reserve a table, for a roaring, mesquite-fired oven produces some of the area's best pizzas as well as exquisite marinated shrimp, fish, and steaks. In addition, the open kitchen serves up steaming bowls of homemade pasta.

The Lighthouse. Atlantic Ave. at 1st St., Rudee Inlet. ☎ **757/428-7974.** Reservations accepted. Sandwiches $8–$11; main courses $16–$25. AE, DC, DISC, MC, V. Mon–Fri noon–10pm; Sat–Sun 10am–11pm. SEAFOOD.

None of the resort area's beachfront seafood restaurants are particular noteworthy, but heavy wood beams create a warehouse effect in this rustic wooden building, and you can usually park free in the lot here. Choice seating is either outside beside Rudee

Inlet or upstairs, where you can see over the raised Boardwalk to the ocean (you'll be looking at sand from the first-floor tables). The menu offers a variety of seafood ranging from freshly caught flounder to live Maine lobster. In addition to traditional Southern dishes like fried fresh oysters, a char-grill perfectly singes the likes of swordfish and salmon steaks. The big draw here, however, is an all-you-can-eat buffet of crab legs, shrimp, crabcakes, and barbecued pork ribs at $24 for adults, $12 for children 7 to 12, and $5 for kids under 6. There's also a big Sunday brunch buffet all year.

✪ **Timbuktu.** Atlantic Ave. at 32nd St. (in Days Inn Oceanfront). ☎ **757/491-1800.** Reservations recommended. Main courses $12–$23. AE, DC, DISC, MC, V. Daily 7am–10am and noon–3pm; Sun–Thurs 6–9pm; Fri–Sat 6–10pm. Closed Mon off-season. Valet parking at dinner. AFRICAN/AMERICAN.

Although Timbuktu offers breakfast and lunch as part of the Days Inn Oceanfront's services to its guests, at night it turns into the venue for accomplished chef Willie Moats's far-reaching cuisine. As befits the name, leopard-print tablecloths, palm-shaped ceiling fans, and camel caravans engraved in glass table dividers set a North African scene behind big windows overlooking the ocean. Likewise, you'll find Saharan dishes such as grilled lamb and curried couscous with a vanilla-mint yogurt sauce on the seasonally changing menus. Or you can choose from more familiar fare, such as prime rib and grilled barbecue chicken. Every offering is expertly seasoned and accompanied by fresh local vegetables.

AT LYNNHAVEN INLET

Henry's. 3319 Shore Dr. (U.S. 60), at Lynnhaven Inlet. ☎ **757/481-7300.** Reservations accepted. Main courses $10–$23. AE, DISC, MC, V. May–Sept, Mon–Sat 11am–11pm; Sun 10am–11pm; Sun brunch 10am–2pm. Off-season, Mon–Sat 5–10:30pm; Sun 10am–10pm; Sun brunch 10am–2pm. From the resort area, take Shore Dr. (U.S. 60) west for about 6 miles to east side of Lynnhaven Inlet bridge. SEAFOOD.

You'll feel as though you're aboard ship in any one of the casual dining rooms or outdoor decks of this bi-level waterfront dining complex. At the front door, an 8,000-gallon cylindrical aquarium rises two stories and holds marine life native to this area. Gray-tile floors, blond-wood tables, white easy chairs, and lots of mirrors create an appealing contemporary setting. Fresh fish is prepared six different ways—grilled, broiled, fried, blackened, Cajun, or poached. Seafood platters, sautéed combinations, and Henry's famous lump crabcakes are all eminently recommendable. Dessert treats include homemade cheesecake.

Lynnhaven Fish House. 2350 Starfish Rd. ☎ **757/481-0003.** Reservations not accepted. Main courses $14–$22. AE, DC, DISC, MC, V. Daily 11:30am–10:30pm. Closed Thanksgiving and Christmas. From the resort area, take Shore Dr. (U.S. 60) to the Lynnhaven Fishing Pier, east of Lynnhaven Inlet bridge. SEAFOOD.

Perched on pilings over the beach, this Virginia Beach institution has fabulous bay views from its wraparound windows. At lunch, a good bet is half a dozen fresh-shucked clams on the half shell with cocktail sauce. Other choices include a crabcake sandwich, shrimp salad on a croissant, seafood pasta salad, or seafood stir-fry. The dinner menu starts off with oysters Rockefeller and selections from the chowder pots. Fresh fish of the day (flounder, sea trout, salmon, red snapper, tuna, swordfish, or rainbow trout) is offered broiled, grilled, steamed, or poached, accompanied by one of nine sauces. All dinners come with a choice of baked potato, sweet potato, French fries, or black beans and rice; coleslaw, house salad, or Caesar salad; and corn muffins and hushpuppies. For dessert, try the moist carrot cake, lavishly frosted, or a refreshing peach Melba. A cafe to the side has outdoor dining beside the fishing pier.

VIRGINIA BEACH AFTER DARK

The prime performing-arts venue here is the 20,000-seat, open-air **GTE Virginia Beach Amphitheater,** inland at Princess Anne and Dam Neck roads (☎ 757/ 368-8888 for schedule, Ticketmaster at 757/671-8100 for tickets). Big-name stars appear here (Jimmy Buffett, James Taylor, Cyndi Lauper, Tina Turner, Hank Williams, Jr., and The Who helped inaugurate its first season in 1997), as well as more highbrow acts like the Virginia Symphony. About 7,500 seats are under cover, with some 12,500 spaces available out on the lawn. Big TV screens and a state-of-the-art sound system let everyone see and hear what's going on. The season runs from April through October.

There are frequent outdoor concerts along the Boardwalk during summer (the visitor information center can tell you when and where). The biggest of all is the annual **American Music Festival,** over Labor Day weekend on the beach at 5th Street. You might catch America or Tanya Tucker on one stage, the Average White Band or Wilson Pickett on another. Tickets are sold on a first-come, first-served basis, or as part of special hotel packages (☎ 800/VA-BEACH).

Hotels and restaurants all along the beach have live music for nighttime dancing during the summer season. Just follow your ears along the Boardwalk. Of particular note are the **Jewish Mother** (see "Where to Dine," above); **Abbey Road Pub & Restaurant,** 22nd Street between Atlantic and Pacific avenues (☎ 757/425-6330), rated the best acoustic club here; and the **Duck-In & Gazebo,** on Shore Drive (U.S. 60) at Lynnhaven Inlet (☎ 757/481-0201), a seafood restaurant with sunset beach parties every Wednesday and Friday during summer.

3 Chincoteague & the Eastern Shore

Chincoteague, 83 miles N of Virginia Beach and Norfolk; 185 miles SE of Washington, D.C.

Miles of uncrowded beaches, countless waterways, abundant wildlife, and downhome cooking and hospitality welcome visitors to the tranquil Eastern Shore. Whether you'd like to take a day cruise to a quaint island out in the Chesapeake Bay, bike along traffic-free back roads, go bird watching in a wildlife refuge, sun and swim on one of America's great undeveloped beaches, or browse little villages with Native American names like Chincoteague, Wachapreague, or Onancock, you'll enjoy the gentle pace of this serene area.

Virginia's 70-mile-long end of the Delmarva Peninsula is bordered on one side by the Atlantic Ocean, on the other by the Chesapeake Bay. The ocean side is shielded by a string of barrier islands, many of them now happily preserved in their natural state by the Nature Conservancy (thus making them impossible to visit without a boat). Fishing towns like Chincoteague and Wachapreague sit inside the barrier islands. On the bay side, creeks cut into the land, creating natural harbors for towns like Onancock, jumping-off point for cruises to the most quaint destination of all, Tangier Island.

SEEING THE EASTERN SHORE

VISITOR INFORMATION   For information about the area, contact **Virginia's Eastern Shore Tourism Commission,** U.S. 13 South (P.O. Box R), Melfa, VA 23410 (☎ 757/787-2460).

GETTING THERE   There is neither airport nor public transportation on the Eastern Shore, so you'll need a car. From Norfolk take I-64 east, or from Virginia Beach take U.S. 60 west, and follow the gull signs to U.S. 13 north and the Chesapeake Bay Bridge-Tunnel, a beautiful 17.6-mile drive across and under the bay ($10 per car).

From the Cape Charles end of the bridge, go north on U.S. 13, a four-lane highway running down the center of the Eastern Shore. To reach Chincoteague, turn east on Va. 175, about 65 miles north of the bridge-tunnel and 5 miles south of the Maryland line.

CHINCOTEAGUE & ASSATEAGUE ISLANDS

With its many motels, inns, restaurants, and proximity to Assateague Island, Chincoteague Island is the most popular base for exploring the Eastern Shore. It sits just south of the Maryland line and is 7 miles long by 1¹/₂ miles wide. Settled by the English in the late 1600s, Chincoteague is famous for its surrounding bays full of flounder, oyster beds, and clam shoals. Marguerite Henry's children's book, *Misty of Chincoteague* (later made into a film), aroused wide interest in the annual pony penning and swim in late July, when pony-size wild horses are rounded up on Assateague Island, forced to swim across to Chincoteague, and sold to benefit the local fire department.

For us humans, wonderful Assateague Island is just a short bridge away from Chincoteague. This barrier island is the site of both the Chincoteague National Wildlife Refuge and Assateague Island National Seashore, which together protect the wild ponies' habitat and 37 miles of pristine beach. Assateague is on the main Atlantic Flyway, and its population of both migratory and resident birds is simply astounding.

While the town of Chincoteague has its share of tourist facilities, it retains much of its old fishing-village charm. Rickety old piers still jut out into the water next to modern motels, and watermen in work boats still outnumber tourists on jet skis. Of the nationally recognized chain names, only McDonald's will be seen on this quaint island—and that occurred only after a long and sometimes bitter fight.

ESSENTIALS

VISITOR INFORMATION   The **Chincoteague Chamber of Commerce,** P.O. Box 258, Chincoteague, VA 23336 (☎ **757/336-6161;** fax 757/336-1241; e-mail: pony@shore.intercom.net), operates a visitor center in the traffic circle on Maddox Boulevard, about a mile before the Assateague bridge. It's open from June to October, Monday through Saturday from 9am to 4:30pm, Sunday from noon to 4:30pm. Off-season, it's open Monday through Friday from 9am to 4:30pm.

AREA LAYOUT   Va. 175 crosses the Chincoteague Channel and dead-ends in the old village at Main Street, which runs north-south along the island's western shore. Turn right at the stoplight to reach the motels, marinas, and bait shops which line Main Street south of the bridge. Turn left at the light for Maddox Boulevard, which heads east from Main Street 9 blocks north of the bridge and goes to Assateague Island. Maddox Boulevard is Chincoteague's prime commercial strip, with a plethora of shops, restaurants, and motels. Church Street goes east 2 blocks north of the bridge and turns into East Side Drive, which runs along the island's eastern shore. Ridge Road and Chicken City Road together run north-south down the middle of the island. On Assateague, there's only one road other than a wildlife drive, and it goes directly to the beach.

GETTING AROUND   This flat land is great biking terrain, and you can rent bicycles at several shops on Maddox Boulevard. **The Bike Depot,** at the Refuge Motor Inn (☎ 757/336-5511), and **Jus' Bikes,** at the traffic circle (☎ **757/336-6700**), are closest to Assateague Island.

SPECIAL EVENTS   In the last 2 weeks of July, the **Chincoteague Fireman's Carnival,** a fun fest with rides, live entertainment, and food, climaxes with the famous **pony swim** across the Assateague Channel to Chincoteague Memorial Park. There

The Eastern Shore

MD.
VA.
Crisfield
New Church
Silva
Chincoteague Nat'l Wildlife Refuge
Assateague Island
13
175
Saxis
Oak Hall
Temperanceville
679
Chincoteague
Sanford
Hallwood
Mappsville
Assateague Island National Seashore
Bloxom
Guilford
316
Nelsonia
Modest Town
Parksley
679
Gargathy Inlet
Tasley
Onancock
Accomac
Metompkin Island
Onley
178
Locustville
Metompkin Inlet
Harborton
Melfa
799
Keller
Cedar Island
180
Pungateague
695
Painter
Wachapreague
Craddockville
182
Wachapreague Inlet
Belle Haven
Quimby
Exmore
Parramore Island
183
Jamesville
Nassawadox
Franktown
Weirwood
Quinby Inlet
618
Birdsnest
Johnsontown
13
NORTHAMPTON
Hog Island
Machipongo
Hog Island Bay
Eastville
Cobb Island Bay
Great Machipongo Inlet
Cobb Island
Cheriton
639
Bayview
Oyster
Sand Shoal Inlet
Cape Charles
184
Wreck Island
600
New Inlet
Capeville
Ship Shoal Island
Kiptopeke Beach
Townsend
Little Inlet
Kiptopeke
Cape Charles
Smith Island
Fishermans Island Nat'l Wildlife Refuge
Cape Charles
Highway
Scenic
13
Chesapeake Bay Bridge-Tunnel
Cape Henry
Virginia Beach

Chesapeake Bay

Atlantic Ocean

Tangier Island
3
Tangier

N

LEGEND
------- Ferry

Chincoteague National Wildlife Refuge 2
Onancock 4
Oyster Maritime Museum 1
Refuge Waterfowl Museum 1
Tangier Island 3
Wachapreague 5

VIRGINIA
Eastern Shore

is no charge for parking or watching the ponies swim. The ponies are herded to Memorial Park on East Side Drive, where the first colt to come ashore is given away, and many are then sold at auction. The swim takes place on the last Wednesday in July; the remaining ponies swim back to Assateague the following Friday. It's all for a good cause—proceeds go to the fire company's ambulance fund. Another top event is the **Chincoteague Oyster Festival,** when you can get your libido going by gorging on fresh oysters during the first week of October. This event is always sold out in advance, so call ☎ **757/336-6161** for ticket information.

EXPLORING THE ISLANDS

✪ Assateague Island

A barrier island protecting Chincoteague Island from the Atlantic Ocean, Assateague Island boasts over 37 miles of pristine **beaches** on its east coast, the northern 25 miles of which are in Maryland. The island is administered by two federal agencies, with the highest degree of protection afforded to wildlife on the Virginia side.

You first enter the **Chincoteague National Wildlife Refuge,** which is open May 1 to September 30, daily from 5am to 10pm; April and October, daily from 6am to 8pm; November 1 to March 31, daily from 6am to 6pm. Owned and managed by the U.S. Fish and Wildlife Service, the refuge accepts the annual entrance passes issued at national parks; otherwise, admission is $5 per car for 1 week, free for pedestrians and bikers.

Bird-watchers know Assateague Island as a prime Atlantic Flyway habitat where sightings of peregrine falcons, snow geese, great blue heron, and snowy egrets have been made. The annual Waterfowl Week, generally held around Thanksgiving, takes place when a large number of migratory birds use the refuge.

The famous **wild horses**—called "ponies"—have lived on Assateague since the 17th century. Local legend says their ancestors swam ashore from a shipwrecked Spanish galleon, but most likely English settlers put the first horses on Assateague, which formed a natural corral. Separated by a fence from their cousins in Maryland, the Virginia horses are now owned by the Chincoteague Volunteer Fire Department, which rounds them up and sells the folds at auction during the last week of July (see "Special Events," above).

Beginning at the visitor center, the paved **Wildlife Drive** runs through the marshes and is the best place to see the horses. **Assateague Island Tours** (☎ **757/336-6155**) conducts 1¹/₂-hour wildlife tours of the refuge, daily from Memorial Day to Labor Day at 10am and 2pm, at least once a day in April, May, and September. These tours cover 14¹/₂ miles and are usually the only way to visit most areas of the refuge other than on foot (the sole exception is the refuge's open house on Thanksgiving weekend, when 7 miles of service roads are open to vehicles). The tours cost $7 for adults, $3.50 for children. Book at the refuge visitor center.

The beach itself is in the **Assateague Island National Seashore,** operated by the National Park Service (☎ **757/336-6577**). You'll find a visitor center, two bathhouses, and summertime lifeguards at Tom's Cove, at the end of the road on the island's southern hook. In addition to swimming and sunning, activities at the beach include shell collecting (most productive at the tip of the Tom's Cove spit of land) and hiking. Biking is allowed on the paved roads and along a bike path beside the road from Chincoteague to the Refuge visitor center, then along Wildlife Drive to the Tom's Cove visitor center.

Note: Only a certain number of vehicles are allowed on the island at any given time. When that number is reached, park rangers stop traffic before the bridge to the island and allow one vehicle to cross only when another departs. Accordingly, it's best to arrive early in summer and on some fall weekends.

Several other **regulations** apply. Pets and alcoholic beverages are prohibited, even in your vehicle. In-line skating is not allowed, and off-road vehicles are permitted only at Tom's Cove. Surf fishing with a Virginia state license is allowed except on the lifeguard beach at Tom's Cove. Climbing and digging in the sand dunes is illegal. No overnight sleeping is allowed anywhere (backcountry camping is permitted on the Maryland end, a 12-mile hike from the Virginia-side visitor centers). And finally, thou shalt not feed the horses.

For **information** about the refuge and visitor-center seasons and programs, write or call Refuge Manager, Chincoteague National Wildlife Refuge, P.O. Box 62, Chincoteague, VA 23336 (☎ **757/336-6122**).

Museums

You'll pass a large airstrip as you drive to Chincoteague on Va. 175—this is NASA's Wallops Flight Facility, a research and testing center for rockets, balloons, and aircraft. The facility also tracks NASA's spacecraft and satellites, including the space shuttles. Across the highway is the **NASA Visitor Center** (☎ 757/824-1344), which explains the facility's history and role in the space program. Kids will get a kick out of seeing a practice space suit from the Apollo 9 moon mission. Admission is free. The visitor center is open from July 4 to Labor Day, daily from 10am to 4pm; March to June and September to November, Thursday through Monday from 10am to 4pm. The center is 5 miles west of Chincoteague.

On Maddox Boulevard, between the traffic circle and the bridge to Assateague, are two small marine-themed museums. The **Oyster and Maritime Museum** (☎ 757/ 336-6117) tells the area's history and the role played by the vital seafood industry from the 1600s to the present, with examples of marine life (some of them live). It's open Memorial Day to Labor Day, Monday through Saturday from 10am to 5pm, Sunday from noon to 4pm. Off-season hours are irregular. Admission is $3 for adults, $1 for children 12 and under.

Virtually next door, the **Refuge Waterfowl Museum** (☎ 757/336-5800) has an interesting variety of antique decoys, boats, traps, art, and carvings by outstanding craftspeople. It's open Memorial Day to Labor Day, Thursday through Monday from 10am to 5pm. Admission is $2.50 for adults, $1 for children under 12.

In the Landmark Plaza on North Main Street, the small but interesting **Island Aquarium** (☎ 757/336-6508) contains a marsh exhibit and touch tanks, where children can handle some of the marine life from local waters. Admission is $3 for adults, $2 for children under 15. It's open Memorial Day to Labor Day, Monday through Friday from 10am to 9pm, Sunday from 1 to 5pm. Call for off-season hours.

CRUISES & OUTDOOR PURSUITS

CRUISES While most visitors head for the beach on Assateague, don't overlook the broad bays and creeks that surround Chincoteague. A good way to get out on them is with **Captain Barry's Back Bay Cruises** (☎ 757/336-6508), which depart Landmark Plaza on Main Street. Barry Frishman moved from upstate New York to Chincoteague and set about learning everything he could about the water and what's in it. Now he shares his knowledge by taking guests out on his pontoon boat for $1^1/_2$-hour early-morning bird-watching expeditions ($15 per person); 4-hour morning or afternoon "Back Bay expeditions" in search of crabs, fish, shells, and clams ($30 per person); champagne sunset cruises ($20); moonlight excursions ($10); and just plain old "Fun Cruises" in spring and fall ($15).

Another way to see the birds at nesting time is on 2-hour nature cruises on the *Osprey* (☎ 757/336-5511), which departs the Town Dock opposite the Fire House on Main Street most evenings from Memorial Day through September, and on

Tuesday, Thursday, and Saturday in October. Prices are $10 for adults, $5 for children. Reservations are required. Purchase tickets at the Refuge Motor Inn on Maddox Boulevard (see "Where to Stay," below).

East Side Rentals & Marina on East Side Drive (☎ 757/336-3409) also offers 1-, 2-, and 3-hour nature cruises priced at $15, $20, and $30 per person, respectively.

FISHING   Before it became a tourist mecca, Chincoteague was a fishing village for centuries—and it still is. Both work and pleasure boats prowl the back bays and ocean for flounder, croaker, spot, kingfish, drum, striped bass, bluefish, and sharks, to name a few species. Among the pontoon party boats fishing the back bays are *Daisey's Dockside II,* at Daisey's Dockside Pier, South Main Street (☎ 757/336-3345), and the *Chincoteague View,* operating out of East Side Rentals & Marina on East Side Drive (☎ 757/336-3409). They charge $30 per person. More expensive are the charter boats that go oceanside, including the *Bucktail* (☎ 757/336-5188), the *Patty Wagon II* (☎ 757/336-1459), and the *Mar-shell* (☎ 757/336-1939). Reservations are essential, so call ahead.

Of course, you can do it yourself, either from a rented boat or by throwing your line from a dock. For equipment, supplies, free tide tables, and advice, check in at **Barnacle Bill's Bait & Tackle** (☎ 757/336-5188) or **Capt. Bob's** (☎ 757/336-6654), both on South Main Street. Marinas on East Side Drive that sell bait and rent boats and equipment include **East Side Rentals & Marina** (☎ 757/336-3409), **Snug Harbor Marina** (☎ 757/336-6176), and **Sea Tag Boat Rentals** (☎ 757/336-5555).

JET SKIING   You can rent these noisy but exciting contraptions at **Snug Harbor Marina** on East Side Drive (☎ 757/336-6176).

HUNTING   The marshes in these parts are perfect for hunting ducks, geese, and brants in the fall (dates of annual seasons are announced the summer before). **Andy's Guide Service** (☎ 757/336-1253) and the **Chincoteague Hunting & Fishing Center,** on Maddox Boulevard (☎ 757/336-3474), offer guide services. Reservations are required.

KAYAKING   The waters around Chincoteague are ideal for sea kayaking, and **Tidewater Expeditions** has early morning and evening trips and an all-day sea clinic, all departing from its shop on East Side Drive (☎ 757/336-6811 or 757/336-3159). Costs for the excursions range from $21 for one-person kayaks to $37 for two-person kayaks. The clinic costs $65 per person. The company also rents kayaks and canoes, starting at $10 an hour, $40 a day.

WHERE TO STAY

If you're looking for a longer-term rental on Chincoteague Island, contact **Vacation Cottages,** 6282 Maddox Blvd., Chincoteague, VA 23336 (☎ 800/457-6643 or 757/336-3720); **Island Property Rentals,** 7065 Main St., Chincoteague, VA 23336 (☎ 800/346-2559 or 757/336-3456); and **Bay Company, Inc.,** 6207 Maddox Blvd., Chincoteague, VA 23336 (☎ 800/221-5059 or 757/336-5490). They all have fully furnished cottages in various locations, including some on the waterfront.

At press-time, no national chain motels were yet on Chincoteague.

Motels

Beach Road Motel. 6151 Maddox Blvd. (P.O. Box 557), Chincoteague, VA 23336. ☎ 800/699-6562 or 757/336-6562. Fax 757/336-1839. 20 rms, 3 efficiencies. A/C TV TEL. Summer $58–$88; off-season $35–$48 double. Additional person $5 extra. AE, DC, DISC, MC, V. Free parking. Turn left at the bridge and drive 8 blocks to Maddox Blvd.

This owner-operated motel offers comfortable rooms in two one-story white-masonry buildings, one with a long front porch. The rooms are immaculate and contain all the basics, including refrigerators and beverage hot pots. The efficiencies include a studio, a one-bedroom cottage, and a two-bedroom mobile home with full kitchen facilities. There is an outdoor pool on the property.

Driftwood Motor Lodge. 7105 Maddox Blvd. (P.O. Box 575), Chincoteague, VA 23336. ☎ **800/553-6117** or 757/336-6557. Fax 757/336-6558. E-mail: driftwood@shore.intercom. net. 52 rms, 1 suite. A/C TV TEL. Summer $83–$96 double, $110 suite; off-season $55–$65 double, $75–$85 suite. AE, DC, DISC, MC, V. From the bridge, turn left on Main St., right on Maddox Blvd.

Along with the Refuge Motor Inn across the road (see below), this gray, three-story shiplap building is the closest accommodation to Assateague Island. Entered from the rear, the motel-style rooms all have balconies facing the road (those on the third floor overlook the marshes). Most contain two double beds, tables and chairs, and full tiled baths. The one suite has two bedrooms, one bath, and a microwave, refrigerator, and coffeemaker. There's an outdoor pool surrounded by shrubs and a picnic area with barbecue grill.

✪ **Island Motor Inn.** 4391 N. Main St., Chincoteague, VA 23336. ☎ **757/336-3141.** Fax 757/336-1483. 60 rms. A/C TV TEL. Summer $88–$150; off-season $58–130. AE, DC, DISC, MC, V. From the bridge, turn left on Main St. to motel on left.

The top motel here, the Island Motor Inn sits right on Chincoteague Channel just north of the business district, giving its spacious rooms great views across the bay to the mainland. Reception is in a new, three-story building whose rooms are better appointed than the standard units in an older, two-story motel block adjoining. In fact, rooms on the ends of this new building have bay windows on their sides, giving them two-way views. All rooms have private balconies, desks, 27-inch TVs, and custom-made furniture. Some also have reclining sofas and baths with phones and pedestal sinks. On the waterside of the property, you'll find a 600-foot boardwalk and boat dock, a covered barbecue area with hammock for lounging, an outdoor pool, and glass-enclosed indoor pool and fitness center (with a trainer on duty during summer). On the road side, owners Reggie and Anna Stubbs have built a charming landscaped garden with lily ponds and benches for relaxing. There's also a guest laundry and a cafe that serves breakfast and lunch.

Refuge Motor Inn. 7058 Maddox Blvd., Chincoteague, VA 23336. ☎ **800/544-8469,** ext. 2, or 757/336-5511. Fax 757/336-6134. 70 rms, 2 suites. A/C TV TEL. Summer $85–$195 double; off-season $55–$110 double. AE, DC, DISC, MC, V. Free parking.

Located between the traffic circle and the bridge to Assateague, this very attractive motor inn with weathered gray siding nestles on beautifully landscaped grounds shaded by tall pines. The care and attention lavished on decor and facilities at this family-owned spot are evident everywhere. Furnishings are charming: Some rooms have colonial-style pieces, bleached-pine headboards, decoys, handmade wall hangings, and all the elements of country style. All rooms have refrigerators. First-floor rooms facing the back have sliding doors to private patios where guests can use outdoor grills. Facilities include an observation sundeck on the roof, an exercise room with sauna, a glass-enclosed pool and Jacuzzi, a children's playground and pony enclosure, rental bikes, a coin-op laundry, and a lobby gift/crafts shop.

Waterside Motor Inn. 3761 Main St. (P.O. Box 347), Chincoteague, VA 23336. ☎ **757/ 336-3434.** Fax 757/336-1878. 45 rms. A/C TV TEL. Summer $95–$150 double; off-season $54– $92 double. Additional person $5 extra; children under 12 stay free in parents' room (limit of

2 children). AE, DC, DISC, MC, V. Free on-site parking. At the bridge entering Chincoteague, turn right; the motel is on the right, about half a mile from the bridge.

All the accommodations at this three-story property feature private wooden balconies overlooking Chincoteague Channel, guaranteeing some breathtaking sunset views. Cream clapboard siding with slate-blue trim has a properly nautical look. Rooms are decorated in comfortable contemporary style. All have coffeemakers and refrigerators. The Waterside also offers a Jacuzzi, an exercise room, a tennis court, and a swimming pool, and it's located right on a fishing and crabbing pier.

Bed & Breakfasts

⚫ **Cedar Gables Seaside Inn.** 6095 Hopkins Lane (P.O. Box 1006), Chincoteague, VA 23336. ☎ **888/491-2944** or 757/336-6860. Fax 757/336-1291. www.intercom.net/user/cdrgbl. E-mail: cdrgbl@shore.intercom.net. 4 rms (all with bath). A/C TV TEL. $130–$175 double. Rates include full breakfast. AE, DISC, MC, V. From the bridge, turn left on Main St., right on Maddox Blvd., left on Deep Hole Rd., right on Hopkins Lane.

Innkeepers Fred and Claudia Greenway offer Chincoteague's most luxurious accommodations at their modern house, which looks out to Assateague Island from a perch beside a marsh-lined creek (this is the only B&B here that enjoys a waterfront location). The building doesn't actually have gables, although an irregularly shaped roof creates gable-like ceilings in the guest quarters. Each guest room has a gas fireplace, ceiling fan, TV with VCR, refrigerator, phone with data port, individual heating and air-conditioning controls, embroidered robes and Egyptian-cotton bed linens, and a bathroom with Jacuzzi tub, hair dryer, toiletries, and separate phone. Most intriguing (and expensive) is the Captain's Quarters, a spacious top-level room with its own deck and winding stairs leading up to a private tower with 360° views over the waterways and islands. Every unit has both inside and outside entries, so you don't have to traipse through the house to get into and out of your room. Served on a screened porch in good weather, three-course breakfasts begin with fresh fruit and Claudia's homemade granola. Out on the lawn, a swimming pool is completely surrounded by screens to keep the mosquitoes away. The Greenways also rent canoes and kayaks to their guests. *Note:* Kids 14 and older can stay in one room; otherwise, this is an all-adult establishment.

Inn at Poplar Corner. 4248 Main St. (at Poplar St.), Chincoteague, VA 23336. ☎ **800/336-8787** or 757/336-1564. Fax 757/336-5776. 4 rms (all with bath). A/C. Summer $135–$149; off-season $109–$129. Rates include full breakfast and afternoon tea. MC, V. From the bridge, turn left on Main St. to inn on right.

This three-story house with wraparound veranda looks like it's been here since Victorian times, but it was actually built from scratch a few years ago by the owners of the Watson House across the street (see below). Floral wallpaper, period antiques, and lace curtains add to the atmosphere. A central hallway is flanked by a formal parlor and a dining room, whose French doors open to the veranda, thus permitting guests of both B&Bs to enjoy full gourmet breakfasts outside during good weather. The two rooms on the front of the second story have bay windows, while the one to the rear has its own private balcony. But the star here is the third story, which has a unique lounge (you have to stoop under the roof to reach a small reading area) and a bedroom with three gables and French doors leading to a huge bathroom. All rooms have window air-conditioning units, ceiling fans, and Jacuzzi tubs, but none has a phone or TV.

Island Manor House. 4160 Main St., Chincoteague, VA 23336. ☎ **800/852-1505** or 757/336-5436. Fax 757/336-1333. www.accomack.com/imh. E-mail: imn@shore.intercom.net. 8 rms (6 with bath). A/C. Summer $85–$120 double; off-season $70–$90 double. Rates include full breakfast and afternoon tea. MC, V. Free parking. From the bridge into Chincoteague, turn left onto Main St. and continue about 1¹/₂ blocks; the inn is on the right.

This older B&B consists of two white-clapboard houses joined by a one-story, light-filled garden room with a lovely brick patio and fountain outside (where guests enjoy breakfast in good weather). Originally, there was only one house, built before the Civil War by two young men. They eventually married sisters, who did not enjoy living under the same roof, so they split the structure and moved the front half next door. Today, both houses have been handsomely restored and are furnished mainly in Federal style, along with 17th-, 18th-, and 19th-century pieces collected by hospitable owners Charles and Carol Kalmykow. In the two first-floor sitting rooms are fireplaces and telephones for guest use.

Miss Molly's Inn Bed & Breakfast. 4141 Main St., Chincoteague, VA 23336. ☎ **800/ 221-5620** or 757/336-6686. 7 rms (5 with bath). A/C. Summer $89–$155 double; off-season $69–$125 double. Rates include full breakfast and afternoon tea. DISC, MC, V. Free parking. Closed early Jan to Feb. From the bridge into Chincoteague, turn left onto Main St. and continue about 1¹/₂ blocks to the inn, on the left.

This charming 1886 Victorian, with a wide wraparound porch, is named for the daughter of the builder J. T. Rowley, known as "the clam king of the world." Miss Molly, who lived in this house until the age of 84, was a resident when Marguerite Henry stayed here to write *Misty of Chincoteague*. Although this is the least upscale of the B&Bs in the area, innkeepers David and Barbara Wiedenheft have decorated all rooms with an agreeable mix of Victorian and earlier antiques, lace curtains, pretty coverlets, Tiffany-style lamps, and bibelots adorning mantels and dresser tops. The parlor and dining room have exceptionally fine Victorian pieces—marble-top tables, a curved sofa, and original newel-post lamps—and Oriental carpets. There are five porches, including a screened one at the rear of the house.

The Watson House. 4240 Main St. (at Poplar St.), Chincoteague, VA 23336. ☎ **800/ 336-8787** or 757/336-1564. Fax 757/336-5776. 6 rms (all with bath). A/C. Summer $85–$105; off-season $65–$85. Rates include full breakfast and afternoon tea. MC, V. From the bridge, turn left on Main St. to inn on right.

Unlike its sibling, the Inn at Poplar Corner (see above), the Watson House actually dates back to the Victorian era, having been built before 1874. You'll pay less on this side of Poplar Street, but you'll also get a much simpler room and a bath just large enough to accommodate a toilet and shower stall (pedestal sinks stand in the sleeping quarters). Nevertheless, Victorian oak furniture and lace curtains supply charm, and two of the rooms have small sitting areas. Guests breakfast at the Inn at Poplar Corner, but afternoon tea is served here, either in the formal dining room or on the wraparound veranda.

Campgrounds

Chincoteague has several family-oriented campgrounds. At the traffic circle, the **Maddox Family Campground,** 6742 Maddox Blvd., Chincoteague, VA 23336 (☎ 757/336-3111; fax 757/336-1980), has 550 campsites, some with views of the Assateague Lighthouse. On the grounds are a pool, playground, pavilion, grocery store with RV supplies, rec hall, laundry room, bathhouses, dump station, and propane filling station. Shuffleboard, a duck pond, horseshoes, crabbing, and bird watching are on site. Rates range from $19 for a tent site to $26.50 for full hookup. Discover, MasterCard, and Visa are accepted.

As its name implies, **Pine Grove Campground & Waterfowl Park,** 5283 Deep Hole Rd. (P.O. Box 8), Chincoteague, VA 23336 (☎ 757/336-5200), sits in a shady pine grove, and has a park-like area where domestic and exotic waterfowl are bred and raised. There are 100 RV sites and 50 tent sites in separate areas, a pool, laundry room, play area, camp store, dump station, and bathhouses. Rates range from $17.50 to $22; MasterCard and Visa are accepted.

WHERE TO DINE

You won't find fine dining here, but you will be served seafood fresh from the boat. The famous Chincoteague oysters are harvested from September to March. The area is also known for flounder, caught year-round.

AJ's by the Creek. 6585 Maddox Blvd. ☎ **757/336-5888.** Reservations not accepted. Bar menu $3–$7; main courses $9–$24. AE, DC, DISC, MC, V. Mon–Sat 11:30am–10pm; Sun 4:30–10pm. ITALIAN/SEAFOOD.

A favorite with locals, AJ's offers dining either on a screened-in patio beside a narrow creek or inside, where candles and dried-flower arrangements adorn a mix of tables and booths (romantically inclined couples can wait for the one private table sitting alone in a corner). The menu offers a mix of Italian-style pastas (the house specialty) and traditional dishes such as fried or steamed shrimp and Chincoteague oysters. The smoked pork flavor overwhelmed the fresh oysters in a rich champagne, bacon, scallion, and cream sauce over linguine, but it was still an interesting concoction. A popular local hangout, the friendly and cozy bar to one side offers sports TVs and its own lunch and snack menu (including sandwiches, shrimp baskets, and small orders of pasta).

Landmark Crab House. Landmark Plaza, 6162 Main St., on the bay. ☎ **757/336-5552.** Reservations recommended on weekends. Main courses $11–$18. AE, DC, DISC, MC, V. Mon–Sat 4:30–10pm; Sun 1–10pm. Closed Dec–Feb. SEAFOOD.

The setting, more than the cuisine, attracts crowds to this crab house at the end of a pier on Chincoteague Channel. Wraparound windows provide panoramic views of small fishing vessels tied up for the evening. The gorgeous Victorian bar, dating to 1897, was brought here from Chicago. The wood-paneled dining room has a nautical motif with ship figureheads, ship models, lanterns, and mounted fish. For an appetizer, you can't beat Chincoteague oysters on the half shell or a bucket of steamed clams. Trips to the salad bar come with all entrees. Landmark specials include half a pound of steamed shrimp with fresh broccoli and hollandaise sauce, soft-shell crabs, and crab imperial. Landlubbers can choose from fresh fried or teriyaki chicken, filet mignon, or New York strip steak. On Friday, Saturday, and holiday evenings, there's piano music in the lounge, and the deck bar has entertainment on summer weekends.

P.T. Pelican's Intercoastal Deck Bar. At Chincoteague Inn, Marlin St. (off Main St., south of the bridge). ☎ **757/336-6110.** Reservations not accepted. Sandwiches and salads $4–$9. DC, DISC, MC, V. Easter to mid-Oct, daily 11am–10pm. Closed mid-Oct to Easter. SEAFOOD.

It's rustic and funky, with a well-weathered lean-to tin roof covering a spacious square bar and beat-up stools, but this establishment right on the Intercoastal Waterway is the most interesting place in town for a lazy waterside lunch—or for whiling away an afternoon chatting with the local watermen who take libation here after crabbing and oystering. You can sit by the water at green plastic tables and order from the bar menu, which features burgers, crabcake sandwiches, sautéed soft-shell crabs, steamed or raw oysters and clams on the half shell, small pizzas, and tasty shrimp and crab salads.

Shucking House Café. Landmark Plaza, 6162 Main St., on the bay. ☎ **757/336-5145.** Sandwiches $3.50–$5; main courses $10–$13. AE, DC, DISC, MC, V. Daily 8am–3pm. Closed Dec–Feb. AMERICAN.

Adjoining the Landmark Crab House and under the same ownership, the Shucking House Café has a cathedral ceiling, windows overlooking the channel, and seating in red-leather-upholstered booths and at small tables. Breakfast options include country ham and biscuits, French toast, and blueberry pancakes. The lunch menu features soups, chowders, sandwiches, and seafood entrees such as crabcake platter and fried shrimp and clam strips. On Sunday, there's a dinner buffet from 11:30am to 3pm.

✪ **Village Restaurant.** 6576 Maddox Blvd. ☎ **757/336-5120.** Reservations suggested on weekends. Main courses $10–$19.50. AE, DISC, MC, V. Daily 5–10pm. Closed 1 day a wk off-season. SEAFOOD.

The garden-like Village Restaurant, with white trellises and floral wallpaper, overlooks a creek and a marsh. You'll enjoy the best traditionally prepared seafood in town here, whether you choose fried oysters, stuffed flounder, or crab imperial. The house seafood platter is piled with fish filet, soft-shell crab stuffed with crab imperial, shrimp, scallops, oysters, clams, and lobster tail. Avoid the blackened fish, which is simply coated with Cajun spices. Non-seafood main dishes include veal Parmesan, fried chicken, and filet mignon. All entrees are served with salad, home-baked bread, and a choice of slaw, potato, rice, or vegetable of the day.

ONANCOCK

In contrast to Chincoteague's somewhat scruffy fishing-town image, the picturesque town of Onancock, 1 mile west of U.S. 13 and Olney, has a more genteel charm dating back to 1690. Situated on Onancock Creek some 2^1/$_2$ miles from the Chesapeake Bay, it has always made its money from agriculture and trading as well as from the bay. The great ferries and ships that once plied between Norfolk and Baltimore put in here, helping to make Onancock a wealthy town. As a consequence, it has stately churches (many with fish-scale shingle exteriors) and fine historic homes built by wealthy traders and bankers.

WHAT TO SEE & DO

It's worth a stop here to visit **Kerr Place,** a stately Federal mansion built in 1799 by Scottish merchant John Shepherd Kerr on Market Street (Va. 179). This two-story brick manor house, now headquarters for the Eastern Shore of Virginia Historical Society (☎ **757/787-8012**), is beautifully furnished with 18th- and 19th-century antiques. Admission is $3. It's open March to December, Tuesday through Saturday from 9am to 4pm (closed holidays).

While here, linger for a bit at the town dock, at the foot of Market Street, and take a look at **Hopkins & Bro.,** a general store built in 1842.

✪ **A CRUISE TO TANGIER ISLAND**   Hopkins & Bro. store is also the departure point for cruises to tiny Tangier Island and its picturesque village of 750 souls out in the Chesapeake Bay. There are no cars on the narrow streets, which seems appropriate to this unspoiled island, discovered by Capt. John Smith in 1608. In fact, the local accent actually hearkens back to Elizabethan English. This is no glitzy resort: Entertainment consists of walking around the island, perhaps chatting with local watermen, and just enjoying the serenity and fresh sea air. In any case, you'll want to eat at **Hilda Crockett's Chesapeake House,** where home-cooked lunches are served boardinghouse-style from 11:30am to 5pm daily for $11.75. You can also stay overnight at Mrs. Crockett's for a reasonable $40, which includes dinner and breakfast. For details and reservations, the address is simply Tangier Island, Tangier, VA 23440 (☎ **757/891-2331**).

The Onancock–Tangier Island ferry operates June through September, daily at 10am, returning at 3pm. Round-trip fare is $18 for adults, $9 for children 6 to 11, and free for children 5 and under. For reservations, call ☎ 757/787-2240.

WHERE TO STAY

The town of Olney, 1 mile east of Onancock on U.S. 13, has a modern **Comfort Inn** (☎ 800/228-5150 or 757/787-7787), one of only two chain motels between Charles City, Va., and Pocomoke City, Md.

Spinning Wheel Bed & Breakfast. 13 North St., Onancock, VA 23417. ☎ **757/787-7311.** 5 rms. A/C. $65–95. Rates include full breakfast. MC, V. Closed Nov–Mar. Free parking. From Market St., turn north on North St.

Every room in this three-story wood-frame Victorian, built around 1890, has an antique spinning wheel, part of an extraordinary collection belonging to innkeeper Karen Tweedie. She and husband David have added other Eastern Shore antiques throughout, including iron and brass beds. Dormer windows have contributed unique shapes to the top-level rooms. Free bikes are available for guests' use.

WHERE TO DINE

✪ **Armando's.** 10 North St., Onancock. ☎ **757/787-8044.** Reservations accepted 5–6pm only. Main courses $8–$16. AE, MC, V. Sun and Tues–Thurs 5–9pm; Fri–Sat 5–10pm. INTERNATIONAL.

Argentine-born Armando Suarez settled in Onancock in 1988 and opened a pizza and sandwich shop. So popular did it quickly become that he opened this fun storefront restaurant adorned with an eclectic mix of pottery, plants, and photos of jazz musicians. Armando's menu is equally eclectic, with some inventive twists such as crab crêpes, shrimp margarita (a slightly piquant tequila sauce), and lobster ravioli "drizzled" with sage, butter, and tomato cream sauce. Armando constantly spins jazz CDs and occasionally has live jazz on weekends.

WACHAPREAGUE

Appearing much like Chincoteague must have looked before its days of tourism, the tiny village of Wachapreague (290 permanent residents) sits on the Atlantic coast mainland just 10 miles from Onancock. It overlooks the marshes and waterways that lie between town and an inlet between ✪ **Cedar Island** and ✪ **Parramore Island**, which protect the bays and marshes here as Assateague does for Chincoteague. At the turn of the 20th century, Wachapreague was a major resort for the likes of Walter Chrysler, actor Ronald Coleman, and former president Herbert Hoover. They were drawn here by the area's excellent hunting and fishing, and they stayed at the grand Hotel Wachapreague, a four-story Victorian palace surrounded by verandas and topped by gabled windows. Unfortunately, the hotel burned down in 1978, but the fishing and hunting here are as good as ever.

Seaside Boat Rentals at the Wachapreague Marina on the waterfront (☎ 757/787-4110) will rent boats for do-it-yourself trips for $60 a day, including fuel and a chart. The marina's bait shop or **Capt. Zed's Bait & Tackle** (☎ 757/787-8060) next door will advise on where the fish are biting. If you decide to go out on your own, do it at high tide, since many channels here are very shallow.

WHERE TO STAY

✪ **Hart's Harbor House and Burton House Bed & Breakfast.** 9 Brooklyn Ave., Wachapreague, VA 23480. ☎ **757/7887-4848.** 10 rms (4 with bath, 6 with toilet and hand basin). A/C. $65–$95 double. Rates include full breakfast. MC. From Va. 180, turn left on Brooklyn 1 block before waterfront.

Born-and-bred Wachapreagers Tom and Pat Hart have turned these two adjacent Victorian houses into a first-rate bed-and-breakfast operation with direct access to the waterfront. Tom salvaged some railing from the Hotel Wachapreague's verandas and used them to build a charming, gazebo-like screened porch on the rear of Burton House (Hart's Harbor House also has a screened porch overlooking the water). Hart's Harbor House's rooms are larger than its neighbor's, but all have baths and attractive Eastern Shore antiques. Guests in the main houses are treated to Tom's country breakfast. The Harts provide free bikes for their guests' use and will arrange cruises, island trips, and hunting and fishing guides. They also have three cottages and a cabin for rent in their back lot, between the houses and the waterfront.

WHERE TO DINE

Island House Restaurant. 17 Atlantic Ave. (on the waterfront). ☎ **757/787-4242.** Reservations accepted. Lunch $3.50–$7; main courses $10–$16. MC, V. Feb–Apr and Nov–Dec, Fri–Sun noon–9pm; May–Oct, daily noon–9pm. Closed late Dec to Jan. SEAFOOD.

Overlooking the marshes, channels, and barrier islands, this shingle-sided building gets its inspiration from the old Parramore Island Life Saving Station, which was built in the 1890s. Raw bar items include fresh Wachapreague oysters from September to March. For a main course, choose from broiled or fried favorites such as soft-shell crabs, crabcakes, and fish.

Appendix: Useful Toll-Free Numbers

MAJOR AIRLINES

American	800/433-7300
Continental	800/525-0280
Delta	800/221-1212
Northwest	800/225-2525
Southwest	800/435-9792
TWA	800/221-2000
United	800/241-6522
US Airways	800/428-4322

MAJOR CAR-RENTAL COMPANIES

Alamo	800/327-9633
Avis	800/831-2847
Budget	800/527-0700
Dollar	800/800-4000
Enterprise	800/325-8007
Hertz	800/654-3131
National	800/227-7368
Thrifty	800/367-2277

MAJOR CHAIN HOTELS & MOTELS

Best Western	800/528-1234
Budgetel Inns	800/4-BUDGET
Clarion Hotels	800/CLARION
Comfort Inns	800/228-5150
Courtyard by Marriott	800/321-2211
Days Inn	800/325-2525
Doubletree Hotels	800/222-TREE
Econo Lodges	800/55-ECONO
Fairfield Inn by Marriott	800/228-2800
Friendship Inns	800/453-4511
Hampton Inn	800/HAMPTON
Hilton Hotels	800/HILTONS
Holiday Inn	800/HOLIDAY
Howard Johnson	800/654-2000
Hyatt Hotels	800/233-1234
Knights Inn	800/843-5644
Marriott Hotels	800/228-9290
Motel 6	800/466-8356

Omni Hotels	800/843-6664
Quality Inns	800/228-5151
Radisson Hotels	800/333-3333
Ramada	800/2-RAMADA
Red Carpet Inns	800/251-1962
Red Roof Inns	800/THE-ROOF
Ritz-Carlton	800/241-3333
Rodeway Inn	800/228-2000
Sheraton	800/325-3535
Shoney's Inns	800/222-2222
Sleep Inn	800/753-3746
Super 8	800/800-8000
Travelodge	800/255-3050

Index

300 Index

FROMMER'S® COMPLETE TRAVEL GUIDES

(Comprehensive guides to destinations around the world, with selections in all price ranges—from deluxe to budget)

Acapulco, Ixtapa & Zihuatenejo
Alaska
Amsterdam
Arizona
Atlanta
Australia
Austria
Bahamas
Barcelona, Madrid & Seville
Belgium, Holland & Luxembourg
Bermuda
Boston
Budapest & the Best of Hungary
California
Canada
Cancún, Cozumel & the Yucatán
Cape Cod, Nantucket & Martha's Vineyard
Caribbean
Caribbean Cruises & Ports of Call
Caribbean Ports of Call
Carolinas & Georgia
Chicago
China
Colorado
Costa Rica
Denver, Boulder & Colorado Springs
England

Europe
Florida
France
Germany
Greece
Hawaii
Hong Kong
Honolulu, Waikiki & Oahu
Ireland
Israel
Italy
Jamaica & Barbados
Japan
Las Vegas
London
Los Angeles
Maryland & Delaware
Maui
Mexico
Miami & the Keys
Montana & Wyoming
Montréal & Québec City
Munich & the Bavarian Alps
Nashville & Memphis
Nepal
New England
New Mexico
New Orleans
New York City
Northern New England
Nova Scotia, New Brunswick & Prince Edward Island
Oregon
Paris

Philadelphia & the Amish Country
Portugal
Prague & the Best of the Czech Republic
Provence & the Riviera
Puerto Rico
Rome
San Antonio & Austin
San Diego
San Francisco
Santa Fe, Taos & Albuquerque
Scandinavia
Scotland
Seattle & Portland
Singapore & Malaysia
South Pacific
Spain
Switzerland
Thailand
Tokyo
Toronto
Tuscany & Umbria
USA
Utah
Vancouver & Victoria
Vienna & the Danube Valley
Virgin Islands
Virginia
Walt Disney World & Orlando
Washington, D.C.
Washington State

FROMMER'S® DOLLAR-A-DAY GUIDES

(The ultimate guides to comfortable low-cost travel)

Australia from $50 a Day
California from $60 a Day
Caribbean from $60 a Day
Costa Rica & Belize from $35 a Day
England from $60 a Day
Europe from $50 a Day
Florida from $50 a Day
Greece from $50 a Day
Hawaii from $60 a Day
India from $40 a Day

Ireland from $50 a Day
Israel from $45 a Day
Italy from $50 a Day
London from $60 a Day
Mexico from $35 a Day
New York from $75 a Day
New Zealand from $50 a Day
Paris from $70 a Day
San Francisco from $60 a Day
Washington, D.C., from $60 a Day

FROMMER'S® PORTABLE GUIDES

(Pocket-size guides for travelers who want everything in a nutshell)

Bahamas	Dublin	Puerto Vallarta, Manzanillo
California Wine Country	Las Vegas	& Guadalajara
Charleston & Savannah	London	San Francisco
Chicago	Maine Coast	Venice
	New Orleans	Washington, D.C.

FROMMER'S® NATIONAL PARK GUIDES

(Everything you need for the perfect park vacation)

Grand Canyon	Yosemite & Sequoia/
National Parks of the American West	Kings Canyon
Yellowstone & Grand Teton	Zion & Bryce Canyon

FROMMER'S® IRREVERENT GUIDES

(Wickedly honest guides for sophisticated travelers)

Amsterdam	Manhattan	San Francisco	Walt Disney World
Chicago	New Orleans	Santa Fe	Washington, D.C.
London	Paris		

FROMMER'S® BY NIGHT GUIDES

(The series for those who know that life begins after dark)

Amsterdam	Los Angeles	Miami	Prague
Chicago	Madrid	New Orleans	San Francisco
Las Vegas	& Barcelona	Paris	Washington, D.C.
London	Manhattan		

THE COMPLETE IDIOT'S TRAVEL GUIDES

(The ultimate user-friendly trip planners)

Cruise Vacations	New York City	San Francisco
Las Vegas	Planning Your Trip	Walt Disney World
New Orleans	to Europe	

SPECIAL-INTEREST TITLES

Arthur Fommer's New World of Travel	Outside Magazine's Adventure Guide
The Civil War Trust's Official Guide to	to New England
the Civil War Discovery Trail	Outside Magazine's Adventure Guide
Frommer's Caribbean Hideaways	to Northern California
Frommer's Complete Hostel Vacation	Outside Magazine's Adventure Guide
Guide to England, Scotland & Wales	to the Pacific Northwest
Frommer's Europe's Greatest	Outside Magazine's Adventure Guide
Driving Tours	to Southern California & Baja
Frommer's Food Lover's Companion	Outside Magazine's Guide to Family Vacations
to France	Places Rated Almanac
Frommer's Food Lover's Companion to	Retirement Places Rated
Italy	Washington, D.C., with Kids
Israel Past & Present	Wonderful Weekends from New York City
New York City with Kids	Wonderful Weekends from San Francisco
New York Times Weekends	Wonderful Weekends from Los Angeles

WHEREVER YOU TRAVEL, *H*ELP IS NEVER FAR AWAY.

From planning your trip to providing travel assistance along the way, American Express® Travel Service Offices are always there to help you do more.

Virginia

Friendly Travel (R)
1506 Belle View Boulevard
Alexandria
703-768-6020

American Express Travel Service
1100 South Hayes Street
Pentagon City
Arlington
703-415-5400

United Travel (R)
9600 I. Main Street
Fairfax
703-978-4404

American Express Travel Service
Tysons Galleria, Suite 3202
1801U International Drive
McLean
703-893-3550

Gibson World Travel (R)
11832 Rock Landing Drive
Suite 208
Newport News
757-873-0606

American Express Travel Service
1412-A Starling Drive
Richmond
804-740-2030

American Express Travel Service
6640 Springfield Mall
Springfield
703-971-5600

Gibson World Travel (R)
279 Independent Boulevard
Virginia Beach
804-499-2333

do more AMERICAN EXPRESS

Travel

http://www.americanexpress.com/travel

American Express Travel Service Offices are located throughout the United States. For the office nearest you, call 1-800-AXP-3429.